DESTINATION
CASABLANCA

DESTINATION
CASABLANCA

Exile, Espionage, and the Battle for North Africa in World War II

MEREDITH HINDLEY

PUBLICAFFAIRS

NEW YORK

PublicAffairs
Hachette Book Group
1290 Avenue of the Americas, New York, NY 10104
www.publicaffairsbooks.com
@Public_Affairs

Printed in the United States of America

First Edition: October 2017

Published by PublicAffairs, an imprint of Perseus Books, LLC, a subsidiary of Hachette Book Group, Inc.

The Hachette Speakers Bureau provides a wide range of authors for speaking events. To find out more, go to www.hachettespeakersbureau.com or call (866) 376-6591.

The publisher is not responsible for websites (or their content) that are not owned by the publisher.

Print book interior design by Linda Mark

Library of Congress Cataloging-in-Publication Data
Names: Hindley, Meredith, author.
Title: Destination Casablanca : exile, espionage, and the battle for North Africa in World War II / Meredith Hindley.
Other titles: Exile, espionage, and the battle for North Africa in World War II
Description: New York : PublicAffairs, [2017] | Includes bibliographical references and index.
Identifiers: LCCN 2017018911| ISBN 9781610394055 (hardcover) | ISBN 9781610394062 (ebook)
Subjects: LCSH: World War, 1939–1945—Campaigns—Morocco. | World War, 1939–1945—Morocco—Casablanca. | World War, 1939–1945—Intelligence service. | France—Foreign relations—United States. | United States—Foreign relations—France.
Classification: LCC D766.99.M6 H56 2017 | DDC 940.54/234—dc23
LC record available at https://lccn.loc.gov/2017018911

LSC-C

10 9 8 7 6 5 4 3 2 1

For my parents, Virginia and Richard,
who instilled in me an affection for books and history.

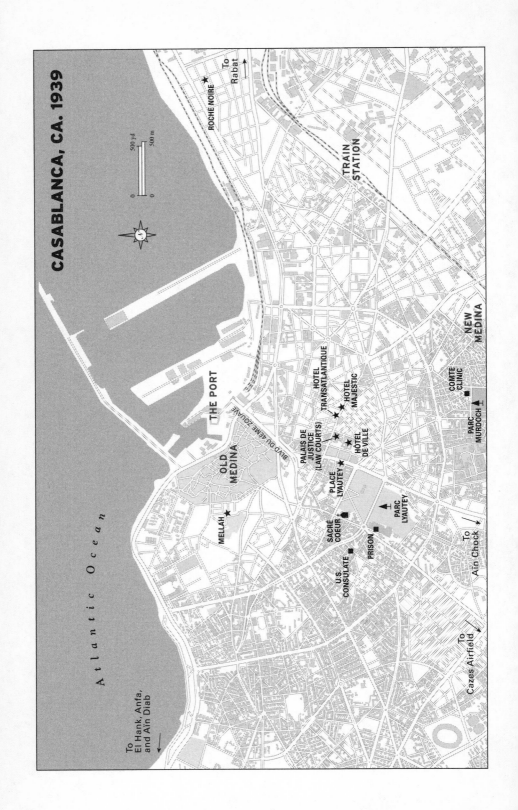

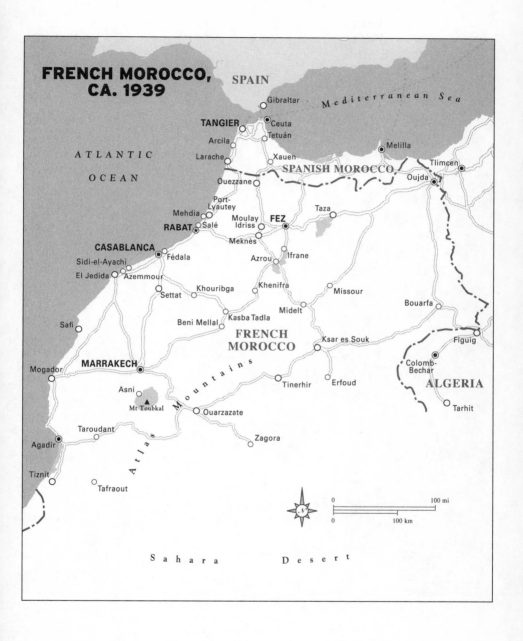

FRENCH MOROCCO, CA. 1939

SPAIN

Mediterranean Sea

ATLANTIC

OCEAN

Gibraltar

TANGIER
Ceuta
Arcila
Tetuán
Larache
Xauen
Melilla
SPANISH MOROCCO
Tlimcen
Ouezzane
Oujda
Port-
Lyautey
Taza
Mehdia
Moulay
FEZ
RABAT
Salé
Idriss
Meknès
CASABLANCA
Fédala
Azrou
Ifrane
Sidi-el-Ayachi
El Jedida
Azemmour
Settat
Khouribga
Khenifra
Missour
Bouarfa
Safi
Beni Mellal
Kasba Tadla
Midelt
Figuig
FRENCH
Ksar es Souk
MOROCCO
Colomb-
MARRAKECH
Bechar
ALGERIA
Mogador
Tinerhir
Erfoud
Asni
Mt Toubkal
Ouarzazate
Tarhit
Taroudant
Zagora
Agadir
Tiznit
Tafraout

Atlas Mountains

0   100 mi
0   100 km

Sahara   Desert

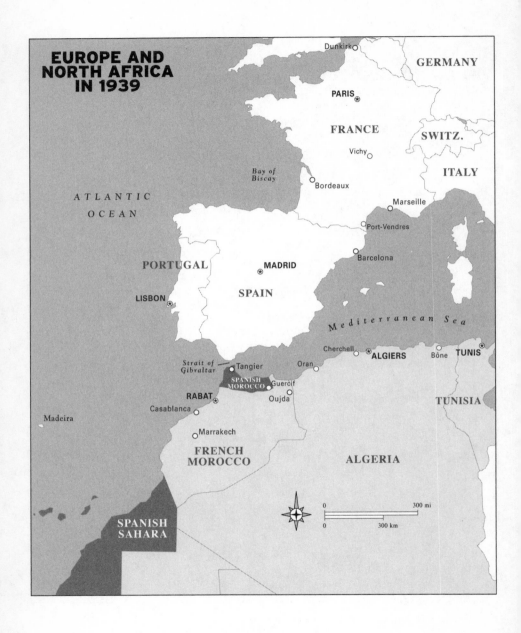

EUROPE AND
NORTH AFRICA
IN 1939

GERMANY

Dunkirk

PARIS

FRANCE

SWITZ.

ITALY

Vichy

ATLANTIC
OCEAN

Bay of
Biscay

Bordeaux

Marseille

Port-Vendres

PORTUGAL

MADRID

Barcelona

SPAIN

Mediterranean Sea

LISBON

Cherchell

Strait of
Gibraltar

Tangier

Oran

ALGIERS

Bône

TUNIS

SPANISH
MOROCCO

Guercif

RABAT

Oujda

TUNISIA

Casablanca

Madeira

Marrakech

FRENCH
MOROCCO

ALGERIA

0   300 mi

SPANISH
SAHARA

0   300 km

Contents

PART II: Torching Morocco

PART III: "Men Pass, France and Morocco Remain"

Prologue

A NTOINE DE SAINT-EXUPÉRY, A TWENTY-NINE-YEAR-OLD PILOT FOR Aéropostale, soared above the terra-cotta Moroccan desert on the edge of Casablanca. As the white city came into focus, he could make out the vast grey-blue reaches of the Atlantic Ocean to the west. He'd regularly been making the run between Casablanca and Dakar in the cockpit of a Latécoère 28, being one of the few pilots brave—or foolish—enough to fly the mail routes between France's African colonies. He'd cheated death at least once too, surviving a crash in the desert. There would be more of those.

Saint-Exupéry's career as a pilot began to take shape some eight years earlier in Casablanca in 1921, where he trained with the nascent French air force. He earned his wings while stationed with the 37th Flight Group at Cazes airfield, located a few miles outside the city. He'd tried his hand as a naval officer and an architect, but neither suited him. In an airplane, however, Saint-Exupéry found his métier. A lumbering man who seemed perpetually out of place, he felt at home in the sky. In Casablanca he learned to fly with a compass, which became his touchstone on the long desert flights that forged his reputation.[1]

After a disappointing sojourn in France, he'd returned to Casablanca in the late 1920s. The bustling port city's thirst for mail from France and elsewhere kept him in the air, but on the ground the streets of the white city offered an array of cafés in which to drink coffee and jot down his latest story between flights. He also spent time running Aéropostale's station at Cape Juby in southern Morocco, where he made sure his fellow pilots arrived and departed in one piece. If one failed to arrive on time, it was his job to search between Casablanca and Cape Juby for the lost man and mail. "I ready myself for great adventure with a certain vanity," he wrote of preparing for a search, "but then a far-away hum announces that the plane will come in, announces that life is altogether more simple than I had thought, that romanticism has its limits, and that the lovely persona in which I have dressed myself is somewhat ridiculous."[2] Saint-Exupéry turned his aerial exploits in French Morocco and beyond into fodder for his first novel, *Southern Mail*, published in 1929.

On returning to Casablanca after a trip to Morocco's southern frontier, Saint-Exupéry once described feeling like one of "the Crusaders arriving in Jerusalem."[3] He was a *colon*, or settler, the name given to the French and other Europeans who descended on Morocco in the early twentieth century. He was also a Christian and a member of the recently installed ruling class in a land long ruled by Muslims. His triumphant language simplifies, in many ways, Morocco's descent into colonialism. France came to Morocco not to convert the masses, although some missionaries would try, but to exploit its resources. The French crusaded not for Christianity but for colonialism and capitalism.

For centuries, the Alaouite dynasty had kept the Europeans at bay, even as foreign powers colonized the rest of the African continent. It was an impressive feat, given Morocco's prime location on the Atlantic coast of Africa. After an assertive push by Germany, France, and Spain at the beginning of the twentieth century, abetted by internal strife, the Europeans carved Morocco up for their own ends. Under the Treaty of Fez, signed in 1912, Spain received the northern quarter of Morocco, the city of Tangier became an international zone, and France took the southern three-quarters of Morocco, including Casablanca. With the establishment of the French Protectorate of Morocco, France now controlled a block of colonies in North Africa stretching from Morocco through Algeria to Tunisia.

French Morocco's first resident-general, Hubert Lyautey, was a skilled colonial administrator and fierce soldier with the heart of a romantic. Bookish by nature, he studied and absorbed Arab customs and language, developing a deep respect for Islam. Even as France imposed its will on Morocco, Lyautey did not want to see Moroccan culture erased. Lyautey pioneered the idea of the "protectorate," a style of government under which the colony retained its traditional cultural and political institutions rather than being assimilated.[4]

Under the French Protectorate of Morocco, the sultan continued to rule the country with guidance from France—meaning, of course, that France ran Morocco's economy, directed its finances, oversaw its defense, and represented its interests abroad. As a representative and descendent of Mohammed, the sultan remained in charge of his Muslim subjects' spiritual lives.

Instead of displacing the powerful families that had ruled Morocco for centuries, Lyautey cultivated their support. The pashas and their families possessed a connection with the Moroccan people and methods of maintaining control over the populace that the French could never achieve with either laws or soldiers.[5]

To bring French Morocco into the twentieth century, Lyautey launched a massive modernization project that transformed the country and Casablanca. He lured some of the brightest minds in architecture, social planning, education, and military affairs to the country to build cities, roads, schools, power plants, ports, and railroads. Modern agricultural techniques also bolstered Morocco's food supply.

In 1919, Edith Wharton accepted an invitation from Lyautey to visit French Morocco and wrote enthusiastically of the transformation underway. "Ten years ago there was not a wheeled vehicle in Morocco, now its thousands of miles of trail, and its hundreds of miles of firm French roads, are travelled by countless carts, omnibuses and motor-vehicles," she wrote in *In Morocco*.[6] Wharton even included an extensive list of Lyautey's accomplishments and applauded "the administrator's genuine sympathy with the traditions, habits and tastes of the people."[7]

UNDER LYAUTEY'S WATCHFUL EYE, a new Casablanca emerged on the coast of the Atlantic. It wasn't the first time the city underwent a transformation. While the town's origins are a little clouded, the first written reference to it appears in the eleventh century, suggesting that it was founded by Zenata Berbers, a Maghreb tribe known for building cities. The town's location and harbor made it a popular trade port during the Middle Ages and the Renaissance, providing ships exploring the western coast of Africa with a place to shelter. The Moroccans called the town Dar el-Beida, but either Spanish or Portuguese traders christened it "Casa Blanca" owing to its whitewashed buildings. The name stuck. Tired of enterprising Casablancans ambushing its ships, the Portuguese razed the town in the fifteenth century and stayed long enough to build a kasbah (or fortress) overlooking the harbor.[8]

In the 1770s, the Moroccan sultan, Sidi Mohammed ben Abdallah, decided to rehabilitate Casablanca and encourage its use again as a port. Even with steady improvements, travelers remained unimpressed with the town, which had grown to 1,000 inhabitants. "Dar Beyda is a small sea-port of very little importance," wrote William Lemprière, an English surgeon. "It possesses, however, a bay which admits vessels of pretty considerable burthen to anchor in it with tolerable safety, except when the wind blows hard at northwest, and they are liable to be driven on shore."[9] The derision continued well into the nineteenth century. "A less attractive spot than Casa Blanca it is difficult to imagine," wrote British botanist Joseph Dalton Hooker in 1878. "Not a tree gives variety to the outline or shelter from the blazing sun. The attempts made by the few residents to cultivate the orange and other useful trees have met with little success; and the eye seeks in vain the gay shrubs that adorn the southern shores of the Mediterranean."[10]

When Auguste Lahure, a Belgian colonel and head of the African branch of the Red Cross, arrived in Casablanca in 1888, he found a disconcerting city of contrasts. The white villas, terra-cotta houses, Arab-style green doors, lush gardens, and minarets climbing into the sky reminded him of Eugène Delacroix's paintings of Morocco. The picturesque charm, however, diminished in the "poor section," where Moroccans lived in houses made of cacti, aloe branches, and found objects and where garbage festered in crowded streets. Morocco's peasants had migrated to the coast in growing numbers, looking for work and escaping the cycle of famine in the interior, where drought and locusts regularly decimated crops. They provided a cheap source of labor for a ravenous city but rarely reaped the rewards.

As the port boomed at the turn of the twentieth century, Casablanca increasingly belonged not to the sultan but to the European powers keen to protect their trading interests. A new crop of money-hungry merchants also arrived, eager to export Moroccan wool, fruit, beans, oil, corn, and animal hides to the continent. "Casablanca was a haven of the uprooted: brash fortune hunters from Europe, Algeria or the Levant eager to pick over the meager bones of Moroccan commerce for their own profit," writes Douglas Porch.[11] The town also lacked the strictures and caste systems that governed the ancient established cities of the interior like Fez and Marrakech, making it easier to turn a profit. Once they did, European merchants could lead a luxurious life for very little money.

THE CASABLANCA THAT SAINT-EXUPÉRY experienced differed vastly from the ramshackle town of the nineteenth century. Lyautey's modernization program had been transforming the city for almost a decade when Saint-Exupéry arrived in 1921 for his pilot training and continued apace until World War II. Yet the remaking of Casablanca from a collection of misbegotten buildings into an orderly city only intensified the disparity between the Europeans and Moroccans.

The port received a massive overhaul, redesigned to be not only an important shipping destination but also a major rail and road hub. "It was truly a battle that had to be fought—a battle against the ocean that had to be tamed by two powerful breakwaters, today Casablanca's pride and joy," wrote Albert Charton of the Institute of Moroccan Studies in 1927. "The port is the lifeblood of this city."[12]

The breakwaters protected ships at anchor from the Atlantic's fickle weather and tides. New wharves and piers made it easier to unload cargo and people, while a transverse jetty was outfitted with powerful equipment for handling phosphates, which became Morocco's most important export.

FIGURE 1. Aeriel view of Casablanca in 1943. The dense area (*upper left*) is the ancient medina. The bottom half of the photo shows part of the modern *ville nouvelle*.
Sueddeutsche Zeitung Photo / Alamy Stock Photo

Two terminals, constructed to handle the large luxury liners the Protectorate hoped to attract with its colorful tourism campaigns, could process up to 1,500 passengers at once, limiting wait times and giving arriving tourists a good first impression of the city.[13] The fishing port, long the domain of vessels that trawled the Atlantic for sardines, also received an upgrade, making it easier to deliver the day's catch to the canning factories. There were also berths for the ships of the French navy, which patrolled the African coast.[14]

Nestled against the port, not quite far enough away to escape the smell of fish and fruit rotting in the midday sun, the ancient medina bustled with tradesmen selling their latest wares and women running their daily errands. Before the French arrived, the medina's walls had reached to the Atlantic, with sea gates to welcome visitors who arrived by water. Canons along the ramparts of the old Portuguese kasbah deterred pirates and other marauders. Now the medina no longer touched the sea as the port's new warehouses and wharves interceded.

Behind its walls, the medina still retained some of its mystery, the winding uneven streets leading to small squares dotted with cafés and family-run

FIGURE 2. Vendors sell pottery and baskets in Casablanca's
ancient medina, ca. 1944. *Portal to Texas History, Hardin-
Simmons University Library, Accession no. 90–06052–116*

shops. Beggars perched on corners, hoping for a scrap or a coin, while servants ran errands for households. The communal ovens that dotted the
quarter produced a steady supply of bread. On narrow streets, plain doors
in high walls opened to reveal exquisitely decorated *riads* that climbed three
stories and enclosed internal courtyards open to the sky. Five times a day,
the voice of the muezzin drifted over the buildings, beckoning the faithful
to prayer. On Fridays, shops closed, and men filled the streets, prayer rugs
tucked under their arms, as they filed toward the mosques.

The French built a wall around the medina, containing its colorful vi-
brancy and pockets of squalor behind stones and mortar. It was a physical
manifestation of Lyautey's belief that Casablanca should have separate European and native quarters.[15] Encased behind another wall was the *mellah*,
the Jewish quarter, whose streets sometimes narrowed such that two people
could barely pass each other without touching shoulders. The majority of
Casablanca's Jews lived in the *mellah*, enduring cramped conditions and, for
many, systemic poverty. During the 1920s, city planners chipped away at the
mellah, encroaching upon its houses, shops, and synagogues as they built
a new Casablanca. The needs of some of the city's poorest meant nothing
compared to the vision and desires of the French.[16]

Around the medina rose the *ville nouvelle*, or new city, the Casablanca
of postcards and tourist posters. The French used Casablanca as a labora-
tory for city planning and design, and architects inspired by the traditional,

FIGURE 3. Rue de Marseille in the *ville nouvelle*, where bicycles, cars, and donkey-led carts shared the road. *Kharbine-Tapabor*

modest whitewashed buildings created a modern white city. Hotels, shops, office buildings, and apartment blocks fanned out north and east of the port and ancient medina. The proportions echoed Paris, with street-level shops and cafés infusing neighborhoods with energy, while offices and the European bourgeoisie inhabited the floors above. Stark white facades, featuring Moorish details and art deco accents, gleamed against the cobalt North African sky. The white exteriors had a downside though: the spring sandstorms coated them with a fine layer of terra-cotta dust that dulled their luster until the rains came to wash them clean.

Jutting out from the entrance to the port, the Boulevard du 4ème Zouaves skimmed the edge of the medina and passed the swanky Hôtel Excelsior before turning into the Place de France, the gateway to the heart of French officialdom. Henri Prost, who worked on plans for extending Paris before joining Lyautey's staff, wanted a central square that brought together the civic and military elements of French rule, while providing a focal point for the city.[17] The buildings of the Place Administrative, as it was known, harmonized with one another, echoing each other's portions and spare ornamentation. Lyautey and Prost deliberately avoided creating buildings that looked like a Moroccan fantasia. Instead the buildings reflected the traditional approach to Arab architecture. "It is a point of honor in Arab construction that nothing should be revealed on the outside, save the profile, contours, and facades," wrote Lyautey in defense of the approach.[18] The spare style only heightened what became a monumental representation of French power.

The post office, which also housed Casablanca's telegraph and telephone exchange, made use of Morocco's tradition of ceramic tile work, with a mosaic of blue and green tiles encircling the building's exterior. The Hôtel de Ville (city hall), where residents came to attend to all matters related to birth, death, and taxes, featured an elegant clock tower that harkened back to a traditional French village. Visitors to the Palais de Justice (law courts), which anchored one end of the square, climbed a monumental staircase and passed through an imposing doorway to enter a grand portico from which to view the entire square. Buildings devoted to military affairs and the administration of trade and commerce flanked the other sides of the complex. At the far end of the square, Sacré-Coeur, an art deco cathedral, provided a place of worship for the 40,000 Catholics who called Casablanca home.[19]

As CASABLANCA GREW, so did its numbers. Between 1916 and 1927, the city's population nearly doubled from 67,000 to 120,000. Europeans, mainly French, poured in, becoming one-third of the populace, and by 1939, the city bulged with 350,000 inhabitants.[20] With their overhaul of Casablanca, the French succeeded in creating an economic powerhouse on the Atlantic coast—a city that attracted Europeans looking to capitalize on the rapidly emerging Moroccan economy and Moroccans seeking new opportunities.

By weaving itself so completely into the city's mental and physical fabric, France ensured that its fate in World War II would dictate, if not disrupt, Casablanca's future. As the war stretched beyond Europe and darkened North Africa, the port that fueled the rise of the new white city became both its most valuable asset and its greatest liability. From its quays, ships would depart, carrying soldiers to fight in France, and ships would arrive, bearing refugees attempting to escape Hitler's advancing armies. But nothing would prepare the city from the arrival of a seaborne American invasion force from across the Atlantic—one sent to liberate French Morocco from the grip of Vichy France.

PART ONE

Collaboration and Resistance

1

The Faraway War

Before they went to bed on Sunday, September 10, 1939, Moroccans moved their clocks and watches forward an hour. When dawn broke on Monday morning, their country would operate on the same schedule as France.[1] The synchronizing of clocks attested to the power of France over Morocco and also to the importance of Morocco to France's impending fight with Nazi Germany.

Ten days earlier, on September 1, 1939, German tanks had rolled into Poland and plunged Europe into war. With greater mobility and superior numbers of troops and armor, the Wehrmacht and Luftwaffe quickly overpowered Poland's valiant, if futile, defense. Taking only what they could carry, more than 200,000 Poles became refugees, fleeing to Lithuania, Romania, Hungary, and France. The Polish government took flight too, heading first to Romania and then, like so many of its people, to France.

On September 3, France and Britain honored their pledge to come to Poland's aid and declared war on Germany. Rather than immediately launching an attack, they adopted a defensive posture that aimed to avoid fighting until the balance of power shifted in their favor. French and British officials believed a "long-war strategy" would allow them to fully mobilize their armed forces and weaken Germany through economic warfare.[2] Years of strategic estimates and planning convinced French and British military planners that they could prevail against Germany if they had time to prepare their forces.[3]

The decision to go on the defensive yielded the curious illusion of war declared but not fought. The French called it *la drôle de guerre*—the Phoney War—the war that wasn't quite a war. For eight months, western Europe lived in suspended animation. All signs pointed to Adolph Hitler's turning west in the spring, after the winter snows melted and the ground grew hard enough for men and tanks to march forward. Until then, they waited and prepared.

As a colony of France, Morocco was expected to contribute to the French war effort by harnessing its economy and providing men to fight for the French army.

The campaign to make Moroccans embrace France's fight as their own began immediately. Mobilization for war began at 12:01 a.m. on September 2.[4] Two days later, on September 4, in Casablanca's mosques and elsewhere, imams read a letter from Sidi Mohammed ben Yusef, the sultan of Morocco, expressing his support for France in her battle with Germany: "From this day forward until the banner of France and its allies is covered in glory, we owe them our unreserved support. We will drive no bargains about supplying them with our resources, we will stint them no sacrifice. We were joined to them in times of peace and plenty and it is only right that we should remain at their side during the trials that they are undergoing, from which they will emerge, we are convinced, both victorious and great."[5]

With literacy low, let alone literacy in French, the most direct way for the sultan to reach his people remained the mosque. Within its walls, the sultan could speak directly to his people. The French, of course, approved his words.

Three weeks later, Sidi Mohammed again pledged his fidelity to France during a ceremony to honor Moulay Idriss, who founded of the Kingdom of Morocco in 788 and brought Islam to the people of the Maghreb. As the sultan uttered his pledge before Idriss's tomb, General Charles Noguès, the current resident-general, stood beside him. By uttering those words next to Noguès for all the world to see, the sultan provided yet another demonstration of his commitment to France—this time camera ready and perfect for printing in the newspapers read by the Europeans who called French Morocco home. The story would also be read out loud in the cafés that populated Casablanca and every city and town, as Moroccan men came together to drink thick coffee, trade gossip, and escape their wives.[6]

In their own way, Sidi Mohammed and Noguès embodied the duality of French Morocco in 1939. In his snowy white robes with the hood pulled over his head, Sidi Mohammed looked younger than his thirty years. Not even the trim beard that framed his face did much to mature his boyish looks. The son of the previous sultan, Yusef ben Hassan, and his Turkish wife, Lalla Yaqut, Sidi Mohammed was reared in Morocco and privately educated by tutors. He ascended the throne in 1927 when only eighteen. The Moroccan

FIGURE 1.1. Resident-General Charles Noguès with Sidi Mohammed and his son Prince Hassan. *AFP / Getty Images*

families who backed his candidacy and the French officials who endorsed it believed they had picked a sultan whom they could manipulate to do their bidding. But from the beginning, Sidi Mohammed demonstrated backbone and spent the 1930s urging reforms. He also played coy with the nationalists who wanted to liberate Morocco from colonial rule, preferring to keep them at arm's length rather than risk the ire of the French.[7]

General Charles Auguste Noguès, a handsome man of sixty-three years, symbolized the French colonial project. A graduate of the elite École polytechnique, Noguès chose a career in the army as an artillery officer. After working for Hubert Lyautey, the first resident-general of French Morocco, during the early years of his administration, Noguès distinguished himself in World War I, earning accolades for his leadership of the 17th Artillery Regiment. Marriage to Suzanne Delcassé, daughter of one of France's most celebrated diplomats, provided both personal happiness and a boost to an already promising career. Noguès soon found himself as comfortable in the drawing rooms of Paris as in the palaces of Morocco's pashas.

Noguès returned to Morocco in 1924, arriving in the middle of the Rif War, a bloody conflict between the Berber tribes of the Rif Mountains and Spain that spanned the early 1920s. When the conflict expanded to embroil the French, Noguès earned high marks from Moroccans for his defense of the ancient city of Fez. Offered the post of resident-general in 1936, he accepted after President Léon Blum convinced him that France would not export the domestic socialism of the Popular Front to Morocco.[8]

The sultan and Morocco's elites welcomed Noguès. They saw in him an heir to Lyautey, who, while disposed to military order, understood the value of Moroccan institutions. Noguès also possessed a deep, abiding love for Morocco that permeated his dealings with its people.[9] Noguès and Sidi Mohammed forged a strong relationship that allowed Noguès to carry out France's policies with his support. Now, in the time of France's need, the sultan would help rally his people to her aid.

ALONG WITH PUBLIC SUPPORT offered by the sultan, a series of *dahirs*, or decrees, designed to put Morocco on a war footing poured forth. While issued under the sultan's signature, the *dahirs* were written by the Residency, the name given to the French administrative center in Rabat. Price controls were implemented, along with a ban on war profiteering. New regulations governing the distribution of food, drugs, commodities, and minerals appeared. For example, those who made or distributed sugar, butter, margarine, condensed milk, coffee, or green tea had to declare their stocks and log all their transactions. The government also had to approve all exports. The Residency intended to keep a close eye on the food supply. Shortages bred unhappiness among the people, which could lead to protests. The administration also wanted to make sure that only France or her allies acquired any minerals, phosphates, lead, and iron, useful for the production of war matériel.[10]

Financial transactions were restricted too. Capital could only be exported with permission of the government. Imports of all merchandise, except gold, were terminated.[11] France extended currency measures to Morocco and its other colonies to protect the franc.[12] Starting in January 1940, Moroccan residents with incomes below 50,000 francs paid an additional 2 percent income tax to help finance the war. Above 50,000 francs, it increased to 4 percent.[13]

The Protectorate could now seize the property of German nationals and German companies who did business in Morocco.[14] It also banned all relations between people living in French Morocco and enemy nationals wherever they lived, along with anyone living either in Germany or its occupied territories. Anyone doing business with Germany or its territories could terminate contracts without legal penalties. Nothing could be imported from Germany. Anyone who supervised or was in possession of enemy property also had to report it within thirty days.[15] The Protectorate's intelligence service also began keeping close tabs on Germans and Italians in French Morocco, along with whom they met and what they said.[16] They, of course, received a helping hand from concerned citizens.[17]

New controls imposed on communications made it easier to spy on the residents of French Morocco. All coded telegrams, except those sent by governments, were forbidden. Businesses that used codes to ward off industrial espionage or individuals who simply weren't keen on clerks at the telegraph office knowing about their private affairs had few alternatives, particularly since their mail was subject to inspection as well. All telegrams also had to be written in French. On top of that, anyone wishing to send a telegram had to show it to the local authorities first. Telephone calls between cities within Morocco by private individuals were banned. Local calls also had to be conducted in French or the regional dialect.[18]

ON NOVEMBER 18, 1939, the throne room at the sultan's palace in Rabat filled with men in their finest attire. The diplomatic corps dressed in their dark suits and perfectly starched shirts provided a stark contrast to the fine cloth of the snowy white robes worn by the Mahkzen, the sultan's advisors. The officers of the French army and navy appeared gaudy beside them, their shoulders decked with gold and silver braid and chests heavy with enameled medals.

They had gathered to celebrate Throne Day (*fête du trône*), a commemoration begun in 1933 to recognize the day Sidi Mohammed became sultan. Originally organized by the nationalists to emphasize the centrality of the sultan to Morocco, the celebration grew in scope as the public's interest increased. What started as a critique of French power in the early 1930s by Moroccan nationalists and a reminder of the country's heritage had evolved into an elaborate Residency-sanctioned event.[19]

At the time of the celebration of Throne Day in 1939, the French had forced the nationalist movement underground and there were no rumblings of a resurgence. If any of its leaders thought about resuming their activities, Noguès made certain the new wartime regulations yielded stiffer penalties for challenging French authority.[20]

The throne room itself was a masterpiece of Moroccan decorative arts. Under foot lay marble tiles overlaid with plush rugs. Two colonnades, one on each side, ran the length of the room. Its double columns soared into arches carved with delicate geometric and botanical patterns. Mosaics rendered in blue, green, and white glass danced along the walls, while a chandelier of Venetian glass floated down from the ceiling. At the far end of the room sat a modest throne, a low-slung chair covered in velvet and adorned with carved legs painted in gold leaf.

On that day, the throne room also included a microphone for the first time. As part of the day's festivities, the sultan and the resident-general would give a speech, which the newspaper then printed. Now, thanks to technology, listeners of Radio Maroc would be able to hear the sultan's voice. Noguès spoke first, recalling the sultan's trip to Lorraine during the summer, where he visited with Moroccan troops poised to defend France. He also praised the resolute attitude and loyalty of the Moroccan people. The sultan again expressed his fidelity to France and offered glowing praise of Noguès for his great knowledge and understanding of Islam and for his stewardship of Morocco in a time of crisis.[21]

As part of the day's events, the sultan's guards performed feats of marksmanship and displays of horsemanship on the grounds before the palace. The bold colors of the guards' tunics, the polished hardware gleaming in the sun, and the elegant lines of their horses provided the pageantry that such a celebration demanded. Their gallant displays reflected a deep appreciation within Moroccan culture for military power and the prowess necessary to defend one's territory and people.

France's decision not to fight—but instead to play a waiting game against Germany—raised questions among the Moroccans about French military might. That worried Noguès, who knew that any sign of weakness would be noted, but he was a prisoner to Paris's decisions. As France went, so went Morocco. He would provide the troops requested by military planners— eventually sending 47,000 Moroccans to France to help with her defense— and trust that France could weather the impending Nazi onslaught.[22]

2

The Twilight

IN THE FALL OF 1939, JOSEPHINE BAKER STEPPED ONTO A STAGE unlike any other she'd graced in her sizzling career. Hoping to improve the morale of the troops who manned the Maginot Line, the massive defensive structure that guarded France's eastern border, the French high command had asked her to perform a series of shows. The bunkers and barracks were a far cry from the blazing lights of Paris's Folies-Bergère or the Casino de Paris where Baker dazzled audiences with her graceful dancing, comedic timing, and barely-there costumes.[1] Her shows gave the troops a reprieve from watching the German border and wondering when the Wehrmacht might strike. Instead, the men hooted and hollered as the thirty-three-year-old Baker sang and slinked her way through a series of French chansons.

Maurice Chevalier, who had made a career of musical comedy in Paris and Hollywood, joined Baker on the tour. The fifty-something Chevalier, sporting his trademark straw hat, insisted on going second, intending to finish the show in grand style. He didn't count on Baker's receiving calls for encore after encore, cutting into his performance time.[2]

The soldiers responded to Baker the same way Paris had ever since the ambitious African-American girl from St. Louis charmed the city with her comedic sensuality. After a hardscrabble childhood in St. Louis, Baker found her way to headline *La revue nègre* at the Théâtre des Champs-Élysées in 1925. The daring show, which featured Baker dancing in nothing but a feather skirt, set Paris talking—and it hadn't stopped since. Parisian society also welcomed Baker, giving her a level of freedom and acclaim that her country of birth could barely imagine, let alone offer. She embraced it all: the men, the jewelry, the clothes, the grand houses. She sauntered down the Champs-Élysées with

FIGURE 2.1. Maurice Chevalier and Josephine Baker meet with French soldiers at the front, November 1939. *Spaarnestad Photo / National Library of the Netherlands.*

her pet cheetah on a leash. She even gave product endorsements. When Casablancans opened their newspapers and magazines, they saw ads for Bakerfix, a *crème* "to keep your hair supple, brilliant, and in place," available at Casablanca's finer salons.[3]

IN DECEMBER, BAKER AND Chevalier returned to the stage together at the Casino de Paris, the legendary red-velvet music hall in the ninth arrondissement. Rationing, curfews, travel permits, sandbags around monuments, sweethearts kissing loved ones farewell, and daily stories about war preparation dampened Paris's joie de vivre. Inside the Casino de Paris, the halcyon days still reigned as people filled the theater to the rafters to see *Paris-Londres*, a revue celebrating Anglo-French friendship. The show—"a new spectacle of rhythm, charm, and beauty"—featured thirty-two "beautiful women" from Paris and London, along with performances by Chevalier, Baker, and Nita Raya. Chevalier opened the review with "Paris Will Always Be Paris," while Baker closed the show with "Mon coeur est un oiseau des îles." The sentimental song, in which she likens her heart a tropical bird, could melt even the hardest soldier's heart.[4]

The opening-night performance of *Paris-Londres* raised money for charity, with Baker's portion going to the French Red Cross.[5] Baker participated in other charity shows, including one at the beginning of February 1940 with Edith Piaf, Alibert, and other music hall icons.[6] During the day, Baker worked in a shelter on the Left Bank for homeless refugees, continuing a long-standing habit of helping those less fortunate than her. "My heart sank at the sight of those exiles, broken body and soul by defeat," she wrote.[7]

Baker also began working for the Deuxième Bureau, the French intelligence service, after being recruited by Jacques Abtey, who sought "honorable correspondents" who could feed his organization information about what they heard and observed: who met whom, who had tense conversations in corners at parties, who struck up unusual friendships. In the aftermath of Germany's invasion of Poland and its alliance with the Soviet Union, France's security services became obsessed with Fifth Column threats. A theatrical agent, Daniel Marouani, suggested that Abtey consider using Baker, telling him, "She is more French than the French." With her extensive social connections and adoring fans, Baker could be a trove of information.[8]

Abtey agreed to meet Baker at Beau Chêne, her home in the Paris suburb of Le Vésinet. There, instead of a starlet, he encountered a woman in a battered hat collecting snails from her garden to feed her ducks. The glamour came next, when Baker invited him to join her in the salon, where a white-jacket-clad servant poured them champagne before a roaring fire. "'France made me what I am,' she told him. 'The Parisians gave me their hearts, and I am ready to give them my life.'" It also didn't hurt Abtey's cause that he sported Nordic good looks—"young, blond, athletic, bursting with life," as Baker described him—and was exactly her type. Baker became both his lover and his student.[9]

"When I gazed deep into my own inner self, I realized that I would be incapable of functioning as a real spy," wrote Baker. "But intelligence work was different. It seemed the perfect way to fight my war."[10] It didn't take long for Baker to start passing along information gleaned at receptions at the Japanese and Italian embassies, parties she personally threw, and other affairs around Paris. "Sometimes," Abtey said, "she would write along her arms, and in the palm of her hand, the things she heard. I told her this was dangerous, but she laughed. 'Oh, nobody would think I'm a spy.'"[11]

As a celebrity and an American, Baker lived a charmed life in Paris, even after the start of the war. That wasn't the case for many of the refugees from eastern Europe who had sought sanctuary in Paris during the 1930s. In the weeks following the invasion of Poland, the Sûreté, the civilian police force, systematically made its way through Paris's refugee community, rounding up writers, artists, and intellectuals. The same impulse that prompted Abtey to recruit Baker—a desire to know if there were any Fifth Column threats within France—led to the mass arrests. Left-wing exiles with Communist ties or sympathies fell under suspicion, even if they preached against the evils of fascism. French authorities feared the Soviets might use these fellow travelers to undermine the Third Republic from within.

For Hungarian-Jewish journalist and aspiring novelist Arthur Koestler, the knock on the door came as he finished his bath on the morning of October 2. He soon found himself at Roland Garros tennis stadium, which had been converted into a makeshift processing center for "undesirable aliens." After nine days of sleeping on a tennis court strewn with straw and huddling under the bleachers, Koestler joined five hundred other prisoners at Le Vernet, an internment camp located southwest of Toulouse.[12] The barbed wire camp was divided into three sections: "A" for those with a criminal record; "B" for political prisoners, and "C" for those who were simply undesirable. Koestler lodged in section C, hut 34.[13]

Even though the Sûreté could point to a thick file documenting his Communist ties, Koestler had publicly fallen out with the party in 1938. Having once seen communism as a positive, modernizing force, he became disenchanted with the Soviet Union after learning that his friends had been subjected to show trials and shot in their aftermath. The Nazi-Soviet Pact of August 1939 further sealed his rejection.[14] Even though Koestler's conversion was real—not some Fifth Column charade orchestrated by Moscow—as far as the French security services were concerned, his long-standing ties to Communists made him questionable.

Koestler lived a grim existence at Le Vernet, his days organized around twice-daily roll calls and manual labor. He was assigned latrine duty, carting foul-smelling waste bins over icy terrain down to the river Ariège.[15] Care packages from friends supplemented the camp's meager daily rations of eleven ounces of bread and watery beef broth. When the prisoners were ordered to suffer the indignity of having their heads shaved, an enraged Koestler insisted on taking the scissors to his lush head of hair first. "I've been wanting to do it ever since I was child!" he told the barber before letting him finish the shearing.[16]

A campaign by his estranged wife, Dorothee, and his girlfriend, Daphne Hardy (Koestler had a complicated love life), to mobilize his influential friends resulted in his release from Le Vernet in mid-January 1940. Those same friends, however, could not secure a visa for Koestler to go to Britain. "It was impulsive and unfair on the part of the Sûreté to clap Koestler into a camp. He is as anti-Nazi as can be, and his one desire is to help the Allied cause in any way he can," wrote Harold Nicolson, head of Britain's Ministry of Information, in a letter lobbying to let Koestler in.[17] MI-5, Britain's domestic security service, refused to budge. It regarded Koestler's past membership with Friends of Socialist Unity, a group with ties to Marxist organizations intent on overthrowing imperialist Britain and France following Hitler's defeat, as grounds for denying him entry.[18]

Upon his return to Paris, Koestler devoted his time to finishing a novel that he started before his internment and continued to work on while at Le Vernet, thanks to an act of kindness by the camp's director. He channeled his anger, claustrophobia, and paranoia into the story of Rubashov, an old Bolshevik who finds himself arrested and put on trial for crimes he didn't commit by the state he helped create. The novel offered a scathing indictment of the Soviet system, while capturing Koestler's own psychological trauma from his imprisonment. As Koestler turned out pages in German, Hardy translated them into English. When they sent off the manuscript to Koestler's publisher in London, they popped a bottle of champagne.

Darkness at Noon, which appeared in bookstores in the fall of 1940, would become one of the most important novels of the twentieth century and make Koestler's international reputation.

Koestler mailed the book on May 1.

Hitler's assault on western Europe began ten days later.[19]

The Sûreté would come again for Koestler, careening him on a path to Casablanca.

3

The Fall of France

IN MID-MAY 1940, CAPTAIN ANTOINE DE SAINT-EXUPÉRY, NOW thirty-nine years old, occupied the cockpit of a Potez 63 as it soared over northwestern France and Belgium. From a height of 33,000 feet, he followed streams of "ghastly whitish jelly" cutting through the landscape. Saint-Exupéry could only see the lines of smoke; he couldn't see or feel the heat of the advancing flames as they licked and then consumed French villages and farms. Diving down close wasn't the job of a reconnaissance pilot. His mission was to stay aloft and use the camera mounted on the plane to capture the progress of the war below.

Click. The German army advanced.

Click. The French army retreated.

Click. The refugees poured south, clogging the roads.

Saint-Exupéry had returned to uniform after the war erupted, wrangling an assignment with the French air force's 2/33 Reconnaissance Group.[1] It was an almost surreal assignment for a man who had become an international literary star only a year earlier, following the publication of *Wind, Sand, and Stars*. The memoir chronicled his time delivering mail for Aéropostale, the precursor to Air France, in northern Africa and South America. He portrayed flying as an almost mystical experience in which man and nature do battle in the air. Saint-Exupéry also captured the crude realities of flight in its formative years—controls freezing, engines cutting out, oxygen evaporating—and his near-death experience after crashing in the Sahara while attempting to break the speed record between Paris and Saigon.[2]

Despite the literary accolades bestowed on him, Saint-Exupéry relished his return to flying as part of a squadron. The young pilots who greeted his arrival with apprehension—living legends were often best viewed from afar—soon found an amiable colleague and, when needed, a mentor. It also didn't hurt that Saint-Exupéry shared with his squadron mates the benefits of fame, including swanky dinners in Paris and use of his De Soto sports car.[3]

Now, instead of flying over the sandy waves of the Sahara or battling the sheer cliffs of the Andes, Saint-Exupéry floated above a springtime countryside ripped to shreds by advancing armies. His major fear wasn't an engine stalling out over the desert but attracting the attention of German antiaircraft guns or Luftwaffe squadrons sent to blow him out of the sky.

ON PAPER, THE BATTLE of France started out as a somewhat fair fight. Germany committed 136 divisions, while the Allies—France, Britain, Belgium, and Holland—mustered 144.[4] Ten of the French divisions, some 73,000 men, or 9 percent, came from France's colonies, including five divisions drawn from North Africa.[5] The men of Morocco, Algeria, and Tunisia who answered the call to defend France manned the Maginot Line or joined the French army in Flanders or along the river Meuse.

On May 10, 1940, the Wehrmacht swooped northwest, around the Maginot Line, rolling its tanks and marching its troops through Belgium and the Netherlands, having already made short work of Luxembourg. France expected to fight the Germans in central Belgium, just as in World War I, and committed the bulk of its army and resources to defending its northeast border. The Germans, however, broke through French lines in the Ardennes on May 15. That same day the Dutch capitulated. Rotterdam lay in rubble, and the Germans threatened to lay waste to Amsterdam.[6]

With the French army crumbling under the German assault, French prime minister Paul Reynaud asked for the resignation of General Maurice Gamelin, who served as commander in chief. To take his place, Reynaud called upon General Maxime Weygand, the seventy-three-year-old commander of the Army of the Near East. After the invasion of Poland, Weygand had been called out of retirement to help solidify the French position in the Middle East. Now he was about to step onto center stage.[7] To bolster the nation's confidence, Reynaud also recruited the aged Marshal Henri-Philippe Pétain to serve as vice premier. Pétain, a French icon, had orchestrated France's victory at Verdun in 1916.[8]

Not content to rely on confused reports reaching Paris, Weygand decided to survey the front lines for himself on May 21 in hopes of targeting Germany's weak spots and organizing an offensive assault. As Weygand flew over German positions, bullets strafed his plane. In Ypres, he attempted to meet with Lord General John Gort, who commanded the British Expeditionary Force, but the effort went awry. Gort hadn't been informed in advance of Weygand's plans, and terrible travel conditions prevented him from arriving in time to meet his French colleague. Hundreds of thousands of Belgian refugees desperate to avoid falling under Germany's control clogged the roads, making it difficult for Allied military forces—including generals—to maneuver.[9]

Unable to return to Paris by plane owing to German bombing raids, Weygand made his way to Dunkirk, braving the roads during an air raid. From there, he caught a torpedo boat to Cherbourg and a train to Paris. Arriving mid-morning the following day, he took a taxi to French army headquarters at Chateau de Vincennes when his personal car failed to appear at the train station. The chaos in northwestern France turned Weygand's survey into a farce, but his findings were grave. The situation, he told Reynaud, was much worse than they had thought.[10]

On May 26, five days after Weygand's survey, the Allies started evacuating troops from Dunkirk in northern France. In the middle of the operation, Belgium capitulated. On June 4, the Germans marched into Dunkirk, having traversed northern France.

The Wehrmacht also continued its surge southwest toward Paris, launching an assault at the river Somme on June 5. The French lines, bruised and bloodied, held at first. Weygand managed to cobble together forty divisions by transferring men from garrisons across France, diverting units from the Alps, and pulling troops off the Maginot Line. Soon there would be no more men to call up. The German army kept growing as more soldiers arrived from the east, amassing one hundred divisions along a hundred-mile stretch.[11]

On June 10, Italy joined the fray, declaring war on the Allies. Later that night, Weygand declared Paris an open city, and the French government packed its bags and fled.

As the Germans moved south, so did the refugees, with estimates suggesting that between 6 million and 8 million people participated in the mass exodus. "They were evacuating. There was no way to house them. Every road was blocked. And still they were evacuating," wrote Saint-Exupéry. "Somewhere in the north of France a boot had scattered an ant-hill, and the ants were on the march. Laboriously. Without panic. Without hope. Without despair. On the march as if in duty bound."[12]

The refugees took to the roads in wagons, lumbering trucks, shiny new cars and old cars wiped of dust and smelling of fresh oil, and any piece of

farm equipment with wheels that would allow them to carry the remnants
of their life. With dismay, Saint-Exupéry watched Orconte, the village he'd
called home while billeted with the 2/33, "go to pieces." For ten days, the
townspeople watched the refugees from the north flow through their village before deciding to join the river. "I do not expect ever to be free of that
clinging, viscous memory," he wrote in *Flight to Arras*.[13] Orconte wasn't the
only town to evaporate. In Chartres, home to the soaring twelfth-century
cathedral, only 800 townspeople out of 23,000 stayed behind. Lille went
from 200,000 to 20,000. In the south, towns and cities swelled as the refugees
arrived. Bordeaux bloomed from 300,000 to 600,000, while Pau exploded,
growing from 38,000 to 150,000.[14]

THREE MILLION PEOPLE LEFT Paris, draining the city of more than half
its population. Josephine Baker continued performing *Paris-Londres* at the
Casino de Paris even as the French and German armies did battle, but the
audiences soon disappeared.[15] She too joined the exodus south during the
second week of June, heading not for Bordeaux or Marseille but for Les Milandes, her chateau in the Dordogne. Along for the ride in the Packard were
her maid Paulette, a Belgian refugee couple she'd been helping, and three of
her dogs. She also packed extra petrol for the trip, storing it in champagne
bottles.[16]

Before she left her house at Le Beau Chêne, Baker arranged for its contents to be packed up, including suits of medieval armor, a gold piano, and her
bed, which had once belonged to Marie Antoinette. Feather pillows, sheets,
towels, and other comforts of home also went onto the trucks. She could buy
another house, but replacing the items that made it her home—that attested
to her rise to fame—would be harder.[17]

The goods eventually arrived at Les Milandes, which burst with people
who had heard of Baker's sanctuary in southwestern France. Among her
guests were members of the Lion family. Baker had married Jean Lion, a
dashing Jewish businessman, in 1937 after a whirlwind courtship. With the
marriage, Baker acquired French citizenship, but also a husband she never
saw. She continued to perform at the Folies-Bergère, returning home close
to dawn, while Lion kept business hours, rising for the day as she retreated
to her bed. Neither wanted to change their schedules or tame their wandering eyes. The marriage also proved disappointing in another way. Baker
desperately wanted a child, but she never conceived. Baker and Lion filed
for divorce after fourteen months. The presiding judge remarked, "Here are
two people who never had a chance to get to know each other." Yet, Baker

found herself once again living with Lion, whom she still cared for, as he recuperated from his battle wounds at Les Milandes.[18]

ON JUNE 14, 1940, German troops marched into Paris. The following day, Verdun fell, and 400,000 French troops surrendered. On June 18, another evacuation from Dunkirk began, with 192,000 Allied soldiers transported across the English Channel; 110,000 of them were French.[19] The German army continued to consume French territory with astonishing speed, reaching south to Lyon and all the way to the Atlantic coast, where they marched into Brest and Nantes.

After meeting with the British, Reynaud and his cabinet traveled to Bordeaux, arriving on June 15. The world associated the ancient Atlantic coast port with French wine, but it had also sheltered the French government in times of strife. The city provided sanctuary from the Germans in 1870 and during World War I—and would do so once again in 1940.

With German troops in Paris and the second evacuation of Dunkirk imminent,[20] the cabinet had to decide whether to continue to fight or agree to an armistice. During the previous weeks, Reynaud had asked his staff to explore the possibility of relocating the government and what remained of the army to North Africa and using the French colonies as a base of resistance. General Charles de Gaulle, the undersecretary of state for national defense and war, reported that only 60,000 men per month could be sent across the Mediterranean, not the 450,000 Reynaud envisioned. Admiral Jean-François Darlan, commander in chief of the French navy, gave an equally depressing report. Transporting that many men required at least two hundred ships, but the bulk of the French navy was dispersed. It would take time to assemble an evacuation fleet. There was also the issue of what to do with the men once they arrived in North Africa. France treated its North African colonies as a recruiting ground for soldiers—not a place to maintain a large standing army.[21]

The discussion about whether to agree to an armistice also revealed the depths of conflict within Reynaud's cabinet and between the politicians and the military. If France decided to surrender, who should bear the burden of culpability? The politicians wanted to blame France's defeat on the military, while the military wanted fault to lie with the politicians.

Weygand opposed the government's fleeing France, which would place the burden of signing a cease-fire on the army. Doing so would bring it dishonor, something Weygand could not stomach. He believed a strong army, in which the people had faith, was necessary to keep France from succumbing to revolution and anarchy. Without it, the Communists and anarchists might step into the void and seize power.

Weygand's views might have been dismissed as the paranoid ranting of a conservative Catholic with royalist leanings who disdained the left-wing politicians of Reynaud's cabinet—had Pétain not agreed with him. Pétain believed France's long-term survival required a formal armistice. "The duty of the government is, whatever happens, to stay in the country or lose its right to be recognized as a government," he told the cabinet. "To deprive France of her natural defenders in a period of general disarray is to deliver her to the enemy." Pétain vowed not to leave the "soil of France" and to "accept the suffering which will be imposed on the fatherland and its children."[22]

With each mile the Germans advanced into France, the chatter among the French cabinet to seek an armistice grew louder. Weygand had even suggested the option as early as May 25. Reynaud remained steadfast, but by mid-June he found himself outnumbered. After making a last-ditch plea to keep fighting, Reynaud tendered his resignation on June 16.[23]

His resignation cleared the way for Pétain to become the new prime minister of France and to petition Germany for an armistice. "It is with a heavy heart that I say to you today that it is necessary to cease fighting," Pétain told the French people by radio. "I have this evening approached the enemy to ask if he is ready to try to find, between soldiers, with the struggle over and in honor, the means to put an end to the hostilities."[24]

The cease-fire went into effect on June 20. It had only taken Hitler's armies six weeks to conquer France. Two hundred thousand French soldiers lay wounded, with another 92,000 dead. Another 1.5 million French soldiers became prisoners of war.[25] French Morocco's bill for defending France: 2,000 dead and 18,000 taken prisoner by Germany.[26]

ON SATURDAY, JUNE 22, shortly after 6:30 p.m., the formal surrender discussions began at Compiègne, a small town fifty miles northeast of Paris. In 1918, the Germans had surrendered to the French at the very same spot. To heighten the French humiliation, Hitler arranged for use of the same railway dining car that had hosted the 1918 ceremony.[27]

The Third Reich's leadership turned out in force for the negotiations, including Field Marshal Wilhelm Keitel, Deputy Führer Rudolf Hess, Air Minister Hermann Göring, and Foreign Minister Joachim von Ribbentrop. General Charles Huntzinger led the French delegation. The two men, Pétain and Weygand, who had argued so passionately for an armistice, did not attend.

Pétain instructed Huntzinger to terminate surrender negotiations with the Germans if they demanded two things: the French fleet or France's colonial possessions. Germany asked for neither. Instead, the Germans would occupy the northern three-fifths of France, including Paris and the entire Atlantic seaboard. France would also pay 400 million francs a day for the privilege of being occupied. French prisoners of war would continue their captivity, but France had to turn over any German soldiers or pilots in their possession, along with any refugees with a history of anti-Nazi activities. Anyone joining a French resistance effort faced the death penalty.[28]

Believing the demands could have been more onerous, Pétain agreed to the terms and split France in two. French Morocco now answered to Pétain's new government.

4

Rebel for the Republic

O N JUNE 24, THE STEAMSHIP *MASSILIA* SAILED INTO CASABLANCA'S harbor carrying twenty-seven political refugees of France's government. Leading the exodus were Georges Mandel, the minister of interior, and Edouard Daladier, the minister of defense and onetime prime minister.[1] Three days earlier, they had left France fearful for their lives and the future of their country. In the wake of Paul Reynaud's resignation and the ascendency of Henri-Philippe Pétain and Maxime Weygand, those who argued against signing an armistice with Germany found themselves in jeopardy, believing reluctantly that if they remained, they would be thrown into prison—or, possibly, shunted in front of a brick wall and a firing squad.

Mandel, a fifty-five-year-old Jewish journalist turned politician, had been one of the most vocal supporters in Reynaud's cabinet of continuing the war. When Reynaud expressed doubts about that tack or started to waver, Mandel kept him steady, a task that became more difficult as June progressed and the drumbeat for an armistice grew louder.

When the government arrived in Bordeaux on June 15, before the armistice was declared, Mandel had established a command center at the local prefect to stay apprised of developments across France. He feared Weygand and others favoring an armistice would continue to fabricate information to advance their cause. To bolster his argument for preserving the army, Weygand had already falsely claimed that a Communist government had been established in Paris. Mandel feared he might try such dirty tricks again.

MANDEL'S BURGEONING RESISTANCE CELL became a threat to Pétain and Weygand's plans to pursue an armistice as well as to the stability of their hours-old government. They grew anxious about reports detailing the stream of people visiting Mandel. When they received information suggesting he had given money and weapons to a gunman, along with orders to assassinate ministers who opposed him, they jumped on the rumor.

On the afternoon of June 17, a tired and pale Mandel ate lunch with Beatrice Bretty, his companion, at Chapon Fin, one of Bordeaux's finest restaurants. The pleasant meal in the dining room filled with diplomats, politicians, and refugees offered a small patch of peace following a frenetic forty-eight hours. As the dessert course arrived, the colonel in charge of the Bordeaux gendarmerie appeared with an arrest warrant. Instead of putting up a fight, Mandel asked if he might be allowed to finish his cognac. The colonel agreed. Upon finishing his drink, Mandel rose to his feet, kissed Bretty's hand, and followed the officer out of the restaurant. General Jules-Antoine Bührer, who had worked for Mandel as the inspector general of the colonial troops, was also arrested.[2]

The restaurant had been packed, and news of Mandel's arrest quickly spread through Bordeaux. Speculation ran rampant, particularly since Mandel's position was supposed to give him immunity from arrest. Was this the beginning of a coup d'état? Did the Germans demand his arrest? As Bordeaux boiled with conspiracies and anger, Pétain realized he had made a serious mistake. That evening, Pétain called Mandel and Bührer to his office, where he informed them that an investigation had revealed the charges to be false. They were free to go.

An angry Mandel refused to let Pétain simply wave the matter away. After accusing Pétain of being the "puppet of his entourage," Mandel demanded an apology. Dissatisfied with Pétain's offering, Mandel dictated one, which Pétain obediently copied down and signed. "I am convinced that the information was unfounded and was designed to provoke disorder. I apologize for the arrest and insist that this unfortunate incident have no further consequences," read the final lines. The apology represented a small victory after a fraught day, but Mandel's arrest demonstrated how perilous his situation had become.[3]

The day before his arrest, Mandel had refused an offer from General Edward Spears, the British military liaison, to help him leave France. Spears wanted him to go to London, where Mandel could speak to and for France as an opponent of the armistice. "Someone whose name was known and carried weight must make them see the shame of accepting defeat while they were undefeated and it was still possible to fight for France," Spears told him.

Mandel also sensed that Spears wanted him to leave because he worried what would become of him once the Nazis arrived. "You fear for me because I am a Jew," said Mandel. "Well, it is just because I am a Jew that I will not go tomorrow; it would look as if I was afraid, as if I was running away."[4]

Now, however, Mandel realized he needed to escape. On June 18, the day after his arrest, he requested to join Lord Lloyd, the British minister for colonies, on his flight back to London. Lloyd had come to Bordeaux to offer British assistance in evacuating the French government and army to North Africa. However, some confusion led Lloyd to believe that Mandel also wanted to bring his companion, Bretty, which the minister considered an extraordinary request and refused.[5]

MANDEL'S ARREST OCCURRED IN an environment of massive uncertainty and anxiety. Reynaud resigned on June 16. Pétain made his radio address on June 17 telling the French people about the request for an armistice. The Germans agreed to discuss terms, but then remained silent and offered no other details for two days. Hitler was busy discussing—or more to the point, dictating—the terms of the armistice with Benito Mussolini. Italy entered the battle late and added little of material value to the fight but nevertheless wanted to claim French territory.[6] The ad hoc arrangements in Bordeaux, the vast unknown of what lay ahead, and the gapping silence amplified an already tense situation.

It also provided opportunities.

During the communications void, a proposal materialized for the French government to depart for North Africa and establish a new government in Algiers. General Charles Noguès, who was in Algiers coordinating French military efforts in North Africa, had been sending a stream of messages urging the government to continue the fight from the colonies. "The army, air force, and navy all demand the continuation of the struggle in order to preserve our honor and keep North Africa for France," he wired on June 17. "If the government has no objection, I am ready to take responsibility, without formal authorization, for the continuation of the war with all the risks that that action involves."[7] Noguès's enthusiasm reflected popular sentiment in France's North African colonies. Regrouping across the Mediterranean and making plans to continue the fight could still save the metropole.

Evacuating the bulk of the French army to North Africa may have been impossible, but key elements of the government could easily leave and establish a new resistance government. A plan coalesced for the president, Albert Lebrun, along with the leaders of France's two legislative bodies, the Senate and Chamber, to leave as soon as arrangements could be made. Pétain, as prime minister, insisted on remaining behind.

As the North Africa scheme materialized, the forces in favor an armistice also regrouped.[8] On the morning of June 20, the Germans finally gave notice of their willingness to receive a French delegation that evening. While Pétain failed to grasp that the mass departure of the government would endanger and potentially void the armistice, Weygand and others did not.[9]

Pierre Laval, the right-leaning former prime minister, undertook the task of keeping President Lebrun in France. As Lebrun made preparations to leave for North Africa, Laval appeared at his lodgings, flanked by a dozen men, and berated the amiable Lebrun. Did the president not realize that if he left, the remaining government would lack authority? Did he realize that taking the seals of state also meant taking the authority to make laws? Did he want to be considered a traitor by his people? Laval ended the verbal assault with a demand that Lebrun resign rather than leave. Humiliated and browbeaten, Lebrun decided to stay in Bordeaux.[10] Those who had already gathered in Perpignan, in preparation for departure for Algiers, including Léon Blum and the Ministry of Colonies staff, were called back.[11]

ON JUNE 21, THE *Massilia* departed for Casablanca, an intermediary stop on the way to Algiers. The ministers and parliamentarians who waited at Le Verdon for their departure had never received word to return to Bordeaux. The assembled group comprised some of the fiercest critics of the armistice. Mandel and Daladier were joined by old friends and allies Pierre Mendès-France, Jean Zay, Michel Tony-Révillion, and César Campinchi. Prominent deputies Paul Bastid, André Le Troquer, and Pierre Viénot also made the trek. Many brought their families with them, including Mandel and Mendès-France.[12]

As the ship sailed south, its passengers fretted about who wasn't onboard. Reynaud, Blum, and Bührer had failed to materialize before the ship weighed anchor, and the poor state of wartime communications made it impossible to determine what had become of them. Even without his core comrades in arms beside him, Mandel remained determined to carry on. When Louis Marin, one of the deputies, questioned why no Pétain supporters had joined them, Mandel brushed his concerns aside. "I have no more confidence in the government than you do, but I must get to North Africa," said Mandel.[13]

For Pétain and his supporters, the departure of the *Massilia* represented a victory: they had succeeded in dispatching their fiercest opponents to North Africa. After the war, Charles Pomaret, who became Pétain's interior minister, characterized the *Massilia* as a trap laid and executed by Admiral

Jean-François Darlan to remove the troublesome opposition. Darlan suggested and made available the *Massilia*. Darlan diverted the ministers to Le Verdon. And Darlan authorized the *Massilia*'s sailing on June 21.[14]

TWO DAYS OUT FROM Le Verdon, in the middle of the Atlantic, the *Massilia*'s passengers learned that France had signed an armistice with Germany. They also received news that their colleagues scheduled to depart from Perpignan would not be joining them. This band of men who felt so certain of their opposition to the armistice now found themselves isolated and alone in the middle of the Atlantic.[15]

The rebels—that is what they became as soon as the armistice was signed—gathered in the *Massilia*'s reading room to discuss their next move. Should they go back to Bordeaux and attempt to influence Pétain's government? Should they sail for Britain? Or should they continue on their current course? Mandel believed the choice was clear: they must sail to North Africa and establish a resistance government with the twenty-seven politicians onboard the *Massilia*. For Mandel, the voyage transformed from a journey undertaken out of fear into a mission to reestablish France.

In his determination to reach North Africa, Mandel received some inadvertent assistance from the ship's captain. Darlan ordered him to deliver the parliamentarians to Casablanca. There would be no course changes.[16]

AS THE REBELS SAILED for Casablanca, the British government gave General Charles de Gaulle, a relatively unknown French solider, a chance to rally the French people.

The advent of war had dramatically changed de Gaulle's fortunes. Once a staff officer maligned by his superiors for his advocacy of tank warfare, he seemed to be one of the few who understood Germany's armored tactics—and with good reason. Hitler had studied and annotated de Gaulle's book advocating a mechanized infantry, while de Gaulle's own superiors ignored it.[17] De Gaulle's appointment to Reynaud's cabinet thrust him into the crucible of the decision making over the armistice, of which he proved a fierce opponent. With the ascent of Pétain and his supporters, de Gaulle feared it was only a matter of time before he too was arrested or shunted off to a distant post where he would be unable to aid resistance efforts.

After de Gaulle made a convincing case to General Spears, the British military liaison, that someone must rally the French people to stand against Pétain's government and inspire the French Empire to join with Britain,

Spears helped him leave Bordeaux. With Mandel still refusing to go to London, de Gaulle offered a pallid but viable alternative. On the morning of June 17, de Gaulle went to the airport acting as if he intended to see Spears off, only to dive into the hatch of the plane as the door closed for takeoff.[18]

On June 18 and 22, de Gaulle took to the BBC airwaves to make an impassioned plea to the people of France. He called upon any soldier, sailor, or skilled worker who could reach Britain to join him in continuing the war. "We still have a vast empire, our fleet is intact, and we possess large sums in gold," he told listeners. "We still have allies, who possess immense resources and who dominate the seas. We still have the gigantic potentialities of American industry."

He also hoped to stir the hearts of any French men or women who had doubts about the armistice. "I say honour, for France has undertaken not to lay down arms save in agreement with her allies. As long as the allies continue the war, her government has no right to surrender to the enemy."[19]

SHORTLY BEFORE 8:00 A.M. on June 24, the *Massilia* sailed into Casablanca's port. News of the armistice came as a blow, but arrival in French Morocco offered a glimmer of hope. Noguès's telegrams suggested that he could serve as an ally in the effort to reconstitute the French government overseas.

But instead of being greeted with open arms, the parliamentarians were confined to the ship. Georges Fourneret, director of the Sûreté, feared that letting them wander around Casablanca when emotions remained raw about the armistice might create a volatile situation. They might encourage the residents of Casablanca to join their cause.[20] Mandel and Daladier eventually received permission to visit the Port Police, where they spoke with Admiral Armand d'Harcourt, who commanded French naval forces in Morocco. When they asked if they were prisoners, d'Harcourt offered an ambiguous but troubling answer: he was awaiting further instructions from Noguès.[21]

Around 11:00 a.m., Jean Morize, the delegate general to the Residency, arrived at the port. After the cold reception of the morning, Morize's warm welcome came as a relief. Morize had worked with Mandel during his tenure as minister of colonies. Over a cordial lunch, Morize provided details about the armistice and told them about de Gaulle's broadcast from London. After lunch, Mandel and Daladier stretched their legs and explored Casablanca under the watchful eye of the Sûreté. As they shopped at the Carnival of Venice hat shop, a lively discussion about the armistice occurred with others in the shop, precisely the kind of exchange Fourneret feared.[22]

Late in the afternoon, Fourneret escorted Mandel and Daladier to the Residency in Rabat, a sixty-mile drive north of Casablanca. They hoped to speak with Noguès, who remained in Algiers, and asked his cabinet chief to arrange a telephone call. While they waited for his return, Daladier paid a courtesy call on Madame Noguès, whom he knew personally. Mandel visited the British consulate, where he spoke with consul general Leonard Hurst. A couple hours later, Mandel and Daladier finally spoke with Noguès. Mandel encouraged him to take action, but Noguès demurred, saying that nothing could be done until more details were known of the armistice. Mandel found it astonishing that Noguès believed what Pétain and the others told him about the nature of the armistice. The longer the conversation continued, the more his anger grew. "Bordeaux represents nothing!" shouted Mandel into the receiver and hung up.[23]

5

Two Men and a Mission

I N London, members of Britain's War Cabinet gathered for a late-night discussion at 10 Downing Street, home of the prime minister. At such meetings, Winston Churchill and his ministers, who represented the scope of military, diplomatic, and domestic concerns, discussed the latest developments in the war and what to do next. The ministers "were the only ones who had the right to have their heads cut off on Tower Hill if we did not win," wrote Churchill.[1]

A telegram from Leonard Hurst, the British consul general in Rabat, recounted Georges Mandel's arrival in Casablanca earlier that day and his intention to establish a resistance government. Mandel and the others planned to depart within twenty-four hours unless Protectorate officials became more hospitable. Another telegram from Algiers indicated that Charles Noguès had yet to make a public statement about continuing the fight from North Africa, but all signs pointed to his falling in line with Pétain and Weygand.[2] There was even a rumor going around Casablanca that he had been summoned to Bordeaux.[3] Another telegram suggested that French resistance could continue in North Africa if the British provided arms and munitions.

Like Mandel, Edouard Daladier, and others who opposed the armistice, the British government wanted the French to continue the fight. In addition to giving Charles de Gaulle airtime, Churchill delivered a blistering radio address aimed at driving a wedge between the Bordeaux government and the French people. He charged that the terms of the armistice would "place not only France but the French Empire entirely at the mercy and in the power of the German and Italian dictators."

For Britain, the French colonies in North Africa appeared the key to carrying on the war against Germany for emotional and practical reasons. A stream of telegrams from Algiers, Rabat, and Casablanca reported on the local French population's support for a resistance government. If given the chance, they would rally behind a strong resistance leader. In the days leading up to the armistice and after, the British wondered if that man might not be Noguès. Along with controlling men and matériel, he commanded the respect of both Europeans and Moroccans. If Noguès did not want to join the resistance, the British had to consider the possibility of staging a coup d'état and replacing him—very possibly with Mandel.

The cabinet decided to send a representative of the British government to Morocco to see what aid could be given. Duff Cooper, the minister of information, volunteered for the job. He and Mandel were old friends, which would inspire trust. Cooper also had a taste for gambling and fast living, which made dashing off to North Africa to establish a new French government precisely his sort of game. The cabinet decided that a military man should accompany Cooper and drafted the eminently practical General John Gort for the job.[4] Along with serving as chief of the Imperial General Staff during the 1930s, Gort had commanded the recent ill-fated British Expeditionary Force in France.

AT 7:00 A.M. THE next morning, June 25, a Sunderland flying boat took off for French Morocco carrying Cooper and Gort. The four-engine seaplane offered the fastest means of traveling the 1,250 miles between London and Rabat.

While Cooper and Gort made their way south, word came from Algiers that Noguès had made a radio broadcast announcing his support for the armistice and offering assurances that the integrity of North Africa would be maintained.[5] Germany's promise to leave the French colonies and the fleet under Pétain's control convinced him not to oppose the agreement. For Noguès, keeping French Morocco out of German hands trumped all other considerations. He lacked the men and matériel to continue the war without support from Bordeaux, which wouldn't help him, or Britain, which could not provide immediate reinforcements. It would be months before a British Expeditionary Force could land in North Africa, and opposition to the armistice among French army and navy officers in North Africa had dwindled once the terms became known. Faced with a lack of support on all sides, Noguès chose to save his career and do what he could to steer French Morocco through the war.[6]

Twelve hours and one refueling stop later, Cooper and Gort touched down on Rabat's Bou Regreg river. The plane's arrival and novelty—flying boats were a rare sight in Morocco—drew attention from onlookers. "The crowd, however, seemed quiet and depressed, flags were flying at half-mast and there was no sign of welcome," wrote Cooper.[7]

A party of French officers passing by on a boat gave Cooper and Gort a ride to the shore, where Brigadier General Eric Dillon, the British military liaison to Noguès, waited for them. Dillon, who had flown in from Algiers, warned them not to expect a favorable reception. Noguès had issued orders to prevent them from seeing Mandel and Daladier.[8] Even as Cooper and Gort made their way south, Hurst had sent a telegram to London urging that their mission be cancelled, given its slim chance of success.

Now that they were there, Hurst tried to arrange for Cooper and Gort to meet at once with Mandel, who remained on the *Massilia* in Casablanca's harbor. As a first step, William Bond, the British consul in Casablanca, was asked to deliver a message to Mandel: Cooper would meet him wherever and whenever he wanted. Within a few minutes of the telephone call to the British consulate in Casablanca, Residency delegate general Jean Morize phoned and informed Cooper that he was forbidden to communicate with Mandel. Morize hoped Cooper would comply and not put him "in the awkward position of having to take action which would be most distasteful to him." The timing of the call suggested to the British that their phone lines had been tapped.

After apologizing for not providing more notice of his visit, Cooper asked to call on Morize at the Residency. When Cooper arrived, he found Noguès's deputy in a "highly nervous and emotional state" but anxious to extend every courtesy. Cooper informed him that he had been sent to French Morocco to determine whether there was any possibility of carrying on the war from North Africa. Morize offered the new French line: any division in the ranks would lead to the collapse of the country. "What yet remained must stick together," said Morize.

When Cooper tried to press him, Morize insisted he must obey his instructions, even if he found them distasteful. "He said that if General Noguès ordered him to shoot himself he would obey, but the orders that he had were even more cruel," wrote Cooper. Noguès ordered him to treat Mandel and the others as virtual prisoners. "The ex-Ministers were old friends of his and he had recently been serving under their orders. But as things were at the present he had no option but to obey his instruction and he counted on me to do likewise," wrote Cooper.

Given the situation, Cooper feared that if he tried to see Mandel, he would fail and possibly provoke an "unpleasant incident." Instead, he sent a coded message explaining the situation—the French couldn't eavesdrop on that—to Casablanca for delivery to Mandel. Cooper hoped Mandel would head for Gibraltar or Britain, and he would provide transport if necessary.[9] Over dinner with Dillon, Cooper and Gort decided that remaining in Rabat or attempting to reach Casablanca was futile. Mandel had also managed to send a message indicating that he was under surveillance and could not meet, which only reinforced their determination to leave. Rather than return to the hotel, where they had been harassed by the police, the Brits decided to spend the night on the river in the Sunderland.

In Casablanca, things grew worse for Mandel and the others. They were barred from leaving the *Massilia*, which was then dragged out into the middle of the harbor. Mandel would not be able to send or receive any messages with the outside world.

WHEN DAWN BROKE ON the next morning, June 26, Cooper and Gort departed for Gibraltar. Once ensconced on the British military base, they discussed next steps with their military colleagues. Telegrams flew to Casablanca stressing the importance of finding a way to help Mandel reach Britain and urging Bond and Hurst to collaborate with the captain of the British destroyer now floating off the coast of Casablanca.[10]

Noguès, who had returned to Morocco, had other ideas. When Hurst asked permission to transfer the passengers on the *Massilia* to a British destroyer, Noguès responded with indignation and outrage. He forbade Mandel to leave for England and instructed Admiral Armand d'Harcourt to prevent any clandestine landing by the British.[11]

The following day—with no sign of Cooper and Gort's return—Noguès allowed the *Massilia* to redock and the parliamentarians to disembark. When Mandel and Beatrice Bretty reached the quay, they discovered five policemen waiting for them. Noguès had issued an arrest warrant for Mandel because of his meeting with Hurst, believing that their conversation had led to Cooper and Gort's trip to Morocco. With his arrest, Mandel entered state custody—and never again regained his freedom.[12]

With Mandel in jail, Britain's hope of his spearheading a resistance government collapsed. On June 28, Charles de Gaulle became leader of the Free French government.[13] "I agree that General de Gaulle might well try by his presence to crystallise the movement here," wrote Hurst upon hearing the news. "In spite of growing criticism of us and him, I consider that by swift action he might still rally the majority to his call."[14]

6

The Evacuees

THE SAME DAY THE *MASSILIA* ARRIVED IN CASABLANCA, ANOTHER
ship docked at the trade pier. The *Mohamed Ali Kebir* carried the last
batch of evacuees from Gibraltar.[1] Within a week of the start of the German
assault on France in May 1940, General Sir Clive Liddell, the governor of
Gibraltar, had asked the War Cabinet for permission to evacuate the civilians.
Britain had governed the slice of land at the confluence of the Mediterranean
and the Atlantic since the eighteenth century, making the care of the 20,000
civilians who called Gibraltar home the responsibility of His Majesty's Government. The families of British servicemen would return to England, while
the Gibraltarians would depart for French Morocco as soon as transport
could be arranged.[2]

On May 21, notices appeared around Gibraltar announcing the evacuation of the elderly and families with children under fourteen. "His Excellency
fully realizes that these steps will cause a great deal of anxiety and inconve-
nience, but they are being taken in the interests of the persons concerned and
in those of the Fortress," read the notice from the governor.[3] Between May
21 and June 24, more than 13,000 residents of the British colony arrived in
French Morocco.

Those Gibraltarians who could afford to pay their own way and arrange
their own accommodations, 328 adults and 166 children, departed on May
21 aboard the *Gibel Dersa*. The following day, the first of the government-
arranged voyages began, with 950 women, children, and old men boarding
the *Mohamed Ali Kebir*. With accommodations below deck limited, the majority of passengers spent the overnight journey sleeping under the stars.

The sudden arrival of the evacuees in Casablanca caused headaches for Protectorate authorities. The hasty and improvised nature of the departure from Gibraltar made it impossible to do proper paperwork. After the first batch of evacuees arrived without visas on the *Mohamed Ali Kebir*, Protectorate officials demanded that all subsequent evacuees obtain visas before departing. In particular, the French worried the Gibraltarians might include Spanish Republicans and wanted them vetted before their departure. They weren't keen to introduce political refugees into Morocco, lest they create trouble. But Gibraltar officials argued that obtaining the visas was impossible, since the list of departing evacuees only became final minutes before the ship sailed.[4]

The first Gibraltarians who arrived in Casablanca received lodgings in four dance halls converted into makeshift dormitories. Curtains hung on wires and temporary walls created cubicles on floors originally designed to host couples swinging to the latest music from Paris and New York. When mattresses weren't available, the families slept on straw. At every site, the bathroom arrangements proved inadequate for the number of people crammed into the buildings. The dislocation and communal living came as a shock to many Gibraltarians, who only a few days before had cooked dinner in their own kitchens and slept in their own beds. Now, they ate mass-produced meals provided by a caterer and stood in line to use a bucket.[5]

As more evacuees arrived, two other dance halls became dormitories. A camp was also established to house nine hundred evacuees in Aïn Chok, an area southeast of town. With lodging in Casablanca running short, Protectorate officials urged Gibraltarians with friends in other Moroccan cities to impose on their hospitality.[6] Soon evacuees were living in Safi, Mazagan (El Jadida), and Oued Zem.

As June progressed and more Gibraltarians arrived in Casablanca, French and British authorities discussed long-term arrangements. The Gibraltarians couldn't camp out in dance halls indefinitely. The evacuees were then classified into three categories: those who could pay for nice lodgings, those who could afford inexpensive housing, and those who would need financial assistance.[7] The French also wanted the British government to pay for the construction of five hundred huts to house between 2,500 and 3,000 Gibraltarians. The camp would be located in Roches Noires, an industrial part of Casablanca close to the docks and known to be a bit dodgy.[8]

THE ARRIVAL OF THE last group of evacuees from Gibraltar on June 24 occurred two days after the signing of the armistice between France and Germany. In the days following, part of the French fleet assembled at Mers-el-Kébir, Algeria. Tied up at the long jetty were four of France's most powerful capital ships: the aging battleships *Bretagne* and *Provence* and the modern battle cruisers *Dunkerque* and *Strasbourg*. Six destroyers and a seaplane carrier also docked. Up the coast, Oran's harbor provided sanctuary for seven destroyers and four submarines. The impromptu gathering represented the second most powerful fleet in Europe after Britain's Royal Navy.

Missing from the gathering were France's two modern battleships, both unfinished but still formidable. *Richelieu* sailed for Dakar, while *Jean Bart* set a course for Casablanca. The French wanted the ships out of the reach of Germany's clutches.

With the advent of the armistice, Admiral Jean-François Darlan, now serving Henri-Philippe Pétain as minister of the marine, reassured his captains and sailors that they continued to sail for France and not Germany. Nor did the French fleet belong to Britain. With an eye to preserving the fleet's integrity, Darlan issued a series of orders to his captains. Demobilized warships must remain French, sail under a French flag, be manned by reduced French crews, and sail from a French port, either metropolitan or colonial. If Germany threatened to seize them, captains were to scuttle their ships, rendering them useless, or sail for the United States. A captain should also take precautions to ward off sabotage and ensure that any former ally attempting to seize a ship would not be able to use it subsequently. And under no circumstances should any captain obey orders given by a foreign admiralty.[9] "To respond to outside interests would lead our territory into becoming a German province," wrote Darlan. "Our former allies are not to be listened to: let us think French, let us act French."[10]

WHEN WINSTON CHURCHILL LOOKED at France's navy, he saw a weapon too powerful for Germany to resist—and he didn't believe Hitler would honor his promise not to seize the fleet. If Germany gained control of the French navy, it could dominate the Mediterranean and cut off Britain's access to the Suez Canal. Without the resources of its empire, Britain could not hold out against the inevitable German assault. Churchill believed the Bordeaux government must be made to see reason and sail the fleet to a safe port, whether neutral or British. If Pétain and Darlan refused, Churchill faced the difficult decision of whether to authorize the sinking of the French fleet. Could Britain attack its former ally?

Churchill, a pugnacious former soldier with a talent for words and a love of drink and cigars, had served as prime minister since May 10. After spending the 1930s as a backbencher who argued in vain for Britain to wake up to the threat posed by Germany, he now shouldered the task of directing the war. "I have nothing to offer but blood, toil, tears and sweat," he told the House of Commons in his maiden speech as prime minister. The speech also offered an unflinching assessment of the task before the people of Britain. "We have before us an ordeal of the most grievous kind. We have before us many, many long months of struggle and of suffering," he warned. Britain would, however, wage war with "our might and with all the strength that God can give us" to defeat Germany. "You ask, what is our aim? I can answer in one word: It is victory, victory at all costs, victory in spite of all terror, victory, however long and hard the road may be; for without victory, there is no survival."[11]

Churchill believed Britain's survival hinged on the fate of the French fleet. After intense discussions, the War Cabinet decided it must give the French three options with regard to the ships now docked at Oran and Mers-el-Kébir. Option one: the French could sail their ships to British ports and continue the fight with Britain. Option two: the French could sail their ships to British ports with reduced crews, after which the crews would be repatriated; at the end of the war, Britain would return the ships to France and pay for any damages sustained. Option three: the French could sail the ships with reduced crews to a French port in the West Indies or Martinique, where they would be demilitarized or entrusted to the United States for the duration of the war.

The instructions sent to Admiral James Somerville, who commanded Britain's Task Force H based in Gibraltar, listed the options and concluded, "If none of the above alternatives are accepted by the French you are to endeavor to destroy ships in MERS EL KEBIR but particularly DUNQUERQUE and STRASBOURG, using all means at your disposal."[12]

ON JULY 3, BRITAIN came for the French fleet. That morning, in a surprise operation, British troops boarded and seized control of all French ships docked in Portsmouth, Plymouth, Falmouth, Southampton, and other British ports. The bounty included two aging battleships, eight destroyers, two light cruisers, and six submarines, along with two hundred smaller ships. British troops encountered resistance on only two ships. Four sailors were killed on the submarine *Surcouf*, while an unsuccessful attempt at sabotage occurred on the destroyer *Mistral*. The success of the operation confirmed for Churchill how easy it would have been for Germany to seize French ships docked in ports they controlled.

As the surprise operation unfolded in Britain, Admiral Somerville and Task Force H sailed into position off the coast of Mers-el-Kébir, Algeria. The ships under Somerville's command included the battleships *Ark Royal* and *Valiant*, the battle cruiser *Hood*, two cruisers, eleven destroyers, and one aircraft carrier. The French, however, did not know of Task Force H's arrival. Somerville staged his ships so they were not visible to sailors on watch, tucking them behind a mountainous outcrop northeast of the port. The armistice prevented the French from using aerial reconnaissance, aiding Task Force H's stealth approach.

While Task Force H moved into place, Captain Cedric Holland, who had served as the British naval attaché in Paris, delivered a document outlining British demands to Vice Admiral Marcel-Bruno Gensoul: Gensoul could either join the British or agree to sink his ships within six hours. Should he choose to do neither, Somerville had orders "to use whatever force may be necessary to prevent your ships from falling into German or Italian hands."[13]

At 10:00 a.m., Gensoul offered a reply. The assurances previously given that no French ships would fall into German hands stood. If the British attacked, the French would defend themselves. He also reminded Somerville, "The first shot fired against us would have the practical effect of aligning the entire French fleet against Great Britain—a result diametrically opposed to that which the British government is seeking."[14]

By noon, the negotiations had reached an impasse, and Gensoul ordered his ships to prepare for action. With all signs pointing to battle, British airplanes dropped magnetic mines at the entrance to the harbor, a strategy designed to bottle up the fleet and prevent it from leaving the port. Discussions continued but with no change in results. Gensoul scrambled to contact his superiors, but the limitations imposed by the armistice on communications between the metropole and North Africa made receiving a rapid response difficult. The French admiralty also happened to be in the midst of relocating to Vichy, the new capital of unoccupied France, providing yet another maddening complication for Gensoul.

As the afternoon ticked away, Somerville decided to force the issue. He gave Gensoul until 3:00 p.m. to come to terms. At 2:40 p.m., Gensoul requested a meeting with Holland. After railing against Britain's foolhardy approach, Gensoul showed Holland a copy of Darlan's order specifying that ships be scuttled or sailed to America. He assured Holland that he would sail the ships to Martinique—but not while under threat of attack from the British navy.[15]

Holland believed Gensoul's stance followed the spirit of the British demands and hoped to convince Somerville of the same. The situation, however,

FIGURE 6.1. "Don't forget
Oran!" says this Vichy propaganda
poster. The British attack on the
French fleet at Mers-el-Kébir
poisoned relations between the
former allies. *Library of Congress*

N'oubliez pas Oran!

quickly deteriorated. Gensoul received from the French admiralty no message other than a notice that all ships at Toulon and Algiers had been ordered
to sail for Mers-el-Kébir and Oran. Britain intercepted the transmission and
warned Somerville to "settle matters quickly or you will have reinforcements
to deal with." Somerville issued another ultimatum: Gensoul had until 5:30
p.m. to accept British terms or his ships would be sunk. For Gensoul, the
reinforcements sailing for Mers-el-Kébir indicated that the French admiralty
wanted him to resist British demands and fight. He resolved, however, to
make the British fire the first shot.[16]

At 5:54 p.m., the British assault began, as *Hood*, *Valiant*, and *Resolution*
opened fire. For the next ten minutes, 144 fifteen-inch rounds rained down on
the harbor and the French ships at dock. The *Bretagne* took a direct hit in her
midsection, causing the magazine to explode. The battle cruiser sank shortly
after 6:00 p.m., sending 977 French sailors and marines to their deaths.

The *Dunkerque*, *Provence*, and *Mogador* all sustained damage and loss
of crew before being run aground. The *Strasbourg* managed to get underway, narrowly avoiding a slew of shells that landed in its now empty berth.
Skirting the mines laid by the British at the mouth of the harbor, *Strasbourg*
and four destroyers made for open water. A bombing run by British Fairey
Swordfish launched from the *Ark Royal* attempted to sink the *Strasbourg*,
but her antiaircraft guns kept them at bay, allowing her to escape to Toulon.

When the smoke cleared, the French had suffered 350 wounded and 1,297 dead. Vichy France no longer commanded the second most formidable fleet in Europe.

FRENCH REPRISALS FOR THE attack at Mers-el-Kébir came swiftly. In Morocco, British ships were barred from leaving port, and some crews were thrown in jail. The telegraph lines to the British consulates in Rabat and Casablanca were cut and guards posted at the entrances. Both Leonard Hurst and William Bond, British consuls, burned their cyphers and archives and made plans to leave the country. Their American counterparts agreed to help seal the consulates and assist any British subjects in need.[17]

On July 6, three days after the attack, Protectorate officials insisted that all Gibraltar evacuees leave Casablanca immediately, or "measures would have to be taken for their protection" against a rising tide of anti-British feeling.[18] French Morocco, like France, seethed with anger against Britain. These sentiments ran particularly high in Casablanca, home to a French naval base. The sailors and their families stationed in Casablanca had known men on the ships attacked, making the assault an affront not only to France but to them personally.[19]

In the wake of the Mers-el-Kébir attack, Governor Liddell warned London that the Gibraltarians might be expelled from French Morocco. The evacuees presented an easy way for the French to exact revenge against the British. Their removal would also absolve Protectorate officials of arranging for long-term accommodations. Liddell, however, reminded his London colleagues, "They cannot be allowed to return here for defense reasons."[20] The Gibraltarians weren't exactly welcome in Britain either. John Anderson, the minister for home security, told the War Cabinet it was "desirable to prevent these refugees from being landed in this country if possible, as we had no means of dealing with them except in internment camps."[21]

The Foreign Office scrambled to find a new home for the Gibraltarians, sending out pleas to British colonies and friends. Portugal would allow 2,500 evacuees to live on the island of Madeira, provided no Republican Spaniards were among their number. They also wanted no publicity.[22] South Africa agreed to accept a small number of evacuees who were "British Subjects of English race" but did not want "Spanish people of Spanish extraction" because they would not be a politically "desirable element to receive in the Union."[23] Mauritius agreed to take 5,000, provided Britain helped import building materials to construct living quarters. In the meantime, the Gibraltarians would have to live under canvas tents.[24] Jamaica said it could put 2,000 in hotels temporarily, but building a camp to accommodate them would take two months. "I regret being unable to be more helpful but it is not perhaps realized that the number proposed is bigger than any town in Jamaica except Kingston," wrote the island's governor.[25]

While telegrams zipped back and forth between London, Lisbon, and Kingston, the problem of how to transport the Gibraltarians was solved by good timing. A convoy of British ships carrying 18,000 French soldiers who wanted to be repatriated began arriving in Casablanca. The ships could turn around and take the evacuees to a new location when the arrangements were finalized.[26]

THE FRENCH HAD OTHER ideas. Gibraltarians, clutching suitcases and bags to their chests, waited on the quay as the first British ships arrived on July 10. "No sooner had the repatriated soldiers disappeared from view than a mass of civilians poured through the dock gates and spilled out across the road leading to the jetty. Black troops forced them forward with rifle butts," wrote Commodore Kenelm Creighton, who commanded the British convoy. "It was plain that the French Admiral, livid after Oran, was intent on using these helpless scraps of humanity to embarrass the British."[27]

Admiral Armand d'Harcourt ordered Creighton's ships impounded. A ship would be allowed to leave only once it had boarded 1,000 Gibraltarians. Creighton pleaded with d'Harcourt and his officers for time to make the ships habitable and to arrange for water, food, and portable kitchens. After fourteen days of soldiers living, sweating, and defecating below deck, the troop ships needed a thorough cleaning. Not doing so placed the passengers' health at risk. The galleys of the ships also weren't designed to produce meals for 1,000 people. Creighton worried about the passengers' safety too. The troop ships, designed to transport able-bodied men who could scurry up and down vertical ladders between decks, could be hazardous or unmanageable for small children and the elderly.[28]

Creighton's pleas for time and consideration fell on deaf ears. As the British and French argued, the Gibraltarians baked under the hot North African sun. Creighton asked if they could wait in an unused warehouse, but the French refused. As the hours ticked by, the mass of evacuees on the docks increased with the arrival of each new busload. It was a humanitarian disaster in the making.[29]

Creighton reported the problems to the British admiralty and announced his intention to sail for Gibraltar. It seemed the only viable solution. "For Heaven's sake don't—we had enough trouble getting them out," wrote Admiral Dudley North, his commanding officer. Governor Liddell again voiced his opposition to their return. Nevertheless, risking his career, Creighton ordered the ships to head there anyway. The six-hour voyage, much of which could be passed on deck, would pose little harm to the evacuees.[30]

By July 13, the evacuees had all returned to Gibraltar, where the British government didn't treat them much better.[31] Governor Liddell refused to let the Gibraltarians disembark, fearing they would not agree to leave again. After a series of protests, he allowed them ashore so the ships could be cleaned and properly supplied. The Gibraltarians, of course, scattered soon after. Twelve thousand were evacuated again, this time to Britain, arriving in time to experience London during the Blitz, before moving on to Northern Ireland. Two thousand went to Madeira under the auspices of Portugal. Another 1,500 crossed the submarine-infested waters of the Atlantic to live in Jamaica.[32]

7

A Painful Surprise

A T THE BEGINNING OF JULY 1940, LESS THAN TWO WEEKS AFTER THE armistice, Marshal Henri-Philippe Pétain's government—no longer welcome in Paris, the seat of kings, revolutionaries, and now Nazis—made the trek from Bordeaux to Vichy. Vichy had become the new capital by elimination. Clermont-Ferrand, the home of tire manufacturer Michelin, didn't have enough space to house the government. Marseille was considered far too shabby and seedy to play midwife to a new France. Lyon, France's second-largest city, bustled with a large working class, which didn't suit the Pétain government's right-wing sensibilities. Toulouse, the home of Aéropostale, lacked good rail connections.

That left Vichy, a pleasant spa town with enough villas and hotel rooms to house 30,000 French bureaucrats on short notice. It also had proximity in its favor, being four hours to Paris by train and only thirty miles to the demarcation line between the occupied and unoccupied zones. As a summer town, it fostered the notion that the nightmare of a divided France would be over by the fall and everyone could return to Paris. That was certainly the goal of Pétain, who likened Paris to "the heart and brain of the nation."[1]

Vichy's mineral baths had attracted visitors since the Roman era, but it became a fashionable destination in the 1860s when Emperor Napoleon III made regular visits. Claiming to benefit from the curative properties of its sulfur springs, the emperor used his holidays as a feint for seeing his mistress. He also ordered the construction of a casino, church, town hall, and train station, transforming the sleepy town into a showcase for Second Empire architecture.[2] After World War I, Vichy became the destination of choice for well-to-do Parisians seeking to escape the city. By day, visitors strolled on the promenade and dined in cafés, taking note of the famous and notorious who came for a cure. Aching feet and other aliments found relief in visits to one of the town's numerous bathhouses. By night, visitors slipped into silk and diamonds to hear the voices of Europe's premiere sopranos and tenors soar in the newly built art nouveau opera house and gamble their fortunes away at the casino.

On July 10, 1940, from the seats of the opera house, what remained of the National Assembly voted to give Pétain the power to revise the French constitution, effectively ending the Third Republic. The following day, Pétain issued a constitutional act abolishing the office of president.[3] Albert Lebrun, whom former prime minister Pierre Laval had cowed into not leaving for North Africa in order to preserve France, was out of a job. Pétain now served as head of the French state, occupying the role of both prime minister and president. Another act gave Pétain the power to appoint and dismiss ministers and pass laws through the Council of Ministers. He also dissolved Parliament. With his handpicked ministers, Pétain would rule unoccupied France unencumbered by the opinions of anyone who might disagree with him.

The Hôtel du Parc, an elegant and expensive hotel in the heart of the city, became the nexus of power in the Vichy government as Pétain took up residence on the third floor and his deputy Laval claimed the floor below. The Colonial Ministry colonized the Hôtel de l'Angleterre, and the Ministry of the Interior set up shop in the casino. As hotel rooms became offices, armoires and bathtubs were pressed into service as makeshift filing cabinets. The improvised quarters became permanent after the Germans reneged on their promise to allow Pétain's government to return to Paris.[4]

The Free French government in London dubbed Pétain's regime "Vichy," turning a word popularly associated with an expensive brand of water, travel posters, and cold soup into a shorthand for collaboration and capitulation. When pronounced by non-French speakers, it even sounded sinister.[5]

As PÉTAIN'S GOVERNMENT SETTLED into Vichy, an unsettling demand arrived from Germany on July 15. Now that Hitler had conquered France, he intended to turn his attention to Britain. To aid this endeavor, Hitler requested construction of eight airfields near Casablanca, in locations to be determined by a German commission. Vichy would provide equipment and personnel for the airfields, along with additional land for antiaircraft batteries. Germany would also have unrestricted use of French merchant shipping, North African ports, and the Rabat-Tunis railroad, along with unfettered access to North Africa's communications network. Vichy authorities would be held accountable for any acts of sabotage. The request was to be fulfilled immediately.[6]

Though he couched the demand in terms of Vichy's aiding Germany's offensive against Britain, Hitler intended the new airfields at Casablanca to fulfill much grander ambitions. Hitler had trashed the Treaty of Versailles, launched a massive rearmament program, and invaded Poland and western Europe as part of his plan to obtain Lebensraum (living space) for the German people. That was only phase one. Hitler's master plan called for three wars: the first against France, the second against Russia, and a third against the United States.[7]

Initially, Hitler regarded the United States as a dangerous opponent, because through immigration it had brought together the best strains of the Nordic race at the expense of Europe. That view changed during the 1930s in the wake of the Great Depression. America's slow recovery led Hitler to believe the country was a racial melting pot hampered by the elevation of mongrel races and Jews to its highest offices. The only hope for the United States was its rescue by Nazi Germany and for German Americans to take their rightful place at the helm of its government.[8] France's rapid defeat and the failure of the United States to come to her aid assured Hitler and his deputies that a war with the United States would end quickly.

By using France's fleet and her naval bases in North Africa, Germany would be able to launch an offensive across the Atlantic. Any offensive also required air power, both for bombing targets and delivering troops and supplies, so Germany needed airbases in North Africa as well. The flying range of airplanes of the era required that trips across the Atlantic be done piecemeal. The northern route from Britain to the United States involved stops in Ireland, Greenland, Canada, and New York. The southern route began in Lisbon and island-hopped, with stops in the Azores and Bermuda, before reaching Miami.[9] Casablanca, however, lay directly across from South Carolina, making it a good staging point for a German assault on the United States. It was also controlled by Vichy, which answered to Berlin, unlike Spain or Portugal. French Morocco was so enticing that as early as 1937, the German navy and air force both sent agents to scout locations.[10]

Despite coveting use of France's North African colonies, Hitler had not made their transfer a condition of the armistice. He feared doing so would delay the conclusion of fighting with France, which would not willingly relinquish its empire, and delay his plans to attack the Soviet Union. Hitler also had little interest in occupying North Africa or making it part of a greater German empire. He considered the region the dominion of France, Italy, and Spain.[11]

BRITAIN'S JULY 3 ATTACK on Mers-el-Kébir changed calculations on both sides. The French used the attack to justify its request that Germany withdraw its insistence that France demobilize its troops in North Africa. "If we do not wish to run the danger of losing to both sides, we must direct the attention of Germany and Italy to the considerable sacrifices to which we are agreeing so that we can defend the honour of our name," wrote Maxime Weygand.[12]

Germany had proved agreeable to the French requests but began to doubt the willingness of Vichy to fight in the wake of events at Mers-el-Kébir. In response, Vichy had severed relations with Britain and launched an attack against Gibraltar that proved more symbolic than effective. On July 6, the British aircraft carrier *Ark Royal* attacked the French battle cruiser *Dunkerque*. German concerns about Vichy's tepid response to British aggression increased after yet another British attack on July 8, this one against the battleship *Richelieu* moored in the harbor at Dakar. *Richelieu*'s stern suffered severe damage.

The events at Mers-el-Kébir and Dakar only confirmed Hitler's longheld view of the French as feckless. When Vichy requested permission to operate its navy as it saw fit—a request lodged the same day as the *Richelieu* attack—he decided to draw the line. He would not allow the French to reassert control at the expense of German aims. The answer from Berlin was no.

PÉTAIN CALLED GERMANY'S REQUEST to establish a foothold in Casablanca "a painful surprise." Only a week before, Vichy had requested a meeting in Berlin to discuss becoming an "associated power." The armistice did not account for its ongoing battle with Britain, an enemy it shared with Germany. Pétain and his advisors had demonstrated a willingness to collaborate, but allowing the Germans a permanent presence in North Africa was another matter entirely.[13]

Weygand, who served as Pétain's minister of defense, was particularly incensed by Germany's demand. General Karl von Stülpnagel, president of the German Armistice Commission, said the French were required to snap their heels together and obey. Weygand, however, had no intention of allowing France to cede so much to Germany so quickly. During cabinet meetings, he helped orchestrate a rejection of German demands. Vichy would provide what the armistice called for "and not a comma more." Pétain backed the recommendation of his cabinet.[14]

The letter sent to Berlin on July 17 cloaked the French refusal in the courtly and overly polite language of diplomacy. It lauded German greatness, while insisting on the need to adhere to the armistice. France refused to become a vassal in its own colonies. "Can such subservience be regarded as an equivalent consideration for the deferment of certain conditions of the Armistice? I think not," read the letter signed by Pétain. "If the French government signs the demands advanced by General von Stülpnagel, it would . . . accept the guardianship if not the supremacy of the German military authorities over a considerable portion of this part of the globe." Germany's insistence on pursuing these demands would necessitate establishment of a "new relationship" between the two countries. "I have a sincere desire that after so many quarrels our countries grow to understand each other better," wrote Pétain.[15]

After submitting the letter, Vichy's leaders awaited the response from Berlin with trepidation. Their relationship with Hitler was too new to know how he might react to a refusal. They might get a tongue lashing, or he might nullify the armistice and march troops into unoccupied France. Instead, Berlin remained silent.

ON JULY 19, THE members of the Reichstag and Germany's senior leadership gathered at the Kroll Opera House in Berlin to listen to Hitler deliver his first speech since October 1939. Instead of hosting a production of Wagner or Strauss, the theater became a carefully staged scene of Nazi power. As Hitler took center stage on the dais, a massive eagle clutching a laurel with a swastika spread its wings on the wall behind him. Enormous white circles inscribed with swastikas floated to the left and right of the eagle. Hitler dressed demurely, a single Iron Cross medal hanging from the chest of his double-breasted jacket. He left the military finery to the generals he had gathered to honor.[16]

For nearly two hours, Hitler delivered a fiery speech, his front lock of hair springing loose as he threw his whole body into the delivery. "In looking back upon the last ten months we are all struck by the grace of Providence that has allowed us to succeed in our great work. Providence has blessed our great resolves and guided us in our difficult matters," said Hitler. The German soldier had triumphed and given the Reich victory in "the most tremendous series of battles in the history of the world."

He was proud to have obliterated the "humiliation and disgrace" of Germany's defeat twenty-two years earlier. France, having refused to make peace with the Fatherland, now lay in ruins, and an "indescribable misery has overtaken that great country and people since that day." The same fate would also befall Britain if it continued to resist. "I do realize that this struggle, if it continues, can end only with the complete annihilation of one or the other of the two adversaries. Mr. Churchill may believe this will be Germany. I know that it will be Britain," said Hitler.[17]

After the speech, however, Churchill and Britain refused to back down or accept Hitler's taunting peace offer, leaving the western front still in play and a powerful opponent on the field. Twelve days later, on July 31, Hitler authorized an attack on the Soviet Union, setting in motion preparations for Operation BARBAROSSA, the largest Germany military operation of the war.[18] One year later, in the summer of 1941, Germany would launch a massive assault on its erstwhile ally to the east.

Rather than respond in a huff or retaliate against Vichy, Hitler chose to let the demand for the Casablanca bases drop. While he objected to French impertinence, he did not want to send German troops to North Africa. The Reich should focus on bringing Britain to its knees, while preparations for the attack on the Soviet Union progressed.[19]

North Africa and the United States could wait a little while longer.

8

Acts of Kindness

IN THE SUMMER OF 1940, BOATS PLIED BETWEEN MARSEILLE AND Casablanca, delivering demobilized French troops back to Morocco. Men in varying states of cleanliness filled the ships. To escape the stench and claustrophobia of the cramped quarters below, Edmund Schechter found it best to pass the time on deck. "I don't remember how or what the food was, but the enforced leisure, the sun, and the feeling of being safe—at least for the moment—helped me recuperate and make a halfway decent appearance when we arrived a few days later," wrote Schechter.[1]

Schechter had joined the French army in one of the auxiliary units reserved for foreign volunteers. His unit was stocked with refugees who had fled Hitler—Jews from Germany, Austria, the former Czechoslovakia, and Hungary, along with socialists, leftists, Catholics, and Protestants who dared to challenge the Reich and earn its ire.[2] When the German onslaught began, Schechter's unit traveled west from Paris in dilapidated railroad cars, inching along the tracks. More than once, the train stopped, and the men dove from the railcars into ditches and under bushes to escape the Luftwaffe's bombing runs. Upon arriving in Quimper, a small town at the western tip of Brittany, Schechter's unit received uniforms, ancient weapons, and no training. His commanding officers also seemed confused about why they were there and what they were meant to accomplish.[3]

After they had been at Quimper more than a week, a German infantry battalion reached their position, having streaked west across France. Schechter was stunned when half a dozen members of his unit dug into their boots and produced identity cards revealing themselves as German agents. After the jaw-dropping disclosure, Schechter held his breath, waiting to see how they would be treated as prisoners of war. Given the informants, the battalion captain would know of their political and racial makeup. The German captain, however, took pains to make sure his prisoners knew he was a soldier and not one of Hitler's goons. He confiscated their weapons but permitted them to keep their personal belongings and stay in their tents. They also received regular meals.[4]

A week into their captivity, the German battalion captain assembled his prisoners and informed them of the Gestapo's impending arrival in forty-eight hours. The announcement puzzled Schechter and his fellow prisoners—the captain had no reason to share such information except to give them a chance to escape. Schechter and his longtime friend Roy Mehler decided to take fate into their own hands. When darkness fell, they disappeared into the woods behind the latrines. "I saw—or I believe to have seen—a man standing, smoking a cigarette, and watching the situation," recalled Schechter. "Whatever, I shall to the end of my days believe it was the captain."[5] After walking for hours, they found sanctuary with a kindhearted Breton couple, who offered them a place to rest, food, and a change of clothes. Shed of their uniforms, they now looked like peasants from Brittany instead of escaped prisoners of war.[6]

For the next week, Schechter and Mehler hitchhiked south, often catching rides on German trucks. "I assumed the psychology of a refugee and had the great idea to do exactly the opposite of what one would expect," said Schechter. "We hitched rides only from German soldiers in German vehicles, because these were the only ones that were not stopped and they were not searched and were not asked for identification papers."[7] They spoke only French, which allowed German soldiers to assume they were French peasants. At the demarcation line dividing occupied and unoccupied France, the duo decided to "play real poker" to foil the checkpoints. The first vehicle that stopped was a van carrying high-ranking German staff officers. The Germans gave the "peasants" a ride across the demarcation line, dropping Schechter and Mehler off in Toulouse's central square. "We could hardly wait for the truck to disappear from sight, before we fell into each other's arms," wrote Schechter.[8]

To celebrate their arrival in Toulouse, the duo ate their first hot meal in weeks. But Schechter's joy was short-lived, as he found himself writhing in pain from a kidney stone. Mehler helped him to the hospital, where Schechter urged him to continue on—there was no telling how long it would take him to recover. Mehler reluctantly parted ways with his friend, making it to Spain and eventually the United States.

After he regained his health, Schechter caught a train to Marseille, France's largest and most important port on the Mediterranean and the gateway to North Africa. The South of France suffered none of the bombs and carnage of more northern parts, remaining untouched except for masses of refugees and soldiers flooding Marseille, hoping to sail to safety or home. "The city was bursting. You could not help meeting somebody you knew on each corner," said Schechter. The telegraph lines still functioned, allowing Schechter to send messages to his family in southern France and his father in Tel Aviv. Within twenty-four hours, his father sent him a telegram informing him of his mother's safe arrival in Casablanca.[9]

Schechter decided to head for Morocco to reunite with her. "There was nothing in the summer of 1940 that was not arrangeable in Marseille," he wrote. Schechter's previous work assisting Jews hoping to book passage to Palestine through "unofficial channels" helped him obtain a set of counterfeit demobilization papers declaring Casablanca his home city. With that, Schechter secured a spot on a troop ship bound for Morocco.[10]

WHEN THE SHIP ARRIVED in Casablanca, thousands of people—mothers, wives, husbands, sons, daughters, lovers—milled around on the dock, waiting to lay eyes on their loved ones. The men returning home to Morocco were lucky. They hadn't fallen defending France's eastern border or been shunted into a prisoner-of-war camp. Schechter picked his mother out of the crowd almost immediately.

Madame Schechter had arrived in Casablanca by accident. When the Germans marched on Paris, Edmund's friends gave her a place in their car and inched along the roads to the Normandy coast. After boarding a ship supposedly bound for Britain, she discovered it was heading south to Casablanca. Instead of getting off at the next port, she decided to continue on to Morocco. Upon her arrival, the local Jewish community helped her secure a room with a kitchen. It also became her son's home for the next seven months.[11]

TWO WEEKS AFTER HIS arrival in Casablanca, Schechter found himself standing in front of a white, one-story building in a quiet square located a few blocks southwest of the Place Administrative. Outside the US consulate, refugees waited in line for their turn to speak with a staff member. Some days, the line ran two hundred people deep.[12]

Since the fall of France, refugees had deluged the American consulate, seeking visas to immigrate to the United States. Obtaining one, however, was an involved and often lengthy process requiring applicants to fill out forms, provide documentation, obtain sponsors, show means of financial support through bank accounts or family connections, and submit to an interview and medical exam. The refugee also had to prove he or she had booked passage on a ship or airplane departing for the United States. For most refugees in Casablanca, that meant a reservation on a ship leaving Lisbon.

The quota system further complicated the process. If a refugee appeared to meet the criteria, the American consulate in Casablanca then wrote to the US embassy in the refugee's country of birth, asking to use part of its visa quota. A law passed by Congress set annual limits on how many people could immigrate to the United States from a particular country. Visas were allocated on the basis of the refugee's home country, not from where they submitted their application. This meant an Austrian refugee, like Schechter, who found himself in Casablanca, was subject to the visa quota for Germany, which now included Austria.[13]

US visa quotas could not accommodate all the Jews and others attempting to flee Nazi Germany and its expanding empire. Other countries across the Atlantic Ocean, including Mexico, Canada, and Cuba, were equally, if not more, tightfisted with visas. Most Latin and South American countries had no consulates in Casablanca at which refugees could apply for emigration.[14]

DESPITE THE LONG ODDS, applying for and then checking on the status of a visa application at the American consulate became part of the daily routine for many refugees. They couldn't work without permission from the Protectorate, which worried that refugees might take jobs from Moroccans. Instead, the refugees wiled away the hours standing in line before retreating to a café.

The sudden deluge of visa requests strained the small staff of the US consulate, which had responsibility for all of French Morocco. Herbert S. Goold, the consul general, and Quincy Stanton, the vice consul, were aided by four clerks and one interpreter.[15] The American community in Morocco was small, numbering only 106 people in 1939, and didn't require much caretaking.[16] The consulate registered the occasional birth and helped replace and renew American passports.[17] Before the war, most of its work focused on helping American businesses that sold their wares in French Morocco, ranging from Douglas airplanes and Singer sewing machines to surgical supplies and radios. Socony-Vacuum Oil Company (the precursor to ExxonMobil) had a strong presence too.[18] Moroccan firms also worked with the consulate to send their goods to New York, filling cargo holds with olive oil, almonds, snails, sheep casings, and animal hides.

The pace of work picked up at the start of 1940 as people and businesses grew anxious and the Phoney War dragged on. Once hostilities started, Goold and his staff became travel agents for Americans attempting to leave North and West Africa. They booked passages, arranged visas, helped transfer money, and answered inquiries about the whereabouts of Americans from anxious relatives. By the end of June, the trickle of refugees seeking visas had become a daily mob.

NOT REALIZING HE WAS supposed to join the queue, Schechter walked through the front door of the consulate. At the receptionist's desk, he asked, to speak with "Monsieur, le Consul General." "Since I had come through the main entrance and spoken to her in fluent French, the receptionist probably assumed that I had reasons of State to see the top man, since visa matters were not handled at that level," wrote Schechter.[19]

After a few minutes, the receptionist ushered Schechter into the office of Herbert S. Goold, the US consul general. Tall and handsome, with silver hair and startling blue eyes, Goold struck Schechter as a "typical American, in the good sense of the word."[20] Upon entering his office, Schechter realized he had made a mistake. He should have been outside in the line with the rest of the refugees. "I'm terribly embarrassed, but I really probably should have come the other way, because what I want is a visa," he told Goold. "If you tell me I should walk out right away, I'll walk out right away."

Instead of fobbing him off on one of the clerks, Goold urged Schechter to sit and tell him his story. Schechter decided to be as open and frank as he could, telling Goold how he came to be in Casablanca, confessing to the fake papers, and expressing his desire to help his mother. "One day I hope again to prove my story," he told Goold when he'd finished. "Right now it's a question that either you believe me or you don't believe me."[21]

"What is it that you want?" asked Goold.

Schechter wanted to give up his fake identity and start the process of obtaining a visa for the United States—but his paperwork was a sheaf of lies. He needed time to contact friends, obtain addresses, and secure affidavits of support. He also hadn't registered with any of the agencies that helped refugees immigrate. "If I start right now, I probably have dozens of Viennese friends who, despite the fact that they left Vienna later than I did, are in the States now, but 'til I get their addresses—I was busy fleeing the Germans and I just don't have any basis for identification," he told Goold.[22] While he waited for letters to make their way back and forth across the Atlantic, he needed a letter from the US consulate to the Casablanca Prefecture saying that he was expecting an American visa, which would allow him to obtain a *permit de séjour*, a residence permit. Without it, Schechter risked being sent to an internment camp.

As SCHECHTER SPOKE, GOOLD listened to his story, watching him intently. When Schechter finished, the consul general got up, went to his desk, and pulled out a piece of stationary bearing the consulate's seal. In his own hand, Goold wrote a letter stating that Schechter had applied for visas for both himself and his mother with the US consulate. As such, they must be available at a moment's notice for consultation. Goold would appreciate if the Protectorate issued temporary residence permits for them. With a mischievous twinkle in his eye, Goold told him, "There are certain letters that even a consul general prefers to write with his own hand and without copies."[23]

Schechter, overwhelmed with gratitude and surprise, could hardly believe his eyes when he read the letter. Goold suggested that he go immediately to the Prefecture and secure the permits. They could discuss the arrangements for the visas another day. Drawing on some of his small savings, Schechter splurged for a taxi to the Prefecture. When he emerged from the police station hours later with the permits in his pocket, he felt as if he'd "drunk four bottles of champagne."

Arriving back at the hotel, he found his mother waiting for him out front. Before he could tell her the good news, Madame Schechter told him that she'd received a visit from Cora Goold, the wife of the US consul general. Her husband had sent her over to check out Schechter's story, a common occurrence, and to see if they needed anything. She had brought with her soap and chocolate, two things in short supply in Casablanca, along with some flowers.[24] Together Schechter and his mother pieced together the stories and the events that had led to their good luck. "I always called this one of the great miracles," said Schechter.[25]

Seven months later, both he and his mother received their visas.

9

The Refugee Club

Edmund Schechter arrived in Casablanca as a demobilized soldier, which entitled him to disembark from his ship. Not every refugee was so lucky. In the wake of the armistice, two hundred ships laden with refugees attempting to stay one step ahead of the Germans had arrived off Casablanca, taxing the port's capacity. For a number of weeks, many vessels dropped anchor outside the harbor. The port simply didn't have enough berths for them. As food and water ran low, conditions on the ships waiting for their turn at the dock quickly deteriorated. The ships, most of which were overcapacity, had only laid in enough food and water for the short trip from Oran, Marseille, or Bordeaux. They hadn't stocked provisions for weeks of waiting to discharge their passengers.

French officials struggled to resupply them, hampered by the unprecedented number needing assistance and the scale of the problem. As ships began to go days without food and water and the July sun baked the metal hulls, some refugees and sailors fell ill or became dehydrated, requiring their evacuation to the shore. Temporary sheds were set up in the port to provide medical care, while the more serious cases were taken to local hospitals.[1]

Once the refugees made it ashore, they presented a new series of challenges. Like the Gibraltar evacuees, they had to be processed and provided with places to stay until they could make other arrangements. It didn't help that the refugee influx coincided with the repatriation of French and Moroccan soldiers from Great Britain, straining Casablanca's housing supply. To accommodate the refugees, the Protectorate established an internment camp in Aïn Chok, an area approximately five miles east of the city center.

The camp had previously served as a quarantine facility for native Moroccans during the typhus outbreak of 1938–1939.[2]

At the beginning of July, George Kelber, a passenger on the SS *Chateau Yquem*, found himself interned at Aïn Chok along with seven hundred other recently arrived refugees. Kelber described the conditions as "tragic." "There are no authorities representatives for the time being in this center, people are getting exhausted, many of them are ill, and hygienic conditions are far from being satisfactory," he wrote. When representatives from the local Jewish community came to visit the camp, the refugees mobbed them, making it hard to discuss anything. "All these people have suffered a lot since four weeks and many of them are morally and physically broken and there is no question of discipline," wrote Kelber.[3]

As large numbers of Jews began arriving from Europe, Casablanca's Jewish community opened their hearts and wallets to provide assistance. By the first week of July, Casablanca's chief of municipal services had accredited representatives from the Jewish community to visit Aïn Chok and work with the refugees.[4] The Committee for Assistance of Foreign Refugees (Comité d'assistance aux réfugiés étrangers) also formed under the leadership of Hélène Cazès-Bénatar, who served as its director.[5]

A stout woman of forty-two with kind brown eyes, Bénatar moved to Casablanca with her family in 1917. She had spent her youth in Tangier, where she received a stellar education at a school run by the Alliance israélite universelle and became the first Moroccan Jewish woman to receive a bachelor's degree. Bénatar then obtained a law degree from the University of Bordeaux and returned to Casablanca to open a law practice, becoming the first female lawyer in French Morocco. After Germany invaded Poland in 1939, she signed up to volunteer with the French Red Cross and trained as a nurse. She also mobilized the Jewish community in Casablanca to volunteer for service in the French army: 2,000 Moroccan Jews signed up to fight.[6] France's quick collapse and armistice with Germany thwarted Bénatar's nursing career, and after hearing de Gaulle's speech from London on the radio, she wrote to the British consulate in Casablanca offering her services.[7] Unable to join up with the Free French and facing a humanitarian crisis in her adopted city, Bénatar founded the refugee assistance committee, running the organization out of the offices of her law practice.[8]

Bénatar's committee helped many of the refugees to leave Aïn Chok. They received accommodations in Casablanca, ranging from a rented apartment or a hotel room with a kitchen to living with a Jewish family that had

FIGURE 9.1. Hélène Cazès-Bénatar organized assistance for refugees stranded in Casablanca. *AJJDC Archives*

generously opened its home. Bénatar's committee also assisted with completing the paperwork for visa applications, signing up with aid agencies, and registering with Protectorate authorities. Those who lacked funds received modest financial assistance. During the summer, the committee had 825 refugees on its rolls.[9]

As THE SUMMER OF 1940 progressed, the crush of refugees in Casablanca began to strain the capacity of the US consulate. "The American consulate in this city has been a club for hundreds of people who couldn't get into the United States or Canada, but who came to tell their stories to us and to each other," wrote Consul General Herbert Goold. "I suppose it was one of the few places where they did not get a cold shoulder, and I do not regret that these forlorn, harassed people felt that at our office, they could at least hear a friendly word. But they have nearly wrecked us."[10]

Within a few weeks, the US consulate had also assumed responsibility for the affairs of Britain, Canada, Australia, New Zealand, and South Africa. If refugees wanted transit or immigrant visas for any of those countries, they too came to the Americans.[11] "It is no exaggeration to state that the bulk of the Europeans and South Americans in distress in this part of the world apparently hold the conviction that an American consulate is a hybrid institution, which partakes of the nature of a Red Cross bureau, a general welfare bureau, a free shipping agency, and a worldwide diplomatic clearing house for all governments — especially for that of a nation in case it has no representation in such an out of the way post as Casablanca or even in the case of an application with no nationality at all," wrote Goold.[12]

The bulk of the refugees who called at the consulate were Belgian, Dutch, French, Czech, Polish, ex-German, and ex-Austrian nationals. In the line outside and in the reception area, French business magnates rubbed shoulders with Amsterdammer diamond merchants. Belgian landowners traded stories with professors from Vienna and Prague. Spanish Republicans demanded help to reach Mexico to avoid going back to Spain, where Francisco Franco's government would send them to prison or the gallows. Polish and Czechoslovak men wanted help reaching Canada to join up with their legions or enlist in the Dominion forces to fight Germany and reclaim their homelands. Some Moroccans visited the consulate too, hoping to leave before the Nazis came to North Africa, but the regulations implemented by the Protectorate to prevent capital from leaving the country proved an obstacle.

Because the refugees who arrived in Casablanca were so varied, Goold had to ask other consulates for portions of their visa quotas. Telegrams flew to US consulates in Germany and Latvia, which had taken over Soviet affairs, asking for visas for Germans, Austrians, and Russians. He wrangled visas for stranded Belgians and Dutch families from the US consulate in Lisbon, which had assumed responsibility for minding visas for those countries after Germany invaded.[13] But even when Goold could get the necessary visas and the refugees passed muster, they often went unused, because there was no way to leave Casablanca.[14]

As the refugees waited in line at the American consulate, they shared stories of their encounters with the Gestapo and time spent in concentration camps at Dachau and elsewhere. "They spread such fear amongst the waiting groups that here were numerous distressful scenes — fainting, hysterical weeping, and frantic men and women groveling on the floor before the desks of the visa clerks," wrote Goold. There were also threats of suicide if visas weren't granted. In one case, a refugee tried to cut his throat after learning his visa application had been rejected.[15]

Goold found local French officials helpful when it came to granting the necessary exit visas. The Casablanca police also exhibited a degree of sympathy for the refugees and their attempt to escape the Nazis, along with a real desire in numerous cases to help the Allied cause. The helpfulness did not apply, however, to the passengers of the *Massilia*. Goold could not grant transit visas for the United States without seeing the parliamentarians and their families. The police refused to allow the passengers to come to the consulate—or Goold or his staff to board the ship.

Refugees who wanted to go someplace other than the United States also found the prospects tough going. British nationals and Czech and Polish refugees with visas for Canada were continually foiled in their efforts to book passage out of Lisbon or charter a boat. Those wanting to go to Latin or South America were also stymied. The local consuls were all honorary, which meant they could not grant visas for permanent residence. The refugees lucky enough to hold immigration visas for Latin or South America had obtained them in Europe. In these cases, the American consulate granted transit visas, which would allow them to travel to their destinations via Lisbon and New York.

There were also fake visas and passports to contend with. Refugees calling on American consulates presented a surprising number of Luxemburg passports. The Portuguese consul general in Vienna had also issued one hundred fraudulent passports between 1934 and 1938.[16]

BETWEEN COLLECTING PAPERWORK AND conducting interviews, the consulate staff tried to steer the refugees away from unscrupulous people looking to capitalize on their misery and desperation. They directed refugees who needed help with housing to Bénatar's committee. They prepared lists of reliable jewel merchants, allowing the refugees to sell precious gems for a fair price. Nazi Germany forbade Jews from taking money out of the country, forcing them to convert their savings into anything portable that they could sell elsewhere. Diamonds, rubies, and emeralds had the added advantage of being easily hidden in hems and bodices.[17] The consulate staff also helped book passage on American Export Lines or another of the passenger services out of Lisbon for a fair price.

Still, the Casablanca port burst with ships unable to depart once they unloaded their cargo, human and otherwise, because of Britain's naval blockade of France and Germany. It was common practice for the refugees to roam the port, chatting up crews in the hopes of securing a berth once the ships received permission to leave. The refugees offered stacks of cash—up to $800—for the chance to sleep on a bunk, on deck, in a lifeboat, or even in the boiler room of a dirty coal ship or a grimy oil tanker. By comparison, a second-class ticket on a passenger ship from Lisbon to New York, which included a shared cabin and regular meals, cost $525.[18]

During the SS *Arena*'s two months in dock, its captain and radio operator did their best to exploit the refugees. The captain, Imre Horvath, made multiple agreements for the ten spots available on his ship. If he thought he could get more money, he tossed aside the last deal. When the spurned refugees tried to get their money back—he had required them to pay upfront—Horvath threatened to denounce them to the Gestapo. If a female refugee wanted a spot on Horvath's ship, he demanded sex, as well as the outrageous fee. The radio operator, Samuel Hakem, also regularly visited the US consulate, offering passage to the refugees waiting in line. Once the refugees paid for their spots, Hakem then tried to shake down the consulate's staff for the necessary visas. He also collected fees from the refugees to make representations on their behalf.

It didn't take long for Casablanca's port police to develop an interest in Horvath and Hakem's activities. Inquiries to France revealed that Horvath possessed a long list of fake identities and might even be a member of the Ustaše, the terrorist group behind the 1934 assassination of King Alexander of Yugoslavia in Marseille. Before the port police could act, the SS *Arena* departed for Takoradi, the main port of Britain's Gold Coast (now Ghana). On board were ten refugees, including Bertha Berner, an Austrian refused an immigrant visa and a transit visa by the US consulate. Horvath and Hakem agreed to take her on as a "stewardess" and intended to collect their fee from her fiancé upon arrival in New York.[19]

IN MID-AUGUST, THE PROTECTORATE issued an order forbidding men between the ages of seventeen and fifty who hailed from Britain, the Netherlands, Czechoslovakia, Belgium, Norway, and Poland from leaving Morocco. Vichy and Germany didn't want men of fighting age reuniting with their home forces. The order stranded hundreds of men from Allied nations.[20] With the legal avenues of departure shut down, their only options to leave became the illicit ones.

10

Keep Your Enemies Closer

O N OCTOBER 19, 1940, AN AIRPLANE CARRYING GENERAL MAXIME Weygand departed from Algiers and made its way southwest over the Mitidja plain in northern Algeria. It was the first time Weygand had flown over what he called "that masterpiece of French colonization." Below him, fields of grain, orange groves, villages, and roads cut patchwork patterns into the landscape. As the plane passed into Morocco, bound for Rabat, the craggy heights of the Atlas Mountains replaced the countryside. "The end of the journey left me with an unforgettable picture of the map of Morocco from the corridor of Taza to its façade on the Atlantic," wrote Weygand.[1]

At 3:00 p.m., the plane touched down at the aerodrome outside Rabat, where a cavalcade of officials turned out to greet him. After a brief ceremony at the airport and some short presentations at the Residency, Charles Noguès escorted Weygand to the palace to call on the sultan. It would be the men's first meeting. During the short audience, Sidi Mohammed once again declared his loyalty to France and praised Noguès's stewardship of Morocco. He also made it known that if France would not defend Morocco against Spain's increasingly bold territorial claims, he would do so himself.[2] Since the beginning of the war, Spain had looked longingly at Tangier and French Morocco, wondering if the conflict might provide the chance to pounce.

WEYGAND ARRIVED IN MOROCCO not as the minister of defense for Vichy but as the delegate general for French Africa, a job created for him by Henri-Philippe Pétain. The governors-general of French North and West Africa now reported to him rather than Vichy. He set up his new administration in the Winter Palace, a crumbling building that had once dazzled as one of Algiers's architectural showstoppers.[3]

Weygand's exile to North Africa resulted from months of bickering among Pétain's cabinet about the future of the regime. The defeat of France at the hands of the Germans signaled to Pétain and his ilk that France needed to be remade and the vestiges of the liberal Third Republic swept away. At the core of the new "national revolution" was a return to the Catholic moral order, which emphasized hierarchy, social order, and traditional family values.[4] The emphasis on Catholicism derived from the personal beliefs of the men who governed Vichy, along with a desire to reclaim France's glory days as a Catholic country that dominated Europe. Under the Vichy regime, order, decree, and compliance would replace democratic government, laissez-faire economics, and the voices of the masses.[5]

Germany did not impose this new vision on France. "Neither diplomats nor soldiers at Berlin cared a fig for Vichy's internal acts as long as order was maintained and French wealth poured into the German war machine," writes Robert Paxton.[6] Even if Vichy's new national program didn't come spoon-fed from Berlin, a strong desire existed among many in Pétain's cabinet to work closely with Germany. Pierre Laval, in particular, courted German officials who decided policy for France, ingratiating himself at every opportunity.[7]

Weygand supported the regime's policies. He believed in education and the importance of family, country, and God. France's plummeting birth rate must be reversed to maintain the nation's vitality and ability to defend itself. He wanted an end to the strikes and trade union activities that marked the 1930s. Suspicious of foreign influences, he believed fewer immigrants should receive citizenship. He worried about the influence of the Free Masons and looked askance at those who occupied themselves with the pursuit of pleasure.[8]

But when it came to Germany, Weygand parted ways with Laval and others in the cabinet. Rather than giving into every German demand, Weygand believed, Vichy should stand firm or at least oppose requests it found distasteful or potentially harmful to its economy, national defense, or people. His own efforts showed this was possible. After the attack on Mers-el-Kébir, Weygand convinced Germany and Italy that the region could not be left fallow, leading to a buildup of French defenses in North Africa. He lobbied successfully for the resumption of air service between Vichy France and North Africa: soon flights departed three times a week for Algiers, once a week to Oran, and once a week to Tunis.[9] He also remained suspicious of German intentions, leading him to authorize the creation of a new army counterespionage bureau. Officially, the Bureau des menées antinationalies

(Bureau for Antinational Affairs) sought information about Communist, Allied, and Gaullist activities; unofficially, it spied on the Germans.[10]

While Weygand supported Pétain's need for a vice premiere—the marshal was no longer a spry young man with boundless energy—he lamented the appointment of Laval, whom he considered "fundamentally untrustworthy" and blinded by anti-British and pro-German sentiments. He also doubted Laval's fitness to steer the country should anything happen to Pétain.[11] Weygand and Laval's constant sparing in cabinet meetings over how much to collaborate with the Germans dismayed Pétain. Their fighting became particularly vociferous in August after Germany seized Alsace-Moselle and imposed occupation policies that banned the French language, enacted anti-Semitic regulations, and drafted French citizens into the Wehrmacht.[12]

To settle the battle of egos, Pétain decided to appoint Weygand as delegate general of the government in French Africa, a new position that combined the political post of delegate general with commander in chief of French forces in North Africa. Weygand had no inkling that anything was amiss until he received the job offer from Pétain on September 5. The marshal billed the newly created position as important to "the fate of Africa." Ever the dutiful soldier, Weygand agreed to take the post.

On October 6, he boarded a plane with his wife to begin the journey to Algiers.[13] "I was in a hurry . . . to leave Vichy, where I felt ill-at-ease, and to regain, with vast horizons, a pure air and well-defined responsibilities," he wrote.[14] He spent half of his first eighty days on the job flying around North Africa, visiting the territories under his rule and meeting the men who now answered to him.[15]

DESPITE CLASHING WITH PÉTAIN and Weygand, Noguès managed to keep his job as resident-general, but he no longer served as commander in chief of North Africa. The post was abolished at the beginning of August 1940. Instead, he was appointed inspector general of France's North African army, which consisted of overseeing its demobilization and adhering to the armistice.[16] By pushing for France to continue the war from North Africa, he had challenged the judgment of Pétain and Weygand.[17] He would have been dismissed if not for his relationship with the sultan and his track record in managing Morocco's complicated politics. Instead, as the price for his impertinence, they did everything short of firing him.

Weygand's appointment to North Africa and his insertion into Moroccan affairs vexed Noguès, adding another level of discord to their rapidly deteriorating relationship. Before Noguès had a direct line to Paris, and then

Vichy, to plead his case or lobby on behalf of Morocco. Now he had to make his appeals to Weygand in Algiers and hope the latter would pass along his concerns to Vichy.

In the face of such an affront, Noguès could have resigned. But he chose to stay on, anxious to keep his beloved Morocco out of German hands at any cost, including his pride. "Our welfare, our families, the future of France and Morocco are at stake," said Noguès in a speech. "Nothing will stop me from protecting them. The stakes are too high to tolerate even the slightest weakness. Everyone must work with dedication and recognize that now is the time for unity, obedience, and duty."[18]

His bad treatment aside, Noguès found much to like in the new Vichy regime. As in Vichy, elective bodies in Morocco were abolished and replaced by appointed councils. Noguès also mimicked Vichy's laws abolishing secret societies and targeted the activities of Communists, Free Masons, Gaullists, and anarchists. New agencies were created to promote the family and sport. Casablanca's newspapers soon burst with stories about the latest soccer, rugby, or boxing match, along with tales of cycling heroics and hockey.[19]

Noguès's decision to continue as resident-general rather than resign was also influenced by General Charles de Gaulle's ill-conceived attempt at the end of September to capture Dakar, the capital of French West Africa (now Senegal). De Gaulle had hoped to wrest Dakar away from Vichy and turn it into a Free French outpost in Africa. The British agreed to support the operation, which had the unfortunate code name MENACE, to bolster the Free French, believing that the colonial betrayal would have political and emotional impact. Dakar also presented a tempting target for another reason: it was now home to the gold reserves of France and Poland, which had been spirited away for safekeeping as France collapsed.

The assault, which began on September 23, 1940, turned into an embarrassing debacle as Vichy forces mounted a vigorous defense of the city. Britain's naval task force failed to crack Dakar's coastal defenses, and de Gaulle baulked at sending French troops into the city to fight other French troops. The incident did little to bolster de Gaulle's reputation, while causing other military officers in North Africa who might have challenged Vichy to think twice.[20]

IN NOVEMBER 1940, WEYGAND made a second trip to Morocco, this time for nine days, during which he inspected troops and garrisons and had a longer audience with the sultan. "At the risk of astonishing and even hurting General Noguès, I made a point of having private interviews with many official personages or administrators, colonists, and industrialists who had expressed a wish to talk to me without witnesses," wrote Weygand.[21] During his meetings, Weygand encouraged Protectorate officials and luminaries to write directly to him in Algiers with their concerns. Behind the scenes, Weygand accused Noguès of failing to fully embrace Vichy's national revolution, of not doing a thorough job of purging the bureaucracy of suspect individuals, including Free Masons, Jews, and those sympathetic to the Free French, and of withholding information.[22]

From the trip's planning stages, Noguès believed it was designed to undermine his authority, and he begged to attend meetings where his presence was expected. By the end of the trip, his fears had been realized. "I do not understand what would make a leader undermine the authority of his subordinate in a country where authority is, more than elsewhere, indispensable, especially in the present circumstances," he wrote.[23] When his complaints to Vichy about Weygand's tactics fell on deaf ears, Noguès decided he had no choice: he would have to take whatever steps necessary to ensure his professional survival, along with the integrity of Morocco and France's empire in North Africa.

If that led to Weygand's downfall, so be it.

11

Mon Legionnaire

As Hungarian journalist Arthur Koestler listened to the Nazi anthem on Radio Paris and heard Pétain's reedy voice announce the surrender, he realized his time in France had come to an end. Only a few weeks before, he had escaped another attempt by the Sûreté to arrest him. With the Germans closing in, French authorities' paranoia increased and the roundups of refugees began anew. Koestler, however, caught a lucky break when the clerk processing him expressed confusion about the reason for his arrest. Koestler had a Hungarian passport, and Hungary remained neutral, so why had Koestler been arrested? Seizing the moment, Koestler blustered his way into getting released, his bravado aided by booze. He'd packed a bottle in his suitcase to help dull his senses to the inevitable return to captivity and had started drinking while waiting for the clerk to call him forward for processing.

Rather than return to his apartment, Koestler hid at the PEN Club and then at the apartment of Adrienne Monnier. As the owner of la Maison des amis des livres, Monnier had boosted the careers of T. S. Eliot, Ernest Hemingway, and Antoine de Saint-Exupéry. Now she would help Koestler escape Paris. Through Monnier's connections at the French Foreign Ministry, Koestler received a travel permit to Limoges. After living in hiding for a week, Koestler and his companion, Daphne Hardy, joined the exodus south in mid-June.[1]

The problem was where to go next. Hardy, a British citizen, could go to the United Kingdom, but Koestler remained betwixt and between. His already perilous situation became even more so after the police in Limoges refused to extend his residence permit because he had failed to obtain the stamp granting him permission to leave Paris.[2] It was only a matter of time before both the French and Germans were looking for him. He needed a plan.

As Pétain's voice faded, thirty-four-year-old Koestler remembered a film with Jean Gabin, in which his character avoids arrest by signing up with the French Foreign Legion. Upon seeing a recruiting station, Gabin enters with no papers and emerges with a *carnet militaire* (military identification) and a new life. When Gabin asks the sergeant if it's really that simple, he replies, "Whatever your past has been, from this moment it is dead. Here nobody will ask you indiscreet questions; in the Legion we are all *des morts vivants*."[3]

A few hours later, Koestler walked into the Legion barracks in Limoges as Arthur Koestler of Budapest, Hungary, and emerged as Albert Dubert of Berne, Switzerland, for the price of five years of service to the Legion.[4]

He also began to grow a moustache.[5]

KOESTLER HAD JOINED, AS the movie sergeant suggested, *des morts vivants*—the living dead. The French Foreign Legion started in 1831 as a military unit for foreign nationals who desired to serve in the French armed services. Instead of swearing allegiance to France, recruits swore (and continue to swear) allegiance to the Legion. They directed their loyalty to their comrades in arms and not to a particular country. Over the years, the Legion gained a reputation for fierce fighting, particularly in Morocco, where it helped France fulfill its colonial ambitions. It also offered a way for a man to reinvent himself or indulge in a spot of adventure. Whether a banker, a nobleman, or a fishmonger, a man could enlist with the Legion under a false name, no questions asked, and disappear into the North African expanse. At the end of five years of service, he reentered the civilian world with a new identity.

Aside from having seen a Legion reinvention tale on the screen, Koestler would have heard stories of Jewish refugees signing up. A law passed in April 1939 allowed refugees who had lived in France for ten years to join the regular French army, but few refugees could claim a decade of residency. For many, joining the Legion became the only way to stay one step ahead of the Germans.[6]

The Legion's leadership, however, fretted that large numbers of Jewish refugees from eastern Europe, many from middle-class backgrounds, might not assimilate into the Legion's ranks or adapt to its rough-and-tumble ways. The Legion's esprit de corps depended on rejecting political ideology, which men who had fled for their lives because their political beliefs often found difficult to embrace. Anti-Semitism also factored in. But even so, as Koestler discovered, an able-bodied man would find acceptance if he proved to the recruiting officer he was serious about joining.[7]

Rather than reporting as ordered to the Legion's depot at Angers, Koestler continued south with Hardy, hoping to make it to Bordeaux and a ship. After numerous rancorous arguments about whether to split up or stay together, fate intervened in the form of a checkpoint. Hardy passed through; Koestler was taken into custody and sent to the military barracks at Bayonne. Hardy carried Koestler's Hungarian passport, since he didn't want to be caught carrying two sets of papers. Now he had no way of proving his true identity should he need it. He was Albert Dubert.[8]

Over the next six weeks, Koestler ruined his feet marching in new boots and abandoned his unit, only to return to it for the safety it provided. He battled fits of depression—the loss the Hardy, the loss of France, fear for his fate and that of his friends—but he rejected committing suicide even though the possibility of one final escape taunted him. "What I find revolting is the sense that the majority of people are able to negotiate the deluge that has overwhelmed Daphne and our friends, while hardly getting their feet wet," wrote Koestler. "Without that I might be happy to swim myself, happy to have saved my life, and perhaps find peace, the nice peace of resignation."[9]

IN EARLY AUGUST, KOESTLER received orders to report to the Legion depot in Marseille for demobilization. He argued with his commanding officer that he had signed up for five years, but there was nothing to be done. The German Armistice Commission had ordered the Legion demobilized, and all foreign enlistees were being turned out.[10]

In Marseille, he bought a good pair of shoes for his still tender feet, took his first hot shower in months, and sent off cables in hopes of discovering if Hardy had made it to Britain safely.[11] He ran into old friends on the street who were startled to find him strutting around in a Legion uniform, complete with the iconic white kepi perched on his head. They shared tales of suicide by other refugee intellectuals—veins sliced, drugs swallowed—to avoid capture by the Germans.[12] Walter Benjamin, the renowned German Jewish philosopher and Koestler's former neighbor in Paris, offered Koestler half of his morphine supply in case he wanted to end things. Benjamin swallowed his pills a few weeks later after failing to gain entry to Spain.[13]

Koestler hoped that by joining the Legion, he would be whisked away to North Africa or anywhere far away from the Germans, but the Legion's demobilization spoiled that plan. Aware of the limitations of his Legion ruse, he tried to get passage to Britain or America, even working with Varian Fry's

Emergency Rescue Committee. Unfortunately, Koestler didn't yet merit assistance from the committee, formed to rescue leading intellectuals from France. He took solace, however, in the news of Hardy's safe arrival in England on a British merchant ship.[14]

At Fort Saint-Jean, the main Legion depot in Marseille—and for all of France—Koestler stumbled upon a group of sixty soldiers from the British Expeditionary Force. After being captured by the Germans near Saint-Valéry, they had escaped and now found themselves interned by the French. The enterprising Koestler made friends with four soldiers who were scheming to escape to North Africa and convinced them to let him serve as their interpreter. With Koestler's help, they obtained Legion uniforms and false papers showing that they were to be discharged in Casablanca.[15]

On September 3, Koestler and the soldiers, who masqueraded as Yugoslavs who couldn't speak French, sailed for Algeria. After three days at sea, they arrived at Oran, where they boarded a train bound for Casablanca. At Oujda, just over the border in French Morocco, the group encountered a French adjutant who wanted to transfer them to a military train. Knowing the fake papers carried by the British soldiers would never hold up to close scrutiny, Koestler plied the adjutant with red wine until he agreed to let them continue on to Casablanca.[16]

KOESTLER AND THE BRITS arrived in Casablanca on September 7 only to discover that the British consulate was closed. Instead, they would have to try their luck with the American consulate, which had agreed to provide aid to British nationals.[17]

The British soldiers obtained emergency certificates, which took the place of their missing passports and, with the help of a "Mr. Ellerman," secured passage on a ship bound for Lisbon. Ellerman, a tall, charming, forty-something man with an elegant bearing, was really Rüdiger von Etzdorf, a German diplomat who loathed Hitler and worked for British intelligence. Ellerman organized escape routes to Lisbon for Allied soldiers who found themselves stranded in Casablanca.[18]

Things were not so easy for Koestler. The only documents he possessed, his demobilization papers, named him as Dubert. Like many Jewish refugees, Koestler also had a complicated passport history. He had started out with a Hungarian passport but obtained a Palestinian passport in 1928 while working in the Middle East. While he was working in Berlin in 1931–1932, his Palestinian passport expired, and he discovered he could only renew it if

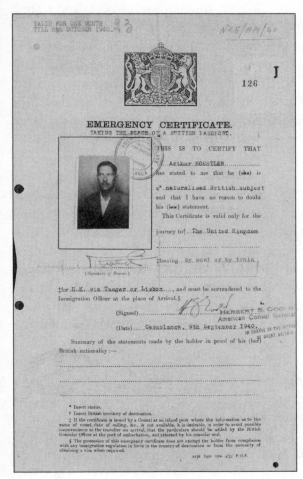

FIGURE 11.1. Arthur Koestler's emergency certificate issued by the US consulate in Casablanca. *National Archives (UK)*

he lived in Palestine for six months. Koestler chose instead to apply for a new Hungarian passport, which he had used ever since.[19]

Koestler decided to ask for an emergency certificate from Britain based on his naturalization in Palestine—which was, after all, a British mandate. This strategy neatly overlooked his Hungarian passport, but his British friends agreed that his situation called for desperate measures.[20] In his meeting with Ellerman, Koestler argued that working for British newspapers in the Middle East should also entitle him to some claim of protection. "The fact that he had been working for British interests gave me the official excuse to include him in the party to be put on board the next ship to Lisbon," wrote Ellerman in his diary.[21]

When he met with Herbert Goold, the American consul general, Koestler played up being a naturalized "British subject" of Palestine, while failing to mention his current Hungarian passport. Koestler must have talked a good game, because Goold issued him a certificate listing him as a "naturalised British subject." By signing the form, Goold attested that he had "no reason to doubt his statement." Koestler now had permission to travel to Britain through Tangier or Lisbon and could leave Morocco on a boat or train. The picture affixed to the certificate shows a slightly weary Koestler, his thick hair slicked down, his cheekbones drawn, with a fully developed moustache. Absent was the cigarette that hung perpetually from his mouth.[22]

AFTER BEING IN CASABLANCA for less than two weeks, Koestler and the Brits boarded *El Mar Azul*, a Portuguese fishing boat bound for Lisbon. Running into Ellerman allowed them to depart Morocco quickly and with relative ease, something few other refugees accomplished. As the ship dodged German U-boats, Koestler battled terrible seasickness, an ominous beginning to what proved a torturous seven weeks in Portugal. While his British friends hopped a flight home, Koestler found himself stranded. Not even a request to join the British army, which was denied, could help gain him the necessary visa.

Koestler joined the ranks of the refugees stranded in Lisbon, who spent their days walking the city, reading in cafés, standing in line at the telegraph office, and calling yet again on their preferred consulate in the hope that a visa might be granted. Koestler sustained himself with money from his American publishers, which paid for a room first at the Hotel Frankfurt and then the Pension Leiriense and kept him in cigarettes and coffee. On the surface he appeared to have a leisurely existence, but a constant feeling of terror marked his days. He called the weeks in Lisbon "worse than anything that went before, worse even than Le Vernet."[23] Koestler lived in fear of arrest not for a minor visa infraction but because of his journalism. During the Spanish Civil War, he had written articles detailing Portugal's support for Franco—articles that cast Portugal in an embarrassing light internationally—and he worried that the regime of Antonio de Oliveira Salazar would finally claim its retribution.

Despite Ellerman's best efforts and those of other prominent Britons, such as newspaper magnate Lord Leighton and Harold Nicolson, director of the Ministry of Information, MI-5 continued to deem Koestler a security risk. The rejection of his visa applications by British authorities, however, came with no explanation, leading Koestler to speculate about the forces working against him. His anxiety level increased when he learned Portuguese authorities might not renew his transit visa when it ran out in fifteen days.[24]

Already consumed by despair, news of Benjamin's suicide prompted him to take the same step. Before swallowing the morphine pills, he wrote out Rilke's "Autumn Poem," which begins with the line "Sir, it is time." Instead of dying in an opium haze, Koestler awoke the next morning and vomited up the remnants of his overdose. Either he'd somehow botched the mission, or time had rendered the pills ineffective.[25]

With a new lease on life, Koestler returned to his pursuit of an avenue of escape, determined not to "fall for the third time into the enemy's hands." By the end of October, it appeared he might obtain permission to go to America, with his passage paid for by the Committee of Publishers. Koestler, however, had his sights set on Britain, where he could join the fight against the Nazis and combat whatever "libelous denunciation" had led MI-5 to blackball him. Determined not to "perish as a victim of red tape or of bureaucratic error," Koestler decided to enter Britain illegally, knowing full well it would lead to his arrest. Transparent about his motives, Koestler informed Sir Henry King, the British consul general, of his plans. Luck once again intervened: Koestler learned that he could claim a vacant seat on a British Overseas Airways flight. He jumped at the chance, with a little help from King. In return for the kindness, Koestler left behind a letter absolving the consul general of any wrongdoing.[26] On November 6, 1940, Koestler stepped onto the tarmac at Bristol's Whitchurch Airport and was promptly arrested—just as he planned.[27]

12

Definition and Concentration

The deluge of refugees into Casablanca in the summer of 1940 continued into the fall. For every refugee able to secure a visa to depart, another took his or her place. What began at the end of June as an ad hoc effort by Hélène Bénatar to assist refugees stranded in the port turned into an organization capable of providing sustained aid to Casablanca's refugee community throughout the war.

A report by Bénatar from mid-September 1940 provides a snapshot of the men and women under her care and the lives upended. Bénatar's committee initially provided assistance to 825 refugees at the beginning of the summer.[1] By September, it still had 813 refugees on its rolls—736 Jews and 77 Gentiles. The refugees hailed mainly from Poland, followed by Austria, Germany, Czechoslovakia, Belgium, Romania, Netherlands, France, the Soviet Union, the Baltics, and Italy. Men between the ages of seventeen and fifty made up the largest group, totaling 406. There were also 47 men over the age of fifty, and 107 boys under the age of seventeen. The women numbered 253.

The refugees practiced an array of professions: there were twenty-five artisans, seventy-six businessmen, ten chemists, twenty-eight diamond dealers, nineteen students, ten writers, fifteen engineers, fifty-five mechanics, twelve doctors, three opticians, four professors, twenty-nine tailors, and eight lawyers. Their ranks also included hairdressers, chauffeurs, manicurists, a police sergeant, a plumber, and one historian. That the middle and upper classes would populate Casablanca's refugee ranks is not surprising, given that a journey from Paris or Brussels would have required train fare or a car, followed by passage on a boat and perhaps a train. By the time they arrived in Casablanca, many of the refugees had taxed their financial resources. Only

358 could pay for all or some of their voyage to the United States or else-where; 455 were indigent.

THROUGHOUT THE SUMMER AND fall, the American Jewish Joint Distri-bution Committee—commonly known as the Joint—kept an eye on Casa-blanca from its offices in Lisbon. The New York–based organization had been providing assistance to Jews around the world for more than two de-cades. Following the advent of Nazi Germany, the Joint increasingly focused its efforts on aiding Jews fleeing Hitler's anti-Semitic regime.[2] After escaping Paris one step ahead of the Germans, the Joint's staff ended up in Lisbon, where it set up a new office. Working through local organizations, it pro-vided relief to the thousands of Jewish refugees swamping the city and ar-ranged transportation to the North and South America.[3]

It didn't take long for written and oral reports, along with pleas for assis-tance, to start trickling into the Joint's Lisbon office from French Morocco.[4] Instead of establishing an office in Casablanca, the Joint offered to provide financial support for Bénatar's committee. She had already demonstrated her enormous talent for organization, and a newly arrived representative would be hard-pressed to match her local connections and political savvy.[5]

By teaming with the Joint, Bénatar's committee received funds to help sustain her operations, heretofore financed by Casablanca's Jewish commu-nity. As fall progressed, it was clear that the number of visas available would not match the number of refugees in need. "It is primarily a question of ob-taining visas to an overseas territory," wrote Joseph Schwartz, who ran the Joint's office in Lisbon. "Once a visa has been obtained it is not difficult to bring the individuals from Casablanca to Lisbon in order to arrange their passage. So far, however, only very few of the refugees there have been able to provide themselves with the necessary visas."[6] The money provided by the Joint would help sustain those refugees who had already run out of money or would soon.[7]

Despite Schwartz's gloomy assessment, he had kind words for Herbert Goold and his staff. "The American Consulate in Casablanca has been most sympathetic and liberal, and has given visas to the United States in instances where it would have been impossible to secure the visas for similar cases in Lisbon," wrote Schwartz. Even so, the majority of refugees had few prospects for emigration. "Unless some country is open for these people, I am afraid that there is very little that can be done for them except to provide some mea-sure of relief in the place where they happen to be" wrote Schwartz.[8]

As Bénatar worked to organize assistance for the refugees who found their way to Casablanca, the foundation of her life as a Jew in Morocco began to crumble.

Under Islamic law, Moroccan Jews were legally defined as *dhimmis*—"protected people"—and required to pay an annual *jizya*. In return they received the protection of the sultan, as dictated by the Quran and the sacred law of the sharia. From its earliest inception, Islam regarded Jews as "People of the Scripture" with their own religious texts. When the Muslim conquerors arrived in North Africa, they allowed Jewish communities to continue practicing their faith, while demanding that the Berbers and other nomadic tribes embrace Islam or face the sword.[9] While protected by the sultan, Moroccan Jews were nevertheless subjected to laws that made them second-class citizens in comparison to Muslims.

The Jewish community in Morocco was hardly monolithic, and the same can be said for that in Casablanca during French rule. Broadly speaking, Sephardic Jews carried on the traditions and language of medieval Spain, from which their ancestors had fled. They excelled in banking and trade, easily adopted imported European customs, and formed the core of the Jewish community's upper class. The middle class comprised white-collar Moroccan Jews who worked as civil servants, teachers, doctors, and lawyers. They benefited from the education provided by the Alliance israélite universelle, a private network of schools for the Jewish community supported by the state. Some also profited from a limited number of spots available to Jews in French schools. The Judeo-Arabs, who formed the largest segment, spoke Arabic and Judeo-Arabic, a blend of Arabic and Hebrew.

With the advent of the Protectorate in 1912, Morocco's Jews saw their status within the political pecking order reduced even further, subordinated to the French, the Europeans, and Muslims. Despite the demotion, or perhaps because of it, many of Morocco's Jewish elite adopted French customs and learned the language. They believed, as the French so often said, that anyone could become French. Nevertheless, the French walked a fine line with the Jews, careful not to grant them any rights that would antagonize the vocal and influential French and European community or breed resentment among Muslim Moroccans. By 1940, the refugees from Europe who lived among Casablanca's Jews told tales of jobs lost, homes and businesses plundered, and relatives arrested in the middle of the night never to be seen again. As the new Vichy regime took shape, the Jews of Morocco waited to see if Henri-Philippe Pétain and his cabinet would follow in Germany's footsteps and enact anti-Semitic legislation similar to that of Nazi Germany.

On October 3, 1940, Vichy issued its first statute concerning Jews, a homegrown decree handed down without pressure from Berlin. The law defined as Jewish a person who had three grandparents "of the Jewish race" or had two Jewish grandparents and was married to a Jew. The law also drastically limited the professions that Jews could engage in, barring them from the civil service and leadership roles in the armed services. Any position that might influence public opinion or shape minds was also now closed to Jews, including teaching, journalism, theater, and the cinema. Finally, Article 9 of the decree specified that similar laws be introduced in Algeria, Tunisia, and Morocco.[10]

Noguès harbored reservations about implementing Vichy's anti-Semitic policies, believing they could disrupt Arab-Jewish relations and the intricate internal political dymanics upon which French rule of Morocco depended. At the same time, he faced pressure from the French community to follow Vichy's mandates. Failure to do so with alacrity spawned telegrams and letters to his superiors complaining about his lack of commitment to Vichy's principles. The challenge posed by the anti-Semitic laws to Sidi Mohammed's authority also worried both the Residency and the palace.[11]

Nevertheless, the sultan issued a *dahir* covering the Jews of Morocco on October 31, 1940. It applied to all Jews as defined by "race" and specified the same limitations on professions and public office. The statute differed from Vichy's in a few aspects. The sultan insisted that Jews who converted to Islam not be subject to the racial definition. Special treatment was also given to Jews who served with honor in the military. Jews who worked for the schools run by the Alliance israélite universelle could continue teaching. The statute also did little to disrupt the internal running of the Jewish community. Rabbis continued to preside over personal matters, such as births, deaths, and inheritances.[12]

Over the following weeks, approximately 280 Jews were dismissed from government service in Casablanca, including clerks, a justice of the peace, postal workers, transport employees, and those who worked for the state-owned water and electric companies. The German-controlled *La Vigie marocaine*, Casablanca's major daily newspaper, also dismissed its Jewish employees. The Protectorate subjected Jewish-run businesses to strict surveillance and made numerous arrests for concealment of stocks and trading in foreign exchange. The Jews of Morocco also officially became classified as an element dangerous to public security. They joined the Communists, Free Masons, and Gaullists as enemies of the state.

After speaking with representatives from Casablanca's Jewish community, Goold concluded that the *dahir* had yet to be applied in its entirety. "From all accounts, it would appear that General Noguès is not more Anti-Semitic than the average French officer," he reported. "The Jews have stated that until recently he showed no signs of being either favorably or unfavorably disposed towards them, while some of his collaborators have stated that he is not likely to press measures against the Jews unless forced to do so." The relative restraint with which the first statute was applied reflected the Residency's acknowledgment of the integral role that Jews played in Morocco's already beleaguered economy. At the same time, Noguès worried about the statute's ability to foster pro-British sentiment among the Jewish community at the expense of positive feelings toward the French.[13]

When France entered the war against Germany, the Jews of Casablanca had donated large sums of money to the war effort. Bénatar organized the recruitment of 2,000 Jewish men of fighting age to serve with the French army. Many sons, fathers, and husbands died defending the Meuse river as part of the First Zouaves. For their support, Vichy France was now rewarding them with the impending destruction of their community.

THE ANTI-SEMITIC LAWS INTRODUCED at the end of October 1940 applied only to Moroccan Jews. The Protectorate had already introduced a *dahir* that provided the mechanisms for dealing with the refugees, Jewish and otherwise, who flooded Casablanca. In January 1940, a *dahir* specified that anyone thought to be a danger to public security or national defense, residing in the country illegally, or unable to leave, despite an expulsion order, could be interned.[14] The *dahir* gave the Protectorate the authority to deal with any elements that might become troublesome in wartime, but it also became an effective tool for corralling any refugees who outstayed their welcome or became a burden on the local government.

At the end of October 1940, the Protectorate opened an internment camp at Sidi-el-Ayachi, a small town close to Azemmour, some fifty miles southwest of Casablanca. It was the first of a network of thirty labor and internment camps throughout French Morocco, twelve of which housed Jews. Before the war, Sidi-el-Ayachi lodged members of the French Foreign Legion. Now it became a dumping ground for Jewish refugees who had outstayed their welcome in Casablanca.[15]

In mid-November, Goold passed to Robert du Gardier, head of Morocco's diplomatic cabinet, a proposal from Casablanca's Jewish community to facilitate the release of some of the internees. If the Protectorate agreed to release the Jewish men interned at Sidi-el-Ayachi, Casablanca's Jewish community would pay for them to live in Meknès, Settat, Mazagan, and elsewhere.

They pledged 200,000 francs for their maintenance and promised that the released men would not become a burden on the state or return to Casablanca.

In passing along the proposal, Goold acknowledged that the US government had no official interest in the matter, but he lent his personal support to the plan. "I write to you in this unofficial manner expressing the hope that something will be done to permit these people to live in the ordinary communities of the country," wrote Goold.[16] The *contrôleur civil* for Casablanca, however, nixed the plan on the grounds that the men could not be released for "reasons of public order."[17]

At the beginning of December, Goold visited the camp at Sidi-el-Ayachi in the company of Guy Capart, a representative of the Belgian Red Cross. "El Ayachi is definitely a prison into which some 160 unhappy people have been forced merely because they were 'cluttering' Casablanca, a city of three hundred and fifty thousand persons," wrote Goold. "Precisely how they were cluttering this city and making it impossible for the Police to carry on I have not been told, but, for the most part they are poor, and either quite without nationality or the citizens of countries which were, not so long ago, the glorious allies of France, but are emphatically not so at the present." In addition to destitute Jews, there were also some twenty Spaniards, whom Goold described as "the most forsaken of all."[18]

At the time of Goold's visit, Sidi-el-Ayachi housed one hundred single men, ten single women, and ten married couples. According to Capart's report, each day the inmates rose at 7:00 a.m. and ate breakfast at 7:30, before departing for a supervised work detail at 8:30. At 11:30, they returned to the camp for lunch, embarking once again at 1:30 p.m. for another work detail. They returned to the camp at 6:30 and received dinner at 7:30, followed by lights out and complete silence at 8:30. Throughout the day, the guards brutalized the internees for any transgression, real or imagined. The camp also lacked sufficient water, creating appalling sanitary conditions.[19]

"After visiting such an establishment, it is difficult to restrain oneself from musing over the very low estate to which Liberty, Equality, and Fraternity have fallen," wrote Goold. "Evidently, they are only words."[20]

13

The President's Secret Envoy

FROM THE MOMENT HE'D SET FOOT IN VICHY, ROBERT MURPHY'S dislike for the new French capital had grown. He came to loathe the town's "Alice-in-Wonderland atmosphere," which required him to conduct business in casinos, music halls, and hotels suites.[1] "All of us felt absurdly isolated in this inbred community, making our diplomatic rounds in this artificial, gaudy, improvised political centre," wrote Murphy in his memoirs.[2] After President Franklin D. Roosevelt recalled US ambassador to France William Bullitt for failing to follow the French government to Bordeaux, the job of keeping up American relations with France fell to Murphy, who acted as the American chargé d'affaires. Despairing of when he might return to Paris, he packed up his possessions, handed over the keys to his apartment, and joined the sad parade of bureaucrats, foreign officials, and sycophants making their way to Vichy.[3]

Murphy established a new US embassy at the Villa Les Adrets, a summerhouse leased from Frank and Florence Jay Gould, a jet-setting American couple who frequented the French Riviera and collected impressionist art.[4] Rather than claim rooms at the Hôtel des Ambassadeurs, where the diplomatic corps congregated, Murphy and the rest of the consulate staff lived at Villa Ica around the corner from the embassy. The arrangement afforded the Americans some privacy and helped them avoid the worst of the gossip mill.[5]

With no US ambassador yet appointed to Vichy—or a Vichy ambassador accredited in Washington—the job of explaining American policy fell to Murphy. A tall midwesterner with a disarming smile and a manner that charmed even the haughtiest of officials, Murphy had spent two decades in the Foreign Service, including a ten-year posting at the US embassy in Paris.

FIGURE 13.1. Robert Murphy, who served as President Franklin Roosevelt's secret envoy for North Africa. *Alamy Stock Photo*

Navigating the viper's nest of personalities that made up Henri-Philippe Pétain's cabinet demanded all of his tact and experience. His first task was to convince Vichy's leadership that the United States had no prior knowledge of the British attack on Mers-el-Kébir—and, in fact, found it deplorable—while also making it clear that American sympathies lay with Britain.[6]

Murphy worked hard to develop cordial relations with Pétain and Pierre Laval, regarding them as the key to France's future. "The old soldier and the suave lawyer-politician had almost nothing in common except their conviction that Germany had won the war and that Frenchmen must somehow adapt themselves to this fact," wrote Murphy.[7] When he questioned Vichy's increasing collaboration with Germany or asserted that the Allies would eventually triumph, he had the feeling that Pétain, the elder statesmen, merely indulged him. "Each time I talked with Pétain he expressed in some way his friendly feeling for the United States, implying that it was only his affection for our country that made him tolerate my rather unwelcome arguments."[8]

As for Laval, Murphy initially believed he would determine the future of Franco-German collaboration. Unlike other Vichy politicians who struggled with the bifurcated France, Laval appeared to thrive in the Vichy hot house. They had met at receptions and parties in Paris before the war, but the politically ambitious Laval never had reason to take an interest in Murphy. Now

Murphy found himself the object of Laval's attentions, giving him ample opportunity to study the Frenchman, whom he considered "the shrewdest, most forceful personal in Vichy." It quickly became clear that Laval's hatred of Britain, which he blamed for French losses in World War I, impaired his worldview. Laval even turned a tour of his château, located in nearby Chateldon, into an extended rant against the British, going so far as to invoke Joan of Arc. Laval's Anglophobia was compounded by a stunning naïveté about Hitler's ambitions—and a smug belief that the German führer could be outsmarted.[9]

AFTER SPENDING MORE THAN two months gazing through the looking glass, Murphy was recalled to Washington at the beginning of September 1940. He arrived just in time to witness the State Department's growing concern about French North Africa, particularly French Morocco. The fall of France and advent of the Vichy regime changed American calculations about the region. Believing the Vichy government a legitimate successor to the Third Republic, the United States immediately recognized it. The early nod to legitimacy helped dispose Vichy officials toward the neutral United States, as they believed the Americans could counterbalance the naked hostility of the British. They regarded the attack on Mers-el-Kébir and Britain's support for Charles de Gaulle's attempt to seize Dakar as evidence of British duplicity. Vichy officials also loathed Britain's economic blockade, which crippled their fragile economy by shutting down imports and interfering with trade between France and its colonies.

Policymakers and military men in Washington looked at the map of French North Africa and wondered if it would be possible to keep the region from falling into German hands. If Hitler seized what remained of the French fleet and established a formidable military presence in Morocco, Algeria, and Tunisia, then Germany could control the Mediterranean and shutdown Britain's lifeline to its empire through the Suez Canal. Casablanca, as the largest port in North Africa, would become a base for the German navy and air force, changing the scope of the battle for control of the Atlantic Ocean.[10]

At the end of October, a stream of intelligence reports began trickling in confirming American policy makers' worst fears. An "absolutely sure source" claimed Germany intended to seize the French fleet, including the battleship *Jean Bart*, docked in Casablanca. North Africa would then be divided up, with Algeria and Tunisia becoming subject to a tripartite Franco-German-Italian mandate. French Morocco, however, would go to Spain.[11] As if to confirm the ominous report, Spain occupied Tangier at the beginning of November 1940 in violation of the 1912 Treaty of Fez, which specified that the city was to remain an international zone. Spain claimed that its occupation prevented Tangier from falling into Italian hands, but the seizure caused panic in both London and Washington.[12] If that wasn't bad enough, a German official had arrived in Casablanca to observe the movement of ships to and from the port.[13] And in mid-November, a new rumor about the *Jean Bart* surfaced, this one claiming the ship was to be transferred from Casablanca to a port on the Mediterranean.[14]

As the rumors combined with Spanish aggression to ratchet up the anxiety level in Washington, one piece of seemingly good news remained: Pétain continued to oppose Germany's peace terms, and his ministers remained divided over whether to accept them.[15] This led the State Department and the White House to start thinking about how to strengthen Pétain's hand. One way to do that was to improve conditions in French North Africa generally and Morocco specifically. Maxime Weygand and Charles Noguès had not been shy about lobbying the United States for closer trade relations.[16]

IN MID-NOVEMBER, MURPHY RECEIVED a summons to a secret meeting.[17] Much to his surprise, he found himself in the Oval Office, seated across from a pair of inscrutable blue eyes, answering a string of questions about the Vichy regime and the men running it. A large map of French North Africa covered President Roosevelt's desk, and smoke curled upward from his ever-present cigarette.

A little more than week before, the American people had elected the fifty-eight-year-old Roosevelt to an unprecedented third consecutive term in the White House. For eight years, the New York–bred, Harvard-educated, Washington-hardened Roosevelt had entered American homes through his radio Fireside Chats. His voice, a friendly, wandering tenor, soothed and inspired a nation pained by but determined to navigate out of the Great Depression. He proposed and ushered through Congress sweeping economic and social programs that bootstrapped the lives of millions of Americans. As western Europe collapsed under the weight of tyrannical fascism, Americans again sought his voice to assure one and all that the United States would continue to build and defend its way of life.[18]

As Murphy spoke to his presidential host, it became clear that Roosevelt was intrigued by the fact the Franco-German armistice left North Africa free from German occupation and control. He had been giving serious thought to how the United States might encourage pro-Allied elements to resist collaborating with the Germans and, if it came to it, stop a Nazi invasion. Roosevelt considered Weygand the key to keeping the Germans from gaining a foothold. As the delegate-general for French North Africa, Weygand commanded more than 100,000 soldiers. If the Germans invaded, Weygand's response would determine the fate of the region. Roosevelt wanted to know more about the general and his long-term plans. He couldn't square in his mind the idea that "this honorable old soldier" could stomach France's subordination to Germany.[19] The president had also read the reports about French North Africa's deteriorating food supply and the need for sugar, tea, petrol, and drugs, particularly in Morocco.[20] He wondered if the United States could use economic aid as a tool to foster pro-Allied sentiment.

Roosevelt had a multitude of questions but few answers. Everything the Americans knew about the situation in French North Africa amounted to hearsay or came through the British, who had their own agenda regarding Vichy. The president wanted someone to go there, verify the claims of shortages, and determine what commodities were needed. He wanted someone to look Weygand in the eye and take his measure. Above all, Roosevelt hungered for an answer to the question of whether French North Africa could remain somewhat independent if the United States provided economic assistance.[21] And he decided that Murphy was the man to do it.

While Murphy came highly recommended by William Bullitt, the former US ambassador to France and a Roosevelt confidante, his Catholic faith helped win him the job. Given the Vichy regime's renewed emphasis on Catholicism, the president believed Murphy's faith would allow him to forge intimate relationships with French officials, especially Weygand. Roosevelt even proposed, with a mischievous wink, that Murphy and Weygand could go to church together. "That suggestion conjured a more amusing picture to me than it apparently did to the President," wrote Murphy.[22]

Murphy entered the White House as a chargé d'affaires but left as the president's special—and secret—envoy to North Africa. Going forward, he would serve as Roosevelt's eyes and ears, communicating anything of interest directly to him. For a career diplomat, the order to bypass the State Department came as a shock. When Murphy asked Undersecretary of State Sumner Welles about the president's instructions, Welles confirmed Roosevelt's penchant for informal relationships and urged him to follow orders.[23]

Less than a week after the meeting with Roosevelt, Murphy returned to Vichy. He planned to stay only long enough to obtain the necessary visas for his trip. According to the official State Department line, Murphy was embarking on a much-needed inspection tour of American consulates in French North and West Africa—a description that fooled no one. He arrived in Vichy to find the government in turmoil, delaying his departure by almost a month.[24]

Vichy's leadership had bickered nonstop over how cozy to become with Germany, but the disagreements reached a crisis point during the final months of 1940. On October 24, Pétain and Hitler famously shook hands—and posed for a notorious picture—in a railway car parked outside the train station in Montoire. Six days later, Pétain announced that the regime was "entering the path of collaboration."[25]

The nature of Franco-German collaboration, however, remained to be determined, as no formal agreement had yet been signed. Vichy wanted improved conditions for French prisoners of war, a relaxation in travel restrictions between occupied and unoccupied France, and a reduction in occupation levies. France paid 400 million francs a day to Germany, on top of providing a long list of commodities and goods regularly demanded by the German Armistice Commission for shipment to Germany and its territories.[26]

In return for making these concessions, Germany demanded Vichy to reclaim French Equatorial Africa, a loose grouping of French territories in central Africa that ran north from the Congo river to the Sahara. By staging a successful rebellion against Vichy in August, the colony had convinced de Gaulle that Africa could serve as a base for the French resistance. In Hitler's eyes, Vichy needed to retake French Equatorial Africa to demonstrate its commitment to its empire and eliminate de Gaulle's influence in Africa. Vichy dithered on setting a timetable for the operation, recognizing that any attack would more than likely provoke British retaliation. Was Vichy really prepared to battle Britain in Africa?[27]

Pétain's cabinet fractured over how much to concede to the Germans. Laval, whose zeal for close collaboration led him to make backroom deals with the Nazis without consulting Pétain, headed one faction. Marcel Peyrouton, the minister of the interior, led the other. Peyrouton believed that as long as Britain remained in the war, Vichy should cooperate as little as possible with Germany. Recognizing he needed to reorder the cabinet to tame the disagreements, Pétain asked his ministers to submit their resignations on December 13. Laval tendered his, smug in the belief that he, above all others, would remain. Much to his surprise, Pétain accepted it, ousting him from power and robbing Germany of its strongest advocate in Vichy. Laval had erred not so much in collaborating with the Germans but in failing to produce real results. With every deal he made, France's predicament grew worse. Angered by the loss of its best ally inside the Vichy government, Germany closed the demarcation line. No one from Vichy was allowed into the occupied zone, putting Paris out of reach.[28]

14

The Agreement

On December 17, 1940, Robert Murphy boarded a 10:30 a.m. Air France flight bound for Algiers, finally embarking on the mission that Franklin Roosevelt had given him more than a month before.[1] Pierre Laval's ouster four days earlier removed the personal and bureaucratic obstacles to his trip, and the required visas were finally issued. Vichy even offered to provide him with a plane, but the State Department told Murphy to decline the offer.[2] Murphy needed the capacity to determine his own itinerary and not depend on a French flight crew loyal to Vichy with orders to report his movements in detail. Along with the small notebooks into which he scribbled memoranda at every meeting, Murphy carried with him a French translation of the Quran, which he was reading to better understand North Africa.

Even though the machinations behind the diplomat's inspection tour qualified as both juicy gossip and political news, the press in the United States and Vichy France downplayed the trip at the request of their respective governments.[3] It made no mention of the forthcoming meeting between Murphy and Maxime Weygand. Both Vichy and American officials feared that any glowing publicity would provoke German ire.[4] Nevertheless, the trip proved noteworthy enough to earn a mention halfway around the world in Saigon's French weekly, *Le Nouvelliste d'Indochine*.[5]

When Murphy landed in Algiers, he discovered that General Weygand was 2,500 miles southwest in Dakar, having embarked on another inspection tour. Rather than wait for his return, Murphy headed out to join him, cramming his tall frame into a trimotor Dewoitine transport plane for two days.[6]

FIGURE 14.1. General Maxime Weygand. *Sueddeutsche Zeitung Photo / Alamy Stock Photo*

Weygand's choice of location for their initial meeting on December 21 made Murphy wonder if the Americans had misjudged the general. He proposed the office of Pierre Boisson, the high commissioner of French West Africa and the man responsible for preventing Charles de Gaulle from turning Dakar into a base for the French resistance. By all accounts, Boisson was an ardent Vichyite, but Murphy found him to be pro-British, pro-French, and anti–de Gaulle—a collection of attitudes that embodied the messy nature of French politics in the winter of 1940. In Boisson's eyes, de Gaulle's attempt to seize Dakar jeopardized France's presence in Africa, which impelled him to defend the city. If de Gaulle had succeeded, Boisson believed, Germany would have immediately occupied North Africa.[7]

Murphy's fears evaporated as the meeting progressed. Weygand and Boisson, who stayed for the discussion, didn't mince words.[8] The three men discussed how the United States could help French North Africa and the many potential obstacles to delivering aid. Vichy might object for fear of upsetting Germany. Berlin might object lest American assistance embolden Vichy to resist German demands. London might object because such aid ran contrary to its economic blockade of Nazi-occupied territories, which included Vichy France and its colonies.

Murphy impressed upon Weygand that Britain would only agree to the deal if strenuous safeguards prevented goods imported from the United States from being reexported to Vichy for use by Germany. Vichy had to guarantee the goods would stay in North Africa. Weygand told Murphy to name his terms—and he would meet them.[9]

Weygand also made his stance toward Germany and Britain clear to Murphy in the presence of Boisson. If Germany invaded North Africa, French forces would resist with every man and airplane available.[10] As for Britain, he wished Winston Churchill and his advisors would follow a different strategy. "Obviously I hope for a British victory. We all do," said Weygand. "My primary job, however, is to keep French Africa intact for France. It is a situation in which the greatest discretion must be exercised. It is a great misfortune that the British feel that everything must be shouted from the rooftops." Weygand wished they would "act intelligently."[11]

It was the beginning of a beautiful working relationship. Weygand left the meeting with an "excellent impression" of Murphy. "Quite apart from his personality, his attitude, and his courtesy, all of which created a liking of him, Mr. Robert Murphy proved in this first exchange of views very candid and very well disposed toward France," wrote Weygand in his memoirs.[12] Murphy left the meeting with answers for Roosevelt: Weygand would defend French Africa from the Nazis, and he wanted American assistance.

FOLLOWING THE MEETING, ARMED with a travel pass signed by the general, Murphy continued his "inspection tour."[13] Instead of staying in Dakar, where he could have spent Christmas Eve slurping down oysters at a rousing holiday party, he headed inland to Gao, a ramshackle town on the river Niger in Sudan (now Mali), which the French were attempting to revitalize.[14]

Christmas Day found a homesick Murphy at a lavish banquet for twenty sheiks hosted by the resident-general. After two decades of towering over pasty-skinned European diplomats in navy and charcoal suits, Murphy was the short man in a room full of imposing black Muslims cloaked in brilliantly colored silk robes. When Murphy discovered that the sheik sitting beside him could speak French, they fell into conversation. Murphy mentioned that he had been reading the Quran to better understand Islamic thought. "I said jestingly that we Americans were impressed by Mohammed's encouragement of multiple wives, because we found that even one wife could present many problems," wrote Murphy. "The chief could not believe that I would joke about such a serious subject. He explained solemnly that he never had the slightest difficulty with his four wives, since he kept them in separate villages about fifty kilometers apart."[15]

After spending the New Year in Tunis, Murphy finally headed for Casablanca and arrived on January 3, 1941.[16] Within an hour of setting foot in the city, he received a phone call at his hotel from Theodor Auer, the senior German official in town, requesting a meeting.[17] Auer oversaw the local office of the German Armistice Commission, which determined what goods the Nazis could extract from Morocco to benefit the war effort. He also directed German intelligence efforts in the country.

When Murphy didn't jump at his request, Auer followed up with a note reminding him of their shared years in Paris, when Auer served as first secretary of the Germany embassy. "Probably you are very busy but if you should find a spare moment for a rendezvous it would certainly give me great pleasure," wrote Auer.[18] Although he remembered Auer as a likeable fellow, Murphy wasn't keen on having him "poking around in my affairs."

After some prodding from French officials, Murphy met Auer at last in the bar of the fashionable Hôtel Transatlantique for drinks. Ensconced in a room adorned from floor to ceiling with green and white mosaic titles, the two diplomatic hands sized each other up. Auer got to the point at once, asking Murphy why he was in Africa. Murphy gave him a spiel about looking for commercial opportunities—the United States was a nation of businessmen, as Auer surely knew—and inspecting the consulates.

Auer didn't buy it for a minute.

"Murphy, I will be more honest with you than you were with me," Auer told him. "I came here for one purpose only, to convince that prize ass in Berlin, our Fuehrer, of the importance of the Mediterranean and of Morocco in particular. Herr Hitler does not seem aware that this area exists. He always looks in every direction except south." Auer had been waging a campaign to have the Italians on the armistice commission replaced with Germans and would soon have enough men to do a proper job. "Notwithstanding Auer's geniality and the highballs, my spirits sank. The last thing we wanted was active Berlin interest in the western Mediterranean," wrote Murphy.[19]

Murphy spent his last night in North Africa in Tangier before catching a flight to Lisbon on January 11. From Lisbon, he pounded out a report outlining what he'd learned.[20] "Above all, I was delighted to meet Frenchmen who were strongly anti-Nazi, who were much more pro-British than I had anticipated," wrote Murphy. He also passed along a plea from Weygand for the British to quit using him as part of their propaganda campaign. Every time a report appeared about his pledging to resist the Nazis or about North

African opposition to the Germans, his job got that much harder. "He would be the happiest man in the world if his name would never be mentioned; almost every time it is mentioned there is a back-fire from the Germans thus rendering his task doubly difficult."[21] After that, the BBC and British press avoided any mention of Weygand's continuing the struggle.[22]

MURPHY'S TRAVELS SPURRED INTENSE discussions in London and Washington about what kind of aid they could provide to North Africa. Both the Americans and the British agreed that strengthening Henri-Philippe Pétain's hand against Germany would help the Allied war effort. The British, however, did not want the program to dilute the effectiveness of its blockade against Germany.[23]

During World War I Britain's economic blockade targeted all sectors of the German economy but became notorious for its success in depriving the German population of food and consumer goods.[24] Hitler, like many right-wing Germans, believed the deprivations experienced by the German people had caused them to revolt against their leaders and demand an end to a war Germany was clearly winning.[25] He manipulated the "stab-in-the-back" myth, as it was popularly known, to orchestrate his rise to power.[26]

Britain believed the blockade had played a critical role in its victory over Germany in World War I—and would help win the current war. If Germany did not have wool, it could not clothe its troops; if it did not have iron ore, it could not build munitions; if it did not have food, it could not feed its soldiers, the German people, or civilians in occupied territories. But in mid-November 1940, the Committee on Allied Resistance warned the War Cabinet that Vichy's continued trade with French North Africa not only diluted the blockade's effectiveness but also reinforced the regime's control over French colonies. "We are not only blunting the spear-head of our own attack," lamented the committee, "but also strengthening the force of the Vichy Government's potential attack against the Free French colonies—or against ourselves."[27]

Through a combination of intelligence gathering and eyewitness reports, Britain and the United States documented the extent of German extractions and Vichy acquiescence during the fall. Germany requisitioned 118,000 quintals of wheat at Moulins. As French officials scoured the countryside counting livestock, villages slaughtered their cattle, sheep, and pigs to prevent them from being requisitioned. Of the 17,000 sheep that arrived in Nice from Algeria, more than 11,000 were routed to Italy with their final destination unknown. In Aix-en-Provence, the supply of potatoes—including those still in the ground—was bought up wholesale. Freeman Matthews, an American Foreign Service officer, personally witnessed German officers checking food shipments arriving from Algeria and received a steady stream of reports from Marseille of large "purchases" of foodstuffs. Vichy even boasted that from mid-September to mid-October more than 200,000 tons of goods from North Africa entered French ports. There was also ample evidence that the Germans and Italians seized as much as 60 percent of the supplies coming from French North Africa.[28]

Nevertheless, the Americans hoped to sway the British to sign off on an economic-assistance program for North Africa, especially French Morocco. It wasn't an impossible request. Roosevelt had just talked Britain into providing milk to children in Vichy, pitching the program as a way "to win over the French people whose sentiment is turning more favorably towards Great Britain and becoming more hostile to joining Germany." He argued such aid would strengthen the United States' hand in dealing with Vichy by showing that the regime could receive assistance as long as it remained friendly to the Americans and refused to help Germany. "I know you will appreciate," Roosevelt wrote Churchill, "that this government has not the slightest intention of undertaking any policy which would weaken or militate against the efficacy of the British blockade."[29] After months of resisting the idea, Churchill agreed to the program at the start of 1941.[30]

Churchill acquiesced to the milk program because the United States played a key role in maintaining a dialogue with Vichy. Providing milk to children was a small price to support diplomatic relations. The prime minister also could not overlook Roosevelt's support for Lend-Lease. In December 1940, Churchill had asked Roosevelt for help securing warships, merchant ships, and aircraft to continue the war. Britain also needed American assistance in escorting supply convoys across the Atlantic. "The decision for 1941 lies upon the seas," wrote Churchill. "The moment approaches when we shall no longer be able to pay cash for shipping and other supplies."[31] Roosevelt's solution was Lend-Lease. The United States would produce the needed armaments and "lend" them to Britain, neatly sidestepping the sticky issue of granting loans, credits, or subsides to a belligerent.[32]

In the early days of 1941, as it stood alone against Hitler in western Europe, Britain regarded the economic blockade as key to its long-term survival. Roosevelt regarded the Murphy-Weygand agreement as another tool to keep Vichy France's dependence on Germany at a minimum. Would the British agree to another concession?

On February 27, 1941, Murphy returned to Vichy with a piece of paper in his pocket. The previous day in Algiers, Weygand had initialed a memorandum of understanding covering the North African Economic Aid Program, otherwise known as the Murphy-Weygand agreement. Under the agreement, the French could not stockpile the goods provided by the Americans and must distribute them to those in need. The supplies also had to be consumed in North Africa. Nothing could be sent to Vichy. The American government would station control officers at ports throughout North Africa to observe the arrival and distribution of the supplies. Finally, if the French violated the terms, the Americans would terminate the agreement immediately.

As a show of faith, Weygand provided a list of German and Italian officials in French Morocco working for the armistice commission. Among the Germans there were twelve officers, sixteen noncommissioned officers, fourteen soldiers, ten mechanics, and two civilians, including Auer. The Italian delegation consisted of twenty-two officers, ten noncommissioned officers, eighteen soldiers, and seven civilians. Charles Noguès assured Murphy that his intelligence service was keeping a close eye on the Germans, tracking their every move. Given the German and Italian delegates' lack of experience with Arab affairs or knowledge of North Africa, Noguès believed it would be some time before they exerted much influence.[33]

Even though Weygand signed off on the terms, Pétain still had to give his blessing, forcing Murphy to once again navigate the surreal world of hotel room offices and ministries run out of former casinos. This time, Murphy had help from William Leahy, the new American ambassador. Leahy arrived in the makeshift capital at the beginning of January after a bitterly cold and treacherous journey by car and train from Madrid. Roosevelt hoped that his military service—Leahy was the former chief of naval operations—would allow him to develop a rapport with Pétain. Leahy was also Roosevelt's man. The two men forged a friendship during World War I when Roosevelt served as assistant secretary of the navy and Leahy oversaw naval transport.[34] "Marshal Pétain is remarkably capable for a man of his age," reported Leahy after their first meeting, "but the burden of work which he has assumed is beyond his physical capacity. He does not appear to have complete confidence in any of his Cabinet."[35]

On March 4, Leahy and Murphy met with Pétain and Admiral Jean-François Darlan to discuss some disquieting developments with regard to North Africa.[36] Laval's spectacular fall in December led to Darlan's ascendency from commander of the French fleet to vice premier. The piercing blue eyes dancing under black caterpillar eyebrows and a tendency to set his hat at a rakish angle belied Darlan's long career as a shrewd operator. Unlike many of Pétain's key supporters, who exhibited royalist sympathies, Darlan came from a family with a strong republican tradition and leftist political connections. During the 1930s, he served in a series of staff jobs, forging alliances with successive liberal governments, which garnered the French navy robust budgets despite the penny-pinching ways of the Third Republic. By the time World War II erupted, the French navy had never been stronger. Under Vichy, Darlan used his political acumen to build an empire of his own. Since becoming vice premier, Darlan had also assumed the roles of foreign minister, minister of information, and minister of the interior.[37]

Leahy began the meeting by mentioning the rumors about petrol moving from North Africa to Italy, a worrisome development given a recent deal to provide Morocco with needed fuel. The United States had arranged the shipment as a goodwill gesture. Pétain claimed to know nothing about the shipments, while Darlan became visibly uncomfortable and launched into a long-winded explanation of why Vichy had to provide the petrol. Leahy reminded them that movement of petrol from North Africa to Germany or Italy would kill the impending economic agreement. He then brought up the growing numbers of Germans in Casablanca, only to have Darlan bat the issue away by saying the armistice agreement required it.

Pétain and Darlan also scoffed at American concerns that Germany might be planning an invasion of North Africa. Pétain believed this would only happen if Germany failed to take Britain. "So you must make up your minds," he told the Americans, "whether you prefer the failure of an attempted invasion of England followed by an unsuccessful invasion of French North Africa, or an attempted invasion of French North Africa followed by an unsuccessful invasion of England." No matter what, Vichy would resist any German incursion into North Africa.

Before Leahy and Murphy departed, they mentioned one other rumor: Weygand would not have his job much longer. When Pétain dismissed such murmurings as gossip, Leahy reminded them that Weygand's presence in North Africa factored into Washington's support for the economic program.[38]

Weygand's arrival in Vichy two days later helped move discussions about the economic agreement along. Over lunch with Leahy and Murphy, Weygand admitted that he had no illusions about the purity of the Germans' intentions: they had come to Morocco to spread propaganda among the native population and spy on the French. When asked about the petrol shipment to Italy, Weygand said he deplored the arrangement but had been forced to comply. He hoped, however, that the economic agreement would allow him to withstand further demands. He also promised to provide the Americans with a detailed report of what North Africa needed soon and confirmed that petrol, auto parts, twine for binding crops, tea, and sugar would top the list.[39]

Vichy, of course, had to consult with the armistice commission, which tried and failed to find a basis for forbidding an agreement with the United States. Instead, the commission attempted to convince Vichy that it would eventually have enough food to feed its people.[40]

On March 11, Pétain and Darlan approved the Murphy-Weygand agreement.[41] Two weeks later, Britain approved it as well, thereby granting the ships traveling from the United States to North Africa passage through the blockade. In fact, Britain wanted the United States to send its observers to North Africa as soon as possible.[42]

15

Visa Problems

JOSEPHINE BAKER HAD BEEN HIDING OUT IN LES MILANDES SINCE escaping Paris following the fall of France. Over the previous few years, she had spent little time at the château deep in the countryside of the Dordogne, but now it became a sanctuary. "How peaceful it was in this beautiful setting," she wrote. "It was hard to believe that elsewhere people were fighting, suffering, dying."[1] The château might have seemed suspended in time, but the radio brought news of the war and the Germans occupying her beloved Paris. Regulations forbidding Jews and blacks to take the stage now banned Baker, once the toast of the City of Lights, from performing. A sign nailed to the door of the Folies-Bergère read, "Access Forbidden to Dogs and Jews."[2]

The radio also delivered the rousing addresses of Charles de Gaulle. "We were deeply moved by the General's voice uttering words we had despaired of hearing, phrases that touched our innermost beings," she wrote. "His ringing tones reflected the indomitable spirit of France itself, which I knew would never die. From that moment on everything seemed possible."[3] Jacques Abtey, the French intelligence officer and Baker's handler, had also found his way to Les Milandes, avoiding the Vichy regime's call to join its ranks. Between hunting and fishing, he made contact with his old boss, Captain Paul Paillole, who was now masterminding an underground intelligence network in Vichy.[4]

In October 1940, a courier arrived from Paillole with an assignment. Paillole wanted Abtey to go to Portugal and make contact with British intelligence. But he remained leery of Baker. "I was afraid that she was one of those shallow show business personalities who would shatter like glass if exposed to danger," said Paillole. Despite his reservations, he agreed to give her a chance.[5]

According to the cover story they devised, Baker was embarking on a tour of Portugal and South America. Given that Germany had swallowed up most of western Europe, it would be logical for Baker, an international star, to look to neutral Portugal and the untouched countries of South America for bookings. Abtey, posing as her ballet master, became the forty-one-year-old Jacques-François Hébert. Abtey, who was really thirty-five, had to be aged because no man under forty was permitted to leave Vichy.[6] To make himself look older, Abtey wore glasses and donned a heavy moustache. Assessing the starlet and her middle-aged ballet master, Paillole declared himself satisfied. "You look good together," he said. "Good luck."

To reach Portugal from Vichy, they needed transit visas for Spain. Baker worked her magic, charming a reluctant Spanish consul in Toulouse into giving them the needed paperwork. She did the same at the Portuguese and Brazilian consulates.

WINDING THROUGH THE PYRENEES by train, the duo crossed over the border from Vichy into Spain on November 23. The information collected by Paillole about the German army in western France was written in invisible ink on the back of Baker's sheet music. Photographs were pinned to the inside of her dress. At the border crossing, Baker, decked out in a stunning fur coat that engulfed her lithe frame, chatted amiably with the Spanish policeman and German agents. The star-struck officials didn't give a second glance to the drab man accompanying her. "You see what a good cover I am?" she told Abtey.[7]

Had Baker and Abtey been discovered with the information they carried, their lives would have been in jeopardy, as would Paillole's fledging resistance movement within French intelligence. "This woman had undertaken, of her own volition, to cover me to the very end, closing the door behind her and binding her fate to mine," said Abtey years later. "I call that courage."

From Madrid, they flew to Lisbon, where Baker booked into the Hotel Aviz while Abtey found lodgings elsewhere. It didn't take long for the journalists to descend upon her, allowing her to talk up her forthcoming South American tour. Meanwhile, Abtey contacted Wilfred Dunderdale, who had until the fall of Paris served as Britain's station chief in the French capital.[8] Along with expressions of appreciation from London, he passed on new instructions: Abtey was to stay in Portugal until he received new orders while Baker returned to Vichy.

At the beginning of December, Baker flew to Marseille, where Paillole debriefed her. He found her faith in the Free French cause a welcome dose of optimism. "The United States is going to enter the war and we're sure to win," she told him.[9] Baker also ran into Frédéric Rey, an old lover and dance partner. He encouraged her do a revival of *La créole* at Marseille's Opéra, rather than return to Les Milandes. Baker had starred in the comic opera, which features music by Jacques Offenbach, to rave reviews in 1934. Along with the lure of returning to the stage, performing the opera would give her a reason to be in Marseille—and Vichy for that matter—while she waited for Abtey to return. The theater's management agreed, thrilled to put Baker on their marquee.[10]

As Baker and Rey got to work recreating from memory the costumes and sets of the previous production, Abtey continued his discussions with British intelligence in Lisbon. Abtey emphasized that he and Baker wanted to be categorized not as spies but as members of the Free French, with the ultimate goal of joining General Charles de Gaulle in London. But that was not to be. Instead, they received a new mission: to go to Casablanca and set up a liaison station, where they would relay messages and intelligence between Vichy and London.

ON CHRISTMAS EVE 1940, the new production of *La créole* opened with Abtey in the audience. On January 15, 1941, the duo received news that they needed to leave for North Africa sooner than expected. Paillole had become anxious about the possibility of the Germans marching into Vichy and wanted them on the next boat to Algiers. Their early departure meant that Baker could not perform the last two shows as scheduled. When they claimed Baker was ill, the suspicious theater manager demanded a doctor's note, which they produced. The fake note asserted that Baker "had a shadow on her lungs, and should leave this cold country as soon as possible." It helped that Baker had been coughing nonstop.

Refusing to leave her animals behind, Baker dispatched a friend to Les Milandes to fetch them. "I can't understand abandoning animals! They would never do it to us," she told Rey. The menagerie consisted of Bonzo, a Great Dane; Glug Glug, a female monkey with a mean streak; Gugusse, a small monkey "nasty as the plague"; Mica, a "suave lionmonkey"; and Curler and Question Marker, two tiny white mice. The animals, along with twenty-eight pieces of luggage packed with costumes and Baker's extensive wardrobe, made the trip across the Mediterranean.[11]

By the end of January, Baker, Abtey, and the menagerie were in Casablanca. As they made plans for Baker to return to Portugal to continue her intelligence gathering, they encountered a roadblock: the Portuguese consulate refused to issue Abtey a visa for Lisbon. Baker even tried the damsel-in-distress argument—"how would I manage the details without him?"—but the consul held firm. Abtey was stuck in French Morocco.

Back at their hotel, they debated about what to do next. "Do you think they may have blown your cover, Jacques?" she asked. Abtey didn't think so, but they needed to press forward. "We decided," wrote Baker, "that I would have to travel to Lisbon alone. Taking my sheet music, of course."[12]

At the end of February, Baker took the train north to Tangier, where she could catch a flight to Lisbon. While in Tangier, she renewed friendships forged during the filming of *Princesse Tam-Tam*, shot on location there and in Tunisia in 1935. She spent a few days at the villa of Abderahman Menebhi, the sultan's brother-in-law, where she also saw Ahmed ben Bachir, the court chamberlain to the caliph of Spanish Morocco. With influential friends and a command of Spanish, Baker was also poised to gather information about Spanish Morocco.[13]

By the beginning of March, Baker was back in Lisbon, where posters with her face plastered walls and kiosks around the city, announcing her upcoming shows. She needed every seat filled; her take of the box office receipts had become increasingly important. Financial restrictions made it difficult to get money from her bank accounts in Paris, putting a damper on her normally extravagant tastes. Between rehearsals, Baker lobbied for a visa for Abtey. She also collected bits of intelligence from sources who found their way to her, along with information she amassed from loose-lipped diplomats and Axis officials. She returned to Morocco at the end of March with messages from Paillole to Abtey pinned inside her bra. And once again, notes written in invisible ink covered the back of her sheet music. She didn't, however, have a visa for Abtey.[14]

For the next few months, Baker flitted back and forth between Casablanca and Lisbon, Seville, Madrid, and Barcelona. Between performances, she accepted invitations to parties and embassy functions, where she hobnobbed with the elite and diplomats. As she bantered over champagne and twirled around the dance floor, she continued her intelligence gathering, transporting the information back to Abtey.[15]

Meanwhile, for those stuck in Marseille without celebrity status, exit visas for the United States, Cuba, and Mexico became prized possessions. So too did a spot on a ship bound for the Americas—and Casablanca became a regular stop on the French Caribbean route between Marseille, Casablanca, and Martinique. Between October 1940 and May 1941, sixteen ships carrying refugees called at Casablanca on their way to Fort-de-France.[16] While it operated, the Marseille-Casablanca-Martinique route ultimately became one of the most reliable ways to leave Vichy France.[17] For Varian Fry, who operated the Emergency Rescue Committee, which focused on helping intellectuals and artists targeted by the Nazis, the route was a godsend. "We couldn't have thought up anything better if we had the power to arrange the route ourselves," wrote Fry. "They not only eliminated the trouble with the transit visas—they also removed the danger of the trip through Spain."[18]

Even as the city still swam with refugees, Hélène Bénatar found her efforts to aid refugees thwarted by the appointment of a new civil controller for Casablanca. The insufficiently pro-Vichy Louis Contard had been sacked and replaced with Georges Poussier, whose allegiance was to Maxime Weygand. On May 16, 1941, Poussier notified Bénatar that her committee represented a threat to the "security of the state" and was being dissolved. He asked that she present herself to the prefect and turn over all her records. Bénatar appeared, as requested, but claimed not to have any records. She also argued that the refugees living in Casablanca still needed help emigrating to North and South America. In response, Poussier told her she was the subject of an internment order.[19]

Bénatar had made many friends over the years, and one of them secured for her an interview with Resident-General Charles Noguès. Upon hearing her predicament, he told her that if she encountered any more trouble with Poussier, she was to inform him immediately. Two days later, Colonel Maurice Herviot, the head of the Sûreté in Casablanca, asked her to come see him. Instead of threatening deportation, Herviot handed her a card, written in his own hand, authorizing her to continue her work. Unable to reconstitute the formal committee, she continued her work with refugees under her own name.[20]

BÉNATAR'S ONGOING REFUGEE WORK would be instrumental in helping the passengers of the ill-fated SS *Alsina*. In January 1941, the ship left Marseille bound for Argentina. Among the passengers were two hundred Spanish Republicans, including Niceto Alcala Zamora y Torres, the former president of Spain. In desperate need of farmers, the Argentine government actively sought to recruit Basques, who had a reputation as good farmers, to emigrate to Argentina. The recruitment campaign gave Spanish Republicans

with Basque heritage a way to leave Vichy. Given Spain's friendly relationship with Germany, they feared it was only a matter of time before they
were rounded up and sent back to Spain, where Francisco Franco's government would gladly have them shot.[21] Also onboard the *Alsina* were Jewish
refugees—Russians, Czechs, Belgians, Romanians, and Poles—headed to
Mexico, the United States, and Argentina.[22] Ninety of the Jews carried visas
issued by Brazil's ambassador to Vichy, Luis Martins de Souza Dantas, in
violation of his government's ban on Jewish immigration.[23]

After the *Alsina*, sailing under a French flag, cleared the Strait of Gibraltar, its captain received orders from Vichy to change course and head for
Dakar. The Royal Navy had seized and intercepted its sister ship, the SS
Mendoza, off the coast of Brazil, and Vichy officials feared a similar fate
might befall the *Alsina*.[24] On January 27, the *Alsina* sailed into Dakar's harbor—and remained there for the next four months, languishing off the coast,
a floating metal jail baking in the hot African sun. The passengers suffered
from malnourishment and disease in the increasingly filthy conditions.[25]

In mid-June, the *Alsina* finally sailed for French Morocco. Upon arriving in Casablanca, the refugees received permission to leave their maritime
prison.[26] At this point the plights of the Spanish Republicans and the Jews
diverged. The Jews were sent to an internment camp until, in July 1941, the
SS *Nyssa* called at Casablanca and two hundred of them left for New York.[27]

Meanwhile, the Spanish Republicans boarded another ship and sailed
back to French West Africa, where they were interned at Rufisque.[28] While
shipping them south decreased the chances of Vichy's handing them over to
Spain, something Noguès did not want to do, it made getting them to Argentina that much more difficult. Small Portuguese cargo ships sailed between
Dakar and Casablanca, but those trips were infrequent and unscheduled.
The Spanish Republicans also could not use the Casablanca-Tangier-Lisbon
route, as entering Spanish Morocco would result in their immediate arrest.

The Residency hoped that the US consulate could secure passage for the
Spanish Republicans, but the Americans could do little except help with
transit visas and other paperwork. No American ships had called at Casablanca in more than fifteen months.[29]

After an agonizing summer, plans finally came together for the Spaniards
to sail to Lisbon on the SS *Quanza*, a Portuguese steamer, and they were
brought back to Casablanca. But when the *Quanza* docked on October 30,
1941, French officials discovered the ship's navicert didn't cover the Spaniards. The captain refused to transport them unless the paperwork was fixed.
H. Earle Russell, who had replaced Goold as the US consul general, sent an
urgent message to the American legation in Lisbon asking for assistance in

updating the navicert, issued by the British embassy there. As they waited to learn their fate, the Spaniards slept on the pier overnight, as no last-minute accommodations were available in Casablanca.[30]

When no response had arrived from Lisbon by the next morning, the captain again threatened to sail without the Spanish Republicans. Robert du Gardier, the Protectorate's diplomatic chief, begged Russell to do something. He feared that if the refugees didn't leave on the *Quanza*, they would be stranded in French Morocco indefinitely and Noguès would be pressured to turn them over to Franco. Russell decided to take the extraordinary—potentially career-ending—step of issuing the navicert himself.[31]

After months of handwringing about arrangements and cruel twists of fate, Russell, du Gardier, and Bénatar watched with satisfaction as the Spaniards boarded the *Quanza*. Before they made their way up the gangplank, Alcala Zamora and other members of his party thanked Russell for his assistance. "In 25 years of experience I have never heard anything more sincere, more heartfelt or more pitiful than the expressions of gratitude emanating not only from these two notables but also literally dozens of less eminent Spanish refugees on board," wrote Russell. "Had the work and risk been far more than they were, these expressions would have repaid me many times over for the efforts of my staff and myself."[32] Alcala Zamora also asked Bénatar to pass along his thanks to Noguès. The president knew that this journey could have ended not in Argentina but in Spain.[33]

At 11:00 p.m., the ship departed for Lisbon. After stops at Vera Cruz and Havana, the Spanish Republicans reached Buenos Aires before the new year.[34]

16

Absent Without Leave

On February 26, 1941, Ted Harris, a soldier in the French Foreign Legion, boarded a train for Casablanca. The young "Englishman" hoped that a trip to French Morocco might finally provide him with a way to sail for Britain and join the fight against the Nazis.

Despite the Franco-German armistice's call for the demobilization of the French Foreign Legion, Harris had remained in uniform and stuck in Algeria. After fighting with his cavalry unit at the Somme, the twenty-four-year-old Harris received orders to report to Port-Vendres for transport back to North Africa. "The journey lasted three days," wrote Harris in his memoir. "Then it was Oran, the camp of the Legion, the German sergeants, the Prussian corporals, the harsh discipline which the war had completely relegated into oblivion. It was like a bitter awakening from a dream into reality."[1] From Oran, they traveled to Sidi-Bel-Abbes, "the great sorting center of the Legion" and its home since 1843. Instead of battling the Germans, Harris spent the next six months serving as squadron secretary and running the commissary. His overly liberal approach to store credit earned him a transfer to a mechanized unit conducting training with World War I–era equipment. It was enough to drive a soldier mad.[2]

Unlike Arthur Koestler, Harris signed up with the Legion because he wanted to fight. He enlisted in the fall of 1939, when it looked like it would be months before Britain faced Germany on the battlefield. As with many a man in the Legion, Harris wasn't really Harris. He had been born Fedor Vladimirovich Minorsky in Petrograd, Russia, in 1916 to Tatiana, a translator, and Vladimir, a sometime diplomat and renowned scholar of Persian and Kurdish. After fleeing the Russian Revolution, the Minorskys settled in

Paris before moving to London in 1933. When he entered the Legion, young Minorsky adopted a new identity, the first of many. He wrote "Theodor Harris" on the inside cover of the diary he kept in prison in Casablanca and published his account of his time in the Legion under that name.[3]

Harris had received his cavalry training at Sidi-Bel-Abbes, which meant he knew plenty of the legionnaires still wandering around the town, scheming for new assignments to make themselves useful. His old friend Jean was shocked to see him alive and well, having been told of Harris's death by a man who claimed to have dug his grave. After the macabre welcome, Harris learned that their mutual friend Peter had also survived and now lived in Casablanca. When Germany invaded Poland, Peter had been on vacation in the South of France. Rather than return home to England, he also impulsively joined the Legion. The two Englishmen cemented their friendship over dinners of couscous from Arab stalls and alcohol-soaked discussions about their mutual desire for adventure.[4]

It didn't take long for Harris to secure a leave pass and a ten-day certificate of accommodation for Casablanca, allowing him to visit Peter. "Casablanca was a revelation to me," he wrote. "It is a wealthy interloping city, where thousands of people live without any ascertainable or any well-defined means of support."[5] Instead of arriving to a rousing reunion, he found Peter bedridden with the flu. With only ten days to plot his getaway, Harris wished Peter well and set to work hatching a plan to get himself to England.

Harris quickly learned to make his inquiries with care. "One had to act with discretion because the town was full of police spies and German agents-provocateurs," he wrote. One scam worked with chilling efficiency. Knowing that men hungered to leave Morocco and join the Free French in London, Vichy agents loitered in cafés, eavesdropping on conversations, waiting for the right moment to suggest a means of escape. The agents then offered to arrange to transport from Fédala, a town just north of Casablanca, to Gibraltar for two hundred francs. After nightfall on the appointed evening, the eager men climbed into a waiting boat. When the boat was full, the agent disappeared and the police materialized to arrest them all.[6]

Harris also visited the American consulate, where he spoke with the clerk who handled British visas. He received no encouragement and went away empty-handed. Unlike Arthur Koestler, Harris didn't have four authentic British soldiers to vouch for him or a master spy waiting in the wings to help.[7]

HARRIS'S VISIT TO THE US consulate and his experience in the cafés pulled him into the orbit of a scheme hatched by Theodor Auer, head of the

Gestapo in Casablanca, to embarrass the Americans. In July 1940, the US consulate had assumed responsibility for British interests in French Morocco, which included helping refugees, stranded nationals, and those in need of financial assistance. From its inception, the office of three clerks struggled to keep up with the heavy workload and ran a "pretty ragged" operation. Herbert Goold, the consul general, and Quincy Stanton, his second in command, also found it difficult to keep a close watch on the office owing to the explosion of their own workload. In addition, the British interests section was located across the street from the American consulate in what was known as the "annex," the old British consulate, which further isolated the office.[8]

At the beginning of March 1941, Robert du Gardier, Morocco's diplomatic chief, informed Goold and Stanton of evidence that Auer intended to entangle the British interests section—and by extension the American consulate—in a scheme to organize clandestine departures from French Morocco. Auer intended to use the scheme as a pretext for demanding the assignment of fifty extra German soldiers to Morocco to watch the Americans. Since Auer had already embarrassed the Belgians with a similar operation and even arrested their consul general, du Gardier feared the Americans might be next.[9]

Goold and Stanton decided to take the warning seriously. Cyril Barton-Smith, a clerk working in the British section, was sent to the interior on a much-needed holiday. French intelligence suspected Thomas Proctor, his colleague, of aiding Auer's scheme. Barton-Smith's absence would isolate him. Shelia Clark, a British citizen and the longest-serving clerk at the US consulate, was put in charge of the office. French intelligence hoped the office shakeup would force Auer to make his move, allowing them to arrest his agents.[10]

Auer failed to act, but Clark's yeoman efforts revealed that things weren't quite above board in the British interests section. Every visitor who asked to see Proctor, and occasionally Barton-Smith, about a "strictly private and confidential matter" was referred to Clark for an interview. Once behind closed doors, the visitors asked about arranging illegal means of departing French Morocco to join up with the British army. They offered to provide information useful to the Free French or British forces. They sought use of the diplomatic pouch to pass secret messages. Surveillance of Proctor revealed very friendly relations with French naval officers and government officials hostile to the Allied cause. He also was terribly indiscreet.

"It was clear that no confidence could be placed in Proctor," wrote Stanton. Goold fired Proctor and replaced him with Leonard Wiggins, an affable Englishman. On holiday in Morocco when the war started, Wiggins was subject to the British government's order that all British nationals of fighting age remain in place until specifically summoned. After the armistice, he was again prevented from leaving by travel restrictions placed on British nationals. Wiggins employment with the US consulate kept him out of an internment camp, and he became a welcome addition to the staff.[11] As for Barton-Smith, he returned from his vacation and was cleared of any wrongdoing. To ensure the British interest section didn't once again become a hotbed of intrigue, Clark continued to oversee it.[12]

AT THE END OF his ten days' leave, Harris decided not to return to Sidi-Bel-Abbes. He had been unable to secure passage from Casablanca, but vowed to keep trying. He bought a new set of clothes in the *mellah* and sent his uniform and other Legion belongings back to Sidi-Bel-Abbes, which would prevent him from being charged with both theft and desertion.[13] "From the moment I had discarded my military uniform I became a deserter," wrote Harris. "The Gendarmerie would take the matter in hand and my description would be sent in all directions with an order to arrest me wherever I might be and return me to Bel-Abbes." Having once been tasked with typing up the descriptions of deserters, Harris took some delight in imagining the squadron secretary filling out the thirty-six different items prescribed by regulation. "I was always inclined to make them somewhat whimsical in order to give the deserters a sporting chance."[14]

Becoming a deserter consigned Harris to a life in the shadows. Along with the police, who would be looking for him, current and former legionnaires crawled the streets of Casablanca. Before he deserted, he had run into two legionnaires he knew. To avoid detection, he stayed in at night and kept away from cafés. He could also retreat to the dark confines of a movie house, which became a favorite place of sanctuary for Casablanca's weary population. The city boasted nineteen movie houses, from the modest 200-seat Chaouia and 300-seat Mondial theaters to the 1,300-seat and 2,000-seat movie palaces of the Rialto and Lux in the *ville nouvelle*, which screened French films and Hollywood productions dubbed in French.[15]

FINALLY THE DAY CAME for Harris to make his escape to England. Peter decided to join him. So did Frank, a cadet pilot with the French air force, whom Harris met during his outings during his first week in the city. Frank, a deserter, had been using forged papers to live in Casablanca under the name "Fernandez."[16]

From Casablanca they caught the 8 p.m. train to Petit-Jean (Sidi Kacem), arriving around midnight. At the desolate station, they each bought a first-class ticket for Souk-el-Arba-du-Rharb, due to arrive in one hour. From that small village, they planned to walk over the frontier into Spanish Morocco. As they waited anxiously on the platform, they did their best to act like they didn't know each other.

Three European men in their twenties buying first-class train tickets to a remote train station in the dead of night piqued the interest of the police detective on duty. Souk-el-Arba-du-Rharb was a favorite destination for those attempting to leave French Morocco without permission. The detective working the train station decided to trail them.[17]

When they reached Souk-el-Arba-du-Rharb, they were arrested and interrogated by the territorial inspector. Harris and Peter, the two Englishmen, decided to say they were brothers—last name Smith—in the hopes that they wouldn't be separated. If that ruse was already shaky, it became more so when the police found a forged good-conduct certificate in Harris's pocket. He tried to say that he had found it on the floor in a café.[18] The inspector didn't buy their stories for a minute.[19]

The next day, the trio were sent back to Casablanca on the train, guarded by the detective who originally spotted them. Installed with his prisoners in a compartment, the inspector trained his revolver on them, making it clear they shouldn't attempt anything foolish, but he kept falling asleep, waking up only long enough to check what train station they were pulling into. Thinking the inspector finally dead asleep, Peter grabbed the envelope with their paperwork and lunged for the door, only to trip over the inspector's legs. He shook himself free and charged into the aisle. The sleep-addled detective gave chase, but Peter jumped from the train before he could catch him. As Peter retreated into the distance, the detective trained his gun on him but declined to shoot.[20]

Upon arriving in Casablanca, the detective delivered Harris and Frank to the main police station, which abutted the Place Administrative. The dire reality of their situation started to sink in when Harris found himself sitting before the chief inspector. Deciding that he needed to come clean to some degree, Harris confessed that he'd served in the Legion. After that the lies started. He claimed he'd entered French Morocco on foot and thrown away the papers proving he had been demobilized by the Legion. During their conversation, Harris told the chief inspector he had studied Arabic in Paris with Régis Blachère, now director of l'Institut des hautes études marocaines in Rabat. The inspector knew him. "It was only a detail, but a coincidence of that kind is sufficient to create a nucleus of confidence in the mind of the doubting listener," wrote Harris.[21]

Peter's life on the run, however, proved short-lived. He was arrested attempting to board a bus in Rabat headed for Casablanca. His arrival only made things worse for Harris, as Peter was known in Casablanca by the last name Fernandez. The tale they told the territorial inspector in Souk-el-Arba-du-Rharb about being brothers was clearly a lie. The now irate chief inspector urged the men to come clean. Harris admitted they weren't brothers, and Peter admitted to not being Fernandez. Harris, however, kept mum on his desertion from the Legion.[22]

WHILE THEY WAITED FOR their hearing before a judge, the trio received provisional freedom. They longed to see friends but realized the police could be using them to learn the identities of other Gaullists. With Casablanca full of refugees, they found it difficult to find a hotel. After wandering around for two hours, inquiring at hotel after hotel, they found a room at Hôtel Normandy, which faced army headquarters. On the hotel registry, they wrote, "Coming from: Just out of prison. Going to: Probably back to prison." The proprietor raised an eye but also knew that with the Protectorate's roundup of British men, their situation wasn't unusual.[23]

While happy to have lodgings, Harris nevertheless worried about running into people who might further puncture his story. Having a room across from army headquarters was not ideal for a man in his position, and it didn't take long before he spotted familiar faces from the Legion. He took back alleys. He avoided sitting in cafés, particularly those known to be pro-Allied. He also started to understand what it felt like to be hunted. "The most difficult thing is to rid oneself of the obsession of being followed, and to find a happy medium between excessive fear and imprudent negligence," he wrote. Ironically, he came to feel safest in the police station, where he had to appear every day to have a piece of paper stamped to attest he hadn't skipped town. Within its walls, he chatted with the chief inspector about his interest in Eugène Vidocq, the nineteenth-century criminal who had founded France's Sûreté nationale, and worked on his Moroccan Arabic with a police interpreter who wanted to improve his English.[24]

After three weeks of probation, the trio decided to try once again to obtain forged papers. The longer they stayed in Casablanca, the worse their chances of escaping internment became. They were also running out of money. "To approach the people capable of procuring that most sought after

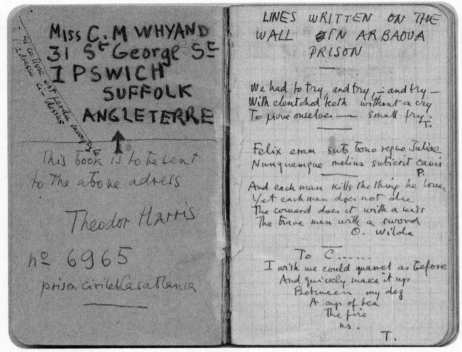

FIGURE 16.1. The inside cover and title page of the diary kept by Ted Harris in prison and afterward. *Churchill Archives Centre,* Diaries of Fedor Minorsky *(alias Theodor Harris),* HARS

article is a more difficult business than one would imagine," wrote Harris. "The main difficulty is to lead up to the subject. Very often it is simply a matter of verbal courage."[25]

Before they could secure new papers, they were arrested.

THE TRIO ARRIVED BEFORE the massive iron gate guarding the entrance to Casablanca's civilian prison, drunk and singing at the top of their lungs. They had convinced their escort, who happened to be Harris's Arabic tutor, to let them have one last meal before going to jail. The warden refused to believe they were his charges until he saw the paperwork. One by one, they were logged into the master register and assigned a number. Harris became "6965." They emptied their pockets and turned over their belongings. A body search came next. In the days that followed, they would also have their hair sheared and photographs and fingerprints taken. The prison's photographer also took a series of body measurements with calipers.[26]

Once the warden logged them in, the progression into the prison began, as eight heavy doors made of iron railings and sturdy locks opened and closed, one after the other. "Every time one of them closed on us I felt a heavy hammer-blow fall on my love for wide open spaces," wrote Harris. "Eventually we arrived at a roundabout of iron bars and there, like tigers in a cage, native warders were pacing about, watching the different corridors."[27] Upon spying the new arrivals, the other prisoners pelted them with questions. Harris quickly realized they were in the section reserved for political prisoners.[28]

The guards pushed them through another set of doors and down a hallway to reach a cellblock, where they were deposited into different cells. Four prisoners resided in each cell, which measured nine feet by eleven feet. In one corner, a cement basin with a copper tap above it served as a toilet and washbasin. Harris's cellmates quickly schooled him in the ways of prison life, including the first rule: do not ask your neighbors or cellmates the reason for their imprisonment. "In the Legion, women are always, or nearly always, the foundation of adventure. In prison, it is always an error of justice, and if the prisoners are to be believed, the judges ought to be in prison in their place," wrote Harris.[29]

Prison life revolved around a strict schedule. At 6:00 a.m., a violent knock on the door served as an alarm. If a prisoner purchased coffee, which he could do once a week on Wednesdays, he received his morning cup. A minimal breakfast followed. They spent mornings cleaning their cells with rags and a pail of water with disinfectant provided by the jail.[30] At 4:00 p.m., they took a walk in the courtyard, which gave Harris, Peter, and Frank a chance to meet up. After the prisoners returned to their cells, it was time for the evening meal. A hearty brown bread with a crisp crust made up for the soup, which consisted of "a few beans in yellowish water, and floating on the surface, some boiled maggots."[31] Around 7:00 p.m., the mattresses, neatly stacked in the corner during the day, covered the floor of the cell. Each cell only had one bed, and the prisoner with the longest tenure claimed it by custom. As the newest arrival, Harris had the spot closest to the toilet. At 9:00 p.m., the lights went out, and prisoners were forbidden to talk. Once a week, on Friday, they received showers. They stole the soap provided by the jail to wash their clothes in the sinks of their cells.[32]

As he had little to do, Harris's attention frequently wandered toward the cell's high-barred window, where he could see patches of sky. "The only joy is to watch the swallows fly in and out through the bars," he wrote. "Their sight brings the perfume of the outside world. They are like messengers of hope. They come and go, they make one dream."[33]

Every prisoner was entitled to a sheet of paper and an envelope. With Frank's help, Peter wrote to a lawyer he knew from his time playing for the Casablanca rugby club.[34] Maître Vaugier agreed to represent them and arranged to have them all transferred to the same cell.[35] Vaugier, however, could do little to dampen the police's interest in the trio. None of them could receive bail because they lacked a fixed residence.[36]

AFTER A MONTH IN prison, Harris, Frank, and Peter appeared before a judge at the Law Courts. "From the covered gallery which runs along the whole building of the Courts, we admired the people in the street and on Place Lyautey," wrote Harris. "After a month in a cell it was like being in a cinema."[37] Maître Vaugier demolished the prosecution's arguments, leading to a mild sentence from the jury. All three men were fined ten francs for circulating in a military zone without permission. Frank, however, continued to face a more serious charge of forgery and the use of forged documents. While Harris and Peter won their freedom, Frank would have to stay in jail.[38]

The day after their release, Harris and Peter visited the food stalls at the new medina. In the 1930s, the French had built an idealized Moroccan marketplace east of the old medina and adjacent to the sultan's palace in Casablanca. French officials wanted to capture the color, variety, and craftsmanship of the old medina, but without the layer of seediness that often pervaded the ancient quarter. In the new medina, tourists and Casablancans could shop for Moroccan food and goods in a more orderly environment. The Habous, as it became known, also showcased the work of Morocco's artisans, providing an easy way for tourists to carry a piece of Morocco home with them.[39] From the food stalls, they bought a feast of black and green olives, radishes, turnips, and other vegetables—the kind of food one came to crave on a diet of soup and bread—and had it delivered to the prison for their former cellmates.[40]

Having spent so much time scheming to reach Britain, Harris realized he had failed to notice the city around him and spent his newfound freedom exploring Casablanca. "There were gardens and monuments, and above all the two native quarters, throbbing with intense life. The *mellah* with its torturous and swarming little streets, with its Jews in black scull-caps, and the new Medina with its covered stairs, where reigns a religious silence." To live and eat, they gave English lessons, mainly to Moroccan Jews, charging between five and twenty francs an hour.[41]

Nevertheless, the obsession with reaching Britain persisted. The chief inspector advised them to lay low and not attract attention—if they reminded the police of their existence, they might end up in a camp. They decided, instead, to obtain new identity papers. With the help of the trainer for the rugby team, Harris and Peter met with a man who accepted their applications with minimal questions. Once they submitted the paperwork, which took three days to be processed in Rabat, Harris started having misgivings. Protectorate officials might ask for more details, which they could not provide. "Three days pass quickly when one has nothing special on one's mind. Three days of suspense are like three years, particularly when Doubt has a finger in the pie. We were nervous," wrote Harris.[42] The dreaded questions came, but they still managed to get their new identity cards.

In the meantime, Frank went on trial for forgery and was found guilty. He received a sentence of two years' imprisonment, commuted to probation. The sentence was then revised by the Residency to a deportation order for the internment camp at Missour.[43]

Missour was one of a growing number of surveillance or confinement camps (*centre de séjour surveillé*) established by the Protectorate to deal with "undesirable" foreign nationals. The camps were located in the interior, far away from urban centers where the French resistance tended to operate. By removing undesirable individuals to camps, the Protectorate hoped to diminish their ability to promote the Allied cause or generally cause trouble. The remote areas also made it difficult for relief organizations and foreign consulates to help those interned. In the fall of 1939, Missour served as a dumping ground for Spanish nationals who deserted their units in Spanish Morocco. After the armistice, it housed men from the Allied nations. Located on a plain overlooking the Moulouya river, Missour was basically in the middle of nowhere. Between it and Casablanca lay the Atlas Mountains; to the east lay the desert expanse of the Moroccan-Algerian border. The closest big city was Fez, 120 miles northeast by road.[44]

Harris's freedom didn't last long either.[45] After the Residency declared him "dangerous to the security of the land, sea, and air forces," he landed back in Casablanca's prison.[46] One week later, he boarded a train with nine other prisoners, under the watchful eye of eight guards, bound for Missour. Resentful of being paraded in public in shackles, he took solace in the fact that he would at least see Frank again.[47]

17

The Apostles

D AVID KING AND STAFFORD REID JUST WANTED A DECENT CUP OF coffee. They had been traveling for more than seventy-two hours before finally arriving in Casablanca at 7:00 a.m. on the overnight train from Tangier. The rattling of the aged train, the repeated shriek of the whistle announcing a new station, and the relentless squawking of the chickens that shared their car left them short on sleep. Stumbling into a café, one that would have looked at home on Champs-Elysées with its rows of tables and chairs, they ordered *petit déjeuner*. Instead of a croissant, they got a slice of crusty bread. Instead of coffee, they got a mixture of ground date pips, caraway seeds, and fig juice. After the first gag-inducing swallow, bread never tasted so good.

In May 1941, Casablanca was awash with color, as fragrant pink moccasin flowers, blue spider lilies, and hot pink verbena blossomed across the city. But getting a cup of real coffee and some sugar to put in it proved next to impossible.[1] Grain and petrol were scarce as well. King and Reid knew about Casablanca's scarcity of basic goods: they had been recruited to serve as American observers charged with inspecting the supplies being shipped to French North Africa under the Murphy-Weygand agreement. They also had another assignment: gathering information about French Morocco for American military intelligence.

DAVID WOOSTER KING DIDN'T end up in Casablanca by accident. In February 1941, convinced it was only a matter of time before the United States entered the war, he began looking for a way to be useful. Through a

108

friend, King received an introduction to Lieutenant Colonel Ralph Smith of US Army Intelligence, who shared his belief that the Americans needed to start gathering information on North Africa.[2] "I told him that I considered England our advance post and North Africa our future plane-carrier and springboard," recalled King in an interview. King believed the United States should be building up its intelligence network now rather than later. Trying to do so once hostilities started would be next to impossible.[3]

That Smith didn't attempt to fob King off says something about the man seeking his assistance. King wasn't your average trust fund blue blood with an entry in the *New York Social Register*. When World War I broke out, he left Harvard and joined the French Foreign Legion, transferring to the US Army when America joined the fight. The war left the wiry, dark-haired King with a body full of shrapnel and a facial twitch near his eye. He spent the 1920s divorced, bouncing between adventures in Africa, Afghanistan, and India, and dabbling in international affairs, including stints as a press liaison for the American delegation at the naval disarmament talks in Geneva (1927) and Lausanne (1928). The 1930s saw him back in New York, where he managed his family's business and investments and collected more wives.[4]

After Smith gave him the go-ahead, King looked around for ways for an American to enter North Africa without raising eyebrows. He quickly discovered that trade had dried up between the United States and North Africa, making an import-export angle impossible. Next he investigated collecting debts for American and Moroccan firms paralyzed by the trade embargo. When that didn't pan out, King approached the Rockefeller Foundation about sponsoring a project in the region, but its representatives were "too solicitous of their good name to cooperate." Finally, using an archaeological dig as a cover was "worse than no cover at all," since the British, French, and Germans had turned that strategy into a cliché. King reported back to Smith that his only hope for infiltration was convincing the State Department to take him on as a consular clerk and moonlighting as an intelligence agent on the side.[5]

At the end of March 1941, King received a telegram from Smith: "Come down here at once. Stop. I think Ive got our wagon."[6] The "wagon" was service as one of the twelve Americans observing the shipments to French North Africa under the Murphy-Weygand agreement. Everyone, from Henri-Philippe Pétain to Maxime Weygand to Charles Noguès to Robert Murphy, understood that the observers would also collect intelligence for the American government.[7] Realizing the typical Foreign Service officer might not be wired for danger or comfortable with intelligence work, the

State Department latched onto the idea of using experienced military officers. Conversations with the heads of Army and Navy Intelligence, however, quickly revealed how little the American military knew about North Africa.

"It must be confessed that our Intelligence organization in 1940 was primitive and inadequate," wrote Murphy. "It was timid, parochial, and operating strictly in the tradition of the Spanish-American War. To the chiefs of the Army and Navy Intelligence groups, North Africa seemed something new, almost another planet." Rather than building its own expertise, the United States had depended for decades on tidbits about the region provided by France and Britain. No qualified Arabic speakers were available either.[8]

After some prodding by the State Department, the military intelligence chiefs came up with a roster of men, including King and Reid, who had military experience, spoke French, and could claim to know French culture. They were businessmen, engineers, and lawyers. None of them knew Arabic or had much, if any, experience with Arab culture. For men who would be observing the comings and goings at North African ports, they also had little experience with ships. "One or two of us, with luck, might be able to distinguish a battleship from a submarine on a particularly clear day," complained Murphy.[9]

King and Reid met for the first time when they reported to Washington for their orientation. William Stafford Reid— "Staff" to his friends—had also offered his services to Smith in the spring of 1940.[10] A graduate of Yale, Reid worked for military intelligence in World War I. After the war, he built a thriving real estate business in New York and was a regular on the social circuit. Despite his classic good looks and flush bank account, he remained a bachelor.[11] Over the course of ten days, King and Reid received briefings on North Africa from military intelligence and learned the full scope of their duties. For the State Department, they were to check the invoices of all ships delivering goods under the Murphy-Weygand agreement. They were also, hypothetically, to check the cargos of all departing ships carrying goods similar to those imported. If one bag of sugar found its way to Vichy or German-occupied territory, the British would stop the import program. Once the American goods were off-loaded, King and Reid were to work with French officials to ensure the supplies were distributed through proper channels and didn't find their way to the black market.

As for their unofficial duties for the army and navy, King and Reid were tasked with collecting intelligence about the German Armistice Commission and the French military in Morocco. They were also to gather information about fortifications, public utilities, railroads, and bridges. If they could manage it, a copy of the order of battle for French Morocco would be nice

FIGURE 17.1. David Wooster King, ca. 1929, during his time in Afghanistan, and W. Stafford Reid, ca. 1943. *King credit: Lowell Thomas. Reid credit: NARA, RG 226*

too. Finally, they were to recruit Frenchmen sympathetic to the Allied cause and foster resistance groups.[12] It was a spectacularly ambitious mission scope to assign to seasoned intelligence agents, let alone to two men whose primary occupation the week before had been minding their investment portfolios and drinking cocktails.

WHEN KING AND REID boarded a Lisbon-bound Clipper in New York on May 5, they did their best impression of Foreign Service officers: dark suits, black homburgs, and leather portfolios firmly tucked under their arms. On the last day of orientation, they learned they would be going over as civilians, using the title "vice consul," rather than as military officers. It had dawned on someone in the State Department that if the United States entered the war, they could be arrested as spies if in uniform.[13]

From Lisbon, they caught a train to Madrid and then hopped a nerve-wracking flight to Tangier, during which the rickety plane struggled to hold together during a violent thunderstorm. Fierce winds buckled one of the plane's wings, forcing the pilot to dump fuel to make it over the Sierra Nevada mountains in southern Spain. Feet firmly back on the ground, they spent the night in Tangier at the El Minzah, a glamorous hotel opened by a British marquis. In the courtyard of the hotel, Reid heard for the first time the Muslim call to prayer.[14]

Once in Casablanca, King and Reid acquired rooms at the Hôtel Transatlantique in the *ville nouvelle*. The American consulate was short on personnel, so with no shipments yet to inspect, they worked as code clerks for five to six hours a day. During their off hours, they explored the city, learning the cafés and bistros and taking note of their clientele. They also started mentally cataloging who worked for the Gestapo, the Service d'order legionnaire, the Parti populaire français, and the Italian Espionage Service.[15] Quincy Stanton, the American consul, invited them over for dinner, allowing them to get to know other members of the diplomatic community. He also arranged introductions to key Protectorate officials.[16]

After staying a few days at the Hôtel Transatlantique, King and Reid realized they needed to find lodgings elsewhere. Too many people were taking an interest in their movements, despite the hotel's unfriendliness to Vichy and German sympathizers. The proprietor greeted every room request from a German with the same answer: "Sorry, there are no rooms. We are booked up with French government officials and refugees."[17] When King and Reid received word that German officials were about to requisition an empty villa in the swanky Anfa neighborhood, they raced to the address, threw their bags through the door, and announced their arrival to the startled Arab caretaker and his wife. Two German officers who rang the bell a short time later were enraged to find King and Reid eating breakfast.[18]

As May progressed, the other vice consuls began arriving in Casablanca, including John Knox, who had attended Saint-Cyr, the French military academy, and served in the French Foreign Legion. Knox began looking up his old classmates and discovered that many held senior positions in the Protectorate.[19] As he reconnected with these men, Knox also introduced them to King, whose own service in the French Foreign Legion put him in high regard. Because of Knox, King made contacts with the French military officers that would reap huge dividends over the next eighteen months.[20]

To get around town, King and Reid relied on bicycles like much of the rest of Casablanca. Gasoline was rationed, and cars, especially ones with diplomatic plates, were conspicuous. A bike also offered an easy way to drop into a sidewalk café for a vermouth cassis or *café noir* should they spot someone worth getting to know. With good tobacco in short supply, an offer of a cigarette provided a natural way to start a conversation.[21]

WHILE KING AND REID settled in, the first ships carrying American goods made their way across the Atlantic. Murphy also returned to North Africa, setting up a base of operations in Algiers, so he could be close to Weygand.[22]

The trade agreement, however, almost faltered at the beginning of June, when news of the Protocols of Paris leaked. Throughout May Admiral Jean-François Darlan had negotiated a deal that would boost Germany's presence in Africa. After a meeting with Hitler at Berchtesgaden on May 11, Darlan reported that the Führer had offered Vichy one last chance of rapprochement with Germany. Only by collaborating with the Reich could France remain a great power in the wake of its terrible defeat. "My choice is made: it is collaboration," wrote Darlan.[23] The resulting deal, signed on May 27, 1941, gave Germany three major concessions: use of Syrian airfields, access to the Tunisian port of Bizerte to provide supplies and logistical support for General Erwin Rommel's Afrika Korps, and establishment of a submarine base at Dakar. In exchange, Vichy would receive the return of World War I veterans currently in German POW camps, easing of travel restrictions between Vichy and occupied France, and reduced occupation payments.

Discussion about whether to approve the deal touched off a series of contentious meetings of Pétain's cabinet at the beginning of June. Weygand led the charge against ratification. Ultimately Vichy devised a list of counterdemands to be fulfilled by Germany before the protocols could go into effect. The list included dissolving the demarcation line between occupied and unoccupied territories and French control of Paris. Stunned by the demands, the Germans backed down—and then became preoccupied by the invasion of Russia, which kicked off on June 22, 1941. The protocols never went into force.[24]

Upon Weygand's return to Algiers from Vichy, an anxious Murphy called upon him, looking for reassurance. News had trickled out of Vichy about the German demands. Weygand looked Murphy in the eye and swore that nothing had changed. North Africa remained in French hands.[25]

WITH THE LATEST CRISIS over Franco-German collaboration averted, Murphy called the vice consuls to Algiers for a meeting in early June. It was time to go to work. Reid, used to being around high-powered men, found Murphy impressive. "Getting along with all sorts of people appeared to be second nature to him," wrote Reid. "His strong constitution was a powerhouse of energy which he applied unsparingly to every job at hand. A striking characteristic of his personality . . . was an engaging smile charged with understanding and friendliness. It swept away trifles and inspired confidence immediately."[26]

After thoroughly interviewing each of the vice consuls and sizing up their personalities, Murphy organized his team. King and Reid remained in Casablanca, joined by C. Denbeigh Wilkes, Franklin Canfield, and Sidney Bartlett. Kenneth Pendar, an antiques dealer, would cover Fez and Marrakech. John Knox was transferred to Algiers, where he teamed up with Harvey Boyd, the former manager for Coca-Cola in Marseille.[27] Harry Woodruff and John Utter staffed Tunis, while Leland Rounds and Ridgeway Knight handled Oran.[28] Because they numbered twelve, they also became known as the "Apostles."

Murphy made assessing the extent of German infiltration their first priority.[29] He also insisted that they work in pairs, believing there was safety in numbers. A vice consul working alone presented an enticing target for German or French intelligence. A distraction or accident could lead to inadvertent abandonment of a diplomatic pouch with classified documents. There would also be two witnesses to any inspection or confrontation with French or German officials. To thwart the ubiquitous phone taps, the vice consuls learned to speak in an elaborate code, using American slang and referring to people by nickname.[30]

Murphy wasn't initially impressed with the men assigned to work for him—and neither were the Germans. A confidential report about them sent to Berlin was positively dismissive: "The vice consuls whom Murphy directs represent a perfect picture of the mixture of races and characteristics in that wild conglomeration called the United States of America," read the report. "We can only congratulate ourselves on the selection of this group of enemy agents who will give us no trouble. In view of the fact they are naturally lacking in method, organization, and discipline, the danger presented by their arrival in North Africa may be considered as nil. It would merely be a waste of paper to describe their personal idiosyncrasies and characteristics."[31]

THE ARRIVAL OF FIVE vice consuls in Casablanca taxed an already struggling American consulate. The staff had yet to recover from the refugee deluge of the fall. To make matters worse, almost four months passed before H. Earle Russell, the new consul general, arrived in Casablanca.[32] A portly, fifty-one-year-old man with round gold-rimmed glasses, Russell had formerly been posted in Morocco, making him a solid choice for the job. Unfortunately for him, he inherited a consulate in chaos. To provide room for new staff, which the consulate desperately needed, a second story was being added to the existing building, turning the offices into a construction zone. The consulate also needed more clerks, especially ones cleared to manage the code traffic between Casablanca and Washington, and secretarial help. The vice consuls were enlisted to help with the coding when they first arrived, much to their dismay, but they would not be available once the economic program got off the ground. The vice consuls would also be writing reports that needed typing in multiple copies, only compounding the problem.[33]

When Murphy visited Casablanca in mid-July, he was so appalled by the personnel situation that he fired off a telegram to the State Department. Given the current staffing, the consulate would be hard-pressed to do the work desired by State, Army, and Navy under the economic plan. "Part of this work relates to the question of German infiltration and it is pertinent to mention in that connection that the German Armistice Commission in French Morocco includes personnel of 204 persons, a large percentage of which is stenographic and clerical," wrote Murphy. "The personnel of our Consulate General at Casablanca does not include one stenographer."[34]

MEANWHILE, KING AND REID became a formidable duo. The arrival of two ships in mid-June freed them from their code work and gave them access to the port. Before the cargo ship docked, they took a small boat out to meet it; they then inspected the cargo and reviewed the paperwork to make sure it matched the telegram sent from Washington detailing the shipment. They also interviewed the captain about the journey over: What ships did he encounter during his voyage? Did the British navy stop him for inspection? Did he see any German submarine activity?

Once the ship docked, King and Reid watched over the transfer of the cargo. Down in the hold, the bags and bales were put into large nets, which were then pulled tight for hoisting to the dock by a crane. The Moroccans who did the manual labor were a rag-tag lot and poorly paid for backbreaking work. When a bag of sugar broke, they scrambled to fill their pockets, with more than one knife drawn.[35] From the dock, the cargo went into secure warehouses for distribution in Casablanca and elsewhere in Morocco.

The inspections and distribution arrangements provided King and Reid with a reason to be at the port, allowing them to gain detailed knowledge of its workings. They mapped the configuration of the warehouses and noted which berths provided homes to commercial ships and the French navy. They learned the habits of the harbor police, along with the location of the mines that defended the entrance to the port. As they walked the docks, they became immune to the pungent combination of raw fish, mashed olives, rotting fruit, and undisposed sewage that engulfed the port each afternoon as it baked in the hot North African sun.

King and Reid also befriended the machinists, painters, and welders who plied their trade among the ships. In exchange for canned milk, cigars, cigarettes, and sugar, these men fed them information about the departures and arrivals of destroyers and cruisers belonging to the French navy. They developed a network of informants to track every repair completed on the *Jean Bart* to gauge when it might be ready to leave port.[36] They also confirmed that Casablanca operated as a repair base for German submarines.[37]

As King and Reid moved around the port, they nevertheless had to be careful. They had a shadow. The French admiralty had requested that Vichy send men specially trained in surveillance to trail them as they worked. Following each visit to the port, a report detailing their movements landed on Admiral Armand d'Harcourt's desk.[38] King and Reid's own reports, which covered everything from the movement of ships in the port to schematics of buildings, were sent by courier to Tangier, where they were forwarded on to Washington and Algiers by diplomatic pouch or secure cable.

By mid-October 1941, only four ships carrying goods under the Murphy-Weygand agreement had docked in Casablanca, with another three on the way. Constant haggling between the British, French, and Americans over the type and lack of shipping to carry the goods across the Atlantic resulted in continual delays. The program had, however, allowed the United States to establish a fledgling intelligence network thanks to the vice consuls. "They have developed more satisfactorily than we could have hoped," wrote Murphy. "They are all sincere, conscientious and willing men."[39]

18

On the Road to Missour

A T THE END OF JULY 1941, STAFF REID AND QUINCY STANTON LEFT Casablanca in a Buick packed with extra gasoline, spare tires, rope, and Michelin maps of Morocco. For added protection, they put a .38-caliber handgun in the glove box. The two men were bound for Missour, the internment camp, on the other side of the Middle Atlas Mountains. The Allied governments had asked the US consulate in Casablanca to check on the condition of their citizens residing in the camp, and Stanton, the consulate's second in command, had volunteered for the assignment. Itching to see more of Morocco than Casablanca's cafés and port, not to mention the code room at the consulate, Reid decided to tag along. After investigating Missour, they would head north to survey the frontier between French and Spanish Morocco. One of Reid's contacts had heard Theodor Auer discussing a possible Spanish incursion into French Morocco, encouraged by the Germans, and a growing number of troops at the border.

At the end of the first day, they reached the Middle Atlas foothills and spent the night in Meknès. The next morning they pushed forward into the mountains, winding their way through thick cedar forests. After stopping for dinner in Ifran, they decided to continue on to Missour, using the night to avoid the blazing daytime temperatures that would engulf them once they departed the mountains and began to skirt the Sahara. To stay sharp on the poorly marked roads, they took turns behind the wheel. As they descended onto a broad, sandy plateau, the road crossed back and forth over the summer-starved Moulouya river. When they weren't driving, Stanton puffed on his pipe, filling the car with tendrils of tobacco smoke, while Reid jotted down his impressions of the terrain and roads to pass along to military planners in Washington.[1]

As the night closed in, Reid felt the air gushing through the car windows grow warmer instead of cooler. Stanton noticed what looked like scrub brush moving across the moonlit landscape. Within a few minutes, sand squalls dampened the beams of the Buick's headlights. Narrow cones of sand reaching ten feet high started to dance around the car before exploding into funnels climbing fifteen feet into the air. With a sandstorm rapidly engulfing them, they stopped the car to wait it out. The sand was relentless, covering the car's interior in a layer of terracotta dust as it seeped in through cracks and vents. It caked over the front and back windshields, blotting out the world beyond. After fifteen minutes the roar of the wind subsided. They tried to open the Buick's doors, only to strain against the weight of the sand drifts surrounding the car. It took half an hour to shovel themselves out by hand and even longer to clean the carburetor intake and dust off the engine before daring to start the motor again—all done by flashlight.

When ready to get going again, they discovered the sandstorm had blotted out the road, rendering their map useless. To find their way to Missour, they followed a series of stone markers that appeared every hundred yards or so—an ancient system developed by the Berbers to mark the caravan routes.

After the harrowing drive, they arrived in Missour around 2:00 a.m. From the small collection of buildings that comprised the village, they picked out what appeared to be an inn and wine shop and rapped on the shutters. The vast silence of the sleeping desert seemed to amplify their knocking. The shutter flung back, revealing a burly man spewing a string of obscenities over the disruption of his sleep. Reid asked for a room, and soon Jean Horwath, the proprietor, appeared at the front door, clutching a lamp and wearing hastily donned pants. Guests were rare in Missour, let alone those who appeared in the dead of night. Horwath invited them into the shop, which featured a sad assortment of bread and sausage along with a small collection of cognac and wine. Reid noticed their host was missing a finger and engaged him in a conversation about World War I. Horwath, a sharpshooter, had lost the digit at the Second Battle of the Marne. For good measure, he also pulled up his shirt and displayed the violent scar across his hip, earned at Soissons. After serving out his five years in the Legion, the Hungarian Horwath had decided to settle in Morocco.[2]

Upon learning that Reid and Stanton were American—so few made it out to that desolate spot—Horwath offered his hand in friendship. The cognac also came off the shelf. Reid pulled out two packs of American cigarettes as his own gesture of friendship, while Stanton offered up two chocolate bars. The conversation turned, as so many did in those days, to the French situation, the predicament of Vichy rule, and how an honorable man might follow his conscience. Reid asked Horwath if he'd seen or heard anything of the Germans in the region. The Hungarian had heard rumors of German engineers about and talk of a landing strip, but nothing definite. As the night ticked away, Reid and Horwath worked out a plan: when Horwath went on his monthly trip to Guercif for supplies, he would pass along anything of interest to the assistant stationmaster, who was an American informant. The information would make its way to Reid.[3]

Horwath led his tired guests across the courtyard, disturbing a shed full of chickens that squawked in protest, to a one-story building. The Americans received the best rooms available, spartan accommodations consisting of an iron bed, a table, a candle for light, and a tin basin with a pitcher for washing. Before they went to bed, Stanton and Reid used a flashlight to search their accommodation for scorpions, anxious to avoid its deadly sting.

The next morning, as Reid and Stanton devoured their breakfast of coffee and coarse bread, they received a visit from "a stocky man in a torn shirt and dirty trousers." The prisoner, whose name was Radou, wanted to know who they were and what news they could give of the outside world. Reid and Stanton were shocked to discover that the prisoners could roam around the village. Radou explained that the warden believed it wasn't necessary to lock them up, because escape was impossible—or at least foolhardy. One could only reach a major town by braving the desert trails, which would lead to death from the extreme temperatures and lack of food and water along the route. Prisoners also ran the risk of stumbling across a Berber tribe, which might not take kindly to Europeans wandering around on its land. Reid and Stanton later learned their guest was a convicted murderer.[4]

ON STANTON'S LIST OF men to interview was Ted Harris. Since his arrival at the camp two months before, Harris had become well versed in the rules and customs that governed that godforsaken place. On his first day in Missour, after an interview with the camp commandant, Harris received a permanent pass, granting him permission to leave the camp provided he returned by 10:00 p.m. every evening. "By the general rules of the camp, we were forbidden to go out before 11 a.m. One had to be back at three and remain inside until six, after which one could go out again," he wrote. The discipline about returning, however, was so lax that the prisoners could drink late at Horwath's café and stumble home at 3:00 a.m. without consequences.[5]

"The camp and the village lead an interdependent life," wrote Harris. "It is certain that the village draws the major part of its income from the camp. If the 120 internees were withdrawn from Missour overnight, it would become a dead place"[6] The camp, which had started life as a military outpost, lay to the southeast of the village. It consisted of two aging stone barracks, an infirmary, and a headquarters of more recent vintage. Behind the infirmary, the refugees started a vegetable garden with mixed results. Nary a tree grew in the desert terrain surrounding the camp. A swimming pool provided relief from the heat, when it was clean, which wasn't often. Despite the availability of water, sanitary conditions were poor.[7]

The internees themselves hailed from across Europe: Spaniards, Belgians, Czechs, Hungarians, Russians, Italians, a Lithuanian, Danes, Germans, Swiss, Dutch, Jews without a nationality, a Rumanian, a Greek, plus the small British colony of nine. Spaniards, who numbered about seventy, made up the largest group, followed by Arabs, of which there were about twenty. A handful of internees with useful trades received permission to live in the town, including a barber, a chemist, a dentist, a baker, and a carpenter. Two Spanish Republicans repaired bicycles, while an Italian anarchist did masonry jobs. The majority of the internees were foreigners whom the Protectorate would love to expel but could not under the terms of the armistice agreement, which required that men between the ages of seventeen and fifty not be repatriated. The camp also included four murderers and three others guilty of serious crimes.

At Missour, the internees bunked four or six to a room. Harris's roommates included Baranoff, a Russian who had served with Franco's forces in Spain but decided to enlist with the French army in Morocco to fight the Nazis when the war broke out. French intelligence believed him to be a Communist spy disguised as a Spanish nationalist.[8] "The Major" was a forty-something bespectacled Brit who carried the patina of empire about him. After a life of adventure, he had settled in Morocco, where he ran a number of businesses. The Protectorate arrested him for distributing Gaullist propaganda.[9] "The Pole," an engineer living in Paris at the time of the French defeat, had joined the refugee exodus south. He managed to make it to Morocco with his wife, only to end up in Missour. René, an ex-legionnaire from Switzerland, had settled in Morocco after fulfilling his five-year contract. The Protectorate interned him for constructing a wireless transmitter, despite his lack of knowledge about electronics. He worked as the camp's smith and shoemaker. He also raised cats, which the prisoners ate in a stew to supplement their paltry diet.[10]

Between the stone construction and the poor windows, daylight struggled to penetrate their room. To add some cheer, they decorated the walls using colored chalk and charcoal. One wall featured a Union Jack and the motto of the Royal Air Force—Per Ardua Ad Astra (through struggle to the stars)—along with a small newspaper photo of the king. The remaining walls featured quotations from the Bible on the evils of wine, passages by Persian astronomer and poet Omar Khayyám, and quotes and observations that the occupants liked. They also marked the wall to keep a running list of what bit them, making hash marks next to "bugs," "scorpions," and "sundry animals."[11]

Harris quickly learned that he had to remain vigilant about the Legion. The camp teemed with former and current legionnaires. The sole Lithuanian was really a German deserter who had been in Harris's squadron at Sidi-Bel-Abbes. They did their best to ignore each other. Harris said a prayer of thanks the day the Lithuanian disappeared and failed to return. His nerves frayed again when he spotted a Swede who had served as his former squadron adjutant in France. By "some extraordinary miracle," he failed to recognize Harris. "I took good care to cross his path as little as possible, but the idea of being at the mercy of his memory was most unpleasant," he wrote. With Frank's help and a set of hand signals, Harris avoided finding himself in the Swede's presence.[12]

STANTON ARRANGED WITH THE camp's staff to meet with the British and Belgian prisoners in the morning. As he interviewed each, the two French officials responsible for the administration of the camp looked on. Stanton was impressed by the prisoners' seemingly humane treatment, given the desolate conditions, which the internees themselves confirmed during their discussions—and not merely because their jailers looked on.

Harris arrived at his interview in a wheelbarrow pushed by Frank, having badly sprained his ankle. With the two camp administrators present, Harris couldn't be truthful about his situation. Revealing that he'd deserted from the Legion would result in transfer to an even worse prison. Stanton offered him reassignment to the work camp at Settat some forty miles south of Casablanca, provided he agreed not to attempt an escape. Harris refused. Aside from believing he was obligated to escape if the opportunity presented itself, accepting the transfer to Settat would cause Protectorate officials to reexamine his file. The less scrutiny he endured, the better. Frank received the same offer during his interview and also refused. While helping to preserve their fake identities, their refusals also earned them the grudging respect of their captors.[13]

When the interviews concluded, the French officials invited the Americans to lunch at what passed for a bistro in the village. Reid judged the food surprisingly good, but the flies gathering on the glasses and utensils after each use turned his stomach. Lunch in a bistro outside an internment camp in Morocco was a world away from a boozy midday meal at Manhattan's 21 Club or the Waldorf-Astoria.[14] When Reid and Stanton returned to the inn to retrieve their bags, they discovered the wine shop packed with a dozen locals who had come to lay eyes on them. Some men expressed their happiness at having American visitors, even going so far as to remove their berets and offer toasts to their health. Others scowled at them from the corner.[15]

RATHER THAN WAIT FOR darkness, Reid and Stanton departed Missour with the sun high in the sky. When he tried to open the door to the Buick, Reid scalded his hand. The heat only intensified as they headed north toward Guercif, and they started to worry about the tires on the car "melting"— becoming too soft to support the weight of the Buick—and running out of water both for themselves and the engine. Even though they wore sunglasses, the glare from the sand roasting in the afternoon sun exhausted their eyes. To battle eye fatigue, they changed over at the wheel every fifteen minutes or so. Desperate for a spot of shade and to replenish their water supply, they set their sights on a French Foreign Legion outpost.

When they tried to cross the Moulouya river at Oulad-el-Hadj, they discovered the bridge had collapsed. At that time of year, the river only ran a foot and a half deep, so they decided to risk driving the Buick across. Worried about stones puncturing the warm rubber of the tires, Reid decided to keep watch from the running board. The arrival of the Buick at the crossing drew the interest of a group of local boys, who were more than willing to help push when the car failed to gain traction in the middle of the river. After they made it safely across, Reid noted in his book, "Heavy military convoys can cross the river bed here at this season of the year without injury to tires. River banks solid and gradual slopes both sides."[16]

After fording the river, they headed for the Legion outpost, happy to see its pink walls and crenelated battlements materialize in the empty landscape. A small village of one-story stucco buildings hewed close to the fort, shutters closed to ward off the blistering midday heat. A faded sign on the door of the bistro read, "Café Beau Geste, Vins et Liquers." They knocked on the door. An old, rotund woman answered and beckoned them inside, dispensing a lecture about traveling at that time of day. Stanton ordered two glasses of Algerian rosé, which appeared at room temperature. They sipped the hot wine, trying not to gag on its cloying sweetness. After a polite amount of time passed, they asked about obtaining some water for the Buick's engine. The proprietor gave them a resentful look but agreed to give them a bucketful. "It might have been easier perhaps to have asked for champagne."[17]

With the hot wine in their stomachs and water obtained for the Buick, they drove on, heading northeast toward a series of old kasbahs perched along the mountains overlooking the plains below. The High Plateau, a mixture of grasslands and semipermanent salt lakes, stretched northeast from the Middle Atlas Mountains into Algeria. Reid immediately saw what had made the location attractive to builders centuries before: defenders could throw down deadly fire onto any approaching force below. He noted the position of the kasbahs on a map.[18]

As they drove on to Guercif, the disappearing sun turned the mountains shades of violet before finally shrouding them in black. This time, the darkness brought not a paralyzing sand storm but a vast blanket of stars and much-needed relief from the heat. Rather than stay in Guercif, they pushed on to Fez, the ancient capital of the Assoulite dynasty. They took lodgings at the Palais Jamai, an old palace once belonging to the sultan's grand vizier and since converted into a hotel. The crisp sheets, plush rugs, and elaborately decorated rooms were a far cry from their accommodations at Missour.

The next morning they headed for the frontier between Spanish and French Morocco to investigate a rumor that Spanish troops were gathering along the border. As they followed the roads north, the desert and mountains gave way to the green fertile lands of French Morocco's breadbasket. Scrub brush and hard earth became fields of wheat and green pastures with grazing sheep. Reid wanted a bird's-eye view of the valley, but that meant entering into Spanish Morocco without visas. Deciding it was better not to ask permission, Reid pushed the accelerator to the floor and blew through the sentry post guarding the border. In the rearview mirror, he saw the sentry, standing in the road, madly shaking his gun at them.

As the sun began to set, they were finally in position to observe the valley below. Much to Reid's relief, there were troops, but nothing like the buildup needed for an invasion. "We spotted some troops in bivouac and a company of infantry going through a close-order drill on a small clearing near a river bank; in the distance a few supply trucks," wrote Reid. They also detected a partially hidden ammunition dump. Reid suspected that whatever operation Auer had been discussing had been called off, and his informant had failed to hear the follow-up.[19]

Spain would not be invading any time soon.

19

The French Conscience

On June 22, 1941, a massive three-story banner adorned with Marshal Henri-Philippe Pétain's face and the words *travail, famille, patrie* (work, family, country) hung from the roof of the Palais de Justice. As Pétain's visage kept watch over Place Lyautey, 10,000 veterans filled the square. They assembled into three sections—French, Moroccan, and mixed—creating the sharp rows their military training had drilled into them. They had come to pledge their allegiance before General Maxime Weygand to the newly formed Légion française des anciens combattants de l'Afrique du Nord (French Legion of Veterans of North Africa).[1]

For months Charles Noguès had fought against the creation, and then growing power, of the Légion des combattants, authorized by Pétain in the fall of 1940 to harness enthusiasm for the national revolution within Vichy. The veterans, united under one organization instead of competing groups, would become foot soldiers in the transformation of France.[2]

The arrival of the Légion des combattants in Morocco only added to Noguès's headaches with Weygand. Its president, General François had no problem going behind Noguès's back and taking his complaints—of which there were many—directly to Weygand. He even made it known that should Noguès's services no longer be required, he would be happy to become resident-general. François's duplicity and ambition only confirmed Noguès's feeling that the organization amounted to a "state within a state." Things deteriorated between the two men such that the veterans would not take the oath to the organization before Noguès—which is how Weygand came to preside over the striking ceremony in Casablanca's central square.[3]

FIGURE 19.1. Members of the French Legion of Veterans of North Africa gather in Casablanca before General Maxime Weygand to swear their allegiance to Vichy in June 1941. *Kharbine-Tapabor*

The same day as the ceremony, Nazi Germany invaded the Soviet Union, tearing up the nonaggression pact signed with Moscow in August 1939. Although the war in the west remained unfinished—Hitler had yet to bring Britain to its knees—the Nazis turned their attention to the Soviet Union, inaugurating what would become the bloodiest front in the European theater of war.

EVEN AS NOGUÈS AND Weygand quarreled over the scope of their authority, they found common cause in attempting to foil future German designs on North Africa, particularly French Morocco. The arrival of a savvy army officer aided their campaign. Like his cadre, Antoine Béthouart had attended Saint-Cyr, graduating in the same class as Charles de Gaulle. Assigned to the infantry during World War I, he fought at Verdun and the Somme and survived despite being wounded three times. He spent the interwar period learning and teaching mountain warfare, in addition to serving a stint as deputy military attaché in Yugoslavia.

When World War II erupted, Colonel Béthouart formed and commanded the High Mountain Brigade, which would fight to secure Narvik, Norway. After being evacuated from Norway to Britain in June, he faced a choice: join Vichy or join de Gaulle. No lover of either, he opted to return to France to face whatever fate awaited his country. "Personally, I affirm and affirm always that the armistice was a grave error, a tragic fault," he wrote in his memoir.

Instead of landing in France, he found himself in Casablanca after his ship was diverted to Morocco in the wake of the attack on Mers-el-Kébir.[4] Noguès welcomed the arrival of such an accomplished soldier and assigned him to command the subdivision at Rabat, which was responsible for defending French Morocco against any Spanish incursion south over the border.[5]

In April 1941, Béthouart was promoted to brigadier general. He also received a new assignment: to serve as the liaison to the German Armistice Commission. Weygand and Noguès wanted him to set up a network to spy on the Germans. Wherever the Germans were in Casablanca—their offices, hotel rooms, apartments, villas—listening devices were installed to surveil their movements.[6] The need for added vigilance against the Nazis increased in May 1941, following the arrival of General Paul Schultheiss to head up the armistice commission. Schultheiss's appointment secured Germany's ascendency over Italy in the administration of French Morocco. Béthouart did his best to keep Schultheiss and his men at a distance, while fulfilling German demands for inspections and information about French military and economic capabilities.[7]

Schultheiss's arrival allowed Gestapo chief Theodor Auer to concentrate on growing his spy network, which the French increasingly regarded with dismay. Auer had learned that plenty of Nazi sympathizers in Casablanca were willing to talk or pass along information. Others, for the right price, would give up names and details. Auer's operation proved so effective that the French attempted to blackmail the Germans into removing him. While visiting Tangier, Auer had a tryst with Franz Duschnitz, an Austrian Jew and "notorious homosexual." Given the Nazi regime's hostility toward homosexuality, Vichy officials believed that Auer's behavior could serve as a pretext for his recall. French intelligence even tried to set up a "honey trap" to gain more evidence of his exploits. Nevertheless, Berlin refused. Auer's operation was too effective. Germany also had no intention of allowing Vichy to dictate its staff.[8]

Noguès, Weygand, and Béthouart had plenty to hide from the Germans. Worried that the day would come when Morocco would need to defend herself from Germany, Noguès and Weygand had embarked on a scheme to keep Moroccan (*goumiers*) troops mobilized and armed while concealing them from the German Armistice Commission.[9] The armistice limited the number of troops France could have in Morocco. To subvert this, Noguès created the *mehallas cherifiennes*, a new internal police force to govern the interior, consisting of 268 French officers, 868 noncommissioned officers, and 24,400 troops.[10] The Protectorate passed off the *mehallas cherifiennes* as an extension of the sultan's traditional guard, a sleight of hand facilitated by German officials' lack of knowledge about Morocco. The *goumiers* were assigned to—or concealed in—Morocco's rural and mountain areas, reaches of the country the Germans expressed little interest in and lacked the staff to police themselves. Those same areas also housed a large cache of military equipment spirited away before the Germans could take inventory. Hidden on farms and squirreled away in caves in the Atlas Mountains were 60 cannons, 50 tanks, 150 cars, 250 trucks, and some 20,000 weapons.[11]

VICHY'S GROWING INFLUENCE IN French Morocco also took the form of a new batch of anti-Semitic laws in the summer of 1941. At the beginning of June, Vichy further tightened the definition of a Jew and imposed sweeping prohibitions against Jewish participation in unoccupied France in business and "liberal, commercial, industrial, or artisanal professions."[12] Worried about the export of similar laws to Morocco, a council of Jews was held in Casablanca on June 23 attended by the grand rabbis of Fez, Rabat, Casablanca, and Marrakech. The Jewish community decided to lobby Noguès for assistance, hoping to stop the promulgation of any further laws. A letter signed by the presidents of Jewish communities of Rabat, Salé, Meknès, and Casablanca reminded the resident-general that the Jews had been loyal and hardworking members of the Moroccan community for 2,000 years and expressed alarm about possible new anti-Semitic legislation. The Jews placed their economic, social, and intellectual future in "his hands." "The French conscience has always been a guide for humanity," said the letter. "Once again, it will decide in favor of divine and human justice."[13]

A new *dahir* reflecting Vichy's policy was supposed to have appeared on July 10 but was delayed by further opposition, this time from the palace. El Mokri, the grand vizier and one of the sultan's most trusted advisors, lodged a protest with Noguès, arguing that the Treaty of Fez, which established the French Protectorate of Morocco, gave the sultan full jurisdiction in religious matters. Moroccan Jews were subjects of the sultan, their status regulated by sharia law. Therefore, anti-Semitic legislation represented a form of interference.[14]

Despite the opposition from the palace and the Jewish community, a new batch of *dahirs* arrived in August. These regulations expanded the list of professions barred to Jews, including real estate, investments, and banking. Jews were also forbidden to serve as reporters, editors, or periodical directors (except for religious or scientific journals). They were banned from producing or directing movies or theatrical productions. Jews in retail trade and handicrafts could, however, continue their businesses. A new quota system also limited to 2 percent the number of Jews who could practice law and medicine. All Jews were also ordered to register and make declarations of their occupations and property.[15] It was everything the Moroccan Jews had feared.

On August 22, another *dahir* appeared barring Moroccan Jews from living in the European sections of cities and outside the *mellahs*, the Jewish ghettos, to which they were required to return by September 22, 1941. Those who refused to move faced both expulsion from their homes and a fine of between 500 and 1,000 francs.[16]

The issuance of the new *dahir* coincided with the arrival in Morocco of Xavier Vallat, Vichy's commissioner for Jewish affairs. In an interview with the press, Vallat praised the new *dahir*. "I am pleased to see that recent orders of the Sultan have already partly solved the Jewish problem in Morocco in accordance with the spirit of Vichy," he said. "Our aim is to eliminate the Jewish influence wherever we find it predominant. French Jews in Morocco will have to conform to the special laws issued for Jews in France, while Moroccan Jews will be kept within limits where they can be useful without the risk of their becoming harmful."[17]

It is not entirely clear, however, how many of the Jews in Casablanca moved their homes or relinquished their professions. In Casablanca, the *mellah* was already stuffed to capacity, with no extra lodgings available to accommodate the large Jewish population living outside its walls. The daunting logistics appear to have foiled the implementation of the removal order in Casablanca—but that was not the case in Fez or Meknès.[18] As a longtime resident of *ville nouvelle*, Hélène Bénatar did not move into the *mellah*. She did, however, lose the ability to practice law. Like many other Jews, she filed a petition for exemption but was denied.[19]

Throughout the fall, the Jews of Morocco continued to look for ways to engage the sultan to help remedy their situation. The sultan expressed his support for the community privately, but they hoped for a public declaration or even a rollback of the laws already implemented.[20] After being assured of an amiable reception, the Jewish community of Rabat sacrificed two oxen before the palace and petitioned for an audience. Sidi Mohammed received them, allowing them to make their appeal for assistance against the destruction of their livelihoods. He also continued to meet with the Jewish community, often in secret, throughout 1941 and 1942.[21]

The Residency also took steps to ensure Vichy's anti-Semitic message reached the public. Newsreels shown before feature films dripped with anti-Semitism. Some featured images of Georges Mandel and other rebel parliamentarians of Jewish ancestry, followed by a statement branding them as traitors who had sold out France and orchestrated her defeat.[22] Casablanca cinemagoers were also cautioned that if they left the theater during the newsreels, which became common practice for half the audience, they would not be allowed back in unless they paid for another ticket. "Thus, all the spectators will be able to watch without disturbance the showing of the news films, the faithful images of the work of national renovation which is being accomplished under Marshal Pétain," said the notice in *Petit Marocain*.[23]

20

Generals on the Ledge

O N OCTOBER 16, 1941, GENERAL MAXIME WEYGAND STEPPED OFF a plane in Vichy, having been ordered to appear by Admiral Jean-François Darlan. Rumors swirled that the Germans had once again asked for his resignation as high commissioner of North Africa. Weygand had heard such rumors before and ignored them. But this time was different. Along with the usual allegations of obstructing German demands, Berlin charged Weygand with conspiring with the Americans to supply French North Africa with weapons. Weygand also knew from his friends in Vichy that Darlan had been working against him for some time, unable to quench his jealousy of Weygand's authority and prestige.[1]

Weygand arrived to discover that Darlan was supposedly absent, but he received a warm welcome from Henri-Philippe Pétain, his old friend and mentor. The following day, their conversation wasn't so pleasant, as Pétain delivered the news that Germany had given Vichy an ultimatum. "My presence in Africa was impossible because of my relations with the Americans," wrote Weygand. Instead, Weygand would be appointed minister of state in charge of preparing a "constitution of the Empire." Weygand refused the post. "My honor forbade me to give up voluntarily a post in which the trust of millions of French and natives made it a duty for me to stay." If the Germans wanted him to leave North Africa, Pétain would have to fire him. Instead, Pétain agreed to write a letter to Hitler voicing his support for Weygand.[2]

With his appointment reaffirmed, Weygand attended to other business in Vichy and made plans to return to Algiers. When he sent word to Darlan of his intention to depart, the admiral's assistant suggested that Weygand be locked up. Outraged by the insubordination of Darlan's man, Weygand complained to Pétain, who mustered enough energy to complain in person to Darlan. Soon Weygand was standing in Darlan's office, watching with angry amusement as Darlan attempted to cover up his chicanery by talking about the weather, their families, anything, his face growing redder by the minute.[3]

Before Weygand returned to Algiers, Pétain showed him the note from Otto Abetz, the German ambassador to Vichy France. Hitler and his advisors considered Weygand's continued stewardship of North Africa "an insurmountable obstacle to a constructive policy between Germany and France." Weygand displayed no indication of wishing to work with Germany and spoke in an openly hostile manner about German plans. Berlin also took offense at Weygand's pronouncement that he wished for Germany's attack on the Soviet Union to "bring disaster to the armies of the Reich and its allied nations." Weygand considered the dispatch and its charges a badge of honor.[4]

THE POSSIBLE DISMISSAL OF Weygand, who had helped orchestrate the economic program for North Africa, concerned the Americans. The gossip around Vichy did little to assuage their concerns. "I won't conceal the fact . . . that ever since Weygand's last visit here and a few weeks prior thereto the question of his status in Africa has been a burning one. It remains so. What will come out of it I do not know," Charles Rochat, the acting secretary general of the French Ministry for Foreign Affairs, told Admiral William Leahy, the US ambassador to Vichy, in an unguarded moment.[5]

In mid-November, Weygand was once again summoned to Vichy, this time by Pétain. Darlan had threatened to quit unless Weygand was relieved. "Either he goes or I go," said Darlan. The pressure from Berlin to dismiss Weygand also continued. Pétain once again proposed relieving Weygand of his military duties, which would allow him to focus solely on political and economic matters. For a soldier, there could be no greater insult. Weygand refused the offer. "So I expected," said Pétain.

A day later, the axe fell on Weygand. A new ultimatum had arrived from Berlin demanding his recall. Berlin wanted assurances of Vichy's commitment to collaboration, and a resignation by Darlan, who supported Franco-German unity, would send the wrong signal. Despite their years of service together and Weygand's role in birthing Vichy in the wake of the collapse of France, Pétain could no longer protect him.[6]

The Vichy Foreign Ministry explained the decision to the Americans as necessary to preserve the empire. "If the Marshal had not made this decision there is every indication to believe that German troop penetration into Africa would have been inevitable and would undoubtedly have occurred very soon," said the *note verbale*.[7] In a meeting with Leahy, a visibly distressed Pétain went even further, claiming that if he had not dismissed Weygand, Germany would have occupied Vichy.[8]

Upon hearing the news, Winston Churchill lobbied Franklin Roosevelt to use what influence the United States possessed to preserve Weygand's command. "It would be disastrous if Weygand were to be replaced by some pro-Hun officer just at the moment when we are likely to be in a position to influence events in North Africa both from the East and from home," wrote Churchill.[9]

Weygand would not be saved; nor would he return to Algiers. Instead, he was sent into retirement, forbidden to work or to leave Vichy.[10] Rather than appoint someone to take Weygand's place, Darlan parceled out his command. General Alphonse Juin, who served as Weygand's deputy, became commander in chief of land, air, and coastal defenses in North Africa. He answered directly to Darlan.[11]

FOR CHARLES NOGUÈS, WEYGAND'S departure represented a victory. For months, he had made his unhappiness with Weygand known in Vichy, finding a particularly sympathetic ear in Darlan. His complaints and recriminations helped Darlan assemble a case against Weygand that the Germans, who had their own objections to his conduct, would champion. Instead of having to funnel everything through Weygand in Algiers, Noguès could now return to reporting directly to the colonial and foreign ministries in Vichy. He regarded Weygand's recall as a delicious comeuppance for a man who had spent months belittling him and undermining his power.[12]

The Germans capped off the ouster of Weygand by reinforcing their presence in French Morocco. The Reich had previously refused to dismiss Theodor Auer, the head of the Gestapo in Casablanca, despite Vichy's attempts to orchestrate his removal. In November 1941, Germany promoted Auer to consul general of French Morocco. The mastermind behind Germany's surveillance network wasn't going anywhere.[13]

The day after Weygand's dismissal, General Paul Schultheiss, head of the German Armistice Commission in French Morocco, ordered his men to appear in public wearing their uniforms and bearing their sidearms. Across the country, men who heretofore had presented themselves to the world as accountants and lawyers stepped out of their homes in Nazi dress and red armbands adorned with swastikas. Weygand had forbidden the Germans to wear their uniforms, but now they would walk proudly down the streets in them.[14]

WEYGAND'S RECALL AND FIRING unsettled the French army in Morocco. Its officers looked upon his removal as an omen that foretold of an invasion and occupation of North Africa by Germany. Weygand had provided a moral compass of sorts with his "defend the empire, but oppose the Germans" stance. By losing their advocate and bulwark against German aggression, French army officers began to realize that the onus of resistance now rested with them.

After Weygand's departure, Dave King received visit a from an envoy of Major General Antoine Béthouart. The general wanted to meet with Robert Murphy. Béthouart was known to be Weygand's man and rumors suggested he was interested in fostering a community of pro-Allied Army officers and corps. Béthouart's recruitment would represent a big coup for the Americans, but it also required careful handling. King sent a coded telegram to Murphy in Algiers, alerting him about the possible contact. Murphy's reply began with "FOR KING PERSONALLY," giving him permission to set up a meeting.[15]

Franklin Canfield, another vice consul, was on code duty when Murphy's response arrived. The thirty-one-year-old Canfield possessed a blueblood pedigree much like that of King, but he lacked the seasoning that came from service in World War I.[16] He had only worked in a law firm and had no experience with intelligence. Ignoring that the telegram was addressed to King, Canfield drove to Béthouart's headquarters in a car sporting US Consulate plates. When Canfield arrived unannounced and asked to see the general, he was informed that Béthouart was away. He then asked a French officer to lunch, one who was known to his colleagues as having dubious allegiances.

Béthouart's staff noted the debacle and informed the general immediately. If they noticed, so too must have Vichy and Germany's intelligence services. Fearing he might be arrested at any moment, Béthouart put a plane on standby for twenty-four hours, so he could leave for Gibraltar at a moment's notice. The experience left Béthouart with a deservedly poor opinion of the Americans. Despite repeated attempts by King and Murphy to engage him over the next ten months, he kept his distance.

Canfield's decision to ignore instructions made him damaged goods in Casablanca. Word of his recklessness traveled among those with resistance sympathies. He was also persona non grata among the Casablanca team. The fiasco with Béthouart wasn't Canfield's only stumble. He and Kenneth Pendar, the vice consul who worked out of Marrakech, raised eyebrows when they threw a cocktail party for the local native leaders. Offering alcohol to devout Muslims demonstrated a striking lack of knowledge or regard for their religious beliefs. Murphy decided to send Canfield to Dakar to replace Frederick Culbert, an Annapolis graduate and war hero, who was being reassigned by the US Navy to Casablanca. When Canfield balked at going to Dakar, he was sent home.[17]

21

Up to the Neck
and In to the Death

ON SUNDAY EVENING, DECEMBER 7, 1941, THE SUN SLIPPED INTO THE Atlantic Ocean, pulling with it the weak light that turned Casablanca into a pale, postcard version of itself during the winter. As darkness closed on the city, 8,300 miles away Honolulu awoke, just starting its Sunday. Like Casablanca, life in the main port of Hawaii revolved around the ocean, but the water rushing onto the sandy beaches came from the tropical Pacific instead of the grey Atlantic. And like Casablanca, Honolulu boasted a key naval base.

On that sleepy Sunday morning, just after 6:00 a.m., 183 planes took off from six Japanese aircraft carriers bobbing in choppy seas north of Pearl Harbor. The fighters, bombers, and torpedo planes constituted the first wave of a carefully planned surprise attack intended to decimate American military strength in the Pacific. While Hitler marched the Wehrmacht across Europe in his quest to build a new German empire, Japan had been pursuing its own imperial ambitions in Southeast Asia. With the Dutch under German occupation and Britain consumed with the fight against Germany, Americans were the only power capable of opposing Japan's plans to seize Singapore, Malaya, and the Philippines. By rendering Pearl Harbor useless as a base and crippling the American fleet anchored there, Japan believed it would have free rein to pursue its conquests.

Shortly before 8:00 a.m., the first Japanese bomb fell. Total surprise had been achieved. Over the next two hours, bombs rained down on Pearl Harbor and the adjoining army air base. By the time the Japanese planes returned to their aircraft carriers, the US Pacific fleet lay in pieces; 188 aircraft were destroyed, another 159 were damaged, and almost 3,500 sailors and soldiers were either dead or wounded.[1] Standing before a joint session of Congress the next day, Franklin Roosevelt delivered a stinging indictment. "Yesterday, December 7, 1941—a date which will live in infamy—the United States of America was suddenly and deliberately attacked by naval and air forces of the Empire of Japan." He asked Congress to declare war on that nation.[2] It complied. On December 11, Germany declared war on the United States—and the United States responded in kind.[3]

After months of pushing the boundaries of neutrality, the Americans had finally joined the war. "No American will think it wrong of me if I proclaim that to have the United States at our side was to me the greatest joy," wrote Winston Churchill in his memoirs. "I could not foretell the course of events. I do not pretend to have measured the martial might of Japan, but now at this very moment I knew the United States was in the war, up to the neck and in to the death."[4]

Churchill believed a face-to-face meeting with Roosevelt vital. He worried that America's pride—and taste for revenge—would lead the American president to give the war in the Pacific priority over the conflict in Europe.[5] After obtaining the approval of the War Cabinet and King George VI to travel, he wrote to Roosevelt on December 9, proposing a conference. "We could review the whole war plan in light of reality and new facts, as well as the problems of production and distribution."[6] Roosevelt demurred, fearing the journey across the Atlantic and its German submarine–infested waters might endanger Churchill's life.[7] He also wanted time to mobilize the country to fight in the Pacific before having to deal with Churchill dogging him about what American entry into the war meant for the British war effort.[8]

Writing back, Churchill dismissed the president's concerns about safety, believing the bigger danger lay in not coordinating strategy immediately.[9] Japan's attack on Hawaii was part of a larger offensive that included assaults on Guam, the Philippines, Wake Island, and Midway Island. Britain suffered ongoing losses from Japanese attacks on Hong Kong and Malaya. Vichy France also weighed on Churchill's mind. How would America's entry into the war effect its relations with Vichy? What would it mean for Hitler's plans for North Africa?

At last Roosevelt relented, cabling Churchill to come to Washington. "Delighted to have you here at the White House," he wrote.[10] Even as he packed his bags, Churchill wondered if the United States might offer to land an American Expeditionary Force at Casablanca.[11]

CHURCHILL WASN'T THE ONLY one making plans. Within hours of the news about Pearl Harbor, William J. Donovan, director of the Office of the Coordinator of Information in the United States, was marshaling his intelligence resources. Six months earlier, he had convinced Roosevelt to let him start an agency that could collate, analyze, and act on the intelligence gathered by the army, navy, State Department, and Federal Bureau of Investigation. As the country ramped up its war effort, Donovan intended to show the president and the military chiefs just how useful an intelligence agency could be. Bags of reports arrived at the White House multiple times a day for the president's review. Donovan also floated schemes that ranged from practical (setting up a regular way to review European newspapers) to downright crazy (a commando raid on the Japanese island of Hokkaido).[12]

Knowing that Churchill was on his way, Donovan urged Roosevelt to include special operations as part of any strategic plans the Allies considered. He recommended the organization of "a guerilla corps independent and separate from the Army and Navy, and imbued with a maximum of the offensive and imaginative spirit." This force would strike the enemy where it least expected and where it was most vulnerable. Donovan believed North Africa to be the perfect place to mount such an operation.[13] He also papered the president with memos advocating using North Africa as a beachhead for an attack on Europe.[14] If the Allies were going into North Africa—and Donovan hoped that was the case—he wanted his men and his organization to be part of it.

CHURCHILL ARRIVED IN WASHINGTON, DC, on December 22, just in time for Christmas. He spent the stormy ten-day voyage across the Atlantic aboard the battleship *Duke of York* drafting strategy memos and reading adventure novels, including one about Napoleon's exploits in Egypt.[15] For the next three weeks, he lived in the White House. The intimate quarters helped cement the growing friendship between the president and the prime minister. The conversation about how to wage war began in the morning, continued through lunch, barreled into the afternoon, lingered with dinner, and faded over late-night drinks. The next day, they picked up where they had left off. Churchill felt no compunction about wandering into Roosevelt's bedroom if he had something on his mind.[16] Roosevelt also sought out Churchill in his quarters. Once he arrived to find the prime minister, pink from the bath, dictating as he walked around the room, seemingly oblivious of his towel's having fallen away.[17]

They also made carefully managed public appearances designed to sell the country on the Anglo-American alliance and the need to help Britain in her battle to wrest Europe from Nazi Germany's clutches. On a bitterly cold Christmas Eve, he helped Roosevelt light the Christmas tree on the south

FIGURE 21.1. In the wake of Pearl Harbor, Prime Minister Winston Churchill spent Christmas at the White House. *Library of Congress*

lawn of the White House and sent out holiday tidings to the American people. "I spend this anniversary and festival far from my country, far from my family, and yet I cannot truthfully say that I feel far from home," Churchill told the crowd.[18] On Christmas morning, the president and prime minister attended church at Foundry Methodist, singing hymns together from the fourth pew.[19] The day after Christmas, Churchill delivered a stirring thirty-five-minute speech before a joint session of Congress, making him the first British prime minister ever to do so. He concluded the speech by praising the partnership and the possibilities of the Anglo-American alliance. "It is not given to us to peer into the mysteries of the future; yet, in the day to come, the British and American peoples will, for their own safety and for the good of all, walk together in majesty, in justice and in peace." As deafening applause engulfed the Senate chamber, Churchill raised his right hand clenched in a fist, but for two fingers flashing his trademark "V" for victory.[20]

The night of the speech, Churchill suffered a heart attack. But rather than agree to abide by the standard treatment of six weeks of bed rest, as recommended by his doctor, he insisted on continuing to work and keeping the incident a secret. The prime minister's determination to soldier on didn't keep him from fretting about his heart when he experienced shortness of breath or felt too warm. On December 29, Churchill flew to Ottawa, where he met with Canada's leadership, delivered another rousing speech, this time before the Canadian parliament, and charmed his way through dinners and receptions. By January 1, Churchill was back in Washington, ready to continue the discussions with the Americans.

THE TRIP TO WASHINGTON wasn't just cocktails, speeches, and informal chats. The day after the British delegation arrived, a series of formal meetings began between the Americans and British to discuss how to coordinate the Anglo-American war effort and map out a strategy for 1942. Roosevelt and Churchill attended some of the meetings, but otherwise their military staffs hashed out the details.[21]

The British breathed a huge sigh of relief when they learned that Roosevelt and his military advisers favored a "Germany first" strategy. As to the question of where to confront Germany, Churchill advocated an offensive in North Africa. If the Allies seized that region, they could use it as a base for attacking the Germans through the Mediterranean. He found the president backed the idea as well. Roosevelt had briefly entertained the idea of sending an American Expeditionary Force to Casablanca during the fall, only to be talked out of it by Chief of Staff General George C. Marshall and Secretary of War Henry Stimson.[22] The president's military staff, however, continued to oppose a North Africa campaign, preferring a cross-channel attack from Britain into northwestern France. For them, North Africa was a potentially expensive and bloody diversion from the real goal of reclaiming France and then Germany.

"There was general agreement that it was vital to forestall the Germans in N.W. Africa and the Atlantic islands," Churchill wired the War Cabinet on Christmas Eve. "The President said that he was anxious that American land forces should give their support as quickly as possible wherever they could be most helpful, and favoured the idea of a plan to move into North Africa being prepared for either event, i.e. with or without initiation."[23]

The First Washington Conference—also known by its code name ARCADIA—continued through January 14. Over the next three weeks, the Americans and British dealt with other issues vital to managing their nascent full-fledged alliance. They agreed to unify their military command structure, allowing for the coordination of land, air, and sea operations.[24] The Combined Chiefs of Staff, based in Washington, became the body through which the Americans and British planned the execution of the war against Germany and Japan. The decision to prioritize unity over parochialism would play a key role in the success of the Anglo-American war effort.[25]

The conference also dealt with strategy for fighting Japan, forming a joint command with the Dutch for the Far East, sending American bombers to bases in England, and signing a declaration against making a separate peace with Germany. Roosevelt and Churchill also quarreled over the British Empire and decolonization, but without any lasting damage to their relationship.

BY THE TIME CHURCHILL and his military advisors boarded the *Duke of York* for the return trip across the Atlantic, Donovan had secured Roosevelt's approval to expand his operation into North Africa. An Allied invasion of North Africa would take months to plan and execute, but he could develop an intelligence infrastructure to support that campaign in the interim. Donovan needed someone who could provide better coordination and oversight of the intelligence work already being done in the region by Robert Murphy's vice consuls. He would also need someone to serve as a liaison with British intelligence and organize guerilla activities.

Donovan found his man in Lieutenant Colonel William Eddy, an erudite, hard-drinking marine with startling blue eyes. Born in Sidon, Syria (now Lebanon), to Presbyterian missionaries, Eddy grew up speaking both English and Arabic. After graduating from Princeton in 1917, he signed up with the Marine Corps' 2nd Division, working as an intelligence officer.[26] His luck ran out at the Battle of Belleau Wood, when a high-explosive shell tore up his right foot. He returned to the front, only to be felled by a nasty case of pneumonia. Eddy fought his way back from the brink of death, but an associated septic infection permanently damaged his hip joint. He would limp for the rest of his life.[27] Upon seeing the stack of combat ribbons from World War I on Eddy's Marine uniform, Major General George S. Patton Jr. remarked, "The son-of-bitch has sure been shot at enough."[28] When World War II dawned in Europe, Eddy resigned as president of Hobart College and returned to active duty with the Marine Corps at the rank of lieutenant colonel. He found his way to Cairo in July 1941, where he served as the US naval attaché.[29]

Eddy agreed to work for Donovan, and at the end of January 1942, he set up shop in a three-room apartment in a wing of the American Legation in Tangier. The United States had occupied the beautiful Moorish-style building, which featured elaborate mosaic floors and a fountain in the inner courtyard, since the sultan of Morocco had bestowed it as a gift in 1821. Eddy marveled at how from the roof he could see the coast of Spain—and on a clear day the Rock of Gibraltar. He found lodgings up the hill at the El Minzah hotel. "I have to climb almost vertically half a mile to get back for lunch and dinner!! The exercise is good for me and ought to help keep me in condition," he wrote.[30]

With Murphy already established in Algiers, Tangier was the logical place to headquarter American intelligence efforts in North Africa. It had direct flights to Lisbon, something Casablanca lacked, and was an easy hop over to the British base at Gibraltar. The British also had a consulate, making it possible to share intelligence in person.[31]

The city's openness also made it a magnet for spies. Eddy learned to live with a shadow, as he had a tail wherever he went. "I know the man who follows me because I have photographs of the 55 Axis agents in Tangier and Spanish Morocco." His telephones were tapped.[32] He even caught an agent attempting to listen into a conversation in his hotel room. "While we were in my room, I felt sure that the dumb sleuth was in the vacant room next door. So I tiptoed out and got the pass-key from the chambermaid, and walked right into the vacant room, and there he was, pretending that he was making repairs in the clothes closet."[33]

Eddy spent the first month crisscrossing French Morocco by train and in a secondhand 1936 Dodge, the best car he could buy, meeting a parade of French and Moroccan officials. He found Charles Noguès to be a "fine looking, courteous gentleman of the old French type, I remember seeing in the other war." During their half-hour chat, Noguès expressed a friendly attitude toward the United States but cautioned Eddy against any activities that might give Germany or Spain a pretext for occupying Morocco.[34] "So now I am officially introduced, accepted, and permitted to sneak about more (or rather LESS) at will," wrote Eddy after the meeting.[35]

Eddy marveled at the warm reception he received during his travels, something he had not expected given his nationality. The Americans were now allied with the British, who occupied a special place of contempt in French hearts for Mers-el-Kébir. Vice Admiral Armand d'Harcourt, commander of the French fleet in Morocco, should have been hostile to him in deference to his boss, Admiral Jean-François Darlan. Instead, d'Harcourt regaled him with stories about the lasting friendships he had forged with Americans during the previous war. He also asked Eddy if he could help him get copies of *Time*, which he missed reading.[36]

As Eddy drove through towns and countryside, Moroccans raised their hats or saluted—sometimes even clapped—when they saw the small American flag flapping from the radiator cap of his car. "Tangier as well as Rabat and Casa, everywhere we go, there is nothing but friendliness for the Americans," wrote Eddy. "The stiff members of a German armistice commission don't count. They have no friends in Morocco and always travel together in a car, like ostracized lepers, for their own safety."[37]

Of course, not everyone approved of Eddy's arrival. British intelligence foiled two attempts to blow up his car.

22

Calling Station Lincoln

THROUGHOUT THE SPRING OF 1942, BILL EDDY TRAVELED BACK AND forth between Tangier and Casablanca, catching one of the trains that ran between the cities daily. "I wish you and all the family could come with me," he wrote his son Jack about the journey. "It is really a beautiful trip through romantic and free scenery with the Riff Mountains arising on the left and with the ocean constantly appearing and reappearing on the right through valleys that lead down to the sea."[1]

One such trip coincided with an official day of mourning for those killed when the Royal Air Force (RAF) bombed the Renault factory in the Paris suburb of Boulogne-Billancourt. Within days of the armistice, the Nazis had seized control of the factory and put its 16,000 employees to work making trucks for the German war effort. By the end of 1942, the plant was scheduled to turn out 13,000 trucks. On March 3, shortly after 9 p.m., three waves of British bombers dropped more than four hundred tons of bombs on the Renault complex, turning the night sky red and gold with fire visible for miles. Despite the RAF's attempts to hit only the factory—bombing runs remained incredibly imprecise—two hundred workers' homes located next to the factory went up in flames. Almost four hundred people died, with another six hundred sustaining serious injuries. The failure of the Germans to sound the air raid alarm compounded the casualties. It was the worst British attack on the French since Mers-el-Kébir in the summer of 1940.[2]

"The only thing I do not like very much about these British attacks on French soil is that they are occasional pinpricks which make the French more and more anti-British, and are not followed up by incessant bombing of German installations in France," wrote Eddy after the meeting. "Either the British should avoid irritating the French, or they should carry the damage to its effective conclusion of total destruction of the objective."[3]

Eddy's practical and tactical mind-set was one of the reasons William Donovan had picked him to head up the North Africa venture. Before Eddy left Washington, Donovan handed him a brief that read like something out of a spy novel. He was supposed to obtain the aid of "native chiefs," cultivate the loyalty of the local inhabitants, organize a fifth column, place weapons caches in strategic locations for use in an Allied invasion, and organize "guerilla bands of bold and daring men."[4] To accomplish his mission, Eddy could draw on $1 million from the White House's secret fund. He also received operational control of Robert Murphy's vice consuls, who had nominally been working for Donovan since the fall of 1941.[5]

As he took the helm of American intelligence operations, Eddy turned to Dave King and Staff Reid to help him accomplish his goals. Aside from being hard workers, King and Reid had succeeded in staying out of trouble, unlike some of their cohorts. One vice consul gambled eye-popping sums of money while socializing with a local pasha. Another squatted in a lavish villa belonging to an American socialite. There was, however, one problem: King and Reid's competitive natures fueled an unhealthy rivalry. They had even ceased to be roommates. At Murphy's urging, Eddy split up their duties, giving them separate areas of responsibility. Reid took charge of communications, while King worked on building up the resistance.[6]

EDDY WANTED TO COMMUNICATE in code with the American consulates in North Africa—Casablanca, Oran, and Algiers—which required setting up a clandestine radio network. A courier service ran between Casablanca, Tangier, Oran, and Algiers once a week, which was good for long reports but bad for conveying information quickly. Eddy chose Casablanca as a testing ground and provided Reid with a Paraset, a small British-made radio transmitter-receiver. The radio's name derived from its purpose: Britain's Special Operations Executive designed the sets for use in the field by resistance groups, dropping them behind enemy lines by parachute. The set had a range of only five hundred miles. Reid, and eventually the others, would wire reports to Tangier; then Eddy would send them on to London using his long-range transmitter.[7]

Eddy picked up the radio while visiting the British installation at Gibraltar. He passed it on to Reid on one of his visits to Tangier, and Reid smuggled the radio back to Casablanca in a diplomatic pouch.[8] That was the easy part.

Now Reid needed an operator—Eddy made it clear that he could not smuggle one in—and a safe location to set up the radio. At the suggestion of another vice consul, Reid met with "Ajax," a former French merchant marine with experience as a radio operator. Ajax, whose real name is lost to history, had done some work for the Americans in Algiers and proved reliable. After two lengthy conversations, during which Reid made sure that Ajax understood the risks, Reid had his man.

With informants lurking around every corner in Casablanca, Reid needed a private and secure location to house the radio and locate the antenna. They first tried using a wine press next to Cazes Airfield, which lay five miles outside Casablanca, but interference from the engines at the nearby hangers made operating the set impossible. The temporary location, however, did generate a new blueprint of the improvements made to the airfield, including new batteries and foxhole trenches for airplanes. Ajax sketched it while working the nightshift as part of his cover.

In mid-March 1942, Reid asked US Consul General H. Earle Russell for the impossible: permission to locate the antenna on the roof of the American consulate. If French authorities discovered the transmitter, the United States would be expelled from Morocco and possibly all of North Africa. Russell wasn't initially keen on the plan but gave his consent after Reid spent two hours pleading his case. Russell later expressed misgivings to Murphy about the arrangement. "Murphy, I hope you know what you are doing. But I should like to make clear that I disapprove of espionage," he said.

A few nights later, as consulate employees slept, an unused water closet and storage room in the back corner of the consulate's basement became a secret—and secure—room for housing the Paraset. The finished room was just large enough to hold a desk, chair, and carpet. Another night saw Reid and Ajax scampering around on the roof, drilling five-inch hooks into the parapet from which to string the antenna wire. They had bartered the hooks from a slaughterhouse in exchange for American tobacco. From the roof, a lead wire snaked down an unused chimney into the basement, where it ran into the secret room.[9]

To foil the gossips and informers, Reid started a program to listen to and record foreign propaganda recordings, most of which aired at night. He bought a Swiss-made radio from the Arcade Radio Shop and had it delivered to the front gate of the consulate in broad daylight. The porter placed the radio on the desk of the consulate's receptionist, from whom Reid would later pick it up. He also let it slip in conversations here and there that he was installing the radio in the cellar to receive daily BBC broadcasts. Anyone who listened to the BBC could be arrested—but everyone in Casablanca tried to anyway. "It was generally conceded that all of us were vitally interested in the progress of the war but had no means of getting this information except from one or two members owning a set," recalled Reid. He then hired Ajax as an interpreter to help monitor the broadcasts.[10]

On March 24, 1942, Reid and Ajax sent the first US-military-coded message from a clandestine station in North Africa. When station "Midway" in Tangier acknowledged the message, Ajax did a dance in the radio room. After station "Lincoln," as Casablanca was known, began trading messages with "Midway," consulate employees never lacked for the latest news from the BBC.[11] Over the next six months, Reid coded and decoded approximately 350 messages, most of the time working alone.[12] "Only one person in Casablanca should do your coding or know how to do it—that is yourself, or some fellow American of your choice," Eddy told Reid.[13]

The French suspected that the Americans were operating a clandestine set but hunted for it to no avail. At night, they patrolled the city with radio detectors, forcing Reid and Ajax to go dark for days at a time. Knowing the wireless sets ran off rechargeable batteries, the French ordered all garages to note the make and serial number of every battery brought in for recharging. Unable to find a friendly garage, Reid tried bringing charged batteries down from Tangier, but the logistics made it difficult to keep the set operational. A foot pedal charger was unworkable too. They finally hatched the solution of using a dynamo charger that hooked up to a car engine.[14]

WHILE REID WAS CODING messages in the cellar, King worked out of a building across the square from the American consulate. The annex, as it was called, made it easy for him to come and go unobserved by the consulate staff. Eddy tasked King with developing a resistance network in Morocco, something he'd been working on even before Eddy arrived.

King built up his network with the help of two women. Shelia Clark, who had previously taken over the British interests section, became his girl Friday. Clark's knowledge of Casablanca and Arabic meant that before long she was doing more than typing memos and filing requisitions. To arrange meetings with his contacts, King needed a courier who could deliver messages without attracting attention. Dorothy Ellis, a British woman who resided in Casablanca prior to the war, became King's most important courier. Ellis supported herself by teaching at the Lycée Jeanne d'Arc, a private Catholic school located next to the American consulate, and giving private

English and French lessons. As she bicycled around the city to and from her various jobs, Ellis delivered messages to King's assets underneath the noses of the Gestapo and Deuxième Bureau. Any agents who intercepted her would have found only innocuous-seeming notes arranging for language lessons. King also considered her highly discrete, so much so that they embarked on an affair.[15]

King also worked closely with Michel Despax, code name "Pinkeye." An Austrian by birth, he had tangled with the Nazis in Vienna, earning himself a thick police file. Preferring freedom to a concentration camp, he headed for France, where he joined the French Foreign Legion as a second lieutenant. When the Legion demobilized in the fall of 1940, he was stationed in North Africa and soon found himself targeted for deportation back to Germany. With the help of a friendly general, he changed his name to Michel Despax, allowing him to hide from Nazi and Vichy officials, and began working with the French resistance in Algiers.[16]

Impressed with what Despax had accomplished, Murphy asked him if he'd be willing to go to Casablanca and help King establish a similar network.[17] As cover, Despax set himself up in Rabat as a businessman who specialized in black market transactions, particularly macaroni, working out of the Hôtel Balima. French officials wrote him off as a shady businessman out to profit from the war, never suspecting him of working with King or masterminding a resistance network.

With the help of his Legion connections, Despax recruited both Captain Albert Breitel, chief of French counterintelligence, and Colonel Maurice Herviot, chief of the Sûreté in Casablanca. Finding other recruits, however, proved a delicate and dangerous task that required patience. "We had a special system of just beginning to talk about the current situation in the country, then we would talk about the French army, and reminisce about France, then we would start cautiously with a slight observation against the Germans and Vichy, and go a little bit nearer," said Despax of his technique. "And after two or three contacts of this kind, we could begin to have a slight idea of whether or not the man was good for something. Then we had to check one man against another." Using this method, Despax built a network of several hundred contacts in the military, government, and commerce. Some of his recruits, however, changed their minds after the German victories began to pile up in the winter of 1941–1942.[18]

King also demonstrated a flare for recruitment. One of his best-placed agents was André Pelabon, code name "Penguin," the technical chief of Casablanca's aviation workshops. Pelabon wasn't an easy recruit. "I spent a whole morning reasoning with him, and he finally decided that the real future of France was in the hands of England and possibly, America in the future, and not in the Pétain government," recalled King. Once he had cast his lot with the resistance, Pelabon delivered a steady stream of information about French aviation capabilities, plans for defending Casablanca and the coast, the schematics for airfields across Morocco, and military gossip. Documents were regularly smuggled out of Pelabon's office, copied overnight, and returned by the next morning, before they were missed.[19]

By December 1941, King and Despax were regularly sending Washington information on current troop levels, updates to the order of battle for Morocco down to the regiment level, and other intelligence of military significance.[20] A contact in the Deuxième Bureau provided lists of ships and cargos coming through the port, which were then cross-checked with the harbormaster. Despax described the work before Pearl Harbor as "relatively easy," but American entry into the war changed the stakes and the demands. Washington wanted resistance cells capable of taking out railroads and bridges. It needed detailed information about the coast from Port Lyautey to Safi for use in planning a possible invasion. It also wanted a list—not just assurances—of French military officers willing to help the Allies.[21]

BEGINNING IN MARCH 1942, King and Despax began to organize civilian resistance groups in Port Lyautey, Casablanca, Fédala, Rabat, Mogador, and Agadir. Groups were formed to seize, protect, and, if necessary, destroy the telephone exchange, powerhouses, and signal stations for the railroad. Gaining control of the railway lines was particularly important, as the French army would use them to bring reinforcements from Fez, Meknès, or Marrakech in the event of an invasion on the coast.[22]

The resistance network operated on the cell system: King and Despax knew the identity of the cell leaders, but they didn't know the men who made up the cells.[23] Despax handpicked the leaders, favoring hardcore anti-Nazi types. With the help of Breitel and Herviot, he sprang legionnaires who had been thrown into internment camps after the armistice for being Jewish, socialist, or anti-Vichy. Many of the men had records that went back to the early days of the Nazi regime, having fled Germany to escape imprisonment. Despax picked men like himself—men with long-simmering grievances who would not be swayed by a pretty speech or deterred by a hard look from a policeman. He also recruited known leftists, including a schoolteacher and a retired army major.[24]

From King and Despax's contacts emerged a scheme proposed by "Colette," which called for using small groups of men to stage a coup d'état in Morocco in preparation for an American landing. Four hundred men would take Casablanca, 185 would take Rabat, and 100 would seize Port Lyautey, with additional men at Meknès and Safi. Colette believed his force could hold Morocco for forty-eight hours before being overpowered by reinforcements. If the Frenchmen succeeded in snatching Morocco from Charles Noguès, Henri-Philippe Pétain, and Vichy, they would reinforce the French bond with the Allies and encourage others to rally to the cause.[25]

23

Robin Hood, Tweedledum, and Tweedledee

WHILE DAVE KING WORKED TO BUILD A MOROCCO-BASED RESISTANCE network, Robert Murphy found himself dealing with the Algiers-based Group of Five, which wanted to pry all of French North Africa from Vichy's grip. The "five" were united in their hatred of Vichy and their right-wing politics. Jacques Lemaigre-Dubreuil, an industrialist with businesses in both the occupied zone and Africa, owned newspapers in France and Morocco. Jean Rigault worked for Lemaigre-Dubreuil as editor of *Le Jour*. Rigault's politics leaned fascist; he wanted the Nazis ousted from France but favored keeping the authoritarian-style regime imposed by Vichy. Colonel A. S. Van Hecke commanded the North African branch of Chantiers de la jeunesse, a paramilitary youth organization established by Vichy. Van Hecke recruited Baron Henri d'Astier de la Vigerie, a young charismatic charmer, to both Chantiers de la jeunesse and to the resistance group. Jacques Tarbé de Santi-Hardouin, a diplomat and sometime member of Maxime Weygand's staff, had met Murphy while negotiating the economic agreement.[1]

The Group of Five chose no leader from their collective, hoping to find one instead—and that man would not be Charles de Gaulle. While they supported any effort by de Gaulle to unseat Henri-Philippe Pétain, they were reluctant to embrace a postwar France in which he played a large role. Lemaigre-Debrueil and Rigault in particular found the presence of socialists and Communists in the Free French organization unsettling. They even went so far as to request that any military discussions not involve the Free French. The Group of Five wanted the United States to provide military support—guns, ammunition, antiaircraft guns, mines—for an operation that would separate French North Africa from Vichy. Once they established a provisional government, the Group of Five wanted the Americans to provide economic aid to ensure its viability.[2]

Murphy's association with the Group of Five later opened him up to charges of fascist sympathizing. But in the winter of 1941–1942, these men provided leadership to a very diffuse French resistance movement in North Africa. They had stepped forward, putting their lives in jeopardy, while looking to Murphy and the United States for guidance and support for their scheme. Murphy dutifully reported their personalities, politics, and plans to Washington, hoping for advice on how to use—or gently dispense with—these men who had found their way to him. The State Department remained silent. With no help from his colleagues, when the Group of Five asked him for commitments, Murphy could only point to Franklin Roosevelt's pledge that the United States wanted to aid those opposed to the Axis.[3]

Although silence emanated from the State Department, the plans proposed by the Group of Five and Colette were forwarded to the army's War Plans Division for evaluation. In the aftermath of the ARCADIA Conference, Allied planners were hard at work assessing their strategic options. Like General George C. Marshall, Major General Dwight D. Eisenhower, the deputy chief of the War Plans Division, considered North Africa "a sideshow." For Eisenhower, serious consideration of a North Africa operation suggested that "amateur strategists" and "prima donnas"—meaning Winston Churchill and Franklin Roosevelt—were conducting strategic planning. Eisenhower believed that politicians should not determine military priorities.[4]

Not surprisingly, the War Plans Division looked at the proposals submitted by Murphy and Bill Eddy with skepticism and a dose of practicality. Eisenhower had the advantage of knowing what the army had (or didn't have) in its stocks and scheduled for the production lines. "The requirements for materiel and ammunition to equip the French North African forces as set forth in this plan are quite large and could not be made available in the near future," wrote Eisenhower at the end of February 1942. Shipping was a problem. He also did not like the idea of putting American lives in the hands of an unknown force. "In an unstable situation as this one would be, to entrust command of participating American forces to French authorities, as indicated in the plan, would be fraught with great danger." Nevertheless, if the people proposing the plan seemed responsible, he recommended continuing discussions to assess their capabilities.[5]

WHILE WASHINGTON DEBATED THE proposed schemes, discussions with the Group of Five continued. During a series of meetings with King in Casablanca, Van Hecke—code-named "Robin Hood"—provided a new invasion plan that used the Chantiers de la jeunesse as advance troops. As the commissaire général for North Africa, Van Hecke commanded 26,000 men divided between five camps—one in Morocco, one in Tunis, and three in Algeria. Vichy started the compulsory service organization for twenty-year-old men as a way to socialize them in the absence of conscription, which had been abolished under the armistice. Teaching young men service, community, and loyalty, while working their bodies and subjecting them to military discipline, also fit nicely with Vichy's focus on family, work, and fatherland.[6]

Van Hecke wanted to turn Vichy's own organization against it. The young men wore a jaunty uniform of a short khaki jacket, baggy pants, and a slouchy, mallard-blue beret, but were not issued weapons. The Group of Five believed that if the Allies armed the Chantiers de la jeunesse, they could take French North Africa. To facilitate the plan, the Allies needed to provide weapons for 26,000 men—and seven motorized divisions and five armored divisions as support.[7]

This new farcical plan also possessed the flaw that had previously troubled Eisenhower: Americans depending on untrained troops. And then there was Van Hecke. A graduate of Saint-Cyr, he had served twenty years in the French army, participating in the campaigns for Fez and Marrakech from 1909 to 1913. After retiring from the army, Van Hecke worked for French intelligence. "He is able, fearless, young, experienced, and enjoys the essential elements of prestige which could be rapidly developed," wrote Murphy. At the same time, the forty-five-year-old Frenchman harbored royalist sentiments and had participated in the 1937 Cagoulard plot to overthrow France's Popular Front government.[8] Did the Americans really want to turn an unrepentant royalist into a major resistance leader?

Eddy and King also didn't like that every time they met with Van Hecke, his demands increased. "Whereas before they needed one or two divisions, they now need a dozen fully equipped," Eddy told Murphy. At a particularly tense meeting, Van Hecke asked for 1 million francs to buy the support of the Moors throughout North Africa in the event of an invasion.[9] Van Hecke also requested 100,000 francs to pay the expenses of members who resigned from their jobs to run the resistance cell. Another payment of 5 million francs would be needed within the next month to finance operations across North Africa.[10]

In mid-March 1942, Eddy and King delivered the news to Van Hecke that the Allies would not be storming the beaches of North Africa anytime soon.

The US Army planners also rejected the plan to use the Chantiers de la jeunesse. Small shipments of guns and ammunition to aid resistance work might be possible. They would, however, be stored at Gibraltar until required by a yet-to-be-planned Allied invasion. Van Hecke took the news badly, making an impassioned plea for using his organization before the opportunity passed. Just to heighten the drama, he claimed that the Parti populaire français, the French fascist party that collaborated with the Germans, had started to make inroads into North Africa.[11]

Murphy shrugged at the table pounding. In some ways, the increasing demands made the Group of Five easier to manage. "We should not forget that we are dealing with a Latin mentality which likes to bargain. It is acutely conscious of the law of supply and demand and its market price is inclined to shift with the breeze," Murphy told Eddy. "The present offer, in my opinion, is puffed out of all recognition, and I have not the slightest doubt that the boys will deflate their demands if we really come down to brass tacks."

As VAN HECKE SULKED, King worked on developing another plan proposed by the Berger brothers, Casablanca businessmen with experience importing goods, to aid an American landing. The duo received the whimsical code names "Tweedledee" and "Tweedledum." This more modest plan called for the resistance groups to take out strategic targets—the power grid, telephone and telegram lines, major bridges—prior to American soldiers' hitting the beaches. It was exactly the kind of thing Eddy had been sent to North Africa to facilitate. To carry out the plan, the group needed small arms. Instead of trying to smuggle them in by landing them at night on an isolated stretch of beach in south Morocco, the Berger brothers would arrange for the weapons to go through customs at Port Lyautey. If the Americans put the weapons on a Portuguese boat, provided manifests, bills of lading, and invoices showing the goods to be of Portuguese origin, and consigned them to the Office of Post, Telegraphs, and Telephones (PTT), the Bergers would do the rest. After the weapons cleared customs, trucks from the PTT would pick up the crates from the warehouse on the dock and drive them into the interior for safekeeping.[12]

In mid-April, Eddy forwarded Tweedledee and Tweedledum's plan to Washington. "The French are determined to resist and asked today 'How soon can you deliver at Port Lyautey: 20,000 antitank mines, 15 kilos each (packed in cases weighing 20 to 30 kilos); 8000 similar mines will be wanted elsewhere later,'" he wrote. William Donovan passed Eddy's memo on to Roosevelt, attaching a warning about the possibility of German breakthrough in Tunisia and, more ominously, an attack on Spanish Morocco.[13] Both were pure speculation, but he knew his audience. Donovan also assured the Joint Chiefs of Staff that shipping the weapons to Port Lyautey was both safe and possible. If they had any doubts, Donovan encouraged them to send their own man to North Africa to investigate.[14]

Once again, the Joint Chiefs of Staff turned down arming a large-scale resistance force in French Morocco. They did, however, encourage distributing "funds judiciously for the purpose of initiating and maintaining guerilla opposition in that area." The Joint Chiefs feared that if the German Armistice Commission intercepted any of the shipments, they would use the weapons as a pretext for seizing the French fleet or forcing tighter military collaboration between the French and Germans.[15] The decision didn't surprise Eddy. He knew British officials lived in fear of losing the French fleet, so it followed that America's top military brass would echo the same anxiety. As he wrote Murphy, "I do not myself share the jitters about the fleet, but policy for me has not been set. They would rather have no groups armed in advance for resistance, than to have danger of present disturbance."[16]

Worried that Eddy would take another rejection hard, Donovan gave him a pep talk. "You must not be discouraged if the authorities here do not go the full way," wrote Donovan. "You must be prepared to meet those obstacles. If we are right it will work out right. In the meantime, you must recognize that I have the fullest confidence in what you are doing and we will back you to our limit."[17]

ON THE HEELS OF the Joint Chiefs' ruling, Murphy finally heard from the State Department about the various resistance schemes and personalities that he had diligently reported. The State Department refused to endorse any plan that might undermine French authority in North Africa. State Department officials worried that the resulting disorder would weaken French prestige in the region and elsewhere. As such, controls were being put in place to prevent dispersal of money to Eddy for any subversive activities without the State Department's approval. "From our point of view, the most worthwhile manner in which this money might be spent would be for the purpose of organizing friendly elements who might be in position to act in our behalf if and when we are compelled to withdraw our forces from North Africa," wrote Wallace Murray, who headed the Near Eastern and African Affairs Division.[18]

The blow dealt by the State Department left Eddy feeling like the "grand work" that he and King had done was "now washed up with the tide."[19] He also understood Van Hecke's frustration with them. "I am heartbroken over the disappointment of Robin Hood [Van Hecke] and Uncle Charlie [d'Astier de la Vigerie] in our co-operation and I do not blame them at all for feeling that we are no good," he told Murphy.[20]

There were, however, limits to Eddy's understanding—and he reached them when he learned of Van Hecke's flirtation with the British. He also discovered that British officials had warned the Joint Chiefs of Staff that Van Hecke and the Chantiers de la jeunesse could not be trusted.[21] Then, there was the very reliable gossip that Britain's Special Operations Executive (SOE), which handled covert and guerilla operations, had made overtures to Van Hecke—and been rejected. It looked to Eddy as if the British had scuttled American plans to work with Van Hecke so that they could step in and take over. All of it made for one angry marine.

"It was a knife in the back, a resentment that we should be dealing with French groups at all, rather than through the British," wrote Eddy of the duplicity. He suggested to Murphy that if the British insisted on behaving this way, the Americans should consider hampering their operations in North Africa. Eddy delivered mail to British agents in Tangier. The British could suddenly find their mail delivery service suspended.[22] Instead of retaliation, Donovan orchestrated SOE's termination of its relationship with Van Hecke.[23]

THE GAME PLAYING BETWEEN the Americans and the British signaled a larger problem with the lack of coordination between Allied intelligence and special operations in North Africa. Competing for assets and information was counterproductive. In mid-June 1942, Donovan flew to London to meet with Sir Charles Hambro, head of SOE. In the unassuming flat at 64 Baker Street that served as SOE's headquarters, they hammered out an agreement. Britain would oversee the Balkans, the Middle East, India, and, at least for the time being, western Europe. They would work together in Southeast Asia, Germany, and Italy. The United States would get the run of China, Finland, and North Africa.[24]

The following day, Donovan won another victory when Roosevelt signed an executive order creating the Office of Strategic Services (OSS), the first US intelligence agency. The name was the president's idea, but Donovan liked it.[25] From here on out, Eddy, King, and Reid would work for the legendary— and somewhat infamous—OSS.

24

Sympathy and Chivalry

WHILE WILLIAM DONOVAN WAS IN LONDON IRONING OUT AN agreement with the British, Bill Eddy journeyed to Washington to present a report to the senior staff of the army's Intelligence Division. Neither he nor Murphy had given up on the idea of fostering armed resistance in North Africa. Eddy's optimistic assessment claimed that 35,000 men in Algeria and 5,000 men in Morocco were prepared to assist an Allied invasion. They only needed weapons. He told assembled officers about the work of the Group of Five in Algiers. He also noted indications that General Alphonse Juin, who controlled the French army in Algeria, was sympathetic to the Allied cause but would not declare himself. "He turns his back and will not say anything so long as the Germans are not brought down on his head," said Eddy.

In French Morocco, Charles Noguès continued his diffidence toward the Allies. "The people do not trust Noguès," said Eddy. "He is a very correct army officer who obeys his superiors. He made one generous gesture towards resisting the Axis and he received no cooperation, so he just isn't going to bother anymore." General Antoine Béthouart, who commanded the Casablanca division, also remained elusive. "General Béthouart will come over to our side if we send an expeditionary force, but he will not commit himself."

The 5,000 men in French Morocco—mostly French with a smattering of Poles, Norwegians, and Spaniards—had been organized into eight cells with the job of carrying out sabotage. The vice consuls had, however, avoided working with the Arab population on orders from the State Department. "The French are very touchy about this and think we might try to turn the

Moors against them," said Eddy. "The French fear what might happen if the Moors were armed." Eddy also dismissed the idea of working with El Glaoui, the pasha of Marrakech, the second most powerful man in Morocco after the sultan and known to play politics. "The Glaoui has not signed on the dotted line for anybody," said Eddy. "He takes money from all because he is so much in debt. It is like pouring money into a bottomless pit, and is useless, at present. At the right time a deal can be made."

Eddy emphasized that French Morocco was the perfect place to use resistance cells to carry out sabotage. "There are only two ways in which Axis reinforcements could be brought in: Spanish Morocco and Taza Pass, and these could be blown up easily by sabotage," he said. As for slipping the weapons and ammunition needed by the cells into the country, he had a solution for that too. A resistance contact owned a seaweed-processing factory at Agadir. He regularly sent boats ten kilometers off the coast to drop nets. When the boats went out, they could rendezvous with ships carrying guns and ammunition and bring the weapons back to port, where they would be stored in the factory's warehouses. From there, the weapons would be distributed to the resistance cells as part of the regular deliveries made by the owner's trucks.

"We don't need to be timid about North Africa," said Eddy. "On the contrary, we should feel that we will lose popularity by staying away." The French were waiting for the Americans to come. He predicted that at least 75 to 80 percent of the French hoped for an Allied victory.[1]

Eddy's briefing, which advocated for covert operations as preparation for an Allied invasion, was an outgrowth of the work done by his team and Robert Murphy in North Africa. Its overly optimistic tone and "can do" attitude reflected a somewhat naive belief that once the resistance groups in Algeria and Morocco had weapons, all the pieces would fall into place. It also played into Franklin Roosevelt's thinking about the need for a major Anglo-American offensive in North Africa, an idea he had refused to relinquish during the previous six months, despite the objections of his military advisers. Like Winston Churchill, Roosevelt loved nothing more than a good scheme.

EDDY'S BRIEFING OCCURRED ONLY a few days before a message arrived from Churchill suggesting a second meeting in Washington. "In view of the impossibility of dealing by correspondence with all of the many difficult points outstanding, I feel it is my duty to come to see you," Churchill wrote Roosevelt on June 13, 1942.[2] "Difficult points" referred to the increasingly parlous strategic position of the Allies in Europe and the need to make some hard decisions about where to focus British and American resources over the next twelve months. The eastern front had become a bloodbath. The Russian army succeeded in pushing the Germans back from Moscow, but Leningrad remained under siege, and the summer campaign season was about to begin. Further south in the Middle East, Britain's Western Desert Force traded blows with Germany's Afrika Korps across the unforgiving reaches of the Libyan Desert in a contest for control of the eastern Mediterranean. Under the leadership of General Erwin Rommel, German forces pushed past Benghazi and laid siege to Tobruk. Egypt and the Suez Canal would soon be within Germany's reach. Something needed to be done about opening a second front in Europe to divert the Germans.

"I find I must be in Hyde Park," wrote Roosevelt, suggesting the prime minister join him for a few days. The two leaders could talk one-on-one at his New York home before formal discussions between their staffs.[3]

With the trip set, Churchill and his aides dashed off to their tailors for summer-weight suits to survive the summer humidity and packed their bags.

BEFORE CHURCHILL ARRIVED, ROOSEVELT assembled his key military advisers: General George C. Marshall, his chief of staff; General Henry "Hap" Arnold, head of the Army Air Force; Admiral Ernest King, chief of naval operations; Frank Knox, secretary of the navy; and Henry Stimson, secretary of war. The Americans needed to clarify their own thinking on the issue of how and when to open a second front—before Churchill arrived full of schemes and plans.

Foremost in the president's mind was relieving pressure on the Soviets. His meetings at the end of May with V. M. Molotov, Joseph Stalin's envoy, confirmed information gathered by Allied intelligence: the Russian position was "precarious" and would continue to deteriorate.[4] Roosevelt pledged to Molotov that the United States and Britain would open a second front in Europe by the end of 1942. But what should that second front look like?

During the previous five months, Roosevelt had pushed for a cross-channel invasion of northwestern France late in the year. Securing the ports at Brest or Cherbourg would give the Allies a bridgehead from which to drive toward Berlin. The American service chiefs disliked the 1942 date. Instead they wanted the same operation (code name BOLERO) but with a spring 1943 start date. Also on the table for discussion was an invasion of North Africa (code name GYMNAST) in late 1942. By seizing Morocco and Algeria, the Allies could reclaim France and attack Germany and Italy via the Mediterranean. Churchill favored the North Africa option and would undoubtedly press its merits when he arrived.

It often fell to Marshall to remind the president of the practicalities of military operations. An assault on North Africa required transporting men and matériel from the United States across the Atlantic Ocean. Even if the ships evaded German submarines and arrived safely, the invasion force still needed air cover. If the Allies invaded northwestern France, Britain could serve as the staging area, making the task of assembling men and matériel far easier. They would only have to transport Allied troops 100 or 200 miles, as opposed to more than 4,000 miles to North Africa.[5]

Marshall also opposed invading France in 1942 because he considered the start date unworkable. But he was far more opposed to a North Africa invasion, regarding it as a distraction from the real objective of opening a second front in western Europe. He believed the United States should pressure Britain to support an invasion of Europe in 1943.

As was typical of Roosevelt's meetings, no one kept minutes for the afternoon session at the White House, but Stimson, an avid diarist, left behind a colorful report. When the president argued for the North Africa option, he encountered "rather robust opposition." "Marshall had a paper already prepared against it for he had a premonition of what was coming," wrote Stimson. "I spoke very vigorously against it. King wobbled around in a way that made me rather sick with him."

Despite their stated objections, Roosevelt asked his advisers to look for solutions to the problems they raised regarding the North Africa operation. "The only hope I have about it all is that I think he may be doing it in his foxy way to forestall trouble that is now on the ocean coming towards us in the shape of a new British visitor," wrote Stimson.[6]

JUST BEFORE MIDNIGHT ON June 17, Churchill and his entourage boarded a Boeing Clipper in Scotland. The late departure diminished the possibility of encountering a Luftwaffe patrol off the western coast of Britain. "The weather was perfect and the moon full. I sat for two hours or more in the co-pilot's seat admiring the shining sea, revolving my problems, and thinking of the anxious battle," wrote Churchill.[7] British forces at Tobruk, a port city in Libya, struggled to keep the Germans at bay. If the city fell, Germany would have use of a strategically positioned port from which to reinforce Rommel's Afrika Korps as it closed in on Egypt.

Among those traveling with Churchill were General Alan Brooke and Major General Hastings "Pug" Ismay. As chief of the Imperial General

Staff, Brooke coordinated Britain's military efforts. A stern Ulsterman with perfectly pomaded hair, Brooke regularly clashed with Churchill over strategic issues. He had no problem disagreeing with the very opinionated prime minister, a trait Churchill appreciated. "When I thump the table and push my face towards him what does he do?" wrote Churchill of Brooke. "Thumps the table harder and glares back at me."[8] Ismay, a politically savvy staff officer, served as Churchill's liaison with the British service chiefs.

Twenty-seven hours later, the Clipper approached Washington, DC, giving the Brits a chance to see the nation's capital from the air. Brooke marveled at the "sight of this beautifully laid out town in the hazy light of the evening." Instead of growing in the hodge-podge manner of London, Washington had been built in an orderly north-south, east-west grid from its inception. "The Potomac looked like a small silver ribbon running through the middle of it," wrote Brooke.[9] As they descended, the Clipper came level with the top of the Washington Monument, prompting Churchill to suggest to the pilot that they not hit the iconic white marble obelisk and abruptly end the Anglo-American alliance. Shortly after 7:00 p.m., the plane touched down on the murky blue waters of the Potomac, docking southwest of the White House. Marshall and Lord Halifax, the British ambassador, met the new arrivals and escorted Churchill's delegation to the British embassy for dinner.[10]

BEFORE LEAVING FOR HYDE Park the next morning, Churchill met with Marshall at the embassy. As predicted, the prime minister expressed reservations about invading northwestern Europe and lobbied for a North Africa operation. Marshall telegrammed Roosevelt immediately to warn him. He also relayed the tenor of the discussion to Stimson. "Churchill was full of discouragement and new proposals for diversions," wrote Stimson. The Americans were going to have to stand firm.[11]

After the meeting, Churchill caught a plane to New York to meet Roosevelt. "The President was on the local airfield and saw us make the roughest bump landing I have experienced," wrote Churchill.[12] Roosevelt, accompanied by his son James, drove Churchill back to Hyde Park in a Ford V-8 convertible modified to allow him to operate it without using his polio-stricken legs.[13] As they drove through the green reaches of the Hudson Valley, the two leaders talked politics while negotiating hairpin turns and careening down narrow roads. Roosevelt got a charge from attempting to lose his Secret Service detail. "He invited me to feel his biceps, saying that a prize-fighter had envied them," wrote Churchill. "This was reassuring; but

I confess that when on several occasions the car poised and backed up on the grass verges of the precipices over the Hudson I hoped the mechanical devices and brakes would show no defects."[14]

Over the next two days, Roosevelt and Churchill talked strategy, taking refuge from the summer heat behind the shades in the president's library. Churchill brought with him a memo outlining the strategic issues they needed to discuss. Britain did not favor a cross-channel operation unless a permanent bridgehead could be established on the Continent. "We hold strongly to the view that there should be no substantial landing in France this year unless we are going to stay." Furthermore, "no responsible British military authority has so far been able to make a plan for September 1942 which had any chance of success unless the Germans become utterly demoralised, of which there is no likelihood."

Arguing that the Allies couldn't afford to "stand idle" during 1942, Churchill pushed for an invasion of North Africa. Britain had flirted with the idea of a North Africa operation in early 1942 but discarded it in the face of Germany's growing control over the Atlantic. Churchill believed that such an operation—bolstered by the military and naval might of the Americans— could force Germany to divert troops from the eastern front. It would also accomplish two major strategic goals: the opening of a second front, which would help take the pressure off the Soviets, and the creation of a new staging area from which to seize control of the Mediterranean and eventually western Europe.[15]

At some point during their Hyde Park sojourn, Roosevelt and Churchill also discussed how the United States and Britain might share research on making an atomic bomb. They agreed to trade information but put no formal agreement in writing.[16]

WHILE CHURCHILL AND ROOSEVELT conspired at Hyde Park, Marshall and Brooke met with the Combined Chiefs of Staff, the body formed by the Americans and British to plan and coordinate the war, to discuss Allied strategy. As usual, the generals and admirals met on neutral territory: an imposing classical revival building at 19th and Constitution Streets NW, which prior to the war had hosted the Public Health Service. Also on hand were Brigadier General Walter Bedell Smith, secretary of the Combined Chiefs, and Major General Dwight D. Eisenhower, who had just been put in charge of the army's new Operations Division. The British comprised Brooke and Ismay along with Field Marshall John Dill, chief of the British Joint Staff Mission. Dill had been packed off to Washington owing to his acrimonious relationship with Churchill, but he got on famously with his American colleagues, particularly Marshall.

It didn't take long for consensus to emerge. The Combined Chiefs favored an invasion of Europe as the basis for future Allied strategy and set a target date of spring 1943 for a full-scale attack in northwestern France. An offensive should only be launched in 1942 if an "exceptionally favorable opportunity presented itself." Otherwise, there were just too many logistical and matériel challenges to overcome. They absolutely did not want to invade North Africa. Nor did they want to invade Norway, another of Churchill's favorite possibilities.[17]

As Marshall summed it up, "To defeat the Germans we must have overwhelming power, and North West Europe was the only front on which this overwhelming superiority was logistically possible. . . . From the military point of view, therefore, there seemed no other logical course than to drive through with the BOLERO Plan."[18]

Despite the unity of opinion, the military men knew they could be overruled. "We fully appreciated that we might be up against many difficulties when confronted with the plans that the PM and the President had been brewing up together at 'Hyde Park'!" wrote Brooke in his diary. "We fear the worst and are certain that North Africa or North Norway plans for 1942 will loom large in their proposals, whilst we are convinced that they are not possible!"[19]

ON THE NIGHT OF June 20, Roosevelt and Churchill traveled back to Washington by presidential train, pulling into Union Station at around 8:00 a.m. the next morning. "We were heavily escorted to the White House," wrote Churchill, "and I was again accorded the very large air conditioned room, in which I dwelt in comfort at about thirty degrees below the temperature of most of the rest of the building." The weather in Washington was, in Brooke's words, "stinking hot."[20]

The arrival of grim news quickly overshadowed the charm of returning to the White House. As Churchill, Brooke, and Ismay gathered around Roosevelt's desk, Marshall appeared with a pink sheet of paper. Roosevelt read it first, before handing it to Churchill. "Tobruk has surrendered, with twenty-five thousand men taken prisoners," read the telegram.[21]

Ismay called the surrender of the British garrison in Libya "a hideous and totally unexpected shock."[22] Seven months earlier, Britain had wrested Tobruk from the Italians; now Rommel had ousted the British. The fall of

Tobruk put the Germans one step closer to seizing Britain's naval base at Alexandria and gaining control of the Suez Canal. Control of the Suez would enable Germany to sever Britain's imperial lifeline.[23]

Churchill didn't want to believe the news. He asked Ismay to telephone London to confirm. "I did not attempt to hide from the President the shock I had received," wrote Churchill. "It was a bitter moment. Defeat is one thing; disgrace is another. Nothing could exceed the sympathy and chivalry of my two friends. There were no reproaches; not an unkind word was spoken."[24]

Another telegram soon arrived from Britain's Mediterranean command. Britain's position in the region had deteriorated such that an air attack on its naval base at Alexandria was possible. With the approach of a full moon—ideal for nighttime bombing raids—the British fleet was heading south of the Suez Canal until the moon waned.

Roosevelt wanted to know how the United States could help. Marshall offered to send the 1st American Armored Division to reinforce the British position in the Middle East, but the troops were only halfway through their training. Next came an offer of three hundred Sherman tanks and one hundred 105-mm howitzers, but that too was problematic. American factories went into overdrive after Pearl Harbor, refitting to churn out the tanks, guns, and munitions required by the war effort. Six months later, the tanks were only now starting to come off the assembly line and slated for use by US Army divisions, which either had no equipment or were using outdated weaponry.[25]

Marshall believed, however, that Britain's immediate need took precedence. "Anybody knowing what it entails withdrawing long-expected weapons from fighting troops just after they have received them will understand the depths of kindness that lay behind this gesture," wrote Brooke.[26]

With Tobruk weighing heavily on everyone's minds, they spent the rest of the day debating Allied strategy. By late evening, Churchill and Roosevelt had gained control of the discussion, insisting that planning for invasions in France and North Africa proceed on parallel tracks. "Provided that political conditions are favourable, the best alternative in 1942 is Operation GYMNAST," wrote Ismay in a summary of the discussions.[27] This meant that of the two possible invasions, North Africa would come first. Roosevelt and Churchill had trumped their service chiefs.

Over the next two days, the Combined Chiefs gathered with and without the president and the prime minister to discuss plans for reinforcing the Middle East, mounting naval operations in the Pacific, and maintaining the shipping lines in the Atlantic. Marshall walked out of a particularly tense late-night meeting after Roosevelt suggested sending American troops into the region between Alexandria and Tehran, declaring it "an overthrow of everything they had been planning for."[28]

Not quite ready to give up, Marshall circled back to the topic of a second front on the afternoon of June 23. Using the memo Churchill had presented to Roosevelt as a springboard, he delivered a blistering appraisal of a North African invasion, deeming it "a poor substitute . . . emasculating our main blow to which we should contribute our utmost resources." Even if the operation proved a success, it "may not result in withdrawing planes, tanks, or men from the Russian Front."

Instead, Marshall pushed for an "aggressive, continuous air offensive": "Such an offensive, followed by the cross-channel operation, would be the best means of taking some of the weight off Russia. As a minimum it would, in our opinion, bring on a major air battle over Western Europe. This air battle in itself would probably be the greatest single aid we could give to Russia."[29]

But Roosevelt and Churchill wouldn't budge. North Africa remained the priority.

ON THE EVENING OF June 23, the British delegation boarded an overnight train for South Carolina. Marshall had arranged for a military demonstration at Fort Jackson, which served as a training ground for 60,000 men. Before they departed, Elmer Davis, head of the Office of War Information, questioned whether Churchill should be seen inspecting American troops in the aftermath of Tobruk. Churchill dismissed Davis's concerns, noting that his opponents would be lucky to round up twenty members of Parliament to support a "no confidence" vote.[30]

The Brits found Washington muggy and uncomfortably warm, but it was nothing compared to the stifling heat and humidity that greeted them when the train arrived at Fort Jackson around 11:00 a.m. The "very hot day" reminded Churchill, who wore an ill-fitting lightweight suit, bow tie, and Panama hat, of his time in India. A military band performed "God Save the King" and "The Star-Spangled Banner," while a battery of motorized field pieces offered a series of booming salutes.

Safe from the sun under an awning, Churchill, Stimson, and the others watched as armored and infantry divisions paraded past. Next came an airborne exercise, with six hundred paratroopers practicing an attack on an enemy position. Churchill was given a walkie-talkie, which he had never used before. While gleefully chomping on his cigar, he avidly followed the operation's progress as the white silk parachutes delivered the soldiers to the ground and the men closed in on their target. The exercise yielded three casualties: one broken leg, one sprain, and a suspected skull fracture. After lunch, field exercises with live ammunition showcased the readiness of infantry, tank, and artillery battalions. Churchill couldn't resist getting into the act: he worked the breech on a 75-mm gun and poked into the packs carried by the soldiers. After the five-and-a-half-hour demonstration, the prime minister, soaked with sweat and caked with a layer of dust, wished he could see more.[31]

"At the end I said to Ismay . . . 'What do you think of it?'" wrote Churchill in his memoirs. "He replied, 'To put these troops against continental troops would be murder.' Whereupon I said, 'You're wrong. They are wonderful material and will learn very quickly.'" Churchill relayed a similar message to Stimson. "I have had considerable experience with such inspection and I can say that I have never been more impressed than I was with the bearing of the men whom I saw," wrote Churchill. "The undemonstrative, therefore grim, determination which was everywhere manifest not only in the seasoned troops but in the newly-drafted bodes ill for our enemies." Churchill, however, did remind his American hosts that it took two years to turn a green recruit into a soldier.[32]

The last day of the conference, June 25, was devoted to finalizing American aid to the British military effort in the Middle East. Since Marshall had made his initial offer of matériel, there had been ongoing discussions about whether sending American troops might be better. Churchill and Roosevelt leaned toward sending troops—it played better politically—while their service chiefs believed tanks and guns would be more useful. In the end, Brooke and Ismay convinced Churchill that the "military aspect of this problem and its advantages outweighed the political considerations."[33]

After the British delegation said their good-byes, they headed north to Baltimore, where the Clipper awaited them for the return trip home. When they arrived at the dock, they found Roosevelt's lead Secret Service agent riled up. Minutes before, his men had arrested an Irish American employee of British Overseas Airway Corporation after someone reported hearing him murmuring Churchill's name over and over. The man carried a fully loaded revolver in his pocket.[34]

A FEW DAYS AFTER the conference, Brooke wrote Marshall, "I have returned with deep gratitude for all your kindness and the conviction that our discussions have gone a long way towards ensuring that close co-operation and understanding so essential between us in the execution of the task we are engaged in." Marshall repaid the compliment: "If nothing else was accomplished during the visit of the Prime Minister I feel that the intimate accord and I believe understanding developed between us justified the trip."[35]

For Brooke, the trip was certainly worth it. "I feel now in much closer touch with Marshall and his staff and know what he is working for and what his difficulties are." He also believed that while disheartening, the surrender of Tobruk had a silver lining. "I always feel that the Tobruk episode in the President's study did a great deal towards laying the foundations of friendship and understanding built up during the war between the President and Marshall on the one hand and Churchill and myself on the other."[36]

On June 27, Roosevelt and Churchill issued a joint statement about the conference. "While exact plans, for obvious reasons, cannot be disclosed, it can be said that the coming operations which were discussed in detail at our Washington conferences, between ourselves and our respective military advisers, will divert German strength from the attack on Russia."[37] The following day, Marshall sent Churchill a telegram informing him that three hundred tanks and one hundred howitzers would be ready to send to the Middle East in two weeks.[38]

Churchill predicted there would be "a beautiful row" about Tobruk when he returned to London.[39] It came in the form of a "no confidence" vote in Parliament. The motion to remove him was greeted with insolent laughter from the assembled members of the House of Commons—and soundly defeated 475–25. After learning the news, Roosevelt wired Churchill, "Good for you."[40]

25

Of Locusts and Missed Ships

DURING THE SUMMER OF 1942, CASABLANCA WAS UNDER ASSAULT AS locusts descended on the city in biblical proportions. "They settled in your hair, they crunched under your feet, the grass in the park was brown with swarms of young locusts, and the branches of the trees were black, with no leaves left," wrote Esti Freud of her encounters with them.

The locusts, the brown-black speckled cousin of the grasshopper, had swarmed from their breeding ground in central Africa on the banks of Lake Chad, northeast across the Sahara, to arrive in Casablanca. The British usually covered the sand where the locusts laid their eggs with crude oil to prevent them from hatching, but the war temporarily halted such measures. Now the insects attempted to devour every inch of green in the city, stripping it bare. The palm trees lining the boulevards became tall poles, their vivid green crowns eaten away. Elaborate gardens given over to vegetable patches to supplement rationing were reduced to nubs. The locusts even ate the moss on sea walls around the port.[1]

BY THE TIME THE locusts descended, Esti and her daughter, Sophie, had been in Casablanca for almost six months. Like other refugees ensnared in the cruel trap of expiring visas and late ships, they found themselves stranded in a city a world away from their bourgeois life in Vienna. Esti had met Martin Freud, the son of famed psychoanalyst Sigmund Freud, in the opening days of World War I. While Martin served as an artillery officer in the Austrian army, they courted by letter and postcard, despite reservations about the match among both their families. Esti's well-to-do Viennese parents

165

worried that the Freuds were too middle-class, while the Freuds fretted that Esti was too pretty. When peace settled on Europe, the couple tied the knot and had two children: Walter and Sophie.

The arrival of the Nazis in Austria turned the Freuds' world upside down. Since coming to power in 1933, the Nazis had made a practice of burning Sigmund Freud's books in public, both for his theories, which were considered sexually deviant and subversive, and his Jewish heritage. "What progress we are making," observed Freud. "In the Middle Ages they would have burned me. Now, they are content with burning my books." In failing health and reluctant to leave his beloved Vienna, Freud had resisted pleas from family and friends to leave Austria, believing he and his loved ones were safe as long as the Nazi madness remained confined to Germany.

After the Nazis seized power in Austria, their gaze soon fell on the Freuds. The Gestapo conducted multiple searches of Martin's house, along with Sigmund's home and office. After the Gestapo detained and interrogated Freud's daughter Anna, he realized his family needed to leave. Well-connected friends managed to secure seventeen exit visas, which necessitated hard choices given the size of the extended Freud family. Four of the visas went to Martin, Esti, Sophie, and Walter. They were the lucky ones. Freud's four sisters stayed behind and fell victim to the Holocaust: three died in the ovens of Treblinka, while the fourth died of starvation in Theresienstadt.[2] When Sophie later criticized her grandfather's theories, her brother told her, "Without Grandfather, the Nazis would have made lampshades of your skin."[3]

Rather than emigrating together, Esti and fourteen-year-old Sophie headed for Paris, while Martin and seventeen-year-old Walter went to London. After arriving in Paris in April 1938, Esti and Sophie carved out a life for themselves, aided by the presence of Esti's sister. Esti longed for an invitation to reunite with the rest of the Freud clan in London, while also turning her eyes toward the United States, where other relatives had begun to gather. When the German army closed in on Paris in June 1940, Sophie and Esti joined the exodus south, each shouldering a single knapsack as they rode their bikes, weaving in and out of the cars and trucks that jammed the roads. They eventually made their way to Nice, which became their home for the next eighteen months. Esti worked at the local hospital, while Sophie struggled to master French and prepare for her baccalaureate degree at the Lycée Jean de la Fontaine.[4]

AFTER MONTHS OF LETTERS to family members pleading for help, the Freuds obtained visas to the United States only days before Pearl Harbor.[5]

In January 1942, they took the train to Marseille, where they joined a group of refugees bound for the United States. The group was organized by the American Jewish Joint Distribution Committee, which handled the daunting travel arrangements and liaised with local officials. Since American entry into the war had closed Spanish ports, the refugee group sailed to Casablanca, where they would catch a ship for New York.

Upon arriving in Casablanca, the Freuds and the other refugees became virtual prisoners of the Protectorate. They were escorted under guard from the ship to the customs house and then onto a bus that delivered them to the Aïn Chok refugee camp outside the city. "The first ride through Casa was very impressive," wrote Sophie in her diary. "I opened up mouth and eyes. Palm trees, veiled women, ragged men with hostile looks were passing by. White houses, cheerful, colorful nature."[6]

The accommodations at the refugee camp, which would serve as home until their ship arrived, were spartan and communal. Mattresses for sleeping were spread on the floor of a large hall. With no netting for protection, the buzzing and stinging of mosquitos made sleep difficult, as did crying children and whispered arguments. The first night, the Freuds slept in their clothes for want of some place private to change and used their coats for blankets. The overhead lights in the hall remained on so that people could find their way to the bathroom at 2:00 a.m.

On their second day in French Morocco, the Freuds received permission to venture into Casablanca. Sophie, who had feared they would be stuck in the camp and never have a chance to explore the city, rode into town on top of the bus so she could soak up the sights. "Casablanca itself is not very unusual. Big, white, bare houses and many broad streets," wrote Sophie. "When the sun hides, everything looks dusty and wretched, but the sun embellishes everything. Everywhere one sells salted almonds. The most beautiful Arab stores are on the Boulevard de Zouaves. There they have magnificent rugs, blankets, slippers, pocketbooks, plates, big cups, and if one could spend three or four thousand francs, one could buy wonderful things."[7]

While dazzled by the old medina and the delights it offered, Sophie found the poverty of the Arab and Jewish quarters disquieting after her sheltered life. "People are covered with a few rags, they lie about somewhere on the street, they seem to have no notion of cleanliness. Perhaps they feel comfortable in their misery. Quite diverse folks walk about—the women are usually covered up to their eyes with a white sheet. Those who are not covered are native Jewish women. One can recognize the Jews by the black caps that they wear but also by their intelligent and more finely chiseled faces. There are many Jews, they are as dirty as the others but they often wear black clothes. Many are blind."

Even as the Freuds explored the city, a cloud of anxiety hung over them. The ship they were to take to the United States, the SS *Serpa Pinto*, had yet to arrive, and their American visas were set to expire in forty-eight hours. The American consul agreed that as long as the Freuds were on the ship by the stroke of midnight on January 24, the day their visas expired, they would not be turned away when they arrived at the port of New York. The *Serpa Pinto* arrived on January 25, twenty-four hours too late. They would have to start the application process all over again.

When Sophie learned of their fate, she cried for a day.

THE FREUDS WERE NOW stranded in French Morocco—without permission to be there. While Esti navigated the Protectorate's bureaucracy, registering their presence and obtaining the required identity cards, Sophie fell ill, waking up one morning with her eyes "glued together with stuff." Esti worried that she had contacted trachoma, a bacterial eye infection rampant in Casablanca that can cause blindness. Sophie's illness turned out to be a mild case of conjunctivitis, and within a few days her eyes had cleared and her fever abated.[8]

Realizing that their position was a little precarious, Esti let it be known that Sigmund Freud's granddaughter was stranded in Casablanca. The family name had helped them in Paris and Nice, so perhaps it could do so again. She also began to appreciate how different life would be in French Morocco as opposed to Austria and France. "There we were, two young women without male protection in a Mohammedan country, a country where women wore veils and were covered from head to toe by a kind of caftan and never seen on the street without the company of husbands or relatives," wrote Esti. "I understood that the most awkward thing one could do was to sit in a coffee house on the main square."[9]

Through Hélène Bénatar, they met the Coriats, a prominent Sephardic Jewish family, who adopted them for the duration of their stay. The Coriats had two daughters, Donna and Flor, who were close in age to eighteen-year-old Sophie. Donna, the oldest, had recently married and moved out of the house, so the Coriats suggested Sophie claim her old bed in the girls' common room. Esti found a flat nearby and had a standing invitation to join the family for lunch. They also secured a spot in one of the Alliance israélite universelle schools for Sophie, which allowed her to continue her studies.[10]

Despite the war, Sophie's time in Casablanca was almost idyllic. Through Flor, she became part of a close-knit group of Jewish friends, which allowed her to enjoy being a young woman of eighteen. There were picnics at the beach and horseback-riding lessons on a friend's farm. She also fell for Roger, a thirty-three-year-old French naval officer and the only non-Jew in her social circle. "He is very tall, over 6 feet, and has magnificent black hair with a natural wave," she wrote in her diary. "He has a beautiful small mouth, a Greek nose and eyes that tilt downwards, like mine. He is a mixture of Gary Cooper and Robert Taylor and every time Mother sees him she is stricken with his beauty and thinks he should absolutely become a film actor. He has a faultless body and attracts me like an irresistible magnet." The chemistry between the lovebirds didn't go unnoticed by the Coriats and her mother, who diligently chaperoned them. The romance ended when Roger's cruiser departed Casablanca in the summer of 1942.[11]

Esti used her training as a speech therapist to organize a school for deaf children, the first of its kind in Casablanca. She devoted her mornings to working with twelve deaf and hard-of-hearing children. In the afternoon, she rode her bike to appointments with paying clients, most of whom were among Casablanca's wealthier Jews. While conducting research at the Library of Casablanca, she met Monsieur Dupree, the recently widowed head librarian, and developed a relationship with him. Dupree even proposed marriage, which Esti declined. She was reluctant to remain in Casablanca, let alone to initiate the sure-to-be acrimonious divorce proceedings with Martin.[12]

THE FREUDS' SOJOURN IN Casablanca was extraordinary in many ways. By the time they arrived, Vichy's anti-Semitic laws regulated what professions Jews could practice, where they could live, and how they could use their severely restricted ration coupons. Casablanca's Jews were also banned from living in the city's European neighborhoods. Instead, they were all supposed to live in the *mellah*, the ancient Jewish quarter rife with poverty.[13]

Despite the Protectorate's anti-Semitic policies, the Freuds' diaries and memoirs don't speak of going without food or being harassed by the authorities. Esti believed that she and Sophie were spared the "unpleasant surprises" that befell other refugees because of her work with deaf children. She heard through the grapevine that the official who oversaw Casablanca's refugee population had taken note of her activities and approved. Her relationship with Monsieur Dupree, a prominent and well-regarded Frenchman, also added another layer of protection. Perhaps the largest factor was their adoption by the Coriats, who were part of the wealthy Sephardic Jewish community. The Coriat family clearly hadn't made the move to the *mellah* — and neither had their friends, who retained their villas on the edge of Casablanca, along with weekend retreats outside the city. If their last name hadn't been Freud, Esti and Sophie very easily could have spent 1942 behind barbed wire in a camp guarded by the French Foreign Legion.

By October 1942, Esti had obtained new American visas, aided by her family members in the United States. Now she just needed transit visas for Portugal, the only place where passage across the Atlantic could still be obtained. While on yet another visit to the Portuguese consulate, Esti met a man in the foyer who was waiting to see the consul. She told him her story. He clearly had some sway, because the visas she and Sophie needed were granted immediately. Esti left the consulate, booked a night train to Tangier, where they could catch a plane to Lisbon, and ran home to find Sophie and pack their things.

The Freuds' life in Casablanca ended just as suddenly as it had begun. At the train station, a group of friends gathered to see them off, while Monsieur Dupree cried on the platform. "My heart broke for Dupree because he seemed so miserable," wrote Sophie.[14] In Tangier, they boarded a twelve-seat airplane for the trip to Lisbon. Sophie found her first plane ride exhilarating, until the landing, when the airplane jumped, hopped, and spun around. She narrowly avoided throwing up on the tarmac. After a short stay in Portugal, the Freuds sailed for the United States on October 23, 1942. "Who would have thought it, we are sailing to America!!," wrote Sophie. "Just now I am sitting somewhere high up on the ship. It seems impossible, fantastic and I could never have imagined this moment."[15]

26

Resistance in Jeopardy

WHILE IN WASHINGTON, BILL EDDY PAINTED A PICTURE OF A robust resistance network in Morocco and North Africa. It was true that things had rapidly grown in the six months since he'd arrived North Africa. He'd set up radio sets in Algiers, Tunis, and Marrakech, as well as in Casablanca and Tangier. Members of the resistance cells were also doing low-level sabotage jobs, such as slipping iodine into the tanks of German trucks to wreck the engines or blowing small chunks of railroad lines. Carleton Coon, a Harvard professor who worked with Eddy in Tangier, developed a sticky bomb that looked like the mule dung so often found on the city streets. It was perfect for blowing out tires.[1]

Plans were also developed to help an invading force seize specific targets along the coast. For example, "Cheesecake," who ran a resistance cell in Port Lyautey, home to an army base and air strip, recognized that he did not have enough men to take on the two regiments of *tirailleurs*, two hundred members of the French Foreign Legion, and some six hundred sailors. Instead, in advance of an American invasion, he would use his team to cut communication lines, destroy ammunition dumps, blow up bridges, and set flares to indicate the position of antiaircraft batteries and coastal defenses.[2]

The civilian resistance cells also continued to draw members from a wide swath of French Moroccan society and politics. There were government bureaucrats, shopkeepers, cooks, restaurant managers, train conductors, traffic commissioners, teachers, port workers, tradesmen, and housekeepers. They might be for or against Charles de Gaulle—the towering general inspired strong emotions—but they were always anti-Vichy and pro-France. Communists, royalists, and fascists, factions that would never have united under the Third Republic, coexisted in the same resistance cells. But enmity toward the British still ran deep because of Mers-el-Kébir; so too did a desire to preserve the colonial order. "If the British come, I will pick up a rifle and shoot until I am killed. If the Americans come, I will welcome them with open arms," said a member of the resistance and the fascist Parti populaire français. "I am a colonist, and I am not a fool. The natives have had enough of privations and want. If we were to fight against the Americans, they would stab us in the back, because they know the only material aid they have had recently came from America."[3]

As the summer turned blazing hot, it became difficult to keep the resistance cells in Casablanca fired up about taking action. Dave King and his number two, Michel Despax, couldn't promise the Americans would be arriving soon. They couldn't promise they would receive guns, hand grenades, or any weaponry. To keep the cells active and focused, they put the members through trial runs. With gasoline in short supply, the resistance did much of its work on bicycles. If tasked with destroying a bridge, the cell bicycled to it during the day and at night, carrying weights equivalent to the explosives they would use and timing how long the journey took. New routes were tested as needed.[4]

With Despax doing much of the recruiting and message delivery, it was natural for the cell leaders to develop doubts about whether he worked with the Americans. King, like all the vice consuls, was a known quantity to French and German intelligence, while Despax continued to cultivate his profiteering persona. To calm their fears, Despax and King arranged for a "review of troops" on the sidewalk in front of the American consulate annex, where King had his office. "The chiefs of our resistance groups and a few men of each group rode by on bicycles, and it gave great encouragement to see them passing by and looking us over, with expressions on their faces which clearly indicated their confidence and determination," recalled Despax.[5]

Resistance activity, with its messages, meetings, and missions, also carried the risk of discovery no matter how careful members were. The French and German intelligence services prowled Casablanca for signs of dissent. So too did members of the Légion des combattants, along with the Service d'order legionnaire, its paramilitary offshoot. At the end of June 1942, French authorities arrested three hundred people suspected of ties to the resistance.

Despite that major setback, King forged on with cultivating his resistance network. In July, he assumed control of a resistance group working to sabotage rubber shipments between Casablanca and France. Its members had avoided being rolled up in the mass arrests at the end of June. When the head of the group, a Moroccan Jew, lost his nerve and resigned, King replaced him with "Mengin," with whom he had served at Verdun. Despite the new leadership, the group fell apart, making anything other than small-scale sabotage impossible. King urged the remaining members focus on small acts, like throwing rubber out of railroad cars as trains made their way to Algiers. They also managed to set fire to a few wagons full of rubber.

The group operated out of the Fortin Moullot stationary store, located at 12 Boulevard de la Liberté, in Casablanca's *ville nouvelle*. After someone tipped off the Gestapo, the police raided the store and discovered that along with stocking the finest paper from Paris, the store also kept on its back shelves pro-Allied propaganda literature and two incendiary bombs. "Life became very agitated," said King of the raid's aftermath. One man was persuaded to take the fall for the bombs, in exchange for a promise to break him out of jail later, which allowed the others to deny any knowledge of resistance activities. Then the group's former leader was arrested and talked— and talked and talked—telling his interrogators that not only did the French general staff in Casablanca approve of his activities but King also served as their ring leader. Colonel Maurice Herviot, head of the Sûreté, arranged for removal of King's name from all police reports, but it was, as King said in his understated way, "an awkward few days." Worried about Mengin's safety, King secreted him away in a clinic, where he was checked in as a patient under observation until arrangements could be made to smuggle him out of the country.

Meanwhile, King also needed to extract André Pelabon (code name "Penguin") from Casablanca after Vichy began to suspect him of passing information about French Morocco's aviation capabilities to the Americans. Pelabon, one of King's best sources, received orders to report to Vichy, and his likelihood of avoiding a jail cell or worse was slim. With Herviot's help, King arranged for a ship docked in Casablanca's port to escape German inspection before it departed. To provide cover for their handiwork, King started a rumor that the Service d'order legionnaire had kidnapped Pelabon.[6]

EVEN AS THE SUMMER doled out setbacks, it also presented an intriguing new possibility for the resistance effort in North Africa. Since the departure of Maxime Weygand, the broader movement had lacked focus and leadership, but a new candidate emerged who could provide both gravitas and prestige.

General Henri Giraud, currently in hiding in Vichy, had made it known that he would be interested in taking command of French forces in North Africa or France. Giraud authorized General Charles Mast, chief of staff of the 19th Army Corps in Algiers, to approach Robert Murphy.[7]

The sixty-three-year-old Giraud was a bona fide war hero with combat experience in North Africa. After graduating from Saint-Cyr in 1900, he commanded units of the Zouaves, the legendary indigenous light infantry, in Tunisia. Upon completing a seven-year tour in North Africa, he earned a spot at l'École de guerre, where he failed to impress then colonel Henri-Philippe Pétain, who judged him lazy, lacking in spirit, and in possession of "a confidence that does not seem justified." Giraud would prove Pétain wrong. During the first weeks of World War I, he led the 4th Regiment of Zouaves in a bayonet charge against the Germans at the Battle of Guise. After the retreating French army left him for dead on the field, German medics found him and sent him to a German-run hospital. He escaped his captors at the end of September with the help of Edith Cavell, a British nurse who helped almost two hundred Allied soldiers reach the neutral Netherlands during the war. Once his wounds healed, Giraud returned to the battlefield, earning victories and commendations.[8]

When the Germans invaded France in May 1940, Giraud commanded the 7th Army, which attempted to stop their advance through the Netherlands. On May 19, he was captured by the Wehrmacht and sent to Königstein, the hulking fortress perched on a cliff above the Elbe river in Saxony. The Nazis turned the fortress into a jail (Oflag IV-B) for high-ranking prisoners of war. After two years of meticulous planning and help from Mast, who also served time in Königstein, Giraud escaped in April 1942. Using a rope made of bed sheets reinforced with twine and copper wire, Giraud clambered down the castle wall and the formidable cliffs below. A rendezvous with French intelligence outfitted him with false papers, clothes, and money. Masquerading as an industrialist—and shorn of his telltale moustache—Giraud spent days riding trains, waiting for the furor caused by his escape to die down. With the German border guards challenging any man who resembled him in height or age, he decided to cross into Switzerland on foot, traversing a mountain trail in the dark. With more subterfuge, he slipped into Vichy, where he lobbied Pétain to join the Allies. Pétain rejected Giraud's plea, but the old man still possessed a backbone: he refused to hand Giraud over to the Nazis. In retaliation, Germany issued an order for Giraud's assassination and arrested seventeen members of his family to use as hostages.[9] Angered by Giraud's escape, Hitler also vented his anger against French POWs, stopping repatriations for sick prisoners, ending camp inspections, and terminating negotiations for release.[10]

Giraud seemed the perfect leader to galvanize the French resistance in North Africa. Not only did his escape turn him into a national hero, but he also hadn't sworn allegiance to Pétain. His dramatic getaway also captured the imagination of Winston Churchill, who believed as early as April 1942 that he might play a key role in an invasion of North Africa.[11]

"According to Mast, General Giraud is heart and soul for the resumption of hostilities against the Axis," reported Murphy to the State Department. Mast also believed that the Americans, should they choose to come to North Africa, could count on the cooperation of at least fourteen divisions, comprising a mixture of French and native troops led by French officers. That was a far cry from the ragtag resistance groups King and the other vice consuls were cultivating. Mast also made it clear that Charles Noguès was not their man in Morocco. Instead, General Antoine Béthouart, whom Murphy and King hoped to engage even after the debacle in January, had been designated as Giraud's representative.

Mast was not ready to make any commitments on behalf of Giraud but suggested that staff talks between Giraud's men and the Americans might occur in the fall. "He stated the opinion which he said is shared by General Giraud and other important French officers, that German defeat is certain, and that the only hope France has to emerge from her humiliating position is the resumption of hostilities at a time when she can expect from the United States adequate and timely military aid," wrote Murphy.[12]

The French military didn't trust de Gaulle, owing to the disaster at Dakar and his seemingly cozy relations with the British. Giraud, however, appeared to be precisely the kind of man to rally the French military and public behind him.

ON JULY 4, 1942, almost one year after Staff Reid and Quincy Stanton made their trek to the Missour internment camp, Ted Harris walked out into the desert, bound for Spanish Morocco. He had planned his escape meticulously, gradually assembling and hiding what he would need to survive the arduous desert trek: a pair of sturdy boots, an Arab shirt, bandages, medicine to battle dysentery, food, and iodine supplements. As he plotted, he mercilessly mocked the other men who attempted to escape and spread the rumor that the British Foreign Office was attempting to obtain his release on health grounds. He exercised in secret to build stamina, while feigning lethargy and illness around his fellow internees. In the year since the visit from the Americans, conditions at the camp had deteriorated. The magnanimous overseer was replaced by a man who enjoyed enforcing arbitrary rules, reading their mail, and stealing what little rations the men in the camp received.[13]

On the morning of July 4, Harris went for a swim in the Moulaya river along with the rest of men in the camp. A lumbering Alsatian belonging to one of the camp's officers romped with them. In the murky water, the dog mistook Harris's head for an object to play with and took a bite out of his scalp. The superficial injury aided Harris's escape plan, as it allowed him to claim he had a headache and retreat from the normal chatter among the men. When darkness finally descended and the camp slept, Harris donned his jacket, hoisted the satchel containing his food on his shoulder, and slipped over the wall behind the latrines. Tucked inside his jacket was the journal he'd kept since his time in Casablanca's prison.

Harris walked for hours, pushing himself through the night into the morning hours without stopping. He wanted to put as much distance as possible between himself and Missour. By slipping away on Saturday night, he bought himself extra time. The post office was closed on Sunday, which meant the camp commander couldn't send a telegram about his disappearance until Monday morning. Despite his good progress, his diarrhea returned. The ailment had plagued him for months, but he was still alive. The same could not be said for his friend Frank, who had contracted typhus from lice and died a slow, painful death in February 1942.[14] Jean, the amiable proprietor of the hotel and café, passed soon after from a heart attack.[15]

For the next ten days, Harris walked through the night and hid during the day, careful to avoid people. He was prepared for the thirst and fatigue but not for the flies that picked at his body. "I have never known flies to sting so hard," he wrote. By Monday, July 6, he had walked 28 miles, a small triumph when more than 170 miles lay before him. "My legs feel like blocks of wood," he wrote. "[I] feel like a tiny insect progressing slowly on a huge map."[16] By the third day, his right knee started to fail. "These marches across the desert are not amusing. My feet are full of thorns which I can't get out. But it's safer not to follow roads or paths."[17] The lack of water—he'd long-ago consumed his supply—played havoc with his body and mind. He dreamed he was being chased by Arabs, but no one appeared on the horizon.

After days of fruitless searches through the lunar terrain, on Friday, July 10, he found water, drawn to a secluded *oeud* by the sound of frogs. "There I undressed completely and lay on my stomach in the shallow water."[18] He knew better than to drink a massive amount of water quickly, but his thirst overwhelmed him. Luckily, his body soaked up the water, then began to sweat it away.

By Sunday, July 11, he had made it to the outskirts of Guercif, and on Wednesday, July 14, he walked into Spanish Morocco. "It's done. I've crossed the frontier! All is well. I have walked for miles and miles, climbing all the time, down precipices and up again. Then I reached a plateau of chaotic rocks, obviously an old glacier. Like a flow of lava. It was the most sinister and lonely walk I have ever taken." Above him, in the black night sky saturated with stars, only the Great Bear witnessed his accomplishment.[19] Harris pushed forward, his sore-covered feet having long since become numb. The bark of a dog cut through the heavy silence. Next came the sound of a bubbling spring, where he took time to bathe.

Instead of hiding when dawn arrived, Harris continued walking, soaking in the startling colors of the desert and the cobalt sky. He followed the cuts in the terra cotta landscape to a group of huts and beyond that a valley. "A handsome old man with a white beard came toward me and took my hand. He was dressed in immaculate robes and had blue, limpid eyes like the torrents of Scotland. 'Welcome,' he said to me in Arabic."

With the help of a guide provided by the old man, Harris arrived later that afternoon in Ain-Zohra, Spanish Morocco. For lunch, he ate a steak with a side of fried potatoes, washing it down with white wine. By July 23, he had made it to Gibraltar, his passage arranged by the local British consul general. From there he sailed home to Britain, disembarking on August 1, almost three years to the day after he enlisted in the French Foreign Legion. "Now, when I walk at night in the silent streets of Cambridge, among the slumbering colleges, imposing as cathedrals, and when I see the Great Bear, I am seized by a desire to return to Africa."[20]

Harris, however, wasn't done with the war. Depending on which story you believe, he enlisted with the Royal Air Force or worked, hush hush, for the Special Operations Executive.[21]

27

A Nerve-Wracking State
of Uncertainty

BY THE END OF JULY 1942, PLANS FOR INVADING NORTH AFRICA HAD
begun to coalesce. The operation became known as TORCH, a moniker
bestowed by Winston Churchill, and would be planned and led by an American headquartered in London. The commander would also answer to the
Combined Chiefs of Staff. The soldier who got the job: Lieutenant General
Dwight D. Eisenhower. For a man who thought he would be asked to retire
at the rank of lieutenant colonel because the small size of America's interwar
army left little room for advancement, the war gave Eisenhower's military
career a second life.

Eisenhower also became a bit of a celebrity, earning regular mentions in
the newspaper—something he never thought would happen. When an old
friend suggested that perhaps she should stop calling him "Ike," his long-
standing nickname, he protested. "Why in the devil should you not call me
Ike?," he wrote. "I have never been called anything else, and as a farm boy, at
least in spirit, I get so weary of the amount of formality that is forced upon
me, that the sound of Ike is pleasing in my ears."[1]

The fifty-one-year-old Eisenhower already crinkled around the eyes
when he laughed, but his new job aged him, adding more lines to his face and
turning white what little hair he still possessed.

EISENHOWER MADE NORFOLK HOUSE, a red-brick neo-Georgian office
building on St. James Square, his base of operations, filling it with a mix

of American and British officers to create Allied Forces Headquarters (AFHQ).[2] There were no strategy papers or handbooks dealing with how to turn the armed forces of two countries into a coherent fighting force, let alone engage in unified planning. Unlike in World War I, the Americans and the British agreed to use a command structure that allowed British officers to issue orders to American soldiers and vice versa. That alone took some getting used to—so would thinking in terms of a grand strategy and not national pride. Eisenhower told the men who worked for him at AFHQ to check their nationalism at the door.

Army chief of staff George Marshall urged Eisenhower to "take the bull by the horns" when it came to setting up AFHQ and diving into the planning for TORCH. "To what extent you can bring about an organization under these circumstances I do not know, but do your best to crystallize matters and get away from committees," wrote Marshall.[3]

Before long Eisenhower and his new staff were up to their eyeballs in frustration. From the outset, the Americans and British struggled with the question of where to invade in North Africa. Targeting Casablanca would help them secure French Morocco. Landings at Oran and Algiers would secure two of Algeria's major cities, while coming ashore further east along Algeria's coast at Phillipeville and Bône would place the Allies closer to Erwin Rommel's Afrika Korps in Libya. The need to split the force between the Atlantic for a Moroccan landing and the Mediterranean for an Algerian landing further complicated the decision.

American planners also continued to have reservations about the wisdom of TORCH, and the mechanics and scope of action demanded by the operation added to their wariness. The Americans had never before attempted an amphibious operation of this magnitude. AFHQ planners wanted to deliver more than 100,000 American troops by ship to North Africa and to start fighting as soon as the men set foot on land. The operation required ships to carry the troops across the Atlantic, along with more ships to protect the convoys and patrol for submarines. A flotilla of landing craft was required to carry the men ashore. Airplanes were needed to conduct reconnaissance and provide air support. Eisenhower found it a challenge to determine the number of men, ships, and planes available. The objectives and available resources seemed to change almost daily, creating what he called "a nerve-racking state of uncertainty."[4]

The British and the Americans also wanted different start dates for TORCH. The British pushed for October 7, while admitting that it might be highly ambitious. The Americans believed TORCH couldn't happen before November 7. The US Navy needed ninety days to prepare the ships, get them into place, load men and supplies, and sail across the Atlantic. The Americans also wanted to give their troops time to rehearse an amphibious landing. It was one thing to lower a landing craft into the water, fill it with twenty men, and send it ashore. It was quite another to put hundreds of landing craft and tens of thousands of men in the water at the same time and coordinate their arrival on shore—which is what TORCH required. The US Army's 2d Armored Tank Division, along with elements of the 3rd and 9th Divisions, also needed time to familiarize themselves with the new M4 tank, which would not be ready until mid-September.[5]

The British preferred sacrificing rehearsal time in favor of speed. The Americans regarded their haste as madness. Landing unprepared, whispered the Americans privately, would be tantamount to the disastrous Union Army outing at Bull Run during the Civil War or Britain's ill-fated Norway campaign in 1940.[6]

AT THE END OF the first week of August, a four-engine Boeing Stratoliner delivered a group of senior US Army and Navy officers from Washington, DC, to London. The men passed the long flight sleeping and talking about hunting and fishing—anything but the war.[7] They marveled at the changing landscape below as the plane flew north over Newfoundland before swooping east toward Ireland and finally Britain. The flight capped off a whirlwind week for Major General George S. Patton Jr. Seven days earlier, he had been summoned from California to Washington, DC, where he learned he would command the Western Task Force, one of three armies that would come ashore during TORCH. He'd barely had time to set up a base of operations at the War Department on Independence Avenue before packing his bags for consultations with Eisenhower in London.[8]

Patton slept off his jetlag at Claridge's, the grand, red-brick luxury hotel in Mayfair, where he received orders to billet. Before the war, the hotel provided a posh playground for London's bright young things; now, it bustled with military and government officials from the Allied nations and provided a temporary home to the exiled kings of Greece, Norway, and Yugoslavia and their families.[9] "London seems just half alive with very few people, even soldiers, about," wrote Patton in his diary after his first look around. "All the women are very homely and wear their clothes badly."[10]

Blunt opinions were the fifty-six-year-old Patton's stock and trade. A balding, still-trim soldier with a gaze that could go from dancing to deadly in an instant, Patton had forged a career out of bravado and tactical brilliance. He and Eisenhower had met as young soldiers in 1919 in Washington,

DC, and forged a friendship that endured through promotions and changes in duty stations. Eisenhower saw through Patton, past the showmanship, the legendary swearing, and the grand antics. "All the mannerisms and idiosyncrasies he developed were of his own deliberate adoption," wrote Eisenhower. "One of his poses, for example, was that of the most hard-boiled individual in the Army. Actually he was so softhearted, particularly where a personal friend was concerned, that it was possibly his greatest fault."[11]

WHEN GIVEN COMMAND OF the Western Task Force, Patton learned he would be charged with taking Casablanca and securing French Morocco. But as AFHQ planners worked through the problems facing them, Casablanca appeared and disappeared from the list of invasion objectives.

There were plenty of reasons for the Allies to seize Casablanca. With the largest port on the Atlantic in North Africa, it could become a logistical hub for the United States. Supplies delivered there from the United States could be routed north to France or elsewhere in the Mediterranean. A railroad line ran northeast from Casablanca, threading its way through the Atlas Mountains and into Algeria, where it pushed through to Oran and Algiers before heading into Tunisia. Delivering supplies to Casablanca would also allow American supply ships to avoid the Strait of Gibraltar, whose bottleneck provided a ripe hunting ground for German submarines. Along with Casablanca, AFHQ planners eyed French Morocco because of the airbase at Port Lyautey, which lay eighty-five miles north of Casablanca. It boasted the only concrete airstrip in all North Africa, providing American bombers and supply planes flying across the Atlantic with a reliable landing spot.[12]

AFHQ planners also believed an invasion of French Morocco would send a strong message to Spain—don't even think about invading—while preventing Vichy from attempting to rally the Berber tribes to attack Allied positions in Algeria. Whether Vichy could have convinced the Berbers to fight for them is debatable, but Allied planners certainly did not relish the idea. From their clashes with France and Spain during the 1910s and 1920s, the Berbers had earned a reputation as fierce opponents skilled in unconventional tactics.[13]

Yet an invasion of French Morocco also pitted the Allies against a serious danger: the Atlantic Ocean. In the autumn, the weather systems over the Atlantic churned up long swells that crashed into the Moroccan coast—swells capable of tossing and smashing a boat full of men to pieces. A good day, when the water calmed, came once every five or six days. Timing an operation for one of the good days was near impossible. The French considered the Atlantic approach so formidable during the autumn and winter months that it sent a portion of the troops assigned to guard the coast in the spring and summer to the interior, believing a seaborne invasion highly unlikely.[14]

As the planning progressed, Eisenhower favored focusing TORCH inside the Mediterranean and leaving Casablanca off the list. The risks of a Moroccan invasion were too high, too dependent on the whims of Mother Nature and the sea. The lack of aircraft carriers to support an assault on Casablanca also troubled him. Any attempt to use the airfield at Britain's base at Gibraltar would tip off the Axis spies who watched the departures and arrivals like hawks. Instead, Eisenhower recommended that an Allied assault on Casablanca come anywhere between three to ten days after an assault on Oran and Algiers.[15]

"We both feel that the operation is bad and is mostly political," wrote Patton after another skull session with Ike. "However, we are told to do it and intend to succeed or die in the attempt. If the worst we can see occurs, it is an impossible show, but, with a little luck, it can be done at a high price; and it might be a cinch."[16]

28

Ms. Baker Comes
to Casablanca

JOSEPHINE BAKER WAS BEGINNING TO WONDER IF HER HEALTH WASN'T a lost cause. She had languished for almost a year in a Casablanca clinic. Her once glamorous life of fabulous clothing, carefree parties, and flowing champagne, all in the service of the Free French, had given way to endless bed rest in a hospital gown.

The trigger for Baker's health crisis remains a bit murky, as she did everything possible to obscure its real origins. According to Baker's own account, she became fascinated with the ability of X-rays to see into the body after having one taken of her chest. While passing through Casablanca upon arriving back in Morocco after one of her trips abroad, she asked a doctor to take an X-ray of her uterus to see if a structural impediment was preventing her from conceiving the baby she so desperately wanted. As part of the procedure, the doctor injected her uterus with contrast fluid. The X-ray revealed nothing amiss internally, which was welcome news.

Baker continued on to Marrakech, happy to be reunited with Jacques Abtey, her lover and partner in espionage, and to return to the luxurious *riad* she called home. Built around an interior courtyard with a fountain open to the sky, the *riad* provided a decadent sanctuary amid the noise and dirt of the boisterous city. As the couple navigated the medina's winding passageways and caught each other up on their adventures, Baker experienced crippling stomach pains. For the next three days, her body burned with fever. Unable to find an ambulance, a worried Abtey borrowed a car, tucked Baker into the backseat, and drove to Casablanca, where he believed the medical care would be superior. Upon arriving, he asked a police officer for the name of the best clinic in the city. The officer referred him to Mers-Sultan.[1] According to the doctors, Baker had developed a raging infection from a dirty needle used to inject the contrast fluid. The infection turned into peritonitis, an inflammation of the membrane covering the inner abdomen, which morphed to septicemia, a bacterial infection of the blood that can lead to organ failure.[2]

There might have been another reason for her illness. According to a nurse who worked in the clinic, Baker delivered a stillborn baby. After the birth, Baker developed a severe infection, which required a hysterectomy. The peritonitis and septicemia that shattered her health followed.[3]

Whatever the cause, treating septicemia in the early 1940s was a difficult business. Sulfa was the only antibiotic then widely available. Penicillin wouldn't be produced in mass quantities outside a lab for another two years.[4] Most people who contracted the condition rarely survived. Somehow Baker clung to life, as the body that once moved with such grace and glee became a fragile shell. She struggled to lift her head. She struggled to speak. Her once glowing skin grew splotchy and waxlike. She found herself on the road to recovery, only to relapse and become even sicker. For every walk among the palm trees and olive groves at Parc Murdoch, which bordered the clinic, she spent weeks in bed. As she languished, Abtey regularly slept on a cot in her room, helping the nurses change her sheets and bathe her.[5]

BAKER'S DAYS OF FLITTING off to Spain and Portugal and returning with bits of intelligence pinned inside her bra or written on sheet music had come to an end. That didn't mean, however, that the duo's work with the Free French was over. While in Casablanca, Abtey made contact with Staff Reid. The day after Pearl Harbor, the two men walked the lush hilly streets of Anfa in the dead of night discussing the implications of American entry into the war and what it might mean for resistance efforts in French Morocco.[6]

Before Abtey could make plans, Christmas and another health scare for Baker intervened, prompting him to stay close to her side. When 1942 rolled around, Abtey found himself dealing with yet another vice consul: Sidney Bartlett, who previously worked for Shell Oil in Paris and served as an ambulance driver for the American Field Service during the 1940 German invasion, became his handler.[7] Abtey had found Reid a calm, reflective man of few words. Bartlett, on the other hand, was a boisterous California boy. "His appearance was rough, but he had an open face," wrote Abtey. "He

FIGURE 28.1. Josephine
Baker in 1931. *Spaarnestad
Photo / National Library of
the Netherlands*

had the lazy gait of a cowboy and spoke American, swallowing half the
words." They got on famously.[8]

Bartlett wanted to use Baker's sick room as a rendezvous point. The clinic's stellar reputation brought French businessmen, German control officers,
pashas, and the bourgeoisie of Morocco through its doors. Anyone could
feign a reason for visiting. Given that Baker was a famous American, a vice
consul's visit to inquire about her health would not raise eyebrows. Abtey
agreed and became an intermediary between the Americans and Colonel
Paul Paillole, who worked for the French resistance while simultaneously
running Vichy's counterintelligence agency.[9]

In July 1942, Abtey once again found himself in need of a new handler
after Bartlett was shipped back to the United States. The divorced Bartlett
had fallen hard for a sweet Frenchwoman he met in Casablanca: "Madame
Escarment." She claimed her father, a captain in the French army, had spent
time as a prisoner of war in Germany, and Bartlett wanted to marry her on
the spot. The other vice consuls begged him to reconsider—where he saw
an innocent girl in need of protection, they saw a conniving seductress. Before vows could be exchanged, madame's husband arrived from Dakar. An

investigation also revealed that she had close ties to members of the German Armistice Commission. Dave King, Bartlett's colleague, believed that a besotted Bartlett had unknowingly supplied the Germans with information. Faced with a possible Gestapo plant in their ranks, Robert Murphy quietly arranged to send Bartlett home.[10]

IN AUGUST 1942, MAURICE Chevalier passed through Casablanca. Unlike his old costar Baker, Chevalier had remained in Vichy, retreating to his villa near Cannes. Like many Frenchmen, he instinctively venerated and supported Henri-Philippe Pétain. "I ask myself: what would he say if he were in my shoes?" Chevalier told a newspaper in December 1940. "How would he behave if he were beneath my straw hat? That's why, for the coming year, I can only make the same wish that our Great Man among the Greats would make." Chevalier continued to perform for audiences in Vichy. His music filled the airwaves of Radio Paris, as new chansons promoting love and the need to rebuild France played along with old favorites.[11] In 1942, he charted a hit song, "The Symphony of the Wooden Soles," which lauded the clacking of women's shoes. Leather shortages in Vichy during 1941 led to women's shoes being made with wooden soles, a challenge to both the ear and French fashion sensibilities.[12]

In September 1941, Chevalier returned to the stage of his beloved Casino de Paris, performing his first show, *Toujours Paris*, in Nazi-occupied France.[13] It would be the first of many performances in Paris in front of audiences packed with Nazi uniforms. Chevalier also traveled to Germany at Vichy's behest to perform for 3,000 French prisoners of war interned at Stalag XI-A, the same camp he endured for twenty-seven months during World War I. While he refused to perform for the German public, the Nazis still won the propaganda battle, rebroadcasting his concert on French and German radio and publishing photos of his performance at the camp that omitted any mention of the circumstances.[14] Chevalier's cozy relations with Vichy and apparent support for Germany made him an enemy of the French resistance. His name, along with those of Jean-François Darlan, Pierre Laval, Maxime Weygand, and others, appeared in *LIFE* magazine as part of a "black list" of Frenchmen accused of collaborating with the Germans. "Some to be assassinated, others to be tried when France is free," read the ominous explanation.[15]

Upon hearing that Baker was in Casablanca, Chevalier wanted to call on his old friend. She refused him, both for health reasons and out of disdain for his choices. Baker considered Chevalier "a man without a soul and without heart."

Upon returning to Paris, an embittered Chevalier falsely reported to a newspaper that Baker was penniless and teetering on the brink of death in Casablanca. He claimed that during their visit, she had clung to him and begged him not to abandon her. "Don't leave me, Maurice," she told him. "I am so unhappy." The story quickly led to reports that Baker had syphilis, and, then over the next few months, that she had died.[16] Langston Hughes, who saw Baker perform in New York and Paris before the war, devoted one of his first columns for the *Chicago Defender* to her death. "The Aryans drove Josephine away from her beloved Paris," he wrote. "At her death, she was again just a little colored girl from St. Louis who didn't rate in Fascist Europe."[17]

A year later, a still very much alive Baker exacted revenge. "Maurice Chevalier is to the stage what Laval is to politics," she told a reporter. "Chevalier and I played together at the beginning of the war to whip up the Anglo-French spirit, but now he is helping Goebbels to keep up German morale."[18]

29

Ballade of the Second Front

O N AUGUST 12, 1942, A LONE AIRPLANE FLYING NORTH OVER THE
Caspian Sea made a course adjustment to head northwest toward Kuiby-
shev, in the Ukraine, in order to avoid flying over Stalingrad, where the Russians and the Germans fought to control the city. It wouldn't do to have the
prime minister of Great Britain shot down by a stray round or an ambitious
Luftwaffe pilot.[1] Winston Churchill had departed Tehran that morning bound
for Moscow and a meeting with Stalin to discuss British and American plans
for a second front in North Africa. With Franklin Roosevelt unable to make the
journey, W. Averell Harriman, the president's special envoy to Europe, came
along to hold up the American end of things. "I feel that things would be easier
if we all seemed to be together," Churchill wrote Roosevelt, requesting Harriman's presence. "I have a somewhat raw job."[2] He didn't relish delivering the
news but believed they owed it to Stalin to tell him in person rather than by an
impersonal telegram. "At least it showed that one cared for their fortunes and
understood what their struggle meant to the general war," wrote Churchill.[3]

They reached Moscow around 5:00 p.m., taking in the domes and spires
of the city as the plane circled above before landing. After an airport ceremony, a car whisked Churchill off to State Villa No. 7, which lay eight miles
outside Moscow. When he rolled down the window to breathe in some fresh
air as they traveled through suspiciously empty streets, he was startled to
discover that the glass was two inches thick. At the villa, the Soviets spared
no luxury for their guest: white-jacketed servants stood by to fulfill every
wish, and tables overflowed with decadent quantities of food and drink. A
spacious underground bunker offered shelter during air raids, while guards
patrolled the area around the villa, ready to challenge anyone who braved

the approach through the dense surrounding woods. Churchill branded his quarters "totalitarian lavishness."[4]

After a bath and some food, a refreshed Churchill returned to Moscow for a 7:00 p.m. meeting at the Kremlin. The complex of churches and palaces encased by an imposing red-brick wall had served as the seat of Russian power since the days of the tsars. When the Soviets came to power, they tried to strip away some of the grandeur, but the elegant bones of past regimes remained. To foil German pilots on bombing raids, the Kremlin's iconic red walls were painted with stripes and its buildings covered with camouflage netting. Even the golden domes of the Eastern Orthodox churches received a coat of paint to dampen their luster.[5]

After years of circling each other as enemies and then cautious allies, Churchill and Stalin finally met face-to-face. The first two hours of the conference devolved into a grim affair as Churchill explained that Britain and the United States would not be invading France in 1942. Stalin peppered Churchill with questions as he tried to understand his allies' thinking, with each answer less satisfactory than the last. Churchill equated telling Stalin that there would be no second front in 1942 with "carrying a large lump of ice to the North Pole."[6] Nevertheless, the icy tone thawed when Churchill turned to the subject of TORCH. Stalin became animated as he turned over in his mind the outlines of the operation and what it could achieve. When he asked about its timing, Churchill explained that it would happen no later than the end of October—possibly sooner—to which Stalin replied, "May God prosper this undertaking."[7]

Churchill explained that if the Allies could seize North Africa by the end of the year, they would be in a position to "threaten the belly of Hitler's Europe." In full salesman mode, Churchill drew a picture of a crocodile, the sly predator who demolishes its prey with a fearsome mouth of sharp teeth, while its scaly hard skin provides protection from its foes. The crocodile, noted Churchill, possesses a vulnerability: its underbelly, where the soft skin allows for easier penetration. Instead of attacking Germany's hard scaly armored skin, they would attack its exposed belly, starting in North Africa. If the British and Americans attempted to invade France, they risked defeat, but an operation in North Africa had a high chance of success—and with it the ability to force Hitler to divert resources from his fight against the Soviets.[8]

Stalin appeared to grasp the military advantages of the operation, particularly its ability to put the Allies within striking distance of Erwin Rommel from the west, but he questioned the political gains. Would the French people understand why the Allies were attacking French colonies in North Africa? What about Charles de Gaulle? "I said that if he were thought helpful he would be used, but at present we thought the American flag was a far better chance of easy entry," wrote Churchill in his report of the meeting. French sentiments towards de Gaulle remained complicated: the French were just as likely to fire on a Gaullist force as on the British. It was unlikely, however, that the French would fire on the Americans.[9]

While the first meeting between Stalin and Churchill finished on a cordial note, discussions the following day became acrimonious as the Soviets again pressed the issue of the second front. The British felt the Soviets had no understanding of the conditions in France, the challenge of conducting amphibious operations, or the available resources. The Soviets felt that their western friends did not understand the urgency of opening a second front to take pressure off their armies struggling against Nazi Germany on the eastern front. North Africa wasn't France.[10]

At one point, the discussions devolved into accusations that the British and Americans lacked the courage to fight the Germans, broke their promises, and only sent the Soviets second-rate equipment. Churchill did his best to rebut the claims without reverting to name-calling, but the allegations nevertheless stung.[11]

AFTER THE DISHEARTENING CONVERSATION, Churchill had little interest in attending the lavish banquet Stalin planned for his guests in one of the Kremlin's state dining rooms, but he dragged himself to dinner anyway. Stalin sat at the center of the table with Churchill on his right and Harriman on his left. The call for toasts started immediately, and the vodka flowed freely—a glass never sat empty for long.[12] After more than three hours, nineteen courses, and endless toasts, the banquet came to a close on the other side of midnight. Churchill and Stalin said their parting good-byes and shared a friendly handshake. As Churchill made to leave the cavernous room, Stalin found him again and personally walked the prime minister through the vast hallways and down the staircases until they reached the front door, where they again shook hands.

Aware that the acrimonious discussions had left Churchill in a foul mood, Stalin decided to practice his own version of personal diplomacy. On Churchill's last night in Moscow, he invited the prime minister for an informal discussion over drinks in his private quarters in the Kremlin. For six hours, the two leaders drank and talked, barreling into the wee hours of the morning. Stalin even introduced Churchill to his daughter, Svetlana, a comely sixteen-year-old redhead, who helped set the table for an impromptu dinner and gave her papa a shy kiss.[13]

Churchill departed the Kremlin at 3:00 a.m., confident that a sense of goodwill had prevailed. "I feel that I have established a personal relationship which will be helpful," he told Roosevelt. And despite the tension and name-calling, he believed that coming to Moscow to deliver personally the news about the second front and TORCH had been the right decision. "Now they know the worst, and having made their protest are entirely friendly," wrote Churchill. "Monsieur Stalin is entirely convinced of the great advantages of TORCH and I do trust that it is being driven forward with superhuman energy on both sides of the ocean."[14]

ON THE FLIGHT HOME from Moscow, Generals Alan Brooke and Archibald Wavell, who had accompanied Churchill to Moscow, camped out in a small cabin at the rear of a Liberator. Designed to deliver bombs, the plane lacked much in the way of comfort or seats, forcing the two generals to sprawl out on the floor. As Wavell madly scribbled notes in his corner, Brooke wondered if he should be working in a similar fashion. At last, Wavell threw a piece of paper across to him. On it, he'd scrawled the "'Ballade of the Second Front' by P. M. Loquitur," a four-part parody of their discussions in Moscow. The mischievous poem closed with

> Prince of Kremlin, here's a fond farewell;
> I've had to deal with many worse than you.
> You took it though you hated it like hell;
> No Second Front in 1942.[15]

Churchill returned from Moscow on August 24 to discover that planning for TORCH wasn't going as he had envisioned. A debate raged over whether to focus on the "inside" (the Mediterranean and Algeria) or the "outside" (Morocco and the Atlantic). Roosevelt, George Marshall, and the US Chiefs of Staff favored a landing in Morocco, which didn't fit with Churchill's Mediterranean strategy. The Americans also preferred a November start date rather than the October 14 date he had promised Stalin.

Unhappy with how things were unfolding, Churchill wrote Roosevelt on August 26 arguing for the need to settle on a date for the operation and make it conform to the deadline, rather than waiting for everything to be ready. Doing so, he asserted, would give Dwight Eisenhower the power he should have as Allied commander in chief. Churchill also wasn't sold on Casablanca. "If it came to choosing between Algiers and Casablanca it cannot be doubted that the former is incomparably the more hopeful and fruitful object," wrote the prime minister. Calling Casablanca "the one most remote from the vital objectives in the Mediterranean," he cited the weather and autumn swells as a reason to avoid Morocco. "Casablanca might easily become an isolated failure and let loose upon us for a small reward all the perils which have anyway to be faced in this great design," he wrote.[16]

The next day, what Churchill called "a bombshell" arrived from Washington. The US Chiefs of Staff wanted the operation to focus on Casablanca and Oran. The Americans believed Casablanca provided a valuable logistical link between the United States and North Africa. They were also thinking ahead, in terms of how to get men and supplies in position for a future assault on southern France and, if Churchill had his way, Sicily and Italy.[17] For Churchill, this new line of thinking challenged the very foundation of the Mediterranean strategy he had sold to Stalin.[18] The Americans didn't seem to understand that "powerful action" inside the Mediterranean was necessary for success.

Desperate for the Americans to buy into British strategy, Churchill launched a campaign to persuade Roosevelt to come around to his way of thinking, kicking off what Eisenhower dubbed the "transatlantic essay contest." For the next two weeks, the prime minister and the president traded a series of telegrams thrashing out the details of TORCH. At one point, a plane stood waiting to fly Churchill to Washington should he deem it necessary to talk to Roosevelt in person.[19] As the discussions dragged into the first days of September, a "deeply perturbed" Churchill considered having a letter hand-delivered to Harry Hopkins, the president's personal envoy, to enlist his assistance in getting the president to see things his way. He couldn't understand why the Americans were so insistent on Casablanca and so reluctant to attack inside the Mediterranean.[20]

On September 5, after eleven testy and argumentative telegrams, Roosevelt and Churchill settled their first spat over wartime strategy. "We agree to the military layout as you propose it," wrote Churchill. TORCH would have three objectives: Casablanca, Oran, and the newly added Algiers, which lay 250 miles east of Oran. The attacks would be made initially by American ground forces led by American commanders with support from British naval and air forces. Roosevelt and his advisors believed an assault led by the British or done in cooperation with the Gaullists would lead to "determined resistance." The Americans would also have charge of relations with French civilian and military authorities.[21]

Upon realizing they'd reached an agreement, Roosevelt cabled, "Hurrah!" Churchill replied with, "Okay full blast."

The Americans were coming for Casablanca.

30

Lieutenant Colonel MacGowan

ON SEPTEMBER 5, 1942, ROBERT MURPHY FOUND HIMSELF FLYING north along the Atlantic seaboard. Upon arriving in Washington, DC, a few days before, Murphy had learned that Franklin Roosevelt wanted to meet with him to discuss North Africa. He expected to make the short walk from the State Department, where he claimed a temporary office, to the White House, sweating under his suit with each step from the late-summer humidity. Instead, the walk became a flight in a small airplane bound for Hyde Park. The president had taken advantage of the Labor Day holiday to escape Washington for four days.[1]

Upon Murphy's arrival, Roosevelt invited him into the library, where they could talk without being interrupted. Harry Hopkins also joined the discussion. He too had escaped to Hyde Park for some relaxation. In a nod to their vacation frame of mind, both Roosevelt and Hopkins wore shirtsleeves and no ties. Over the course of the afternoon, Roosevelt dominated the conversation. He took pleasure in personally telling Murphy about TORCH, the outlines of which had been settled the day before, and the deliberations leading up to the decision. "The North African expedition appealed to his sense of adventure, especially as it involved a major naval operation," wrote Murphy.

Roosevelt understood the competing allegiances and political complications the Allies would create with the invasion. Without Henri-Philippe Pétain's approval of the operation—which would not be forthcoming—American troops could face resistance from the troops loyal to Vichy. Allied victory would come through overwhelming military force or by convincing Charles Noguès and the other colonial administrators to surrender. Defection was only possible if the French commanders distinguished between

193

allegiance to Pétain and fidelity to France—and chose France. Following an Allied victory in North Africa, Roosevelt did not want to endorse or recognize any particular person or group as the leader of France. He believed the French people should decide that question after the war. "You will restrict your dealings to French officials on the local level, prefects, and the military," Roosevelt told Murphy. "I will not help anyone impose a Government on the French people." Murphy would use this credo to guide his dealings before and after TORCH.[2]

Roosevelt sent Murphy back to Washington with orders not to tell anybody in the State Department about TORCH, because "that place is a sieve." Given that more leaks seemed to come from the White House than State, Murphy found the president's instructions amusing but also troubling.[3] When Murphy expressed reservations about the order—he didn't like having to conceal a major secret from his boss, Secretary of State Cordell Hull—Roosevelt brushed them aside. "Don't worry about Cordell. I will take care of him; I'll tell him our plans a day or so before the landings," said Roosevelt.

As HE MADE THE rounds in Washington over the next few weeks, Murphy found that North Africa had gone from an exotic place of postcards and adventure movies to the subject of intense study. At the State Department, War Department, and Bureau of Economic Warfare, he provided details about the French, the Spanish, the Berbers, the local French resistance cells, transportation lines, and whatever else might be on the list.

Murphy's meeting with Henry Stimson, secretary of war, was removed from the official calendar, and arrangements were made to conceal his arrival and departure. Having gotten wind of a project involving North Africa, a newspaper columnist published a piece speculating about an operation. Stimson didn't want to add to the gossip. At the meeting with Stimson, which also included Chief of Staff George Marshall, Murphy learned about the misgivings among America's military leadership for TORCH. Stimson and Marshall didn't conceal their disappointment in the prioritization of North Africa over a cross-channel operation. Marshall also discounted the idea that French assistance could help TORCH and worried about the "danger of confiding our plans to Frenchmen."[4]

BEFORE HE HEADED BACK to North Africa, Marshall decided that Murphy should visit Dwight Eisenhower in London. Given that Murphy had become a minor political celebrity, Marshall feared he might be recognized if he flew to London on a commercial flight, which would encourage reporters to dig around even more. His solution was for Murphy to become "Lieutenant Colonel MacGowan." "Nobody ever pays any attention to a Lieutenant Colonel," said Marshall.[5]

To further conceal Murphy's movements, Marshall arranged for him to travel to Britain on September 15 as part of the Ferry Command, which delivered airplanes to Britain from factories in North America. When the aerial convoy touched down at the airfield in Prestwick, Scotland, Murphy was startled to hear someone calling his name. "Why, Bob! What are you doing here?" The voice belonged to Donald Coster, who had worked for Murphy as a vice consul in North Africa up until a month before.[6] Before Coster knew what was happening, he was arrested and carted off under the orders of Colonel Julius Holmes, a member of Eisenhower's staff. By recognizing his old colleague, Coster had inadvertently drawn attention to Murphy's top-secret trip to England. "Fortunately, there were thousands of Bobs in the Army, some of them doubtless lieutenant colonels, so no harm was done," wrote Murphy. Just to be safe, Coster was kept under lock and key until after the invasion.[7]

FROM SCOTLAND, MURPHY TRAVELED to a military airfield on the outskirts of London and then by car to Telegraph Cottage. The Tudor-inspired house, nestled on a quiet road in Kingston-upon-Thames, served as Eisenhower's retreat from the grind and politics of Norfolk House. Taking advantage of the fine fall weather, Murphy and Eisenhower began their discussions under a towering pine tree in the yard. Other members of Ike's staff joined them as the day progressed.

"Murphy, I saw, was tall, slightly stoop-shouldered, and talked more like an American businessman canvassing the ins and outs of a prospective merger than either diplomat or a soldier," wrote Captain Harry C. Butcher, Eisenhower's personal aide. Murphy did his best to describe the people and places they knew from reports and telegrams. He also fielded questions about troop strength, defenses, training, and equipment. "Murphy impressed us all as an honest reporter who delivered his story objectively," wrote Butcher.[8] The military men may have been impressed, but Murphy became aware of his "own appalling ignorance of military matters," for which he apologized.[9]

At sunset, the air grew chilly, and they retreated inside to the living room and the warmth offered by the coal-burning fireplace. A dinner of soup fortified them, along with copious cigarettes. As the discussions continued late into the evening, a cloud of blue-grey smoke floated above them, unable to push past the blinds and window curtains pulled tight to heed blackout rules.[10]

From the outset, it was clear to Murphy that Eisenhower's staff had little knowledge of the region. "I was the only person at that London conference with prolonged experience in Africa itself, and from questions asked I could see that Eisenhower and some of his officers had mental pictures of primitive country, collections of mud huts set deep in jungles," wrote Murphy. He explained that North Africa didn't resemble the lush jungle of the Rudyard Kipling stories they read as boys; rather it looked like California, with its profitable farmland, soaring Sierra Nevada Mountains, desert expanses, and bustling coastal cities. Algiers and Casablanca also offered plenty of "creature comforts." Given the terrain, Eisenhower wanted to know if his men needed winter underwear. Murphy said yes, especially in the more elevated reaches of Algeria and Morocco. Thousands of American soldiers had Murphy to thank for their long johns during the coming winter.[11]

Like Marshall, Eisenhower harbored doubts about TORCH, considering it a risky operation with untested men and too many unknowns. Eisenhower had a list of questions for Murphy. How would the French react? What would Spain do when the Americans set foot in Morocco? Would it invade from the north? Murphy had no clear-cut answers for those questions—only ifs, thens, and maybes. If the French opposed them, the fight could be long and bloody. If they laid down their weapons, the Americans could be battling Erwin Rommel in Tunisia in no time. If Spain invaded, they could be stuck in Morocco helping the French defend their colony. Murphy predicted things would end up somewhere in between.[12]

Eisenhower also shared Marshall's opinion that the French resistance in North Africa would be of limited use. Having evaluated some of the resistance proposals from Dave King and Murphy earlier in the year, he was familiar with the cast of characters and their capabilities. Murphy still held out hope that members of the French military leadership in North Africa would step forward and bring with them a sizable number of army divisions and air force squadrons. General Antoine Béthouart, who headed the Casablanca division, might be induced to help them under the right circumstances. Murphy also had positive discussions with General Charles Mast, who commanded French divisions near Algiers. Even so, French army officers valued loyalty above all else. Joining the resistance and helping the Americans required renouncing their oath of fidelity to Pétain, which would make them traitors in the eyes of some of their comrades. They would not make such a decision lightly.

Believing surprise essential to the success of the operation, Eisenhower ordered Murphy to withhold information about TORCH until four days before the Allies were scheduled to land. Murphy argued that his French contacts were as interested in ousting Vichy and the Nazis from North Africa as the Allies, but Eisenhower stood firm. He would have four days—and four days only—to transmit information about the invasion and coordinate the activities of the local resistance cells across a 2,000-mile stretch of territory.[13]

31

Baggage Compartment

IN MID-SEPTEMBER 1942, BILL EDDY, HEAD OF THE OFFICE OF STRATEgic Services (OSS) in North Africa, asked Staff Reid, his diligent communications man in Casablanca, to make the six-hour journey north to Tangier. They had things to discuss that they could only talk about in person. Like Robert Murphy, Eddy had been to London and received a briefing on TORCH.

Instead of booking into a hotel, Reid bunked with Franklin Holcomb, Eddy's very earnest number two, in a villa located four miles outside Tangier. Gasoline rationing and sky-high prices forced many Tangierines to close up their villas and live full-time in apartments in the city. Holcomb had taken advantage of the cheap rent and owners looking for a good tenant to secure a house outside the city, allowing him to escape the grime and crush of Tangier. The American Legation in Tangier, which provided OSS with a home, bordered the medina and lay a few streets over from the Grand Socco, the open-air market teaming with snake charmers, vegetable sellers, storytellers, and carpet dealers. Adventurous buyers could also find drugs, gambling, and prostitution. At the far edge of the market, the red, white, and black Nazi flag hung from the Mendoubia, the palace that once housed the sultan's representative in Tangier and now provided a home for the German consulate. When Spain reclaimed Tangier, it welcomed Germany with open arms.[1]

At 3:30 a.m. on September 12, Reid bolted awake, ripped from sleep by the sound of heavy gunfire coming from Spanish batteries in town. Was Tangier under attack? He tried to turn on the lights only to find the current switched off. As he stood in the dark trying to figure out what to do next, the drumbeat of brass pots and tom-toms filled his room, along with fragments shouted in Arabic. From the window, Reid could see people running down the road. Convinced that a military offensive was afoot, he stumbled through the house to Holcomb's room and rousted him. When Holcolmb, who slept like the dead, was finally awake, he too became alarmed by the sounds filling the house.

But it wasn't an invasion. It was the beginning of the holy month of Ramadan, which Holcomb's cook helpfully explained. The people of Tangier, including some overly enthusiastic Spanish battery commanders, were celebrating the first breakfast before dawn on the first day. For the next month, Muslims would fast from sunrise to sunset. Both Reid and Holcomb had been oblivious of the onset of a major religious holiday in a predominantly Muslim country, despite working as intelligence officers. Their alarm and cluelessness amused Eddy, who knew well the rhythms and customs of the Islamic calendar, having grown up in the Near East.[2]

LATE THE FOLLOWING EVENING, a car with false license plates driven by a Moroccan member of Eddy's staff picked up Reid and delivered him to another villa nestled in the hills outside Tangier. Like Holcomb, Eddy had rented the isolated retreat to escape the claustrophobia of life in a city where his every move was reported in triplicate by German intelligence, but he also relished it beauty. "It is really lovely, old Moorish decorations and carved woodwork, tricky stained glass windows, tiled floors on which I have no doubt dancing girls did the Harem rhumba years ago," he wrote.[3]

Reid found Eddy waiting for him. The ex-marine had removed his jacket and rolled up his shirtsleeves. "Sit down." Eddy motioned Reid to a chair at a table where empty glasses stood ready. He unscrewed the cap on the scotch bottle and poured them both a drink.

"I am now going to give you the approximate date of D-Day for the forthcoming American invasion," said Eddy. "This is a momentous occasion and we will celebrate this by a pledge that I will exact from you that under no conditions, even pressure, will you divulge this historic secret."

Eddy gave Reid the job of handling radio communications in Casablanca—and ensuring that they remained open—during the invasion. Eddy and Dwight Eisenhower, who would be based at Gibraltar, would need reports about how the American effort progressed. Reid would also have to process messages for Dave King, who would be coordinating resistance activities.

"With these instructions, we clicked glasses with the hope and expectation that the American operation would be a success," wrote Reid.[4]

REID SET UP TWO new secondary radio stations on the theory that they would soon have to shut down the one at the US consulate for security reasons. Murphy had smuggled the new transmitters into North Africa by diplomatic pouch on his return from Washington.[5]

Reid found a new spot in an apartment next to the waterfront—and not more than two hundred yards from the battleship *Jean Bart*. The building's owner, a Moroccan Jew, let Reid know a few months before that he was interested in helping any way he could. The owner suggested they locate the transmitter in the chicken coop on the apartment building's roof.

To give Ajax, Reid's crack radio operator, a reason to visit the building and the roof, they established a small carpenter shop next to the coop. The walls of the shop would also shield the radio and the transmitter. "To avoid suspicion with the French at this time, you always had to have some excuse for your presence more than once at any specific locality," wrote Reid. Carpentry work was at a premium in Casablanca, so it would make sense that an enterprising carpenter would seek out and rent such a space for his business.

Reid located a second station in a small house not far from the Casablanca railroad station. A "for rent" sign had hung on the house for a few weeks before he inquired about it on behalf of the US consulate, explaining they needed it for extra storage. Thrilled by the interest, the estate agent offered the house to Reid with a seven-day cancellation clause.[6]

LIKE REID, DAVE KING had a secret meeting with Eddy at which he received the job of coordinating resistance cells for the day of the invasion. Despite the setbacks of the summer and the increased scrutiny of his movements, King continued his efforts to recruit French army officers, using his service in the French Foreign Legion to earn their trust. When scouting around at Casablanca's watering holes, he often appeared in a drunken haze, which made him seem harmless to those uninterested in joining the Allied cause. Of course, the drunk American would try to recruit them, they could tell themselves and anyone who inquired about their conversation—except King wasn't drunk.[7]

King kept hoping that one of his new connections would lead him back to General Antoine Béthouart, who continued to shun the Americans.[8]

AS PLANS FOR THE invasion coalesced, King received an inquiry from Washington about securing the services of a pilot familiar with the river leading to Port Lyautey Air Base, a notoriously difficult patch of water to navigate.

The base, which had the only concrete airstrip in North Africa, lay six miles inland from the coast, but reaching it by water required navigating twelve miles of the Sebou River, which made a series of treacherous twists inland. If such a pilot existed, George Patton wanted him sent to Washington to brief the US Navy and possibly aid them during the invasion.[9]

King knew just the man: René Malevergne, a World War I veteran and former chief pilot of Port Lyautey, who had no love for Vichy. After connecting with a resistance cell in Rabat, he became involved in a plot to liberate forty Belgian pilots interned in Morocco. The ill-planned British intelligence operation led to his arrest and a trial in Vichy, France. Malevergne was found "not guilty," and the Residency allowed him to return to Morocco in December 1941, provided he did not reside in the Mehdia and Port Lyautey region. Vichy officials feared he might rekindle his work with the resistance.[10]

Malevergne found a job working for Charles Chenay, who owned a cannery and also moonlighted with the resistance. As part of his job for Chenay, Malevergne surveyed the arrival of fishing boats in ports along the Moroccan coast. That information and anything else he observed found its way to King, who gave his new informant the code name "The Shark."[11] By the spring of 1942, Malevergne was also helping OSS smuggle weapons and communications equipment into Morocco.[12]

King cast around for ways to smuggle Malevergne out, but nothing would quite do the trick. Shipping traffic had dropped to a trickle, and Casablanca's port operated under increased surveillance following the addition of more than fifty customs officials.[13] With the port out, the only option appeared to be to sneak him over the border into Spanish Morocco for delivery to Tangier. The perfect means to do so arrived in Casablanca in mid-September in the form of Gordon Browne, Holcomb, and a Chevy. Browne and Holcomb, who both worked for Eddy in Tangier, had spent the previous couple of weeks driving around French Morocco photographing the Taza corridor, a vital strategic passageway between the Riff and Atlas Mountains.[14] Holcomb also held a diplomatic passport, which subjected him to less scrutiny at the border between French and Spanish Morocco.

King wired Eddy for approval to enlist Browne and Holcomb's help. Eddy granted it but cautioned against using false papers. Malevergne would need to be smuggled out of French Morocco in the "baggage compartment."

Through a mutual friend, King arranged a meeting with Malevergne, which is how the pilot found himself standing in King's villa in Anfa one evening. The two men knew each other's names but had never met before.

King explained the mission and asked Malevergne if he was ready to leave. Malevergne said yes, and they sealed the deal with a glass of whiskey.[15]

WHEN THE MEN GATHERED at King's villa on the day of their departure, they discovered the compact Malevergne, who stood five feet, four inches, couldn't fit into the trunk of Browne's car. But he would fit into the small trailer Browne and Holcomb used to carry extra petrol for their trip. Malevergne could squeeze between the now empty fuel drums.

King thought the trailer would work just fine, but Holcomb protested, arguing that it wasn't a baggage compartment—and Eddy had said "baggage compartment." "Young Holcomb," as King referred to him, was a captain in the Marine Corps and used to following orders to the letter. His father also happened to be the commandant of the Marine Corps. King believed in flexibility; his whole life had been one big improvisation. The argument over the definition of "baggage compartment" and the need to sometimes stretch orders grew heated until Browne intervened.

"Do they want the man badly?" asked Browne.

"You're God damn right they do," replied King.

"What the hell is the argument?" said Browne. "Let's go."

Malevergne, who spoke only a smattering of English, found it hard to keep up with the rapid-fire argument. When he asked Chenay if he still got to go, Chenay replied yes.

"I like King," said Malevergne. "He looks like a diplomatic gangster."

They backed the trailer into the villa's garage, away from prying eyes, and made a nest for Malevergne. A thick Moroccan rug provided some padding against the hard metal floor. Once Malevergne found a comfortable position, they covered him with gunnysacks. A tarp then went over the whole trailer. As they said their good-byes, King cautioned Browne and Holcomb to stop every now and then to make sure Malevergne wasn't being asphyxiated.

The trio set off at around 4:00 p.m. for Tangier, which lay two hundred miles north. Outside Casablanca, they rescued Malevergne from his cramped quarters, installing him in the back of the car buried under some rugs.[16] Twenty miles south of the border, they pulled off the road to eat dinner, which King had kindly provided. Once the sun dropped below the horizon, they returned Malevergne to the trailer and drove for the border.

As they waited for border control agents to inspect and process their papers, a dog took a keen interest in the trailer. Knowing the game was up if Malevergne was discovered, Browne tried to shoo the dog away with small stones—to no avail. Then he remembered a half-opened tin of ham in the car leftover from dinner. As the dog lapped up the unexpected feast, it lost interest in the trailer.

Once safely in Tangier, they stashed Malevergne at Eddy's villa outside the city. For Eddy, who had become a bit jaded by all the political machinations of the resistance cells, meeting Malevergne restored his faith. "I have never met a finer Frenchman, about fifty, a veteran of the last war where he was in sectors close to the ones I served in," wrote Eddy. "And here he is again giving up everything when he was told he was needed. When I tried to thank him he said, 'Not at all, I serve France and I can serve her best now by helping you, because your cause is ours.' It is an inspiration."[17]

From Tangier, Malevergne was smuggled across the strait to Gibraltar and put on an airplane to the United States. When Eisenhower found out about the extraction, he was furious, believing that, had it gone wrong, it could have tipped the French and Germans off about the North Africa invasion. But as far as French authorities in Morocco knew, Malevergne was bumming around the Grand Atlas, having followed orders to leave the coast.[18]

32

We Need a Hero

ON OCTOBER 21, THE SUBMARINE HMS *SERAPH* SURFACED IN THE dark off the coast of Algeria near Cherchell, a small town about fifty-five miles west of Algiers. Major General Mark W. Clark of the US Army trained his binoculars on the beach looking for an isolated villa with a light burning in a second-story window. When the signal was confirmed, Clark and his team would venture ashore with the help of three British commandos for a meeting with General Charles Mast, deputy commander of 19th Army Corps in Algeria and French resistance stalwart. With less than three weeks to go before TORCH, the Allies still held out hope of obtaining French assistance.[1]

Clark hadn't come alone. With him were Brigadier General Lyman Lemnitzer, one of Ike's senior planners; Captain Jerauld Wright, the US Navy's liaison; Colonel Archelaus Hamblen, an expert on logistics and supply; and Colonel Julius Holmes, who had charge of civil affairs for TORCH. On only a few days' notice, the group had traded the smog and fog of London for the pungent confines and claustrophobia of a Royal Navy submarine to make the trip east from Gibraltar to the sun-washed Algerian coast. When it was safe, the submarine surfaced for fresh air and the chance to run at ten or twelve knots before plunging again below the surface, where it crawled along at an agonizing two or three knots. To ward off boredom, Clark and his team played endless rubbers of bridge and added cribbage to their repertoire after a few lessons from the Brits. At an angular six feet, two inches, Clark found the cramped quarters of the *Seraph* hard on his head. He also didn't relish having "literally to crawl on all fours" to use the "head."[2]

The forty-six-year-old Clark served as Dwight Eisenhower's deputy in London. Clark knew the plans for TORCH inside and out, which made send-

FIGURE 32.1. Major General Mark Clark—"Wayne" to his friends—led the secret mission to Cherchell, Algeria. *Library of Congress*

ing him on a secret mission to meet Mast a terrifying prospect. If the French captured Clark, the mission, not to mention his life, would be in jeopardy. The son of an army officer, Clark secured a spot at West Point, where he struck up a friendship with an upperclassman by the name of Eisenhower. When George Marshall solicited names to head up the army's War Plans Division in the aftermath of Pearl Harbor, Clark recommended Eisenhower. When Eisenhower needed help setting up his command in London, he asked for Clark, who had a talent for planning and organization. His rapid wartime promotion provoked grousing among his fellow officers, including General George Patton, who considered Clark "more preoccupied with bettering his own future than in winning the war."[3]

When Robert Murphy sent a telegram pleading for urgent staff talks with Mast to discuss a possible collaboration with General Henri Giraud, Eisenhower once again called on Clark, confident in his ability to represent his sensibilities and take the measure of the men who claimed to offer assistance.

In the early-morning hours of October 22, the submarine came within visual distance of what Clark believed to be the rendezvous point but delayed going ashore. Too much was at stake to risk showing up in the wrong place. Instead, they would spend the day conducting reconnaissance of the coastline using the submarine's periscope and try again that night.[4]

THE WHOOSH OF THE waves hitting and then retreating from the beach below cut through the silence of the night. Murphy stood on a bluff searching the Mediterranean for signs of Clark and his team. They had turned on the light, as planned, to signal the submarine. Now it was just a matter of waiting for Clark to materialize out of the dark sea.

Keenly aware that Eisenhower and the rest of Allied Forces Headquarters would feel better about TORCH's chance of success if they could count on the support of the French military, Murphy had decided to make the trek to Rabat upon his return from London. Charles Noguès had always been friendly to Murphy and receptive to American overtures—all while refusing to backtrack on his pledge to defend Morocco from any incursion, whether by the Axis or the Allies. Given the impending invasion, Murphy decided to make one last attempt to lure Noguès over to the Allied side. "I knew that this shrewd soldier, with several decades of experience in Morocco, familiar with all the intricate problems of the region, would be of incalculable assistance if only he would change his mind," wrote Murphy.[5]

Noguès extended every diplomatic courtesy during their meeting, including inviting Murphy to dinner. The opportunity to speak with the resident-general away from the phalanx of courtiers provided just the opportunity Murphy needed. During their private postdinner conversation, Murphy outlined in detail the Americans' rapidly expanding military output. The mobilized economy ran on all cylinders, churning out guns, tanks, airplanes, and ships, all of which would allow the United States to fight a global war. Hundreds of thousands of soldiers and sailors were being drafted and trained for fighting overseas. Murphy then floated the possibility of the United States' using its military muscle to send 500,000 troops to North Africa. Would that interest Noguès?

"Do not try that!" cried Noguès. "If you do, I will meet you with all the firepower I possess. It is too late for France to participate in this war now. We will do better to stay out. If Morocco becomes a battleground, it will be lost to France!"

The general's explosive and emotional reaction gave Murphy his answer: the Americans would have to look elsewhere for help.[6]

WHILE NOGUÈS REMAINED OBSTINATE, Murphy found himself courted in the weeks running up to TORCH by two other Frenchmen: Admiral Jean-François Darlan and General Henri Giraud. Darlan, the man who worked so hard to orchestrate greater collaboration between France and Germany, had been secretly sending messages to Murphy expressing an interest in working with the Americans. Darlan's overtures weren't entirely unexpected. He had dropped hints to American ambassador William Leahy for the past thirteen months, making it known that if the Allies appeared in North Africa with an army capable of taking on Germany, Vichy would not oppose them. Leahy considered Darlan "a complete opportunist," an assessment Murphy shared.[7]

Before Leahy departed Vichy for good in April 1942, he paid one last call on Darlan at this office in the Hôtel du Parc. Despite Darlan's recent demotion in the face of Pierre Laval's triumphant return—Vichy's cabinet was nothing short of an evolving high-stakes soap opera—he wanted Leahy to know that he still controlled Vichy's defenses. France would not use its fleet against the United States. Darlan also sought to maintain a good relationship with the United States but insisted on keeping his distance from Britain, which he loathed to his core.[8]

Upon Leahy's exodus, Darlan started courting Murphy through an intermediary in Algiers, claiming that French North Africa would fight Germany once the United States provided the necessary matériel to ensure victory. Alain Darlan, Darlan's son and a naval officer, also regularly spoke with Murphy. Unlike his cagey father, the younger Darlan presented himself as very pro-Allied in his conversations with Murphy.[9]

Murphy's reports about Darlan's overtures failed to generate any interest at the State Department during the spring and summer of 1942, but that changed with the decision to launch TORCH. Eisenhower's staff was interested in what aid Darlan might be able to provide to the "extremely precarious" invasion, but Darlan was still Darlan, one of the most loathed men in Europe and the United States.[10]

The second Frenchman courting Murphy was General Charles Mast, who represented General Henri Giraud. Mast had approached Murphy on Giraud's behalf in the summer, and the discussions had continued into the fall. Conversations with Mast revealed Giraud would participate in a North Africa campaign, provided it was an American-only operation and the Americans also landed simultaneously in France. Giraud also wanted command of all troops in the North African theater, both American and French, to demonstrate French sovereignty. Eisenhower, however, refused to entertain discussions about command. It was too early for such decisions—the Americans hadn't set foot in North Africa yet, and whether French forces would participate remained to be seen. In response to Giraud's demands, Murphy passed along expressions of general American support, prompting a request by Mast for staff talks.[11]

SHORTLY AFTER MIDNIGHT ON October 22, Clark and Lieutenant Norman Jewell, skipper of the *Seraph*, again trained their binoculars toward the shoreline, searching for the signal to come ashore. They had spent a restless day submerged off the coast, popping up the periscope for short stints to survey the beach to verify they were in the right place. Two hours before, at 10:00 p.m., the coast remained black, prompting a frustrated Clark to bet each of his men $10 that the light would not appear.

He was going to have to pay up.

Clark and his team clambered down the side of the submarine and into the small kayak-like boats that would take them the remaining two miles. The two-person folbots folded down to the size of a suitcase, allowing them to be passed through the submarine's hatch and assembled on deck. When the team had paddled within two hundred yards of the beach, one boat went ahead to scout, while the others bobbed in the Mediterranean, waiting for the signal to proceed. A few minutes later, a flashlight signaled "okay" in Morse code from the beach.[12]

Clark and the rest of his team rode the surf in, only to find themselves alone and exposed. Spying a steep bluff that offered protection, they dragged their boats and gear toward it. A figure sporting a baseball cap, turtleneck, and sneakers emerged from the twisting olive trees perched on the edge of the bluff.

"Welcome to North Africa," said Murphy.

Out of breath and relieved to be in the right place, Clark's mind blanked on the speech he'd prepared in French. "I'm damned glad we made it."

Murphy led the way up a steep rocky path to the crumbling whitewashed, red-roofed villa that would host their discussions. The house belonged to Jacques Teissier, a member of the French resistance. With Mast and his associates not due until dawn, Clark caught a few hours of sleep in an upstairs bedroom, gladly falling into a rumpled bed, but not before instructing the British commandos accompanying him to make themselves scarce when the French arrived. This was supposed to be a purely American affair.[13]

GENERAL MAST AND HIS staff arrived around 6:00 a.m. on October 23, having driven from Algiers. Mast managed a few words of English—"Welcome to my country"—before retreating to his native tongue. Clark could get by in French, and what he couldn't manage, Murphy and Holmes could fill in. Over a breakfast of coffee, sardines, bread, and jam, they began discussing the military situation in North Africa. Clark found Mast's sincerity compelling. It was clear that the Frenchman would do anything required to make an Allied operation a success. Mast's earnestness made it all the more difficult for Clark and Murphy to lie to him. Neither was authorized to reveal that American forces would be storming the beaches of Morocco and Algeria in sixteen days. Instead the Americans led their French counterparts to believe they had months to prepare for a spring invasion. The subterfuge generated hard feelings in the weeks and months to come.[14]

Mast pressed for clarification of Giraud's role. The French wanted assurances that Giraud would command both American and French forces. Clark demurred, explaining that it was impractical to make decisions in the initial planning stages of an operation, but Giraud would receive an overall command "as soon as possible." They also discussed the possibility of Darlan's participation in an operation, an idea that Mast could not stomach. Mast believed Darlan's attempt to join the Allied cause stemmed from naked opportunism rather than conviction. The Allies didn't need Darlan. Giraud would rally France's African army and air force—and the navy would fall in line behind him.[15]

As THE AMERICAN AND French officers talked, members of Mast's staff kept watch at the windows and walked around the house, scouting for signs of trouble. Everything remained quiet through the morning. Around noon, they broke off discussions for a lunchtime meal of "chicken cooked with a hot Arab sauce," along with oranges and red wine. After Mast returned to Algiers, lest his prolonged absence raise suspicions, his staff stayed on for the afternoon to talk strategy and logistics. The discussions benefitted from the stacks of reports brought by the French, outlining troop positions, naval deployments, supply depots, and more.

In the midafternoon the phone rang, delivering a heart-pounding warning: the police were on their way. With astonishing speed, the French officers stripped off their uniforms and donned civilian clothes before disappearing out the villa's doors and windows. Clark rushed upstairs to rouse the sleeping British commandos.

"Where can we hide?" asked Clark.

Teissier ushered them onto the patio, where he pulled up the trapdoor to the wine cellar. Clark and the others scrambled down the stairs into the dank cavern, bringing with them the bags of valuable and damning French documents. When the door shut, they were plunged into darkness, but they could still hear every word being said above. Each footstep toward the trapdoor made their hearts beat faster.

Clark perched at the foot of the stairs, weapon drawn, waiting for the moment the trapdoor opened.

A REPORT OF POSSIBLE smuggling activity in the area—footprints leading from the beach to the house had been spotted—drew the police to the villa. Instead of black market booze and coffee, the police found the remnants of a raucous party, courtesy of some energetic acting by Murphy, Teissier, and a few members of Mast's staff who had remained. They clinked bottles. They sang songs. They even confessed to having had some women upstairs. After Murphy sheepishly revealed his identity to the police, he begged them not to embarrass him. Think of his career![16]

The policemen stomped and poked around the house for almost a half hour, before returning to town for further instructions. Despite Murphy and Teissier's best efforts, a shred of doubt remained.

When it was safe, Murphy popped open the trapdoor, which had been hidden by a strategically placed crate. "This is Bob. They've gone, but they'll be back."

Fearful that the police would soon return, Clark and his team headed for the beach, temporarily hiding the boats among the olive trees on the bluff while they surveyed the waves. The rising surf was too high for their small boats to negotiate, endangering their chance of making a rendezvous with the *Seraph*. Undaunted, Clark and one of the British commandos decided to test their luck, stripping down to their T-shirts and briefs. When the first breaker flipped their boat, they lost their paddles, along with Clark's pants and his money belt stuffed with gold pieces, which he had decided against wearing lest the weight drag him under. While they waited for the surf to subside, they retreated to the sanctuary of the olive trees.[17]

As midnight approached, a cold and hungry Clark ventured back to the house for some food and clothing. An already skittish Teissier became even more so as he outfitted Clark with some too-small sweaters and supplied him with bread and wine. He became outright frantic when tires crunched on the gravel and the glow of headlights filtered through the windows of the shadowy villa. The police had returned. Teissier begged Clark to leave—now!—but not by the well-worn path to the beach. The new route required Clark to drop ten feet down to the bluff on his already bloody bare feet.

After waiting through most of the night, an increasingly restless Clark decided they had to risk a dash for the submarine. Daylight would not improve their situation. Murphy lent a hand, wading into the Mediterranean to help steady the precarious wooden boats so the men could climb into them. Clark and Wright, the navy man, ventured forth first and found a break in the surf that allowed them to clear two hard-charging waves before gliding to calmer water. Their colleagues weren't so lucky: the waves tossed all of them into the sea. Their briefcases and musette bags stuffed full of material provided by the French went in too.

Tired and wet, the men rowed forward, desperate to find the *Seraph* in the watery black landscape. After what seemed an eternity, the outline of the submarine materialized. By some miracle seamanship, Lieutenant Jewell managed to maneuver the *Seraph* within three-quarters of a mile of the beach without tearing up her keel.

As the last boat carrying Colonel Holmes came alongside, it knocked against the steel haul. Water gushed through the crack in the boat's wood frame. Holmes barely made it up the ladder before the boat sank, taking his musette bag full of documents down with it.[18] The bag contained letters from Murphy, which, if found, would reveal his presence at the meeting and place him in danger. Clark wanted to stay and look for the bag, but with dawn approaching Jewell recommended they submerge lest they further jeopardize their mission. Once on board, Clark sent a message to Murphy via Eisenhower to warn him of the potential disaster brewing. He also authorized two much-needed rounds of rum for his men and the crew of the submarine.

The boat and musette bag never washed up—only Clark's pants and raincoat.[19]

PART TWO

Torching Morocco

33

Zigzagging

A S THE CRISP AUTUMN AIR ENFOLDED THE PORT OF HAMPTON
Roads, Virginia, on the morning of October 24, 1942, the USS *Augusta* weighed anchor and slipped into the column of ships filing out of the harbor. From the deck of the heavy cruiser, Lieutenant General George S. Patton Jr. stood at the railing and watched as the ship sailed past Fort Monroe and glided her way through a minefield. As the column passed through the buoyed channel, soldiers hung off the railings, watching the Virginia coastline retreat before their eyes and the blue water of the Atlantic stretch out before them.[1]

The ships sailing that morning were the last members of Task Force 34 to depart for French Morocco. After months of planning and haggling over the mechanics of the invasion, Patton now depended of the US Navy to deliver his 33,000 troops across the submarine-infested Atlantic to the Barbary Coast. When the last ship had left port, the convoy sailed northeast as if headed for Britain.

To disguise the sailing of 102 ships bound for Morocco, task force commander Rear Admiral Henry Kent Hewitt—"Kent" to his friends—orchestrated a series of staggered departures. Nazi agents watched the traffic to and from naval bases and U-boats patrolled the Atlantic seaboard. The longer Germany failed to notice the American fleet headed for Morocco, the safer the journey for the ships and the greater the likelihood of maintaining the element of surprise. Five submarines, which served as scouts, had left a week before from Connecticut. The Covering Group, consisting of the battleship *Massachusetts*, two heavy cruisers, and four destroyers, departed from Casco Bay, Maine. The first convoy of troop transports and warships left Hampton Roads on the afternoon of October 23, heading south toward Bermuda. Meanwhile, the Air Group, consisting of five aircraft carriers, nine destroyers, a light cruiser, and an oiler, plied the waters off Bermuda, having been sent there on exercises earlier in the month.[2]

Many of the captains sailing out of Hampton Roads didn't know their final destination until Hewitt conducted a predeparture briefing on October 23. They also had the pleasure of listening to Patton tell them he had serious doubts the navy could deliver his troops on time and in one piece. "Never in history has the Navy landed an army at the planned time and place," he told them. "If you land us anywhere within fifty miles of Fedhala and within one week of D-day, I'll go ahead and win. . . . We shall attack for sixty days, and then, if we have to, for sixty more. If we go forward with desperation, if we go forward with utmost speed and fight, these people cannot stand against us."[3]

Over the next four days, from October 24 to 28, the submarines, Covering Group, Air Group, and two troop convoys altered their courses until they united as a single force in the middle of the North Atlantic. "The day set for the rendezvous was sunny with a slight mist on the horizon," wrote Air Group commander Rear Admiral Ernest McWhorter. "Everyone strained their eyes to sight the convoy. At last, out of the haze loomed a ship, then another, and another until it was no use counting them. We swung into our formation with the signal lights blinking from halfway around the horizon."[4]

The rendezvous constituted an amazing feat of seamanship, not only in its planning and execution but because many of the ships had sailed directly out the shipyard, crewed by sailors on their first cruise. When assembled, Task Force 34 covered a stretch of ocean twenty by thirty miles wide. Five lines of ships, organized into nine columns spaced 1,000 yards apart, formed the heart of the convoy. The Covering Group served as the advance guard, while the Air Group protected the rear. Around the edges, destroyers patrolled for submarines.[5] To limit the chance of detection, the convoy operated under radio silence and used the centuries-old method of communicating orders between ships using signal flags. An order could be delivered from the *Augusta*, Hewitt's flagship, to the entire fleet in ten minutes. To avoid using light signals at night, course changes were signaled before sunset.[6]

Such a precise rendezvous was to be expected from Hewitt, who had forged a career on seamanship and mathematics. A Jersey boy from Hackensack, he graduated from the US Naval Academy in 1906. In the run-up to World War I, he had circled the globe with the Great White Fleet, served as executive officer on a destroyer, and taught mathematics at the academy. During the war, he earned the Navy Cross for escorting convoys across an Atlantic teaming with German U-boats. The interwar years again saw him alternating between ship duty and teaching mathematics at the Naval Academy. While transporting Franklin Roosevelt to Buenos Aires for the 1936 Pan American Conference, Hewitt struck up a friendship with the ship-crazy president. With the outbreak of World War II, Hewitt, now a rear admiral, commanded the Atlantic Fleet Task Groups, which conducted neutrality patrols and escorted convoys. The dangerous crossings had the potential to draw the United States into the war. When Roosevelt and Chief of Staff George Marshall needed a man who could assemble the fleet for TORCH—and stand up to Patton's bluster—they called on Hewitt.[7]

PATTON'S APPRECIATION FOR HEWITT grew as they crossed the Atlantic. "The Admiral has just started zig-zagging," wrote Patton in his diary. "I like him better all the time."[8] Sailing in a zigzag pattern made it harder for submarines to track a ship. While Hewitt tended the fleet, Patton battled boredom, an affliction that affected every rank. "Having nothing to do, some of my people worry," wrote Patton in his diary. "I could myself, but won't. It is hard to realize that in 10 days I shall be up to my neck in work." To keep trim and fit, he used a rowing machine and held onto the dresser while he ran in place for three hundred steps. He read the Koran to better understand the Moroccans and tore through detective and adventure novels. He judged *The Sun Is My Undoing* by Marguerite Steen, a best-selling novel about the slave trade, "pretty sticky."[9]

Patton's tight quarters were luxurious compared to those of his troops, who bunked in every nook and cranny across the fleet. His men battled seasickness. Harold Taylor, a communications sergeant from Fort Wayne, Indiana, sailing aboard the USS *Elizabeth C. Stanton*, considered himself lucky not to be green, like so many of his comrades in the 15th Infantry, 3rd Division. "It was an unbelievable sight to walk around the deck and see the large convoy of ships around us as we made our way across the rough Atlantic," he wrote in his memoir.[10] When the men weren't sleeping or standing in line for a meal or the head, they passed the time reading, attending church services, and playing card games. "Many of my comrades engaged in below deck poker games," wrote Taylor. "The same ones always won and the same ones seemed to always lose. I knew better than to get involved. I couldn't see gambling away what little military pay I received."[11]

AS THE FLEET MADE its way across the Atlantic, Dave King began his own countdown, readying his resistance cells in Casablanca, Port Lyautey, and

FIGURE 33.1. Major General George S. Patton and Rear Admiral H. Kent Hewitt share a laugh onboard the USS *Augusta. Naval History and Heritage Command*

Rabat to aid the American invasion. French intelligence noticed the lights burning through the night in his office and at the American consulate, along with couriers coming and going at all hours. When a high-placed friend with the French police sent word of aroused suspicions, King realized he would have to tell a half-truth. A flat denial would only generate more attention. He crafted a story using a rumor circulating around Casablanca for months: the Americans were worried about a large squadron of German planes—possibly three hundred!—amassing in Tunis, believing it prefigured an airborne invasion. As a precautionary measure, the consulate was burning its semisecret papers at night and sending others to Gibraltar by diplomatic pouch. The French bought the story.[12]

With the help of some friends at the Residency in Rabat, King also kept an eye on German telegram traffic, trying to gauge whether Berlin had an inkling of the American convoy's approach. It did not. The Germans believed the Allied ships crossing the Atlantic and departing from England were bound for either Malta or Dakar.[13]

On Wednesday, November 4, King wrote out individual sets of instructions for the resistance cells at Port Lyautey, Rabat, Fédala, Casablanca, Safi, and Marrakech. The orders covered two scenarios—if French troops did not fight back, and if French troops opposed the Americans — and included a list of objectives to carry out to aid the invasion. He informed the cells of practice alerts from Saturday morning through Monday morning.

King handed the orders for Port Lyautey and Rabat over to Michel Despax, his trusted number two, for delivery. The orders, however, never made it the Port Lyautey cell. Despax passed them on to a French army major in Rabat for delivery, but the major decided he was too important to play errand boy for an American vice consul.[14]

ON THURSDAY MORNING, NOVEMBER 5, another of the Apostles arrived in Casablanca. Kenneth Pendar had driven like mad from Algiers to deliver a package into the hands of his colleagues at the Office of Strategic Services. After calling Staff Reid and vice consul Ernest Mayer into the conference room, Pendar revealed that he had a letter from Roosevelt to Charles Noguès, along with one from the president to the sultan. Robert Murphy asked that Mayer and Reid deliver the letters on the morning of the invasion, one hour before American troops came ashore. Reid protested the assignment. He handled the wireless traffic for the Casablanca station, and if he went to Rabat, no one would be available to do the coding and decoding. Pendar, however, thought that Murphy's orders superseded any given by Bill Eddy. Reid grudgingly agreed.[15]

Around 10 p.m. on Friday, November 6, General Antoine Béthouart ordered that King be brought to him for questioning. Even though he received copies of the letters between General Henri Giraud and Murphy, Béthouart knew next to nothing about the mechanics of the American operation. Yet, he had been ordered to "facilitate" the Allied invasion, maintain order in Morocco, and seize the government from Noguès.[16]

When two agents from the Sûreté appeared and ordered King to come with them, he thought he was being arrested. Instead, he found himself sitting across from Béthouart, who found it amusing to see him looking "white as a sheet." "My dear King, no need to make that face, we're in the same boat," Béthouart told him.

King relaxed, only to have the balding general with the precise moustache fire off a string of questions. Where were the Americans going to land? What did the invasion force consist of? King confessed that the staff officer tasked with briefing him in person had never arrived, having failed to obtain the necessary visas to enter Morocco. King, however, could relay what he knew. He had been told to prepare the resistance groups for action in three places—Mehdia–Port Lyautey, Fédala-Casablanca, and Safi—indicating that the Americans planned to come ashore at those three points.[17]

Béthouart didn't think much of the American plan and ordered King to send a telegram suggesting an alternative: Americans troops should come ashore at Rabat, Salé, and Mazagan, where he would arrange for them to encounter little resistance and receive support from French troops under his command. He cautioned against landing at Fédala, as the autumn tides made navigating the harbor treacherous.

"It seems to the French unnecessarily dangerous to proceed with such an attempt under fire of the shore batteries and warships and submarine attacks," reported King. Béthouart also argued against a frontal attack on Casablanca and Port Lyautey as part of the first stage of the operations. "All these ports will certainly be on guard, ready for action, and will fire on sight."[18]

After shunning American overtures for months, Béthouart wanted Patton, Hewitt, and Dwight Eisenhower to redo their assault plans two days before the invasion. Camped at Gibraltar with Eisenhower, Eddy responded that Béthouart's suggestion "conforms closely" to the planned American operation. He would pass Béthouart's recommendations along to Patton but cautioned that it was too late to change the invasion plan. The exact time of landing would depend on the weather, but "your friends must be ready from this instant on to render specific assistance at all points you have mentioned."[19]

After Béthouart finished second-guessing the Americans, he started making plans of his own. French troops under his command would occupy Rabat, surround the Residency, and take Noguès into custody two hours before the first American soldier hit the beach. The Garde mobile would arrest the German Armistice Commission, while Moroccan troops secured the Allied consulates against retaliation by German and Vichy sympathizers.[20] Troops loyal to Béthouart would also occupy the telephone, telegraph, and radio stations in Casablanca and Rabat to paralyze any attempts to send reinforcements. Once he had control of communications, Béthouart planned to install a new command structure across Morocco comprised of pro-Allied officers.[21] If all went according to plan, the Americans would have the French welcome they so desperately wanted.

Since Béthouart's scheme hinged on timing, he wanted to know how King would learn that the invasion would proceed as planned. King explained that the BBC would broadcast a series of messages over its French and North African programs. Forty-eight hours before the scheduled start of the invasion, King needed to listen for mentions of "Robert": "Robert is on time" or

"Robert will be with you soon" or "Robert is delayed."[22] To make sure he caught the message, King posted six people at locations scattered around the city. The redundancy ensured someone would hear the message despite the French navy's ongoing attempts to block the BBC's signal.[23]

Béthouart's decision to join the fight had a downside for King: it rendered many of the plans for his resistance cells obsolete. If Béthouart's men were going to seize the communications centers in Casablanca and Rabat, King's cells wouldn't have to do it. Keeping both plans in operation could lead to clashes between pro-Allied groups. King telegraphed Eddy asking for guidance. "Unless I hear to the contrary shall instruct my groups to carry out orders you sent me doing my best to avoid clash or incident," he wrote. In the end, most of the plans devised during the previous year were tossed aside. King's resistance cells went dark to avoid spoiling Béthouart's scheme.[24]

WHILE KING HAGGLED WITH Béthouart, Task Force 34 moved into position off Morocco. The fleet arrived unscathed despite German submarines hunting around its edges during the final days of the voyage. A high north wind battered the ships, turning the waves choppy and causing Patton to fret about how the rough seas and high surf would affect the beach landings. Then the weather cleared. "This morning it is very quiet and cool, almost too good to be true. Thank God. I hope He stays on our side," wrote Patton.[25]

As the hours ticked down, Patton outlined for his 33,000 troops, in a written message passed throughout the fleet, the task that lay ahead. He warned his men that they might meet with opposition from the "French African Army, composed of both white and colored troops." "It is regrettable to contemplate the necessity of fighting the gallant French who are at heart sympathetic toward us, but all resistance by whomever offered must be destroyed," wrote Patton. Any surrendering French soldiers they should treat with the utmost respect. "Remember, the French are not Nazis or Japs." During the landing, each soldier should remember his training and work without regard for sleep or food. "A pint of sweat will save a gallon of blood." The eyes of the world would be watching them, and the invasion could not falter. "You must succeed—for to retreat is as cowardly as it is fatal. Indeed, once landed, retreat is impossible," wrote Patton. "Americans do not surrender."[26]

On the morning of November 7—less than one day before the start of the invasion—the Southern Attack Group peeled away and sailed toward Safi. At 3:00 p.m., the Northern Attack Group broke away from the main fleet and headed north for Mehdia and Port Lyautey.[27] With a direct attack on Casablanca impossible because of its naval and shore defenses, the Americans were landing troops in the north at Mehdia and Port Lyautey and south at Safi, to converge on Casablanca in a classic pincer movement.

That left Patton with the Center Attack Group to take Fédala, which lay twelve miles north of Casablanca, and a seemingly interminable wait. He tried to get some sleep, knowing it would be sparse in the coming days. He paced. Once again, he found solace in reading. "Fortunately I found a detective story, 'The Cairo Garter Murders,' by Van Wyck Mason," he wrote in his diary. "I have just finished and will start to worry, or should I feel utterly confident?"[28]

34

Robert Is on Time

Everything proceeded as planned for the Moroccan invasion—everything except the question of French leadership. On the eve of torch, Generals Dwight Eisenhower and Mark Clark found themselves sitting across from General Henri Giraud in the bunker under Gibraltar. A submarine had picked Giraud up off the Côte d'Azur two days earlier, and his appearance bore the marks of a cramped journey. Deep creases marred the hang of his grey suit, and his normally sprite handlebar moustache drooped. But as soon as the office door closed and the red "Do Not Disturb" light sparked to life, Eisenhower and Clark discovered that the rumpled man in need of a shave possessed a stubborn streak as long as the Loire.[1]

Giraud had come to Gibraltar to discuss his role in torch. After the meeting at Cherchell, Robert Murphy received permission to tell General Charles Mast that the American invasion would occur not in the spring but in less than ten days. Mast took the news hard, charging the Americans with deceit and a lack of faith in their potential French allies. When Mast relayed the news to Giraud, the general declared that he would be unable to leave France before November 20. With Giraud refusing to budge on his timeline despite pleas and assurances, Murphy went so far as to suggest delaying the invasion by two weeks. The answer from Washington was a resounding no. Instead, Eisenhower and his staff devised a scheme to bring Giraud to Gibraltar so they could talk general to general.[2]

The discussion began with the Americans proposing that Giraud resume his previous rank of general, with dominion over French troops. Giraud, however, had other ideas. "As I understand it, when I land in North Africa,

FIGURE 34.1. Generals Dwight Eisenhower and Henri Giraud, ca. 1943. *Library of Congress*

I am to assume command of all Allied forces and become the Supreme Allied commander in North Africa," he declared.

Clark gasped.

Eisenhower seethed but maintained his reserve. Giraud had just proposed taking his job. "There must be some misunderstanding," said Ike.[3]

Clark wracked his brain to figure out what could have given Giraud the notion that they would simply hand him the top command. He had been so careful during his conversation with Mast—or so he thought.[4]

For the next three hours the three generals engaged in a tortuous discussion about rank and command made trickier by the language gap. Eisenhower had a rickety understanding of French. Giraud spoke no English. Clark muddled through in his French and played interpreter when the translator retreated in exhaustion.

Giraud wanted the freedom to carry out his own strategic and tactical plans. All Allied troops on North African soil as of November 10 would come under his control, as would men landed after that date. He also wanted to move quickly into France and proposed using the entire Allied air force headed for North Africa to seize Sardinia and invade France's southern coast. As for command, Eisenhower would act as his second, making administrative arrangements and tending to reinforcements and supplies. He also refused to be beholden to the Combined Chiefs of Staff. Eisenhower would have to deal with them.[5]

Eisenhower and Clark attempted to reason with Giraud. They noted that he had been promised a command, and provisions had been made for long-term collaboration. But the current operation would benefit from his going to North Africa, as soon as it was safe, and taking command of the French forces willing to rally to his side. Giraud refused to consider such a role, claiming that "his countrymen would not understand and his honor as a soldier would be tarnished."[6]

For his part, Eisenhower was willing to recognize Giraud as "the leader of the French effort to save North Africa and restore France" and give him all the honors due to the senior military leader in the region. On one point, however, Eisenhower would not budge: he would not allow Giraud to "issue operational orders" to him.[7]

Exhausted and frustrated, the generals adjourned for dinner. Discussions resumed at 10:30 p.m., dragging on for another two hours. Eisenhower tried to convince Giraud that the time to act was now. Giraud continued to worry about what French people, what his family, would think of him, if he did not lead the invasion. Clark marveled at his obstinacy in demanding command of an operation that the Americans and British had planned and were about to execute.[8]

When it became clear after midnight that there was no way to resolve the impasse, Giraud announced his intention to return to France the same way he arrived. "Oh, no, you won't," said Clark, "That was a one-way submarine. You're not going back to France on it."[9] Giraud knew too much about Allied plans. He wasn't going anywhere until Eisenhower and Clark deemed it safe.

Their bodies buzzing with tension and lack of sleep, Eisenhower and Clark slowly realized that Giraud was playing a waiting game. He wanted to see how the invasion fared, how much French blood was spilled. "He realizes he can do nothing with respect to the landing itself and can gain no credit from it, no matter what happens," wrote Ike to the Combined Chiefs. "His method of gaining time is to insist upon a point which as a soldier he is well aware the Allies cannot accept at this moment." A successful first day of TORCH, Eisenhower predicted, would put Giraud in a more conciliatory mood.[10]

As he headed off to bed that evening, Giraud's final words to the Americans summarized the situation perfectly. "Giraud will be a spectator in this affair."[11]

Reporting the outcome of their six-hour discussion to London and Washington, Eisenhower couldn't hide his frustration. "Eagle [Clark] and I are bitterly disappointed, principally because of the help Kingpin [Giraud] could have rendered except for his intense personal ambition and ego and because we know that the Combined Chiefs of Staff and the two governments were counting strongly on him for constructive assistance," wrote Ike.[12]

WHILE EISENHOWER AND CLARK grappled with Giraud, Dave King waited in Casablanca for news of the invasion. He made the rounds of his listening posts to no avail, ate a hurried dinner, and returned to the American consulate's annex.[13]

He also loaned a car to Lieutenant Merglin, a French army officer working for the resistance. Merglin had turned up early that morning asking if King knew of a car with a reserve gas tank that could travel to Fez and back. King did—his personal car—but was leery of loaning it out. After some hemming and hawing, Merglin confessed why he needed a car: Antoine Béthouart had tasked him with kidnapping General Georges Lascroux, the general officer commanding Morocco, to prevent him from calling up troops during the planned coup. Now that, thought King, was worth the loan of his automobile. King arranged for someone to drive his car, which he fondly called "Prudence," to a street behind French army division headquarters and leave it there with the keys in the ignition. The kidnapping operation went off without a hitch later that day.[14]

Staff Reid spent the afternoon setting up a courier service between the house where Ajax, Reid's radio man, operated the secret transmitter and the consulate. An auto mechanic known as "Captain X" agreed to serve as a courier between Reid and Ajax. Using a motorcycle and a full tank of gas, Captain X would bring the messages that Ajax received to Reid for decoding and deliver any coded messages in need of transmission back to Ajax. Worried about his safety, Reid provided Captain X with grenades and sidearms for protection. To get Ajax through the night, Reid supplied sandwiches, a .45 with two clips, a flashlight, and extra candles. As darkness approached, Reid moved his operation from his secret lair in the basement to the second floor of the consulate. He no longer needed to conceal his activities.[15]

As THE CLOCK TICKED past 8:30 p.m., the words King longed to hear drifted out of the radio. "Robert is on time."

The Americans would be coming ashore at 4:00 a.m.[16]

King dispatched one of Béthouart's men to convey the news to the general. At around 9:30 p.m., another message delivered via the BBC indicated the invasion would be delayed by an hour.

When he tried to personally deliver the news to Béthouart—and catch a ride to Rabat—King discovered the general had already left. Béthouart's staff, however, assured him that plans had been made for Casablanca. General Raymond Desré, Béthouart's old friend, now commanded the city. He gave his word of honor that he would carry out Béthouart's plans, should anything happen to him.[17]

While King chased after Béthouart, Michel Despax slipped off to inform Captain Albert Breitel, who commanded the Garde mobile, of the impending American invasion. Breitel had been charged with arresting the German Armistice Commission, a mission he would relish, as Gestapo head Theodor Auer had lodged numerous complaints against him, jeopardizing his job and his life. Despax also spread the word among the resistance cells he and King had worked with in Casablanca.

Upon returning to the American consulate after his futile attempt to rendezvous with Béthouart, King decided the moment had finally arrived to tell Consul General H. Earle Russell about the impending invasion. He had loathed keeping the consul in the dark for so long, especially given Russell's support for the vice consuls' orders, but orders were orders. Russell wasn't to know until the very last minute.

The consul general took the news well—he was more excited about the invasion than angry over any affront to his ego. King apologized for not telling him sooner, as he knew Russell would have liked to get his wife, Josephine, out of harm's way.

"That's all right, Mr. King," Russell told him. "Mrs. Russell and I have been through a lot together, and I don't think she'd go anyway."[18]

35

The Best Laid Plans

I N THE AFTERMATH OF HIS MEETING WITH DAVE KING, ANTOINE Béthouart had methodically and carefully organized the men he knew to be loyal to him and sympathetic to the Allied cause. Men who had said in hushed conversations that they would support the Allies if they landed in North Africa now had a choice: to cower or to act. Béthouart lived in terror of his plans coming to light. The more people who knew, the harder the secret was to keep—especially when it involved a coup d'état.

An envoy flew to Marrakech to make certain General Henry Martin, who commanded the air base and the district, received a briefing on the impending invasion. Colonel Joseph Magnan, who commanded Rabat's colonial infantry regiment, received a summons to Casablanca. Magnan burst with happiness when he learned of the plans. When he informed the officers of his regiment of their charge—they would surround the Residency on the night of the invasion—not a single man objected.[1] Béthouart also recruited General André Dody, commander at Meknès, and General Auguste Lahoulle, commander of the French air force in Morocco. Béthouart couldn't, however, depend on assistance from his naval colleagues, as the French navy remained firmly pro-Vichy. To them, he said nothing.

Béthouart's plan hinged on the Americans' storming the beaches at 2:00 a.m. in Rabat—jeopardizing its success from the outset. Either King's message about the new start time failed to reach him or he ignored the information. Béthouart also believed the Americans would revise their invasion plans based on his recommendations. As a seasoned soldier, he knew the folly of altering a massive operation at the last moment. Yet his hubris convinced him that the Americans would come ashore at Rabat.

As the clock closed in on 2:00 a.m., Béthouart set his plan in motion. He ordered Colonel Magnan to deploy his colonial troops around the Residency. Then, the phone line from the Residency to the outside world was cut. Béthouart and his band of resistors believed they had trapped Charles Noguès inside with no way to call for reinforcements.[2]

Next, a letter delivered to Noguès informed him of the Allied invasion. Béthouart wanted Noguès's diplomatic chief or his military chief to bring the missive to the resident-general, but one wasn't home and the other refused. Instead, the task fell to Captain Guy de Verthamon, who also happened to be Madame Noguès's nephew. Before Verthamon departed to make his momentous delivery, Béthouart told him, "If you fail, it will be a catastrophe for Morocco and also for France." Verthamon understood his mission—and was willing to suffer the wrath of his uncle.

At 2:00 a.m., Verthamon entered the Residency and threaded his way through darkened corridors. His boots echoed in the quiet gloom as he transitioned from tile to plush Oriental rugs and back again. After rousting Noguès from sleep, Verthamon gave him Béthouart's letter. At the same moment, Vice Admiral François Michelier in Casablanca also received a copy.[3]

The letter informed Noguès of the Allied invasion of North Africa and the imminent arrival of the Americans off the coast of Rabat and elsewhere in Morocco. Acting under Henri Giraud's orders, Béthouart was assuming command of Morocco's military forces. He urged Noguès to join the Allied cause. "I would be infinitely grateful if you would give me your support," wrote Béthouart. To prove it wasn't a hoax, Béthouart included copies of letters between Giraud and Robert Murphy. Having sworn to protect Morocco from all invaders, Béthouart had just committed an act of treason. In Noguès's eyes, he had also done something far more unforgiveable: Béthouart had betrayed the French army, its traditions, and his comrades. The first made him a misguided traitor; the second rendered him detestable.

Noguès found Béthouart's claims farcical. The Americans lacked the transport capabilities to invade North Africa. And everyone knew it was lunacy to conduct amphibious operations along the Atlantic coast during fall and winter. The tides and weather would rip transport crafts to pieces. Béthouart's recklessness enraged Noguès. If French forces appeared weak, the Moroccans might decide to stage another uprising. But most of all, Noguès worried what Hitler and his advisors in Berlin would think. If the Americans landed in Morocco and the French didn't mount a defense, Germany would have cause to attack. A German occupation of Morocco was the last thing Noguès wanted.[4]

He also faced another immediate problem: Morocco's coastal defenses had gone into hibernation. With the onset of autumn, a portion of the troops that guarded the coastline in the spring and summer now resided in winter barracks in Meknès, Fez, and Taza. A recent transfer of troops to Dakar had also depleted Morocco's overall strength. Vichy's planners had believed that any Allied assault in Africa before the spring of 1943 would occur in West Africa.[5]

Using a secret phone—one that neither Béthouart nor King's contact at the phone company knew about—Noguès called Michelier. The admiral reported that he too had received notice of Béthouart's misguided plans. Michelier, however, assured him that no foreign ships floated off the coast of Morocco.[6] Even though Noguès's brain screamed that Béthouart, one of his most trusted officers, had been duped, years of training as a soldier told him that he could not ignore the possibility of an American invasion.

At 2:10 a.m., Noguès ordered a general alert.[7]

Telegrams went out to Algeria and Tunisia to inquire about the imaginary Allied invasion. The commanders of French military forces at Meknès and Marrakech also received orders to disregard any instructions received from Béthouart. Noguès cautioned them against participating in what he regarded as a "military mutiny."[8]

An hour later, the telegraph machine spit out the bad news: the Allies had attacked Algiers. Next came word of Allied troops coming ashore at Oran. Admiral Jean-François Darlan, in Algiers to visit his dying son, cabled a message vowing to fight and defend North Africa from the Allies.

Noguès, however, remained puzzled. If the Allies were invading Algeria, surely they were also attacking Morocco. He asked Michelier for another update. The admiral reported that there wasn't "a single ship within 100 kilometers of the Moroccan coast."[9]

At the very moment Michelier told Noguès the American invasion force did not exist, the USS *Massachusetts* made a ninety-degree turn to prevent the French spotters combing the waters off the coast from seeing her.[10]

STAFF REID SPENT THE evening holed up on the second floor of the American consulate in Casablanca, decoding messages. Earle Russell found him there at around 11:00 p.m. and announced that he knew about the invasion. The consul general quickly forgave Reid for keeping the news from him. Soon they were dining on a midnight supper of sandwiches, fruit, and coffee delivered by Josephine Russell. She'd also been let in on the secret.

They pulled the blinds of the consulate tight to hide the lights burning late but left the windows cracked to allow the sounds of the city—and any

rumblings of military action—to filter in. A half hour before midnight, the
trio heard the night watchman challenge Russell M. Brooks, the consulate's
second in command, at the front gate. A few minutes later, Brooks, sporting
a white dinner jacket, appeared in the doorway of the office that had become
an impromptu command center.

"What in the hell kind of a midnight party is this being pulled off in the
office here?" asked Brooks. He raised his eyebrows and gave Russell a knowing look. "Mr. Russell, I am surprised to see you and your wife engaged in
this nocturnal spree. Isn't this stretching it a little bit at a consular post? Why
the candles? Why these side-arms and all my desk-pencils with the points
broken!!?"

Russell told Brooks to sit down, poured him a glass of whiskey, and told
him about the invasion. After draining the glass, Brooks announced that he
needed to warn his wife. He couldn't call with the news, so he'd have to go
home. Russell and Reid vetoed that idea, going so far as to hold him down in
his chair. Brooks's wife, a flamboyant French woman, loved to gossip, and all
of Casablanca would know of the Americans' arrival before dawn.

Around 1:00 a.m., Captain X, serving as Reid's courier, appeared at the
consulate on foot, having left his motorcycle a few blocks away so as not to
attract attention. He'd learned from a reliable source that members of the
Service d'ordre légionnaire (SOL), the French fascist organization, planned
to raid the consulate in the next few hours. Reid immediately devised a plan
of defense. He handed Douglas Read, another consulate staff member, a .45
revolver and told him to cover the main entrance from a window on the left.
Reid would cover the entrance from the right, while Brooks hurled grenades
at the attacking SOL members.[11]

Russell, however, put a stop to the scheme. If the SOL—or the French
army—stormed the consulate, resistance would likely get them killed. The
building wasn't designed as a bunker, and they would be outnumbered. In
the event of an attack, they all agreed to surrender rather than fire on French
troops or civilians. Even so, they carried sidearms "just in case."[12]

Shortly after 2:00 a.m., Ernest Mayer arrived to pick up Reid for the drive
to the Residency in Rabat to deliver Franklin Roosevelt's letters to Noguès
and the sultan.[13] Russell again intervened, arguing that Reid's time would be
better spent manning his radio than spending two hours in a car. "Nobody
but you knows the codes and if some important directive came through in
your absence and you never returned, we would be at a big disadvantage,"
he told Reid. Having opposed the assignment from the beginning, Reid consented to stay, provided Russell assumed full responsibility for overriding

Robert Murphy's orders.[14] Russell agreed and tasked Philip H. Bagby, another vice consul, with accompanying Mayer.

As Mayer and Bagby drove north, Reid, Russell, and the others kept watch at the consulate, alternating black coffee with an occasional slug of whiskey to stay awake. A little after 3:00 a.m., dozens of armed men on bicycles appeared outside the consulate's walls. On their left arms, they wore white brassards emblazoned with the letters "SOL," signaling their allegiance to the fascist group. They rode round and round the consulate but never launched an attack.[15]

The stream of bicycles paled in comparison to the crush of military vehicles that soon overtook the boulevards on either side of the consulate. Car after car of military-grade Citroens raced by, roaring their engines as they headed for the port and army barracks. Motorcycles zoomed past too, along with trucks bursting with soldiers. With space at a premium, some officers clung to the sides of cars, feet perched precariously on the running boards. As the procession grew, shutters along the facing streets popped open and heads appeared in windows as residents searched for the reason their sleep had been ruined.

As they stood in the garden of the consulate watching French forces mobilize around them, the Americans began to understand that the French intended to fight. They would not greet the American troops coming ashore as liberators. For Reid, the sight of headlights catching the metal of bayonets already affixed to the end of French guns brought back memories of the Great War and all its carnage. He fought back a choking sensation.[16]

Before dawn, they built a fire in one of the offices, closed the windows to prevent the smoke from leaking out, and burned the strip codes used to encrypt and decrypt messages, instructions, and charts.[17]

BÉTHOUART HAD TOLD THE Americans to come ashore in Rabat, and so that's what he believed they would do. But the Americans hadn't appeared. No task force of destroyers and aircraft carriers floated off the coast. No troops stormed the beaches. Every minute that ticked by without their arrival jeopardized his coup d'état and gave Noguès the advantage.

At around 4:00 a.m., Vice Consuls Mayer and Bagby arrived in Rabat to deliver Roosevelt's letters to Noguès and the sultan. Going first to Béthouart's headquarters to determine the progress of the coup, they learned that Noguès remained inside the Residency and refused to communicate with Béthouart or anyone involved.

Béthouart decided to drive the Americans to the Residency himself in the event that Noguès actually showed his face. With his men in control of the streets around the Residency, they had no trouble driving up to the front gate. Bagby and Mayer informed the guard of their mission and asked to see Noguès. The guard refused them entry. Instead, a few minutes later, Robert du Gardier, Noguès's diplomatic chief, appeared. Through the bars, Mayer and Bagby explained their mission. Again, they were refused entry. Du Gardier, however, agreed to take possession of the letters from Roosevelt. Before he retreated into the Residency, he conveyed one final message to the Americans at the gate. Noguès intended to "defend Morocco against all comers."[18]

Shortly after 6:00 a.m., with no sign of the American troops in Rabat, Béthouart and his men were arrested.[19]

36

Safi

JUST AFTER 6:00 A.M. ON NOVEMBER 7, THE SOUTHERN ATTACK Group, commanded by Rear Admiral Lyal Davidson, peeled away from the main American convoy. With the light cruiser *Philadelphia* in the lead, the complement of twenty-four ships formed into three columns, their engines humming at ten knots as they sailed southwest on a course of 156 degrees true. Shortly after 7:30 a.m., *Philadelphia* relinquished her leadership duties, passing them to the battleship *New York*, which hoisted its guide flag against the hazy morning sky.[1]

The Southern Attack Group was headed for Safi, a sleepy port town of 26,000 that lay 150 miles south of Casablanca. The Americans chose Safi because the design of its harbor made it possible to offload the fifty-one Sherman tanks that George Patton had transported across the Atlantic. Weighing 68,800 pounds each, the tanks couldn't be brought ashore just anywhere. The only other suitable port was Casablanca—and Patton expected he would need the tanks' mobile firepower to take the city. The Americans also needed to unload Major General Ernest Harmon and his 6,428 officers and men. Once they secured Safi, Harmon and his force would head north to rendezvous with Patton for the assault on Casablanca.[2]

Seizing Safi would also help the Americans secure southern Morocco. A main railway line and highway ran ninety-five miles southeast from Safi to Marrakech, home to an airbase and a French army installation. With Safi in American hands, the French would find it difficult to send reinforcements north.[3]

As the Southern Attack Group continued its southwesterly course, a ship materialized on the horizon shortly after 10 a.m. When the mystery boat failed to answer a series of radio hails, the destroyer *Quick* went to investigate. Much to Davidson's relief, the ship wasn't French or German, just a Finnish fishing vessel with a broken radio and a startled crew. The Americans had maintained the element of surprise for the moment.

THE AMERICANS WEREN'T THE first to approach Safi from the sea. In the early sixteenth century, Portugal attempted to lay claim to the region, building a squat cylindrical stone kasbah—or fort—to protect its trading colony. The Portuguese were ousted after three decades, but the fort endured, standing guard over the harbor from its perch on the rocky cliffs.[4] When the French took over Morocco, they expanded Safi's harbor to accommodate the large ships required to export phosphates.[5] Along with the new three-hundred-yard-long Phosphate Pier, the French built a mile-long jetty that extended northwest from the shore. The resulting triangular-shaped breakwater provided ships with shelter from the tumultuous Atlantic, while making it easy to close and guard the port. All ships entering the harbor had to pass through a channel five hundred feet wide.[6]

The Portuguese didn't situate the kasbah overlooking the port simply for the ocean view. Its planners knew that shore batteries—groups of guns placed to allow them to fire into the harbor and out to sea—could menace any invading naval force. Five hundred years later, the principle still held, which is why the French installed heavy artillery to guard the port.

Despite intelligence reports suggesting Safi was garrisoned with 1,000 troops, Major François Deuve only possessed 450 men and fifteen obsolete light tanks with which to defend the town. But while Safi's coastal defenses harassed the Americans, Deuve could call up reinforcements from Marrakech. Within ten hours, another 1,400 cavalry and 2,000 infantry troops, along with tanks and armored cars, could arrive.[7] If the Americans wanted to seize the port, establish control of the docks, and clear the French from the beachhead, they had to work fast.[8]

A LITTLE BEFORE MIDNIGHT, the Southern Attack Group queued up eight miles off Safi, the pitch-black ocean shrouding its presence. Scattered lights to the east hinted at a city deep in slumber. Six transport ships formed a line parallel with the coast, while *New York*, *Philadelphia*, and ten destroyers fanned out to create a protective net around them.[9]

Onboard the transport ships, the process of unloading the men began as the clock hands ticked into the early hours of November 8. The crews

FIGURE 36.1. The narrow entrance to the port at Safi. *Naval History and Heritage Command*

worked with as little light as possible so as not to give away the American fleet. Landing craft were hoisted over the side and down into the water. The motors powering the winches echoed through the night, but the hum failed to carry to the coast. Once the boats were in position, nets were thrown over the side of the ship. On the journey across the Atlantic, the troops practiced climbing up and down the nets, but the men hadn't made the descent in the dark with sixty-pound packs strapped to their backs while dealing with preinvasion jitters. As delays unloading the men and equipment accumulated, it became clear to Major General Harmon that he would have to push H-hour, the time at which the transports departed for the beaches, from 3:30 a.m. to 4:00 a.m.[10]

While the troops transferred to the landing craft, a team of five men from the 47th Infantry departed the submarine *Barb* on a mission to locate the bell buoy marking the edge of Safi's breakwater. From their perch at the bell buoy, the team would use infrared flashlights to direct the ships carrying the amphibious assault troops through the narrow harbor opening. A miscalculation by the *Barb*'s captain resulted in the team's being launched miles from their target, forcing them to spend the next few hours paddling their way toward the shore. With the team from the 47th Infantry out of position, the job of guiding the ships into the port fell to Ensign John J. Bell after his own mis-adventure. Around 2:00 a.m., Bell was dispatched from the destroyer *Harris* in a rubber boat to rendezvous with *Barb* to collect intelligence from her re-connaissance of one of the landing beaches. Unable to find the submarine, he steered his rubber boat toward the bell buoy, reaching it just after 4:00 a.m.[11]

As Bell got his bearings, the aged destroyer *Bernadou* sailed south to-ward Safi's harbor, hugging the cliff walls to avoid detection. As she closed on the narrow opening, the signal "VH" flashed from the shore. *Bernadou* was being challenged. Not knowing what the signal meant or the correct response, the captain guessed and sent the same signal back. As the minutes ticked by without a rumble from French defenses, it seemed the signal had been accepted. But when *Bernadou* sailed through the mouth of the harbor, the French opened fire, lobbing 75-mm shells from the battery at Front de Mer and spraying a cloud of bullets from the machine-gun nests burrowed in the cliffs.[12]

Bernadou responded by shooting a flare heavenward, unfurling an Amer-ican flag across the night sky. The glow cast by the flare only illuminated the *Cole*, sitting outside the breakwater. The rest of the Southern Attack Group, miles from the coast, remained shrouded in darkness.[13] As the flag vanished, the embers forming the Stars and Stripes flaming out, the Americans won-dered, would the French continue to fight once they knew who was there? Dwight Eisenhower had ordered American forces not to fire until fired upon. He wanted to give the French every opportunity to lay down their weapons and join the Allied cause. But once fired upon, the Americans were to fight until Morocco was theirs.

The French answered with a star shell flare, which temporarily saturated the harbor and coast with brilliant light. The French admiralty had alerted Major Deuve that the enemy might be lurking off the coast, sending a signal from Casablanca at 2:30 a.m. saying "Danger," followed by "Alert" at 3:27 a.m. But without any way to constantly flood the harbor with light, Deuve could only guess at what lay in wait in the darkness. Now the flare showed the outlines of the first wave of American landing craft as they headed toward beaches. Further out, the ships of the Southern Attack Group rocked on the swells. As darkness reclaimed the harbor, white tendrils arched through the sky as rounds fired from Batterie la Railleuse whistled toward the American destroyer *Mervine*.[14]

"Batter up!" barked the radios of the Southern Attack Group, signaling that the Americans had been fired upon. At 4:39 a.m., Rear Admiral David-son gave the order to unleash the force of the American fleet: "Play ball!" *Philadelphia* and *New York* trained their sights on Batterie la Railleuse, spitting fire into the cool morning air as their 6- and 14-inch guns discharged their rounds.[15]

The American barrage was defensive but also intended to divert French attention from the harbor, where *Bernadou* continued her run, barreling past the Phosphate Pier. To clear her way forward, the destroyer sprayed the fairway, dock, and kasbah with her 20-mm and 3-inch guns, generating a cloud of smoke, masonry, and metal.[16] At 4:45 a.m., *Bernadou* glided on to the Petite Jettée. Nets dropped from the port bow, allowing the men of Company K, 47th Infantry, to climb down and become the first American troops to set foot on Moroccan soil. Within minutes they were exchanging gunfire with the French Foreign Legion.[17]

"*Cole! Cole!* Come in!" squawked the radio, urging the other American assault destroyer to enter the port. After almost missing the entrance in the dark, *Cole* found her way to her berth, turning the rest of Company K, specially trained in night fighting, loose on Safi.[18]

By 5:30 a.m., American landing craft reached the beaches north of the port, dispersing men with sea legs and sweaty palms onto the dark coast. As they advanced from the beaches, French and Moroccan troops attempted to pick off the shadowy figures with machine-gun bursts and sniper fire.[19]

While another wave of troops and equipment streamed toward the coast, *New York* zigzagged as it dodged rounds from Batterie la Railleuse. The French targeted the thirty-year-old ship, starting with a salvo at 6:40 a.m. Over the next hour and twenty minutes, *New York* lobbed sixty 14-inch rounds up the cliff at the battery, which returned three hundred of its own smaller caliber. At around 8:00 a.m., *New York* landed an indirect hit—the round bounced from the ground into the fire-control station—killing the men inside. Within an hour, the battery ceased firing, and American troops spiked the guns later that morning. By 11:00 a.m., all of Safi's batteries were silent.[20]

At 9:20 a.m., more American troops came ashore eight miles south of the city. They landed unopposed except for strafing of the second wave of boats by a lone French plane. Despite fears that the French air force would scramble from the base at Marrakech, the skies remained clear for the rest of the day.[21]

BY MID-MORNING, THE AMERICANS controlled Safi's port, telephone exchange, post office, and oil storage tanks. French snipers, however, continued to harass the landing craft as they made the beaches. When American troops moved into town, they encountered stiff resistance from the barracks that served as the headquarters for the local garrison. Instead of leveling the compound, the Americans opted for isolation and intimidation, surrounding and training heavy artillery on the barracks. Eisenhower wanted as many French troops kept alive as possible—so they could live to fight another day for the Allies.[22]

While they worked their way through Safi block by block, the American soldiers became objects of fascination for the local population. Moroccan men gathered to watch the exchange of shells between the batteries and ships. They clustered on street corners to follow the fighting between American troops and the French Foreign Legion, seemingly unafraid of the bullets whizzing past. In the afternoon, men gathered on the beaches, offering to help unload landing craft, exchanging their backs and brawn for a cigarette or a can of food. The enterprising among them spirited off rations and ammunition when the Americans weren't looking.[23]

At 1:30 p.m., the seatrain *Lakehurst* sailed into Safi's harbor, dropping anchor at the Merchandise Pier. Within ten minutes, its crew had unloaded its first vehicle. Over the next forty-two hours, the crew worked nonstop to offload 169 vehicles, including Harmon's fifty-one tanks.[24] As the mechanics worked their magic, the tanks that Patton so badly wanted for the assault on Casablanca rumbled to life on the dock. A few hours later, the cargo ship *Titania* docked at the Phosphate Pier. As the crews of both ships moved supplies and matériel from the hold and onto the docks, French snipers, camped out on a bluff east of the port, fired on them intermittently, bouncing bullets off the surrounding buildings and corrugated roofs.[25]

Realizing that he could no longer hold out against the Americans swarming his town, Major Deuve surrendered Safi at 3:30 p.m. The Americans had taken the town in eleven hours with minimal casualties. Ten men died and seventy-five were wounded. Rear Admiral Davidson would attribute the success of the landing to "Divine Providence, good weather, surprise, retention of the initiative, and accurate and overpowering gunnery."[26]

Now Major General Harmon and his men just had to get to Casablanca.

37

Fédala

A LITTLE AFTER MIDNIGHT ON NOVEMBER 8, 165 MILES UP THE coast from Safi, the Center Attack Group moved into position eight miles off the coast of Fédala. Casablanca's harbor was too well guarded to attempt a frontal assault, so the Americans were coming ashore twelve miles north of the city. Intermittent rain and high winds rocked the transport ships as they tried to maintain their four-row, four-column formation. The depth of the ocean floor prevented the ships from dropping anchor, forcing them to heave to now and again to maintain their position.[1]

The transports closest to the coast—*Wood*, *Jefferson*, *Carroll*, and *Dickman*—disembarked their men first, lowering landing craft down onto the heavy swells.[2] The churning ocean swung the nets out from the sides of the ships, making it difficult for the men, their legs stiff from the long, confined voyage, to find the next rung down. Some men prayed and some cursed as they took the last long step, willing their feet to find the boat waiting below.[3]

Despite their jitters, the men were ready. "A spirit of restlessness and subdued eagerness was in evidence," wrote the executive officer of the destroyer *Wilkes*. "All expressed their desire for action. None had any doubt as to our success in overcoming any opposition. It was a good sign."[4]

As the landing craft went into the water, the radios of the Center Attack Group started picking up the broadcasts announcing the Allied invasion. Beginning at 1:30 a.m., the BBC broadcast messages every half hour, in English and French, from Dwight Eisenhower and Franklin Roosevelt. Eisenhower urged the French armed forces not to fight. To signal their intention not to do so, the French should point their coastal searchlights into the night sky; after dawn, they should fly the French tricolor and the American flag, one above the other. Roosevelt spoke to the people of North Africa, his French fine-tuned by the BBC sound engineers to sound less schoolboyish and more stately. He assured listeners, "We come among you solely to destroy your enemies and not to harm you." He begged them not to obstruct Allied efforts.[5]

As the voices of their commanding officer and commander in chief floated through the night, Admiral Kent Hewitt and General George S. Patton resigned themselves to the French being alerted to their presence. Patton had fought to have the broadcasts delayed, but Eisenhower refused. Allied troops were coming ashore at Algiers and Oran in advance of the Moroccan invasion. Knowing the broadcast was coming didn't stop Patton from losing his temper and mimicking Roosevelt's bad French.[6] They scanned the coast, hoping to see the searchlights pointed high into the sky. But the lights remained off, leaving the Center Attack Group to do its work in the dark.

OF THE THREE LANDING beaches in Morocco, Fédala served as the lynchpin of the American invasion. Patton intended to land the bulk of his force there for the attack on Casablanca. The battle plan called for 19,870 troops and officers, 1,701 vehicles, and 15,000 tons of supplies, off-loaded over a span of four days. If Center Group floundered—or failed—the Moroccan expedition would be a bust.

The Americans chose Fédala for its proximity to Casablanca. The town of 16,000 lay nestled in the southern sweep of a bay formed by the headland of Cherqui at the top and Cape Fédala at the bottom. The French had turned the fishing port into Morocco's primary petroleum storage facility, building twenty massive tanks to house the nation's oil supply.[7] Fédala was also known as a resort town, an easy drive or train ride from Rabat or Casablanca for a short getaway, where visitors could sink their toes in the sand, gamble in the oceanfront casino, play a round or two of golf, place a bet at the racetrack, and summon room service at the European-style Hôtel Miramar.[8] The coastal road and railroad line, running north to Rabat and south to Casablanca, formed the eastern edge of the town.

Intent on guarding their oil supply, the French installed a set of coastal defenses that could menace the American troops coming ashore. Cape Fédala had two 75-mm guns capable of firing rounds 9,000 yards. At Batterie du Port, four 100-mm guns could lob rounds 15,400 yards. On the Cherqui headland at the top of the bay, the French installed at Batterie du Pont Blondin four 138.6-mm (5.4-inch) guns, which could hit a target 20,000 yards away. For extra protection, there were also antiaircraft batteries next to and on the golf course.[9]

FIGURE 37.1. One of the landing beaches at Fédala after the first day, littered with boats and equipment smashed by the surf. *Naval History and Heritage Command*

As LANDING CRAFT FILLED the Atlantic, three scout boats, each carrying a five-man team equipped with infrared flashlights, ventured ahead to mark the landing zones.[10] Like others before them, the Americans were coming to Fédala for the beaches, landing at four points along the two-and-half-mile coastline that stretched from Cape Fédala to Batterie du Pont Blondin.[11]

The scout parties guided the first wave of boats to shore between 5:15 and 5:25 a.m.[12] As the landing craft rode the waves, the coastal searchlights snapped on, their white beams cutting through the violet morning sky.[13] The lights pointed up for a moment—and then fell to earth, frantically searching the beaches and the ocean beyond. The beams found the landing craft closing in on the beaches, the men struggling with their packs as they stepped onto waterlogged sand, and transports queued up to deliver more men. The beams roamed for five minutes before a burst of machine-gun fire from an American armed support boat shattered the searchlights and plunged the coast back into darkness.[14]

The French now knew the Americans were there.

With dawn rapidly approaching, the Americans redoubled their efforts, hoping to secure the beaches before the vanishing darkness turned soldiers from ghostly figures into solid targets. By sunrise at 6:55 a.m., the Americans had landed 3,500 troops and secured the beach.[15]

The men in this early wave had the job of silencing the coastal batteries. As long as these were active, they endangered the transports and men coming ashore. One battalion landing team was tasked with capturing Batterie du Pont Blondin, located east of the Nefifikh river. Another was charged with taking out the batteries on Cape Fédala. To ensure American airplanes would not be harassed, a reconnaissance team would seize the antiaircraft batteries adjacent to the golf course. And should the French get any ideas about reinforcing Fédala, they would find the roads and bridges to the city occupied by an American battalion.[16]

As dawn broke, the French opened fire—from a machine-gun battery at Cape Fédala, from the main coastal battery, from the battery at Pont Blondin—aiming for the scout boats, landing craft, and transports. Commander E. R. Durgin, watching the assault from the bridge of the *Wilkes*, radioed, "Firing from Fédala and Sherki. BATTER UP!"

That was all Captain Robert Emmet, commander of Center Group, needed to order, "Play ball!"[17] Starting at 6:20 a.m., *Brooklyn*'s 6-inch guns breathed fire and smoke as they hurled 757 rounds over eighty-five minutes at Batterie du Pont Blondin. When the battalion landing team moved in to seize the battery, they found the French garrison huddled in the latrine, the only building still standing.[18] Meanwhile, *Wilkes* and *Bristol* took out Batterie du Port, as *Augusta* provided covering fire.[19]

Silencing the battery at Cape Fédala proved more of a challenge. The Americans wanted to preserve whatever oil remained in the tanks, so they couldn't use the same tactics deployed by *Brooklyn*. Over the course of the morning, the Americans fired on the battery, with *Wilkes*, *Swanson*, and *Ludlow* teaming up and working in conjunction with *Bristol*, *Edison*, and *Boyle*. Four hours later, the battery fell silent.[20] Despite efforts not to bomb the oil storage tanks, at least one took a hit early in the morning, coating the shoreline in a layer of heavy black smoke that mixed with the morning fog.[21]

Hoping the French would see reason, Patton tasked Colonel William H. Wilbur, a Francophile West Point graduate, with delivering a letter to General Antione Béthouart, who commanded the Casablanca garrison, urging him to surrender. Word of Béthouart's attempted coup had not made it to Patton. Wilbur came ashore in one of the first waves, surviving French fire, only to find his jeep unusable. Commandeering a small car, he made his way south to French lines, flying a white flag of truce to mark him as friendly. Granted safe passage by a French officer, Wilbur continued on to Casablanca. As he made his way through the city, people waved and cheered as they noticed the other flag he carried with him: the Stars and Stripes.

When Wilbur failed to find Béthouart at army headquarters, he ventured on to the Admiralty, where he discovered the courtyard stacked with bloody French marines, casualties of the American assault. He left empty-handed. The French weren't ready to negotiate.[22] After making his way back to American lines, Wilbur helped direct the attack on the battery at Cape Fédala.[23]

With the Americans making steady progress, Patton and his staff made plans to leave *Augusta* and go ashore at 8 a.m. In preparation, their gear was loaded into a landing craft, which was hoisted on a crane, ready to be lowered into the sea below at a moment's notice. As the naval action heated up, Patton sent an orderly to retrieve his beloved white-handled pistols from the boat. A few minutes later, *Augusta* opened fire on the French ships emerging from Casablanca's harbor. "The first blast from the rear turret blew the leading boat to hell and we lost all our things except my pistols," wrote Patton in his diary.

With his gear at the bottom of the Atlantic, Patton remained on *Augusta*'s bridge, with a front-row seat for the only full-scale naval battle in the European theater during the war.[24]

38

Off the Coast of Casablanca

THE NAVAL BATTLE OF CASABLANCA BEGAN WITH AIRPLANES. AT 6:15 a.m., thirty miles northwest of the city, Fighter Squadron 9 began launching Grumman F4F Wildcats, one by one, off the decks of the *Ranger*. As each engine fired, the propeller at the front of the plane spun to life, drawing circles in the hazy morning air. After being catapulted forward, the Wildcats broke the end of the deck, briefly sinking toward the ocean, before rising up to rendezvous with the rest of the squadron. Once assembled in the air, the squadron headed northeast up the coast to Rabat and Salé to bomb the airfields, destroying seven planes and fourteen bombers belonging to the French air force.[1]

Fighter Squadron 41 climbed into the sky next, heading for Cazes airfield, five miles outside Casablanca. The French were waiting for them, having scrambled sixteen planes. A dogfight broke out as planes from both sides climbed, turned, dived to avoid machine-gun fire, and fought for optimal position for the perfect shot. The French lost eight planes in the air and another fourteen on the ground.[2]

At 7:00 a.m., Dauntless dive-bombers, also launched from the *Ranger*, arrived in the sky over Casablanca. The boom-boom of the antiaircraft batteries in the harbor greeted their arrival, dotting the sky with small clouds of black smoke. The bombers dodged the shells as they headed for the submarine pens and French admiralty buildings that lined the port, their locations carefully noted after months of reconnaissance by the Office of Strategic Services.[3] Three submarines sank at their moorings; the remaining eight got underway, commanded by their executive officers. Their captains perished when American bombs exploded on the docks.[4] The planes also blanketed

FIGURE 38.1. A Grumman F4F-4 Wildcat fighter takes off from USS *Ranger*. The Wildcats would target the port, French ships, and surrounding airfields. *Naval History and Heritage Command*

the commercial harbor, sinking ten ships and sending more than forty crew-members to a watery grave.[5]

While the American squadrons flew their sorties, the Covering Group—the battleship *Massachusetts*, heavy cruisers *Tuscaloosa* and *Wichita*, and four destroyers—moved in to prevent the French navy from leaving the harbor and to neutralize the shore batteries. Hoisting their battle ensigns—the Stars and Stripes to identify them as American—they pushed their engines toward twenty-five knots.[6]

For centuries, the white lighthouse at Point El Hank had announced to ships making their way along the Barbary Coast that they had found Casablanca. Now it served as the starting point for the Covering Group's sweep past the harbor. Just after 7:00 a.m., the American ships, guns at rest, sailed past Casablanca, waiting for the French to make the first salvo. The French had turned El Hank into a battery, stationing four 194-mm guns and four 138-mm guns there, but the American ships passed unmolested.[7]

A few minutes later, six rounds splashed 6,000 yards off *Massachu-setts*'s starboard bow, sending columns of water one hundred feet into the air. Since the armistice, the Americans and British had fretted that *Jean*

Bart, the formidable French battleship anchored in the harbor, would leave Casablanca and join the German navy. Now here she was, still moored but serving as a powerful battery, using her modern range-finding equipment to train her four 15-inch guns on the American ships.[8]

The salvo from *Jean Bart* was just what Admiral Robert C. Giffen needed to unleash the Covering Group on Casablanca. He picked up the radio and barked, "Play ball!" As the *Massachusetts* let go the first salvo, smoke and fire discharged from the barrels of her 16-inch guns as the shells took flight. The roar of the guns and their recoil shattered the windows on the bridge, forcing officers and sailors to duck to avoid the glass.[9]

Over the next half hour, the Covering Group loaded and unloaded its guns along the harbor and coast, turning back for another pass when it reached Fédala. The French returned fire, training their coastal batteries, along with the *Jean Bart*, on the American ships.

The *Jean Bart*, however, was no match for the *Massachusetts* and *Tuscaloosa*. Using her 16-inch guns, *Massachusetts* unfurled nine salvos of six to nine shots each. Five rounds hit *Jean Bart*: the first pierced an empty magazine, the second damaged the control station and made a hole in the hull below the waterline, and the third and fourth hit but failed to detonate. The fifth shell landed around 7:20 a.m., striking the forward turret, only to bounce off its mount and fly into the city. The French admiralty recovered the round and displayed it as a trophy at its headquarters. Although the shell didn't explode, it jammed the turret, silencing *Jean Bart*'s guns for the next eight hours. It had taken the Americans all of sixteen minutes to knock out the battleship.[10]

WHEN THE COVERING GROUP halted fire around 8:15 a.m. to turn and make another pass, the French used the lull to launch six destroyers—*Albatros*, *L'Alcyon*, *Brestois*, *Boulonnais*, *Fougueux*, and *Frondeur*—along with the superdestroyer *Milan*. While the ships left the harbor, *Milan*'s chaplain, having arrived too late to board, said a prayer for the men while shells exploded around him on the pier.

The French destroyers queued up in formation and sailed toward the area off Fédala where American troops continued to disembark from the transport ships. As the destroyers made their way northwest, Wildcats from the *Ranger* sprayed their bridges with bullets, killing or wounding senior officers. As medics tended injuries and chaplains pronounced last rights, the French continued to sail forward. At 8:30 a.m., they began shelling the American landing crafts, sinking one.[11]

Task force commander Admiral Kent Hewitt unleashed *Brooklyn*, *Augusta*, *Wilkes*, and *Swanson* on the French destroyers. An officer aboard one of the transports, helpless as the French advanced on his position, described the swarming of American ships as "the most beautiful sight he ever saw." As the Americans lobbed 5- and 6-inch rounds toward the French destroyers, those that fell short sent green and red splashes of water into the air. The rounds had been colored-coded for tracking purposes. The French returned fire, then retreated toward the harbor, obscuring their progress from American gun sights with a smoke screen.[12]

"I was on main deck just back of number two turret leaning on the rail when one [shell] hit so close that it splashed water all over me," wrote George Patton in his diary.[13] The splash covered his leather jacket in yellow film, residue from the dye packet included in the shell. When Patton's aide stepped forward to clean it off, the general grumbled, "Leave it there. This will stay on the #$%& jacket as long as I am able to wear it."[14]

As the clock struck 10 a.m., the battle reached a frenzy. The Covering Group made its way back east, putting it within range of two French destroyers. From five miles out, *Massachusetts* and *Tuscaloosa* scored hits on the *Fougueux*, sending the ship to the bottom of the ocean.[15] Four torpedoes carved shallow trenches through the blue water as they advanced on *Massachusetts*. Steering between them, *Massachusetts* escaped the assault, with one torpedo coming within fifteen feet of starboard. The torpedoes came next for *Tuscaloosa*, launched by *Méduse*, a French submarine plying the rocky depths outside the harbor. *Tuscaloosa* also steered clear.[16]

With the Covering Group dodging torpedoes, three French destroyers again headed for the American transports. *Brooklyn* moved to intercept them, dodging five torpedoes en route, while *Augusta* provided covering fire, but a wall of smoke obscured the French ships. *Brooklyn* and *Augusta* then found themselves under fire from the French destroyers, forcing them to sail figure eights and zigzags, anything but a straight line, to dodge the onslaught. As the French rounds missed, one after the other, red, yellow, and green columns of water erupted from the ocean.[17]

At 10:35 a.m., *Massachusetts* and *Tuscaloosa* joined the fray, firing on the *Boulonnais*. Forty-five minutes and eight 6-inch shells later, the battered French destroyer, having rolled onto its side, sank into the Atlantic.[18]

Around 11:00 a.m., *Augusta* and *Brooklyn* sent the *Primauguet* limping back to port with five hits below her waterline. *Milan*, hit at least five times, soon followed.[19] Next *Augusta* turned on *Brestois*, delivering blows that sent her slinking to the harbor jetty. As she listed at a twenty-degree angle, Wildcats from the *Ranger* sprayed her hull with bullets. With her crew unable to pump out the water seeping in through scores of tiny holes, *Brestois* sank just before midnight.[20]

Now only three French ships remained in service—*Frondeur*, *L'Alcyon*, and *Albatros*—while the Americans continued to operate at full force. At 11:15 a.m., French destroyers decided to focus their efforts on *Tuscaloosa* and *Wichita*, but the Americans put up a smoke screen. Unable to spot their targets, the French ships plied back and forth, waiting for the smoke to clear. *Wichita*, however, edged within range of the shore battery at El Hank and at 11:28 a.m. took a round. The shell destroyed living quarters on the second deck and left fourteen sailors in need of medical care. Ten minutes later, just as the fires had been put out, *Wichita* evaded three torpedoes. *Tuscaloosa* and *Wichita* inflicted damage too, sending *Frondeur* sulking back to port. The Wildcats finished her off, leaving the ship floating like a dead carcass in the harbor.

Meanwhile, *Augusta* squared off against *Albatros*. The French destroyer suffered two blows—taking one round on deck and one below the waterline—but continued to fire on *Augusta*. Bomber planes from the *Ranger* joined the fight, dodging the French destroyer's antiaircraft battery to deliver two bombs to its midsection. Water poured into *Albatros*'s fire room and one of her engine rooms. Another shell from *Augusta* destroyed the other engine room. *Albatros* was now dead in the water.

At 11:45 a.m., the fighting came to a halt, spurred by a piece of bad intelligence. American troops on shore at Fédala sent word that a cease-fire must be observed as they negotiated with the local French commander. As it turned out, the French commander had authority to surrender only Fédala—and Admiral François Michelier knew nothing about the cease-fire. During the lull, Hewitt sent *Tuscaloosa* and *Wichita* to investigate a report of an enemy ship south of Casablanca and intercept if necessary. The last thing the Americans needed was Vichy sending reinforcements from Dakar.[21]

Word also came from Safi that the Americans had taken the beach and the rest of the town would soon be in American hands. After enjoying lunch, Patton and his staff climbed into a landing craft and rode the waves to the beach off Fédala, finally setting foot on Moroccan soil shortly before 1:30 p.m.[22]

Around 1:00 p.m., a car packed with three Americans and one French prisoner raced south along the highway stretching from Fédala to Casablanca. Behind the wheel was marine Lieutenant Colonel Francis Rogers, one of

Admiral Hewitt's men. Next to him sat Colonel William Wilbur, who held a white flag out the window. Colonel Hogard "Hap" Gay, Patton's chief of staff, rode in the backseat, along with a prisoner, a French lieutenant colonel from the 11th Algerian Tirailleurs. Despite his wish to lay down arms, the French officer had no authority to surrender Fédala, even though the Americans controlled the city. The only person who could do that was General Antoine Béthouart.[23] Patton, therefore, had decided to try once more to convince the French to surrender. Having already been to Casablanca once that morning, Wilbur volunteered to go again.

To avoid becoming a French target, Rogers pushed the pedal to the floor, hitting seventy miles per hour on the speedometer. Wilbur, who had charge of the flag, struggled to keep their safe passage hoisted. Every five minutes he yelled at Rogers to ease up. "For Christ's sakes, Rogers, slow down—you're breaking my arm!"

As they barreled toward Casablanca, a French platoon with weapons trained on the car came into view on their left. Ahead of them, a French lieutenant stepped into the middle of the road, holding his hand up, shouting for them to stop. With a pistol pointed at his ribs, Rogers explained in his best French that they were headed into Casablanca to visit Béthouart. The lieutenant lowered his weapon, smiled, and offered a salute. "Go right ahead," he said.

Before they reached the center of Casablanca, they passed through another four barricades. At a checkpoint run by a company of Senegalese soldiers, the Americans turned over their weapons and ammunition. Rogers even had to relinquish his utility knife. Now they had only their wits and a white flag to see them through.

Unlike Wilbur, Rogers didn't have to ask for directions. He easily found his way to French military headquarters, aided by a 1938 visit to Casablanca and some preinvasion study of the city's layout. Upon arrival, they encountered a group of staff officers who were the picture of dejection. They relayed the news of General Béthouart's arrest and Admiral Michelier's assumption of supreme control of the city. The French army officers couldn't have surrendered if they'd wanted to.

One of the French officers agreed to escort the Americans to Admiralty headquarters. When they arrived at around 2:00 p.m., Rogers spoke with the guard on duty. The guard was a marine. Rogers was a marine. Next thing they knew, the French marine left to fetch the officer of the day, who in turn disappeared back into headquarters to deliver news of their mission to Michelier and his staff.

Within a few minutes, a French lieutenant commander appeared. Upon coming within speaking range of the Americans, he snapped to attention, offered a salute, and declared that Michelier wanted nothing to do with them. Rogers and Wilbur attempted to change his mind. Surely the admiral knew of their superior position, the arrival of American troops, and their overwhelming naval force? Still standing at attention, the French lieutenant commander replied, "The Admiral absolutely refuses to have anything to do with you." As soon as the words left his mouth, the boom of a salvo from El Hank rattled the headquarters. The timing couldn't have been better. The lieutenant commander's eyes brightened. "Voilà votre réponse!"[24]

Realizing the futility of arguing, the Americans returned to their car and started back toward Fédala, dropping the French army captain off at his headquarters along the way. At the barricade manned by the Senegalese troops, they reclaimed their weapons. Upon arriving in Fédala, Rogers caught a boat out to *Augusta* and personally relayed the details of the mission to Hewitt. Grabbing a map of the harbor, a "distinctly annoyed" Hewitt asked Rogers to indicate which building housed the Admiralty. Hewitt made it a primary target for his dive-bombers.[25]

As THE SUN CLIMBED high into the autumn sky, a haze of black smoke lay over Casablanca and the surrounding ocean. A light breeze blew but could do little to clear the soot-saturated air.

Admiral Michelier used the respite to organize a third sortie, sending out three untested ships: *La Grandière*, an *aviso-colonial* (a modern-day sloop), and two *aviso-drageuers* (coastal-patrol minesweepers). At 12:45 p.m., the French ships headed in the direction of the transports bringing American troops ashore. At the same time, two new French destroyers, *Tempête* and *Simoun*, sailed back and forth in the harbor entrance, taunting the Americans to brave El Hank's wrath and take a shot at them.[26]

From Hewitt's vantage point on the bridge of the *Augusta*, the French looked poised once again to menace the American transports still sending men ashore at Fédala. He ordered *Augusta* and *Brooklyn* to close in on the three French ships. The French tried to hold them off with a smoke screen, but *La Grandière* was hit. *Massachusetts* then turned her guns on the *aviso-drageuers* but had to withdraw after ten minutes because she was running low on ammunition. *Wichita* and *Tuscaloosa*, which had returned from chasing the phantom ship, took her place. Though hassled by gunfire, neither ship sustained any damage. They also failed to sink their prey.

Meanwhile, a tug pulled *Albatros* onto the beach at Roches Noires, just north of the port, depositing her alongside *Primauguet* and *Milan*. The three ships lined up in a row, provided a tempting target for the Wildcats, which tore them to pieces. A direct hit to *Primauguet*'s bridge killed the captain and eight officers.[27]

At 3:30 p.m., the Covering Group made one final pass for the day on El Hank, unleashing a salvo against the shore battery. The lighthouse and the battery remained standing. As the battle ended, the harbor filled with French sailors from abandoned ships clutching to rafts and lifeboats paddling toward the quay and dry land. Maneuvering among the debris and skirting the floating bodies of their dead comrades made for a slow and painful journey.[28]

THE FIRST DAY OF the Naval Battle of Casablanca raged for almost eight hours. The superior strength of the Americans, along with the element of surprise, led to a lopsided scorecard. The Americans suffered only minor damage. The French scored one hit on destroyers *Murphy* and *Ludlow*, cruisers *Wichita* and *Brooklyn*, and battleship *Massachusetts*. On board *Murphy*, three sailors were killed and another twenty-five wounded.

The French fleet was decimated, turning the waters in and around Casablanca into a graveyard of ships and men. Of all the French ships to engage with the Americans, only *L'Alcyon* survived unscathed. Four destroyers lay at the bottom of ocean, while *Jean Bart*, *Primauguet*, *Albatros*, and *Milan* were no longer seaworthy. Eight submarines had either sunk or gone missing. French casualties were high as well: 490 sailors killed and 969 wounded. Writing seventeen years later, Rear Admiral Paul Auphan called it "a battle of annihilation."[29]

While the Americans ruled the waters off the coast of Casablanca, the French still controlled the port and city. At El Hank, the four 138-mm coastal-defense guns remained operational. Repairs also began on *Jean Bart*'s turret to restore her four 194-mm guns to working order. Mobile batteries were rolled into and around Casablanca as well.[30] Sailors without a ship received guns and orders to help defend the city.[31]

The French would not give up Casablanca without a fight.

UP THE COAST AT Fédala, the Americans controlled the town and coast. Abandoned landing craft lay strewn along the beach, hulls crushed on the rocks or damaged by strafing from French planes. When all was said and done, the Americans had succeeded in landing 7,750 troops on that first day.[32]

After inspecting the port and the town, Patton and his staff retreated to the Hôtel Miramar. Having been hit by American bombs, it lacked running water and electricity, giving the normally swanky accommodations a primitive feel. Behind blackout curtains, Patton and his staff dined on fish and cheese by candlelight, washing it down with champagne.

"God has been very good to me today," wrote Patton in his diary before turning into bed.[33]

39

The American Consulate

As the hands on their watches crept past 4:30 a.m. on November 8, Staff Reid and Earle Russell stood on the roof the American consulate surveying a dark city. The blackout regulations always made the night hours gloomy and desolate, but that morning the city wore an extra shroud. One of Dave King's resistance cells included members of the senior staff of the PTT (Postes, télégraphes, et téléphones). They had arranged to cut the power to the city two hours before American forces were scheduled to come ashore, turning Casablanca into a collection of indigo and violet shadows as its whitewashed buildings picked up the faint light of the stars overhead and the piercing headlights of army vehicles streaming through the streets. As the minutes crept by, a layer of mist descended on the city.

Five-thirty came and went with no sign of the invasion force. The Americans were an hour late.

At around 6:00 a.m., Russell's nerves began to fray, and he started to wonder what would happen to them if the assault was called off at the last minute.

At 6:30 a.m., the buzz of an engine overhead cut through the Sunday morning quiet. A single plane flew over the city, leaving a trail of paper in its wake as thousands of leaflets bearing the American flag and Franklin Roosevelt's picture floated down. Reid and Russell scooped up a few and retreated inside to read them by candlelight. The leaflets bore a message from Dwight Eisenhower on behalf of Roosevelt—written in French on one side and Arabic on the other—assuring the people of Casablanca that the Americans had come as friends to liberate them from the tyranny of German and Italian rule.[1] A few minutes later, the French batteries in the harbor opened fire, the guns roaring as they discharged their rounds.

FIGURE 39.1. Flyers with a message from Eisenhower in French and
Arabic blanketed Casablanca on the morning of the American landings.
Courtesy Michel and Zellige Teuler

The Americans had arrived.

Over the next hour, French police and military units swarmed the streets
around the consulate. Members of the Garde mobile armed with machine
guns descended from transport trucks and fanned out along the exterior
fence. At 7:30 a.m., an Admiralty staff car arrived. Commander Jean Champel, who had served as the French admiralty's liaison officer to the US consulate for the past few months, appeared outside the gate that ran the length
of the driveway into the consulate's courtyard. Russell had ordered the gate
locked to prevent the French from waltzing in unannounced. Peering between the brass bars, Champel informed Russell that a state of war had been
declared between Vichy France and the United States and all members of the
consulate's staff would henceforth be considered prisoners. Everyone was to
remain inside the consulate or on its grounds. French soldiers would patrol
the perimeter to ensure compliance. As Champel departed, a French army
unit arrived and set up antiaircraft guns across from the consulate. To anchor
the guns, they hammered steel pegs into the pavement.[2]

Only the sight and sound of American Wildcats roaring overhead as they
flew toward Cazes airfield made being held prisoner within the consulate tolerable. Reid scrambled back up the ladder to the roof to watch the assault un-

fold. From there, he could see the harbor on one side and Cazes airfield on the other. As gunfire from the shore batteries filled the air, American and French planes engaged in ferocious dogfights, drawing circles and zigzags across the hazy morning sky. White silk parachutes dotted the sky as pilots bailed out of damaged planes.[3] As the dogfights died out, Reid turned his attention to the harbor, where the American navy unleashed salvo after salvo, and the French replied. "By 9 o'clock Sunday morning the whole port area of Casablanca looked like the smoking cone of a volcano in full eruption," wrote Reid.[4]

When the French naval and coastal batteries opened at the same time, the deafening roar of the guns shook the consulate, rattling the windows and shutters. The boom-boom-boom of the antiaircraft batteries across the street, which opened fire whenever an American plane appeared overhead, provided a countertempo. The sound of fighting from the port prompted an exodus to the east, where safety seemed to beckon. From the top floor of the consulate, the Americans watched Moroccan families scramble down the streets, juggling what they would carry. Some stuffed their possessions into baskets and strapped them to donkeys and camels. When a salvo flew, the noise reverberating across the city, the Moroccans sought shelter in the nearest doorway, often leaving their animals standing helpless in the middle of the road. Meanwhile, French families in the neighborhood around the consulate retreated behind their shutters, hoping the wood and dark interiors could keep the war at bay.[5]

Around noon, Josephine Russell attempted to approach the main gate to the consulate. She and Mrs. Brooks, wife of the consulate's second in command, had packed baskets of food to bring to their husbands and the rest of the staff. The French guards refused them entry and made them leave the baskets for inspection. Only after the guards inspected each sandwich and thermos of coffee for secret messages did the baskets pass through the gate.[6]

Nor would the guards allow Ernest Mayer and Philip Bagby, returned from their mission to deliver Roosevelt's messages to Rabat, into the consulate. Admiralty orders specified that no one was to leave or enter during the hostilities. Through the bars of the front gate, Mayer and Bagby delivered the news to Russell and Reid that their mission had failed. They hadn't been allowed to see or speak to Charles Noguès.[7]

Russell, Reid, and Dave King knew it was only a matter of time before the French came to inspect the consulate. The first demand arrived at around 2:00 a.m. in the form of Major Souard, accompanied by several members of the Garde mobile. Souard insisted that he and his men be allowed to inspect the building and the adjoining annex for Reid's hidden and illegal radio. After trying for months to shut down the transmitter, the French now had cause and opportunity to search the consulate.

Russell protested furiously, reminding Souard that the consulate was still American soil, only to finally give in. Russell knew full well that the radio and transmitter had been removed, so the search would be futile. But what else might they find? Souard's men moved methodically through the two-story consulate, pulling up rugs, prying open drawers, peeking behind pictures, and breaking into locked closets. Russell, however, refused to open the safe. After a furious exchange of words, Souard agreed to accept Russell's word that no radio sets were hidden inside.[8]

Reid shadowed one of the policemen up to the second floor, following him as he peered into closets and rustled through drawers. As the Frenchman went about his work, Reid remembered a box of grenades sitting on the shelf in the supply room. While the policeman dismantled Russell Brooks's office, Reid slipped down the hall. Spying a carton full of excelsior, Reid buried the grenades in the box and placed the carton in full view on the lower shelf. He rejoined the policeman, who appeared unaware that his shadow had momentarily disappeared.

When they reached the supply room, Reid held his breath as the policeman rummaged through the jumbled shelves full of stationary, blotters, and office equipment. The Frenchman's eyes latched on to the carton, which had a catsup label plastered on the outside. "You Americans still like luxuries?" he asked. Reid bit his tongue, deciding a smart retort would not help the situation. It worked. The policeman moved on, choosing instead to investigate the contents of an unused desk.[9]

It took Souard and his men a half an hour to complete the search of the consulate's main building. When they were done, they ventured across the courtyard to the annex, which was King's domain. King met Souard at the door, hand on his sidearm, and refused him entry. If Souard wanted in, he'd have to ask Russell for permission and obtain his written consent. The major stomped away, only to return with the required permission a few minutes later. "Souard came in and was just about as disagreeable and cutting as a man could be without actually insulting me," recalled King.

Souard informed King that he was under orders to look for radios and asked for someone to show his men around. Despite the frosty exchange, King volunteered to play escort, only to have Souard refuse. He wanted King where he could keep an eye on him. The escort job fell instead to Shelia Clark, King's trusted associate. As soon as Souard's men were out of earshot, the major revealed that he was for the Allies and started peppering King with questions and advice: Did King really have any sets? If King told him where they were, he would direct his men elsewhere. Have the Americans landed at Safi yet? How's it going at Fédala? Souard also warned King to hide any arms. There would be a weapons search later that afternoon. King was shocked but grateful to discover a new ally.

When Souard's men returned, they reported that they had been unable to find any radios and asked if the major wanted them to search the cupboards in offices. Souard waved them off—King had confided that he stashed his suitcase radios there—and they left the annex.[10]

The Americans had passed their first test.

WHEN JOSEPHINE RUSSELL RETURNED to the consulate later that afternoon, she brought a new batch of coffee—and two messages for Reid. Deciding she was harmless, the guards allowed her to approach within speaking distance of the gate. She let Reid know a message awaited him at the bottom of the thermos. Reid hadn't heard from Captain X, his courier, since before the start of the invasion and worried his trusted messenger was either in jail or dead. When he dumped the coffee out, Reid found a message dated five hours earlier from Bill Eddy, who was at Gibraltar with Eisenhower. They wanted a progress report on the invasion. A note from Ajax said he couldn't contact either Gibraltar or Tangier.[11]

Reid marveled at the risks both Captain X and Josephine had taken to deliver the messages. Now he needed Josephine to continue her skullduggery. Reid wanted her to complain of pain in her ankle, which would require the assistance of Dr. Anton Rublev, the consulate's doctor. Rublev had sought sanctuary at the consulate after being rousted from sleep by the French military vehicles gunning their engines as they headed for the port. Now he found himself an accidental prisoner. With the help of some colleagues, Reid made a commotion to distract the guards, allowing Russell to pass along the plan to his wife. Josephine played her role brilliantly, but the guards wouldn't allow the doctor to examine her. Instead, Rublev asked her questions in French through the gate before passing through the bars some ointment to rub on the joint and a bandage for her ankle. Inside the bandage, Reid hid a coded message to Captain X on a thin slip of paper.[12]

As Souard predicted, Lieutenant Merglin, a member of the French resistance, appeared at the consulate around 4:00 a.m. bearing a signed order from Noguès authorizing him to search and seize any cars and stocks of gasoline owned by the consulate. The French wanted to make it impossible for the Americans to plot a midnight getaway.[13]

Once he completed his search of the consulate, Merglin and his men moved over to the annex. "The poor boy looked as if he had been told to kill his own pet dog," recalled King upon seeing Merglin's face in his doorway.

Once again, Sheila Clark led the Frenchmen around the annex, which left Merglin and King alone. The lieutenant told King he was "desolé" to have to search the annex, but he could not refuse the order and maintain his appearance of loyalty to the Protectorate. King assured him he understood the predicament.

During their search, Merglin's men uncovered a car and an illegal radio set in the garage, both of which they would have to take into custody. They also discovered that the car didn't match the one registered to King.

"You have another car, haven't you? No. 7995MA8? Where is that?" Merglin trembled as he asked the questions, aware of his men watching the confrontation. King had loaned the car to Merglin and his compatriots to kidnap General Georges Lascroux the day before.

King looked him straight in the eye. "I don't know. It was stolen in front of the Consulate yesterday."

Merglin breathed an audible sigh of relief and assured him the car would be found and returned to King.[14]

WITH THE INSPECTIONS SEEMINGLY done for the day, Russell and his staff concentrated on destroying what remained of the strip code instructions and the strips themselves, along with all confidential correspondence.[15] Meanwhile, King built a defensible position in the annex—arranging a room with a barricade, no windows at his back, and a clear line of fire on the door and the consulate's gate. Should the French decide to storm the consulate, he would not go down without a fight.[16]

When night descended, a rosy glow tinged the sky as the soot-saturated air reflected the fires that burned around the port. The power to the city remained off. Reid and Russell had been up for almost thirty-six hours, their eyes bleary and their brains sluggish from fatigue. Using some wool blankets delivered by Josephine Russell on one of her trips, they stretched out on the marble floor of the consulate's lobby, "conforming to a pattern of a first class morgue."[17] As they drifted off to sleep, finally allowing their bodies to override the coffee, whiskey, and adrenaline that had sustained them, they could hear the faint echoes of the American guns at Fédala.[18]

40

Mehdia and Port Lyautey

A s the final hour of November 7 struck, the eight transport ships of the Northern Attack Group began maneuvering into position off the coast of Mehdia, a resort town at the confluence of the Sebou
River and the Atlantic Ocean. Located eighty miles north of Casablanca,
Mehdia was the third landing beach for the American invasion of Morocco.
Over the next hour, the transports tried to cue up according to plan, but
they couldn't achieve the precision of their counterparts to the south. First
they misjudged their initial location; then a series of misguided orders failed
to correct the bad positioning. At 12:36 a.m. on November 8, the group
commander decided the transports were close enough to the planned staging position to start unloading boats and men.[1] It was not a good omen for
the start of the operation.

While the Northern Attack Group worked in the darkness, a convoy of
French steamers emerged from the Sebou River, passing between the Americans and the coast. The convoy's escort, the SS *Lorraine*, signaled to the
Americans, "Be warned. Alert on shore for 5 a.m." The warning was welcome but also tainted. One of the American ships observed the French signal station asking *Lorraine* for information about the boats floating off the
coast—"Quels sont les bateaux?" She most likely answered, "American."
Not long after, Dwight Eisenhower's Kansas twang and Franklin Roosevelt's
patrician vowels crackled from the radios of the Northern Attack Group as
the ships picked up the first Allied broadcasts.[2]

"My heart sank," Major General Lucian K. Truscott Jr. later wrote. "If
the French were not now alert and waiting at their guns we would indeed be

lucky!"[3] Truscott, a World War I veteran and crack polo player with a face that could be Hollywood handsome or craggy, depending on the angle, was in charge of the Mehdia–Port Lyautey operation.

Uneasy about losing the element of surprise and frustrated by his inability to get reliable reports on the progress of the unloading, Truscott decided to survey the situation himself. Shortly after 3:00 a.m., a net was flung over the side of the transport *Henry T. Allen*, and Truscott scrambled down into a waiting boat. As he sailed between the transports, sailors and soldiers were startled to see the general materialize out of the dark, not quite trusting their eyes.[4]

TRUSCOTT AND HIS FORCE of 9,000 were coming ashore at Mehdia because it served as the gateway to Port Lyautey, home to the only concrete airstrip in North Africa. The Americans wanted the airstrip, along with the port and control of the roads and railroads that ran north from Casablanca through Port Lyautey up past Fez and into Algeria.[5] But to get to Port Lyautey, they had to conquer Mehdia's kasbah and control the Sebou River, which stood in their way.

The Sebou River begins high in Morocco's Middle Atlas Mountains and winds north through Fez before turning west and twisting its way to the Atlantic Ocean. At Mehdia, its crystal blue water rushes into the salty grey Atlantic, making an attractive location for a trading outpost. In the fifteenth century, the Portuguese claimed the town as their own, building a fortress on the bluff overlooking the river to guard the harbor. The kasbah boasted a formidable gatehouse and thick crenellating stone walls that looked as if they could still withstand invaders from the sea. After the Portuguese departed, Mehdia became a favorite place of refuge for Spanish, English, and Barbary pirates seeking shelter from the Atlantic and navies set on revenge.[6] As other Moroccan ports grew in prominence over the next few centuries, Mehdia slowly crumbled until the French arrived.

Twelve miles up the Sebou River from Mehdia—six by land—the French built Port Lyautey, a modern port and airfield nestled in the hairpin curve of the river. The airfield was home to an infantry regiment, artillery battalions, and some cavalry. To protect the port, French added a honeycomb of trenches and other defensive works to the marshland between Mehdia and Port Lyautey. The Sebou offered another layer of protection for Port Lyautey: it ran shallow, churning sandbars and silt, which made it difficult to sail any ship with a deep draft up the river. As an extra measure of security, the French had suspended a wire net across the river.

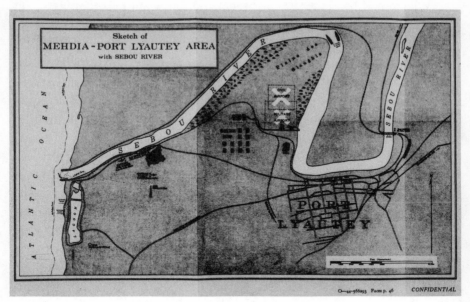

FIGURE 40.1. Mehdia-Port Lyautey Area. *National Archives*

As Truscott sailed between the eight transport ships, he discovered that they were anywhere from one to two hours behind schedule for putting landing craft and men into the water, jeopardizing the planned 4:00 a.m. start time.[7]

Having also lost the element of surprise, Truscott had to decide whether to stick with the plan or devise a new one. He forged ahead, grudgingly delaying the start of the operation by another half hour. The sooner his men were on the beach, with darkness as their ally, the better their prospects for success. The battle plan called for American troops to come ashore at five locations along a ten-mile stretch of coastline around Mehdia. After securing the beachhead, three landing battalion teams would launch an assault on the airfield at Port Lyautey.

At 5:15 a.m., American troops began landing along the coast, darkness still shrouding their arrival. A party of sixteen men divided among three scout boats also made its way to the mouth of the Sebou, charged with cutting the net that blocked the river.[8] The window of opportunity for the Americans lasted until the creeping morning sun gave the French murky targets to shoot at. With that, the shore battery opened fire on the beach, discharging flashes of red into the sky. Meanwhile, a searchlight found one of the scout boats on the Sebou. The French sprayed the net-cutting party with machine-gun fire, flashes of white light crackling across the river as the Americans retreated. Another machine-gun nest riddled the arriving landing craft with bullets.[9]

As dawn bathed the town, the beach, and the ocean in soft golden light, the French became more aggressive. The kasbah battery targeted the destroyer *Roe*, barely missing, before turning its sights on the transports and the landing parties. Rear Admiral Monroe Kelly ordered, "Play ball!" *Savannah* and *Roe* unloaded their guns, sending "great chains of red balls" streaking toward the shore. The battery fell silent for the moment, only to awake later in the day to resume its harassment.[10]

The morning light also brought the French air force, which had scrambled from the Rabat-Salé airfield. The French pilots tore up the beaches with bullets, punching holes into men and boats. They tried to sink *Roe* and *Savannah*, to no avail.[11] The French pilots didn't have the sky to themselves for long, as planes from the *Ranger* and *Sangamon* joined the fray. By 9:00 a.m., the American pilots had shot down nine French planes and chased the others away.[12]

Hoping for a short engagement, Truscott tasked two pilots, Colonel Demas F. Craw and Major Pierpont Hamilton, with delivering a letter to Colonel Charles Petit, commander of the 1st Moroccan Tirailleurs at Port Lyautey, urging him to cooperate with the Americans. Truscott composed the letter and had it translated into French. To add a bit of ceremony, the letter was written in Old English script on a scroll and sealed with ribbons and wax. Craw and Hamilton also wore their dress uniforms, brass and leather polished to shine.[13]

After escaping the beach and dodging bullets from three low-flying French planes, Craw and Hamilton loaded into a jeep and headed down the road toward Port Lyautey. Craw sat in the front holding a French tricolor and an American flag. Hamilton sat in the back clutching a white flag of truce. As they came over a small hill, a French soldier opened fire, peppering Craw's chest with bullets. While Craw bled to death in the jeep alongside the road, Hamilton was taken prisoner and delivered to Petit's headquarters at Port Lyautey. Petit gave Hamilton a friendly reception but admitted he had no authority to surrender French troops.[14]

Things continued to go badly. Coming ashore five miles too far north, the 3rd Battalion Landing Team had to march the long way around to Port Lyautey. The 2nd Battalion Landing Team attempted to seize the kasbah, only to have to take cover from the rounds being lobbed by *Roe* and *Savannah* at the battery harassing the transports.[15] When the Americans finally advanced on the fortress, they discovered the French had reinforced the skeleton force with additional troops from Port Lyautey. The French pushed the Americans back onto the beach. The destroyer *Dallas* attempted twice to deliver an amphibious detachment up the Sebou but failed both times. The first time she was unable to bypass the net and boom; the second, she tried to plow through but had to retreat when the French showered her with artillery rounds.[16]

Truscott tried to follow the course of the assault from the *Henry T. Allen*, but the communication system collapsed. Messages were getting through only in fragments, if at all. Naval radio channels were overloaded. Reports from the coxswains returning from delivering troops to the beaches offered conflicting accounts, adding to the confusion. Around 3:00 p.m., the general and part of his staff boarded a landing craft and rode the heavy surf toward the beach south of Mehdia. Once on land, Truscott's jeep immediately became stuck in thick, heavy sand—and would stay there. Commandeering a half-track, he spent the next few hours, radio in hand, driving along the beach and surveying the terrain on foot, attempting to coordinate his men.[17]

Truscott's reconnaissance efforts did little to improve a dismal American situation. As night fell on November 8, the French still controlled the kasbah, part of the riverbank, and the approaches to Port Lyautey. They had also moved tanks into the woods along the road to Rabat. The net across the Sebou remained in place. Damaged boats, abandoned equipment, and waterlogged soldiers separated from their units covered the landing beaches. To avoid the shells from the French batteries, the Northern Attack Group moved thirty miles off the coast—instead of the original eight—slowing down efforts to land additional troops and badly needed artillery. The ocean also churned, generating waves that reached fifteen feet, making it increasingly difficult for the landing craft to discharge their cargo and retract safely.[18]

On the voyage over, Truscott had held daily meetings to review possible situations and best solutions, but none of the scenarios echoed the tactical morass the Americans now found themselves in.[19] They were in serious trouble.

Sitting alone on a sand dune, listening to waves pound the beach, Truscott considered this next move. More than anything he wanted a cigarette. Soldiers were banned from smoking at night to avoid inadvertently giving away their position. But they hadn't seen a French plane since the morning. How dangerous could it be? "I lit one," wrote Truscott. "In a matter of moments, I was glad when other glows appeared as other lonely and uncertain men sought the comfort of tobacco. They would have been surprised to know that the Commanding General had been the first to violate the blackout order."[20]

41

Vichy

A T 7:00 P.M. ON NOVEMBER 8, SOMERVILLE PINKNEY TUCK, US chargé d'affaires in Vichy, received a summons from Pierre Laval. Tuck had been serving as the senior American representative in Vichy ever since Admiral William Leahy's return to Washington, DC, in May. In the ensuing months, Tuck had prodded Henri-Philippe Pétain and Laval on the subject of how Vichy would respond should the United States enter the war and set foot in French North Africa. To all such inquires, Pétain's spine would stiffen as he insisted that France would defend her colonies from all interlopers, including the United States.[1]

Earlier that morning, as TORCH got underway, Tuck called on Pétain and handed him a message from Franklin Roosevelt in both English and French. The Frenchman learned of the invasion of North Africa with a mixture of "astonishment and sadness" and wrote to the president in reply. He reminded Roosevelt of his pledge to defend France's empire from any aggressor. "You knew that I would keep my word," wrote Pétain. "In our hour of trial, I have, in asking for an armistice, preserved our Empire, and it is you, who, acting in the name of a country to whom we are bound by so many memories and ties, come to take so cruel a step." With France and her honor in jeopardy, Pétain ordered his military commanders to defend North Africa. Despite the tense words, Pétain shook Tuck's hand as they parted, a smile on his face. Tuck couldn't help but notice that Pétain hummed as he returned to his office.[2]

This new summons from Laval could only mean one thing: Vichy intended to sever diplomatic ties. Wasting no time, Laval informed Tuck that, at a meeting of the cabinet that afternoon, Vichy had decided to terminate relations with the United States. The American attack on North Africa left them no choice.

"He said that in conveying to me this momentous decision he wished at the same time to assure me of his sincere regret," wrote Tuck. "The fact that our troops had landed on the soil of French North Africa could not be viewed in any other way but as an act of aggression and for this reason it was no longer possible to maintain diplomatic relations between our respective Governments."[3]

42

Convergence

THE AMERICANS PASSED THEIR FIRST NIGHT AT SAFI WITHOUT INCIdent. On the beach, Major General Ernest Harmon's men dug foxholes and retreated into the ground for some well-earned sleep. At the pier, unloading of the *Lakehurst* and *Titania* continued through the night. Darkness gave the men working on the docks a reprieve from French snipers, but the sheer volume of cargo to unload presented its own challenges. It would take the crew of the *Lakehurst*, working nonstop, forty-two hours to offload 169 vehicles, including Harmon's fifty-one tanks. They would need another sixty hours to unload the 22,086 cans of gasoline and oil, 14,392 cases of ammunition and high explosives, and 1,727 cases of rations.

When the French realized they were being invaded, they destroyed the powerhouse at the pier, making it impossible for the Americans to use the cranes. After spending two days tracing electrical lines and attempting to rebuild the unfamiliar system on their own, the Americans decided to ask for help. The local governor referred them to the port director, who recommended a skilled engineer who lived on the outskirts of town. With the engineer's help, cranes were soon hoisting three to six tons of cargo at a time from the ships onto the docks.[1]

The Americans also knew they had been lucky. The Southern Attack Group could protect the ships in dock against submarines, but attack from the air was another matter. The skies remained quiet on the first day, after a much-feared attack originating from the air base at Marrakech failed to materialize. Instead, three French reconnaissance planes watched over the Americans as they unloaded tanks and other supplies.[2]

The French, however, did not stay away forever.

Just after dawn on November 9, a French air force squadron based in Marrakech headed for Safi, hoping to catch the Americans groggy and unaware. When the pilots arrived, they discovered the town and adjacent coast shrouded in a thick fog bank. The French had finally come out to fight, but they couldn't see their targets. The Americans on the ground couldn't see the planes circling above them, but the buzz of their engines had no trouble cutting through mist.

One French pilot decided to take a chance and plunged below the cloud ceiling for a low-level bombing run. The bomb missed the *Lakehurst*, whose crew worked to unload Harmon's tanks, and hit a small warehouse nearby. The boom of the explosion ripped through the port. As fire engulfed the warehouse, the smoke mixed with the fog, thickening the damp morning air with ash and soot—then the secondary explosions started. The warehouse served as an ammunition dump, and as the fire licked the rounds, they ignited as well. The lone bomb killed five men and wounded ten.[3] For his daring, the French pilot received a spray from an American antiaircraft battery, which sent him crashing into the beach north of town. The Americans didn't see or hear from the French air force for the rest of day.[4]

While the Merchandise Pier burned, American lieutenant commander Joe Ruddy was airborne, almost ninety-five miles inland, surveying French movements in Marrakech. Ruddy had spent eight hours in the air the day before, conducting reconnaissance for Harmon, and would log another nine hours that day. He stocked his plane with extra gear—"a murderous-looking knife, pistols, a rifle, a shotgun, a garrote, a special knapsack of home comforts, a small camera, and 7 by 50 binoculars"—should he need to put his plane down in hostile territory. While making a pass over the Marrakech airfield, Ruddy attracted antiaircraft fire. He retaliated by dropping two bombs, neither of which exploded.

The French attack on Ruddy's plane made the airfield fair game—at least according to the *Santee*'s skipper. That afternoon, eleven bombers and two fighters headed for Marrakech. The last thing Harmon's tanks needed as they made their way north was harassment by the French air force from the rear.[5] The American pilots who conducted the raid reported that they set fire to the hanger and destroyed twenty aircraft.[6]

At Marrakech, the French had a sizable garrison under the command of General Henry Martin, who once served as Henri Giraud's chief of staff. If Antoine Béthouart's plan to seize control of Morocco had gone as planned, Martin would have claimed Marrakech in the name of the resistance.[7] But with Béthouart in jail and the coup aborted, Martin had to respond to the stream of orders flowing from his superior officers, which included launching a counterattack against the Americans. He executed those orders in a very leisurely fashion.[8] The Americans didn't lay eyes on the troops Martin sent to reinforce the French garrison at Safi until mid-afternoon on November 9. Almost a day and a half had passed since Harmon and his men hit the beach—and Marrakech was only ninety-five miles away.

A convoy of fourteen French troop trucks came within fifteen miles of Safi before planes launched from the *Santee* strafed them to a stop. At around 4:00 p.m., American planes attacked another French convoy, this one numbering more than three dozen vehicles. Pushing further inland along the road to Marrakech, the pilots attacked a third French convoy, this one a ragtag group of trucks, horse-drawn vehicles, and soldiers on foot.[9]

While the pilots from the *Santee* tore up the road to Marrakech during the afternoon, the tanks and artillery of the 1st Armored Landing Team drove out to meet the assembling French force, while the 47th Infantry stayed behind to guard Safi. Streaming past the Bouguedra crossroads, fifteen miles out from Safi, the Americans took out a machine-gun post and trundled on down the road until darkness called a halt to the advance. The 1st Armored Landing Team dug in for the night.[10]

HAVING PASSED THE NIGHT at the Hôtel Miramar, General George Patton awoke before dawn on November 9, anxious to tackle whatever challenges the second day in Morocco provided. With Fédala secure, the most pressing problem was getting the remaining men and equipment ashore for the attack on the city of Casablanca. More than 160 landing craft of a possible 330 were either wrecked or missing as a result of the first day's operation.[11] When Patton ventured down to the beach, he discovered a jumble of broken landing craft, strewn equipment, and troops either still asleep or lying about—and his officers appeared to be doing little to bring order. Major General John B. Anderson, who should have been up and ordering his men about, had yet to leave his bed.

With the beach a mess, Patton ordered all incoming landing craft diverted to Fédala's port, where the arrival of new troops and equipment wouldn't add to the chaos. It would also prevent landing craft, loaded down with troops, from braving the rollercoaster ride to the beach as the Atlantic tossed up twelve- and fifteen-foot waves. Patton's message came too late for one boat. He watched it crest a wave, turn end on end, and dump the men, weighted down with packs, into the cold water. All sixteen drowned. "We only found three—they were a nasty blue color," wrote Patton in his diary.

Patton also had little patience for the men who scampered for cover when the French air force strafed and bombed the beach. When one soldier assumed the fetal position, teeth chattering away, Patton "kicked him in the arse with all my might and he jumped right up and went to work." Patton wasn't impressed with the men under his command, be they officers or enlistees. "As a whole the men were poor, the officers worse; no drive. It is very sad. I saw one lieutenant let his men hesitate to jump into the water. I gave him hell. I hit another man who was too lazy to push a boat. We also kicked a lot of Arabs."

With things progressing slowly at Fédala, Patton decided to return to *Augusta* and pay Admiral Kent Hewitt a visit. "He ordered the doctor to give me a drink as I had had no food," wrote Patton. "I needed it."[12]

Things on the beach might have been a mess, but pilots from the *Ranger* were already wreaking havoc on French attempts to reinforce Casablanca. One group shot up a convoy of fifty vehicles headed there. Others dropped bombs on the batteries around Casablanca. In the afternoon, they attacked another convoy headed for the city, dodging machine-gun fire from French troops determined to defend themselves. Dogfights unfolded throughout the day as American and French pilots battled for control of the skies. Despite the French pilots' skill, their aged Dewoitine planes made it hard to match the agility and speed of the American Wildcats. By the end of the day, the Americans ruled the skies above Fédala and Casablanca.[13]

ANDERSON MAY NOT HAVE been up as early as Patton would have liked, but by 7:00 a.m. four battalions under his command were heading for Casablanca. While planes from the *Ranger* patrolled above, Anderson's men worked their way south, dodging the mines surrounding the approaches to the bridge spanning the Nefifikh river. Instead of coming out to meet the approaching American force, the French diverted forces north to Port Lyautey. The lack of a skirmish proved a blessing for Anderson as he halted his advance in order to avoid getting too far ahead of his transportation and communication lines.[14]

MAJOR GENERAL LUCIAN TRUSCOTT passed "a grim and lonely night" on the beach at Mehdia, but the arrival of dawn on November 9 boosted his spirits. The rising sun gave his men light by which to work and a chance to finish their mission.[15] While things looked better to Truscott in the morning, in reality the American position at Mehdia had further deteriorated over-night. The Americans remained miles from the airfield they had come to secure. As Truscott and his men slept on the beach or caught some shuteye further inland, the French spent the night moving in troops and tanks from Meknès and Fez. The skeleton force holding the kasbah also received rein-forcements, as did the units defending the airfield.[16]

Truscott, however, received no reinforcements overnight. The heavy waves and surf long feared by Allied planners materialized, making it im-possible to land more men, heavy weaponry, and tanks. The beaches had also turned into impromptu parking lots, as the trucks, jeeps, and light tanks mired in wet sand piled up along the narrow strip of land.

Shortly after dawn, the French launched a counterattack, attempting to push the Americans out of Mehdia and back onto the beach. The Americans had fought hard to keep their precarious toehold in the town, and now they might lose that too. Taking the kasbah remained a key objective, but the lighthouse soon became a trophy as well. Worried about putting his men in danger, Truscott decided against having *Savannah* unload its guns on the ancient walls of the kasbah. He thought the risk of friendly fire too high.[17]

The real danger to Truscott's expedition, however, came from the ar-mored French column and two infantry battalions closing in from the south. If the French broke through, the Americans might lose the beach altogether. The job of holding off the French advance fell to Colonel Harry Semmes, who commanded the 3rd Armored Landing Team. During the middle of the night, the eight light tanks under his command managed to make it off the beach, rumble around the lagoon, and up the road that led to the highway running from Port Lyautey and Rabat.

A little after 6:00 a.m., Semmes and his men engaged a company of French infantry lodged in the woods beside the road, inflicting heavy casualties. A half hour later, as the sky began to lighten, they spied a group of French tanks advancing up the highway that ran north from Rabat. Outnumbered, Sem-mes ordered his men to take up a front-facing position on a small ridge over-looking the road. He hoped the tactic would allow the superior front armor of the American tanks to take the brunt of any salvos from the 37-mm guns on the Renaults. A lack of radio communications also handicapped Semmes and his team. Somewhere on the journey from the United States to French Morocco, the radios in the tanks had become inoperable, forcing them to rely on visual commands.[18]

As rounds flew back and forth, Semmes feared for his men's survival. His small contingent could only hold out so long against the overwhelming French force. At last, help came from above. Artillery rounds rained down on the area where the French tanks assembled, throwing up clouds of earth and metal. Aided by airplanes serving as spotters, *Savannah*'s guns pummeled the French force, destroying four tanks and scattering the rest in a quest for safety. For Semmes and company, the incoming naval gunfire was both heaven-sent and nerve-racking. Their French opponents were between one hundred and three hundred yards from them, an uncomfortably close distance.[19]

With the sun up for only an hour, Truscott arrived on the scene to find smoke billowing from the smoldering Renault tanks and singed, broken bodies scattered on the ground. These were the first French dead he'd seen. Coming alongside Semmes's tank, Truscott noticed two unexploded armor-piercing rounds lodged in its khaki-colored armor. The colonel had been lucky. Semmes, however, appeared unruffled, even energized, as he surveyed the wreckage before him. He "had the pride of a halfback who had just plunged through the opposing line for a touchdown," wrote Truscott.[20]

Truscott ordered tanks and antitank guns from the 70th Tank Battalion and 60th Regimental Cannon Company to reinforce Semmes's force. At around 9:00 a.m., they repelled another French armored advance. By late afternoon, Truscott's southern flank was secure enough that he could order units of the 70th Tank Battalion to head north to help with the American advance on the airfield.

In mid-morning, word came that the French force holding the kasbah wanted to negotiate surrender terms. The French officer who delivered the overture received an escort back to his lines and instructions to convey to his superiors that the Americans would like to meet at noon. Buoyed by the good news, Truscott and his staff retreated to a rundown casino on the beach to discuss surrender terms. Less than a day had passed since Truscott's envoys had been shot and imprisoned. Eager to make a good impression, Truscott borrowed a razor to scrape the stubble from his face and brushed the sand and grime from his uniform.[21]

When the clock hands passed noon, the designated meeting time, and the French failed to arrive, Truscott wondered if he'd been duped. Adding to his unease was the failure of the French to cease fire. The French officer offering the peace deal had also disappeared. Realizing there was "something peculiar about the incident," Truscott wrote a note to the French commandant, conveying his regret that his emissary hadn't made it across the lines and reaffirming his willingness to meet anytime during daylight hours. He dispatched the letter under a flag of truce, only to have the French fire upon the messengers and send them scurrying back behind American lines. Truscott later learned that a resourceful English-speaking French officer desperate to orchestrate his escape had invented the offer to parlay. "We had been gullible enough to send him back to his own lines with better information concerning us than he could have obtained by even a successful reconnaissance," wrote Truscott.[22]

WHILE SEMMES GUARDED THE road from Rabat and Truscott prepared for the surrender meeting, some seven miles to the northeast, Major Percy McCarley and his men attempted to move inland and secure the much-desired airfield at Port Lyautey. The Americans encountered little resistance as they picked their way through a lightly wooded area. That changed in mid-afternoon, when they crested a large hill known as Mhignat Touama. The French were waiting for them, having camped out on the highway to the northeast and in an adjacent elevated wooded area. Mortar rounds and heavy machine-gun fire now pinned down the Americans. Hoping to press their advantage, the French moved to attack the American flank from the east. McCarley countered and held fast with the help of a barrage from 105-mm howitzers. As the howitzers unloaded their rounds, the air cracked, and smoke wafted from the canons. The arrival of ten tanks from the 70th Tank Battalion, which had left Semmes, changed the momentum in favor of the Americans. Some well-placed rounds, courtesy of the US Navy, dispersed French troops along the highway, while American airplanes took out French machine guns.

As the Americans prepared to again push forward toward the airfield, they got a stomach-churning reminder of the dangers of air support. McCarley's men didn't mark the edge of their advance with the requisite yellow smoke grenades, leading an American pilot to drop two bombs on his fellow soldiers below. Friendly fire killed more men when artillery rounds landed on their position. The chaos and dismay that followed led McCarley to stay put.[23]

As darkness fell, the American position remained bleak. They had failed to take the kasbah or the lighthouse—and struggled to maintain their foothold in the town. They also hadn't seized the airfield. Truscott sent a message to Patton, letting him know that if his men failed to take the kasbah in the morning, he would need reinforcements.[24]

"Our second night on shore was not a cheerful one, although for me it was less grim and dismal than the night before," wrote Truscott. "Someone produced K rations and an alcohol stove and made coffee, my first food on shore." As night crept forward, a heavy band of clouds concealed the stars overhead, while sniper fire crackled across the beaches and around the kasbah. Just after midnight, the sky opened up, drenching Truscott's men and their spirits.[25]

WITH THE AMERICANS SWARMING along the coast, Charles Noguès and his staff decamped 130 miles inland to Fez on the morning of November 9. Nestled into the foothills of the Atlas Mountains, Fez was home to a sizeable garrison and located at a major crossroads, which would allow for coordination of French forces. Vice Admiral François Michelier remained in control of Casablanca and all military and naval forces in that district.[26]

The Americans had yet to cut the telegraph line to France, allowing Noguès to report to Vichy that Morocco remained in French hands. He did not shy away from confessing that keeping the Americans at bay would be difficult, but he believed the people of Morocco were ready to make the "necessary sacrifices." Reporting that the Americans had destroyed the bulk of the French air force, he requested reinforcements.

Noguès was also given charge of troops and operations in western Algeria. The Allies seized Algiers on the first day, but the countryside remained in French hands. Noguès's command authority now extended to the southern provinces of Algeria, which bordered Morocco.

Even as he issued orders to counteract the American advance, Noguès dismissed his subordinates' suggestion that he ask for a truce. "I did not have the right to give the ceasefire order before having the authorization of my superior at Algiers or my superior at Vichy," he later claimed. Even as his beloved Morocco slipped out of French control, he clung to strict military protocol.[27]

43

Lowering the Flag

On the morning of November 9, the American consulate awoke to the thunderous roar of guns from the harbor. The walls shook, and the floor felt like it would drop out from underneath them. The Americans and French had renewed their battle at first light. Staff Reid and Earle Russell had passed an uneventful night: there were no midnight raids by the French, no attempts to storm the consulate.[1]

As they wondered what new problems the second day of the fighting would bring, Dave King surveyed the streets around the consulate from his perch in the annex. The Garde mobile still manned the perimeter. The antiaircraft guns remained at the ready across from the consulate. Sounds of distant fighting began to drift their way. None of this surprised him. The parade of children, some alone, some with their parents, did—they walked up to the doors of the Lycée Jeanne d'Arc, the school across the street, as if it were merely another Monday morning.[2]

A little after noon, a shell crashed near the consulate, shattering the windows. The errant round came from the Center Attack Group's bombardment of the French admiralty's headquarters. Rear Admiral Kent Hewitt was paying Vice Admiral François Michelier back for his treatment of the American delegation. Not long after, an American bomb crumpled the French navy's wireless tower.[3]

Since becoming prisoners in the consulate, King, Reid, and Russell had wondered what the French had in store for them. The answer arrived shortly after 5:00 p.m., when French officials presented Russell with an order, signed by Charles Noguès, dictating the transfer of the American consulate staff to Kasba Tadla, a small town at the foot of the Atlas Mountains some 130 miles southeast of Casablanca. The transfer, scheduled for midnight, would ensure the "safety" of the Americans during the intensifying hostilities. Any staff and family members not already inside the consulate would be brought there for deportation.[4]

Shocked by the blatant violation of diplomatic protocol, Russell argued up a storm with the French officers who delivered the order. Accommodations at Kasba Tadla, little more than a motley collection of buildings that had grown up around an old fort, would also be inadequate. If their safety was really the motivating factor, the French should simply deliver the consulate staff to Fédala, a mere fifteen miles away, and turn them over to the American troops there.

The French army officer tartly noted that Vichy France had terminated relations with the United States. He urged Russell and his staff not to resist, as force would be used to execute the orders. Snapping his feet together and raising his hand in a salute, the Frenchman finished with, "We are at war, Your Excellency, and we shall take whatever precautions are necessary to insure victory of French forces."[5]

Despite Russell's bluster, news of French intentions came as no surprise. Earlier in the day, Major Souard had passed along word of a possible deportation order, sparking an intense debate among the consulate staff. Should the Americans resist or acquiesce and hope for the best? The decision required deciphering French intentions. Did Noguès really have their safety in mind, or did he intend to use them as hostages? Or, worse yet, would he arrange for something to happen to them on the ride to Kasba Tadla? The journey would provide the fascist Service d'ordre legionnaire (SOL) with the perfect opportunity to attack.

Reid preferred to fight over being shot "like a rat in the trap," while King was prepared to make a stand in the annex. Souard begged them not to resist, believing the SOL was looking for any excuse to attack. To provide the Americans with some protection, Souard was arranging for men loyal to him to precede and follow the convoy. He also promised that if an opportunity arose to blunder into Major General Ernest Harmon's column as it made its way north from Safi, his men would deliver the consular staff into the hands of American troops.[6] Delivery of the deportation order turned a hypothetical discussion into reality. Taking into account Souard's assurances, Reid and King grudgingly decided not to resist, a choice endorsed by Russell, albeit reluctantly.

As HE WOULD BE abandoning his post, Russell asked for permission to send a message to Georges Criblez, the Swiss consul, requesting that he assume responsibility for American affairs. While they waited for Criblez to arrive, darkness descended on Casablanca. As the last of the autumn light faded, a rosy glow from the fires still burning in the port tinged the night sky.[7]

Shortly after 6:00 p.m., Criblez's car appeared at the consulate gate, and he was escorted inside by three French guards. Unlike the Americans, who had slept in their clothes, Criblez appeared crisp and clean in his black and white evening dress, having been diverted to the consulate en route to a dinner party being thrown in his honor.

"Mr. Criblez, it is my painful duty at this tragic hour to be compelled to surrender American rights in a country where we have been so long accredited to the court of the Sultan and to the government of France exercising Protectorate authority," said Russell. Before the assembled staff, who held candles and flashlights to illuminate the courtyard ceremony, Russell handed over the keys to the consulate and asked Criblez to seal the building after their departure. Any break in the seals affixed to the doors, windows, and safe would indicate that someone had tampered with American property. The Stars and Stripes was lowered from the flagpole, then folded in half twice, before the traditional final folds rendered it a triangle representing the tricornered hat of the American Revolutionaries. Russell passed the flag to Criblez for safe keeping until the Americans could once again raise it over the consulate.[8] Criblez fought back tears as he shook Russell's hand, swearing to notify both the Swiss and American governments immediately.[9]

Criblez's departure coincided with the exhaustion of the Americans' supply of candles and flashlight batteries. For the rest of the evening, they negotiated the cobblestones of the courtyard and the consulate's rooms and stairs by memory and touch.

WITH THE BUS SCHEDULED to depart at midnight, the French allowed Reid and the others to return home to fetch clothing, but only if accompanied by a police officer to guarantee their return. Reid and his roommate, Len Wiggins, the affable Englishman who worked in the British interests section, piled into a car, along with their police shadow. As they made their way through Casablanca's dark streets toward Anfa, the car meandered back and forth across the road. Reid soon realized their driver was soused, having decided to deal with the advent of war by drinking wine.

Reid and Wiggins had shared a lease on a pink-stuccoed villa in the upscale Anfa neighborhood since July. When Wiggins pitched the idea of being roommates, he touted the villa's size, the housekeeper's cooking, and a respect for Reid's privacy. (Wiggins knew about Reid's work for the Office of

Strategic Services.) The villa's location, however, sold Reid on the notion. On one side stood Villa Maas, one of the largest and most pretentious villas in the city and home to Gestapo head Theodor Auer. Any high-ranking Nazi official visiting Casablanca stayed there. Across the road another villa, designed to resemble a pagoda, housed members of the Italian Armistice Commission. From the terrace, Reid could smell the lemon and eucalyptus trees in the garden—and watch the road that led to Villa Maas. From the back windows, he could often hear the Italians talking.[10]

As they approached their villa, they noticed pajamas and boots scattered across the lawn in front of the pagoda and a pair of silk stockings floating from one of the windows. The Italians had beat a hasty retreat. They arrived at their house to find the grounds patrolled by French soldiers. After their police escort gave the password, a guard at the door allowed them inside. Reid was relieved to find most of the house intact. German soldiers from Villa Maas had fired their machine guns at the house, smashing windows and splintering the doors to the terrace. Bullets also riddled the dining room wall. Things, however, could have been very different. In the garden next to the lemon tree sat an unexploded shell lobbed into the city by the US Navy. The Arab couple that minded the house were also safe, although the wife refused to emerge from the cellar. She had been in hiding since the German firing spree.[11]

When Reid and Wiggins went upstairs to retrieve some clothing, they looked for a means of escape and reluctantly decided it was futile. Even if they managed to make the two-story drop onto the flagstones below without breaking a leg, they would have to foil their guards. The guards were armed; Reid and Wiggins were not.[12] They tried plan B: get their police escorts drunk and convince them to either let them go or join them in a dash for American lines. That didn't work either. While the Frenchmen enjoyed Reid's whiskey, it failed to change their disposition.[13]

REID AND WIGGINS ARRIVED back at the American consulate, suitcases in hand, half an hour before midnight. A small crowd—anxious Americans and twitchy French policemen—milled around a large bus parked in front of the bronze gates, flashlights casting their silhouettes and making masks of their faces.[14]

King had also joined the crowd, pacing back and forth on its edge. Earlier in the evening, a French policeman had slipped him a card bearing the words "This man is OK. Pinkeye." Vouched for by Michel Despax, the policeman then delivered a message. He told King that a car would be waiting for him around the corner, one street over, at a quarter to midnight. It was just the chance King had been waiting for. So that Russell wouldn't panic at his absence—and bring attention to it—King informed him of his plan to bolt. Russell wished him good luck and asked him to alert the American military as soon as possible about French plans for the consulate staff.

After a few minutes, the French policemen ignored King's pacing, writing him off as a man suffering from nervous frustration. When the officer on the perimeter turned his back, King made a run for it, sprinting down the street and around the corner. The promised car was there—and waiting inside were Captain Albert Breitel, Captain Chevalier, and Lieutenant Merglin. The trio hauled King into the car and headed for Aïn Diab, a small beachfront community on the outskirts of Casablanca, using their credentials to sail through the checkpoints erected around the city. Once there, King spent the night at Merglin's house.[15]

AFTER A BRIEF ROLL call, Reid and Wiggins climbed onto the bus, stashing their suitcases and belongings where they could find room. The French had told the Americans to bring as much as they wanted. Doctor Anton Rublev, Ernest Mayer, and Shelia Clark were on board as well. Sixteen members of the consulate staff and their families would make the trip, while five others, overlooked in the Protectorate's records, stayed behind. In the melee of people and luggage, King's absence went unnoted. Once everyone had taken a seat, French policemen armed with submachine guns took up positions in the rear of the bus and alongside the driver. Earle Russell, Russell Brooks, and their wives piled into Russell's big black Buick, which he had convinced the French to allow him to use.[16]

With everyone finally stowed away, they departed at around 12:45 a.m., the ancient bus lumbering through the deserted neighborhood. A few hundred yards down the Boulevard d'Armade, the driver slammed on the brakes, sending passengers and luggage flying forward. They had reached one of the many checkpoints that had popped up around the city. When the machine-gun-toting sentry asked for identification, the driver replied, "Ce sont les cochons du Consulat d'Amerique. [These are the pigs from the American consulate.]" Reid traded worried looks with his colleagues.

As the driver and sentry engaged in a lengthy discussion about paperwork and orders, Reid and Mayer noticed groups of men armed with small flashlights digging into the dirt in the road ahead. Few of Casablanca's streets were paved, even the grand boulevards. The bus's headlights caught the diggers' white armbands, emblazoned with the letters "SOL." The

French fascists were planting road mines! When the bus was finally allowed to proceed, the sentry directed it onto the pedestrian path lining the center of the boulevard. As it barreled through the tunnel of palm trees, branches scraped and whipped its exterior.[17]

The Americans had avoided the mines, only to be trailed by groups of SOL members on bicycles. The bus's slow progress and checkpoint stops made it easy for their tormentors to keep pace, hurl insults, and occasionally show their weapons. Despite their bravado, the SOL men failed to attack the bus, preferring bluster to combat. After hours of harassment and creeping through the dark city, the bus found the highway that led southeast to the Atlas Mountains and rumbled into the interior of Morocco.[18]

ACROSS THE ATLANTIC IN Washington, DC, the White House issued a press release announcing that Vichy France had severed relations with the United States. "I regret this action on the part of M. Laval," said Franklin Roosevelt. "He is evidently still speaking the language prescribed by Hitler. The Government of the United States can do nothing about this severance of relations on the part of the Vichy Government. Nevertheless, no act of Hitler, or of any of his puppets, can sever relations between the American people and the people of France. We have not broken relations with the French. We never will."[19]

44

Aux Armes, Citoyens!

HAVING OUTRUN HIS LOGISTICAL LINES, MAJOR GENERAL JOHN Anderson halted the advance of his men six miles north of Casablanca on the afternoon of November 9. Eight hours later, he was ready to move on the city. Shortly after midnight on November 10, Anderson renewed his advance. He knew the Americans had to avoid taking Casablanca building by building. The narrow labyrinthine streets of the medina and the *mellah* would give the French a natural advantage. Casablanca's beautiful palm-tree-lined boulevards were also perfect for deploying tanks.

The French, of course, expected the Americans and stationed troops at the city's perimeter. The half circle started north at Table d'Oukacha, dipping south to the crossroads where Route de la Grande Ceinture and the road to Marrakech met, before sweeping north again to finish at the formidable battery at El Hank. Along the eastern reaches of the perimeter, the French positioned artillery to harass Anderson's advancing force. Sailors who survived the naval battle on November 8 took up weapons and joined army units to defend the city. "Let every soldier or civilian, do his duty calmly in his place," Noguès told the citizens of Casablanca. "Le Maréchal, France, and Morocco are counting on you."[1]

As the sun came up on November 10, Anderson's men, bleary-eyed from lack of sleep, received their first taste of sustained opposition. Heavy enemy fire—artillery, grenades, machine guns—along with a widespread breakdown in communications scattered American troops pressing against the French perimeter. As American causalities mounted, more than three companies lost their commanding officers. Forced to withdraw, the Americans sought cover to regroup, taking shelter in buildings, huddling in ditches, and darting under bridges.

As if the French artillery barrage from the perimeter wasn't dangerous enough, rounds started arriving from off the coast. In mid-morning, two French corvettes slipped out of Casablanca's harbor and past the US Navy's patrol. The corvettes shelled American troops in the vicinity of Table d'Oukacha until the heavy cruiser *Augusta*, aided by four destroyers, chased them back into the harbor.[2]

Augusta's pursuit of the corvettes drew the ship closer to the shore—and within range of *Jean Bart*'s guns. Believing they had put the powerful battleship out of commission on the first day of fighting, Rear Admiral Kent Hewitt and his sailors were astonished—and rattled—when rounds began flying toward them. The French had worked furiously during the previous two days to repair the ship's guns, disguising their efforts by leaving them in the same position as when they jammed. When the Americans trained their glasses on *Jean Bart*, she still looked disabled.

The newly restored guns now tracked *Augusta*, lobbing ten two-gun salvos against the American battleship. The shots landed uncomfortably close, drenching *Augusta*'s crew on deck and on the bridge with yellow-tinged salt water.

Hewitt was having none of that. In mid-afternoon, a squadron of nine American planes assaulted *Jean Bart*, dropping 1,000-pound bombs on the French battleship. Two landed direct hits, tearing a massive hole in her haul. "No more *Jean Bart*!" declared the squadron leader after the fireball climbed into the sky.[3]

As the sun sank into the Atlantic, smoke once again tinged the sky around Casablanca's port. Anderson's battalions had also reached French defenses east and south of the city. The Americans seized the railroad line between Fédala and Casablanca, making it easier to move south the men and supplies now swelling Fédala's docks and beaches. Trucks dislodged from the wet sand also rolled toward Casablanca, stuffed with ammunition and other supplies.[4]

Now Anderson only needed Major General Ernest Harmon to arrive with his tanks from Safi, and Casablanca would belong to the Americans. Despite great gains over difficult terrain, Harmon's force was still fifty miles south of Casablanca and on the wrong side of the Oum er-Rbia River on November 10. Even though he lagged behind, his advance north meant the French wouldn't be reinforcing Casablanca with troops from Marrakech anytime soon.[5]

HOPING TO USE DARKNESS to gain a tactical advantage over the French position at Mehdia, Major General Lucian Truscott's men engaged in a series of operations as November 9 turned into November 10. As night descended, clouds gathered, dumping rain that made the beaches and marshes surrounding Port Lyautey even more treacherous under foot. The clouds also blotted out the sky, robbing the Americans of any starlight to guide their way.

As the Atlantic roiled off the coast, a demolition team departed from the *Clymer* at 9:30 p.m. for the mouth of the Sebou River, clinging to the sides of their rubber boat as they rode the angry waves forward. The Americans were going to try once again to cut the net. As long as it remained in place, the US Navy couldn't sail up the river to Port Lyautey. With darkness as its ally, the American boat passed through the mouth undetected and continued up the river under the noses of the French troops guarding the shore. The demolition team cut the cable and lowered another man into the water to check that no other obstructions remained. In the gloom, the team tripped a signal wire, which opened the boom—and brought down a hailstorm of French gunfire. As the river popped with bullets, the Americans retreated to the waters of the Atlantic with eight casualties.

Another company of men successfully slipped across the Sebou, only to lose their bearings in the black of night. They dug in and waited for daylight. Two more companies ousted the French troops guarding one end of the Port Lyautey Bridge, but they couldn't hold their position and suffered casualties under heavy artillery fire. To ensure the French couldn't use the bridge, a machine-gun platoon stayed behind, while the rest of the detachment retreated to tend to its wounded.

Major Percy McCarley's battalion landing team made another attempt to approach the airfield from the southwest. The operation called for three companies to swing past Port Lyautey, but the intense darkness caused them to veer toward the compound instead of away. They walked right into a machine-gun outpost. With bullets spraying into the night, McCarley's team scattered, seeking cover in the marshes.

A core part of Truscott's 60th Regimental Combat Team managed to regroup and, at around 4:30 a.m., approached what they believed to be a barracks on the outskirts of the military installation at Port Lyautey. After stationing men at all exits, they called out for the occupants of the blacked-out building to surrender. Bursting in, the Americans quickly realized they had stormed a café filled with French soldiers enjoying a glass of wine or a cup of coffee. Seventy-five Frenchmen surrendered without a fight. Another one hundred prisoners were soon rounded up.[6] By mid-morning of November 10, both the 1st and 7th Regiments of Moroccan Tirailleurs had surrendered, giving the Americans control of the roads leading to Rabat and Mehdia.

Things also appeared to be looking up for the Americans south of Port Lyautey. Having slogged through the rain and mushy ground to arrive at the edge of the military base, McCarley and the remnants of Company B encountered a group of French soldiers who wanted to surrender. To the west, the remainder of McCarley's midnight raiding party also fared well. Having joined up with the 70th Tank Battalion, the remaining members of the 1st Battalion Landing Team advanced on the airfield just after daylight and reached its outskirts just after 10:45 a.m.

AROUND 4:00 A.M., *DALLAS*, an aging destroyer, began fighting the ebbing tide to enter the mouth of the Sebou River. Heavy rain fell, adding a layer of gloom to the operation and making the unfamiliar water even more treacherous. On board, she carried seventy-five army raiders tasked with carrying out an assault on the airfield. With the kasbah still in French hands, a direct attack was impossible. An incursion via the river became Truscott's best play.

As *Dallas* passed between the jetties around 6:00 a.m., René Malevergne took the helm. King had smuggled the veteran river pilot out of Morocco in August for precisely this job. Now he steered the destroyer through the Sebou's mercurial currents, which made sport of tossing ships against the rocky shore or grounding them on sandbars. As the sea broke astern, the ship yawed violently and headed for a dangerous patch of shoal water. Malevergne steered the ship clear in what the *Dallas*'s commanding officer, Lieutenant Commander Robert Brodie Jr., described as a "masterful" piece of seamanship.[7]

As *Dallas* approached the boom, a fortified chain strung across the river to prevent ships from sailing up river, Malevergne and Brodie quickly realized that the cutting team had cleared a path where the water ran too shallow for the destroyer to pass. Before Malevergne could maneuver the ship to deeper water, *Dallas* became stuck in the mud, vibrating from stem to stern as its propellers dug into the river bottom. The floundering ship, now visible in the pale morning light, provided the French battery at the kasbah with the perfect target. While *Dallas* pushed its engines to the brink to try to slog free, a round landed thirty yards "dead ahead," sending up a terrifying splash. Another shell landed starboard, hitting so close that the impact jolted the stern of the ship out of the mud.[8]

The liberated *Dallas* cranked her engines to eighteen knots and rammed her way through the boom, surging up the river toward Port Lyautey. She had evaded those two French shells—but the French weren't done. A 75-mm gun chased her progress, splashing rounds into the water, while machine-gun fire from a ridge overlooking the river carpeted her deck. *Dallas* returned fire, quieting the French. From off the coast, the destroyer *Kearny* lobbed rounds inland, neutralizing a French battery that posed another threat. *Dallas* emerged from the French gauntlet with astonishingly little damage to ship or crew, prompting one of her officers to claim, "The hand of God was right around us!"

In an attempt to block the Americans, the French had sunk two steamers in the channel. Malevergne steered *Dallas* right between them. After safely making a hairpin turn in the river, *Dallas* headed south toward Port Lyautey, while two American planes from *Savannah* tracked her progress from above. Just after 7:30 a.m., *Dallas* fell victim to the shallows of the river, becoming hopelessly stranded in the mud. The French seized on her paralysis and opened fire, landing shells within ten yards of the ship. Within minutes, *Dallas*'s 3-inch guns and a few bombs dropped from her airborne escort had quieted the French position.[9]

As rounds fell around them, the army raider detachment scrambled over the side into rubber boats and made for the airfield. I Company, stranded north of Port Lyautey since losing their way in the dark, also sprang into action. The sight of *Dallas* barreling past their position had boosted the men's spirits.

By 8:00 a.m., the Americans controlled the airfield. By 10:30 a.m., P-40s launched from the decks of the Northern Attack Group's aircraft carriers were landing on its concrete airstrip.[10]

The French, however, hadn't given up yet. French troops still manned the batteries guarding the Rabat-Tangier highway and held the Port Lyautey Bridge. With the help of airborne spotters, *Texas*, *Eberle*, and *Kearny* lobbed rounds inland to neutralize them. By noon, the Americans controlled the city of Port Lyautey, along with the high ground southwest of the airfield, from which the French had so ably menaced them.[11]

For his "extraordinary heroism" in piloting the *Dallas*, Malevergne became the first Frenchman of the war to receive both the Navy Cross and the Silver Star. Brodie also received the Navy Cross for safely delivering the army detachment, which had changed the course of the battle for Port Lyautey's airfield.[12]

FROM THE BEGINNING OF the assault on Mehdia, the kasbah had bedeviled the Americans. Its reign of terror, however, came to an end on the morning of

November 10. Approaching from the south, the 2nd Battalion Landing Team neutralized the French machine-gun nests around the fortress and ousted pockets of entrenched French soldiers. Finally standing before its massive gates, the Americans attempted to pierce them at point-blank range with 105-mm artillery guns. The gates held firm, denying a new generation of invaders entry.

During the previous few days, Truscott had hesitated to call in an air strike on the kasbah, not wanting to endanger his troops fighting in close quarters with the French throughout the town. His reluctance evaporated when the French rained machine and rifle fire down on his men from the ramparts. Enough was enough.

After placing smoke shells around the perimeter, Truscott and his men retreated from the kasbah. Following the tendrils of smoke to their target, eight American dive-bombers swooped down. The ground rocked and eardrums vibrated as bombs exploded near the front gate, engulfing the fortress in a cloud of earth, stone, and smoke. After the last plane peeled away, the Americans rushed the gates, capturing the kasbah and 250 French prisoners within minutes.[13]

Throughout the day, the Americans continued to fight to secure the area around Port Lyautey. As evening approached, Truscott received an overture from Brigadier General Maurice-Noël-Eugène Mathenet to discuss surrender terms. But Truscott refused to talk unless the French produced Major Pierpont Hamilton, captured while en route to deliver a letter to Colonel Charles Petit. Around 10:00 p.m., a French jeep carrying Hamilton raced across the airfield at Port Lyautey as a bugle squawked the notes signaling cease-fire. Using a radio provided by the men of Company C, 70th Tank Battalion, Hamilton spoke with Truscott, assuring him he was alive and well. A surrender meeting was arranged for 8:00 a.m. the next morning in front of the gates of the kasbah.[14]

BY THE AFTERNOON OF November 10, Noguès had started to understand that he would have to relinquish Morocco to the Americans. Still camped out in Fez, he remained miles from the fighting, relying on a stream of reports to keep apprised of the progress of the French defense effort. The reports made for dismal reading. The Americans continued their advance on all fronts, and Casablanca would soon be theirs. Noguès, however, felt that he could not offer a cease-fire to the Americans without authorization from Vichy. His reluctance was both personal and political. He feared the personal repercussions of acting without authorization from his superiors, even if the state of the battlefield told him Morocco had been lost. After all, his one attempt at independent action in 1940—when he urged France to continue fighting from North Africa—had almost cost him his job. He also believed the longer Morocco held out, the better Vichy's negotiating position with the Allies would be.[15]

With communications a jumble, he sent a personal envoy, Captain Gaston Baitaille, to brief Henri-Philippe Pétain in person about the state of affairs in Morocco. He acknowledged that the Americans possessed the troops and matériel needed to control the country, while the French effort had dwindled to "sacrificial missions." Even though French troops fought "magnificently," they lacked the desire to carry on against the Americans. "Their feelings would have been very different had the aggressors been English," he wrote. Civilians also wished for a cessation of hostilities before the destruction wrought by both sides threatened the country's economic future. The longer the fighting endured, the more likely civilians would become casualties.

Despite the depressing state of affairs, Noguès did not suggest surrender. "As long as I am at the helm, your orders, which are those of France, will be obeyed," he wrote. The other message he wanted delivered to Pétain he would not put on paper. His envoy would deliver it orally: if Pétain wanted to save North Africa, he must agree to a cease-fire.[16]

After Baitaille departed, a rumor reached Noguès that Admiral Jean-François Darlan had issued orders on behalf of Pétain to stop the fighting. The third-hand report required confirmation, a difficult undertaking given the cut telegraph lines and lack of a direct phone line from Morocco to Vichy. As he waited for verification, Noguès telephoned General Georges Lascroux, the general commanding officer for French Morocco, to warn him of the impending cessation of hostilities. Shortly after 6:00 p.m. on November 10, the commanders in Casablanca and Marrakech received orders by radio to cease fighting.

Noguès finally heard the text of Darlan's orders around 7:00 p.m., the words coming over a phone line from Oujda. He instructed Vice Admiral François Michelier to arrange a meeting with Lieutenant General George Patton the next day. Michelier, angry that his ships lay at the bottom of the ocean, wanted to continue fighting, going so far as to telegraph Vichy behind Noguès back. He too was told to surrender.[17]

45

The Return

NESTLED IN AN OUTCROP OF LAND SOUTH OF CASABLANCA KNOWN as the Corinche, the beachfront enclave of Aïn Diab provided a manageable retreat from the crush of the city center. The salty smell and lulling rush of the ocean onto the beach replaced the stench and cacophony of the port, cars, horse and donkey carriages, and street vendors hawking their wares. There, as a guest at Lieutenant Merglin's house, Dave King spent the day hiding from French authorities, receiving a steady stream of visits from his French resistance contacts. He was gratified to hear that a major who had pledged not to fight the Americans had surrendered himself and his battalion without firing a single shot.[1]

At around sundown Captain Albert Breitel and several other members of the resistance returned to Merglin's house with news of Lieutenant General George Patton's declaration: if the French continued to resist, he would bomb Casablanca the next morning. Throughout the operation, the Americans had restricted their focus to military targets, doing their best to avoid residential areas. If the French didn't surrender, civilians would become fair game.[2] Patton's logic struck King as a "terrible psychological error" that would lead to thousands of civilian deaths.

Hoping to talk Patton out of his foolhardy plan, King decided to make a break for the American lines. Breitel knew of an ambulance heading to Rabat that evening and suggested King pose as a stretcher bearer. A uniform was produced, and King swapped his civilian clothes for the regulation attire.

Before King departed, his French resistance comrades asked if he understood what would happen if the French caught him. He did. He would be taken prisoner—or shot on the spot. King assured them that he understood the risks. Words failing him, he stoically shook the hands of the men who had risked their careers and lives for him over the previous months. The silence between them conveyed everything: duty, honor, thank you, good luck.

The job of driving King to the ambulance fell to Breitel. "We will know if you are stopped," Breitel told him in the car. "We know where they will put you, and we'll shoot your way out for you, if it takes the last man of us. We won't let you die at the post."

But King never made it past the first sentry, who had received orders not to let any traffic through. Not even Breitel could supersede the order. They returned to Merglin's house and, after tossing around options, decided to try to meet up with General Ernest Harmon's men coming north from Safi.

The journey south proved slow going as they threaded their way around the mines, traps, and barricades laid to thwart the American advance. King noted their locations so he could pass the information along to Harmon's men. When they reached Mazagan without spotting any sign of Harmon, they decided to sweep around Casablanca and meet up with the Americans north of the city. But a chance encounter with an American staff officer with news of the cease-fire cut their journey short. Instead, they drove back to King's house in Casablanca. After cutting the seal on the door, placed there by the Swiss consul, they popped open a bottle of champagne and drank to the impending American victory.[3]

DESPITE TRAVELING ONLY 140 miles to Kasba Tadla, the bus carrying the American consulate staff didn't arrive until 7:00 a.m. on November 10. Day three of the American invasion was just beginning.

News of their arrival electrified the town of 5,000, drawing a small crowd of gawkers within minutes. Yet curiosity quickly turned to derision as the townspeople started flinging insults at the Americans. Kasba Tadla had provided many sons and husbands to the French navy, some of whom now lay at the bottom of Casablanca's harbor. Staff Reid noticed at least a dozen young French girls dressed in black, pressing handkerchiefs to their eyes.

After assessing the situation, Earle Russell demanded to see André Trouvé, the *contrôleur civil* for the region, and was taken to his home. Trouvé rose from his sickbed to meet with him. Having only learned of the Americans' impending arrival a few hours before, Trouvé requisitioned the main hotel in town, ironically named the Hôtel des Alliés, and two rooms in the Cercle des officiers, along with whatever other accommodations were available. He also contacted Admiral François Michelier and Georges Poussier, the *contrôleur civil* for Casablanca, letting them know about the insufficient accommodations in Kasba Tadla and asking if the Americans could be lodged in another town. Both men sent Trouvé a negative response. The Americans were to stay put.[4]

The Russells received the keys to the hotel's bridal suite, which featured an elaborate canopied bed and a gaudy painting of the Temptations of Saint Anthony in a heavy gold frame. Reid was billeted in a house a few doors down. An old farmer answered the door and directed him to a room on the ground floor facing a poultry yard. Tired to his bones, he fell onto the rock-hard mattress and promptly fell asleep.

REID AWOKE AT AROUND 4:00 p.m. to find two roosters and several hens staring at him. After he chased them away and cleaned up, he stumbled back to the hotel where Russell and the others were engaged in a heated discussion. While the Americans slept, Charles Noguès had ordered them moved to Marrakech. Then another telegram arrived ordering their transport to Azrou, which lay 110 miles northeast of Kasba Tadla. Although the accommodations would be better, the last-minute change in plans made Russell suspicious. Trouvé, sympathetic to their situation, provided further grounds for Russell's unease. He confessed to learning that the Americans' final destination was Ourzazate, where they would be imprisoned in one of the many forts that dotted the town.

Suspecting they were now being held as hostages, Russell refused to leave Kasba Tadla until he received more information about Noguès's plans for them.[5] They hadn't sought protective custody, they hadn't asked to go to Kasba Tadla, and they certainly weren't going to become hostages if they could avoid it. Trouvé sent along Russell's protest, and the wait for a reply began.[6]

As the telegrams traveled back and forth between Kasba Tadla and Fez, Trouvé extended every courtesy. He invited Earle Russell, Russell Brooks, and their wives to join him for dinner and to enjoy his hospitality for the night. Though genuinely touched by the kind treatment Trouvé extended to his staff, Russell couldn't accept such a gesture from a French official, no matter how much he wanted to. Trouvé found the refusal shocking at first but came to understand Russell's quandary.[7]

While the Americans dined at the hotel, a messenger arrived from Trouvé requesting Russell's presence. As the minutes ticked by while they waited for Russell to return, Reid and others debated what new tricks Noguès and his cronies might dream up. Their speculations were fortified by more wine after they moved from the dinner table to the bar, which had filled with townspeople eager to get a look at the Americans.

Around 9:00 p.m., Russell burst through the front door, accompanied by a gaggle of military and civilian personnel. Reid immediately noticed Russell's red face—a face he'd seen when he'd angered the affable diplomat—and feared the worst.

Russell picked up a glass and tapped it with a butter knife. The room fell silent as all eyes turned him. Addressing the room in French, he announced the cease-fire. "The war between us is over!"

Pandemonium broke loose in the bar. "Tables were over-turned," wrote Reid. "The same people who a few minutes ago had only bitterness and scorn in their hearts for us, now grabbed us, pushed us around in ecstasy of sheer joy." The bar's proprietor announced that drinks were on the house. Champagne corks popped one after the other as the bottles were passed around to fill and refill glasses. An accordion player soon appeared. As the opening verses of "La Marseillaise"—"Allons enfants de la patrie, le jour de gloire est arrivé!"—filled the room, caps came off, and the French men and women stood at attention, belting out the words with gusto until the last note.

Much to Reid's disappointment, the accordion player didn't know "The Star-Spangled Banner."[8]

46

Gentlemen's Agreement

SHORTLY BEFORE 2:00 A.M. ON NOVEMBER 11, A CAR CARRYING FOUR French soldiers—two officers and two enlisted men—barreled down the highway from Rabat to Fédala, making no attempt to hide its progress. As its headlights cut through the dark, notes from a bugle drifted out of the windows, and white flags flapped against the car. Arriving at an outpost of the US Army's Company G, 30th Infantry, stationed northeast of Fédala, the French soldiers requested directions to the Western Task Force's headquarters. Instead, the Americans gave the car a personal escort.

Upon arriving at the Hôtel Miramar, the French officers explained their mission to a Colonel Horbart Gay, George Patton's chief of staff. General Georges Lascroux had tasked them with delivering a cease-fire order to General Raymond Desré, who now commanded the Casablanca division. Gay gave them safe conduct and a warning: if they didn't return bearing a French agreement to negotiate an armistice, American bombs would start raining down on Casablanca starting at 7:30 a.m.[1]

With Major General Lucian Truscott's men still in the throes of securing Mehdia and Port Lyautey and General Ernest Harmon's tank corps still miles from Casablanca, use of naval air and gunfire offered Patton his best option for taking Casablanca quickly and avoiding house-to-house fighting. A little old-fashioned competition also spurred Patton's desire to secure the city. Communications with Gibraltar had been spotty since the invasion began, but one telegram that managed to arrive indicated that Patton lagged behind his cohorts. "Dear Georgie—Algiers has been ours for two days," wrote Dwight Eisenhower on November 10. "Oran defense crumbling rapidly with navy and shore batteries surrendering. The only tough nut left is in

291

your hands. Crack it open quickly and ask for what you want." Eisenhower knew how to motivate Patton. At the bottom of his personal copy of the message, Ike commented, "Will he burn!"[2]

As the wee hours ticked toward dawn, the Americans waited for the French to officially notify them of surrender. Patton's staff heard multiple reports of cease-fire orders, but no flag of truce had appeared; nor did a senior French official come as an envoy. At 4:20 a.m., Colonel Kent Lambert, Patton's intelligence officer, woke him to say that the French had ceased firing at Rabat and Port Lyautey. When Lambert suggested calling off the attack, Patton refused. "It was too late, and besides it is bad to change plans," he wrote in his diary.

As the sun began to rise, *Augusta*, *Cleveland*, and *New York*, along with several other ships, maneuvered into place off the coast of Casablanca, preparing their guns for the assault on the city.[3]

The French surrendered at 6:40 a.m.

Before TORCH began, Patton had said that he would take Casablanca in four days. He did it in seventy-four hours. "A nice birthday present," wrote Patton, who turned fifty-seven that day.

At 7:30 a.m., Major General John Anderson and his men entered Casablanca with orders to attack if they faced any resistance. As thousands of American soldiers marched into the white city, Patton and his staff held their breath. It was one thing for a country's leadership to surrender; it was another for the order to travel down to the smallest unit. They also had no way of knowing what the Service d'ordre légionnaire or another fascist group might do.

"No one stopped him," wrote Patton of Anderson. "But the hours from 7:30 to 11:00 were the longest in my life."[4]

BEFORE DAYBREAK, STAFF REID, Earle Russell, and others rose from their beds in Kasba Tadla and shook off the previous night's wine to start the journey back to Casablanca. They hoped to return before the Western Task Force entered the city for its victory march. André Trouvé dismissed the ramshackle bus that had brought them there and arranged for army vehicles and drivers to take them back to Casablanca. Reid traveled in the first car with Mrs. Russell Brooks and Len Wiggins, while Earle Russell and Josephine followed in their Buick. The rest of the staff trailed behind.

As the American consulate caravan made its way west along the highway, roadblock sentries stopped them, only to wave them on as soon as Reid's chauffeur cheerfully announced, "Americans!" Approaching the military airfield outside Casablanca, Reid marveled at the devastation wrought by the Americans. "All over the field were the battered hulks of twisted and still smoking ruins of French planes," wrote Reid.[5] Off in the distance, he noticed a line of khaki-colored figures advancing toward them. The US Army was closing in on the airfield. "It was a thrill to shake every depth of emotion," wrote Reid. "One year and a half preparing, organizing . . . waiting and hoping the Army would come. Now the climax. No shame to stop the tears in every eye."[6]

A column of American tanks rumbling up the highway brought Reid's car to a stop. The chauffeur, a "veritable speed maniac," had outpaced the consulate caravan by several minutes, making them the lone car on the road—a lone car with French army markings. A hatch popped open on one of the tanks, and a colonel and three soldiers scrambled out. As they approached Reid's car, they drew their .45's.

"Who in the hell are you?" asked the colonel. "What are you French civilians doing in the battle zone?"

"Colonel, we are Americans and belong to the U.S. Consulate at Casablanca," said Reid. "We have been held in captivity and are now on our way back to the city."

Unconvinced, the colonel told his crew to cover them while he checked out the story. Russell's black Buick pulled up behind Reid's car, and he too faced a barrage of questions from the colonel. After Russell announced his identity and presented his papers, the colonel let out a hearty laugh.

"Go to it, boys, you're in the right alley now!" said the colonel, waving them on.[7]

As they approached the outskirts of the city, they noticed a smattering of Casablancans lining the streets in anticipation of the US Army's arrival. After the caravan crossed the last bridge into the city, Reid attached a small American flag to the reflector mirror. At the sight of the flag, people on the sidewalk cheered. The cheers—"Voilà les Américains! Voilà les Américains!!"—continued as they inched toward the city center, battling the crowds now filling the streets. Flowers rained down onto Reid's car and through the open windows. When the cars entered the square in front of the consulate, the crowd went wild, cheering and clapping. Children and young men clung to tree branches, having climbed high to get a better view. A swarm of French police worked to hold back the crowd. American soldiers stood guard outside the bronze consulate gate, which Casablancans had threaded with red and white roses. Two flags—one American and one French—painted on cardboard hung from the bars too. Reid and the others struggled to fight back tears as they exited their cars. After being carted off at gunpoint to an uncertain fate, they had returned to a hero's welcome.[8]

FIGURE 46.1. The staff of the US consulate return from their imprisonment at Kasba Tadla to a square full of cheering Casablancans. *NARA*

Georges Criblez, the Swiss consul, soon appeared, pushing his way through the crowd to reach them, a huge smile plastered on his face. Overjoyed to see Russell, Criblez embraced him and kissed him on both cheeks. Also present were the commissioner of police, along with several other officials from Casablanca's regional government. After retrieving the key from Criblez, Russell unlocked the main gate and popped the seals on the front door of the consulate. Everything was just as they had left it.[9]

Reid and the consulate's aged porter, Sam, wasted no time rushing up to the roof, where they raised the American flag. When the Stars and Stripes unfurled against the crisp, blue autumn sky, the crowd below let out a roar.[10] Someone started "La Marseillaise," and soon the square filled with hundreds of voices singing the revolutionary anthem. A less hearty, but no less heartfelt, singing of "The Star-Spangled Banner" followed.[11]

SHORTLY AFTER 6:00 A.M., Dave King was rousted from bed by his resistance cohorts. They had a problem: Vice Admiral François Michelier had agreed to the cease-fire but neglected to send a flag of truce. They wanted King to go to Fédala and use his clout to convince Patton to call off the bombardment.

King dressed quickly and joined his cohorts in the waiting car. They tried to get around the American flank and head north, only to be foiled at every turn. Finally they ran into an American staff officer who delivered the news that Casablanca would not be bombed.

Seeing an American tank column snaking its way into the city, King followed its progress and discovered Generals John Anderson and William Eagles at French division headquarters. Although Patton had aborted the bombardment, King had another worry: the impending executions of General Antoine Béthouart and his staff. Even as the French defended Morocco from the Americans, they managed to hold a court-martial and find Béthouart guilty of treason. Rumor had it that their sentences were to be carried out that day.

King caught a ride to Fédala with Anderson, who was escorting Rear Admiral Pierre-Jean Ronac'h, commander of naval forces for French Morocco, and General Raymond Desré, commander of the Casablanca division, to the armistice ceremony. Upon arriving at the Hôtel Miramar, King met other members of the senior leadership of the Western Task Force, including Patton and Rear Admiral James Hall, who served as Kent Hewitt's chief of staff. Patton seemed uninterested in Béthouart's fate, believing it an internal French problem. King had better luck persuading Hall that something must be done to spare their resistance friends a gruesome fate. With Hall's help, King convinced Patton to include in the armistice agreement an order declaring that no one would be executed for his role in the invasion without American approval.

With Hall, Anderson, Eagles, and a few other high-ranking American officers in tow, King visited Ronac'h, who served as the intermediary between a very angry and depressed Michelier and the American high command. Ronac'h also had reason to hold a grudge against the Americans: he had orchestrated the *Jean Bart's* escape from German hands in June 1940 only to have American bombs rip her to shreds.

When King informed Ronac'h of the order, the rear admiral sneered that he was unaware of any executions scheduled in the Casablanca-Rabat sector. King told him the order applied to all of Morocco, including Meknès, where Béthouart sat in prison. Playing coy, Ronac'h declared he had no jurisdiction over those divisions. King made clear that the Americans would still hold him responsible for any ill fate that befell Béthouart. Shaken by the veiled threat, Ronac'h reached for the telephone.

As he waited for the call to go through, Ronac'h surveyed the men accompanying King and asked why he had brought with him a bunch of helmeted, tommy-gun-carrying noncommissioned officers.

"I am very sorry. Let me present General Anderson, General Eagles . . . " said King, rattling off the names of the men standing behind him.[12]

The phone call saved Béthouart to fight another day.[13]

THE ARMISTICE CEREMONY BEGAN with lunch. Upon learning that Resident-General Charles Noguès could not attend the proceedings until mid-afternoon, Patton arranged for a meal at a brasserie in Fédala. A shell from an American destroyer had ruined the kitchen in Hôtel Miramar. When Hewitt arrived at the restaurant, he found a dozen high-ranking officials from both sides: Patton, Michelier, and members of their respective staffs. Colonel William Wilbur served as an interpreter, along with Major Francis Rogers from Hewitt's staff, but their services were rarely needed as most of the French officers spoke English.[14]

Hewitt considered the armistice an army matter but decided to venture ashore when he discovered that Michelier would be attending. The admiral found himself uncertain about how to address the man whose fleet he'd sunk only a few days before. He opted for the straightforward approach: Hewitt stuck out his hand—which Michelier took—and told him that the Americans "had come as friends and old allies, and that it was with the greatest regret that we were forced to fire on the tricoleur."

Michelier looked Hewitt in the eye. "Admiral, you had your orders, and you carried them out. I had mine, and I carried them out. Now, I am ready to cooperate in every way possible."

Over a surprisingly cordial lunch, Hewitt asked about port facilities in Casablanca, which the Americans needed to start making use of. "You have not seen it! *C'est une cimitière!*" said Michelier.[15]

FOR THE ARMISTICE PROCEEDINGS at 2:00 p.m., Lieutenant General George Patton erred on the side of formality, believing there was "no use kicking a man when he is down, particularly a potential ally."[16] When Noguès, Michelier, and the rest of the French military high command arrived at Hôtel Miramar, an honor guard greeted them, and Colonel Gay personally escorted them inside. "This made a very happy impression upon them and was, I believe, a precursor of the excellent entente which has existed ever since," wrote Patton.[17]

Many of the men who gathered in the hotel's smoking room for the conference had served in the Great War. For the French officers, November 11 represented the end of four years of brutal fighting that had resulted in millions of deaths at places like the Somme and Verdun. It represented the triumph of the French and the Americans, along with the British Commonwealth, over Germany and Austria. Now that date would have a new meaning: American victory over French forces in Morocco. What would that victory look like?

FIGURE 46.2. Resident-General Charles Noguès is escorted up the steps to Hôtel Miramar by Colonel Hogard Gay, Patton's chief of staff. *Naval History and Heritage Command*

Patton decided that the two sets of surrender terms drafted before the invasion no longer made sense. One set assumed that the French greeted the Americans with open arms; the other assumed the complete destruction of French military power. Patton believed circumstances called for something in between. "French Morocco is a protectorate and not a province, and its local security therefore depends on retaining the prestige of the French army," he wrote. With only 33,000 men, the Americans were in no position to occupy French Morocco and replace the French administration. Nor did Patton believe that the French really wanted to fight the Americans. "I felt that most of the time they bombed the ocean rather than the beach."[18]

Patton opened the meeting by congratulating the French on their gallantry, which helped to generate goodwill. But the mood in the room quickly soured as Colonel Wilbur read out the harsh surrender terms that applied if the French resisted the American invasion. They called for the Americans to occupy Morocco and seize control of its government and military. Noguès vigorously protested, arguing that the Americans were incapable of governing Morocco. He also hinted at the possibility of an "Arab uprising" if the Americans displaced the French.[19]

With the French rattled and angry, Patton changed tack and now portrayed himself as their friend. Instead of using the terms dictated by Eisenhower, he presented his own, characterizing them as a "gentlemen's agreement." The French military would be confined to barracks but not disarmed. The Americans would be free to occupy any cities, areas, or installations they needed to ensure security and facilitate future Allied operations. Both sides would exchange prisoners and claim their dead. Retaliation against individuals who aided the Allies was forbidden without Eisenhower's approval. The "gentlemen's agreement" would stand until the armistice agreement covering all of French North Africa, then being negotiated in Algiers, was signed. Realizing he had received a gift, Noguès agreed to the terms. French Morocco, for all intents and purposes, remained his.[20]

To close out discussions, Patton played, in his words, "a very nasty trick" on the French. "Gentlemen, we have now settled everything, but there is one disagreeable formality which we should go through." Worried looks reappeared on French faces. Patton then produced some champagne and suggested they drink a toast to the termination of hostilities and the resumption of Franco-American friendship. "They drank $40 worth of champagne, but it was worth it," wrote Patton.[21]

During the meeting with Noguès, Patton acted without Eisenhower's approval. A few days later, he wrote to Ike, explaining the logic behind his approach. "Had I insisted on disarming the army and removing the navy from the ships and shore batteries, I would have dealt such a blow to the prestige of the French that I am personally convinced a revolution would have eventuated." He realized he was taking a chance, but "the end justifies the means."

"We do not wish to occupy this country and pacify it," wrote Patton.[22]

SHORTLY AFTER THE ARMISTICE ceremony, Colonel John Ratay, Patton's military intelligence assistant, asked Staff Reid to assist with a mission. The Americans had received a report of a riot in Casablanca's Jewish quarter, and Ratay was being sent to investigate. The last thing the Americans needed was for the Arabs and Jews to start fighting among themselves.

When they arrived at the Place de France, adjacent to the old medina, Ratay spied a tank and suggested they mount up. Reid squashed that idea, pointing out that the tank couldn't navigate the narrow streets. They would have to proceed on foot. With Reid in his civilian clothes and Ratay in his uniform, they formed a colorful duo. "Colonel Ratay looked the part of a

Roman gladiator wearing a battle helmet and a wide mustache that added
a touch of fierceness," wrote Reid. Like Patton, Ratay favored wearing his
pistols swinging from both sides of his belt.[23]

Reid and Ratay entered the old medina through the main gate and followed the winding streets toward the *mellah*. They weren't alone. A group of
Moroccans started following them, and with each step forward, their number
grew. "Don't pay any attention to that," Ratay told Reid. "I've handled Arab
crowds before during riots. Just show 'em who's the boss."

After navigating a tight passageway, they arrived in the *mellah*, entering a small square lined with two-story stucco buildings. A body lay on the
ground beneath the awning of a souk. Groups of men huddled in conversation dotted the square, while the sounds of women sobbing drifted down
from the balconies and windows above. Behind them, the passageway filled
with men.

Reid felt a touch on his shoulder and turned to see Sidney Nahon, a Jewish employee of the American consulate, standing beside him. He'd heard
that Reid and Ratay had gone to the *mellah* and came to tell them to clear
out. "There will be reprisals and bloodshed," said Nahon. He urged them
not to become "mixed up in this thing."[24]

The warning failed to impress Ratay. "I don't leave this place until every
Jew and Mohamedan here realizes that the Americans have taken over now
and we represent law and order," he said. "If they shoot us, our tanks will
blow these walls down!"

Nahon decided not to stick around, leaving Reid and Ratay, hand on his
weapon, standing in the square. After about five minutes, Ratay decided that
he'd done enough posturing and could leave. As they made their way out, the
crowd of men who shadowed them slowly parted to let them pass. "I never
saw anything like it before," wrote Reid.[25]

An investigation by American officials later determined that a riot started
shortly after the cease-fire was announced. Excited about the American victory, Jews took to the streets, clapping and shouting, "We are the victors! We
are the victors!" Fascist elements unhappy with their pro-American celebration encouraged a group of young Arabs to attack the Jewish men with clubs.
Rumors of wholesale slaughter and mutilation ran rampant through the city,
becoming more lurid with each retelling.

In describing the incident to the State Department, Earle Russell blamed
the Jews. "It is to be feared that the Jews on this occasion largely brought
their trouble upon themselves, inasmuch as immediately after the suspension
of hostilities they became very much in evidence upon the street, shouting,
clapping their hands and crying out," he wrote.[26]

47

Algiers

O N THE EVENING OF NOVEMBER 7, ROBERT MURPHY PERCHED NEXT to a radio in his office in Algiers, listening to the BBC. As events played out in Morocco, another drama unfolding simultaneously in Algiers would have profound consequences for the aftermath of TORCH. Like Dave King and Staff Reid, Murphy waited for the signal that TORCH was about to begin. Unlike in Casablanca, the resistance cells had not been ordered to stand down and were poised to act on receiving word that the invasion was a reality. During the few previous days, Murphy had coordinated with the resistance groups in Algeria, particularly the Group of Five, which had been the subject of much hand-wringing in Washington and London. Now those men would spring into action, securing key points around Algiers and serving as guides on the dark beaches. The fear that things could go horribly wrong nagged at Murphy, prompting him to burn papers, destroy codes and ciphers, and put his affairs in order.

After the BBC announcer confirmed the Allies were off the coast, Murphy and Kenneth Pendar, one of his vice consuls, headed for 26 Rue Michelet, the home of Henri Aboulker, a Jewish doctor, and the unofficial headquarters of the resistance in Algiers. As they made their way across town, they passed people heading to the movies, waiting for buses, and dressed for dinner, just as they would on any Saturday night. The sense of normalcy was both reassuring and unsettling.[1]

Shortly after midnight, the resistance fanned out across Algiers, seizing police stations, rail terminals, power stations, and military headquarters. A major piece of the plan, however, was missing: General Henri Giraud. General Charles Mast and his Group of Five cohorts had promised that the triumphant arrival of General Giraud in North Africa would inspire the French military to unite behind him, disavow Vichy, and join the Allied cause—but Giraud had failed to materialize. Murphy sent frantic radio messages asking about Giraud's whereabouts, only to learn he was at Gibraltar and would arrive shortly. It didn't make sense that Giraud wouldn't come to Algiers. Only later did Murphy learn that he had been in the bunker at Gibraltar arguing with Dwight Eisenhower and Mark Clark about who would command the Allied war effort in North Africa.[2]

As the clock hands ticked well past midnight, Murphy decided to call on General Alphonse Juin, the highest-ranking French army officer in North Africa. Murphy knew Juin harbored Allied sympathies and hoped to enlist him to deliver Algiers—better yet, all of North Africa—without the Americans firing one bullet. He had less than two hours to make his case before the Americans were due to hit the beaches in Algeria.

After talking his way past the Senegalese guards posted outside Juin's house, Murphy convinced a servant to roust the general from his bed. Dressed in pink striped pajamas, his hair sprouting wildly, Juin padded into the drawing room. As Murphy delivered the news of the invasion, Juin started to pace, shaking off his grogginess with each step. Only a week earlier, Murphy assured him that the United States had no intention of invading North Africa, a pledge Juin welcomed since it would save him from having to defend Algeria. Now, tens of thousands of American soldiers floated off the beaches around Algiers and Oran. Murphy asked Juin to issue orders instructing French troops not to fire on the Americans coming ashore.[3]

"Who invited the Americans?" asked Juin.

"Giraud," said Murphy.

Juin continued to pace, turning over the implications of Giraud's arrival.

"If the matter were entirely in my hands, I would be with you," Juin told Murphy. "But, as you know, Darlan is in Algiers. He outranks me and no matter what decision I might make, Darlan could immediately overrule it."

Admiral Jean-François Darlan's unexpected presence in Algiers complicated an already sticky situation. After visiting French Morocco for an inspection tour at the end of October, Darlan traveled to Algiers to see his son Alain, who sought treatment for poliomyelitis. He arrived in secret and retreated to the hospital room where his son battled for his life.

"Very well," said Murphy, "let us talk with Darlan."[4]

TWENTY MINUTES LATER, DARLAN arrived at Juin's villa. The return of Pierre Laval to Henri-Philippe Pétain's good graces had circumscribed

Darlan's power, but he still served as commander in chief of Vichy's armed forces and outranked every French military and naval officer in North Africa. He also remained one of the most hated men of the war. Officials in Washington and London loathed him for collaborating with the Germans and willfully lying about Vichy's intentions and policies. The American and British people despised him too, their hatred stoked by the media's gleeful portrayal of Darlan as a Hollywood-style villain. Knowing his reputation, Franklin Roosevelt nevertheless authorized Murphy to work with Darlan should events in North Africa require it. Avoidance of bloodshed between French and American troops would be worth any public relations fallout from dealing with a notorious collaborator.[5]

Nineteen months had passed since Murphy last laid eyes on Darlan in Vichy. Now the short, balding admiral yelled at him, his face turning an angry purple as he spewed invectives in rapid-fire French.

"I have known for a long time that the British are stupid, but I always believed Americans were more intelligent," spat Darlan. "Apparently you have the same genius as the British for making massive blunders!" As he paced the room, he sucked on his pipe, leaving tendrils of smoke in his wake. Murphy walked with him, shortening his long gait to match Darlan's staccato march, offering every argument he could muster for joining the Allies.[6]

After a half hour of quarrelling and pacing, Darlan remained unconvinced. His own skin aside, Darlan hesitated to align with the Allies because of the inevitable German reprisals on Vichy and Occupied France. Hitler would see Vichy's failure to defend North Africa as a betrayal and exact vengeance. Murphy reminded Darlan that he had vowed to join the Allies if the Americans appeared in North Africa with a formidable force of men, tanks, and airpower. That army had arrived.

"I have given my oath to Pétain and preserved allegiance to the Marshal for two years," said Darlan. "I cannot revoke that now. This premature action is not at all what we have been hoping for."[7]

If Pétain gave his blessing to cooperating with the Allies, Murphy asked, would Darlan do so as well? Darlan said yes and agreed to write a message for the *maréchal*.

When Juin and Darlan attempted to leave the villa for Fort l'Empereur, where they would send a message to Pétain and assess whether Murphy was telling the truth about the invasion, a group of resistance fighters stopped them. While the men paced and debated inside, the resistance displaced Juin's guard, stationing forty of its members around the villa. Men with guns lurked in the shrubbery and behind walls. Murphy, unaware of the plan to surround the villa, found the turn of events disconcerting. The resistance fighters' insistence on serving as informal jailers, however, gave him the opportunity to play for time with Darlan and Juin. Since the Frenchmen were trapped, Murphy offered to have Pendar deliver the text of the telegram to the fort instead. Darlan and Juin agreed, handing him a sealed envelope.[8]

Instead of delivering the telegram to Fort l'Empereur, Pendar took it to the resistance's headquarters on Rue Michelet. When they popped open the seal, Pendar discovered that Darlan, true to his word, had informed Pétain of the American invasion and Murphy's entreaties. Darlan also pledged to defend North Africa.

The telegram was not sent to Vichy.[9]

WHILE MURPHY, JUIN, AND Darlan waited for a reply from Pétain, the clock worked its way past 2:30 a.m., the Americans' planned arrival time in Algiers. As the city slumbered, quiet reigned, darkness muffling the port's noisy, sun-washed daytime persona. Three o'clock came and went. So did four. Still no sign of the Eastern Task Force or Giraud.

As paranoia enveloped him, a stressed and sleep-deprived Murphy wondered if he'd confused the time or even the day of the invasion. He'd slept so little since returning from Cherchell and the meeting with Clark and Mast. The previous four days of activity only compounded it. Finally allowed to tell his resistance contacts about the impending invasion, he encountered an exhausting mix of angry excitement and recrimination.

As 6:00 a.m. approached with no sign of the Eastern Task Force, worry and anxiety coursed through Murphy's body, tightening every muscle. Darlan, earlier a cauldron of rage and spite, grew more relaxed and smug with each passing minute. The changed dynamic led Murphy and Darlan to have a blunt conversation about political and strategic chessboard before them. After Murphy recounted the story of how Giraud became involved, the admiral shook his head.

"Giraud is not your man," said Darlan. "Politically he is a child. He is just a good divisional commander, nothing more."[10]

Shortly after 6:30 a.m., a ruckus in the garden halted their conversation. When Murphy stepped outside to explore the source of the commotion, more than four dozen members of the Gardes mobile confronted him. Rumors of Juin and Darlan's imprisonment ran rampant through Algiers, and the military police had come to liberate them. Shoving a gun barrel into Murphy's back, the soldiers marched him over to the porter's house, which became an impromptu jail. As Murphy stepped through the door, a voice behind him suggested he should be shot. Pendar, already inside, didn't hear the ominous

proposal but couldn't help but notice Murphy's ashen face, even as the affable Irishman offered assurances that everything would be fine. When one
of the Senegalese soldiers guarding the door offered him a cigarette, Murphy
wondered if the gesture was a small, final act of kindness before a wall and a
bullet.[11]

"I came within an ace of being shot as the military police at that moment were not interested in explanations," wrote Murphy months later.[12] His
guardian angel appeared in the form of Juin, who rescued both him and Pendar before anything deadly occurred.

In the aftermath of the uproar and the change in guard, Juin and Darlan
learned that the message for Pétain had not been sent. Pendar was again dispatched to the Admiralty to arrange for its transmission.

This time, the message went to Vichy.[13]

DARLAN BELIEVED MURPHY HAD exaggerated the American operation—
that it might even be pure fantasy—but the reports flooding in told a different
story. In Morocco, the US Navy battled the French fleet outside Casablanca's harbor, while American soldiers swarmed the beaches of Safi, Fédala,
and Mehdia. The Center Task Force had also landed on the coastline around
Oran and proceeded toward the city with little resistance. Outside Algiers,
the Eastern Task Force, a combination of American and British troops, had
made landfall and closed in on the capital. By 8:40 a.m., the Americans controlled the aerodrome at Maison Blanche, which served as the primary military field for Algiers.[14]

Darlan also received a telegram from Pétain. The marshal gave him freedom to act in his name, pushing responsibility for dealing with the Americans back onto his shoulders. Whatever unfolded in Algiers, Darlan's neck
was on the line.[15]

AT AROUND 3:00 P.M., Darlan returned to Juin's house seeking Murphy's
assistance in contacting the general in charge of the American force engulfing
Algiers. Murphy agreed to act as intermediary and accepted the offer of a car
and driver, along with a white flag, for the journey to the beach.

As Murphy made ready to leave, the sound of gunfire floated over the
walls of Juin's villa. When he poked his head out of the gate, Murphy spied
a platoon of American soldiers advancing along the wall, weapons drawn,
squeezing off rounds as needed. Waving the white flag, Murphy approached
the platoon and explained who he was. Even with Murphy's midwestern ac-

cent, the lieutenant remained skeptical, but he allowed him to come closer. Upon learning the lieutenant's last name was Geiser, Murphy said, "You are the best looking Geiser I have seen in a long time!" Now convinced that Murphy was "a bona fide American," thanks to the terrible joke, the lieutenant provided Murphy with an escort for his mission.

When Murphy arrived at the landing beach, the first officer he stumbled upon wasn't American but British and, even more astounding, the son of the prime minister. Captain Randolph Churchill delivered Murphy to Major General Charles Ryder, commander of the Eastern Task Force. Ryder welcomed the news that the French wanted to discuss a cease-fire. Murphy offered to give him a lift to French headquarters, which the general gladly accepted. As in French Morocco, the beaches in Algeria had turned into parking lots, as anything with wheels quickly bogged down in the wet sand.[16]

Upon arriving at Fort l'Empereur, the rumpled and sleep-deprived duo of Murphy and Ryder were escorted to a chamber packed with fifty French officers. Above their precise collars and gleaming medals, the military and naval men wore grim masks of resignation. As they made their entrance, an American bomb dropped nearby, rattling the room. Ryder's face broke into a smile. "How wonderful!" said the general. "This is the first time since World War I that I have been under fire."

A sea of stern faces stared back at him.

Murphy introduced Ryder to Juin, and within a matter of minutes the two generals agreed to a cease-fire covering Algiers starting at 8:00 p.m., after which Algiers would be subject to American occupation.[17]

The Americans and British had conquered Algiers, the jewel of France's North African empire, in less than one day.

48

The Darlan Deal

O N THE MORNING OF NOVEMBER 9, AS FIGHTING CONTINUED IN
Morocco and around Oran, Major General Mark Clark boarded a
plane bound for Algiers. As Clark's party—two B-17 bombers escorted by
thirteen Spitfires flying in close formation—headed east across the Mediterranean, it skimmed the cerulean blue water at a height of five hundred
feet. After the dim confines of the underground bunker at Gibraltar, Clark
relished the chance to drink in the fresh air and wide sky. Donning a helmet
and a pair of goggles, Clark popped open the panel over the radio room and
watched the coast of Africa materialize. In case the flight ran into trouble,
Clark and his men carried special identification papers in French and Arabic,
along with belts stuffed with gold pieces to buy whatever help they needed.
The journey to Algiers, however, proved uneventful. The same could not be
said of the four days that followed.

At the very moment Clark's plane touched down at Maison Blanche
airfield outside Algiers, a dozen German Junkers flew overhead bound for
the harbor in search of American ships unloading supplies at the docks. The
French may have agreed to a cease-fire, but the Germans had not. Dodging
antiaircraft fire, the Junkers dropped their bombs on the port, only to find
themselves in a skirmish with the American Spitfires, which gave chase. The
sky above Maison Blanche morphed into a battlefield as the dogfight drifted
back toward the airfield. And just as Clark's B-17 finished taxiing, slow and
vulnerable on the ground, one of the Junkers dropped a stick of three bombs,
which landed within a hundred feet of the plane's tail. The roar of the explosion was followed by the whine of a Junker barreling down on them. Caught
by the flak from the antiaircraft guns, the plane plummeted toward Clark's

B-17, forcing him and his fellow passengers to make a mad dash for cover. The Junker shattered into pieces at a thousand feet, raining metal down on the airstrip.[1]

After such a dramatic arrival, the luxurious surroundings of the Hôtel Saint Georges provided a welcome oasis. Perched on a hill and surrounded by a lush botanical garden, the hotel had greeted well-to-do travelers with its French spin on Arab fantasia since the late nineteenth century. The owner harbored Allied sympathies, and Robert Murphy had arranged with him for the hotel to become the new home of Allied Forces Headquarters. The Americans quickly nicknamed it "George Sank."

Ensconced in Clark's suite, Murphy briefed him on the developments of the previous thirty-six hours: Admiral Jean-François Darlan was in Algiers, and General Henri Giraud did not have the backing of North Africa's military leaders.

Clark exploded. "This really messes things up!"

That very morning Lieutenant General Dwight Eisenhower and Giraud had reached an agreement specifying that Giraud would serve as part of an overall American command. In a radio broadcast, Eisenhower expressed American support for Giraud's leadership. "General Henri Giraud has arrived in Algiers from France," Eisenhower told listeners. "It can be expected that his presence there will bring around a cessation of scattered resistance."[2]

"We've got to put Giraud back into this business right away," said Clark.[3] If Giraud did not claim a position in the French leadership of North Africa, the Americans would look foolish. Clark's own reputation was also at stake because he led the meeting with Giraud's men at Cherchell and participated in the discussions at Gibraltar.

Desperate for sleep, Clark decided to retire for the night and tackle the thicket of French politics into which he'd been thrust in the morning. Eisenhower had sent him to Algiers to negotiate an immediate cease-fire to preserve American and French lives, not to debate the future of France.

"What a mess! Why do soldiers have to get mixed up in things like this when there is a war to be fought? It's awful!" he wrote in his diary before turning in.[4]

RECOGNIZING HE NEEDED HELP negotiating the labyrinthine politics of North Africa, Eisenhower asked Franklin Roosevelt for permission to appoint Murphy as his civil affairs officer. Ike could concentrate on defeating the Germans in Tunisia, while Murphy dealt with the political and economic aftermath of the Allied invasion. Murphy was also the closest thing the Americans had to an expert on French North Africa. One of Murphy's first jobs in his new role would be to explain the current political situation to Giraud.[5]

The renegade general had made his way to Algeria earlier in the day, arriving at Blida airfield, some forty miles outside Algiers, accompanied by three French staff officers.[6] A radio message by Giraud broadcast the day before urged the Army of Africa to join with the Americans and stated his intention to resume command. "I ask for your confidence," said Giraud. "You have mine. We have only one passion—France—and only one goal—victory. Remember that the Army of Africa holds in its hand the destiny of France." But the officers and noncommissioned officers did not rally behind him. They still looked to Vichy.[7]

Murphy dreaded the upcoming conversation with Giraud. Nothing they promised him was coming to pass. The meeting, however, went better than expected. Giraud listened to his explanation of how circumstances had evolved. "Giraud evinced no surprise when I told him that Darlan and Juin blamed him for jumping the gun," wrote Murphy.[8] Unlike Darlan, a rabid political animal, Giraud harbored no political ambition. He wanted only to preserve French sovereignty and ensure the Frenchmen played a role in operations on French soil.

ON THE MORNING OF November 10, two days after the Americans arrived in North Africa, a platoon of American soldiers surrounded the perimeter of the Hôtel Saint Georges. Inside, a small conference room burst with French generals and admirals, along with Clark and his staff. Clark sat at the head of the long table that dominated the room, with Admiral Darlan on his left and General Alphonse Juin on his right. The military leadership of French North Africa filled out the remainder of the chairs. Missing from the conclave was Charles Noguès, who continued to battle George Patton in Morocco. Giraud was also absent, as he lacked the authority to issue orders in North Africa. Murphy and Colonel Julius Holmes, who had been at Cherchell, acted as interpreters when needed. Captain Jerauld Wright, another Cherchell veteran, was also on hand. Commodore Royer Mylius Dick served as Britain's observer. The French refused to shake his hand.[9]

Clark immediately got to the point: Was Darlan prepared to sign the cease-fire? "It will cover all French North Africa," said Clark. "It is essential that we stop this waste of time and blood."[10]

Darlan evaded the question, asserting that he awaited instructions from Vichy, which would be forthcoming after the Council of Ministers met that afternoon. He lacked the authority to enter into negotiations without Henri-Philippe Pétain's permission. As he gave his answers, he repeatedly pulled out his handkerchief and wiped away the perspiration gathering on his balding head. The beads of sweat, along with his watery eyes, sprang from anxiety but also from lack of sleep. Unlike Clark, Darlan had not gone to bed, opting instead to track the increasingly grim reports of France's military position around Oran and in Morocco.

Clark didn't buy it. "Here is an opportunity for all Frenchmen to rally and win the war," he said. "Here is your last chance!"

For the next half hour Clark and Darlan argued heatedly through their interpreters. Perched in the seat of power, Clark banged on the table to emphasize his points and threw in choice English phrases that left little doubt about his intentions. He didn't care a lick about French politics. He wanted the fighting to stop and that's what he would get.

"Tell him that Pétain is nothing in our young lives," Clark directed the interpreter. "He has today broken relations with the United States and declared this landing as an act hostile to France. He ordered resistance. As far as we're concerned, we don't recognize any authority of Pétain in North Africa."[11]

Clark asked why Darlan couldn't sign the armistice if he was confident that Pétain would agree to a cease-fire. Darlan claimed he was bound by an oath to the *maréchal*. When Clark suggested he would simply have Giraud sign the armistice, Darlan claimed that the troops wouldn't obey Giraud. As a member of the resistance, he was considered a traitor.

Frustrated with the admiral's evasions, Clark threatened to throw Darlan into a cell at Gibraltar, where he could wait out the remainder of the war. Darlan later complained to Murphy that Clark had spoken to him like a junior-grade lieutenant, not a five-star admiral. The condescending tone was nothing compared to what Clark called Darlan in private: a yellowed-bellied son of a bitch.[12]

After thirty minutes, Clark and Darlan remained at an impasse, prompting Juin to suggest they break for a recess. "Give us five minutes to ourselves, and we'll talk it over," he told the Americans.

It was becoming abundantly clear to Clark, Murphy, and the other Americans that the work done by Giraud, General Charles Mast, and their resistance colleagues—the intelligence provided, the meeting at Cherchell, the decision to put their lives on the line in the hours before the Americans appeared—meant little to those who had not done the same. Darlan, Juin, and the other Vichy collaborators didn't admire Giraud—they disdained him and had no intention of uniting behind him. They viewed Giraud and his resistance cohorts as traitors, much in the same way that Noguès considered General Antoine Béthouart and his band of resistors turncoats. The French generals and admirals gathered in the conference room at the Saint George had sold their souls to Vichy, but they still possessed the power to command troops and enact a cease-fire. If Clark wanted to end the fighting and head for Tunisia, where Erwin Rommel and the Afrika Korps awaited, he would have to deal with them—Darlan in particular—however distasteful.

Five minutes later, Clark and others returned to the room. Instead of a fight, the Americans received acquiescence.

"We will sign," said Juin.

Darlan issued a cease-fire order covering all ground, air, and naval forces in Morocco, Algeria, and Tunisia. He also assumed authority over French North Africa "in the name of the marshal." All civil and military officials were to remain at their posts and continue to exercise their duties.

When news of Darlan's deal with Clark reached Vichy, Pétain approved it. The Germans, who monitored French communications, also learned of the deal and threatened reprisals unless Pétain reversed himself and ordered the Vichy government in North Africa to continue to resist. Pétain changed course, rejecting the deal and appointing Noguès as the new commander in chief of French forces in North Africa. Despite Pétain's back pedal, German and Italian forces marched into unoccupied France.

When Darlan learned that Pétain had stripped him of his authority, he informed Clark that he must revoke the cease-fire order.

"Damned if you do," said Clark.

"Then I must consider myself your prisoner," said Darlan.[13]

As THINGS BEGAN TO unravel in Algiers, a message arrived from Pétain for Darlan via a secret naval code, one that the Germans couldn't read. The marshal continued to have faith in Darlan and approved of his actions. Pétain's vote of confidence, along with the news of Germany's occupation of Vichy, galvanized Darlan, Juin, and the others. Now able to rationalize fighting with the Allies as an honorable course, they issued orders for all French troops in North Africa to resist any military action against French positions by the Axis.[14]

After Eisenhower received news of Germany's occupation of Vichy, he encouraged Clark to work with Darlan and Juin to convince Admiral Jean-Pierre Esteva, the resident-general of Tunisia, to seize all German men and material in that country. "I am hopeful that Clark can bulldoze Darlan, Kingpin [Giraud], and Juin into bringing the French forces in Tunisia over to our side," Eisenhower reported to Washington. "Those forces are strong enough to destroy every Axis soldier and airman in the territory if we could only make them move. . . . We are leaving no stone unturned in order to secure every possible advantage out of the rapidly changing situation."[15] On the afternoon of November 10, Darlan ordered Esteva to seize all German men and matériel in Tunisia.[16]

Eisenhower also had one more item on his wish list: bringing what remained of the French fleet over to the Allied side. The British had spent the previous twenty-eight months obsessing about its fate and praying that it would not fall into German hands. Britain's attack on Mers-el-Kébir fractured relations with the French to such a degree that the Allies had to obscure any British participation in TORCH. Worried that Darlan had waited too long to galvanize the French navy, Eisenhower sent a personal message to the fleet inviting it to join the Allies.[17]

ONE MAN STILL SAT on the sidelines. When Giraud learned that Darlan had issued the cease-fire, he considered it an affront. As the presumptive commander in chief of all French forces in North Africa, that honor should have fallen to him. Despite his dismay, Giraud also recognized that events in Algiers had spun out of control—to a degree beyond which he cared to assume responsibility. His short time in Algiers had provided a crash course in the political landscape of French North Africa, and he wanted nothing to do with it. During a meeting with Murphy and Clark, held in a car with just the three of them to ensure their privacy, Giraud offered to serve under Darlan.[18]

That same evening, Darlan and Giraud met for the first time since the arrival of the Allies. Since the invasion, they had lived on parallel tracks: Darlan operated at the center of the action with the full backing of the French military structure, while Giraud stayed with the leaders of the resistance in Algiers's Arab quarter. Now the two men came together to forge an agreement: Darlan would serve as a "high commissioner" for French North Africa, while Giraud commanded French troops.[19]

"You can now see I have two Kingpins, but hope to wiggle out of it somehow," Clark wrote Eisenhower. "I deemed it of utmost importance to secure an order which would be effective to cease hostilities everywhere."[20]

Giraud's decision not to challenge Darlan provided a temporary solution to the question of French leadership in North Africa. But the Americans still had a major problem: no Frenchman with any authority in Algiers would sign an armistice.

Darlan wouldn't do it. Giraud couldn't do it. They needed Noguès.

ON THE MORNING OF November 11, faced with the destruction of Casablanca and news of developments in Algeria, Noguès ordered French forces in Morocco to cease fire. Later that afternoon, he met with Patton at the Hôtel Miramar and signed an armistice covering Morocco. That evening he flew to Algiers. Like his French colleagues, Noguès felt the strain and stress of the previous four days, his body struggling to cope with the lack of sleep. He now also bore responsibility for French North Africa.

Upon arriving in Algiers, Noguès found his way to Clark's office in the Hôtel Saint Georges and demanded a meeting. As Pétain's commander in chief for North Africa, Noguès believed Clark owed him the courtesy of a private conversation. Clark, however, disagreed. "I do not recognize either you or Pétain," said Clark. If Noguès had any doubt as to the meaning of Clark's words, the American's icy stare telegraphed the contempt behind them.

Now that Noguès had arrived, talks about the future of French North Africa could resume. Once again, the French and Americans assembled in the conference room. Clark opened the conversation by outlining Allied objectives and how the French could help. He also made it clear he would throw anyone who resisted or failed to provide assistance into the brig on an American ship in Algiers's harbor. After an hour, Clark asked for Giraud to be admitted to the meeting.[21]

Noguès had intentionally snubbed Giraud on his arrival. Working the hotel lobby like a good career politician, Noguès greeted old friends and former colleagues with hearty handshakes and kind words. When Giraud stepped forward with his hand extended, Noguès turned away. "I do not know a general in dissidence," said Noguès. Now Clark insisted that Noguès not only acknowledge Giraud but also shake his hand. Noguès complied, but the gesture lacked any trace of warmth.

With Giraud's presence, the meeting, which started out on a cordial note, quickly spiraled into discord. Clark and his staff left the French to argue among themselves. Noguès's impending arrival had offered the promise of resolution, but now he became the problem. He refused to recognize the power-sharing agreement between Darlan and Giraud, thereby rejecting the armistice.

When the meeting broke up, Juin decided to make Noguès's stonewalling public. He chose the hallway outside the conference room as his venue, ensuring both the Americans and French would hear. "Enough of your dirty politics Noguès," said Juin. "Now we are going to fight the Germans."[22]

Noguès's obstinacy only compounded the growing dread among Clark, Murphy, and other Allied officials in Algiers: Darlan held the key to getting the armistice signed. Juin would not act without first consulting him. Noguès had refused to stop fighting in Morocco until he received Darlan's cease-fire order. Had it not arrived, Patton would have bombed Casablanca to rubble. Esteva, the resident-general of Tunisia, made it clear he would only obey Darlan. Meanwhile, Mast, Giraud, and Béthouart were regarded as traitors by their colleagues. Giraud also became convinced that only Darlan could unite French forces in North Africa and bring them over to the Allies. And despite the arrival of the Allies, the population of French North Africa hadn't risen up and revolted against Vichy.

Given the choice the Allies now faced—whether or not to make an agreement that would keep a notorious Nazi collaborator in power—Eisenhower would have to bless the deal.[23]

49

Crooks and Turncoats

ON THE MORNING OF NOVEMBER 13, LIEUTENANT GENERAL Dwight Eisenhower and Admiral Andrew Cunningham, the highest-ranking British officer on Ike's staff, flew from Gibraltar to Algiers.[1] Bad weather had prevented them from coming the day before to help Mark Clark deal with the "exasperating" French personalities. Eisenhower found it hard to muster any sympathy for the anguish that permeated the French deliberations in Algiers. As far as he was concerned, the French could "get together and come with us and be the future Marshals of a greater France, or they would go into oblivion." Eisenhower also worried that any sign of discord might encourage Moroccans, Algerians, and Tunisians to challenge France's authority. France's control of its colonies depended on its projection of force. Its administrators could not be seen behaving like petulant children angry about not getting their way.[2]

Shortly after Eisenhower and Cunningham arrived, Clark and Robert Murphy briefed them on the situation, filling in details they could not share in telegrams. It was the first time Eisenhower and Murphy had been together since they sat under the tree in Ike's yard two months earlier. Now Eisenhower was about to experience the politics and personalities of French North Africa that Murphy had tried so hard to convey.[3]

When Eisenhower met with the French, he saw for himself the psychology at work. He found the cult of personality around Henri-Philippe Pétain shocking. "Everyone from the highest to lowest attempts to create the impression that he lives and acts under the shadow of the Marshal's figure," wrote Eisenhower, attempting to explain the phenomenon to his colleagues in London and Washington. "The Civil Governors, Military leaders and naval commanders will agree on only one man as having an obvious right to assume the Marshal's mantle in North Africa. That man is Darlan." Even Henri Giraud had recognized Jean-François Darlan's claim as heir apparent and modified his own ambitions. "The resistance we met initially was offered because all ranks believed this to be the Marshal's wish and for this reason the Kingpin [Giraud] is deemed to have been guilty of at least a touch of treachery in urging non-resistance to our landing," wrote Ike.[4]

Given the circumstances, Eisenhower could either arrest Darlan as a collaborator or sign an agreement keeping him in power to save American and French lives. The Allies could occupy all of French North Africa and replace the French administration or concentrate their efforts on beating the Germans in Tunisia. They could bring the Pétain-worshiping French forces over to the Allied side or continue to fight them and potentially lose what remained of the French fleet.

Eisenhower had only to say no and the deal would dissolve.

"The whole matter has now become a military one," Murphy told Eisenhower. "You will have to give the answer."[5]

Eisenhower decided to make a deal with the devil.

AT 2:00 P.M., EISENHOWER met with Darlan, Charles Noguès, and Alphonse Juin. Ike informed them that he accepted the armistice agreement hashed out with Clark on one condition: the French would attack the Germans.

Darlan gave his consent and vowed to adhere to the agreement "scrupulously"—but while he "heartily" agreed with defeating the Germans, he also worried about the reconstruction of France. Eisenhower acknowledged his concern but again emphasized the expectation that the French would "get in and pitch."[6]

The armistice agreement approved by Eisenhower allowed France to maintain administrative and military control of its North African colonies, provided that its officials cooperated with the Allies. Darlan would oversee French North Africa, thereby allowing the Allies to use the colonies as a base for fighting the Germans and Italians. The Allies would receive unfettered access to French ports, bases, and airfields. Giraud would lead French forces with Alphonse Juin as his deputy, while Vice Admiral François Michelier, who fought so tenaciously against the US Navy in Casablanca, would lead its naval forces. Noguès would remain resident-general of Morocco. Eisenhower pointedly made no commitments as to the future of leadership of France and no promises to Darlan about his future role.

EISENHOWER ASKED MURPHY TO return with him to Gibraltar to help draft a series of telegrams explaining the logic and circumstances behind what became known as the "Darlan Deal." Opting for expediency, Eisenhower chose not to send its terms to Washington or London for review. Instead, he used the authority given to him by Franklin Roosevelt to deal with any French official necessary to aid the cause of Allied victory. In Eisenhower's mind, enlisting the French in the war merited any resulting public and political firestorms. The decision was his and his alone. Ike also knew he might very well be fired.[7]

An exhausted Murphy slept through the nerve-racking landing at Gibraltar. Arriving late in the evening, the plane circled the darkened military base below, looking for the runaway. "I saw no way out of a bad predicament and still think the young lieutenant pilot must have depended more upon a rabbit's foot than upon his controls to accomplish the skillful landing that finally brought us safely down," wrote Eisenhower.

After dinner, Eisenhower, Murphy, and the others worked on writing the cables outlining the terms of the deal. In his plain-spoken style, Ike described why they had opted to work with Darlan. "The actual state of existing sentiment here does not repeat not agree even remotely with some of prior calculations," wrote Eisenhower. "Salient fact is that the agreement reached is only alternative to disorder and passive possibly active resistance, of which results would be disastrous."[8]

Knowing his decision would be controversial, Eisenhower justified it in terms of military expediency. "I realize there may be a feeling at home that we have been sold a bill of goods, but I assure you that these agreements have been arrived at only after incessant examination of the important factors and with the determination to get on with military objectives against the Axis to advance the Allies in winning this war," he wrote. If the Allies did not work with Darlan, any chance of quickly seizing Tunisia would evaporate. He also emphasized that Darlan would not be unsupervised. Giraud would keep an eye on him, as would Clark and Murphy. Eisenhower would also be moving from Gibraltar to Algiers within a matter of days. He too would watch over Darlan.[9]

The initial announcement of the Darlan Deal omitted Giraud's role because of the lingering hostility toward him in French North Africa. While good for French politics, the omission merely emphasized Darlan's centrality. Darlan had also wanted to include a disavowal of Charles de Gaulle—neither he nor his London-based government would be recognized in French North Africa—but Eisenhower squashed the idea. No mention of de Gaulle was made.[10]

When the British learned about the Darlan Deal, cables full of rage and disbelief flew from London to Gibraltar and Washington. The arrangement so worried Winston Churchill that he intended to send an emissary from de Gaulle to Algiers to "fix things . . . with KINGPIN." To head off that scheme, Eisenhower wrote to Churchill, promising that he had not cast Giraud aside. "Please be assured that I have too often listened to your sage advice to be completely handcuffed and blindfolded by all of the slickers with which this part of the world is so thickly populated," wrote Ike.[11]

Churchill also wrote Roosevelt to express his concerns. "The more I reflect upon it the more convinced I become that it can only be a temporary expedient justifiable solely by the stress of battle," wrote the prime minister. "We must not overlook the serious political injury which may be done to our cause not only in France but throughout Europe by the feeling that we are ready to make terms with local Quislings. Darlan has an odious record." He reminded Roosevelt that "it is but yesterday that French sailors were sent to their death against your line of battle off Casablanca and now for the sake of power and office Darlan plays turn-coat."[12]

The Foreign Office fired off an equally strong note to the State Department, warning of the "grave political dangers" ahead. It wanted to know the United States' long-term plans for governing North Africa and Darlan's role in them. It also questioned whether the Americans fully grasped how damaging the deal was to morale in France and other occupied countries, not to mention to the Allies' reputation. "There is above all our own moral position," noted the Foreign Office. "We are fighting for international decency and Darlan is the antithesis of this."[13]

Eisenhower, Clark, and Murphy had drastically misjudged the emotional and moral response to their pragmatic decision. Ike and Clark were political neophytes looking to get the job done, while Murphy's immersion in French North African politics obscured his broader judgment. At the same time, the Americans had made no plans for replacing the Vichy administration, having believed that they and Giraud's men would be welcomed as liberators.

The intensity of the public firestorm around the Darlan Deal forced Roosevelt to issue a statement on November 17. The 450-word text used the word "temporary" five times to describe the arrangement with Darlan. "The present temporary arrangement in North and West Africa is only a temporary expedient, justified solely by the stress of battle," it read. The pact was necessary owing the "stress of battle" and "the vital factor of time." Roosevelt emphasized that the future of the French government remained to be decided. "We are opposed to Frenchmen who support Hitler and the Axis. No one in our Army has any authority to discuss the future Government of France and the French Empire."[14]

Darlan, smarting from the sting of public disavowal, complained to Clark. "Information from various sources tends to substantiate the view that

'I am only a lemon which the Americans will drop after they have squeezed it dry,'" he wrote.[15] The admiral's lament forced Roosevelt to send a private message praising French assistance and conveying his hope "that the splendid cooperation would continue."

Even as the outcry threatened to obscure the accomplishments of the first American outing in the European theater—the securing of Morocco and Algeria in four days—Eisenhower had no regrets. Within days of the end of hostilities with the French, the ports of Casablanca, Oran, and Algiers were already becoming Allied supply hubs. The French shared a trove of intelligence on Tunisia, which would aid the Allied advance against the Afrika Korps. Arrangements were being made for delivery of shipments of sugar, tea, oil, and cotton to Morocco and Algeria. "Once the population looks to us as their benefactors, I can tell all the turncoats and crooks to go to hell," wrote Eisenhower.[16]

WELL AFTER THE MEMOS and cables written at the time, Eisenhower, Clark, and Murphy all justified the Darlan Deal in their memoirs. Even in hindsight, they had no reservations about it. Eisenhower emphasized that the Allies could not afford to replace the French administration wholesale, while noting the arrangement was always intended as a temporary measure.[17] Murphy noted that Roosevelt had made the decision to subordinate French politics to winning the war. "The Good Lord knows we needed a military success in 1942," he wrote. "We could not discuss this publicly at the time, and the storm of charges that the United States was foisting Darlan on postwar France had to go unanswered then." Murphy also believed that Eisenhower deserved credit for shouldering the responsibility for a difficult decision. "A less courageous man might have become alarmed by the outcry."[18]

Clark, still stinging from the criticism almost a decade later, offered a full-throated defense. "I took a great deal of blame later for dealing with a collaborator in North Africa," wrote Clark. "There is only one real answer that I can give—as Ike's deputy, I was charged with fighting a war, or, more specifically, with preventing a war against the French and getting on as rapidly as humanly possible with the war against the Axis in Tunisia. That meant I was trying to save American, British, and French lives—a great many of them. That meant that every day, every hour, was important not only to ending French resistance but in getting our forces into French Tunisia, some four hundred miles to the east. And to carry out this mission, I was ready to deal with anybody who could do the job."[19]

PART THREE

"Men Pass, France and Morocco Remain"

50

Aftermath in the White City

CASABLANCA SURVIVED THE AMERICAN INVASION RELATIVELY UN-scathed except for the port, where scarred and burned-out ships littered the quays and approaches. Stray shells from barrages launched by the US Navy landed in the city when they overshot their marks, but the overall damage to the town was relatively minimal. Had Charles Noguès not asked for a cease-fire on the morning of November 11, the Americans would have reduced the city to rubble, as the Portuguese once had. Instead, the twisty streets of the old medina still held their secrets close, while the white apartment blocks and manicured boulevards of the *ville nouvelle* basked in the afternoon sun.

While the city remained standing, it would take a few days for it to re-claim its rhythm. As the fighting unfolded, the majority of Casablanca's inhabitants sheltered in their homes. They couldn't flee west—the Atlantic Ocean and the US Navy blocked that route. Heading east meant ventur-ing into the interior, whose desert reaches and craggy mountains promised a cruel existence for the unprepared. To the north and south French and Amer-ican troops were amassing and fighting. With the battle over, Casablanca's civil controller encouraged businesses to open their doors again on Thurs-day, November 12. Secondary school students should make sure they'd done their homework because their teachers would expect them in class. Elemen-tary schools would resume on Friday. Concerns about possible mischief and protests led to a ban on public assembly and an order closing all cinemas until further notice. All citizens were to be in their homes by 7:30 p.m. and observe strict blackout rules.

The invasion disrupted the schedule for purchasing rations, but the con-troller assured that deliveries—and shopping—would resume soon. In the meantime, Casablancans needed to collect and use the purified water provided at stations around the city. The fighting had damaged the city's purification plant, making it impossible to deliver filtered water to taps.[1]

THE RESIDENCY ALSO EMBARKED on a campaign to sell the new regime headed by Jean-François Darlan. With the help of the *La Vigie marocaine*, Casablanca's largest daily newspaper and unofficial government mouthpiece, the Residency spun a new tale of hope and eventual victory.

Throughout the fighting *La Vigie marocaine* had served up a string of proclamations about the progress of the war and Vichy's determination to fight the American aggressors. It printed Henri-Philippe Pétain's pledge to Franklin Roosevelt that Vichy would defend itself, along with Pierre Laval's telegram to Noguès saying that France counted on him to defend Morocco.[2] Pronouncements lauded Noguès's handling of French defenses and the sacrifices made by French and Moroccan soldiers and sailors, while downplaying the rapid American advance. The paper even found space to print a notice proclaiming the Service d'ordre legionnaire's support for purifying France and her colonies of their infection with "Jewish lepers."[3]

By November 11, *La Vigie marocaine* could no longer deny that the Americans had conquered French Morocco and Germany had gobbled up Vichy. "By order of the resident general the hostilities have ceased in Morocco," screamed the headline in large type. Below it appeared the text of Hitler's Radio Paris broadcast justifying German troops marching into Vichy—and below that appeared Pétain's protest against German actions.[4]

On November 12, as Noguès debated the future of North Africa with Mark Clark in Algiers, a proclamation by him appeared on the front page calling for "dignity, duty, and unity." Fighting with "legendary bravado," French forces had never wavered from their oath to defend France. In the face of defeat, French Morocco could hold its head high. Noguès assured the people of Casablanca that even though the Americans had triumphed, nothing in French Morocco would change. The bonds between France and the sultan remained as strong as ever. "We should all remain close around the one who saved us at Verdun, symbolizing eternal France; around His Majesty the Sultan, who in these days of ordeal, gave the representative of France his complete and loyal support," read Noguès's proclamation. Even in the wake of defeat, Noguès continued to bind Pétain and the sultan.[5]

The front page of the Saturday, November 14, edition trumpeted Darlan's appointment as high commissioner of French North Africa, which had Pétain's and Noguès's blessing. A triptych of pictures of Noguès, Pétain, and

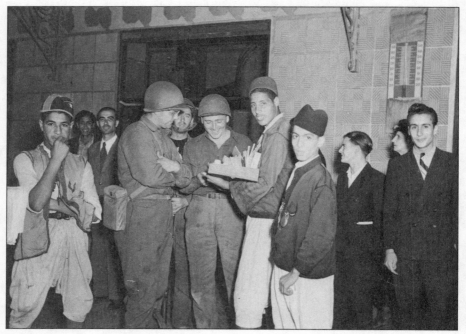

FIGURE 50.1. US soldiers on the street with Casablancans, ca. 1943. *Naval History and Heritage Command*

Darlan stretched across the page. Through a proclamation, Noguès passed his authority to Darlan, who accepted it in the name of the marshal. The Pétain cult that so flummoxed Dwight Eisenhower remained alive and well.[6]

THE RESIDENCY WANTED TO sell the idea that everything in Morocco was as it had been under Vichy. In some ways, that was true. Military chiefs kept their commands, soldiers remained at their posts, and political and administrative functionaries would continue to do their jobs. But the citizens of Casablanca could hardly fail to notice that the city swarmed with Americans.

Before the war, there were fewer than 110 Americans in the entire country. But the Western Task Force had disgorged 33,000 American soldiers into French Morocco, now concentrated mostly between Casablanca and Rabat. Casablanca teemed with thousands of American soldiers and sailors with close-cropped hair, speaking English with accents that ranged from the flat cadence of the Midwest to the twang of Texas, from New England's dropped *r*'s to the South's elongated vowels. The incessant slaughtering of the French language added to the cacophony as the Americans tried out the phonetic crib sheets they'd been given:

Do you speak English? (*Parlez-vous l'anglais?* / Pare lay voo lan glay)
A cup of black coffee (*Une tasse de café noir* / Eune tahass duh *ca*fay nwar)
I want this souvenir (*Je veux ce souvenir-ci* / Juh vuh suh *suv* near sea)
General Giraud (Général Giraud / Jay *nay* ral *Gee* row)[7]

The more adventurous soldiers tried out the Arabic phrases printed on the back.

Hello (Peace to you) (*Sa-laam a-lai-kum*)
Thank you (*Ka-tirr kh-irak*)
How much does this cost? (*Kid-dash*)[8]

With housing in short supply, the men of the Western Task Force pitched their triangular pup tents around Casablanca, occupying parks, squares, and the empty reaches at the perimeter of the city.[9] The Stars and Stripes flapped in the wind alongside the French tricolor.

ON NOVEMBER 14, MAJOR General George Patton relinquished his quarters on the USS *Augusta* to take up residence in Casablanca. Sailors gathered along the railings, hanging over the side to get one last look at the general. As Patton made his way down the gangplank, they sent him off with a boisterous cheer. "I was later told this was spontaneous and seldom accorded to a non-naval person," wrote Patton.[10]

The six-story art deco Shell Building in the *ville nouvelle* became the nerve center of the Western Task Force. Patton set up shop in the director's office, an ornate paneled room with an imposing desk, on the third floor. After a short stint at the Hôtel Majestic—which still lacked running water—Patton eventually moved into Villa Maas, the "small marble palace" that once housed Theodor Auer and hosted a string of Nazi visitors.[11]

In the aftermath of the invasion, Patton switched gears from fighter to administrator. As commander of the Western Task Force, he now oversaw the US Army's informal occupation of French Morocco. "While I am convinced that Noguès is a crook," Patton told Eisenhower, "I believe that I can handle him."[12] Patton's job was to secure the region so that it could become the logistical hub that Allied planners envisioned. The points where the Americans came ashore on November 8 became the centers of their administration. From Port Lyautey, General Lucian Truscott minded northern French Morocco, keeping an eye on the coast, along with Fez, Petitjean, and Meknès on the interior. The 47th Infantry minded southern Morocco from its headquarters in Safi, sending regular patrols to Marrakech, Mogador, and Mazagan. Patton kept watch on Casablanca, Fédala, and Rabat, with the help of General Ernest Harmon.

Under the agreement signed with the French, the Americans had use of and controlled all military facilities. The US Army set about not only employing those bases and airstrips but also improving them. They cleaned up the damage inflicted during the fighting, while bolstering defenses, roads, railways, and other infrastructure. They paid special attention to the logistical lines connecting Casablanca to Oran and Algiers.[13] Eisenhower was desperate for better lines of communication between Gibraltar and Casablanca and between Algiers and Casablanca. The delayed cables and lost messages were maddening.[14] The Americans also dictated all flights in and out of Morocco.

ON THE MORNING OF November 12, the USS *Augusta*, Task Force 34's flagship, sailed into Casablanca's port, past the burned out hull of a French destroyer blocking the approach. As the battleship negotiated the entrance, Rear Admiral Kent Hewitt noticed French sailors standing at the ready next to the antiaircraft guns. "Had there been any breach of faith on the part of the French, we would have been in trouble," wrote Hewitt. But with the help of tugboats and a French pilot, the *Augusta* safely maneuvered into her berth on the port side of Phosphate Pier and dropped anchor.[15]

Warned by Vice Admiral François Michelier that the port resembled "une cimitière," Hewitt now saw for himself the devastation. A line of charred merchant vessels listed against the main pier, while a capsized passenger ship lay prone at its end. A massive hole had been punched into the side of the battleship *Jean Bart*, once feared by the Allies and the subject of so many intelligence reports. The battered dock house looked ready to crumble at any moment. Outside the port, more damaged French ships littered the coast, having been beached to prevent them from sinking into the Atlantic's hellish depths.

Task Force 34 needed to clear the port of the wreckage in order to finish unloading its supplies and make way for the next convoy, due in less than a week. This necessity took on extra urgency after German submarines began to hunt the American ships waiting off Fédala for their chance to unload. On the evening of November 11, the same day as the armistice, U-173 torpedoed the *Joseph Hewes*, sinking the ship and killing her captain and several sailors. It also struck the *Hambleton*, killing nine men, and put a twenty-five-foot hole in *Winooski*.

With the help of La Royale (the nickname for the French Navy), the Americans cleared eight of the sixteen berths, allowing their ships to drop anchor.[16] As the massive cranes set to work hoisting cargo out of the holds, American soldiers, French marines, and Moroccan stevedores provided the muscle needed to wrestle the goods onto trucks and railcars. Flyers went up around the port and elsewhere in Casablanca in French, English, and Arabic, advertising the need for men. In exchange for his sweat, a laborer could purchase extra rations of tea, sugar, rice, cotton fabric, and petrol from American stocks. With rationing still in effect in Casablanca—and little on the shelves to buy—extra rations were better than money.[17]

After four days with no sign of the U-boats, a torpedo struck the transport *Electra* on November 15, fifteen miles off the coast of Fédala.[18] The loss of the transport and its sailors cast a grim shadow over an otherwise successful operation. It also reminded the Americans of the need to remain vigilant in the aftermath of victory.

THE QUAYS IN CASABLANCA'S port still groaned under the weight of American cargo when another convoy arrived. On November 18, ten days after American troops first set foot in French Morocco, Task Force 38 (UGF-2) queued up off Casablanca. The convoy, consisting of nine transport ships, nine cargo ships, and a naval escort, had departed Staten Island, New York, on November 2.

If the convoy that delivered Patton and his men to Morocco was devised to conquer, Task Force 38 was formulated to support the United States' informal occupation. It transported 3,000 engineering troops to construct whatever the Western Task Force required, 1,700 members of the Signal Corps to establish and maintain communications networks, and 2,000 quartermaster troops to establish gas depots, supply outposts, bakeries, and laundry facilities. Another 4,000 men would see to transportation, while 4,800 men attended to ordinance. There were 1,800 medical personnel and three hospital units to care for the wounded evacuated from the front lines in Tunisia. Much to the delight of the men, the hospital staff included female nurses. Another 6,300 men would establish the XII Air Support Command, which operated initially out of Cazes airfield outside Casablanca. There was also staff for a post office, censorship bureau, and administrative support for the Western Task Force's headquarters. All told, Task Force 38 delivered another 31,790 Americans to Casablanca.[19]

Eisenhower, who was on hand to witness the transport ships' unloading of 30,000 troops in thirteen hours, relished seeing the Americans and French working together. "I value this aid more than the active participation of their troops," he wrote Washington.[20] The cooperation he witnessed only confirmed for him the wisdom of the Darlan Deal. "We have these advantages

FIGURE 50.2 As American ships unload in the port, the supplies pile up on the docks. *Naval History and Heritage Command*

through the influence of the entire group through which we have worked," he wrote.[21]

After the troops came the supplies. Boxes, crates, and drums of every size and shape hoisted out of ships' holds added to the towers of provisions already overwhelming the piers. Ammunition sat on top of food, which lay next to oil drums. There weren't enough trucks or train cars to keep up. Then the rain came. The November sky opened up and drenched the port and the supplies, turning an already chaotic enterprise into a wet slog.[22] One army private lost his life when accidentally struck by a truck and thrown into the harbor.[23] Working to the brink of exhaustion, the Americans unloaded 36,000 tons of supplies in ten days.[24]

Before the year was done, three more convoys of men and supplies arrived in Casablanca.[25]

A LITTLE LESS THAN two weeks after the cessation of hostilities, Patton declared his command healthy. His men were in generally good spirits and adapting to their new environment. "When they first got here they were extremely sloppy, probably due to excessive fatigue, but within the last two days our efforts at smartening them up have borne fruit, and shortly, I believe they will be a credit to any country."[26]

The arrival of the second convoy also provided something for the American GIs to eat other than K rations. The US Army erected kitchens and started running chow lines at locations around Casablanca. Some troops suffered from diarrhea, most likely from drinking the local water. They were reminded to use their purification tablets and only to fill their canteens at water locations declared safe by the army's engineers.[27]

With so many soldiers in and around Casablanca, rules developed to guide their conduct and maintain order. All GIs were to "habitually observe the highest standard of neatness, military courtesy, and soldierly bearing." If an American soldier or sailor misbehaved and the Shore Patrol or Military Police were not available, the local police could arrest him. Any disrespect or resistance toward French officials doing their duty was considered a "serious breach of discipline, and will be dealt with accordingly."[28]

The US Army also controlled how many soldiers roamed around Casablanca, with only 5 percent of men from a unit allowed on leave at any one time. While out and about, they were required to show respect for Arab customs. To help the soldiers understand Moroccan culture, the War Department provided them with a fifty-page pamphlet, which included warnings against entering mosques and offering a Muslim an alcoholic drink. The sternest language was reserved for women. "Never stare at a Moslem woman. Never jostle her in a crowd. Never speak to her in public. Never try to remove the veil. This is most important," said the pamphlet.[29]

Sections of the old medina and the new medina were declared off limits due to the presence of the plague. Leave passes expired at 10:00 p.m., and all men had to return to their units by that time. All enlisted personnel were required to leave stores, restaurants, and entertainment venues by 9:30 p.m. While on leave, GIs were not allowed to carry guns or ammunition; nor could they carry knives or dirks. Leave passes could also be refused to any soldier who failed to look presentable.

Meanwhile, the arrival of the Americans provided opportunities for people to make money, particularly off vice. Soldiers and sailors were also warned to be on their guard against people misdirecting them to "respectable" homes instead of the promised bordellos. The language and cultural barriers resulted in angry and embarrassing exchanges on both sides. "The motives of such persons may well be enemy-inspired to incite general disorders or to arouse the Arab population against us," read the cautionary memo issued to all units. "These incidents will surely result in killings or attempted killings. All men will be warned against this."[30]

51

Cheerful and Effective Cooperation

Successful relations between the French and Americans required, in Lieutenant General Dwight Eisenhower's words, "mutual cooperation and development of unified effort." He believed the Americans needed to make a concerted effort to win over the French. "Atmosphere of optimism, confidence, friendship for French and faith in them is now mandatory," he wrote. Everything should be done to cultivate "prompt, cheerful, and effective cooperation."[1]

In French Morocco, Ike wanted Major General George Patton to set and keep high standards of behavior for American forces. "We should raise our standards, smartness, discipline, saluting and courtesy to the maximum extent," he told Patton. "Nothing could have a better effect in winning the confidence of the population and professional elements of the French defense forces. At times we will have to suffer irritations with a smile on our faces."[2]

Even as he preached the gospel of cooperation, Eisenhower knew challenges lay ahead. One of those challenges was Charles Noguès. The resident-general's response to his new circumstances would determine the success of the American occupation of French Morocco. In a letter sent a few days after their November 13 meeting in Algiers, Eisenhower wrote of wanting to move beyond "our late difficulties" and to dispel any resentment between Frenchmen and Americans. He did not want the men who had aided the American invasion persecuted either legally or professionally.

"As you explained to me at Algiers, the French Army, because of its high sense of duty, felt compelled to fight us in spite of its own real sentiments and

inclinations, and naturally it deeply resented any sympathy with its opponent," wrote Eisenhower. "But I am sure you will agree with me that nothing
could be gained now by permitting this type of difference to occasion more
trouble or difficulty. Obviously we should let bygones be bygones."[3]

Eisenhower asked that Noguès's demonstrate his commitment to moving
forward by immediately releasing General Antoine Béthouart and his compatriots. Béthouart had escaped a firing squad but remained in jail. Ike made
the request for clemency directly to Noguès, rather than going through his
superior, Admiral Jean-François Darlan. "I am giving Noguès a chance to
show me the color of his money," Eisenhower told Patton. "His response
will be a test of his cooperation."[4]

Noguès grudgingly agreed "to avoid any misunderstanding which might
be damaging to the common task." He made clear, however, that he did so
with reservation and continued to insist that Béthouart had "committed a serious offense against discipline and military honor, an offense which, in any
army worthy of the name, should be punished."[5]

Within a few days, Béthouart was in Algiers, serving as General Henri
Giraud's liaison officer with Allied Forces Headquarters. General Charles
Mast also came out of the shadows, into which he had retreated during the
negotiations with Darlan, to serve as chief of staff for Giraud.[6] They were the
lucky ones. Despite an order issued on November 19 by the French North
African Commission declaring "full and entire amnesty to all persons who
favored Allied action in North Africa," those who did not have Béthouart
and Mast's connections remained in jail two days later.[7]

The Americans would continue to ask about many of them two months
later.

"We left Casablanca, a city which combines Hollywood and the Bible at
9:45 and proceeded toward Rabat," wrote Patton. On the morning of November 16, Patton headed north to Rabat for his first meeting with Noguès since
the armistice and an audience with the sultan. Noguès realized that, as with
Maxime Weygand, he would have to manage Patton in order to continue to
rule Morocco the way he wanted. Protocol practicality dictated that Patton receive an introduction to the sultan, which Noguès would arrange with plenty
of Moroccan spectacle to dazzle the status-conscious American general.

As Patton traveled the road between Casablanca and Rabat, he took in
the stretches of farmland dotted with sheep and cattle. Ever the tank commander, he couldn't help but note the terrain. "The country after passing
Fédala is the finest tank country I have ever seen being rolling and open with

here and there stone farms which would make infantry strongpoints, but would be useless against the 105," he wrote.[8] Patton noted with satisfaction the collection of destroyed French trucks and burned-out armored cars littering the side of highway.

Patton stopped first at the Residency for a meeting with Noguès. General Ernest Harmon, who commanded American troops around Rabat, wanted Patton to arrive accompanied by an escort of scout cars and tanks, but Patton thought arriving in a tank "would appear boastful," so he dismissed them.

Noguès, however, did not skimp on the pageantry. A battalion of Moroccan cavalry resplendent in red uniforms, along with Noguès's personal bodyguard, greeted Patton in the courtyard. "Both guards were very impressive," wrote Patton, "and each had its own field music, consisting of French trumpets, drums, and a brass umbrella with bells around the edge which continually rotated during the playing of the ruffles and flourishes." At the same time Patton deemed the guards relics of a bygone era. "It was rather pathetic to think that one of the light tanks in the escort, which I had turned down, could have easily destroyed all of the splendid creatures standing at salute," he wrote. While the guards had been for show, the antiquated equipment used by French troops in Morocco had stunned the Americans.

Twenty minutes later, the two generals proceeded to the audience with Sidi Mohammed. Patton was a well-traveled man for the era, having spent time in Latin America and Europe, but nothing in his experience prepared him for what he encountered at the palace. Throughout the day he would fall back on biblical explanations to make sense of what he was seeing.

Reaching the wall that surrounded the palace grounds, their entourage passed through a gate. After another half mile, they approached a second wall pierced by a towering horseshoe arch, outlined with elaborate tile work and just big enough for a wagon—or a modern automobile—to pass through. One by one the cars carrying Noguès, Patton, and their entourage pulled into the courtyard of the palace where a parade of Moroccan guards and troops awaited them. "Black troops dressed in red coats, red bloomers, and white gaiters, and armed with rifles, were drawn up completely around the square," wrote Patton. "I should think that at least 400 men were present."

The spare exterior of the whitewashed palace was nothing compared to the lavish interior, with its plush carpets, intricate tile work, and colorful mosaics in shades of blue, green, and terra-cotta. Upon entering, Noguès and Patton were met by Si Mammeri, the sultan's chief of protocol. "He was dressed in a white robe with a hood and wore underneath it a silk headdress embroidered in gold," wrote Patton. "He has the most enormous set of gold inlaid teeth I had ever seen, and a scraggly beard." Si Mammeri led them up three flights of stairs to the throne room, pausing to remove his shoes before entering. Patton, however, kept his boots on.

A "most distinguished looking group of men" dressed in fine white robes filled the left side of the long room. Patton dubbed them the "twelve apostles and some reserves." The men, who wore traditional Moroccan vestments, were the pashas of Morocco and some of the most powerful men in the country. Patton's introduction to them would have to wait until after he met the sultan, who was seated on a platform at the far end of the room.

Patton followed Noguès's lead, giving a bow upon entering, then another halfway down the hall, and finally a third on standing before the sultan. Sidi Mohammed rose from his throne and shook hands with Patton and Noguès, after which he invited the two generals to sit on the gold-painted Louis XIV chairs positioned on the right side of the throne. Patton had the honor of sitting closest to the sultan.

Speaking in Arabic, Sidi Mohammed instructed Si Mammeri to tell Patton in French how glad he was to meet him. Using an interpreter, Patton declared his happiness that the French and Americans were once again reunited and "assured him that our one desire was to unite with his people and the French in making common head against the enemy."[9] The sultan offered the same wishes, while also telling Patton that he hoped American soldiers would respect Muslim customs and institutions.

"I told him that such an order had been issued in forceful language prior to our departure from the United States and was going to be enforced," wrote Patton. "I further stated that since in all armies, including the American army, there might be some foolish persons, I hoped that he would report to me any incidents of sacrilege, which some individual soldier might commit." The sultan assured Patton that he had faith that no such incidents would happen, but if they did, he would let him know through Noguès. Patton concluded his audience by complementing the sultan on the beauty of Morocco and the "discipline of its citizens."[10]

PATTON RETURNED TO RABAT on November 18 to attend the Throne Day festivities at the palace. Morocco's changed circumstances made celebrating the holiday honoring the sultan's ascension to the throne even more necessary. As before, Noguès honored Patton with pageantry. A mounted escort accompanied them on the journey from the Residency to the palace. "The men were mounted on white stallions, with white capes and blue hoods thrown back, white turbans, red coats with brass buttons and brass frogs," wrote Patton. Trumpeters played as they made their way to the palace, where the Moroccan units continued to impress the former cavalryman. "On reaching the palace, a whole regiment of cavalry was drawn up," he wrote. "One squadron was equipped with lances. This regiment and the escort had the finest mounts I had ever seen."

From the courtyard, they were led into the throne room by two guards, each armed with a "very long and very curved scimitar in a red Moroccan scabbard." This ceremonial throne room burst with people—Morocco's pashas, other regional chiefs, high-ranking French officials, and the diplomatic corps. The prince, who had developed a fascination with Patton, sat in the chair closest to his father. Noguès sat next to him, with Patton in the third position. Noguès read a statement in French praising the sultan and his rule. Si Mammeri translated it into Arabic. The sultan then read his response in Arabic, which was translated into French.

As the messages flew back and forth, Patton decided that the United States was "playing too small a role." Despite being the occupying power, the Americans had not been asked to offer a message of congratulations or given a role in the ceremony. When Noguès stopped speaking, Patton stepped forward and offered his own remarks. He presented Franklin Roosevelt's complements on the occasion of the anniversary of sultan's accession to the throne. Patton's highly diplomatic and appropriate remarks heavily mirrored the text of a note soon to be delivered to the sultan from Roosevelt.

"I wish to assure you that so long as your Majesty's country, in cooperation with the French Government of Morocco, cooperates with us and facilitates our efforts, we are sure, with the help of God, to achieve certain victory against our common enemy, the Nazis," said Patton.

He reminded the sultan and those gathered of the long history shared by Morocco and the United States, including the gift of the building that housed the American legation in Tangier. In a nod to France, he cited the friendship that had existed between that country and the United States since the days of the American Revolution and George Washington. He closed by thanking the sultan for his subjects' cooperation with the Americans.[11]

As was the tradition, the remarks offered by Noguès and Sidi Mohammed were printed in *La Vigie marocaine* with a headline celebrating them as an affirmation of "Franco-Moroccan solidarity." The paper printed Patton's words in the bottom corner, accompanied by a picture of him at the Residency with Noguès.[12]

ANCHORED AT THE FAR end of Casablanca's central administrative square, Sacré-Coeur resembles an ice palace rising out of the desert. The sharp lines and white facade of the cathedral continue inside, with even the nontraditional stained glass windows framed in white. On the morning of November 23, the cathedral served as a place of healing for both the French and the Americans with the holding of a high mass to honor the dead. The stark white church became a sea of military uniforms and black suits and dresses as French and American officials, military and civilian, filled the pews, along with the families of the dead and the citizens of Casablanca there to pay their respects. At the front of the church lay two biers, one draped in a French flag and the other in an American flag. At the end of the service, conducted by both French and American men of God, honor guards hoisted the biers on their shoulders and solemnly walked the caskets down the center aisle, with Noguès and Patton following behind.

From the church, the worshipers and mourners traveled to the Ben M'Sik Cemetery, where French Moroccan and American honor guards greeted their arrival. Freshly dug graves containing fallen soldiers and sailors dotted the landscape. "We walked about half a mile through the cemetery and halted between two flagpoles, American on the right and French on the left, each with the colors at the truck," wrote Patton. After Noguès and Patton placed a wreath at the hastily made monument commemorating the dead, the somber notes of the French version of "Taps" filled the cemetery, while the French flag was lowered to half mast. As the band played "La Marseillaise," the flag was raised again. The ceremony was repeated for the American flag with "The Star-Spangled Banner." Noguès and Patton then walked among the graves, stopping to salute those buried. Each grave was marked with a white cross, and in the case of the Americans, with dog tags. The names would follow later.[13]

"The whole affair was very solemn, and when I made the remark to General Noguès that I thought the intermingling of French and American blood had produced a very sacred sacrament, he seemed pleased and moved," wrote Patton.[14]

OVER THE NEXT SIX weeks, after the initial rush of adrenaline and activity following the landings had subsided, Patton busied himself with his role as commander of the Western Task Force, now an informal occupying force. "Today I had lunch at Rabat with Noguès, Boisson, et all. And they acted just like old friends," he wrote. "Of course I know and they know that I know that they are only friendly through self-interest but it works well."[15] Content to let Noguès keep running the country as he saw fit—much to the dismay of the State Department—Patton focused on ensuring his men were well trained and ready to fight in the next campaign. He made sure that French Morocco, which now functioned as a massive American supply depot, remained secure. He also tried to stay removed from the intrigues at the Residency by getting out of Casablanca and Rabat and exploring the country. Between his French and his well-earned reputation as a warrior—a trait valued by Moroccans— Patton charmed the country at the parades, ceremonies, and reviews held in his honor.[16]

Even as he went on boar hunts with the pasha of Marrakech, shopped for carpets, and collected antique canons and swords, he turned his eyes toward Tunisia, wondering when and if he would get a chance to prove his mettle once again. His Moroccan adventures couldn't stave off his melancholy at not being part of a campaign. The day after Thanksgiving, which he celebrated at the US consulate with three helpings of mincemeat pie, he confided his pain to his wife, Beatrice, in a letter. "I have the most awful blues today," he wrote. "Nothing seems to be happening and I just sit. I suppose it is because I want to go on and have nothing to go on with. I also heard that Clark got a M.H. [Medal of Honor] for riding in a submarine. I don't believe it but still it is not pleasant." Although he was going "mad," he told her not to worry about him.[17]

52

Hope and Delay

At the end of November 1942, Inge Ruth Lueck eagerly awaited her release from the internment camp at Sidi-el-Ayachi. The arrival of the Americans gave the thirty-five-year-old German hope that maybe soon she could leave the barracks that had been her home for more than a year. Her chest still rattled from the remnants of the whooping cough picked up the previous summer from one of the children she taught in the camp.[1]

Lueck's road to Sidi-el-Ayachi began in 1933 when the Gestapo threw her husband, a German socialist, out the window of his Berlin apartment. After watching in horror as he dropped from sight and hearing his screams of terror filter back, she attacked the Gestapo officer who meted out the punishment, pounding him with her fists. The assault earned her a trip to prison, where she lay battered from the first of many rounds of interrogation, unable to be at her husband's side when he finally succumbed to his injuries two days later. Released from prison in 1934, she sought refuge in the Saar, a coal-rich patch of land on the Franco-German border, governed by the League of Nations under the Treaty of Versailles. When the Saar's population voted overwhelmingly to reunify with Germany in January 1935, Lueck headed for Paris.[2]

As she built her life in the City of Light, the psychological terrors of her incarceration receded, but she still carried the physical scars. She suffered from terrible stomach cramps, a legacy of the punishment doled out by a Gestapo goon with iron-heeled boots. She found work as a private secretary and fell in love again with a Frenchman. He proposed just before the war started, but before they could marry, he was drafted into the army, and she was sent to Gurs, an internment camp in southwestern France on the edge of the Pyrenees. She survived the harrowing conditions there and was released in June 1940. Her fiancé wasn't so lucky. He died defending the very country that had interned his betrothed. Hoping to stay one step ahead of the Germans, Lueck made her way to Morocco, where she landed in another internment camp, this time outside of Marrakech. From there she was transferred to Sidi-el-Ayachi, which became a favored dumping ground for German-born foreigners. By the fall of 1941, at five feet, nine inches, she had withered to just 107 pounds.[3]

Unlike many of the refugees she was interned with in French Morocco, Lueck didn't have family or friends in the United States to help her with the visa process. Instead, a woman who befriended her in the camp became her advocate from afar. Eva Szamatolski, who departed Sidi-el-Ayachi and Morocco on a Cuban visa with the help of her family in New York and the American Jewish Joint Distribution Committee (Joint), wrote letters to the American Friends Service Committee (AFSC) in Philadelphia, pressing Lueck's case. "I could not have survived Morocco without Inge," wrote Szamatolski. "She is one of the few truly valuable women, who one simply must help."[4]

As a Gentile, Lueck could not benefit from the network of private agencies that helped Jews emigrate from Europe. Instead, AFSC (the Quakers) and other Christian relief and refugee agencies became the lifeline for non-Jews stranded in Casablanca or Lisbon.

Szamatolski recruited Sherwood Haynes, a physics professor at Brown University, to provide an affidavit of support, which was vital to Lueck's visa application. While living in Paris before the war, Haynes had tutored Szamatolski in English, and she wrote to him about Lueck's visa struggles. When a family crisis made it impossible for Haynes to do the affidavit, which required the signer to pledge financial support to prevent the refugee from becoming a burden on the state, he nevertheless committed to providing the money for her passage and visa application.[5]

When Leslie Heath arrived in Casablanca in the fall of 1942 to serve as AFSC's man on the ground, his list of refugees to check on included Lueck's name. On a tour of Sidi-el-Ayachi in September 1942, he finally had a chance to meet the woman who had been the subject of so many letters. "She takes pride in her school teaching, and showed me some photographs that were taken of her little class of about 20 to 25 children, when General Noguès visited the camp several months ago," wrote Heath. "She also seems somewhat depressed, which is not surprising. She is a woman of considerable poise."[6]

After the arrival of the Americans, Lueck sent a cable to Szamatolski in Cuba, telling her that she could obtain release from the camp when she acquired money for living expenses.[7] Lueck didn't know it, but AFSC had a visa application ready to file, but the State Department had suspended all North African cases because of the lack of transportation facilities in the wake of TORCH.[8] The Friends had found two professors at Penn State to provide affidavits of financial support. Haynes would pay for her passage and the visa application.[9] When Christmas rolled around, however, Lueck would still be at Sidi-el-Ayachi, where she helped organize a party and program for the children who remained.

RUTH LUECK WAS ALSO on Hélène Bénatar's list.[10] After the Residency dissolved her committee, the Moroccan-Jewish lawyer with boundless energy and kind eyes had, as a private citizen, continued her work with refugees and those pressed into the labor camps. It didn't matter if they were Jewish, Catholic, French, German, Austrian, or ex-Legionnaires on their third identity—Bénatar believed in helping them all. Wagering that the arrival of the Americans offered a chance to spring people from the camps, she made inquiries with French officials about the numbers involved. Once they left the camps, the internees would need help finding housing and jobs and starting their new lives—and Bénatar intended to provide it. She had not been allowed to visit the camps as a private citizen, and public information about them remained scarce. Despite multiple inquiries, Bénatar still didn't have a good handle on the number of internees requiring assistance at the end of November and described the situation as "chaotic."[11]

The Joint also saw the American landings as an opportunity to help Jews interned in Morocco and offered to finance Bénatar's work.[12] Bénatar made clear that not all of those helped would be Jewish, a condition to which the Joint agreed. Any hope for a quick and favorable solution to the refugee problem, however, was quickly dashed. Emigration remained at a standstill, and it became clear that the process of emptying the camps would take months, not weeks.

At the beginning of December, Bénatar learned that 250 internees still resided in Sidi-el-Ayachi. The authorities would liberate seventy Poles and Czechs as soon as housing was found for them—they were liberating internees from the Allied nations first. The remaining Germans and Austrians, most of them stateless, along with the Spaniards would be released after vetting. The Americans did not see a problem with releasing the Germans and Austrians, but the French dragged their feet, now considering them enemy aliens. In a few short weeks, stateless refugees like Inge Ruth Lueck went from being interned because their visas had expired to being held because they were born in or had ties to Germany or Austria.

Bénatar also learned from friends in the French government that more than seven hundred men were interned in work camps across Morocco. (That number would turn out to be deceptively low.) The French, however, did not intend to release them immediately. Instead, they hoped to continue to profit from their sweat and muscle by enrolling them in either the Labor Corps or the French army.[13]

As the internees began to trickle out, Bénatar worked with AFSC and HICEM, another Jewish organization, to provide aid.[14] Upon leaving the camps, the refugees needed new clothing, a place to live, and money to tide them over until their first paycheck, along with medical care. Jobs were arranged and the paperwork for visas updated or started from scratch. Soon their efforts grew to encompass internees not just from Sidi-el-Ayachi but from Mogador, Marrakech, Buerguent, Kasba-Tadla, Meknès, Missour, and Oued Akreuch. In January 1943 alone, Bénatar's group assisted forty-nine men, thirty-nine women, and thirty-one children in Casablanca, along with more than thirty-five internees who continued to reside at Sidi-el-Ayachi.[15]

THE RESIDENCY HAD SPENT more than two years obscuring the presence of the camps and their residents. Even as the Americans and British pressured the French to empty them, the French still attempted to expand the numbers of men interned. In the aftermath of the Allied landings, Admiral Jean-François Darlan ordered the internment of all Italians deemed dangerous because of their connections with the Italian Armistice Commission or ties to the Fascist Party.[16] At the beginning of December 1942, the scope expanded to encompass all Italian men between the ages of eighteen and sixty, including those born in Morocco of parents with Italian heritage who had never naturalized. Regarding the Italians as dangerous to internal security, the French believed they were within their right to utilize Italian labor. After all, French citizens had to provide wartime service.

As space became available in the camps, French authorities summoned the Italians. In the Casablanca region, they interned 2,647 Italian men, mostly in a camp established in the Roches Noires section of the city. Fortunately, at the end of January 1943, the French started to release some of the Italians, granting liberty to those over age forty-eight or in ill health. They discharged others with a brother, son, or father serving in the French army or whose freedom could aid the war effort. The United States' Psychological Warfare

Branch arranged for the release of five Italians to work on radio broadcasts to Italy.[17]

"What seems to be reasonably clear is that no Italian was released if he was anti-fascist, if he was a Jew, or if he was engaged in a business or profession in which he was in competition with the French," wrote Frederick Culbert, one of Robert Murphy's vice counsels.[18]

As the camps filled up, the Americans recognized that they would have to do something about the Italians too.

53

Loyalty

Dave King had spent thirty months in Casablanca on behalf of the American government, learning its ins and outs. Among the French, he knew who supported Vichy, who supported the Allies, and who claimed to support Vichy but harbored Allied sentiments. He laid the groundwork for the invasion of the Western Task Force by collecting maps of the coastline and charts of the harbor. He regularly arranged to steal the order of battle for French Morocco, which listed the locations of all the military units in the country and their mobilization sequence. With the help of his band of resistance fighters, he scouted targets and provided whatever information the planners in Washington and London desired.

Now that the Americans had arrived and the invasion was a done deal, King found his expertise and contacts unwelcome. "From the moment that the Western Task Force had set up its HQ in Casablanca, our role was reduced to zero," observed Michel Despax, one of King's key agents. "Nobody asked us our opinions, and nobody would take our advice, in spite of our two years' experience in Morocco." The arrival of the Western Task Force abruptly rendered the Office of Strategic Services (OSS) peripheral. The US Army simply didn't know what to do with the OSS agents or how to thread them into the rigid army intelligence structure.[1]

King had particularly strong opinions about whom the Americans should work with, opinions that did not jive with Major General George Patton's decision to look the other way when it came to collaborators. He watched with dismay as the US Army hired Frenchmen he knew to be pro-Vichy without doing cursory background checks. He butted heads with Patton over the general's refusal to help the imprisoned French officers who had aided the invasion. Patton claimed he could do nothing; they would have to let justice take its course. King protested that letting the Frenchmen rot in jail damaged American prestige. "Don't bother your pretty little head about that," said Patton. "It'll all come out all right."

When King threatened to hide an army major wanted by the French authorities for aiding the landings, Patton forbade it. Instead of arguing, King shut up. Rather than conceal the major in his house, King lodged him with Staff Reid and Len Wiggins in Anfa, knowing that neither French nor American authorities would search the villa. King eventually cleared the major's name, and he went on to fight with distinction in Tunisia and Italy.[2]

The run-in with Patton, however, sealed King's fate. He returned to Washington at the end of December 1942, taking with him a trove of knowledge about French Morocco that could not be easily replicated.

The more politically astute and less hotheaded Reid remained in Casablanca, helping set up a new OSS station at the beginning of January 1943. He hadn't run the resistance cells, however, and didn't know the vast network developed by King. Fortunately, Despax agreed to continue working with OSS as well, providing much needed experience in a station that would soon consist primarily of recent arrivals.[3] There was plenty of work to do. The landings put the German and Italian armistice commissions out of business, but Axis sympathizers remained behind. The border between Spanish and French Morocco also needed watching. The Americans had just gotten their foothold, and the last thing they needed was the Spanish crashing down from the north.[4]

Fred Culbert, another vice consul turned OSS agent, managed to gain Patton's trust. In his chic top-floor apartment, Culbert hosted gatherings that brought French and American officers together in a social setting. The parties were held on Patton's orders; the general believed that informal gatherings would help bridge any lingering hard feelings. But when the accountants in Washington started squawking about the liquor and food bills, Patton had some explaining to do.[5]

"DEATH TO THE TRAITOR Darlan!" screamed the graffiti scrawled on the walls around Algiers, defacing the whitewashed buildings. The threats were more extreme versions of the sentiment pervading Allied Forces Headquarters (AFHQ) as the Allies came to doubt Admiral Jean-François Darlan's usefulness and grew weary of the controversy surrounding him. His desire to preserve French honor and sovereignty turned Franco-American cooperation into a painful enterprise. The French fleet also remained in Toulon, within the Germans' reach, much to Eisenhower's consternation.

There were also mind-boggling errors in judgment. Darlan asked for an honor guard of two hundred Coldstream and Grenadier Guards to participate in a celebration of the Battle of Austerlitz. Napoléon Bonaparte's victory over Austria and Russia on December 5, 1805, is considered one of his finest moments as a general. But celebrating his victory over an ally, the Soviet Union, to say nothing of his subsequent battles with Britain, was inappropriate.[6]

As December came to a close, Darlan seemed to tire of serving as high commissioner of French North Africa. He mentioned to more than one person that he might resign and suggested to Robert Murphy that he might do so on more than one occasion. "Please tell your President that any time he decides I am more of a liability than an asset to him, I will gladly step down," he told Murphy.[7]

On December 23, at a holiday luncheon for the senior Allied and French leadership, Mark Clark broached with Madame Darlan the idea of traveling to Warm Springs, Georgia, to visit their son, who had recently traveled there to receive treatment for polio. Franklin Roosevelt invited the young man to convalesce there after learning of the younger Darlan's battle with a disease he knew personally. It was a small act of kindness during a volatile period, but one designed to build trust. The president was also a father.

"I think it could be arranged for Admiral Darlan to go, too, if he chooses," said Clark. The admiral nodded, appearing to consider the idea. "I would like to turn this thing over to General Giraud; he likes it here and I don't."[8]

After lunch, Darlan invited Murphy back to his office to discuss a number of lingering issues. Before he dug into the stack of paperwork, Darlan's mood turned serious.

"You know, there are four plots in existence to assassinate me," he said. "Suppose one of these plots is successful. What will you Americans do then?"

He then rattled off a list of possible replacements. It included Charles de Gaulle, but Darlan cautioned against bringing him to North Africa. It might be too soon. He also mentioned Henri Giraud but once against asserted that he was nothing more than "a good divisional commander."

As he listed other possibilities, Murphy couldn't help but notice his detachment. Tiring of the morbid discussion, Darlan grabbed the stack of papers and began to discuss them with Murphy one by one.[9]

WHEN DWIGHT EISENHOWER LEARNED that Darlan was knee-deep in the negotiations in Algiers during TORCH, he swore up a storm. "Je-e-e-e-e-suss

Ch-e-rist!!" he drawled. "What I need around here is a damned good assassin!"[10] On Christmas Eve, he got his wish.

After enjoying a leisurely holiday lunch, Darlan returned at around 3 p.m. to his office in the Summer Palace, where he encountered Fernand Bonnier de La Chapelle. The twenty-two-year-old student with monarchist sympathies was waiting patiently for him in the anteroom of his office, smoking a cigarette to pass the time and calm his nerves. Using a Rubis revolver, which he had first fired only that morning, Bonnier shot Darlan in the face and chest. After putting another round in the thigh of Darlan's aide-de-camp, he attempted to escape through the window. But before he could disappear into the palace grounds, a spahi cavalryman pulled him back inside, while another knocked away the gun.[11]

Upon learning of the shooting, Clark and Murphy raced to the hospital, arriving a few minutes after Darlan died in surgery.[12] "The Little Fellow looked calm and quiet," wrote Clark. "I couldn't help thinking that maybe this was a relief to him after the terrible 'hot seat' he had been occupying for the last month and a half."[13]

A hastily convened military tribunal held on Christmas Day found Bonnier guilty and condemned him to death. The casket had been ordered before the trial even began. The following day, Bonnier faced a firing squad, insisting until the end that he was a hero. "They will not shoot me," he told a priest. "I have liberated France."[14]

Darlan would have approved of the pageantry marking his funeral. On Christmas Day, his body lay in state in the Government House, surrounded by the tricolor and floral wreaths; spahis and *tirailleurs* stood guard as more than 8,000 people passed by to pay their respects. The following day, a black hearse delivered his body to Cathédrale St. Phillipe for a funeral mass attended by French officials, the AFHQ leadership, and other mourners. At the end of the exceedingly long service, Eisenhower, Giraud, and the others saluted Darlan's body, while eight French sailors carried it down the cathedral steps. As they made their way to the chapel of the Summer Palace, a procession designed to show Allied unity trailed behind, including a regiment of Zouaves, spahis riding white horses, a British color guard, and members of the American 34th Division.[15]

Darlan's assassination and the quick trial and execution of his killer immediately generated wild theories about who had arranged the killing. Everybody in Algiers seemed to have a reason to want Darlan dead. The anti-Vichy elements saw him as a traitor to France. The pro-Vichy elements questioned his loyalty for working with the Americans and British. Other theories pointed to Britain's Special Operations Executive, or the Office of Strategic Services, or the Gestapo. Yet another theory cast blame on French royalists, suggesting they killed Darlan to restore the monarchy by installing the comte de Paris, pretender to the French throne.[16]

Whoever orchestrated the assassination freed the French, Americans, and British of a troublesome problem. The killing brutally severed the chord with Vichy. "Admiral Darlan's death was, to me, an act of Providence," wrote Clark. "It is too bad that he went that way, but, strategically speaking, his removal from the scene was like the lancing of a troublesome boil. He had served his purpose, and his death solved what could have been the very difficult problem of what to do with him in the future."[17] Winston Churchill felt the same. "Darlan's murder, however criminal, relieved the Allies of their embarrassment at working with him, and at the same time left them with all the advantages he had been able to bestow during the vital hours of the Allied landings," he wrote.[18]

But Darlan's assassination also presented a serious problem: who to put in charge. The French leadership in Algiers started lobbying for Clark to send for Charles Noguès. Instead, Clark demanded that news of the assassination be withheld from him. With Eisenhower away meeting with the troops, Clark imposed a news blackout until the situation could be sorted out. He wanted to buy time to convince Giraud to become the new high commissioner of French North Africa. Giraud consented, but he still wanted a military command.[19]

As THE ALLIES MOVED further east into Tunisia, anxiety increased about the vulnerability of the supply lines extending from Casablanca and Gibraltar into Algeria. So too did concern over a possible invasion of French Morocco by Spain. In December 1942, the US War Department created the Fifth Army, with Lieutenant General Mark Clark as its commander. The Fifth Army combined elements of the Western and Center Task Forces that had participated in TORCH, including the I Armored Corps in French Morocco, the II Army Corps in Western Algeria, and the XII Air Support Command. Clark would also oversee the military and political affairs of French Morocco and western Algeria.[20]

Patton, who deeply resented Clark's military success, now reported to him in his role as commander of the I Armored Corps. His days as the most powerful American in Morocco were over. Clark would also inevitably start siphoning off Patton's men to build his new army. It already irked Patton that Clark, eleven years his junior, had an additional star. Now Clark had his own army.[21] "It makes me mad but there is nothing that can be done about it," wrote Patton.[22]

After almost two months in the hot house of Algiers, Clark welcomed the chance to escape the intrigues of Allied Forces Headquarters and the sniping among the different French factions. He would have preferred a chance to test his mettle at the battlefront in Tunisia, but Eisenhower needed his organizational talents. Clark had designed the system that allowed the US Army to ramp up quickly after Pearl Harbor, and Eisenhower hoped he could work the same magic with the new Fifth Army. Clark also knew what kind of man Noguès was, having seen him in action during the armistice negotiations in Algiers. That insight would provide a valuable corrective to the administration of Morocco after Patton's cozy relationship with the resident-general.[23]

Rather than set up shop in Rabat or Casablanca, Clark chose Oujda, a town just over the border from Algeria, as his headquarters. "It is centrally located, with a good airfield, good roads and railroads, and signal communications. There is also another reason that influenced me strongly. There are no politicians here," Clark told his officers. The distance would help prevent him from developing a chummy relationship with Noguès and his staff. The campus of a girls' school on the outskirts of town became home to the Fifth Army, formally activated by Clark on January 5.[24]

French Morocco now had a new overseer.

54

Air Commodore Frankland and Don Quixote

As 1942 LOGGED ITS LAST DAY, SAILORS, SOLDIERS, AND CASABLAN-cans shuffled into a warehouse next to the port. They came to celebrate New Year's Eve and the dawn of 1943 with the drum tap of torso punches and the crunch of fists smashing into jaws. A few weeks before, Lieutenant Commander Albert M. Witwer Jr., a Methodist chaplain for the US Navy, had organized the first boxing matches in the warehouse, which also doubled as the officers' mess hall and a place of worship. Boxing, which needed little equipment except for some gloves and mouth guards, provided an easy way for the men to show their mettle or cheer on their mates. As the popularity of the fights grew, the Navy's Seabees built a collapsible, regulation-size boxing ring that could fit over the mess hall's tables—and be spirited away before breakfast the next morning.

Father Witwer had made the journey to Casablanca with the Western Task Force, providing spiritual guidance to the men before and after the invasion. Sports were a natural way for a man of God to bond with his flock, and the forty-year-old Witwer was also a bit of a jock, having lettered in track in college. During his tenure in Casablanca, Witwer would also organize basketball and softball leagues for American soldiers and sailors.[1]

With the New Year's Eve fight card, the new boxing ring received its first workout. The first pair of boxers, drawn from American soldiers and sailors in Casablanca, bumped gloves at 8:00 p.m. Just stepping into the ring earned a fighter two cartons of American cigarettes; winning earned him even more. A Navy lieutenant who had boxed for the University of Virginia served as referee.[2]

The men were still slugging away at 3:45 a.m., when a Luftwaffe bombing run offered its own New Year's fireworks. German bombers dropped sixteen five-hundred-pound bombs on Casablanca, aiming for the port where US Navy ships dominated the berths. As the first bomb exploded, the rain-soaked sky filled with the glow of searchlights and crisscrossing pink tracers from rounds fired from the antiaircraft batteries. At one point, a thermite round lit up the sky for twenty minutes, sending tentacles of fire across the city. Awakened by the initial explosion, George Patton scrambled up to the roof of the Hôtel Majestic for a better view. When the bombers made another run, American ships docked in the port joined the fray. "It was better than the greatest Fourth of July demonstration possible to imagine," wrote Patton.[3]

When dawn came, Patton walked the surrounding neighborhood to assess the damage. The bombs had left craters "the size of an average bedroom" in the streets. The port escaped unharmed except for damage to a warehouse, but a close-by residential area suffered substantial devastation, with more than fifty Moroccans dead and even more injured. Patton wrote a letter of condolence to the pasha of Casablanca and offered up 100,000 francs to help the Arab families who had lost their homes and loved ones.[4] Casablanca had just suffered its first German attack of the war.

ACROSS THE ATLANTIC OCEAN, another party was in full swing. To celebrate New Year's Eve, President Franklin D. Roosevelt gathered together the generations of his family and a few close friends for his annual holiday party. World War II had scattered his many sons and nephews, turning them into sailors and aviators, but boisterous laughter and remembrances still flowed, filling the White House with equal parts joy and melancholy. At midnight, the president raised a glass of champagne and offered a toast to "the United States of America and to United Nations Victory."[5]

The entertainment for the evening was a new release from Warner Brothers: *Casablanca*. The movie, set in the city of the same name, revolves around a love triangle between Rick Blaine, a world-weary barman and sometime gun runner; Ilsa Lund, a jaded ingenue torn between duty and love; and Victor Laszlo, a charismatic resistance leader desperate to escape the Nazis. Seeking a way to leave Casablanca, Laszlo and Lund find their way to Rick's Café Américain and inquire about purchasing on the black market two letters of transit, which would allow Laszlo to escape Europe and the Nazis once and for all. Captain Henri Renault, a Vichy officer, is also on the hunt

FIGURE 54.1. Still from the film *Casablanca,* featuring Paul Henreid, Ingrid Berg-man, Claude Rains, and Humphrey Bogart. *A.F. Archive*

for the letters after he learns of their theft from two dead German couriers. The Nazis soon arrive on the scene to threaten Laszlo with imprisonment in a concentration camp.

The movie also delves into the plight of refugees in Casablanca. Blaine's high-class café serves as a meeting place for the displaced. "Everybody comes to Rick's," says Captain Renault. At the tables, sipping wine and gambling in the casino, are those refugees who still have money or are looking to make more. Another slate of refugees—German, Russian, Czech, French—work as waiters, bartenders, and singers in the café. The specter of Vichy intern-ment for holding expired papers—or supporting the resistance—hangs over all of them. They long to be on next plane for Lisbon.

The movie's clever dialogue—"Round up the usual suspects," "Of all the gin joints in all the towns in all the world, she walks into mine," "Here's looking at you, kid"—elevated it above other films trying to capitalize on the war. So too did its subtle portrayal of headline issues, such as Vichy col-laboration and the plight of refugees. In a legendary scene from the movie, Laszlo leads the patrons of Rick's in an emotional rendition of "La Marseillaise," drowning out a group of Germans singing a Nazi anthem. There's also nothing quite like the cinematic Casablanca, a mysterious city teeming with refugees, governed by the black market, and ruled by the whims of Vichy and Nazi officials.

It was pure coincidence that Warner Brothers had shot a film set in a city that was now the site of a major Allied victory. The studio had planned for *Casablanca* to appear in theaters in late spring of 1943. The war changed all of that when, thanks to newspaper headlines about American exploits in North Africa, "Casablanca" became a buzzword. Warner Brothers moved the movie's debut up, premiering it at the end of November 1942, and put it into wide release in early 1943. *Casablanca* made a respectable showing at the box office but dominated the Oscars, winning for best picture, best director, and best screenplay.[6]

ONLY A HANDFUL OF people at the Roosevelts' party knew that the word "Casablanca" would soon take on another significance. At the end of November 1942, Roosevelt suggested to Winston Churchill that a meeting between the three Allied leaders to discuss strategy would be in order. Now that the United States and Britain had a toehold in North Africa, what should they do next? The president suggested meeting in Cairo or Moscow.[7] Churchill replied with Iceland.[8] Roosevelt, however, had no interest in going anywhere cold. "I should prefer a secure place south of Algiers or in or near Khartoum," wrote the president. "I don't like mosquitoes."[9]

The next step was to ask Joseph Stalin, who, as Churchill predicted, declined. "To my great regret however I will not be in a position to leave the Soviet Union," Stalin wrote Churchill. "Time presses us and it would be impossible for me to be absent even for a day as it is just now that important military operations of our winter campaign are developing." The gory battle between the Russians and the Germans for control of Stalingrad, begun in August, still raged; it would ultimately consume almost 2 million men on both sides. Given the ongoing slaughter on the eastern front, Stalin's telegrams of regret included the inevitable question about opening a second front in western Europe in the spring of 1943. Churchill and Roosevelt demurred on an answer for the moment.[10]

Even with Stalin abstaining, Roosevelt and Churchill decided that they and their staffs should still get together, as a slew of issues required discussion. Knowing the American public and press would kick up a fuss if he left the country, Roosevelt pushed for North Africa. "One mitigating circumstance would be the knowledge that I had seen our military leaders in North and West Africa, and that is why I think it would be best if we could meet somewhere in that neighborhood instead of Khartoum," wrote Roosevelt. "Incidentally, I could actually see some of our troops."[11]

Just after Christmas Day 1942, representatives of both Roosevelt and Churchill scouted locations around Casablanca and Fédala for the conference, which received the code name SYMBOL.[12] They considered the Hôtel Miramar in Fédala, where Patton held the armistice meeting with Charles Noguès, only to dismiss it because of the bomb damage and "squalid surroundings." Instead, they recommend Anfa, the well-do-to Casablanca suburb. "It consists of a hotel surrounded by a group of excellent villas situated five miles south of Casablanca and one mile inland," reported Dwight Eisenhower. The layout of the neighborhood also made it possible to set up a tight security perimeter.[13]

Having settled on Casablanca as the conference location, the president and prime minister couldn't resist picking out their own code names for their forthcoming adventure. Churchill decided to be "Air Commodore Frankland," while Roosevelt and his close advisor Harry Hopkins opted for "Don Quixote" and "Sancho Panza."[14]

55

Round Up the Usual Suspects

On January 12, 1943, a B-24 Liberator departed England before midnight and headed south, the plane's four engines buzzing as
its propellers cut through the night air. Instead of conducting a submarine
patrol or hauling cargo to Egypt, the bomber carried Winston Churchill and
part of his entourage bound for Casablanca.

From the beginning of their discussion about the conference, Churchill
and Franklin Roosevelt had decided their meeting should remain secret until
its conclusion, requiring extreme subterfuge to assemble everyone in French
Morocco.[1] Organizers took steps to conceal their departures and provide
cover stories. The absence of so many top-ranking British military officers
from London at one time would not go unnoticed. According to the carefully
crafted cover story, some of the service chiefs would be attending low-level
staff talks in Cairo to discuss future operations in the Middle East. Others
heading to Casablanca would come down with a cold or some other ailment,
preventing them from appearing in public. Deputies and secretaries would
answer correspondence and telephone calls as if they had consulted their
superiors. Conference attendees made social engagements for the week of
January 16 to 21, which their staffs would then cancel owing to the "pressure
of business." When it came time to depart for Casablanca, they would leave
London individually. A pileup of admirals and generals at the train station
would not go unnoticed either.[2]

After the bone-chilling flight from wintry England, Churchill and his delegation appreciated the warmth of the North African sun. The crisp blue sky,
whitewashed buildings, and sprightly palm trees provided a much-needed
antidote to grim and grey London; so too did the orange and lemon trees

heavy with fruit, the yellow and purple pansies dotting the gardens, and the fuchsia and amethyst bougainvillea flowing over and down the walls.[3] "Conditions most agreeable," wrote Churchill to London, reporting on his arrival. The appearance of his son, Randolph, who served on the Tunisian front with the British Special Service Brigade, further bolstered his spirits.[4]

Churchill's mind and disposition thawed as he ambled down the hill from his villa in Anfa for walks on the beach with Sir Dudley Pound, admiral of the fleet, and other members of the British Chiefs of Staff. Watching the Atlantic toss up waves that reached heights of fifteen feet before crashing on the craggy coastline also illustrated for him why so many landing craft had pitched their men into the water and ended up smashed to pieces on Moroccan beaches during the invasion.[5]

CHURCHILL ARRIVED TO FIND an Anglo-American colony in the middle of the lush Casablanca suburb. The job of making the conference arrangements had fallen to Mark Clark and George Patton, who spent two weeks squaring everything away. The Anfa Hotel, a four-story art deco building with lines that mimicked a luxury sailing ship, served as the conference headquarters. Perched on a hill overlooking the Atlantic, the white hotel appeared as if it might surge forward into the sea below. Two months before, the hotel housed the German Armistice Commission; now it became Allied Central. Fourteen of the nearby villas were secured to house Churchill, Roosevelt, and the Allied military leadership. The owners, residents, and their servants were displaced in the run-up to and for the duration of the conference. Those servants who stayed were not allowed to leave until the conclusion of the conference. Roosevelt's villa, selected in part for its maneuverability by wheelchair, also received an upgrade: its swimming pool became an impromptu air-raid shelter.

Triple barbed wire surrounded the makeshift Anglo-American colony—known as "Anfa Camp"—and American soldiers stood guard around the perimeter. Everyone was required to show a pass—no exceptions—at the two entrances to the camp.[6] Guard dogs also prowled the perimeter, happy to take a bite out of both the British and American delegations.[7] Antiaircraft batteries, camouflaged to appear less imposing, dotted the camp, while spotters kept watch for enemy aircraft from the roofs of the hotel and villas. Patton feared the Luftwaffe might return for another bombing run during the conference.[8]

Anfa Camp also boasted its own phone system, courtesy of the US Signal Corps, and a small store next to the bar on the hotel's ground floor doled out

FIGURE 55.1. The Anfa Hotel became the headquarters for the Casablanca Conference. *Naval History and Heritage Command*

cigarettes, chocolate, toothpaste, soap, razors, and anything else a traveler
might have forgotten. The US Army also laid in personnel, food, and drink
for the conference, controlling every bite served. Roosevelt even transported
his own water supply all the way from Washington.[9]

To record the conference proceedings, the American and British delegations both brought their own secretarial pools, turning the hotel's conference
and dining rooms into a sea of typewriters.[10] A courier service also ran between Anfa Camp and the HMS *Bulolo*, a "specially fitted headquarter ship"
docked at a close-by pier. The ship served as a floating library for the British
delegation and functioned as the conference's communications hub.[11]

Even with all the security in place, the American and British delegations
received stern warnings about the need for vigilance. TORCH had decimated
Germany's intelligence network in Casablanca, but the conference offered
ripe pickings for remaining agents or enterprising individuals. Attendees
were urged to use common sense, whatever their rank, to safeguard the conference proceedings. They shouldn't rely on locks or assume walls and doors
were soundproof. No leaving "secret" waste or papers in unoccupied rooms
either. Despite the steps taken to secure the telephone system, conversations
conducted in a loud voice still drifted through doors and windows.[12]

354 DESTINATION CASABLANCA

CHURCHILL'S FLIGHT TO CASABLANCA took all of nine hours, but Roosevelt's spanned days. Worried about security and potential negative press about the president's leaving the country during the war, not to mention flying, the White House and Secret Service took elaborate measures to conceal his departure. The Secret Service picked up the baggage of people traveling with Roosevelt at their homes to avoid it accumulating in their offices or at the White House. The Secret Service then delivered it to the train carrying Roosevelt's entourage to Miami. The crew from the USS *Potomac*, the president's yacht, also replaced the train's staff.[13]

At 10:30 p.m. on January 9, Roosevelt's train departed Washington from the underground station at the Bureau of Engraving and headed north— before doubling back and heading south for Miami, where two Pan Am Clippers waited. After Pearl Harbor, the US government pressed Pan Am's luxurious fleet of flying boats into military service. The Clippers, which took off on water instead of land, offered luxurious accommodations—tables for eating, lounge areas, and sleeping compartments—which made long-haul flights almost civilized.[14]

Twenty-seven hours later, Roosevelt's train arrived at Military Junction in Miami under cover of night. Before dawn on January 11, Roosevelt kissed his wife, Eleanor, who had made the journey south with him, good-bye and headed for the Pan Am hanger, where he was transferred to the Clipper. Joining Roosevelt onboard were Harry Hopkins, who served as the president's personal envoy; Captain John L. McCrea, his naval aide; Admiral William Leahy, head of the Joint Chiefs of Staff; Rear Admiral Ross McIntire, the president's doctor; and a handful of Secret Service agents. A second Clipper carried the remainder of Roosevelt's staff.[15]

"I sat with him, strapped in, as the plane rose from the water and he acted like a sixteen-year-old, for he has done no flying since he was President," wrote Hopkins in his diary.[16] Roosevelt had just become the first president to travel by airplane while in office—and the first one to fly out of the country.[17]

As was common with transatlantic flights in that era, the Clippers hopped their way to Africa, starting with a stop in Trinidad. Leahy, battling a bad cold, stayed behind when the planes departed the next morning for Brazil, touching down only long enough to take on fuel for the next leg across the Atlantic. At 6:30 p.m. on January 12, the Clippers began their 2,100-mile transatlantic flight. The US Navy kept watch below, while the Clipper pilots maintained radio silence to avoid revealing their location.[18] As they sped across the Atlantic, the cocktails flowed, and "everybody was feeling pretty good," wrote Hopkins. Exhausted from the grueling travel schedule, the group turned in early, but the rough air made sleep a fitful enterprise. Nevertheless, after spending his first night on a plane, Roosevelt awoke in good spirits and good health. With hours still left in their journey, the passengers read, talked about the upcoming conference, and played cards. Hopkins even taught McIntire how to play gin rummy.[19]

At around 4:30 p.m., the Clippers touched down in the mouth of the river at Bathhurst (now Banjul), Gambia, where the USS *Memphis* awaited them. They were almost there: Casablanca was only another 1,800 miles to the north. When all was said and done, it took Roosevelt almost five days to reach the white city.

At the end of the long journey, the president was rewarded with the smiling face of his son, Lieutenant Colonel Elliott Roosevelt, who served in the Army Air Force as a reconnaissance officer. The thirty-one-year-old would act as his father's military attaché during the conference.[20]

By 7:00 p.m., Roosevelt was ensconced in Villa Dar es Saada, his home base for the conference. Hopkins fetched Churchill, who was staying fifty yards away in Villa Mirador. "He was in fine form but looked older," wrote Hopkins of the prime minister.

The two leaders talked for an hour over drinks before sitting down to dinner with members of their military staffs and Robert Murphy. In typical Roosevelt and Churchill fashion, the conversation and drinks flowed. At 1:30 a.m., they doused the house lights, a tardy concession to the blackout rules. "We sat around the table with faces lit by 6 candles," wrote Captain John McCrea, Roosevelt's naval aide. "The PM and President in that light and surroundings would have made a wonderful picture." At 3:00 a.m., they finally headed for bed.[21]

"It gave me intense pleasure to see my great colleague here on conquered or liberated territory which he and I had secured in spite of the advice given him by all of his military experts," wrote Churchill years later in his memoir.[22]

56

The Work Begins

As Franklin Roosevelt made the last leg of his journey to Casablanca, the Combined Chiefs of Staff assembled in a conference room at the Anfa Hotel on Thursday, January 14. The discussion, which kicked off at 10:30 a.m., was the first of eighteen formal meetings over the next ten days. The generals and admirals would also hold countless informal conversations on walks, during lunches and dinners, over cocktails, and on car trips along the Moroccan coast to points of interest. The president and prime minister would also offer their own suggestions over meals and cocktails.

Holding up the British end of things were Field Marshal Sir Alan Brooke, Admiral of the Fleet Sir Dudley Pound, and Air Chief Marshal Sir Charles F. A. Portal. Field Marshal Sir John Dill, Chief of the British Joint Staff Mission in Washington, was also on hand. General George C. Marshall, Admiral Ernest King, and Lieutenant General Henry H. Arnold represented the Americans. The Washington Conference in June 1942 had helped the British and American service chiefs get to know each other beyond the cold type of letters and reports. Now those relationships would be tested as they debated how to proceed during 1943.

While the chance to escape Washington and London gave the conference a *Boys' Own* adventure feel, the slate of issues on the agenda provided a harsh reminder of the state of the war. By the end of the conference, the Combined Chiefs needed to decide on the next phase of operations in the European and Pacific theaters. They also had to allocate resources—men and matériel—between both theaters. In the European theater, the British wanted to pursue the "soft underbelly of Europe" strategy outlined by Winston Churchill in Moscow, which would mean striking across the Mediterranean from North Africa into Italy or the Balkans. The Americans wanted to refocus on a cross-channel operation to reclaim France. Both strategies hinged on guessing when Germany might falter on the eastern front against the Russians. They also needed to determine a strategy for finishing the Allied assault in Tunisia. The spring campaign season rapidly approached, and the Nazis would not leave Africa without a brutal fight.

The British came to Casablanca prepared to do battle, having mapped out their strategy and drawn up position papers. The HMS *Bulolo* also served as their secret weapon, its library providing any fact or figure the Brits might need to make their case. The Americans arrived with incomplete plans. After spending so much time opposing TORCH, the Joint Chiefs of Staff finished out 1942 arguing among themselves whether to abandon the Europe-first strategy to focus on the Pacific, where American loses continued to mount. While the European theater had become an Anglo-American affair, the Americans shouldered the overwhelming majority of the war effort in the Pacific. By the end of December 1942, the Joint Chiefs had settled their differences and again united behind the Europe-first strategy, but they weren't quite prepared to argue with the British over next steps.[1]

It was going to be a long ten days.

UNLIKE THE COMBINED CHIEFS of Staff, who stayed in Casablanca for the duration of the conference, Dwight Eisenhower could only spare one day away from Algiers and Allied Forces Headquarters. He counted on Marshall to brief him afterward about anything he needed to know.

On the afternoon of January 15, Eisenhower found himself on the hot seat as the Combined Chiefs discussed the current state of the North African campaign privately and then with the president and the prime minister. After the quick successes of TORCH, the Allied offensive in North Africa had bogged down, dashing hopes of claiming Tunisia by the start of 1943. Wet weather turned the roads into rivers of mud, making it impossible for trucks and tanks to navigate. When the ground hardened in early March, Eisenhower wanted to strike at the Germans from the south. Eisenhower and General Harold Alexander, who was advancing on the Germans from the east with the British Army, needed to coordinate their operations in order to squeeze Erwin Rommel and the Afrika Korps.[2]

The Allies had come to North Africa to create a beachhead to reach across the Mediterranean and into southern Europe. Once they had secured Tunisia and completed construction of more runways in Algeria—the ground had to be reinforced with steel netting or it would crumble—they would be able to launch bombing raids on Italy and the Balkans.[3] Casablanca had yet to become the supply hub planners hoped for. The port facilities were fantastic, but only nine hundred tons of matériel a day moved north to Algeria owing to the lack of railway cars.

Eisenhower also reported that French troops had started to make a solid contribution, but were poorly trained and underequipped. Alphonse Juin had been very helpful, but Henri Giraud was "dictatorial by nature and seemed to suffer from megalomania." While initially hopeful about Giraud's stewardship of French North Africa, Eisenhower believed he lacked the skills to manage the civil government in the region for the long term. Giraud possessed "no political sense and no idea of administration." Ike confessed that he had found it easier to deal with Jean-François Darlan.[4]

EISENHOWER ALSO SPOKE PRIVATELY with Roosevelt in the afternoon. He found the president optimistic and almost lighthearted, which he attributed to the commander in chief's escape from the crush of Washington.[5] During their conversation, Roosevelt asked Eisenhower to tell him about the French generals, who still remained only names in reports. The president also fretted about France's postwar position and the fate of her colonies. "He speculated at length on the possibility of France's regaining her ancient position of prestige and power in Europe and on this point was very pessimistic," wrote Eisenhower. "As a consequence, his mind was wrestling with the questions of methods for controlling certain strategic points in the French Empire which he felt that the country might no longer be able to hold."[6]

Frustratingly for Eisenhower, Roosevelt did not always grasp the Allies' role in North Africa. The president spoke in terms of occupation and compelling the French and local populations to act in accordance with Allied wishes. "It was necessary to remind him that from the outset we had operated under policies requiring us to gain and use an ally—that, far from governing a conquered country, we were attempting only to force a gradual widening of the base of government, with the final objective of turning all internal affairs over to popular control." Roosevelt would correct himself—and then go back to speaking like a conqueror. The president did agree, however, that the French should not receive the military equipment they desired unless they continued to work with the Americans on strategy, provided access to French bases, and purged officials whom the Americans found suspect.

Thankfully for Ike, Roosevelt did not fret about the slow progress made by the Allies in Tunisia since December, believing that their fortunes would turn.[7] Nor did he chide him for the Darlan Deal and its subsequent fallout. Instead, Roosevelt quoted sentences and paragraphs from the cable Eisenhower had sent explaining the deal's rationale. It had been, Roosevelt told him, "most useful in calming fears that all of us were turning Fascist."[8] Given the North African quagmire, Eisenhower half expected to lose his job, but there was no talk of that, much to his relief.

Despite the whirlwind nature of his trip, Eisenhower felt the journey to Casablanca was worth it. "I cannot tell you how valuable it was to me to have the chance to talk to the President and yourself and to the Combined Chiefs of Staff, particularly General Marshall," he wrote to Harry Hopkins. "There is no doubt that great good will come out of your meeting there, and I often regret that you people who are occupying the top positions cannot get together with greater frequency."[9]

Although he made only a brief appearance, Eisenhower benefitted from the discussions held by the Combined Chiefs of Staff at Casablanca. Believing a new command structure was necessary to allow for better coordination of the North African and Mediterranean theaters, the chiefs appointed Eisenhower as supreme commander. In his new role, he would command the forces already under Allied Forces Headquarters, along with Britain's Eighth Army, which was rapidly advancing west across Libya toward Tunisia.[10]

ROOSEVELT FINALLY MET HENRI Giraud two days later, on January 17. Mark Clark had arranged the meeting and attempted to sell the president on Giraud after learning of Eisenhower's sharp assessment. He assured Roosevelt that Giraud remained "head and shoulders above other Frenchmen who were seeking power in North Africa." Not only was the general a symbol for France, but he had also proven cooperative when "dealt with firmly."

Clark considered the meeting between the president and Giraud a disaster. Roosevelt didn't like using the interpreter and tried to converse in French. "This was a dismal failure since Giraud merely became more and more puzzled as the President rattled on in his rusty French," wrote Clark. "Finally, we had to get an interpreter to try to end the confusion."

During the meeting, Giraud pressed hard for the Americans and British to supply the French with guns, tanks, and planes. When Roosevelt asked where the troops would come from, Giraud suggested the French army could recruit tens of thousands of colonial troops. His officers would train them. Roosevelt was dismayed to learn that the mythical 250,000 troops waiting to fight for the Allies still needed to be armed and trained.

The president also tried his hand at brokering a deal between Giraud and Charles de Gaulle. He suggested that Giraud could serve as commander in chief with de Gaulle as his second in command. They could appoint a third person to handle the political matters. "Maybe we could get someone else out of France or someone who has taken refuge in Switzerland," said Roosevelt. Turning and smiling at Clark, the president asked, "Do you want to make another secret submarine trip, General?" Clark was not interested.

After the meeting with Roosevelt, Clark took Giraud over to meet Churchill. The president suggested the Clark stick around to see what happened, but the prime minister's aides quickly shunted him off to the side. "Next day, when I told Mr. Roosevelt I was diplomatically kicked out, he grinned and said that was what he had expected," wrote Clark.[11]

57

To the Bitter End

ALITTLE BEFORE NOON ON SUNDAY, JANUARY 17, A SERIES OF CARS pulled up outside the gate of Franklin Roosevelt's villa. Three generals emerged and, after showing their identification to the guard on duty, proceeded toward the two-story house. Instead of meeting the president of the United States at the Residency in Rabat on his home turf, Charles Noguès had journeyed, accompanied by Major General George S. Patton and Brigadier General William Wilbur, to the makeshift Allied colony that had sprung up overnight in Casablanca.

A few days earlier, Roosevelt had presented Wilbur with the Congressional Medal of Honor for his "conspicuous gallantry and intrepidity in action above and beyond the call of duty" in wading through enemy lines to arrange a cease-fire and subsequent command of a platoon that captured a French battery. He had also been promoted from colonel to brigadier general, earning his first star.[1] If Wilbur was an example of an ideal soldier, Noguès had come to represent its antithesis.

For Roosevelt, the interview with Noguès represented a chance to finally meet the man whom he had read so much about in the reports from Robert Murphy, Mark Clark, and Dwight Eisenhower. Here was the man who fought so hard to defend French Morocco against Patton's forces. And here was the man who refused to sign an armistice agreement that included Henri Giraud. Roosevelt also wanted to meet Noguès because he'd gotten an earful from Winston Churchill about the resident-general. Charles de Gaulle considered him a traitor who should be serving time in jail—not governing French Morocco.[2]

As introductions were made, Roosevelt studied Noguès. The silver-haired general wore his winter uniform of dark olive twill with its jacket belted at the waist and pants tucked into glossy, knee-high leather boots. "I am very pleased to meet you, General, and I must say that you look exactly like your photograph," said Roosevelt.

Noguès thanked the president for his invitation and noted that he and all of French Morocco where honored and surprised by Roosevelt's presence. Despite the activity in Anfa, the Americans had kept the exact nature of the conference secret from Noguès until it became necessary to reveal the presence of Roosevelt and Churchill. The Americans had found yet another way to wound his pride.

The discussion started out with Wilbur serving as translator, but soon Roosevelt and Noguès were managing in French, with Noguès overlooking the president's grammatical stumbles. Any pretense that the meeting was a courtesy evaporated quickly. Roosevelt intended to take Noguès's measure, starting with a dig about Vichy collaboration. The president inquired as to the status of the Germans in French Morocco, trusting they had made a permanent exit. Noguès, who characterized the Germans as "haughty and overbearing," said he welcomed their departure. Those members of the German Armistice Commission who failed to escape now resided in internment camps.[3]

Patton extolled the good working relationship between the Americans and the Residency, giving fulsome praise to Noguès's cooperation. The camaraderie between the two generals only confirmed reports of their chummy relationship.[4] For his part, the president said that he believed the press had made too much fuss over the supposed discord between the Americans, British, and French in North Africa. The time for "name calling is now over," said Roosevelt.

He then returned to the hunt and brought up the issue of political prisoners. The Americans and British were unhappy with Noguès's reticence in releasing those interned because of their politics or religion. Noguès sidestepped the problem of languishing Gaullists by pivoting to the Jews. He explained that most of the Jews had been discharged from the camps, but they remained anxious to see a quick restoration of their rights, which had been stripped away by Vichy.

Robert Murphy, who also attended the meeting, stepped into the discussion to clarify what Noguès meant by "rights." Despite the Allies' arrival two months before, Vichy's anti-Semitic laws remained on the books. French, American, and British officials worried about Muslim public opinion in Algeria and French Morocco turning against the Jews, leading them to endorse a slow approach to repeal. The cautious approach alienated the Jews, who, as

Murphy explained, were "very much disappointed that 'the war for liberation' had not immediately resulted in their being given their complete freedom." In particular, Algerian Jews waited anxiously for restoration of their voting rights, something Moroccan Jews had never been granted.

Roosevelt brushed aside the issue of the vote, noting that no elections loomed. France would not decide its future government until the conclusion of the war and the defeat of Nazi Germany. In the meantime, Roosevelt believed, "the whole Jewish problem should be studied very carefully and . . . progress should be definitely planned." The president proposed limiting the number of Jews practicing medicine, law, and other professions to the percentage of Jews in the population. Roosevelt believed that his plan would dispel the "specific and understandable complaints" of the Germans, who believed that Jews overly dominated the professions.[5]

Roosevelt's suggestion echoed the policies of Nazi Germany and Vichy France—but he didn't believe what he was saying. Indeed, the proposal ran counter to how he conducted his career and his administration. Roosevelt had appointed Jews to run the Treasury Department (Henry Morgenthau) and to the Supreme Court (Felix Frankfurter). Sam Rosenman served as a trusted advisor and speechwriter and became White House consul in October 1943. New York lawyer Ben Cohen was a member of Roosevelt's "Brain Trust," along with Frankfurter, and had helped write the Lend-Lease legislation. Critics of the New Deal sarcastically called it the "Jew Deal," referring to all the Jews who received appointments during Roosevelt's first administration.[6] Roosevelt had also inquired about the status of the North African Jews in early December, urging Jean-François Darlan to repeal Vichy's anti-Semitic measures.[7]

From the reports streaming into Washington, Roosevelt knew that the role of Jews in North Africa and their relationship to the Arabs remained a touchy subject for French colonial officials. A show of sympathy offered the best way to test Noguès's feelings on the subject. Noguès took the bait. He agreed with Roosevelt that limits should be placed on the role of Jews in the professions and civic life. "It would be a sad thing for the French to win the war merely to open the way for the Jews to control the professions and the business world of North Africa," said Noguès.[8]

Noguès, of course, was adept as playing to his audience, so it's possible that he too made a calculation and said what he thought Roosevelt wanted to hear. Even so, the resident-general had not been lobbying Algiers to modify Vichy's anti-Semitic legislation in French Morocco.

During the meeting, Roosevelt asked for Noguès's advice on another matter. The president wanted to invite the sultan to dinner. Would that be appropriate? Both Noguès and Patton agreed that the palace would welcome the invitation. The president could pay the sultan no higher complement. Noguès suggested that breaking bread together was viewed as the equivalent of becoming blood brothers or serving together in combat. He agreed to facilitate delivery of the invitation.[9]

SINCE THE BEGINNING OF the conference, the Combined Chiefs of Staff had met every day, often twice. The Americans and the British also gathered separately, sometimes with the president and prime minister present. On Monday, January 18, everyone assembled for a meeting in Roosevelt's villa at 5:00 p.m. to discuss points of agreement and what remained outstanding.

After seven days of intense discussions, the Combined Chiefs settled on a series of priorities for 1943. Combatting German submarines in the Atlantic to keep the supply lines open between the United States and Britain remained a top a priority. They also reconfirmed the "Europe-first" strategy, which prioritized the fight against Germany over Japan. The Allies would strike at Germany from North Africa, concentrating on Sicily, Italy, Greece, and Crete to draw German forces away from the eastern front. While doing so, they would also continue to draw up plans for a cross-channel invasion of France. A massive air offensive conducted from the United Kingdom against Germany would aim to destroy infrastructure and undermine morale. They also wanted to persuade Turkey to enter the war on the side of the Allies to gain access to its air bases, which would aid operations against Romania. In the Pacific, they sought to oust the Japanese from Rabaul and New Guinea and to prioritize an operation to retake Burma.[10]

George Marshall explained to the group that the decision to invade Sicily and then Italy stemmed from the presence of large numbers of Allied troops in North Africa. Churchill's vision of North Africa as a stepping-stone into southern Europe had come to fruition. But Marshall also wanted it understood that attacking Sicily and Italy would delay a cross-channel invasion of France.[11]

Over the course of their discussions in Casablanca, the Americans raised concerns about whether the British would continue to fight following the defeat of Germany. They would welcome more assistance with the Pacific theater, and Churchill made clear that following Germany's defeat, Britain would devote all of her resources to helping the United States fight Japan. The prime minister believed this to be not only in Britain's interest but also a point of honor. Churchill even offered to enter into a formal treaty with the United States, an idea that Roosevelt brushed aside—Churchill's word was enough. The president did, however, want Britain's help in obtaining a commitment from the Soviet Union that it too would turn its attentions on Japan after Germany's defeat.[12]

Having agreed on Anglo-American priorities for 1943, the Combined Chiefs now had to figure out how to accomplish them all with the men, ships, and matériel available.

DURING THE MEETING, THE military chiefs also clamored for an update on the Giraud–de Gaulle situation. News of Henri Giraud's presence spread through Anfa Camp like wildfire. Would de Gaulle also be joining them? "De Gaulle had said that he would not meet Giraud in an atmosphere dominated by the High Command of the United Nations," Churchill told the chiefs. Given his attitude, Roosevelt and Churchill needed to decide whether to keep supporting de Gaulle's movement.[13]

Churchill's measured response to the Combined Chiefs paled in comparison to his private words to Roosevelt. "I tell you, Mr. President, General de Gaulle is most difficult to deal with. We house him. We feed him. We pay him. We pamper him, and as best we can, we put up with his truculence and insults, but he refuses to raise a finger in support of our war efforts," said Churchill during one of their skull sessions. "He insists that he is entitled to a military command. I ask you, Mr. President, what sort of military command could either of us give him?"

Roosevelt acknowledged the problem but said they still needed to get de Gaulle and Giraud to work together. "Winston, this is a shotgun marriage," said the president.[14]

Anxious for de Gaulle to come, Churchill sent a stream of telegrams to London, begging and then chiding him. "The fact that you have refused to come to the meeting proposed will in my opinion be almost universally censured by public opinion and serve as a complete answer to any complaints," wrote Churchill. "There can of course be no question of your being invited to visit the United States in the near future if you reject the President's invitation now. My attempt to bridge the difficulties which have existed between your Movement and the United States will have definitely failed." Foreign Secretary Anthony Eden also personally visited de Gaulle; yet the general remained steadfast in his refusal. Churchill became so annoyed by de Gaulle's obstinacy that he threatened to replace him as head of the French Liberation Committee.[15]

58

Uneasy Lies a Head
That Wears the Crown

O N THURSDAY, JANUARY 21, ONE WEEK INTO FRANKLIN ROO-
sevelt's stay in Casablanca, the president got his wish to see American troops in the field. He had wanted to go to the front lines in Tunisia, but George Marshall and Dwight Eisenhower vetoed that idea on the grounds that flying from Casablanca to Algiers was too dangerous. The Luftwaffe regularly attacked the transport planes that flew between the two cities, and adding a fighter escort would only draw more attention. The president also wanted to see the blackened shell of the *Jean Bart* in Casablanca's harbor, especially after Winston Churchill's gleeful description of his own outing.[1] "FDR wanted to visit [the] harbor but Secret Service would not let him," wrote George Patton in his diary. "They are a bunch of cheap detectives always smelling of drink."[2] Roosevelt had to settle for inspecting Patton's troops around Rabat and a visit to Mehdia.

At 9:20 a.m., the president's motorcade departed his villa, headed for the outskirts of Rabat. Roosevelt's Daimler occupied the center position in the fifteen-car convoy, flanked by jeeps carrying Secret Service agents. Above them, American airplanes traced their progress and kept an eye out for enemy aircraft.

As the new commander of the Fifth Army, Mark Clark drew escort duty. He'd spent the previous few days going over the arrangements to make sure everything was in order. Clark, who had no trouble wrangling French generals, agonized over the prospect of spending the day making small talk with Roosevelt. He needn't have worried. "The President started

FIGURE 58.1. Roosevelt reviews troops as Clark looks on from the back seat of the jeep. *Library of Congress*

out asking questions and I don't believe he stopped all day," wrote Clark.[3] Patton rode in the car behind with Harry Hopkins, who, he discovered, he genuinely liked. "He is extremely intelligent and very well informed. To my surprise he is quite war-like and is in favor of discipline," wrote Patton.[4]

Outside Rabat, Roosevelt was transferred to a jeep for the review of troops. On a dusty plain, with a sea of pup tents as the backdrop, the troops from armored, infantry, artillery, quartermaster, and reconnaissance battalions filed past. Trucks and tanks rumbled by, and men marched in formation with their guns perched on their shoulders. "It was a good day for review," wrote Clark. "A stiff wind made the flags and banners stand out smartly and the outfits were polished and alert, so the President had a fine time, seemed pleased with what he saw, and showed his pride for what they had accomplished."[5]

After the parade, Roosevelt's jeep rolled slowly past the men standing at attention. Many of the soldiers could not disguise their surprise when they recognized the distinguished-looking man in the gray fedora hat.[6]

Wearing a sweater under his suit jacket to ward off the cold, the president ate lunch outside under the overcast sky, sharing a wooden table with Clark and Hopkins. The meal consisted of boiled ham, sweet potatoes, green string beans, fruit salad, bread, butter, and jam, with coffee to wash it down. As they ate, the 3rd Division Artillery Band serenaded them with popular favorites, including "Chattanooga Choo Choo," "Deep in the Heart of Texas," and "Alexander's Ragtime Band."[7] After the plates had been cleared, Roosevelt asked for a mess kit as a souvenir, forcing Clark to run to the kitchen to find one. "I'll have them put it in the Smithsonian Institution," Roosevelt told Clark as he flashed a big grin.[8]

The president's review of the troops continued after lunch, and Patton beamed with pride at the display. "Our troops put up a really fine appearance," he wrote. "I have never seen so many troops so well turned out or looking so fit."[9]

From Rabat, they headed north toward Mehdia, where Roosevelt received a briefing on the fight for Port Lyautey on a ridge overlooking the kasbah. Major General Lucian Truscott's men had ousted the French from the ancient fortress two months before, but a French flag once again flew from its blackened ramparts. A few hundred yards away, the American soldiers who had died during the invasion lay in a newly built cemetery on a high bluff overlooking the Atlantic Ocean. The sound of the waves crashing on the shore provided a peaceful backdrop for the solemn ground. The cemetery also caught the winds off the ocean, making it difficult for Clark and Captain John McCrea, Roosevelt's naval aide, to lay the large wreaths of orange flowers brought to honor the dead.[10]

ON FRIDAY EVENING, JANUARY 22, the Americans and British wore black tie for the first and only time during their stay in Casablanca. They had spent most of the conference rambling to and from each other's villas within the bubble of Anfa Camp with little need for formal attire. Dinner with the sultan, however, required a good showing. Churchill opted for all black, while Roosevelt donned a white dinner jacket. Harry Hopkins dressed for evening too, but poor Robert Murphy had to make do with a dark suit, having not thought to pack his tuxedo.

Sidi Mohammed, dressed in fine white silk robes, arrived at Roosevelt's villa at 7:40 p.m. accompanied by his son, the grand vizier, and his protocol chief. Charles Noguès, Patton, Lieutenant Colonel Roosevelt, and Captain McCrea rounded out the party of twelve.

The sultan presented Roosevelt with a gold dagger in a beautiful inlaid wooden box. For Eleanor, he offered a gold tiara encrusted with emeralds, sapphires, and rubies, along with a pair of gold filigree bracelets.[11] Hopkins

FIGURE 58.2. Roosevelt hosted a dinner for Sidi Mohammed at his villa. *From left to right front:* Sidi Mohammed, Roosevelt, Churchill. *Back row:* Patton, Murphy, Hopkins, Prince Hassan, Noguès, El Mokri, Si Mammeri, Elliott Roosevelt, and McCrea. *Franklin D. Roosevelt Library*

found the jewelry gaudy, likening it to "kind the gals wear in the circus, riding on white horses." The idea of the no-nonsense First Lady wearing the tiara at a White House function elicited a wink and smile between father and son. Although the gift did not suit Eleanor and would have been out of place in Washington, the sultan's generosity was undeniable. Roosevelt presented his own gift to the sultan: a signed photograph of himself in a heavy silver frame engraved with the seal of the president of the United States.

Murphy had made the dinner arrangements, taking pains to adhere to Islamic dietary laws, including no pork. In consideration of the sultan, the attendees also refrained from smoking and from the ritual of predinner drinks, drinks during dinner, and drinks after dinner. Orange juice and water were served instead of wine. Churchill, Roosevelt, and Hopkins, however, downed a few drinks before the sultan's arrival.[12]

At dinner, the sultan sat to the right of Roosevelt. "The President began the serious conversation by expressing sympathy with colonial aspirations for independence, and soon he was proposing to the Sultan that arrangements should be made after the war for American-Moroccan economic cooperation," wrote Murphy.[13] They also discussed how the sultan might tap into Morocco's natural resources to improve the education and health of his subjects, with the president suggesting that outside interests should not be allowed to obtain concessions that did not benefit Morocco.

The sultan latched on to this idea. He was keen to develop Morocco's natural resources but remained dependent on French and British engineers. He needed trained engineers and scientists among his own people who could do the work. Roosevelt suggested training Moroccans through an educational exchange with leading American universities. "The Sultan nodded," wrote Elliott Roosevelt. "If it had been etiquette, he would have taken notes, names, and addresses of universities, right there on the spot."[14]

Seated at the far end of the table, Noguès craned his neck, hoping to overhear what Roosevelt and the sultan discussed. The bits he heard made him "restless."[15]

As the sultan and Roosevelt ambled along in French, Churchill's mood soured. The prime minister's French wasn't stellar, which made being his usually boisterous self difficult. From what he could glean, Roosevelt was dabbling with the one issue that caused animus between them: colonialism. Churchill believed that after the war both France and Britain would keep their colonies, while Roosevelt believed that European colonialism had run its course. Now, here was Roosevelt discussing ways in which American investment might help the sultan accomplish his vision independent of the French.

Everybody noticed Churchill's bad humor. Hopkins described him as "glum," observing, "A good time seemed to be had by all, except the Prime Minister."[16] Patton went further: "Churchill was very rude, the President was great, talking volubly in bad French and really doing his stuff."[17]

During dinner, a royal marine appeared and indicated that Churchill was urgently needed. The prime minister returned after twenty minutes, during which he appeared to have had a quick drink or two.[18] "I have a feeling Churchill cooked that up beforehand, because I saw the dispatch later and it certainly wasn't one that required the Prime Minister's attention at the dinner," wrote Hopkins.[19]

After dinner concluded, Hopkins remarked to Murphy that Noguès appeared uneasy, which he attributed to the imminent possibility of losing his job. Murphy doubted that was the cause. "Perhaps the President's approaches to the Sultan also aggravated Noguès' fears about American designs on the French empire," he said. "From the point of view of any imperialist— including De Gaulle and Churchill—the President's conversation with the Sultan could seem subversive."[20]

It could also be encouraging, as evidenced by the sultan's mood following the dinner. On the drive to the grand vizier's villa in Anfa, Sidi Mohammed spoke effusively to Patton about Roosevelt. "Truly your president is a very great man and a true friend of myself and of my people. He shines by comparison with the other one," he told Patton. "This has been the happiest day of my life and one I shall always remember. I shall be very worried until I hear that the President is safely home."[21]

THROUGHOUT THE DINNER WITH Roosevelt, Noguès strained to catch snippets of anticolonial sentiment here and there, but he would have been outraged to learn of the conversation that took place the next day, when the sultan's grand vizier, El Mokri, and his protocol chief, Si Mammeri, paid a call on Harry Hopkins. El Mokri had asked Patton to arrange the meeting without telling the British about it. The palace wanted to broach a few issues with the president in private. If Hopkins could not agree to such a condition, then it would be better not to have the meeting.[22] Hopkins promised to respect the grand vizier's wishes and that Roosevelt alone would learn of their conversation. The only other person in the room was Brigadier General William Wilbur, who served as Hopkins's translator.

The grand vizier wanted to present four issues to the president. First, what were the United States' intentions toward French Morocco? The arrival of the Americans had unsettled the country's political equilibrium. France no longer appeared the strongest power, particularly next to the Americans. Both Vichyites and Gaullists had also questioned Noguès's authority. Where did the Americans fit into this picture? "In order to determine his future policy the Sultan would like to know the permanent policy of the U.S. in regard to Morocco," the grand vizier told Hopkins.

The sultan also worried about the Jews in Morocco. When the German Armistice Commission arrived, it had demanded that Jews be treated as they were in Germany, but the sultan had refused. Moroccan Muslims and Jews had a long history of living together, and he would not support such extreme policies. As long as the status quo held—with Jews subordinated to Muslims—there would be "no Jewish question in Morocco." Some Jews, however, thought the American troops' arrival would result in the elevation of Jews to positions of authority over Muslims. "This must not be," said the grand vizier.

The third question concerned supplies. Morocco needed food, clothing, and machinery. The Americans had promised shipments of these. When would the supplies start arriving?

Finally, the sultan believed the war would end with an American victory. "When the time arrives to discuss the conditions of the peace it is the Sultan's intention to throw himself in the arms of Mr. Roosevelt," said the grand vizier. "Provided Mr. Roosevelt will accept him and his country." The sultan wanted to hold a plebiscite about French rule. "The Sultan is certain that all his people both in French and Spanish Morocco will be in agreement and wish to place their future in Mr. Roosevelt's hands," said the grand vizier, who wished particularly for this issue to remain secret.

Upon hearing the list of questions, Hopkins told the grand vizier that he felt comfortable responding to the sultan's concerns, given his familiarity with Roosevelt's views. During the previous four years, Hopkins had served as Roosevelt's roving political envoy, going where the president couldn't. He was privy to every political decision. He also knew very well that the United States had only one formal policy toward Morocco at that moment: it must remain stable so as not to distract from the battle in Tunisia.

Hopkins told the grand vizier that the United States intended to fight until the Allies had defeated Germany and Japan. "The war will be pursued until Germany, Italy, and Japan agree to unconditional surrender," said Hopkins. The American army would not remain in Morocco—it would not fail, like some countries, to depart after the restoration of peace. Nor did the United States intend to exploit Morocco and her resources. Instead, it wanted closer economic relations, aided by the new advances in sea and air travel. He could not give firm answers on the state of the promised supplies for Moroccan civilians but noted that matériel for troops took priority.

Roosevelt also did not deem it necessary to change the present government of Morocco. "The President knows that the people of Morocco are concerned," said Hopkins. "They should not be unduly so." The choice of Casablanca as the location for the conference occurred by chance, but the publicity surrounding the meeting should aid Morocco in the future. "The President has been profoundly impressed, and his visit will be of great benefit for he has become a warm friend of the Sultan and his country," said Hopkins.[23]

If Sidi Mohammed sought an ally to dethrone the French, he did not find it in Roosevelt—at least not at that moment. Roosevelt—and Hopkins—would never promise to oust the French, especially when things remained so unsettled in North Africa and for France. Nevertheless, the new relationship with the United States would provide the sultan and Morocco with more maneuvering room in the future. The long-term question for Sidi Mohammed was how to play the United States off France and Britain to gain the independence he and his country craved. The United States could be a valuable new friend.

59

The Horse Race

A S THE DINNER WITH THE SULTAN WOUND DOWN, ROBERT MURPHY slipped out to meet a new guest. After delaying until the last possible moment, General Charles de Gaulle had consented to travel to Casablanca.[1]

The towering former tank commander with a toothbrush mustache arrived earlier that day with a long list of grievances, which included not being informed of TORCH until it was underway and being excluded from participation in the operation itself. Then there was the deal with Admiral Jean-François Darlan, who was at least now out of the way. More recently, de Gaulle had felt slighted when Franklin Roosevelt asked him to postpone a planned trip to the United States in the wake of Darlan's assassination. The reason for the cancellation became clear when he learned of the president's meeting with Winston Churchill in Morocco.[2] Despite the opportunity to meet Roosevelt and finally talk face-to-face with Henri Giraud, de Gaulle felt the trip would not benefit him. "If I must go to the Anfa conference to enter a race wearing the British colors while the Americans backed their own entry against me, the resulting comedy would be indecent, not to mention dangerous," he wrote.[3]

But after prodding by the Foreign Office and stern telegrams from Churchill, de Gaulle sulked his way to Casablanca. His arrival in Morocco received no pomp. A small delegation headed by William Wilbur received him at the airport and took steps to conceal his presence. Before departing the airfield, Wilbur smeared the car windows with a muddy rag. De Gaulle also received the same size villa as Giraud to prevent charges of favoritism.

"It must be good to be back again among your own people," said Murphy in an attempt at polite conversation. Murphy knew from gossip that de Gaulle did not think much of him.

De Gaulle exploded. "I never would have consented to stay in this house, surrounded by American barbed wire and bayonets, if I had not been informed that it is owned by a Dane, not by a Frenchman!" The general found the arrangements at Anfa Camp—the barbed wire, the sentries, the Americans staffing his residence—an outrageous affront. "In short, it was captivity," wrote de Gaulle. "I had no objection to the Anglo-American leaders' imposing it on themselves, but the fact that they were applying it to me, and furthermore on territory under French sovereignty, seemed to me a flagrant insult."[4]

Knowing that relations between the United States and the Free French needed to improve, Murphy trod carefully with his next words. "We all are happy that you are here. While I would not presume to advise you about French and North African politics, I feel I should say that it would be very helpful to everybody concerned if you could come without making legalistic conditions," said Murphy. "I am certain that if you do, you will have complete control of the French political situation within three months, because General Giraud is interested solely in his military command and has no political ambitions."

De Gaulle's mouth curled into a half smile. "Political ambitions can develop rapidly. For example, look at me."

The spark of humor thawed relations between the two men. For the next thirty minutes Murphy briefed de Gaulle about Roosevelt's policy toward France, how the United States came to be involved with Giraud, and possible means of future cooperation between the two French generals.

De Gaulle listened intently and asked no questions. Instead, when Murphy finished, he offered a warning. "I am not empowered to make any binding decisions while in Casablanca."[5]

AFTER THE SULTAN DEPARTED Roosevelt's villa, Murphy walked de Gaulle over to meet to president. The two leaders knew each other only through newspaper accounts, diplomatic reports, and gossip. Sitting on a long couch in the villa's main salon, they quickly settled into in a discussion about the future of France and its colonies. The president wanted their first meeting to be intimate, without anyone else interceding, so they spoke without the aid of interpreters. As Roosevelt turned on the charm, de Gaulle remained aloof.[6]

De Gaulle believed that the French people should have the right to choose their leader—convinced, as he was, that French North Africa would give him popular support—while Roosevelt believed that the contingencies of the war demanded putting aside political considerations until its end. Roosevelt characterized the situation in French North Africa as a "trusteeship." "The only course of action that would save France," he said, "was for all of her loyal sons to unite to defeat the enemy, and . . . when the war was ended, victorious France could once again assert the political sovereignty which was hers over her homeland and her empire."

De Gaulle found Roosevelt's approach to France's predicament unreasonable. Frenchmen, not the leaders of Britain and the United States, needed to decide the fate of France now, in the heat of battle. Despite his qualms about Roosevelt's stance, de Gaulle opted not to quarrel with him. "We took care not to meet head on, realizing that the clash would lead to nothing and that for the sake of the future, we each had much to gain by getting along together," wrote de Gaulle.[7]

Throughout the meeting, de Gaulle felt a sinister undercurrent to their conversation. As his eyes surveyed the room, he noticed shadows on the second-floor balcony and curtains moving at the edges. Despite Roosevelt's assurances, they didn't appear to be alone. Acting of their own accord, the Secret Service had decided that de Gaulle posed a serious threat and concealed themselves around the room, tommy guns at the ready. "None of this hokus pokus had gone on when Giraud saw the President and it was simply an indication of the atmosphere in which de Gaulle found himself at Casablanca," wrote Harry Hopkins, who also noticed something odd afoot. "To me the armed Secret Service was unbelievably funny and nothing in Gilbert and Sullivan could have beaten it."[8]

Although the meeting ended on a cordial note, Roosevelt found the discussion unsatisfactory. He considered de Gaulle's attitude too rigid, too focused on French national politics at the expense of the immediate war effort. The French republic could not rise again until liberated from the Nazis.[9]

Churchill's meeting with de Gaulle proved less cordial. The acrimony marking their cable exchange continued in person. "I had a very stony interview with de Gaulle, making it clear that if he continued to be an obstacle we should not hesitate to break with him finally," wrote Churchill. "He was very formal, and stalked out of the villa and down the little garden with his head high in the air."[10]

Even though frustrated in the extreme by de Gaulle's stubbornness, the prime minister respected the "unconquerable Frenchman." "He had no real foothold anywhere. Never mind; he defied all. Always, even when he was behaving worst, he seemed to express the personality of France—a great nation, with all its pride, authority, and ambition," wrote Churchill. "It was said in mockery that he thought himself the living representative of Joan of Arc, whom one of his ancestors is supposed to have served as a faithful adherent."[11]

DURING THE FINAL MEETINGS between the Combined Chiefs of Staff on January 23, Churchill and Roosevelt approved a blueprint for the war in 1943. Looking back on the work done over the previous ten days, Churchill noted, "It was the first instance he knew of when military leaders had remained together so long, free from political considerations, and had devoted their full thought to the strategic aspects of the war."[12]

At the top of the list was defeating the U-boats in the Atlantic to maintain the flow of supplies to support the war effort in Britain, North Africa, and the Soviet Union. They would also invade Sicily to secure communications in the Mediterranean. From there, they would jump over to Italy and work their away up its boot to dispatch Benito Mussolini. The Italian campaign would also force Germany to divert resources from the eastern front. From bases in the United Kingdom, the Allies would launch an intensive air assault on Germany and begin building the force needed to conduct a cross-channel assault. And they would calibrate continuing operations against Japan in the Pacific and Far East to ensure the Allies could take advantage of any opportunities that might present themselves in Europe.[13]

THE TEN DAYS OF diligent work and compromise contrasted sharply with the de Gaulle–Giraud drama. Roosevelt and Churchill hoped that when the conference ended, they could announce a new chapter in French unity, but that was not to be after the discussions between the Frenchmen proved fruitless.

De Gaulle refused to enter any arrangement that might further deplete French sovereignty. He did not like Roosevelt and Churchill's power sharing scheme. Under the plan, Giraud would continue to control French forces, while de Gaulle received the title "General of the Army." A third general would attend to political and civil affairs in North Africa. De Gaulle found this unacceptable, believing it would allow Giraud to amass power with Roosevelt's assistance. In de Gaulle's eyes, Roosevelt's support for Giraud aided the president's plan to keep France in pieces, thereby allowing the United States to dominate the postwar landscape. He also found Giraud's willingness to continue to work with Henri-Philippe Pétain's supporters, men like Charles Noguès and Alphonse Juin, morally suspect. How did Giraud intend to unify France and guard French interests when his supporters were Vichy collaborators?

Giraud offered a simple answer: while de Gaulle focused on politics, he concentrated on reassembling a French army that could return to France and vanquish the Germans. The Americans agreed in principle to equip as many units as Giraud could field, and he planned to have twelve divisions within six months. What army did de Gaulle command?

De Gaulle thought that Giraud was missing the point. Unity should be the first priority, along with the creation of a government to provide central leadership. He proposed an alternative in which he would form and lead a government in Algiers. "[From] the very first this central authority must condemn Vichy, proclaim that the armistice was always null and void, and identify itself with the Republic and, in the eyes of the world, with the independence of France," de Gaulle told Giraud. As the leader of the Free French, he had the backing of the French people and the moral authority to serve as their leader. He would then give Giraud command of an army and orders to liberate France from Germany's grip.[14]

Giraud refused de Gaulle's offer. He believed that de Gaulle continued to confuse hatred of the Germans with his own personal popularity. He also remained in the best position to fight the Germans. The standoff continued.

60

Unconditional Surrender

FROM THE VERY BEGINNING OF THEIR DISCUSSIONS ABOUT THE conference, Franklin Roosevelt and Winston Churchill had decided to exclude the press—partly for safety reasons and partly to allow them to work without scrutiny of their every move. Secrecy would also help them orchestrate a "shotgun marriage" between Henri Giraud and Charles de Gaulle.[1]

Toward the end of the conference, Allied Forces Headquarters invited a group of approximately fifty journalists to Casablanca, promising them a history-making event. With space short in Anfa Camp, the journalists received lodgings at the Excelsior, an upscale hotel on Casablanca's main thoroughfare across from the entrance to the old medina. They were instructed not to talk about their assignment in front of hotel employees or others in Casablanca. They were also told to behave as if their rooms were bugged. The Excelsior's bar had been a favorite hangout for the German Armistice Commission, and the current extent of Nazi infiltration of the hotel staff remained unclear. To help with security, the US Army temporarily took over the hotel's switchboard and kitchen.[2]

On January 24, the final day of the conference, the journalists assembled on the lawn behind Roosevelt's villa. Four white chairs sat empty before the scrum of reporters. Shortly after noon, the door to the villa opened, and Churchill, de Gaulle, and Giraud walked out, while Roosevelt was carried to his chair. The whirling of film and clicking of cameras quickly replaced the murmurs of disbelief. The brilliant North African sunshine that morning made flashbulbs unnecessary.[3]

"When the Press reporters saw us both they could scarcely believe their eyes, or, when they were told we had been there for nearly a fortnight, their ears," wrote Churchill.[4]

FIGURE 60.1. Giraud, Roosevelt, de Gaulle, and Churchill gather for one of the war's most awkward press conferences. *Library of Congress*

With Giraud and de Gaulle failing to reach an agreement, there would be no headlines touting a new, unified French war effort. But photographs showing American, British, and French leaders together would galvanize Allied propaganda efforts. As Giraud, Roosevelt, and Churchill traded small talk and offered occasional smiles for the cameras, a solemn-faced de Gaulle smoked a cigarette. A photographer wanted more—something that didn't smack of a command performance—and urged Giraud and de Gaulle to shake hands. The generals ignored the suggestion, until the president prodded them. "Why not shake hands?" said Roosevelt. "You two Frenchmen are loyal to your country, and that warrants a cordial handshake anytime."[5]

They stood, de Gaulle pulling the cigarette from his mouth and holding it to the side, and managed a fleeting handshake. Unable to capture the moment, the photographers called for them to do it again. The second shake was no less awkward.[6]

After Giraud and de Gaulle departed, Churchill moved over to sit by Roosevelt and talk further with the reporters and war correspondents gathered before them. Roosevelt began by reading a background statement and then spoke from some notes for about fifteen minutes. During this short speech he uttered a phrase that became synonymous with the conference: "unconditional surrender."

"I think we have all had it in our hearts and heads before, but I don't think that it has ever been put down on paper by the Prime Minister and myself, and that is the determination that peace can come to the world only by the total elimination of German and Japanese war power," said Roosevelt. "Some of you Britishers know the old story—we had a General called U. S. Grant. His name was Ulysses Simpson Grant, but in my, and the Prime Minister's, early days he was called 'Unconditional Surrender' Grant. The elimination of German, Japanese and Italian war power means the unconditional surrender by Germany, Italy, and Japan. That means a reasonable assurance of future world peace."

As Roosevelt envisioned it, "unconditional surrender" meant not the annihilation of the German, Italian, and Japanese populaces but "the destruction of the philosophies in those countries which are based on conquest and the subjugation of other people."[7]

When the president mentioned "unconditional surrender," Churchill's head whipped toward him.[8] The prime minister's reaction suggested that he found the phrase surprising—a perception that grew after the war, when the concept of "unconditional surrender" became somewhat controversial. Critics charged that its pursuit dragged out the war unnecessarily because it prevented a negotiated peace. At one point, Churchill suggested that he had never heard the phrase until it came out of Roosevelt's mouth at the press conference. In his memoirs, he backtracked on that claim somewhat, while continuing to imply that the policy had not been approved in advance.[9]

Churchill may not have expected Roosevelt to utter the words, but the idea of "unconditional surrender" had been thoroughly discussed at the conference. The minutes of a Combined Chiefs of Staff meeting attended by Churchill note that he uttered the phrase himself. The prime minister had also consulted with the War Cabinet about making an "unconditional surrender" declaration part of a plan to assure the United States that Britain intended to fight to the finish beside its ally. Churchill even suggested issuing a press release saying that "the United Nations are resolved to fight to the bitter end, neither party relaxing its efforts until the unconditional surrender of Germany and Japan has been achieved," but the idea was nixed.[10]

Roosevelt would later tell Harry Hopkins that he hadn't planned on announcing "unconditional surrender" as Allied policy. "We had so much trouble getting those two French generals together," said Roosevelt, "that I thought to myself that this was as difficult as arranging the meeting of Grant and Lee—and then suddenly the Press Conference was on, and Winston and I had had no time to prepare for it, and the thought popped into my mind that they had called Grant 'Old Unconditional Surrender,' and the next thing I knew I had said it."[11]

In his memoirs, Churchill noted that he had disagreed with Roosevelt's decision to announce the policy, but to make that quarrel public before a pack of journalists would have damaged the war effort.[12] There could be no visible fractures in the Anglo-American alliance. Instead, Churchill opened his own remarks to the press by saying, "I agree with everything the President has said." He also emphasized the importance of his friendship with Roosevelt. "Well, one thing I should like to say, and that is — I think I can say it with full confidence — nothing that may occur in this war will ever come between me and the President. He and I are in this as friends and partners, and we work together. We know that our easy, free conversation is one of the sinews of war of the Allied Powers."[13]

FOLLOWING THE PRESS CONFERENCE, the British and Americans hit the road for Marrakech and one last spot of adventure. Churchill believed it would be a pity for Roosevelt to come all the way to French Morocco and not see the sun set over the Atlas Mountains. The best place to do that, in Churchill's estimation, was in Marrakech. When George Marshall caught wind of the scheme, he tried to squash the expedition to Morocco's interior, believing it an unnecessary security risk, but Churchill persisted with the scheme.

For Churchill, Marrakech represented everything exotic about North Africa. He sold the city as "'the Paris of the Sahara,' where all the caravans had come from Central Africa for centuries to be heavily taxed en route by the tribes in the mountains and afterwards swindled in the Marrakesh markets, receiving the return, which they greatly valued, of the gay life of the city, including fortune-tellers, snake-charmers, masses of food and drink, and on the whole the largest and most elaborately organised brothels in the African continent." Presented with such a colorful portrait, and one last chance respite from the pressures of Washington, Roosevelt agreed.[14]

Shortly after 1:00 p.m., the caravan of cars departed for Marrakech. As they headed south, the whitewashed buildings of Casablanca gave way to patches of farmland and the stark, craggy terra-cotta landscape of the interior. American troops stood guard along the highway, while airplanes surveilled from above. The party stopped for lunch alongside the road, dining al fresco on a rocky patch of land, as armored cars patrolled the surrounding area and Secret Service agents kept watch. The British delegation provided the feast of boiled eggs, mincemeat tarts, and generous pours of wine and scotch.[15]

Upon arriving in Marrakech, Roosevelt, Churchill, and select members of their staffs took up quarters in La Saadia. The glamorous villa, nestled into an olive grove, belonged to the widow of the industrialist Moses Taylor and was one of the few properties owned by an American in Morocco. Kenneth Pendar, one of Murphy's vice consuls, used La Saadia as his base of operations in the city. The villa's salmon walls gave way to a lavish interior of blues, greens, and yellows that showcased Moroccan craftsmanship. Black marble fountains gurgled in the two inner courtyards, which bloomed with orange trees, geraniums, and bougainvillea. The Americans and Brits marveled that each bedroom had its own bathroom, replete with a sunken marble bath. The rest of the party stayed at the luxurious Hôtel Mamounia, which had crawled a few months earlier with members of the German Armistice Commission.[16]

While their staffs explored Marrakech's famous central square and labyrinthine souk, Churchill and Roosevelt ascended the villa's six-story tower to watch the sunset. Two Secret Service agents carried Roosevelt up the narrow staircase in a chair. With the tower's platform short on space, the others quickly cleared out, leaving the two leaders alone to take in the landscape before them, highballs in hand. They had spent the previous ten days in a stark white city, breathing the salt air blown in by the wintery Atlantic. Now before them lay a desert city rendered in shades of pink, peach, and terra-cotta, accented by the riotous green tufts of palm trees. The sky provided another feast of color as it dissolved from cobalt blue into ochre and rose. From their perch, they watched Moroccans mounted on camels and mules arrive and depart through the city's main city gate and the sun sink behind the snow-capped Atlas Mountains. As dark descended on the city, the bells and lights atop the minarets of Marrakech's mosques began to chime and flash, signaling the call to prayer. Only the swift arrival of the desert's nighttime chill forced Roosevelt and Churchill down from their roost.

Dinner started at 8:00 p.m. and lasted until midnight. Pendar's cook, with stocks provided by the army, provided a feast of lobster, pâté, and filet mignon. The meal finished with an elaborate, three-foot-tall confection of pastry and spun sugar in the shape of the tower of Marrakech's main mosque. "We had a very jolly dinner, about fifteen or sixteen, and we all sang songs," wrote Churchill. "I sang, and the President joined in the choruses, and at one moment was about to try a solo. However, someone interrupted and I never heard his." After the leisurely feast, the group, together for one last time, wrote telegrams, including one to Stalin, and drafted reports summarizing the conference. [17]

Since they worked until well past 2:00 a.m., Roosevelt told Churchill not to get up to see him off on the morning of January 25. Never one to follow directions, the prime minister appeared at dawn, chomping on a cigar and wearing his favorite jumpsuit, along with a bathrobe and slippers, and drove with Roosevelt and the others to the airfield in Marrakech. Churchill even boarded the plane and made sure Roosevelt was settled, while "greatly admiring his courage under all his physical disabilities and feeling very anxious about the hazards he had to undertake."

Churchill spent another two days at Villa Taylor, catching up on correspondence and indulging in his love of painting. From the tower, he painted "the only picture I ever attempted during the war."[18]

IN THE DAYS FOLLOWING the conference, the British and American leaders filtered home to London and Washington. While pleased with his men's performance, George Patton was happy to have everyone leave. "You will probably have read in the papers and seen on the movie screen that for the last ten days we have been very busy entertaining the leading lights of the world," he wrote his old secretary. "It was very amusing but was not war. Personally, I wish I could get out and kill someone."[19]

Before Roosevelt left Africa and embarked on the arduous journey back to the United States, he took a trip up the Gambia River on a tugboat built in Bay City, Michigan, and delivered to British Gambia as part of Lend-Lease. He also had lunch with Edwin Barclay, the president of Liberia. After touching down in Brazil, Roosevelt met with President Getuilo Vargas. A week later Brazil entered the war on the side of the Allies.[20] There was also an inflight celebration of Roosevelt's sixtieth birthday.

Roosevelt arrived back in Washington on January 31, having been away from the White House for twenty-two days. Four days later, on February 3, the Battle of Stalingrad concluded with the surrender of the German army. The Russians handed the Germans a decisive and devastating defeat, but one that came with a high cost in men and matériel. Only time would tell if the strategy of attacking through the Mediterranean from North Africa, agreed on at the Casablanca Conference, would provide the assistance that Stalin craved.

For the British, the Casablanca Conference represented a victory. They had triumphed over American objections to focusing Anglo-American efforts on the Mediterranean and delayed a cross-channel invasion of France by one more year. For de Gaulle, his appearance in Casablanca, albeit at Churchill's insistence, represented a turning point in his campaign to unify France. By declining to become Giraud's second in command, he preserved his freedom of action, allowing him to continue to pursue his vision. "The unproclaimed victory which De Gaulle won at the Casablanca Conference was a great step forward in his plan to assure France the largest possible share in Allied conquests, including full restoration of the French Empire," wrote Robert Murphy. "The miscalculation which all of us at Casablanca made about De Gaulle was our belief that winning the war had top priority with him, as it did with us."[21]

61

The Club Scene

FOR JOSEPHINE BAKER, THE AMERICANS' ARRIVAL IN MOROCCO provided a much-needed jolt of energy. The United States, whose audiences once rejected her, would also provide the spark to reignite her career. After her months of illness in the Comte Clinic in Casablanca, the arrival of her sometime countrymen to liberate her beloved France seemed an answer to her prayers.

In the aftermath of the fighting, as Casablanca teemed with fresh-faced US soldiers and sailors, Baker departed for Marrakech, finally feeling well enough to leave the confines of the clinic that had been her home for the past nineteen months. She took a suite at the Mamounia, trading the austere hospital room for the hotel's luxurious Arabian fantasia. Her body, however, wasn't as sturdy as she thought, and she fell ill from paratyphoid, a salmonella infection that mimics typhoid's symptoms.

Baker wasn't the only one ill at the Hôtel Mamounia. Ollie Stewart, a reporter for Baltimore's *Afro-American*, languished in his room, sick from a bout of food poisoning. "I hope you will not be as sick as the woman who sings, Mademoiselle Baker," remarked a hotel staff member while checking on him. Upon hearing this, Stewart's reporter instincts kicked in: Baker was supposed to dead.

Marshalling all his strength, Stewart dragged himself around the hotel until he found Baker's room and saw for himself that the woman who had once enchanted Paris was indeed alive.[1] "Josephine Baker is safe," reported the *New York Times* on December 6, printing an Associated Press story that ran across the country.[2]

AFTER HER STAY AT the Hôtel Mamounia, Baker returned to the *riad* she had happily occupied in Marrakech's native quarter, once again a guest of Si Mehebhi. Sidney Williams, director of the Red Cross programs for African Americans stationed in the European theater, found her there. Williams, who had worked for the Urban League in St. Louis and Cleveland before the war, was the American Red Cross's first African-American director.[3] Charged with running a Liberty Club for black GIs in Casablanca, he wanted Baker to perform at its opening in February 1943.[4] The US armed services were segregated, but at the Liberty Club white and black troops could mingle. Along with breaking down barriers, the club would provide GIs with a more wholesome way to spend their off hours than Casablanca's seedier pursuits.[5]

While Baker liked the idea of performing for African-American troops and inaugurating a club that brought the races together, she worried about stepping back onto the stage. Her body had yet to recover from her recent and long-term illnesses, and she struggled to stand for long periods. Her doctor advised against performing, urging her to keep to her bed, but the draw of constructive activity was too great. "How could I best advance the cause? Suddenly I knew," she wrote. "In order to present a united front to the enemy, we would have to be true allies, oblivious of color and origins. Surely I could help by launching the Liberty Club."[6]

After endless months in the hospital, Baker found sitting in front of her makeup table a disconcerting experience. Her cheekbones jutted from her thin face, and her skin lacked its characteristic glow. Her arms and legs had shriveled to "matchsticks," prompting her to pick a well-worn blue polka-dot dress to cover them. She still, however, possessed the thousand-watt smile that transformed her from vamp to comedienne with the curl of her lips. As curtain time approached, the sweat on her brow warned her not to overdo it. The incisions in her stomach were still healing.

That night, the Liberty Club burst with white and black GIs and officers, along with Mark Clark, all dying for a chance to see the legendary Baker—and she delivered. She sang three songs, starting with a Negro lullaby to honor her roots before moving on to a Gershwin song to demonstrate, in her words, "the poetry of the American soul." She closed with "J'ai Deux Amours" ("I Have Two Loves"), a song that helped make her famous and became a chanson staple when she recorded it in 1930. "I have two loves / My country and Paris / By them always / My heart is ravished," she sang. Baker chose the song to emphasize that she now thought of herself as French—and France, as a land of liberty, must be restored to her people.[7]

"It was obvious after the first song that the old time magnetism was still there," wrote journalist Kenneth Crawford, who was in the audience. The three-song set zapped Baker's energy—she grew dizzy—and as soon as the thunderous applause died, she retreated backstage and collapsed onto the couch. After a short rest, Baker rallied for the postperformance festivities, which included coffee and apple pie with the soldiers. While talking to Crawford, she told him of her love for Paris. "I couldn't leave French territory," she said. "It would have been like leaving a sinking ship. I am no rat. I have to be as good as I can for these American soldiers. I hope they'll like me."[8]

She had one more performance to deliver that night. Clark threw a reception in her honor at the Anfa Hotel, which had served as the headquarters for the Casablanca conference. "For the first time since the fighting had begun, I did what I did so well: I made an entrance," wrote Baker. "The entire press corps was there. No one would be able to say I was dead or half dead now!" The party reminded her of the prewar days in Paris. Men in dinner jackets chatted with women in glitzy, décolleté gowns, draped in jewels.[9]

"That night Josephine was reborn to life," said Jacques Abtey, her sometime partner in espionage. Baker was once again a star. She accepted compliments. She smiled. She flirted. And when her body gave out, she fainted into the arms of George Patton.[10]

The Liberty Club in Casablanca became a favorite destination for American soldiers—black and white—in North Africa. "The music there was hotter, the coffee better, and the welcome warmer," wrote Crawford. Williams, its director, also figured out how to make an honest-to-goodness American hamburger, a meal that a homesick soldier would walk miles for.[11]

THE AMERICAN RED CROSS Liberty Club on Rue Chevalier de Valdrome was just one establishment run by the Americans and British for their troops in Casablanca. There was also the Allies Club on the Boulevard de Paris and an American Merchant Seaman's Club on the Boulevard de la Liberté.[12] All formed part of the Allied governments' attempt to provide wholesome entertainment for the troops in Casablanca.

The February 1, 1943, issue of *LIFE* featured the navy-sponsored Airdale Club, housed in a villa requisitioned from an Axis sympathizer. The cover story, a photo essay titled "Date in Casablanca," follows Jim, a naval aviator, and Nikki, a "pretty, wellborn refugee," on an afternoon date. The couple dines on a $2 lunch of hardboiled eggs, beans, herring, and African red wine "cooked by Casablanca's best chef, Papa Gouim, late of Paris and the SS *Normandie*." They walk hand in hand in the medina, which is "safe enough during the day." "But all whites quit the streets at sundown," warns the caption. Nikki bargains with a merchant, but Jim doesn't want to buy

Photo by Eliot Elisofon / LIFE Premium Collection / Getty Images

a brass coffee pot. They meet up with Jim's friends at the Airdale Club. As the day fades, Jim and Nikki take a horse-drawn carriage down to the beach, where they climb along the craggy coast with El Hank watching over them. As they sit perched on a rock with the waves crashing around them, he lights her cigarette: "America's greatest gift to North Africa." Dinner is a small picnic of wine, oranges, and Jim's Field Ration D chocolate bar, another prized item.[13]

With Jim's naval officer's uniform and Nikki's rolled hair and red lipstick, the couple created a glamorous and chaste tableau in an exotic city—one that was picture (and propaganda) perfect for *LIFE*. But American troops on leave in Casablanca could also delve into the sordid. Anything could be bought for price in Casablanca as its residents attempted to make money off the Americans swarming their city. With francs in their pockets, servicemen could easily spend the day getting soused at one of the approved bars—or dodge the military police to frequent one of the city's forbidden areas.

A sailor might also find himself doing something he regretted, as Houston Jones, a sonar operator on the subchaser SC-525, learned the hard way. The earnest, self-described "country boy" from Pelham, North Carolina, with one year of college under his belt, enlisted in the navy after Pearl Harbor and arrived in Casablanca in March 1943. One afternoon he found himself on the town with four of his new shipmates, men he still knew very little about beyond their capacity for alcohol. After a drink at the Opera Bar, his already very drunk shipmates insisted they join him on his planned sightseeing adventure. Rather than explore Parc Lyautey, however, the sailors wanted to find women. Finding female companionship for a price was not difficult as women fell back on prostitution in the face of poverty and wartime hardships. Casablanca was also home to the notorious Bousbir, a government-sanctioned red-light district at the edge of the city.[14] The MPs, however, tried to keep soldiers and sailors out of the brothels and discouraged them from accepting solicitations off the streets.

When a man driving a horse-drawn carriage offered the group some fun, the sailors climbed in. Waiting for them behind the carriage's closely drawn curtains was a "high-class" French woman in need of extra money. "My conscience told me to keep walking toward the park, but since the vehicle was headed in that direction, I climbed up and sat by the driver, an Arab who spoke French," wrote Jones. As the carriage made its way through the city, the park failed to appear, while the laughter and boisterous conversation inside the carriage grew louder. When they reached the outskirts of the city, the driver stopped by a group of trees. Jones had assumed they were going to the woman's home but instead was presented with a blanket on the ground.

Jones watched with dismay as his shipmates disappeared behind the trees and emerged some ten minutes later, giving a thumbs-up, and urging the next man on. "If I had known where I was, I would probably have run away, and when I heard the command, 'O.K., Jones,' I almost blurted out that I didn't want to lose my virginity on a whore," he wrote. "But that would have exposed me as the wimp that I really was, a disgrace to my uniform. I have never felt more unworthy than when applause met my emergence from the woods." When they returned to the city, Jones, still a novice drinker, soaked himself until curfew at Charle's Bar, hoping to wash away his shame.[15]

From that point on, Jones sought out other shipmates whose interests aligned more with his own—more sightseeing and less drinking and whoring. The club for enlisted men run by the American Red Cross also became a sanctuary, not just for the cold Coca-Cola and doughnuts but for the hot showers, which weren't available on his ship. He frequented the Vox, taking in its run of Office of War Information–approved movies. "Nearly seven decades later, I still remember how smitten I was by Lena Horne in *Cabin in the Sky* and *Stormy Weather*, and as a red-neck from the segregated south, I marveled that a Negro could look and sing so beautifully," wrote Jones.[16]

Certain bars, like Opera Bar and Charle's Bar, were designated "approved" not only to control the mayhem of troops on leave but also because Casablanca still crawled with fascists on the prowl for information.

The Jockey Bar, a favorite watering hole of the German and Italian armistice commissions, continued to cater discretely to a pro-Axis clientele. The owner, Victoria Camensuli, a Corsican by birth, provided a backroom or cellar for meetings among the like-minded in need of privacy. She also eagerly chatted up the Americans who found their way into her establishment, trolling for useful tidbits of information. When Spanish refugees who had obtained jobs at the port stopped in for a glass of wine at the end of the day, she turned her attentions on them. They would have been disturbed to know that Dr. Ribes, head of the pro-Franco movement in Morocco, regularly claimed a table there.[17]

The barbershop at 23 Boulevard Jules Ferry also served as "a place of observation and espionage for the organization directed by Dr. Ribes." Juan Carillo, its forty-something proprietor and a longtime Casablanca resident, became a supporter of Franco following the outbreak of the Spanish Civil War, spreading propaganda, recruiting for Franco's army, and helping buy goods for Spain. After the French authorities expelled him, Carillo headed to Spanish Morocco, only to return to Casablanca as secretary of information services for the Spanish Falange, a post he still occupied. Carillo openly bragged about keeping a list of all the Spanish Republicans hiding in Morocco—which he intended to hand over to Franco when Germany conquered Morocco. He looked forward to the day when they were shot. The Residency tried to expel him again, only to have the pasha of Rabat intervene on his behalf.

Carillo's barbershop, "fitted out with some luxury," attracted American officers and noncommissioned officers with lodgings close by. Inside they could settle into a chair for a shave and haircut, escaping their dreary pup tents and the noise of the city. As the steam towels softened their beards and relaxed their defenses, Carillo chatted them up, learning about their jobs and gleaning other tidbits of information. His daughter, a comely young woman of about twenty, also regularly walked out with American soldiers.[18]

62

Leadership

"THIS PLACE IS VERY INTERESTING AND AMUSING, BUT I AM TIRED OF being a peacetime soldier, even in Africa," wrote George Patton to his sister.[1] Patton hungered for glory, and Morocco hadn't been kind to his career. When Dwight Eisenhower sent George Marshall a list of his outstanding commanders from TORCH, he did not include Patton's name. Patton had taken the longest to secure his objective. He had ignored Eisenhower's instructions for the armistice, choosing instead to give Charles Noguès a "gentleman's agreement."[2] Although he did a fine job of training his men and organizing the Casablanca Conference, his laissez-faire approach to dealing with Noguès had given the resident-general too free a hand. Patton's relations with Noguès were, in Robert Murphy's words, "embarrassingly cordial" and became fodder for the newspapers back home, compounding the already bad press about the Darlan Deal.[3]

At the beginning of March 1943, Patton received a chance at redemption when Eisenhower tapped him to take over US II Corps in Tunisia. The inept and eccentric leadership of Lieutenant General Lloyd Fredendall had resulted in the Americans receiving a pasting at the hands of the Germans at the Kasserine Pass and Sidi-Bou-Zid. After the quick and heady victories of TORCH, the defeat served as a wakeup call. Eisenhower relieved Fredendall of his command and brought in Patton to inspire the troops and instill discipline. "For such a job, Patton had no superior in the Army," wrote Eisenhower.[4]

Using every leadership trick he'd learned over the past three decades, Patton transformed II Corps from a dirty, disorganized outfit into a tidy unit that ran on schedule and followed military protocol. Ten days after he took command, the 1st Infantry Division—known as the "Big Red One" for the red number on its shoulder patches—captured a key position, beginning a reinvigorated American assault against the Germans. Now Patton would see if he could take Sfax and move the Allies one step closer to ousting the Germans from Tunisia.[5]

Personal glory aside, Patton had another reason for wanting to defeat the Germans. His son-in-law, John Knight Waters, had been captured at Sidi-Bou-Zid and now sat in a POW camp in Germany. The news shook Patton to the core. "I could not feel worse," he wrote.[6]

FROM HIS NEW PERCH in Oujda on the far eastern border of Morocco, Mark Clark set about creating training programs to prepare American soldiers for future operations. Allied planners had yet to decide what those operations might be, other than invading Sicily and Italy, but Clark's orders specified that he was "to prepare a well organized, well equipped, and mobile striking force with at least one infantry division and one armored division fully trained in amphibious operations." He would also be helping to organize, train, and equip French forces.[7] Despite the uncertainty surrounding the next operation, Clark set to work, aided by Brigadier General William Wilbur, who served as his director of training. (Unlike Patton, Wilbur had received a promotion for his role in TORCH.) Eight training centers were established in Morocco and Algeria to focus on airborne assault, invasion techniques, tank warfare, and air observation, along with providing programs for engineers and field officers. A separate training center was established for French troops.[8]

"A history of North Africa also should point out the opportunities for training which North Africa offered under near battle conditions," wrote Clark. "This was invaluable for the big operations to come."[9]

As part of his new duties, Clark conducted an inspection tour of French Morocco at the end of February, including a requisite stop in Rabat, where Noguès and the sultan turned on the pageantry for their new overseer. Clark returned the gesture in mid-March. During one of their chats, Si Mammeri, the sultan's protocol chief, had mentioned that the sultan was "very much interested in American battleships." When the USS *New York* docked in Casablanca's port on March 18, Clark arranged for a tour. *New York* had sailed from the Brooklyn Navy Yard on March 5, carrying 36,400 troops and 52,700 tons of supplies to Casablanca.[10]

On the evening of Sunday, March 21, the Moroccan flag flew from the *New York*'s main mast beside the Stars and Stripes. Even while anchored in her berth at the Jettée Delure, the battleship projected power, running 573 feet from stem to stern, with a beam that climbed ninety-five feet into the air.

Outfitted with ten 14-inch guns and twenty-one 5-inch guns, the *New York* made for a fearsome opponent—as French forces discovered at Safi during TORCH. But that night, the battleship was on a diplomatic mission. The practice of rendering honors only in daylight hours was being suspended owing to the sultan's schedule.

With seamen lining the rails, the band struck up a tune to welcome the sultan shortly past 8:00 p.m. As the music floated over the dock, Sidi Mohammed, dressed in pristine white robes, boarded the battleship. White canvas stretched from the dock to the captain's gig to guide his way and preserve his shoes from the grime that covered even a freshly scrubbed battleship after a long voyage. After the honors were rendered and the ship's guns offered a roaring salute, the sultan embarked on his tour, exploring the ship down to its lower decks. Caring not a lick about getting dirty, he climbed into turrets and tested the gun sights. He marveled at the engine rooms and other machinery, asking detailed questions about their inner workings. After the tour, Captain A. L. Hamblin, the ship's commanding officer, hosted the sultan and the other guests, which included Clark, Noguès, El Mokri, and Si Mammeri, for dinner.[11]

As Clark said good-bye to the sultan's party on the dock, Si Mammeri told him, "His Majesty wants me to tell you that this has been one of the happiest moments of his life."

Clark broke into a smile. "Tell him that for a fellow who has a hundred and twenty wives, that is saying something."[12]

EVERYWHERE HE WENT, CLARK received a warm reception, but a disconcerting apathy lurked behind the smiles and pageantry. The people of French Morocco were increasingly dispirited about the war and indifferent toward the Americans. They had plenty of reason to be.

Even though the Americans had occupied French Morocco for more than four months and promised to restore freedom to the people, Vichy legislation reigned supreme. Indeed, not until mid-March 1943 did Henri Giraud issue eight ordinances designed to sweep away the laws enacted by Vichy. The ordinances declared the laws, decrees, and rules issued after June 22, 1940, null and void. They repealed racial and discriminatory laws and reinstated local and regional councils and assemblies. They also revoked prohibitions against belonging to secret societies, including the Free Masons. Elections, however, would not be held until the liberation of France.

The new ordinances did not mean Vichy laws would evaporate overnight. Instead, they would remain valid until a commission could evaluate their impact. It was the ultimate French delaying tactic.[13] Noguès also reminded the Americans that the sultan could not sign a blanket *dahir* rolling back every decree issued during the previous thirty-three months. Even so, by the end of March, municipal assemblies had been reestablished, along with advisory groups on industry, commerce, and agriculture. The government council, an appointed body that advised the resident-general on national policy, was revived as well. Noguès promised that *dahirs* lifting restrictions on secret societies and revoking anti-Jewish laws would shortly follow.[14]

Dismantling the Vichy machinery was a step in the right direction but failed to address the larger problem of leadership. Noguès and his administration had set the tone for the country—and the message emanating from the Residency was reticence. Under Vichy, Noguès became adept at impeding requests he did not like. Now he used the same strategy with the Americans and Giraud's Algiers government. The Residency-controlled press dragged its heels on publishing articles highlighting the combined war effort. Efforts to promote Charles de Gaulle, Giraud, and the Free French were stymied, while the Residency allowed the insignia and slogans of the Légion française des combattants, the Vichy veterans' organization, to remain up in all public buildings.[15]

In Casablanca, all roads of distrust ran right to the Automobile Club of Casablanca, the most exclusive private-membership organization in French Morocco. Before the war, it served as a hub of anti-Allied sentiment. In 1941 the club's members, most of whom also happened to belong to the Légion française des combattants, elected Jean Theil to a three-year term as president. Theil openly courted the Germans and Italians when they were in Casablanca; now he turned his attentions to the Americans. When the US Army made noises about taking over the luxurious club for use by its own officers, the membership quickly formed a "Cerle Inter-Allie" and set about cultivating the American and British officers. Theil also hosted lavish receptions at his Anfa villa for Allied officers. His successful courting of the Americans, both for business and information, sent a message to Casablanca's elite that Vichy collaborators still held sway in the city.[16]

Henri-Philippe Pétain's face still looked out from walls and windows in government buildings, and propaganda promoting him also regularly appeared. While the Americans understood that Pétain's popularity would not disappear overnight, they found the Residency's insistence on continuing his cult of personality perplexing. For Noguès, however, Pétain existed separately from Vichy. "Frenchmen did not wish to hear him reviled, since they think of him as a personage entirely apart from the Vichy Government who had done his best to alleviate French suffering, but they recognized that what he said now was of no consequence, since he was in fact a prisoner," said Noguès in a rare interview with American reporters. In the wake of the

German occupation of unoccupied France in November 1942, Pétain handed over this power to Pierre Laval, becoming a virtual prisoner of the Germans in Vichy. His prison may not have had bars, but rumors about his physical confinement by Germany ran rampant.[17]

To help forge a new path—and stomp out the Pétain cult—Giraud ordered in mid-March that all busts, public displays, and declarations of the marshal be removed.[18] Clark, however, thought that only made matters worse. The decree, issued without explanation, generated confusion among the people of French Morocco about how to think of Pétain. For almost three years, the Residency had promoted him as an heir to Hubert Lyautey, the first resident-general and father figure of the French Protectorate. Clark urged Giraud to issue a statement explaining that with Pétain's imprisonment by the Germans, it was no longer practical for the government or the people to maintain ties with the *maréchal*.[19]

A pattern of discrimination against officers with pro-Allied sentiments also began to emerge. Colonel Maurice Herviot, director of public security, was relieved of his duties on February 10. Herviot had worked with Dave King before and during the TORCH landings to aid the resistance. He was replaced by Colonel Ferdinand Taillardat, who had headed the police in Paris for ten months under the direction of General Carl-Heinrich von Stülpnagel, the German military governor of occupied France.[20] Officers with excellent campaign records who spoke in favor of the Allies or de Gaulle also found themselves slated for retirement after reaching the service limit for their rank. At the same time, officers from the same regiments, who espoused pro-Vichy sentiments, received promotions to the next grade, thereby keeping them in the army for another five years. Pro-Vichy reserve officers with less experience and training were also promoted over pro-Allied officers.[21]

The purge of the officer corps of those with Allied sympathies occurred in tandem with the arrival of some of de Gaulle's men. Officers who found themselves answering to Free French officers felt pangs of jealousy and the anger that comes with frustrated ambition. The men who served with de Gaulle had earned coveted promotions, allowing them to advance faster than those who had served in Morocco. Those left behind sneered that, for the Free French, combat amounted to drinking at the bar of London's Savoy Hotel.

Clark's staff and the US consulate in Casablanca regarded Morocco's leadership as the root of the problem. Men who vilified de Gaulle and Giraud—and put Pétain on a pedestal—continued to run the country, despite their sound defeat by the Americans. Such a predicament could only instill confusion and unease in the populace. "They will not have their heart in the common struggle so long as they are governed by the men of Vichy who they believe to be ready to stab them in the back," wrote one American officer.[22]

63

Emptying the Camps

Eight days after the end of torch, during his statement about the Darlan Deal, Franklin Roosevelt spoke about the internment camps operating in French Morocco and Algeria. "I have requested the liberation of all persons in North Africa who have been imprisoned because they opposed the efforts of the Nazis to dominate the world," he said.[1] Despite the president's dictum, Allied Forces Headquarters didn't push too hard. Keeping an eye on Jean-François Darlan and getting the offensive in Tunisia off the ground consumed Dwight Eisenhower, Mark Clark, Robert Murphy, and their British counterparts. When they did ask, they got a series of excuses: The French had to investigate every internee prior to release. The internees had nowhere to go; they were destitute and the Allied armies had taken up all the available housing. The internees were political fanatics or common criminals or Communists.[2]

By the beginning of 1943, the Allies had tired of French excuses. On January 6, 1943, Eisenhower issued an order creating the Allied Joint Commission on Political Prisoners and Refugees in French North Africa.[3] The Joint Commission, staffed by Americans and Brits and backed by the political muscle of Allied Forces Headquarters, was charged with emptying the camps. The French claimed that "there were no persons still detained on account of sympathy shown for the Allied Cause before November 8, 1942." Whether that was true remained to be seen.

Just as the commission began its work, *New York Times* correspondent Drew Middleton filed a report from Morocco with an explosive claim: "French Morocco is a confused, dizzy country where the American flag flies near concentration camps." Middleton's story, which gave Allied officials heartburn, was accurate. The Stars and Stripes flew over US Army supply depots and transit camps for soldiers, which were sometimes located near internment camps established by the French Protectorate. (It's important to note that "concentration camp" in the lingo of the era meant "internment camp." The term would later become shorthand for the camps where the Nazis exterminated more than 6 million Jews.) The resulting public uproar, which seemed to confirm charges that the Allies were working with collaborators, placed even more pressure on the Joint Commission to fulfill its mandate.

WHEN HOOKER DOOLITTLE, THE new American consul general at Rabat, asked Charles Noguès about the continued operation of the camps at the beginning of March 1943, the resident-general claimed there were no "concentration camps" in Morocco. When Doolittle winced, Noguès corrected himself, noting that there were some "workers' camps," where residents were well fed, well housed, and well paid. Doolittle refused to let Noguès off the hook. Before leaving the meeting, he obtained a promise from Noguès to produce a list of all those interned.[4]

On March 10, French and American officials met to discuss how many people remained in French Morocco's camps and why, using the list prepared by the Residency as a starting point. The French claimed to have released 1,398 people since the Allied landings, turning Belgians, Brits, Poles, and Yugoslavs over to their governments. According to the French, 1,563 people remained in camps or in a work-release program. (This number excluded Axis nationals, Italians, and non-European natives.) Spanish Republicans made up approximately 80 percent of prisoners. Most of the 114 Jews had earned a spot in the camps because of expired residency permits and an inability to obtain exit visas. Another 296 people with suspect politics or deemed a threat to public security might have done anything from telling someone that they wanted to join the Free French to holding membership in the Communist party to actively plotting against the Residency.[5]

Unwilling to trust the French at their word, the Joint Commission sent a field team of American, British, and French officers, along with a representative of the International Red Cross, to inspect the camps in both Morocco and Algeria. During March, the team made its first call in French Morocco at Bou Arfa, a penal and forced-labor camp in the northeastern part of the country. In April, they visited Missour, Sidi-el-Ayachi, Djerada, Settat, Im Fout, Casablanca (Roches Noires), and Oued Akreuch and paid a second call on Bou Arfa. Of the camps visited, only Missour and Sidi-el-Ayachi operated as internment camps, with the rest functioning as forced-labor camps.[6]

The Joint Commission discovered that the majority of the men remaining in the camps were Spaniards who had fled the Spanish Civil War.

Using the information gathered by the Joint Commission's field team, Eisenhower and his staff forced Henri Giraud to issue an order "suppressing" the camps for political internees at the end of April. All political prisoners arrested before November 8, 1942, would be released. Those arrested after the Allied landings would be subject to a special investigation.[7]

IN THE SPRING OF 1943, a rumor circulating in Algiers claimed that Robert Murphy, Eisenhower's head of civil affairs and Roosevelt's onetime personal envoy, was helping the French keep the internment camps stocked with prisoners. He was also said to be conspiring with the French to ensure they had enough interned men for the construction crews building the Trans-Saharan Railway.

Kenneth Crawford, a forty-something war correspondent who learned his trade writing for New York and Washington newspapers, smelled a good story.[8] If true, the gossip would confirm the most sinister portrayals of American treachery in North Africa. Everybody told Crawford that he wouldn't be allowed near the camps—but that only made him want to investigate more. Much to his surprise, during their first interview, Murphy not only agreed to let Crawford go but also suggested that other reporters make the trip. More press coverage of the situation would provide more ammunition for bullying the French.[9]

Meeting Murphy was a revelation for Crawford. The stories coming out of North Africa painted him as a fascist snob who refused to rub shoulders with the masses. One reporter even claimed the angle at which Murphy wore his hat revealed an antidemocratic bent. But instead of a die-hard fascist, Crawford found "a quiet, almost diffident man of large, loose-jointed frame and facile mind," who still carried the patina of his Wisconsin upbringing. In fact, Murphy confessed to finding his depiction as a fascist puzzling as he had always considered himself politically liberal and prone to root for the underdog.[10]

"Murphy had come to the perfectly sound conclusion that the way to deny stories that he himself was standing over political prisoners in the Sahara with a black-snake whip in his hand and blood in his eye, was to permit correspondents to go see for themselves," wrote Crawford.[11]

Crawford turned out to be the only reporter who wanted a tour, which is how he found himself on an airplane bound for Bou Arfa in Morocco with S. H. Wiley, the American consul in Algiers and a member of the Joint

Commission. Bou Arfa, a penal and forced-labor camp, lay on the eastern edge of French Morocco's frontier with Algeria. The pilot picked the camp out of the desert expanse by following a stretch of railroad tracks to a plateau, which hosted "a forlorn group of sun-baked buildings." The camp's superintendent and his peg-legged assistant met them at the makeshift airstrip. After lunch, the superintendent turned them over to their guide, José Campos Peral, former editor of *Lucha*, a Republican newspaper in the Andalusian city of Almeria. The French had interned him on his arrival in North Africa in June 1940.[12]

Peral walked them around the camp, which consisted of rows of mud-brick dormitories, a machine shop, a jail, a dining hall, and a recreation hall. The prisoners slept on cots they made with their own hands from wood scraps and chicken wire. After the Americans began investigating the camps, the prisoners received an increase in pay and their "freedom." "Technical freedom in Bou Arfa was meaningless," wrote Crawford. "The camp is surrounded by razorbacks which could be scaled only with difficulty and even if one got out of the bowl it would be hundreds of miles through the desert to civilization."[13]

When Crawford visited the camp, it contained about five hundred émigrés—roughly four hundred Spanish and an assortment of Poles, Czechs, and other Europeans who had not been released in the fall.[14] Before leaving, Crawford and Wiley attended a funeral for one of the Spaniards. "Every one in the camp, both jailers and prisoners, walked silently from the barracks to a burial ground a mile distant," wrote Crawford. "Leaders of the procession bore a rough wooden coffin on their shoulders. They lowered it into a hole in the desert, covered it over and led the procession back to the camp." The silent ceremony was the camp's own version of a hero's send off.[15]

Next, Crawford and Wiley toured camps in Algeria. As the week progressed, Crawford came to respect Wiley, who proved a multilingual warrior in a yellow tie. "His sympathy and patience in dealing with the refugee problem was heartening for an American to see," wrote Crawford.[16] Instead of American villains, Crawford found two diplomats doing their best to remedy a terrible situation.

TO HELP EMPTY THE camps, Allied Forces Headquarters recruited three men with ties to the American Friends Service Committee (AFSC) to join its civilian affairs team. Eric Johnson, a recent arrival from the Quakers' Lisbon office, became the Joint Commission's secretary. An athletic man with dark hair and horn-rimmed glasses, Johnson functioned as both cagey bureaucrat and cheerleader. He quickly learned how to outmaneuver the French while dispensing a warm smile and kept his team's spirits up in the face of numerous roadblocks.[17] Kendal Kimberland and David S. Hartley, two other AFSC staff members, labored out of Casablanca on behalf of the Joint Commission.[18] Kimberland, tall with thinning sandy-blond hair and grey eyes, worked as an economist before the war and took a no-nonsense approach to his job. He also had a talent for taking French officials from no to yes.[19] Hartley operated at a deliberate pace, sometimes to the frustration of his colleagues, but his honesty earned the trust of the very suspicious Spanish internees.[20]

"We have plenty of power behind us," Johnson wrote his colleagues. "This job can now be done quickly. If anyone stands in the way, I think we're in a position to put a good deal of pressure on him. And your mere assertion of power should cause the mighty to quaver."[21] The "power" Johnson referred to belonged to Eisenhower, Murphy, and the British resident minister Harold Macmillan, all of whom had grown impatient with French dithering.

Giraud's decree specified that the Residency could continue to hold *ressortissants de l'Axe* (Axis nationals), a provision it used to its advantage. The Joint Commission, however, decided that the term "Axis national" meant any person in good standing with an Axis country. It did not mean refugees, Jews, antifascists, or former members of the International Brigades. A number of Germans, Austrians, and Poles, particularly those of Jewish heritage, who fought with Communist paramilitary units, known as International Brigades, against Franco in the Spanish Civil War had found their way to French Morocco.[22] As a first strike, the Americans demanded dossiers on all the internees imprisoned for political reasons. The Residency would have to release them or show cause as to why it had not.

As Johnson, Kimberland, and Hartley reconciled the Residency's lists of internees with the prisoner lists logged by the field team on its camp visits, they discovered 250 detainees not included on the French lists. The Americans surmised the Residency wanted to hang on to the prisoners as a source of cheap labor. It didn't matter if they were antifascists or Jews, if they were from Germany or Austria or Spain, the French considered them potential prisoners of war because of their nationality. "In short, it is believed that the administration has not demonstrated that it is always in sympathy with the ideals of freedom and non-discrimination for which the United Nations are said to be fighting," wrote Kimberland.[23]

Allied Forces Headquarters wanted the camps emptied by June 15. Before they could depart, the internees needed either employment or a commitment from friends and family to provide for their maintenance. The men had a variety of options: They could enroll in the French Foreign Legion or the Corps franc, an option few took. They could also sign up with the British Pioneer Corps, another option rarely taken. They could accept contracts for normal wages with their current employers. For internees at Bou Arfa and other work camps, that meant signing up for more backbreaking labor in extreme temperatures. At Bou Arfa, the men would continue working the manganese mine at Kenadza, a prospect few relished. The company building the Trans-Saharan Railway also offered contracts. "The great majority of the men had been working for the companies under conditions of forced labor even since 1940, and were anxious to get away above all from the South into districts where the climate is less severe, and where they would be able to lead a more normal life," stated the Joint Commission's report.[24]

The most attractive option for the internees was a six-month contract working for the Americans. The US Army needed labor to finish construction projects, both planned and underway, so using the men from the internment camps solved two problems. The French and the Americans had also started competing for workers, with the Americans generally losing out to the French. "The Army proposes to go around to the camps and have the men sign the contracts on the spot, and to employ all of them who can work, and to do it at once," wrote Johnson. The Americans were interested in anyone with a strong back, but skilled workers—mechanics, electricians, masons—were particularly prized. The contracts served as proof of employment and secured an internee's release. Recognizing that not all the internees would be able to work, the Joint Commission also hatched a plan to take over Sidi-el-Ayachi as a home for the "lame, the halt, and the blind."[25]

In addition to obtaining work contracts, the Spaniards initially had the option of going to Mexico, but the plan faltered over visa negotiations. Those Spaniards harboring strong political views also remained reluctant to depart for Mexico, preferring to stay close to their homeland in case fortune cast Francisco Franco out and they could return.[26]

THE FILM *CASABLANCA* IS populated with refugees. There's Sascha, the Russian bartender, and Carl, the German-speaking waiter. Annina, a young Bulgarian woman with doe eyes, is ready to sell her body to obtain the necessary exit visas for her and her husband. A Dutch banker who frequents Rick's Café Américain claims to have run "the second largest banking house in Amsterdam." Then, of course, there is Victor Laszlo, the Czech resistance hero, and his charming wife, Ilsa Lund, who are on the run from the Nazis.

The real refugees were the actors themselves. Paul Henreid, who plays Laszlo, fled Austria and was declared "an official enemy of the Third Reich" for his anti-Nazi views.[27] Conrad Veidt, who snarls as Major Heinrich Strasser, had been a major German silent-film star but escaped with his Jewish wife to Britain when Hitler came to power.[28] Peter Lorre, whose creepy Signore Ugarte sets the plot in motion, left Germany after the Nazis purged the film industry of Jews.[29] Helmut Dantine, who plays the oblivious Bulgarian husband, spent time in an Austrian concentration camp as penance for his anti-Nazi views.[30] Madeleine Le Beau, who sulks as Rick's discarded girlfriend Yvonne, and Marcel Dailo, who has a bit part as Emil the croupier, fled France after the armistice.[31] S. Z. Sakall, a Hungarian Jew whose portly, affable Carl provides some comic relief, departed his native Hungary after it joined the Axis in 1940. It was the second time he'd fled the Nazis, having already given up a career in German film. Sakall forged a career in Hollywood as a loveable character actor, but his three sisters were not so lucky. They died in a Nazi extermination camp.[32]

Given that *Casablanca* featured actual refugees, it was fitting that Warner Brothers donated 500,000 francs ($9,000) to the American Jewish Joint Distribution Committee in May 1943 to support Hélène Bénatar's work in French Morocco.[33] Throughout the spring, as the Joint Commission exerted its political muscle and the internees trickled out of the camps, Bénatar provided a safety net on the outside. She helped them acquire new identity cards, obtain ration cards, and find doctors. She gave maintenance guarantees, pledging to cover living expenses, which secured release for refugees like Ruth Lueck, interned at Sidi-el-Ayachi.[34] Bénatar also served as an employment agency, helping those who did not want to work for the Americans find work with private businesses.[35]

The sudden influx of newly liberated internees into Casablanca at the end of May further strained the already overstretched housing supply, making finding accommodations a daunting task. Some internees obtained temporary quarters in one of two homes Bénatar used as boarding houses. With assistance from the United States' Office of Foreign Relief and Rehabilitation Operations, Bénatar also embarked on a renovation of Luna Park, a former dance hall located in Aïn Seeba on the eastern edge of Casablanca. When completed, the main hall and its two smaller buildings would house up to 150 people. Refugees completed the renovations with construction materials provided by the US Army.[36]

The numbers Bénatar helped changed each month as the refugees on the rolls found their footing in Casablanca and newly released internees arrived. At the end of May 1943, Bénatar provided direct assistance to thirty-seven adults and eighteen children in Casablanca and to fifty-seven adults and eighteen children in Sidi-el-Ayachi. She also provided subsidies to refugees in need in Safi, Marrakech, and Mogador. In total, Bénatar's had 199 adults and forty-six children under her care.[37]

Bénatar continued to assist refugees into the summer and fall.[38] The need for her help would not disappear anytime soon. While shipping traffic between Casablanca and the United States gradually improved, the chances of getting an immigrant visa for Cuba, Mexico, or the United States remained slim. Despite including all the needed documents and testimonies of financial support, Ruth Lueck's visa application was turned down by the State Department. She was stranded in Casablanca for the foreseeable future.[39]

EVEN AS THE JOINT Commission made progress emptying the camps, it did not meet the June 15 deadline. Liberating individuals interned for political reasons proved difficult, especially since the French remained reluctant to provide information about them. On June 20, the chief of Morocco's military cabinet finally gave the Joint Commission a roster of all political internees detained before November 8. The Americans were stunned to see that the list ran to 152 names.

Kimberland asked for a meeting with the Residency to discuss the internees. He wanted to sort them into three categories: (1) those who should be liberated immediately, (2) those for whom the Residency had provided sufficient reason to continue their incarceration, and (3) those for whom the military cabinet provided insufficient justification for internment. "I am getting adept at shrugging my shoulders, and if the boys don't convince me that so and so should really be held, I am simply going to shrug my shoulders and put down number three," wrote Kimberland. "Hope it works."[40] Throughout July, Kimberland pressed the French and shrugged his shoulders, until only twenty-five "dangerous types" remained imprisoned.[41]

The Joint Commission also arranged for the release of a group of Spanish Republicans held in the prison at Port Lyautey. With their liberation, all internees placed in camps before November 8 had been freed except for the "hard-core" cases.

It had taken seven months.[42]

64

Why Have You Not Left?

"WHY HAVE YOU NOT LEFT?" ASKED *LIBERATION!*, A GAULLIST newspaper, at the end of March 1943. Its open letter to Charles Noguès pulled no punches. "Since the 8th of last November, there are hundreds of women, mothers, wives, sisters, and children who weep. There are young men who are lying forever within the earth due to your senseless criminal orders. And one can no longer even say that they have died for any purpose. You have sacrificed them against the country's chief interest."[1]

The open letter appeared four days before a Gaullist rally in Casablanca that Noguès attempted to suppress to no avail. Organized by the non-Vichy, nonfascist French War Veterans of Morocco, the demonstration was scheduled for the afternoon of Sunday, March 28. More than a week before the march, Noguès threatened to arrest all the participants. When that didn't dissuade the organizers, he made sure French security forces blanketed the city. He ordered eight battalions, the entire police force of Casablanca, and the Gardes mobiles to be on duty that afternoon. He also ordered the Permanent Tribunal to convene to hear summary trials for those arrested. There would be no appeals. Pierre Parent, head of the veterans group, told Noguès that he was overreacting. The resident-general, however, refused to back down.[2]

Noguès expressed concern to the Americans about the Jews participating in the demonstration, worrying that the presence of a large Jewish crowd might rile up Arab Moroccans. Germany could also use it for propaganda purposes. Noguès warned that if one demonstration occurred, he might not be able to stop a second.[3] Despite his hardnosed attitudes and concerns, however, Noguès would not be in Casablanca that day, leaving Vice Admiral

François Michelier to deal with any trouble. As a precaution, the US Army ordered troops confined to barracks.[4]

The demonstration took place as scheduled. Walking from the Place Administrative toward the Shell Building, the crowd shouted in favor of Charles de Gaulle and bellowed for the removal of Noguès and Michelier. Upon reaching the street leading to the headquarters for the Western Task Force, the marchers found Senegalese troops blocking their way and dispersed. Aside from a few isolated scuffles between the protestors and the police, the demonstration remained peaceful. "All indications now a Gallop poll would reflect an overwhelming majority of French people who want Noguès removed from office," read an Office of Strategic Services report about the demonstration.[5]

Newspapers in French Morocco rarely, if ever, printed criticism of the resident-general. Now, an upstart newspaper had publicly called for his ouster, and people had marched through Casablanca demanding his removal. It was an unsettling development for a man used to exerting complete control.

"WHY HAVE YOU NOT LEFT?" The Americans had asked themselves the same question as their frustration with Noguès grew. As long as Noguès, in Mark Clark's words, "played ball," he remained useful. When that ceased, so too would the Allies' willingness to tolerate him.

To all questions about mobilization, internees, or any other issue, Noguès increasingly gave one response: The old leftist forces of the Popular Front had reemerged to bedevil his work and force his ouster. The Gaullists also sowed feelings of unease among the Moroccan people, making them question the Residency's authority, which made it harder to do his job. Noguès believed Kenneth Pendar, one of Robert Murphy's vice consuls, and Ernest Mayer, a member of the US consulate in Casablanca, were encouraging the leftist thinking permeating Moroccan society. He claimed they meddled in local politics—unlike the British consul general, William Bond. To anyone who would listen, he complained about the Americans and lauded the British.[6]

In April, Noguès took his complaints to Allied Forces Headquarters (AFHQ) in Algiers, embarking on a dangerous gambit to play the Americans and British off each other. Noguès made the rounds, talking to Murphy, British resident minister Harold Macmillan, and finally Dwight Eisenhower.

In his meeting with Murphy, Noguès complained about "the hostile attitude of the American consular and civilian officials in French Morocco." He had a cordial relationship with Clark's Fifth Army but could no longer say the same about the US consulate. "He insisted that Morocco, under his administration, is making the maximum war effort, but that he is continually dogged by a small French minority of self-seekers." With the help of American civilian authorities, these self-seekers continually attacked and embarrassed his administration in their quest to restore the leftist liberal Popular Front. If not for these "troublemakers," Morocco's war effort would be running at full throttle.

Murphy suggested that, not having dealt with public criticism for some time, Noguès might be exaggerating its importance. He noted too that public opinion played a large role in American and British politics. Noguès, however, rejected any similarities. "He will not for a moment admit that he personally is the target and that his continued presence as head of the French administration is causing difficulty and effervescence," wrote Murphy.

Murphy also reminded him that much rancor over his actions at the time of the invasion still lingered. "I was confident that some of my compatriots would never understand why he had acted as he had; that they and I considered that he bore a great responsibility which resulted in the loss of lives of both Americans and Frenchmen, as well as extensive property damage," wrote Murphy. "I said that, speaking for my own people, those things are not easily forgotten." The men about whom Noguès complained had either been interned by him (Mayer) or had a front-row seat to his antics in Algiers (Pendar). Noguès countered that any American with such sentiments should be removed. Ever since his arrival in Algiers on November 11, he had acted in French North Africa's interest and helped foster a "benevolent neutrality."

Murphy refused to let him off the hook, pointing to "his penchant for intrigue" and calling out his attempt to sow discord between the Americans and British. "My conversation with General Noguès confirms the conviction which I have had for a long time that he is unreliable, insincere, and an obstructionist. It is obvious that for some time past he has made a desperate effort to placate American sentiment and to ingratiate himself with us by the shopworn method of social attention," wrote Murphy. "In my opinion, General Charles Noguès's heart is not in this war; he lives in constant fear of the bogey of Communism and the return of the Popular Front in France, and he has completely lost any idea of liberalism and a reasonable play of public opinion."[7]

The same day Noguès met with Murphy, he also met with Macmillan—and tried out the same line of attack. He claimed the Americans were troublesome and the British more sympathetic to the difficulties he faced. Macmillan reminded him that British and American policy remained one and the same. "At this he winced a little and switched off on to other subjects," wrote Macmillan. Noguès also brought up the French army's sentimental allegiance to Henri-Philippe Pétain. Its officers found it hard to reconcile their reverence for Pétain with their desire to fight to free France from German shackles. "I said that we must look to the future, and not to the past," wrote Macmillan. "In my opinion, if any officer had honest and conscientious objections based on his sense of loyalty to the Marshal, the most honourable thing he could do would be to resign."

Like Murphy, Macmillan concluded that Noguès had been on a "fishing expedition" and had hoped to goad him into saying something unfavorable about the Americans. "I am sorry that General Noguès does not speak English because he might get some fairly idiomatic replies from the Commander-in-Chief if he tries this sort of stuff on him," wrote Macmillan.[8] Eisenhower would have no patience for such antics.

The meeting Noguès desperately desired with Eisenhower, the supreme Allied commander in North Africa, took place on Friday, April 16. He again reiterated his complaints about the American vice consuls and their relationship with left-wing elements. "Their activities," Eisenhower reported, "are contributing to misunderstanding, suspicion, and opposition to himself." Noguès argued that he had been doing his best on behalf of the Allied cause. If Eisenhower and Franklin Roosevelt thought he was doing a bad job, he would resign.

Eisenhower told him that he would investigate the accusations. From the beginning, it had been his policy not to interfere in local politics. The Allies' commitment to Henri Giraud to support the local French administration had not waivered. When Ike asked Noguès if he had raised these same issues with Giraud, Noguès offered a vague response. When Murphy asked for details about specific incidents, Noguès became evasive and promised to supply information later.[9]

WHILE NOGUÈS'S CAREER WAS on the rocks, Josephine Baker's was breathing new life. "For the first time in two years, Josephine Baker will dance," screamed an ad in *La Vigie marocaine*. Baker decided to make her official comeback at the Rialto Theater on April 30 in a benefit for the French Red Cross. Accompanying her on stage was Frédéric Rey, her former dance partner and lover. With Rey's help, Baker mined the trunks of costumes she had brought with her to North Africa two years before. As they opened each case, they found only disappointment: moth holes ruined once colorful and elegant dresses. Together they salvaged bits and pieces to create new costumes, taking care to hide Baker's still achingly thin limbs.[10]

On a warm, spring Thursday night in Casablanca, military officers, government officials, and Casablancans filled the Rialto's seats. For the show, a curtain was drawn across the projection screen, and the theater was filled with greenery and Allied flags. Baker delivered a cavalcade of costumes, transforming from a Brazilian into an Asian and then into a Breton villager. For her final number, she sang "J'ai Deux Amours" swathed in a "floating red and blue crepe grown." An audience member remarked that she had cloaked herself in "the colors of Paris."[11]

The tricolor dress and the song became the highlights of her ensuing tour of North Africa. After her performance at the Liberty Club, she had struck a deal with Allied Forces Headquarters: she would perform for free, but AFHQ had to pay for her travel and lodging. It didn't take long to map out a tour and put together a band. From Casablanca, she departed for Algeria, where she gave several shows daily for the troops. Baker's terms were simple: no civilians and no admission charge. She and her band traveled by jeep and truck. She used an army tent for a dressing room, and for a stage, whatever would raise her up so the boys in the back could see her. When she performed in a field, antiaircraft searchlights provided stage lighting. Every show ended with "La Marseillaise," "God Save the Queen," and "The Star-Spangled Banner," with the troops adding their voices to hers.[12]

Baker wasn't above delivering a lecture or two while she had the stage. On the subject of venereal disease, she made a frank plea that delivered more punch than the words of a medic or chaplain. "I want you to look at me," she told the men, "as your mother, your sister, your sweetheart. I'm your family. You are going around exposing yourselves to these diseased girls and you can't miss getting sick." She told African-American troops, frustrated by their relegation to service jobs behind the lines, to bide their time. "As for getting mad because of race prejudice, wait till the war is over. I will come back to the States and join in the fight to break down segregation, but let's win the war first," she said. When she could, she also got in a few words about her hero, Charles de Gaulle, whom she regarded as the undisputed leader of the Free French.[13]

After more than three years, Baker was back entertaining the troops in support of her beloved France. Instead of performing for French soldiers at the Maginot Line, she was singing for Free French troops in the North African desert. Instead of sleeping in a bed that once belonged to Marie Antoinette in a mansion in a Paris suburb, she curled up on a cot in a tent in the North African desert.

She couldn't have been happier.

65

I Leave Morocco My Heart

A N ILLITERATE YOUNG WOMAN WHO BELIEVED THAT GOD SPOKE through her had helped change the luck of French forces under siege by the British at Orléans in May 1429. Even as she suffered from an arrow wound, Joan of Arc helped rally the French to secure a victory over the British. Her bravery, along with her faith, became a touchstone for the French army. Her subsequent capture by the British and trial for heresy, which culminated in her death at the stake, only amplified the legend. Over the next six hundred years, Joan of Arc became part of France's cultural fabric and a patriotic symbol. In 1920, France declared the second Sunday in May, the *fête de Jeanne d'Arc*, a holiday in her honor.

Joan of Arc was called into service once again, this time in French Morocco, on Sunday, May 9. The French and Americans decided to use her namesake holiday to celebrate the rearmament of French forces with American matériel. Charles Noguès believed it "necessary to impress native Moroccans with the favorable course of the war." He imagined something on par with Bastille Day or the Fourth of July in grandeur and pageantry. The festivities would include military parades in major Moroccan cities, featuring French, Moroccan, British, and American troops, and thanksgiving services in churches.[1]

Noguès wanted to celebrate the arrival of the French supplies while also sending a message to the Moroccans: Though defeated, the French were roaring back with the help of the Americans—and they were here to stay.

In October 1942, the French had promised to field an army of 250,000 men, and the celebration on the *fête de Jeanne d'Arc* represented the culmination of their project. Nevertheless, the Americans and British found their troops still woefully unprepared for battle, and in March 1943 the Combined Chiefs of

Staff agreed to equip and train French forces in North Africa themselves. They would use French forces to finish off the Axis in Tunisia, hold North Africa after Allied victory, and fight in forthcoming operations in Europe.[2] The job of organizing and training French and Moroccan forces stationed in French Morocco in the use of the new equipment fell to Mark Clark and his Fifth Army.[3]

On March 19, a convoy departed New York and Hampton Roads bound for North Africa, carrying 126,151 tons of matériel for the French. Four of the convoy's fifteen ships docked at Casablanca on April 11, while the remaining eleven ships sailed on to Algiers. The jeeps, trucks, tanks, and anti-aircraft guns arrived in pieces, requiring improvised assembly lines.[4]

As teams worked around the clock in Casablanca and Algiers to turn the scattered parts into whole machines and armaments, the clash between the Allies and the Axis in Tunisia reached its conclusion. After almost six months in North Africa, the green Americans were turning into a seasoned fighting force, growing in strength and agility with each passing week. The Americans and the British had also learned some hard lessons about working together that would see them through the next phase of the war. And while the Allies evolved, the once superior Axis forces frayed, strained by supply droughts, courtesy of Allied assaults on their convoys from Sicily.

By mid-April, the Axis occupied only a small patch of land in northeastern Tunisia. Over the next few weeks, the dueling armies bled into the sand as they fought for inches, yards, and miles. The Germans retreated— and retreated again. By May 1, the Americans, aided by French and Moroccan units, had arrived within twenty miles of Bizerte. On May 6, the British closed in from the east, entering Tunis. German soldiers surrendered in such large numbers that they clogged the roads, impeding the American and British forces' advance. Soon the Allies had more than 275,000 German prisoners of war on their hands. The impending collapse of the Germans and Italians in Tunisia became something else to celebrate on the *fête de Jeanne d'Arc*.[5]

THE MAIN CEREMONY KICKED off at the Place Lyautey on May 9 shortly after 4:00 p.m. After the presentation of colors, regiments of French, American, British, and Moroccan troops marched down the Avenue d'Amade, along with veteran and patriotic groups. Clark delivered a short speech, handing over the mechanized equipment to the French army. "The victory of the Allied armies at Tunis and Bizerte is a harbinger of future events. As we together chased the enemy from Africa, we will drive him out of metropolitan France," Clark told the crowd. He also promised that a united French army would soon march down the streets of Berlin.[6]

The review started again as French troops paraded by in light and medium tanks, tank destroyers, half-tracks, jeeps, troop-carrying trucks, amphibious cars, and mobile antiaircraft batteries. P-38 Lightnings and P-40 Warhawks roared overhead, filling the square with the hum of their engines. Still more infantry troops followed, including contingents of American and French troops, a detachment of the Royal Air Force, Moroccan cavalry, and finally a special cavalry guard in honor of Generals Clark and Noguès.

Crowds lined the parade route, which ran from the Avenue d'Amade to the Place de France, before turning right down the Boulevard de la Gare and breaking up at the Place Albert Premier. Allied flags hung from the windows, the red, white, and blue blocks of color popping against the stark white art deco buildings of the *ville nouvelle*. As each new contingent appeared, cheers when up from the crowd.

Despite the event's careful scripting, the ceremony soon gave way to protest. When the resident-general and admiral appeared on the reviewing stand, members of the crowd shouted, "Down with Noguès!" and "To the scaffold with Michelier!" They also targeted Casablanca's civil controller with chants of "Down with Poussier!" The strains of "La Marseillaise" and Free French songs rang through the square, and the taunts returned when Noguès and Michelier departed the stand.

When the last section of the official parade left the square, the protestors joined in, led by a man holding a placard emblazoned with "Front National de Liberation" and the Cross of Lorraine. As they marched, the protestors dropped flyers asking people to rally in front of the American and British consulates. But the protest failed to gain momentum as participants were soon engulfed by people attempting to find their way home from the parade, along with an onslaught of cars, wagons, and buses. Instead of using force to disperse the marchers, French officials let the traffic reclaim the avenues that had been blocked. Later, about five hundred people appeared outside the consulates, offered a few cheers, and dispersed.[7]

THE DEMONSTRATION AT THE *fête de Jeanne d'Arc* celebration was the second in three days. On Friday night, May 7, the Vox theater had hosted a gala premiere showing of *Desert Victory*. Produced by Britain's Ministry of Information, it tells "the story of the rout of Rommel in Africa by the British 8th Army . . . with the most thrilling scenes ever taken under fire!"[8] The hour-long film chronicles the first British victory of the war at El Alamein in November 1942, using footage shot by the British army's photographic unit and supplemented with captured German footage.[9]

As the audience, which included French and Allied officials, along with prominent Casablancans, left the theater afterward, an anti-Noguès demonstration greeted them. "Vive de Gaulle! Vive l'Amérique! Vive la France! Vive l'Angleterre!" cried the demonstrators. French officials closed the Vox the following day. *Desert Victory* continued its run at another theater, packing in moviegoers from 9:30 a.m. to 10:30 p.m.[10]

The protests at the screening and the parade were just the beginning. A few days later, vandals bombed the Légion française des combattants for the second time in a week. The first attempt failed to inflict damage, but the follow-up wrecked the entrance and the office. A shop near the Plaza Hotel in downtown Casablanca displaying Henri-Philippe Pétain's picture had its window smashed in overnight. Pétain's picture was vandalized. The following day, another shop suffered the same fate.[11]

"Disorder seems to be increasing, not only in frequency but in violence," wrote Ridgeway Knight, one of Murphy's vice consuls. "The sponsors, the Front de la Liberation, and other sundry Gaullist-leftist groups, seem to be gaining in boldness, doubtless because of the lack of repressive measures." Knight warned that the attacks made Casablancans fearful of a return to the public disorder that had characterized the Popular Front era, but the French army felt powerless to do anything to stop it. "The people doing the disorder are placing themselves in an indefensible position," wrote Knight. "They are attacking Noguès while he's with the Americans and British—also creating a desire on the part of the population for order."[12]

The disturbances continued during the last two weeks of May. Vichy supporters joined the fray, defacing with black paint the Allied flags painted on the side of the building housing the US Psychological Warfare Board. The building had housed the propaganda arm of the Légion française des combattants before Henri Giraud ordered it disbanded. It abutted the French Officers Club and lay two hundred feet from US Military Police Headquarters, making the vandalism all the more shocking.[13] Petitions also flooded Casablanca, demanding Charles de Gaulle's appointment as head of the provisional French government.[14]

Alongside the critiques of Allied and French policy, a nationalist movement was also beginning to revive. The influence of its proponents remained to be seen, but the rhetoric pumped out in American radio broadcasts, speeches, and other propaganda promoting freedom and liberty had not gone unnoticed. Nor had the discourse about the evils of despotism and tyranny. "A perfectly conventional American Fourth of July speech may be made to sound like a rousing cheer for Moroccan Nationalism," warned Lieutenant Colonel Arthur Sutherland, Clark's head of civil affairs. He urged his team members to keep an eye on their tone. "Morocco is essentially a French colony, and rightly or wrongly, the French feel that they should not lose it even in the interest of freedom, etc. for the Moroccan natives."[15] A narrow margin existed between praising American institutions and encouraging Moroccans to seize them for themselves.[16]

AFTER MONTHS OF TRYING to bring Henri Giraud and Charles de Gaulle together, the Americans and British finally got their wish at the beginning of June with the first meeting of the French Committee of National Liberation (Comité français de la libération nationale). De Gaulle agreed to form a government with Giraud, but his cooperation hinged on a series of demands, which included a purge of leaders with Vichy ties. He believed the dismissals were necessary "to indicate clearly that France has never left the war and that she repudiates Vichy entirely." Noguès topped the list.[17]

Giraud objected vehemently but in the end could not save the resident-general. "Ever since the start of our interviews and conferences, General de Gaulle's attack against you was more ferocious than against anyone else," Giraud wrote Noguès on June 3. "You can guess his arguments. General Georges and I have defended you as best we could. This morning in committee a vote was taken and we were beaten. I must ask for your resignation as resident general of Morocco."[18]

Noguès consented, "Bien sûr." His letter of resignation painted his departure as an act designed to solidify French unity. "Several times since the beginning of your talks with General de Gaulle and in particular at the time of the last meeting of the War Committee, I signified that I placed French unity above all other concerns, and offered to retire if my departure would facilitate an agreement which is indispensable," he wrote. "I confirm that I place my office at your disposal, being happy to aid in this way the reunion of all French forces for the liberation of our country."[19] Gabriel Puaux, former high commissioner for Syria and Lebanon, would take his place.

On June 4, the day before the announcement of his retirement, Noguès made his last public appearance at Oujda with Clark, reviewing troops and watching a parachute demonstration. He endured the rigors of the day despite a painful injury to his leg, acquired from a fall, earning the respect of the American officers. Even at the age of sixty-six, the general still had grit.[20]

The next day, news of his retirement appeared in the newspapers and on the radio. Once again, Noguès controlled the narrative, insisting he was retiring rather than resigning. He was a soldier and had completed his mission. "It is with a peaceful heart that I say farewell to you; the essential part of the mission which France confided to me in Morocco has been accomplished," said his public farewell message. "The Protectorate, when I took it in hand, was passing through a period of alarming unbalance. Order and prosperity have been reestablished." With the Axis threat no longer hanging over North Africa and Morocco's integrity assured, he could pass the country to another's hands.

His message also addressed the dilemmas he faced as war engulfed France and her colonies. "The most painful sacrifice which Duty forced me to make for the country was, in June 1940, to accept the Armistice and to make those accept it whom I had urged to resist to the end." One last time, he portrayed himself as a patriot and a soldier doing his duty—and as the man who had kept the Germans from invading Morocco. "On November 8, *we* had to keep our word. We did so with sorrow. In acting thus, we escaped German intervention."[21] The farewell note, with its last grasp at justification, also had a bittersweet tinge. Morocco loomed large in his life; his service there had made his career. He had embraced its people and traditions in a way few men with his power would have dared. "I have always considered Morocco my second country. I leave it my heart," he wrote. "Men pass, France and Morocco remain."[22]

To those who asked, Noguès claimed he had earned a good rest and would retreat from public life. He planned to live "in a quiet corner, somewhere outside of Morocco" but remained mum about his long-term plans. His immediate future involved a trip to Portugal to undergo treatment for malaria, during which Mme. Noguès would wait for him in Tangier.[23] That trip became permanent with denial of his request to retire to Tangier or Algeria.[24]

After making a final call at the Residency on behalf of the State Department, Ernest Mayer, the American consul general whom Noguès claimed was his bête noire, observed that the resident-general had never shaken his opinion that the United States was "a nation of bluffers and incompetents." Although the landings and US occupation of Morocco had given him a chance to observe and study the Americans over six months, "he does not yet seem to understand what makes us tick."[25]

Noguès's leave-taking from the US Army was a little more sentimental. On June 9, Lieutenant Colonel Arthur Sutherland called on him to convey Clark's good wishes on his retirement. Despite their differences, Clark understood what Noguès was leaving. The army was its own kind of family, and to depart in the middle of a war carried extra freight. Noguès "appeared to be greatly touched," wrote Sutherland. The night before, Noguès gathered with his staff to drink a glass of champagne to the future success of the Allied war effort. Pointing to two cases of Mumm Cordon Rouge Champagne from his own wine cellar, Noguès told Sutherland he hoped Clark would do the same. Given the scarcity of champagne in North Africa, it was a generous gift. After the war, Noguès said he hoped to meet Clark in Paris, where they could toast "to a well won victory."[26]

Conclusion

O N AUGUST 6, 1943, GENERAL CHARLES DE GAULLE ARRIVED IN French Morocco. Seven months before, Brigadier General William Wilbur had spirited him away from the airport outside Casablanca, his presence concealed by mud-smeared car windows, to a compound guarded by Allied soldiers. The French and Moroccans learned of his presence at the Casablanca Conference only from radio reports, newspaper stories, and newsreels released after its conclusion.

This time, the press catalogued his every move, beginning with his arrival by airplane in Rabat. The sultan and resident-general received de Gaulle with all the grandeur and pomp reserved for a head of state.[1] Behind closed doors, he spoke with Sidi Mohammed, noting the sultan's desire to modernize his country and perhaps assume the mantle of its leadership independent of the French. De Gaulle took note of the young sultan's aspirations, while attempting to forge the beginning of a friendship with him. "I believed I should take the Sultan Mohammed ben Youssef for precisely what he was, a man resolved to become great, and that I should show myself to him for what I was, the leader of a France that was his suzerain but disposed to do much for those who stood by her," wrote de Gaulle.[2] Now was not the time, de Gaulle believed, for France and Morocco to part ways.

"Impatiently, Casablancans wait," announced the headline in *La Vigie marocaine*'s article reporting on de Gaulle's movements in Rabat.[3] On Sunday, August 8, the wait was finally over. A city draped in banners and flags welcomed him with open arms. Since the beginning of the war, the Place Lyautey had held a panorama of ceremonies to promote the reigning power. During Vichy, it hosted a swearing-in ceremony for the Légion

414

de combattants, the notorious veterans group. Following the Allied land-ings, it served as the backdrop for a display of France's new military might, courtesy of the American industrial complex. Now, it became a stage for de Gaulle to assume the mantle of French authority in Morocco. After a parade of troops had honored him, he addressed the sea of Casablancans cheering his name and crying, "Vive la France!" De Gaulle assured the crowd that French unity had secured the forthcoming victory over the Germans and the restoration of French grandeur. He lauded the "great voice of Casa-blanca," which spoke out with fervor of "her confidence and her hope" in France's future and the role of the empire in it.[4]

For three years, circles in London and Washington had spat de Gaulle's name in frustration, while those in a divided France and her North African colonies had whispered it with hope. The word "Gaullist" described the full range of resistance toward Vichy and Nazi Germany and became a swear-word uttered with contempt by the men who ruled Vichy and French Mo-rocco. But now "Gaullist" also conveyed legitimacy. At the beginning of June, after months of negotiations, Henri Giraud and de Gaulle had agreed to share leadership of the newly created French Committee of National Liberation.[5]

A FEW DAYS LATER, on Friday, August 13, de Gaulle attended a gala in Al-giers to raise funds for the new French committee. The baroque opera house burst with men and women in their finest, who had paid to support the cause and lay eyes on de Gaulle. They also came for another reason: Josephine Baker, back from the dead, had agreed to perform.

Before the show, Baker embarked on a last-minute plan to honor France and de Gaulle in grand style. She envisioned a tricolor flag emblazoned with the Cross of Lorraine, the symbol of the French resistance, unfurling from the ceiling at the end of the evening. With the help of a friend, she found the fabric in Algiers shops, no easy task given wartime austerity, but had less than a day to have it made. Baker convinced the mother superior of the local convent to put her charges to work for de Gaulle and France. Wielding their needles in patriotic fervor, the nuns finished the flag with little time to spare.[6]

When it came time to perform, she floated onto the stage dressed in white. Baker, who had sung before royalty, politicians, and every celebrity imagin-able, stumbled on the words to "J'ai Deux Amours." The presence of her idol, de Gaulle, only yards away rattled her confidence. At intermission, she found her way to de Gaulle's box. "He introduced me to Madame de Gaulle," she wrote of their meeting. "He seated me next to her, in his own seat. I can still see Madame de Gaulle . . . discreet and simple, in her grey lisle stockings, her little flat shoes. She called me, so kindly, 'Nasty little Gaulliste.' General de Gaulle is a great, tall man. . . . I like when you have to raise your head to look at a man." As a token of his appreciation for her work, de Gaulle gave her a tiny gold Cross of Lorraine designed by Cartier.[7]

At the end of the evening, when "La Marseillaise" played and Baker's eighteen-foot flag descended, the crowded roared with applause.

The massive tricolor flag soon became part of Baker's act. Over the next eighteen months, as she traveled around North Africa and Italy doing shows for Allied troops and fund-raisers for the Free French, she helped to raise more than 3 million francs. In recognition of her efforts, the Women's Auxiliary of the French air force made her a sublieutenant; she wore its blue uniform with the same swagger and pride she once reserved for mink coats and diamonds. After the war, as Baker struggled to regain her strength following an operation on her intestines, Élisabeth Boissieu, de Gaulle's daughter, visited her Paris hospital room. Boissieu bestowed on Baker the Medal of Resistance in honor of her work for the Free French and passed along a personal note from de Gaulle. In the decades that followed, Baker continued to perform and became a prominent civil rights activist. She also finally had the family she so desperately craved: she and her fourth husband, Jo Bouillon, adopted twelve children.[8]

De Gaulle's relocation from London to Algiers spelled the beginning of the end of Giraud's power. De Gaulle's force of personality and a brilliantly executed power grab orchestrated throughout the summer and fall led to Giraud's resignation at the beginning of November. There would still be fights with the Allies, but de Gaulle's leadership of France was secure.[9] When the Allies marched into Paris at the end of August 1944, he assumed control the city—and became chairman of the new provisional government of the French republic. Having turned his back on the collaborationist government when he boarded a plane in June 1940, he now presided over the dissolution of the last vestiges of Vichy France.

IN THE SUMMER OF 1943, the Roosevelt Club opened in Casablanca. It took its aesthetic cue from a traditional British gentleman's club but worked to promote Moroccan nationalism. Its founder, Abdelatif Sbihi, editor of the *La Voix nationale*, wanted a place to bring the Arab Moroccan elite and American military officials together—away from the prying eyes of the French. Between rounds of drinks and cigars, Sbihi and others hoped to educate the Americans about the Moroccan fight against French rule. One of the first Moroccans to join was the sultan's younger brother.[10] Sidi Mohammed also quietly signaled his support for the nationalists when he enlisted a well-regarded nationalist to tutor to his fourteen-year-old daughter. The nationalist cause would gain momentum after two long-standing political rivals, Abdelkhalek Torrès and Mekki Naciri, cast aside their differences and began working to renew the network of supporters that had lain dormant since the 1937 crackdown. They also sent a letter to Franklin Roosevelt demanding the end of the French Protectorate, lower taxes, and the restoration of political liberties.

By the fall of 1943, Moroccan nationalism had emerged from whispered exchanges and backroom meetings into the public square, creating a serious problem for the Allies. On one hand, the Atlantic Charter contained lofty rhetoric about self-determination; on the other hand, there was French prestige to consider. An imperialist to his core, Winston Churchill would not preside over the dissolution of the French Empire. Roosevelt and the State Department also decided that France's value as an ally outranked that of an independent Morocco. Washington believed that de Gaulle would be more amenable than the sultan to letting the United States keep a strong military presence in the country after the war. The United States could say none of this publicly, especially when Morocco's predicament ran counter to the Atlantic Charter. Instead, Secretary of State Cordell Hull explained to those who asked that Morocco would gain independence when its leaders could govern themselves properly.[11]

On January 11, 1944, fifty-nine Moroccans signed and published a manifesto declaring the birth of the Istiqlal (Independence Party) and calling for a constitutional monarchy overseen by Sidi Mohammed. The signatories wanted the sultan to negotiate Morocco's independence and to represent her at the postwar peace conference. The manifesto was vague and idealistic, but all the signatories agreed on its broad outlines.[12]

Unlike Charles Noguès, who understood that the nationalists had to be heard before being repressed, Gabriel Puaux, the new resident-general, responded swiftly and unforgivingly. He exiled any minister who voiced support for the Istiqlal and also tried to strong-arm the sultan into publicly denouncing the party. When that didn't work, he threw eighteen of the signatories into jail on the bogus charge of "consorting with the enemy." The arrests kicked off a series of riots across Morocco. In Rabat, crowds stormed the Residency. In Fez, women poured boiling water from the roofs onto police officers attempting to suppress the demonstrators. The riots in Casablanca led to bloodshed. As the violence faded, Puaux ordered the security services to hunt down those behind the protests. Some were tortured for information; others were summarily executed.[13]

It would take more than a decade, but the nationalist movement revived during World War II would ultimately triumph and eject the French from Morocco. Forced into exile in 1953, Sidi Mohammed returned and reclaimed the throne in November 1955. In February 1956, he embarked on negotiations with France to end the French Protectorate and secure Moroccan independence. Spain also relinquished most of its Moroccan territory, including Tangier, helping to reunite the country. In 1957, Sultan Mohammed ben Youssef was crowned King Mohammed V of Morocco. The current king, Mohammed VI, is his grandson.

As THE SULTAN PURSUED Moroccan independence, Noguès and his lawyers fought to restore the former resident-general's reputation. In November 1944, the provisional French government established the High Court of Justice to try those ministers accused of *indignité nationale* (national unworthiness)—or collaboration.[14] In 1947, while Noguès lived in Portugal, the court found him guilty, sentencing him in absentia to twenty years of hard labor and confiscation of his property.

In 1954, he returned to France and attempted to clear his name. The trial, which took place in October 1956, resurrected ghosts from his Vichy past, starting with Madame Beatrice Bretty, the companion of Georges Mandel. She testified about Noguès's failure to support the rogue parliamentarians in the summer of 1940 and Mandel's imprisonment. Despite their rivalry, Maxime Weygand sang his praises. Alphonse Juin explained the events in Algiers and the confusion over authority during the chaotic days following the Allied invasion. Antoine Béthouart spoke of Noguès's refusal to believe an American invasion force was off the coast of Morocco, along with his own subsequent arrest, court-martial, and internment. Hélène Bénatar spoke of Noguès's tacit support for her work with refugees. She did not, however, discuss the legislation enacted against Moroccan Jews like herself. Over four days, these witnesses and more drew a picture of a man who loved French Morocco and France but appeared to have malleable principles. The portrait confirmed the American nickname for him: "No-Yes." Throughout the trial, Noguès insisted that his desire to save French Morocco from occupation by the Nazis had guided his actions.[15]

The court again found Noguès guilty of "national unworthiness" but suspended his sentence. He lived out the rest of his life in Portugal, providing discreet advice to the French government about Morocco. Noguès's friendship with Sidi Mohammed transcended his time in Morocco, enduring until the king's passing in 1961. Following Noguès's death a decade later, King Hassan II, who as a young man sat on Noguès's knee at military reviews, sent a delegation to his funeral in France.[16]

Compared to some of Vichy's leaders, Noguès received gentle treatment. Weygand's trial began in May 1945 and didn't end until May 1948. After three maddening years, during which Weygand demolished every charge thrown at him, he was exonerated.[17] Henri-Philippe Pétain's trial began in July 1945 and resulted in a guilty verdict in August. In consideration of his age, de Gaulle commuted his sentence of death to life imprisonment, allowing the eighty-nine-year-old marshal to spend his remaining six years on the Île d'Yeu, a desolate island off the western coast of France.[18] Pierre Laval was not so lucky. After he attempted to escape to Spain, Francisco Franco handed him over to the Allies. He stood trial in October 1945 and was sentenced to death the same month. To avoid the firing squad, he tried to commit suicide, but the poison failed. After his stomach was pumped, Laval was shot.[19]

THE WAR SERVED AS a catalyst for the careers of the Americans who found their way to Morocco and North Africa. Staff Reid, who left Casablanca in the spring of 1943, found himself stranded in Washington when a medical exam revealed a heart murmur. After months of frustration, he finally convinced his superiors at the Office of Strategic Services (OSS) that he was hale and hearty. They sent him to Yugoslavia, where he worked with Tito and the partisans.[20] Dave King returned to Casablanca in the fall of 1943 after almost nine months away. He arrived to find his once thriving spy network destroyed by the careless actions of the OSS agents who succeeded him. Within weeks, he and Michel "Pinkeye" Despax were back in action, recruiting new sources and restoring relationships. By the end of the year, he had recruited a cadre of men for training to be sent to France as part of underground efforts leading up to the Allied invasion of France in June and August 1944.[21] Colonel William Eddy, their superior out of Tangier, would trade Spanish Morocco for Saudi Arabia, becoming the US envoy extraordinary and minister plenipotentiary. In February 1945, Eddy served as the translator for the landmark meeting between Franklin Roosevelt and King Abdul-Aziz aboard the USS *Quincy*.[22]

After the war, Eddy returned to Washington and served as the special assistant to the secretary of state for research and intelligence. He would also help draft the National Security Act of 1947, which created the Central Intelligence Agency (CIA), successor to the OSS, which Harry S. Truman dissolved at the end of the war.[23] Although the OSS itself did not survive the postwar drawdown, the idea that the United States needed a professional clandestine service did. Many of the men and women who had worked for the OSS filled out applications to work for the CIA, including Dave King.[24]

The American military presence in Morocco steadily declined in 1943 as units transferred to the Tunisian front or eastern Morocco and Algeria to train for the invasions of Sicily and Italy and then finally to conduct Operation HUSKEY (Sicily) in July and Operation AVALANCHE (Italy) in September. Casablanca, however, remained an important supply hub for the Allies for the remainder of the war. Following the end of hostilities in Europe in May 1945, it became a pivotal stopover in "Green Project," the US Army Air Corps' ambitious plan to rapidly transport men home. For three years, Casablanca had served as a funnel for soldiers going to war; now Cazes airfield served as a gateway home as tens of thousands of men boarded C-54s for the journey back to their families and friends.[25]

The assaults on Sicily and Italy realized the idea of North Africa as a springboard into southern Europe, although it would not be the soft underbelly that Churchill envisioned. The Allied campaign for Italy, in which French and Moroccan units also participated, became a brutal, bloody slog up the boot. The campaign also revealed Mark Clark to be a disastrous battlefield commander. When the landing at Salerno faltered, he fired his corps commanders. Then came the debacle at Anzio, where American loses rivaled those suffered by the British at Gallipoli in World War I.[26] In June 1944, Clark disobeyed an order to finish off Germany's 10th Army, choosing instead to march into the abandoned city of Rome, a decision that resulted in more American casualties. "Ambitious, ruthless with subordinates, profligate with the lives of his soldiers, unsympathetic to the difficulties of other Allied armies, and more impressed with style than substance, Clark possessed little of Eisenhower's empathy or capacity to put the interests of the alliance ahead of his own," write historians Williamson Murray and Allen Millet. "For Clark, military effort was directly proportional to the number of casualties."[27]

George Patton, of course, had his own reservations about Clark, but Patton's behavior also became a major liability. Throughout his career, his tumultuous disposition and unedited speech earned him fans and foes, but he vilified himself during the Sicily campaign when he slapped two soldiers hospitalized for battle fatigue, which he believed a form of cowardice. The act was a troubling failure of leadership. Dwight Eisenhower demanded that Patton apologize, which he did privately to the soldiers and to his troops. Ike also attempted to suppress press coverage of the incident, but news of the assaults leaked stateside, creating a firestorm in the press.[28] Eisenhower yanked

Patton from the battlefield for nearly ten months, before allowing him to return to combat as part of the Allied invasion of France in the summer of 1944. With generals possessing Patton's tactical mind in short supply, he received one final chance. Patton chased the Germans all the way to Berlin. Instead of dying on the battlefield, which he would have liked, he succumbed to injuries sustained in car crash on the way to hunt pheasant near Speyer, Germany, in December 1945.[29]

Robert Murphy continued oversee civilian affairs for Allied Forces Headquarters until 1944, when he moved, at Eisenhower's request, to Italy to serve as the American representative on the Allied Control Commission. After the defeat of the Nazi regime, Murphy became a political advisor to the Office of Military Government in Germany, helping administer postwar reconstruction. A stint as ambassador to Belgium followed. In 1952, Harry Truman appointed him the first postwar ambassador to Japan. Murphy also helped negotiate the armistice that ended the Korean War.[30] For a man who began as a code clerk during World War I, he forged a career he could scarcely believe.

The war would also be the making of Dwight Eisenhower. Following the victory at Tunisia and the successful invasion of Sicily, Roosevelt promoted him to supreme commander of the Allied Expeditionary Force, tasked with planning and commanding the invasion of France across the English Channel. Operation OVERLORD, which began on June 6, 1944, would liberate western Europe and put the Americans and British on the path to Germany. In August 1944, the Allies marched into Paris. In May 1945, they marched into Berlin. After the war, Eisenhower became military governor of Germany, before returning to Washington serve as chief of staff of the army, overseeing the drawdown of the forces he had wielded. In 1948, he became president of Columbia University, only to return to uniform in 1950 to serve as the supreme commander of the North Atlantic Treaty Organization. In 1952, with millions of Americans declaring, "I like Ike," Eisenhower became the thirty-fourth president of the United States.

FOR THE 3,000 OR so refugees who still found themselves in Casablanca in the summer of 1943, life remained a challenge. "Living costs are high and wages are low. Food is not the most serious problem," wrote an American Friends Service Committee representative in Casablanca in 1944. "Clothing at almost any price is virtually unobtainable. Because of the increased population and of the requisitioning of hotels and buildings by the military authorities, American and French, the problem of lodging is extremely acute.

All this means that the refugee, though usually able to earn his living, needs most of his earnings to meet the daily expenses of food and lodging. He lives along from day to day, but his future is far from secure."[31]

In 1944, the North African Refugee Center opened outside of Fédala. The center, created under the auspices of the US Foreign Economic Administration but transferred to the United Nations Relief and Rehabilitation Administration (UNRRA), cared for stateless refugees arriving from France. In July 1944, the camp housed 625 refugees.

Hélène Bénatar's talents for organization and providing aid did not go unnoticed. In 1944, she became a liaison officer for UNRRA in Algeria, working with displaced persons. After the war, she served as the American Jewish Joint Distribution Committee's delegate for North Africa, covering not only Morocco but also Algeria and Tunisia. Bénatar increasingly focused her energy on Zionism and, after the establishment of Israel, on helping Moroccan Jews emigrate. In the years following Moroccan independence, she eventually settled permanently in Paris, where she continued her work as a lawyer and advocate for Moroccan Jews.[32]

Unlike other Jewish communities that found themselves under French and German rule, the Moroccan Jewish community survived the war largely intact. There were no roundups. There were no deportations to killing centers. Their escape from the Holocaust is popularly attributed to resistance by Sidi Mohammed and his advisers, and, in the decades since the war, the sultan's role has assumed almost mythical proportions—even though he failed to prevent the implementation of Vichy's less-extreme anti-Semitic policies.[33]

Nevertheless, departures from Morocco like Bénatar's were not uncommon. The wartime experience of the Moroccan Jews revealed in stark and disquieting ways the fragility of their existence and led to a massive exodus during the postwar years. The newly independent Morocco's emphasis on Arab-Islamic policies also contributed to their concern. At the beginning of World War II, 240,000 Jews lived in Morocco. Now the community numbers around 3,000.[34]

THE WHITE CITY ENDURES. Today Casablanca boasts a population of more than 3 million, up from 350,000 during World War II, and continues its reign as the largest African port on the Atlantic. A town once easily covered by bicycle or horse-drawn carriage has evolved into a sprawling and vibrant African city, complete with a modern tramway system and the largest shopping mall on the continent.

And yet, traces of wartime Casablanca remain. The old medina, *mellah*, and colonial *ville nouvelle* (although it's not exactly the "new town" anymore) still hug the port, which acts as the country's commercial engine. Rooms are available at the Hôtel Transatlantique and the Excelsior, as are drinks in the bars where Allied and Axis spies hunted recruits and traded secrets. A poster for the film *Casablanca* occupies a permanent spot on the marquee of the Rialto movie house. The Place Administrative, with its array of government buildings, continues to serve as a focal point for the city and is undergoing a massive redevelopment, including the addition of a theater and an underground parking garage. (Like every major metropolitan city, Casablanca is short on parking.) Sacré-Coeur, the art deco cathedral at the end of the square, has lost its luster, abandoned by the Catholic Church in the wake of independence.

Casablanca has swallowed up Anfa, once an oasis outside the city, though the suburb still retains its leafy, exclusive ambiance. The Anfa Hotel, which provided housing for the German Armistice Commission and served as the headquarters for the Casablanca Conference, has been converted to condos. A modern international airport outside the city has supplanted Cazes airfield. The old air control tower still stands but will be knocked down as construction of a new tech corridor advances.

If you find yourself in Casablanca and venture into the old medina and walk the streets of the colonial city—and squint away the modern signs and satellite dishes hanging from the windows—it's possible for a moment to imagine what 1940s Casablanca might have been like.

Just be sure to have your papers in order.

Postscript: Film Versus History

I F YOU PICKED UP THIS BOOK, YOU MIGHT BE A FAN OF THE CLASSIC film *Casablanca*. Before ending this narrative, I would be remiss if I didn't delineate some differences between history's Casablanca and Hollywood's version. If you haven't seen the movie, this is your last chance to close the book and avoid plot spoilers. If you want to know more, let's adjourn to Rick's Café Américain.

"I bet they are asleep in New York. I bet they are asleep all over America," says Rick Blaine (Humphrey Bogart), an American gunrunner turned barman. Hollywood's *Casablanca* is set in December 1941 in the days before the Japanese attack on Pearl Harbor. Rick's presence would have been unusual in the white city. So too would Sam's (Dooley Wilson), the drummer who faked his way with a piano. Before the war started, there were only one hundred or so Americans in all of French Morocco—missionaries, representatives of American companies, and of course diplomats, along with their spouses and children. After the fall of France in June 1940, most Americans cleared out except for the diplomats. Only one African-American was registered with the US consulate in Casablanca, a down-on-his-luck jockey named Sam, who served as the consulate's night watchman.

The motley collection of refugees who work at Rick's café—Russians, Germans, Austrians, Dutch, French, Spaniards—reflect the refugee population of Casablanca. Carl (S. Z. Sakall) and Sascha (Leonid Kinskey) could have worked for Rick. The government of history's French Morocco, however, preferred that well-paying jobs go to local residents first. Any refugee who wanted to work needed permission from French authorities. With steady incomes, regular visits to the prefecture to renew visas, and influential benefactors, men like Carl and Sascha could avoid the internment camps. And plenty of refugees who landed in Casablanca with money in their pockets could have afforded to drink and gamble at Rick's. If they were smart, they would have saved their francs: they could be stuck in Casablanca for years.

"Waiting, waiting, waiting, I will never get out of Casablanca," mutters one refugee. The characters' obsession with visas is exactly right. A Bulgarian bride is willing to trade her body for a visa before Rick intervenes and helps her secure money for a bribe. In history's French Morocco, the frustration of applying for visas and awaiting their approval often led to desperate acts. Suicide was not uncommon. Getting exit visas to leave French Morocco was generally the easiest step for refugees, as the Residency was happy to see them leave. The hard part was obtaining a transit visa for Portugal, the gateway to North and South America. A blank transit visa for Portugal would have fetched serious money on Casablanca's black market, as would an immigrant visa for the United States, Cuba, Brazil, or Mexico. Refugees who bought counterfeit visas risked being turned away or interned when they landed on the other side of the Atlantic.

As for Rick's café itself, the closest thing to the club in history's Casablanca was probably the lavish bar at the Hôtel Transatlantique, which poured generous cocktails and hosted hot jazz. The owners were also pro-Allied, making it a safe place for those with resistance sensibilities to talk over drinks. The fictional clientele in Rick's Café Américain appears to be a mix of well-to-to Europeans and Moroccans, along with French, Moroccan, German, and Italian soldiers. That would have been unusual, as Moroccans and Europeans did not mix socially in public for the most part.

The film locates Rick's café next to the airport. In reality, Rick's would have been in Casablanca's ancient medina or *ville nouvelle*, close to the port. In one scene, Rick and Captain Louis Renault (Claude Rains), fictional head of the Sûreté, share a drink at a table perched beside the club's front door, watching the planes take off against the night sky. Actually, Cazes airfield was five miles outside of the city, and night flights were banned for security reasons. Nor could you get a flight from Casablanca to Lisbon. Instead, you had to take the train north to Tangier and hop on a flight from there.

"Of all the gin joints in all the towns in all the world, she walks into mine," laments Rick. She, of course, is Ilsa Lund (Ingrid Bergman), his Paris sweetheart. Like so many others attempting to escape the Nazis, Ilsa and her husband, Victor Laszlo (Paul Henreid), end up in Casablanca. They find their way to Rick's, hoping to contact Signor Ugarte (Peter Lorre), who has killed two German couriers and stolen letters of transit signed by Charles de Gaulle. The letters would give whoever held them free passage throughout the French Empire. Such letters of transit did exist. General Maxime Weygand gave Robert Murphy one for his inspection trip of French Africa. But such a letter signed by Charles de Gaulle would have been worthless in French Morocco. De Gaulle, during the time in which the movie is set, had no authority in French North Africa, and Vichy had branded him a traitor. Presenting those letters of transit to a French official would have resulted in a one-way trip to an internment camp or worse.

"I blow with the wind. And the prevailing wind happens to be from Vichy," says Captain Renault. At the end of *Casablanca*, Renault tosses a bottle of Vichy water into the trash, signaling that he has made his choice. Faced with a new regime, many actual French officials and soldiers made accommodations to keep their jobs, but some risked their lives and careers to aid the resistance. For example, the screenwriters had no way of knowing that Colonel Maurice Herviot, actual head of the Sûreté in Casablanca, worked to undermine Vichy in small and big ways. He helped Hélène Bénatar with her refugee work and arranged for American vice consul David King to avoid jail and worse after dealings with the resistance caught the attention of the wrong people.

We can't depart Hollywood's *Casablanca* without discussing Victor Laszlo's leading café patrons in a rousing rendition of "La Marseillaise." The scene provides the emotional heart of the movie. German major Heinrich Strasser's (Conrad Veidt) outrage at the song and the passionate reaction it inspired is not misplaced. During the war, the French national anthem, written during the French Revolution, carried extra political freight. Germany outlawed performance of "La Marseillaise" in occupied France, regarding it as a danger to order. Vichy France didn't ban the song outright but did change a few verses to reflect the regime's sensibilities. It also required that any time it was sung, a song honoring Henri-Philippe Pétain be performed immediately afterward.

The making of *Casablanca* also has its own fascinating history, which I can only touch on briefly in this book. To learn more, crack open Noah Isenberg's *We'll Always Have Casablanca* and Aljean Harmetz's *The Making of Casablanca*.

Hopefully, you aren't shocked—shocked!—at the differences between Hollywood's and history's Casablancas. Even with the discrepancies, the core of the film's story holds true. The morality play that unfolds perfectly captures the real choices that real people faced in Casablanca. As the war progressed, the city became an important destination for those attempting to escape the grip of the Nazis and make their way to Lisbon. A ticket to Casablanca could offer a path to a new life or to an internment camp. Orders to report to Casablanca might end with glory or death. A stay in Casablanca could be the beginning of a beautiful friendship or the end of an affair.

Here's looking at you, kid.

Acknowledgments

THIS BOOK HAD BEEN PERCOLATING EVER SINCE I STUMBLED ACROSS MENTIONS of visa troubles and internment camps in French Morocco while working on another project almost two decades ago. Every time I caught a showing of *Casablanca* on Turner Classic Movies, I would remember those documents and my brain would start popping again. "What was really going on there?" Every historian knows how that ends: a deep dive into the books and archives because we need to know.

I am grateful that my agent James Hornfischer answered the query that landed in his email box. The publishing process for a first-time author can be nerve-wracking and serpentine, but he made everything transparent and less intimidating. Jim also understood from the beginning what kind of book I wanted to write. He didn't ask me, unlike another agent, if I wanted to write "boy history" or "girl history." (I'm *still* gobsmacked by this years later.) I couldn't ask for a better advocate than Jim, who is an accomplished historian in his own right. You should read him too.

I feel very lucky to have landed at PublicAffairs. Clive Priddle and Jane Robbins Mize have been a dynamic editing duo. Their close reading and insightful comments improved the book at every step. My sincere appreciation to them and the PublicAffairs team, especially Sandra Beris, Jennifer Kelland Fagan, Melissa Raymond, and Katherine Haigler. Special thanks to Mike Morgenfeld for making the maps and Kristina Fazzalaro for working her publicity magic.

Research for this book was supported by a General and Mrs. Matthew B. Ridgway Military History Research Grant. It allowed me to spend a productive week at the US Army Heritage and Education Center at Carlisle Barracks, Pennsylvania. I am also indebted to the archivists at the Hoover Institution, the Library of Congress, the American Jewish Joint Distribution Committee, the National Archives (College Park), the National Archives (Kew), Churchill College, and the Centre des archives diplomatiques de Nantes. Their expertise regularly set me off on new trails of research. I owe a particular debt to the U.S. Holocaust Memorial Museum, whose collections provided material central to this book. Ronald Coleman was especially helpful, keeping me in stacks of documents from the museum's archives.

The granddaughters of Herbert and Cora Goold shared materials from their family archive. In the end, the material didn't make it into the book because of space considerations. But I am happy that I was able to tell the official side of the Goolds' life in Casablanca, giving readers a taste of their compassion and generosity.

The National Endowment for the Humanities, my employer, gave me time off to conduct archival research through a program that encourages its employees to continue their scholarship. Writing a book like this while having a full-time job is a recipe for no sleep and a bloodstream made of coffee. I will be forever grateful that David Skinner didn't blanch when I asked for four months of leave without pay to finish writing. He encouraged and supported this project from the beginning.

Writing can be a lonely occupation with only dead people and the glow of your laptop for company for hours on end. That makes friends and colleagues who nudge you along by email and text, induce laughter at lunch, and know your pop culture sweet spots so precious. Thank you to Jason Rhody, Jennifer Serventi, Paula Wasley, Amy Lifson, Anna Maria Gillis, Perry Collins, Brett Bobley, Ann Sneesby-Koch, Eva Caldera, Jeff Hardwick, Marc Ruppel, Andrea Heiss, Rachel Poor, and Mark Burr.

There's nothing quite like the support of fellow historians and writers who can commiserate about the bleary eyes that come from staring at microfilm, faded documents, and the flashing cursor on the screen. They understand when you tell them that you teared up in despair after reading letter after letter from refugees pleading for help to leave Casablanca and the bleak existence of the internment camps. They nod knowingly when you are bursting (or texting) with joy because of an amazing archival discovery. They get it when you say you want to throw your laptop out the window, because you're on draft eleven and the chapter still isn't quite right and online shoe shopping would be more productive at this point.

Holly Tucker, Vanessa Beasley, Christine Jones, and Eric Larsen were virtual (and sometimes in-person) cheerleaders. Rebecca Erberling shared her knowledge of American refugee policy and all things archives. Gary Krist, Karen Abbott, and Margaret Talbot were always quick with a bon mot and sage advice. Jeremi Suri and Daniel Schroeter shared their historical expertise. Peter Sokolowski kept me in jazz and checked my French translations. Jennifer Howard, Anne Trubek, and Mark Athitakis commiserated about writing and life, while offering encouragement and good cheer. Farran Smith Nehme and Deborah Harkness reminded me of the importance of combining grace with persistence.

Russell Wyland has always believed in me and gave important feedback early on. The same can be said of Jason Parker. Robert Hoffman helped me sharpen my prose at crucial junctures. He also reminds me to keep looking down the road.

Sara Wilson and Melissa Klug are the sisters I never had—grounded, funny as hell, and no compunction about smacking me upside the head when needed. Brenda Copeland not only gave me a place to stay in New York, but also encouraged me to follow my gut on this project.

You can only learn so much about an era and a city by reading documents and looking at maps and pictures. I spent weeks walking the streets of the old colonial parts of Casablanca and finding the places frequented by the people who populate this book. The manager of the Hôtel Transatlantique kindly gave me a tour, even though I wasn't staying there. I was almost arrested while taking pictures of the old American consulate. (I didn't know it was forbidden, *monsieur. Vraiment.*) Like so many refugees, I took the train to Tangier. I watched the sun set over the Atlas Mountains from a rooftop in Marrakech's old medina in the vein of Roosevelt and Churchill. I walked on the beach between Fédala and Mehdia during the autumn, the same time of year as Operation TORCH, and watched as the waves churned and smashed against the craggy coast. The Americans were so very lucky. On my visits to Morocco, I had the incredible fortune of staying with Michel and Zellige Teuler. Michel's family has lived in Casablanca since the 1930s, when his grandfather came to Morocco to build a telephone system for the city. I will always treasure my time writing in their beautiful garden and will be forever grateful for their hospitality and friendship. *Merci beaucoup!*

While finishing the book, I spent a week at the Inn at Antietam in Sharpsburg, Maryland. The owners, Miriam and Will Cunningham, fortified me with hearty breakfasts and coffee for writing sprints. If you find yourself in Maryland, stop in.

This book also would not have been possible without the investments made by the governments of the United States, France, and Britain in scholarship and government archives. I benefitted from edited volumes of documents from leading figures of the era, including Dwight D. Eisenhower and George C. Marshall. My work in the archives was made possible by the collection, preservation, and cataloguing of a mountain of personal papers, government documents, films, and newspapers. A nation's historical record does not persist without resources devoted to its care.

In closing, I am obligated to say that the views of this book do not reflect the views of my employer, the US Government. Any errors are also mine alone.

This book is dedicated to my parents. My mom, Virginia, has been a source of love and support throughout the entire journey. I promise to call more often now that the book is done! My dad, Richard, a veteran of World War II in the Pacific, didn't live long enough to see me become a historian, fancy degree and all, but this book would have been just his thing. I imagine him sitting in his recliner, reading glasses perched on his nose, cigar in one hand, book in another. A scotch-on-the-rocks rests nearby. Cheers!

Notes

ABBREVIATIONS

CADN = Centre des archives diplomatiques de Nantes
FDRL = Franklin D. Roosevelt Library
FRUS = Foreign Relations of the United States
HIA = Hoover Institution Archives, Stanford University
LOC = Library of Congress
PDDE: The War Years = The Papers of Dwight D. Eisenhower: The War Years
LOC, Patton Papers = Library of Congress, Manuscript Division, George S. Patton Papers
NARA = National Archives and Records Administration (US)
TNA = National Archives (UK)
USAHEC = US Army Heritage and Education Center
USHMM = US Holocaust Memorial Museum

PROLOGUE

1. Schiff, *Saint-Exupéry*, Kindle Location 1969.
2. Schiff, *Saint-Exupéry*, Kindle Locations 369–371.
3. Schiff, *Saint-Exupéry*, Kindle Location 1986.
4. Singer and Langdon, *Cultured Force*, 198–202.
5. Hoisington, *Casablanca Connection*, 5.
6. Wharton, *In Morocco*, 8.
7. Wharton, *In Morocco*, 90.
8. Cohen and Eleb, *Casablanca*, 22.
9. Lemprière, *Tour from Gibraltar*, 50.
10. Hooker and Ball, *Journal of a Tour in Morocco and the Great Atlas*, 68; Cohen and Eleb, *Casablanca*, 24.
11. Porch, *Conquest of Morocco*, 149.
12. Albert Charton, "La politique des ports du Maroc," quoted in Cohen and Eleb, *Casablanca*, 124.
13. Hoisington, "The Selling of Agadir," 316.
14. Cohen and Eleb, *Casablanca*, 126.
15. Taraud, "Urbanisme, hygiénisme, et prostitution," 98.
16. Cohen and Eleb, *Casablanca*, 120.
17. Cohen and Eleb, *Casablanca*, 95, 470.
18. Lyautey, *Paroles d'action*, 450.
19. Cohen and Eleb, *Casablanca*, 102–109.
20. Cohen and Eleb, *Casablanca*, 90. For an extensive breakdown of Casablanca's population dynamics in the colonial and postcolonial era, see Adam, *Casablanca*.

CHAPTER 1

1. Letter No. 79, Hurst (Rabat) to FO, September 11, 1939, TNA, FO371/23117.

2. Young, "La guerre de longue durée"; Gibbs, *Grand Strategy*, 1:657–684; Butler, *Grand Strategy*.

3. For the most insightful analysis of the development and radicalization of this strategy, see Imlay, *Facing the Second World War*.

4. Telegram 1751, Noguès to Controleur Civil, Casablanca, September 1, 1939, CADN, 11MA/900.

5. Pennell, *Morocco Since 1830*, 254.

6. Letter, Hurst to Halifax, October 3, 1939, TNA, FO371/23117.

7. Zisenwine, *Emergence of Nationalist Politics in Morocco*, 124–125.

8. Hoisington, *Casablanca Connection*, 20–28.

9. Singer and Langdon, *Cultured Force*, 225–226.

10. Letter No. 75, Hurst (Rabat) to FO, August 29, 1939; "Arrêté résidentiel" of September 1, 1939, Bulletin Officiel No. 1401 bis, September 3, 1939, TNA, FO371/23117.

11. Telegram 17, Rabat to FO, September 11, 1939, TNA, FO371/23117.

12. Telegram 73, Gascoigne (Tangier) to FO, September 19, 1939, TNA, FO371/23118.

13. Letter 107 E, Hurst to FO, November 8, 1939, TNA, FO371/23117.

14. Letter No. 79, Hurst (Rabat) to FO, September 11, 1939, TNA, FO371/23117.

15. Letter, Hurst (Rabat) to FO, September 15, 1939; "Dahir du 13 Septembre 1939," Bulletin Officiel, No. 1402 ter, September 14, 1939; Letter No. 81, Hurst (Rabat) to FO, September 18, 1939, TNA, FO371/23117.

16. See multiple "De source qui se présente bonne" for September 1939 in CADN, 11MA/900.

17. Letter 1878, Courtin to Director of Political Affairs, September 9, 1939, CADN, 11MA/900.

18. Letter, Hurst (Rabat) to FO, September 11, 1939, TNA, FO371/23117.

19. Zisenwine, *Emergence of Nationalist Politics in Morocco*, 124–125; M. Thomas, *The French Empire Between the Wars*, 301.

20. Letter, Blanch (Fez) to FO, December 16, 1939, TNA, FO371/23117.

21. Letter 108, Hurst to FO, November 20, 1939, TNA, FO371/23117; Wyrzten, *Making Morocco*, 162.

22. Pennell, *Morocco Since 1830*, 255.

CHAPTER 2

1. "Music-Halls," *Le Matin*, May 25, 1937; Folies-Bergère ad, *Le Figaro*, May 8, 1937.

2. Baker and Bouillon, *Josephine*, 118.

3. Bakerfix ad, l'Afrique du Nord illustrée, February 16, 1935, annex.

4. Baker and Chase, *Josephine Baker*, 225; Rearick, *The French in Love and War*, 248; "Music-Halls," *Le Matin*, November 27, 1939; "Music-Halls," *Le Matin*, November 28, 1939.

5. "Gala de bienfaisance," *Le Journal*, November 30, 1939.

6. Ad for gala "pour nos soldats," *Le Journal*, January 30, 1940.

7. Baker and Bouillon, *Josephine*, 118.

8. Baker and Chase, *Josephine Baker*, 226–227.

9. Baker and Chase, *Josephine Baker*, 226–227; Baker and Bouillon, *Josephine*, 118.

10. Baker and Bouillon, *Josephine*, 118.

11. Baker and Chase, *Josephine Baker*, 226–227.

12. Scammell, *Koestler*, 177; Cesarani, *Arthur Koestler*, 157.

13. Scammell, *Koestler*, 178.

14. Interrogation Report of Arthur Koestler, Cannon Row Police Station, November 8, 1940, TNA, KV2/1273; Cesarani, *Arthur Koestler*, 145.

15. Koestler, *Scum of the Earth*, Kindle location 2014 of 3922.

16. Quoted in Cesarani, *Arthur Koestler*, 159; Scammell, *Koestler*, 178.

17. Letter, Nicolson to Collinson, March 16, 1940, TNA, KV2/1273.

18. Extract from Home Office file K/7411, April 22, 1940; Letter, Baok to Paris Passport Control Officer, May 7, 1940; Letter, Hart-Davis to Passport and Permit Office, March 4, 1940; Letter, JEB to Vivian, January 26, 1940, TNA, KV2/1273.

19. Scammell, *Koestler*, 182.

CHAPTER 3

1. Saint-Exupéry, *Flight to Arras*, 54.
2. Saint-Exupéry, *Wind, Sand, and Stars*, 138–145.
3. Schiff, *Saint-Exupéry*, Kindle location 7271.
4. Roberts, *The Storm of War*, 39.
5. M. Thomas, "The Vichy Government and French Colonial Prisoners of War," 663.
6. Jackson, *France: The Dark Years*, 118; Roberts, *The Storm of War*, 44.
7. Weinberg, *A World at Arms*, 122–123, 129.
8. Lazareff, "The Fall of France," 69.
9. Jackson, The Fall of France, 62.
10. Lazareff, "The Fall of France," 69.
11. Lazareff, "The Fall of France," 71.
12. Saint-Exupéry, *Flight to Arras*, 68.
13. Saint-Exupéry, *Flight to Arras*, 69.
14. Jackson, *The Fall of France*, 174; Jackson, *France: The Dark Years*, 120.
15. Baker and Bouillon, *Josephine*, 119; "Music-Halls," *Le Matin*, March 16, 1940; Rose, *Jazz Cleopatra*, 185.
16. Haney, *Naked at the Feast*, 218; Rose, *Jazz Cleopatra*, 185.
17. Baker and Chase, *Josephine Baker*, 228–229.
18. Rose, *Jazz Cleopatra*, 176; Haney, *Naked at the Feast*, 216.
19. Roberts, *The Storm of War*, 58.
20. Roberts, *The Storm of War*, 58.
21. Jackson, *The Fall of France*, 121–122.
22. Jackson, *The Fall of France*, 123.
23. Jackson, *The Fall of France*, 136–138.
24. Jackson, *The Fall of France*, 143.
25. Roberts, *The Storm of War*, 59.
26. Pennell, *Morocco Since 1830*, 255.
27. Roberts, *The Storm of War*, 59.
28. Jackson, *France: The Dark Years*, 107–108.

CHAPTER 4

1. Favreau, *Georges Mandel*, 412.
2. Favreau, *Georges Mandel*, 404; Sherwood, *Georges Mandel and the Third Republic*, 254; Rollin testimony, January 20, 1949, Rapport fait au nom de la commission charge d'enquêter sur les événements survenus en France de 1933 à 1945, 4:1396.
3. Quoted in Sherwood, *Georges Mandel and the Third Republic*, 254; Lebrun testimony, June 1, 1948, Rapport fait au nom de la commission charge d'enquêter sur les événements survenus en France de 1933 à 1945, 4:998.
4. Spears, *Assignment Catastrophe*, 316–317.
5. War Cabinet Conclusions, WM(40)173, June 20, 1940, TNA, CAB65/7/68; Favreau, *Georges Mandel*, 406; Sherwood, *Georges Mandel and the Third Republic*, 255.
6. Roberts, *The Storm of War*, 56.
7. Sherwood, *Georges Mandel and the Third Republic*, 259.
8. War Cabinet Conclusions, WM(40)173, June 20, 1940, TNA, CAB65/7/68.
9. Quoted in Sherwood, *Georges Mandel and the Third Republic*, 257.
10. Quoted in Sherwood, *Georges Mandel and the Third Republic*, 257; Gates, *End of the Affair*, 265–267.
11. Sherwood, *Georges Mandel and the Third Republic*, 257; Testimony of Marin and Monnet, June 8, 1947, Rapport fait au nom de la commission charge d'enquêter sur les événements survenus en France de 1933 à 1945, 4:1431–1432.
12. Testimony of Madame Bretty, October 23, 1956, in *Le procès du général Noguès*, 132; Sherwood, *Georges Mandel and the Third Republic*, 256.

13. Testimony of Louis Marin, July 26, 1945, in *Procès du Maréchal Pétain*, 217–218.

14. Sherwood, *Georges Mandel and the Third Republic*, 256.

15. Testimony of Madame Bretty, October 23, 1956, in *Le procès du général Noguès*, 132.

16. Favreau, *Georges Mandel*, 414; Sherwood, *Georges Mandel and the Third Republic*, 258.

17. Fenby, *The General*, Kindle location 1771.

18. Spears, *Assignment Catastrophe*, 304, 321–322.

19. Recording of de Gaulle speech, June 22, 1940. See http://www.bbc.com/news /10339678.

20. Testimony of Yvan Martin, October 24, 1956, in *Le procès du général Noguès*, 39.

21. Favreau, *Georges Mandel*, 415.

22. Favreau, *Georges Mandel*, 416.

23. Testimony of Yvan Martin, October 24, 1956, in *Le procès du général Noguès*, 42; Favreau, *Georges Mandel*, 417.

CHAPTER 5

1. Churchill, *Their Finest Hour*, 11.

2. Telegram 35, Algiers to FO, June 24, 1940, TNA, FO371/24328.

3. Telegram 88, Casablanca to FO, June 24, 1940; Telegram 80, Tangier to FO, June 23, 1940; Telegram 24, Rabat to FO, June 23, 1940, TNA, FO371/24328; Telegram 334, Gibraltar to FO, June 23, 1940, TNA, FO371/24329.

4. War Cabinet Conclusions, WM(40)180, June 24, 1940, TNA, CAB/65/7/75; Churchill, *Their Finest Hour*, 189.

5. Telegram 37, Algiers to FO, June 24, 1940, TNA, FO371/24328.

6. Telegram 303, Dillon to War Office, June 23, 1940; Telegram 3, Dillon to War Office, June 25, 1940; Telegram 23, Rabat to FO, June 23, 1940; Telegram 35, Algiers to FO, June 24, 1940, TNA, FO371/24328; Hoisington, *Casablanca Connection*, 176–177; Telegram 9, FO to Rabat, June 24, 1940, TNA, FO371/24328.

7. "Visit to French Morocco," Report by the Minister of Information, WP(40)225, June 27, 1940, TNA, CAB/66/9/5.

8. Telegram, FO to Rabat, 25 June 1940; Telegram 35, Rabat to FO, 25 June 1940. TNA, FO371/24328.

9. "Visit to French Morocco," Report by the Minister of Information, WP(40)225, June 27, 1940, TNA, CAB/66/9/5.

10. "Visit to French Morocco," Report by the Minister of Information, WP(40)225, June 27, 1940, TNA, CAB/66/9/5.

11. Sherwood, *Georges Mandel and the Third Republic*, 260.

12. Testimony of Madame Bretty, October 23, 1956, in *Le procès du général Noguès*, 134–136.

13. War Cabinet Conclusions, WM(40)185, June 28, 1940, TNA, CAB/65/7/80.

14. Telegram 50, Rabat to FO, June 28, 1940, TNA, FO371/24328.

CHAPTER 6

1. Finlayson, *The Fortress Came First*, 232.

2. W. Jackson, *The Rock of Gibraltarians*, 274–275; Note 2959, Directeur d'affaires politique à chef du cabinet diplomatique, May 10, 1940, CADN, 1MA/15/707.

3. War Cabinet Conclusions, WM(40)124, May 16, 1940, TNA, CAB/65/7/19; Finlayson, *The Fortress Came First*, 2–6.

4. Finlayson, *The Fortress Came First*, 10.

5. Finlayson, *The Fortress Came First*, 12.

6. Finlayson, *The Fortress Came First*, 12.

7. Finlayson, *The Fortress Came First*, 15.

8. Finlayson, *The Fortress Came First*, 21.

9. Gates, *End of the Affair*, 334.

10. Adams, *Years of Deadly Peril*, 194.

11. Winston Churchill, "Blood, Toils, Tears, and Sweat" speech, May 13, 1940. See http://www .winstonchurchill.org/resources/speeches/233–1940-the-finest-hour/92-blood-toil-tears-and -sweat.

12. War Cabinet Conclusions, WM(40)191, July 2, 1940; Telegram 0103, Admiralty to Force H, July 2, 1940, TNA, CAB/65/8/3.

13. Gates, *End of the Affair*, 355; Churchill, *Their Finest Hour*, 202–203.

14. Gates, *End of the Affair*, 356.

15. Gates, *End of the Affair*, 358.

16. Gates, *End of the Affair*, 358.

17. Telegram 131, Tangier to FO, July 7, 1940; Telegram 112, Tangier to FO, July 3, 1940, TNA, FO371/24329; Telegram 135, Tangier to FO, July 8, 1940; Telegram 136, Tangier to FO, July 8, 1940, TNA, FO371/24454.

18. Telegram 127, Gascoigne to FO, July 6, 1940, TNA, FO371/24329.

19. Telegram 131, Tangier to FO, July 7, 1940, TNA, FO371/24329.

20. Telegram 364, Gibraltar to Sec State Colonies, July 3, 1940, TNA, FO371/24454.

21. War Cabinet Conclusions, WM(40)197, July 8, 1940, TNA, FO371/24454.

22. Telegram 385, FO to Selby, July 9, 1940; Telegram 404, Selby to FO, July 10, 1940; Telegram 270, Sec State Colonies to Gov Gibraltar, July 11, 1940; Telegram 425, Lisbon to FO, July 15, 1940, TNA, FO371/24454.

23. Telegram 396, High Commissioner in Union of South Africa to Colonial Office, July 9, 1940, TNA, FO371/24454.

24. Telegram No. 130, Colonial Office to Mauritius, July 9, 1940; Telegram 178, Mauritius to Sec State of Colonies, July 13, 1940, TNA, FO371/24454.

25. Telegram 339, Gov Jamaica to Sec State Colonies, July 7, 1940, TNA, FO371/24454.

26. Letter, Makins to Castellane, July 5, 1940, TNA, FO371/24329; Telegram 127, Gascoigne to FO, July 6, 1940, TNA, FO371/24329; Telegram 128, Gascoigne to FO, July 6, 1940, TNA, FO371/24329.

27. Quoted in Finlayson, *The Fortress Came First*, 33–34.

28. Telegram, FOCNA to Admiralty, July 10, 1940, TNA, FO371/24454.

29. Finlayson, *The Fortress Came First*, 34; Letter, Hurst to Morize, July 9, 1940; Letter, Hurst to Noguès, July 11, 1940, CADN, 1MA/15/707.

30. Telegram 85, FO to Tangier/Rabat, July 11, 1940, TNA, FO371/24454.

31. Note 2567, Le commissaire spécial du port à directeur de la sécurité publique, July 13, 1940, CADN, 1MA/15/707.

32. Stockey and Crocott, *Gibraltar*, 69–70.

CHAPTER 7

1. Vinen, *The Unfree French*, 47.

2. http://www.napoleon.org/en/magazine/museums/files/Vichy.asp.

3. Jackson, *France: The Dark Years*, 112.

4. Jackson, *France: The Dark Years*, 142.

5. Vinen, *The Unfree French*, 48.

6. Goda, "Hitler's Demand for Casablanca in 1940," 491; Goda, *Tomorrow the World*, 17.

7. Weinberg, "Hitler's Image of the United States," 1010.

8. Weinberg, "Hitler's Image of the United States," 1012–1014.

9. Budd, "Global Networks Before Globalisation"; Hindley, "Glamorous Crossing."

10. Goda, "Hitler's Demand for Casablanca in 1940," 493.

11. Motadel, *Islam and Nazi Germany's War*, 74.

12. Goda, "Hitler's Demand for Casablanca in 1940," 495.

13. Paxton, *Vichy France*, Kindle location 1117.

14. Singer, *Maxime Weygand*, 120; Metzger, *L'empire colonial français dans la stratégie du Troisiéme Reich*, 259.

15. Paxton, *Vichy France*, Kindle location 1133.

16. Descriptive details are from photos in the Getty Images photobank.

17. "My Last Appeal to Great Britain, A GREAT EMPIRE WILL BE DESTROYED" by Adolf Hitler, Chancellor of Germany, speech made to the Reichstag, July 19, 1940, in *Vital Speeches of the Day*, 6:617–625.

18. Metzger, *L'empire colonial français dans la stratégie du Troisiéme Reich*, 261.

19. Goda, *Tomorrow the World*, 31.

CHAPTER 8

1. Schechter, *Viennese Vignettes*, 153.

2. Schechter, *Viennese Vignettes*, 146.

3. Schechter, *Viennese Vignettes*, 146.

4. Schechter, oral history, 8.

5. Schechter, oral history, 9.

6. Schechter, *Viennese Vignettes*, 149.

7. Schechter, oral history, 9.

8. Schechter, *Viennese Vignettes*, 151.

9. Schechter, oral history, 10; Schechter, *Viennese Vignettes*, 151.

10. Schechter, *Viennese Vignettes*, 152–153.

11. Schechter, *Viennese Vignettes*, 153.

12. Schechter, *Viennese Vignettes*, 157.

13. Breitman and Kraut, *Refugee Policy and European Jewry*, 57, 64–66. Breitman and Litchman, *FDR and the Jews*, 102. "Aid for Refugees Favored by AFL," *New York Times*, March 26, 1938.

14. List of consulates in Casablanca, 1940, NARA, RG 84, Entry UD 2997, Box 31.

15. Living quarters statement, January 1940; Letter, Goold to Sec State, January 5, 1940, NARA, RG 84, Entry UD 2997, Box 31.

16. Casablanca Post Report, January 17, 1939, NARA, RG 84, Entry UD 2997, Box 24.

17. Application for passport, Jeannette Ruth Smith, April 20, 1940 (born December 20, 1939); Report of birth, Jeannette Ruth Smith, April 17, 1940; Application for passport amendment, Ellis Dent Shannon, June 21, 1940, NARA, RG 84, Entry UD 2997, Box 32.

18. Letter, Langer to American Commercial Attaché, February 20, 1940; Report, Radio Market in French Morocco, February 23, 1940, NARA, RG 84, Entry UD 2997, Box 38.

19. Schechter, *Viennese Vignettes*, 157.

20. Schechter, oral history, 12; Schechter, *Viennese Vignettes*, 158.

21. Schechter, oral history, 12.

22. Schechter, oral history, 13.

23. Schechter, *Viennese Vignettes*, 158.

24. Schechter, oral history, 13. Schechter, *Viennese Vignettes*, 159.

25. Schechter, oral history, 13.

CHAPTER 9

1. Report, "Refugee Situation in Casablanca and Transit Visa Rush," August 13, 1940, NARA, RG 84, UD 2997, Box 36.

2. Report, "Refugee Situation in Casablanca and Transit Visa Rush," August 13, 1940, NARA, RG 84, UD 2997, Box 36; "Enquêtes sur les prisons et les camps d'internement," Rapport définitif No. 52, Annexe No. 14, USHMM, ITS, 2.3.5.1, folder 19b, Doc. No. 82371199.

3. Letter, Kelber to AJJDC Lisbon, July 6, 1940, AJJDC Archives, Roll 745.

4. Attestation, July 5, 1940, USHMM, 68.115M, Folder 2, frame 90.

5. Letter, Bénatar to Chief of Municipal Services, July 9, 1940, USHMM, 68.115M, Folder 1.

6. Bénatar bio. USHMM, 68.115M, Folder 1.

7. Letter, Bénatar to British consulate, June 18, 1940, USHMM, 68.115M, Folder 1.

8. Letter 54, Schwartz to New York, August 12, 1940, AJJDC Archives, Roll 745.

9. Report by Commission de refugiés, September 17, 1940, AJJDC Archives, Roll 745.

10. Report, "The Present Position" by Goold, August 12, 1940, NARA, RG 84, Entry UD 2997, Box 35.

11. State Department circular, no. 193, October 25, 1940; Telegram 25, Hull to Goold, July 4, 1940; Telegram 97, State to Bern, July 8, 1940, NARA, RG 84, Entry UD 2997, Box 35.

12. Report, "Refugee Situation in Casablanca and Transit Visa Rush," August 13, 1940, NARA, RG 84, UD 2997, Box 36.

13. Letter, Ward (Riga) to Goold, September 10, 1940; Telegram 25, Goold to Lisbon, September 25, 1940; Telegram 22199, Harrison (Berlin) to Goold, November 6, 1940, NARA, RG 84, UD 2997, Box 36.

14. Telegram 22199, Harrison (Berlin) to Goold, November 6, 1940; Letter, Cunningham (Berlin) to Goold, November 22, 1940; Telegram, Casablanca to Lisbon, December 9, 1940; Letter, Ward (Riga) to Stanton, December 9, 1940, NARA, RG 84, UD 2997, Box 36.

15. Report, "Refugee Situation in Casablanca and Transit Visa Rush," August 13, 1940, NARA, RG 84, UD 2997, Box 36.

16. Letter, Moore to Staff, July 30, 1940; Letter, Messersmith to Staff, January 26, 1940, NARA, RG 84, UD 2997, Box 36.

17. USHMM, "Emigration from Germany."

18. Letter, Goold to SecState, September 4, 1940, NARA, RG 84, UD 2997, Box 36.

19. Letter, Goold to Sec State, September 4, 1940, NARA, RG 84, UD 2997, Box 36.

20. Telegram, Casablanca to London, August 10, 1940, NARA, RG 84, Entry UD 2997, Box 35.

CHAPTER 10

1. Weygand, *Recalled to Service*, 275.

2. Weygand, *Recalled to Service*, 276; Informations générales, Ministére des affaires étrangères, no. 9, October 29, 1940, 28.

3. Weygand, *Recalled to Service*, 272; *Cook's Practical Guide to Algeria and Tunisia* (London: T. Cook & Son, 1908), 71.

4. Paxton, *Vichy France*, Kindle location 2654.

5. Paxton, *Vichy France*, Kindle location 2689.

6. Paxton, *Vichy France*, Kindle location 2689.

7. Singer, *Maxime Weygand*, 123.

8. Singer, *Maxime Weygand*, 124.

9. Singer, *Maxime Weygand*, 120.

10. Kitson, *The Hunt for Nazi Spies*, Kindle location 692.

11. Singer, *Maxime Weygand*, 124.

12. Singer, *Maxime Weygand*, 126; Weygand, *Recalled to Service*, 266.

13. Informations générales, Ministére des affaires étrangères, no. 7, October 15, 1940, 23.

14. Weygand, *Recalled to Service*, 267.

15. Weygand, *Recalled to Service*, 273–282.

16. Hoisington, *Casablanca Connection*, 181.

17. Weygand, *Recalled to Service*, 275.

18. Hoisington, *Casablanca Connection*, 182; *La Vigie marocaine*, August 12, 1940.

19. Hoisington, *Casablanca Connection*, 191–192. See the change in the reporting of sports in *La Vigie marocaine* between July 1940 and July 1941.

20. M. Thomas, *The French Empire at War*, 75–77.

21. Weygand, *Recalled to Service*, 280.

22. Hoisington, *Casablanca Connection*, 187.

23. Hoisington, *Casablanca Connection*, 187.

CHAPTER 11

1. Scammell, *Koestler*, 184; Cesarani, *Arthur Koestler*, 162.

2. Scammell, *Koestler*, 184.

3. Scammell, *Koestler*, 185; Koestler, *Scum of the Earth*, Kindle locations 2545–2546.

4. Koestler, *Scum of the Earth*, Kindle location 2545.

5. Koestler, *Scum of the Earth*, Kindle location 2618.

6. Porch, *The French Foreign Legion*, 443.

7. Porch, *The French Foreign Legion*, 446–447.

8. Interrogation Report of Arthur Koestler, Cannon Row Police Station, November 8, 1940, TNA, KV2/1273.

9. Quoted in Scammell, *Koestler*, 188.

10. Koestler, *Scum of the Earth*, Kindle location 3519.

11. Cesarani, *Arthur Koestler*, 167.

12. Koestler, *Scum of the Earth*, Kindle location 3542.

13. Cesarani, *Arthur Koestler*, 167; Koestler, *Scum of the Earth*, Kindle location 3533.

14. Scammell, *Koestler*, 189.

15. Scammell, *Koestler*, 189.

16. Scammell, *Koestler*, 190.

17. Telegram 112, Tangier to FO, July 3, 1940; Telegram 131, Tangier to FO, July 7, 1940, TNA, FO371/24329; Telegram 135, Tangier/Rabat to FO, July 8, 1940, TNA, FO371/24454.

18. Scammell, *Koestler*, 190; West, *The A to Z of British Intelligence*, 135; Stevenson, *Spymistress*, 210–211.

19. Interrogation Report of Arthur Koestler, Cannon Row Police Station, November 8, 1940, TNA, KV2/1273.

20. Interrogation Report of Arthur Koestler, Cannon Row Police Station, November 8, 1940, TNA, KV2/1273.

21. J. Smith, *British Writers and MI5 Surveillance*, 131–132.

22. Emergency Certificate issued to Arthur Koestler, September 9, 1940, TNA, KV2/1273.

23. Quoted in Scammell, *Koestler*, 191.

24. Interrogation Report of Arthur Koestler, Cannon Row Police Station, November 8, 1940, TNA, KV2/1273.

25. Scammell, *Koestler*, 192.

26. Cesarani, *Arthur Koestler*, 170; J. Smith, *British Writers and MI5 Surveillance*, 131–132.

27. Letter, G. S. to Herbertson, November 25, 1940, TNA, KV2/1273.

CHAPTER 12

1. Report by Commission de refugiés, September 17, 1940, AJJDC Archives, Roll 745.

2. Bauer, *American Jewry and the Holocaust*, 25.

3. Bauer, *American Jewry and the Holocaust*, 43–48.

4. Telegram 103, AJJDC Lisbon to Jointdisco, July 12, 1940; Letter, Kelber to AJJDC Lisbon, July 6, 1940; Telegram 109, Jointdisco to AJJDC Lisbon, July 12, 1940; Telegram 126, Lisbon to Jointdisco, July 14, 1940; Telegram 159, Jointdisco to Lisbon, July 23, 1940; Telegram 200a, Lisbon to Jointdisco, July 27, 1940; Letter 54, Schwartz to New York, August 12, 1940, AJJDC Archives, Roll 745.

5. Letter, Troper to AJJDC New York, December 2, 1940, AJJDC Archives, Roll 745.

6. Letter, Schwartz to AJJDC New York, November 29, 1940, AJJDC Archives, Roll 745.

7. Letter, Troper to AJJDC New York, December 2, 1940, AJJDC Archives, Roll 745.

8. Letter, Schwartz to AJJDC New York, November 29, 1940, AJJDC Archives, Roll 745.

9. Laskier, *North African Jewry in the Twentieth Century*, 12.

10. Yahil, *The Holocaust*, 173.

11. Schroeter, "Vichy in Morocco," Location 5682.

12. "Le statut official des juifs au Maroc," *Bulletin Officiel du Maroc*, October 31, 1940; Satloff, *Among the Righteous*, 31.

13. Memo, "Status of Jews in French Morocco Under the Dahir of October 31, 1940," December 1940, NARA, RG 84, UD 2997, Box 36. Assaraf, *Mohammed V et les Juifs du Maroc*, 129–131.

14. Laskier, *North African Jewry in the Twentieth Century*, 66.

15. "Enquêtes sur les prisons et les camps d'internement," Rapport définitif No. 52, Annexe

No. 14, USHMM, ITS, 2.3.5.1, folder 19b, Doc. No. 82371199; Laskier, *North African Jewry in the Twentieth Century*, 64; Satloff, *Among the Righteous*, 210.

16. Letter, Goold to du Gardier, November 15, 1940, NARA, RG 84, Entry UD 2997, Box 37; Survey of American Interests in French Morocco, January 29, 1941, NARA, RG 84, Entry 2997, Box 49.

17. Letter, Contrôleur Civil Casablanca to Goold, December 10, 1940; Letter, du Gardier to Goold, December 10, 1940, NARA, RG 84, Entry UD 2997, Box 37.

18. Letter, Goold to Sec State, December 4, 1940, NARA, RG 84, Entry UD 2997, Box 37.

19. Report by Guy Capart, "Centre d'hébergement d'Azemour," November 30, 1940, NARA, RG 84, Entry UD 2997, Box 37.

20. Letter, Goold to Sec State, December 4, 1940, NARA, RG 84, Entry UD 2997, Box 37.

CHAPTER 13

1. Murphy, *Diplomat Among Warriors*, 76, 80; Riding, *And the Show Went On*, Kindle location 2273.

2. Murphy, *Diplomat Among Warriors*, 80.

3. Letter, Jack to Murphy, July 8, 1940, HIA, Murphy Papers, Box 8.

4. "A History of the Official American Presence in France," IIP Digital, US Embassy, http://photos.state.gov/libraries/france/45994/irc/uspresenceinfrance.pdf; Riding, *And the Show Went On*, Kindle location 2273.

5. Weisbrode, *The Atlantic Century*, 67.

6. Murphy, *Diplomat Among Warriors*, 78–79.

7. Murphy, *Diplomat Among Warriors*, 81.

8. Murphy, *Diplomat Among Warriors*, 82.

9. Murphy, *Diplomat Among Warriors*, 83.

10. Telegram 866, Vichy to State, November 1, 1940, *FRUS*, 1940.

11. Telegram 82, State to Algiers, October 26, 1940, *FRUS*, 1940.

12. Telegram 3638, London to State, November 5, 1940, *FRUS*, 1940; Telegram 613, Madrid to State, November 5, 1940, *FRUS*, 1940; Telegram 3672, London to State, November 7, 1940, *FRUS*, 1940.

13. Telegram 185, Casablanca to State, November 3, 1940, *FRUS*, 1940.

14. Telegram 708, State to Vichy, November 12, 1940, *FRUS*, 1940.

15. Telegram 82, State to Algiers, October 26, 1940, *FRUS*, 1940.

16. Telegram 904, Vichy to State, November 6, 1940.

17. The date for this meeting is an educated guess. As the meeting was to be secret, there is no mention of Murphy in the White House logs or official record of the meeting. But based on a memo that Murphy wrote to himself, telegrams coming out of Vichy and Morocco about possible aid programs, and an entry for Sumner Welles in the White House usher's diary, November 13 is the most likely date. Memorandum by Murphy, undated, HIA, Robert Murphy Papers, Box 46; Entry for November 13, 1940, "Franklin D. Roosevelt Day by Day," FDR Library, http://www.fdrlibrary.marist.edu/daybyday/daylog/november-13th-1940.

18. Kennedy, *Freedom from Fear*, 463; Fireside Chat, "On the Works Relief Program," April 28, 1935; Fireside Chat, "On the Bank Crisis," March 12, 1933; Fireside Chat, "On National Defense," May 26, 1940 (http://docs.fdrlibrary.marist.edu/firesi90.html).

19. Murphy, *Diplomat Among Warriors*, 94.

20. Telegram 42, Dakar to State, October 31, 1940, *FRUS*, 1940.

21. Murphy, *Diplomat Among Warriors*, 94, 100.

22. Murphy, *Diplomat Among Warriors*, 95.

23. Murphy, *Diplomat Among Warriors*, 96–97.

24. Letter, Long to Murphy, November 15, 1940, *FRUS*, 1940; Murphy, *Diplomat Among Warriors*, 98.

25. Jackson, *France: The Dark Years*, 173.

26. Jackson, *France: The Dark Years*, 149.

27. Jackson, *France: The Dark Years*, 174.

28. Jackson, *France: The Dark Years*, 155.

CHAPTER 14

1. Murphy, *Diplomat Among Warriors*, 98; "Itemized Schedule of Travel and Other Expenses," December 17, 1940, to January 31, 1941, HIA, Robert Murphy Papers, Box 45. The dates in Murphy's memoir for his inspection tour are sometimes off a day or two from the expense report. In such cases, I have opted to use dates on the expense report.

2. Telegram 1110, Vichy to State, December 10, 1940, *FRUS*, 1940; Telegram 831, State to Vichy, December 11, 1940, *FRUS*, 1940.

3. Telegram 1158, Vichy to State, December 19, 1940, *FRUS*, 1940.

4. Telegram 1158, Vichy to State, December 19, 1940, *FRUS*, 1940.

5. "Le voyage de M. Murphy," *Le Nouvelliste d'Indochine*, December 22, 1940.

6. Murphy, *Diplomat Among Warriors*, 99.

7. Murphy, *Diplomat Among Warriors*, 104.

8. Telegram 91, State to Algiers, November 13, 1940, *FRUS*, 1940; Telegram 183, Algiers to State, December 7, 1940, *FRUS*, 1940.

9. Weygand, *Recalled to Service*, 370; Telegram 14, Lisbon to State, January 14, 1941, *FRUS*, 1941, 2:209.

10. Murphy, *Diplomat Among Warriors*, 101.

11. Telegram 14, Lisbon to State, January 14, 1941, *FRUS*, 1941, 2:207.

12. Weygand, *Recalled to Service*, 369.

13. Travel pass issued on Weygand's authority, December 24, 1940, HIA, Robert Murphy Papers, Box 45.

14. Letter, Dakar to Murphy, December 27, 1940, HIA, Robert Murphy Papers, Box 45.

15. Murphy, *Diplomat Among Warriors*, 108–109.

16. "Itemized Schedule of Travel and Other Expenses," December 17, 1940, to January 31, 1941, HIA, Robert Murphy Papers, Box 45.

17. Murphy, *Diplomat Among Warriors*, 106.

18. Letter, Auer to Murphy, January 2, 1941, HIA, Robert Murphy Papers, Box 46.

19. Murphy, *Diplomat Among Warriors*, 107. Note 66, Noguès to Directeur des Affaires Politiques, January 22, 1941, CADN, 11MA/900/49.

20. Travel expense list, December 17, 1940, to January 13, 1941, HIA, Robert Murphy Papers, Box 8.

21. Telegram 19, Lisbon to State, January 17, 1941, *FRUS*, 2:213.

22. Telegram 106, State to Vichy, February 1, 1941, *FRUS*, 2:216.

23. Telegram 46, State to Vichy, January 15, 1941, *FRUS*, 1941, 2:101; Memcon by Villard, December 18, 1940, *FRUS*, 1940, 2:632.

24. Herwig, *The First World War*, 286–289, 295–296.

25. Bell, *A History of the Blockade of Germany*, 672; Offer, *The First World War*, 45–53. For a detailed account of the effects of the food shortages, see Davis, *Home Fires Burning*.

26. Weinberg, *Germany, Hitler, and World War II*, 71.

27. "Breach in the Blockade of Metropolitan France and French Colonies," Committee on Foreign (Allied) Resistance, CFR(40)83, November 9, 1940, TNA, PREM3/74/10.

28. "Reports Regarding Enemy Levies on North African Produce Imported into France," October 19, 1940, TNA, FO837/1227; Telegram 650, Matthews to Hull, September 27, 1940, *FRUS*, 1940, 2:550–551; Telegram 727, Matthews to Hull, October 9, 1940, *FRUS*, 1940, 2:551–552; Telegram 730, Matthews to Hull, October 10, 1940, *FRUS*, 1940, 2:552–553.

29. Telegram R-19x, FDR to WSC, December 31, 1940, in Kimball, *Churchill and Roosevelt*, 1:117–118.

30. Telegram 25, London (WSC) to State (FDR), January 3, 1941, *FRUS*, 1941, vol. 3; Telegram 39, Vichy to State, January 11, 1940, *FRUS*, 1941, vol. 3.

31. Telegram C-43x, WSC to FDR, 12[?] December 1940, in Kimball, *Churchill and Roosevelt*, 1:87–111.

32. Kimball, *Most Unsordid Act*, 107–117.

33. Telegram 249, Leahy to Sec State, February 28, 1941, *FRUS*, 1941, 2:226; Telegram 1015, Washington to FO, March 5, 1941, TNA, FO371/28475.

34. Dallek, *Franklin D. Roosevelt and American Foreign Policy*, 251.

35. Letter, Leahy to Roosevelt, January 25, 1941, *FRUS*, 1941, vol. 3.

36. Telegram 10, Hull to Leahy, January 6, 1941, *FRUS*, 1941, 2:90–91.

37. Paxton, *Vichy France*, 109.

38. Telegram 268, Vichy to State, March 4, 1941, HIA, Robert Murphy Papers, Box 47.

39. Telegram 284, Vichy to State, March 9, 1941, HIA, Robert Murphy Papers, Box 47.

40. Telegram 272, Vichy to State, March 6, 1941, HIA, Robert Murphy Papers, Box 47.

41. Telegram 207, State to Vichy, March 7, 1941; Telegram 290, Vichy to State, March 11, 1941, HIA, Robert Murphy Papers, Box 47.

42. Telegram 1275, FO to Washington, March 29, 1941, TNA, FO371/28475.

CHAPTER 15

1. Baker and Bouillon, *Josephine*, 119.

2. Baker and Chase, *Josephine Baker*, 234.

3. Baker and Bouillon, *Josephine*, 119.

4. Rose, *Jazz Cleopatra*, 186.

5. Baker and Bouillon, *Josephine*, 120.

6. Rose, *Jazz Cleopatra*, 187.

7. Baker and Chase, *Josephine Baker*, 234–235.

8. Richards, *Secret Flotillas* 60; Rose, *Jazz Cleopatra*, 187.

9. Baker and Bouillon, *Josephine*, 121.

10. Baker and Chase, *Josephine Baker*, 236.

11. Baker and Chase, *Josephine Baker*, 237; Baker and Bouillon, *Josephine*, 122.

12. Baker and Bouillon, *Josephine*, 124.

13. Baker and Chase, *Josephine Baker*, 239.

14. Baker and Chase, *Josephine Baker*, 240; Baker and Bouillon, *Josephine*, 125.

15. Baker and Chase, *Josephine Baker*, 241.

16. Jennings, "The Best Avenue of Escape," 37.

17. Fry, *Surrender on Demand*, 187.

18. Fry, *Surrender on Demand*, 187.

19. Testimony of Hélène Bénatar, October 24, 1956, in *Le procès du général Noguès*.

20. Testimony of Hélène Bénatar, October 24, 1956, in *Le procès du général Noguès*.

21. Letter, Tuck to Sec State, July 25, 1941, NARA, RG 84, Entry 2997, Box 49.

22. Lesser, *Welcoming the Undesirables*, 13; Memo on French Steamer SS *Alsina* by Herman F. Reissig, USHMM, 1997.A.0050. Reissig worked for the Spanish Refugee Relief Campaign.

23. Bartrop, *Resisting the Holocaust*, 52.

24. Memo on French Steamer SS *Alsina* by Herman F. Reissig, USHMM, 1997.A.0050.

25. "European Refugees Stranded at Dakar," *New York Times*, March 3, 1941.

26. Letter, Tuck to Sec State, July 25, 1941, NARA, RG 84, Entry 2997, Box 49; "High Seas: The White Sepulcher," *Time*, December 1, 1941. *Personnages douteux debarquant de l'Alsina*, June 16, 1941, CADN, 11MA/900/83.

27. Letter, Russell to Sec State, September 11, 1941, NARA, RG 84, Entry 2997, Box 49.

28. Aide memoire, September 11, 1941, NARA, RG 84, Entry 2997, Box 49; "Dr. Brutzkus, OSE Head, Arrives Here," *Jewish Telegraphic Agency*, April 27, 1941; "600 More Refugees Saved by JDC Reach New York," *Jewish Telegraphic Agency*, August 11, 1941; "Refugee Ship at Havana," *New York Times*, September 23, 1941.

29. Aide memoire, September 11, 1941, NARA, RG 84, Entry 2997, Box 49.

30. Telegram, Russell to Lisbon, October 31, 1941, NARA, RG 84, Entry 2997, Box 49.

31. Certificate regarding embarkment of eighty-four passengers on the SS *Quanza* at Casablanca, October 31, 1941; Letter, Childs to Gascoigne, November 1, 1941; Letter, Russell to Sec State, November 3, 1941; Letter, Childs to Russell, November 1, 1941, NARA, RG 84, Entry 2997, Box 49.

32. Letter, Russell to Sec State, November 3, 1941, NARA, RG 84, Entry 2997, Box 49.

33. Testimony of Hélène Bénatar, October 24, 1956, in *Le procès du général Noguès*.

34. "Zamora on His Way to Argentina," *New York Times*, November 30, 1941.

CHAPTER 16

1. Harris, *Escape from the Legion*, 9.

2. Harris, *Escape from the Legion*, 13–17.

3. C. E. Bosworth, "Minorsky, Vladimir Fed'orovich," *Encyclopædia Iranica*, July 20, 2004, http://www.iranicaonline.org/articles/minorsky-vladimir (accessed May 15, 2016); Prison diary of Fedor Minorsky (alias Theodor Harris), Churchill Archives Center, HARS, file 6.

4. Harris, *Escape from the Legion*, 12.

5. Harris, *Escape from the Legion*, 22–23.

6. Harris, *Escape from the Legion*, 23.

7. Harris, *Escape from the Legion*, 23–24.

8. Telegram 206, Stanton to Sec State (125.283H3), May 21, 1941; Letter, Russell to Sec State (125.283H3), February 19, 1942, NARA, RG 59, Dec File 1940–1944, Box 846.

9. Telegram 791, Gasciogne to FO, November 26, 1940; Telegram 922, Gasciogne to FO, December 16, 1940; Telegram 937, Gasciogne to FO, December 17, 1940; Telegram 922, Gasciogne to FO, December 27, 1940, TNA, FO371/24286.

10. Telegram 94, Casablanca to Sec State, March 6, 1941, NARA, RG 59, Dec File 1940–1944, Box 846.

11. Letter, Stanton to Sec State, April 1, 1941; Letter, Russell to Sec State, February 7, 1942, NARA, RG 59, Dec File 1940–1944, Box 846.

12. Telegram 206, Stanton to Sec State, May 21, 1941, NARA, RG 59, Dec File 1940–1944, Box 846.

13. Harris, *Escape from the Legion*, 25.

14. Harris, *Escape from the Legion*, 25–26.

15. List of moving picture theaters in Morocco, June 14, 1941, NARA, RG 84, Entry 2997, Box 49. Number of movie theaters in Casablanca: 19. The largest, the Vox, sat 2,000. The Rialto sat 1,300; Lux, 1,000; Empire, 1,150; Regent, 1,100; Rio, 1,000; Monte Carlo, 1,000; Imperial, 1,000; Triomphe, 500; Colises, 500; Apollo, 500; Medina, 400; Eden, 800; Moulin de la Gaiete, 400; Mondial, 300; Chaouia, 200; Notre Dame, 300; Familia, 500; Goya, 400.

16. Harris, *Escape from the Legion*, 22.

17. Harris, *Escape from the Legion*, 26–27.

18. Harris, *Escape from the Legion*, 29.

19. Harris, *Escape from the Legion*, 31.

20. Harris, *Escape from the Legion*, 34.

21. Harris, *Escape from the Legion*, 39.

22. Harris, *Escape from the Legion*, 39.

23. Harris, *Escape from the Legion*, 44.

24. Harris, *Escape from the Legion*, 45.

25. Harris, *Escape from the Legion*, 47.

26. Harris, *Escape from the Legion*, 62.

27. Harris, *Escape from the Legion*, 51.

28. Harris, *Escape from the Legion*, 51.

29. Harris, *Escape from the Legion*, 53–55.

30. Harris, *Escape from the Legion*, 59.

31. Harris, *Escape from the Legion*, 55–56.

32. Harris, *Escape from the Legion*, 55–59.

33. Harris, *Escape from the Legion*, 57.

34. Harris, *Escape from the Legion*, 61.

35. Harris, *Escape from the Legion*, 63–64.

36. Harris, *Escape from the Legion*, 66.

37. Harris, *Escape from the Legion*, 73.

38. Harris, *Escape from the Legion*, 74.

39. Cohen and Eleb, *Casablanca*, 216–220.

40. Harris, *Escape from the Legion*, 74.

41. Harris, *Escape from the Legion*, 79.

42. Harris, *Escape from the Legion*, 81–82.

43. Harris, *Escape from the Legion*, 88.

44. "Missour," Rapport définitif No. 52 (Camps d'Afrique du Nord), December 27, 1951, USHMM, ITS, 2.3.5.1, folder 19b, Doc. No. 82371123; Letter, Chef du Cabinet Militaire to Chef du Cabinet Diplomatique, December 19, 1939, CADN, 1MA/15/706.

45. Harris, *Escape from the Legion*, 92.

46. Harris, *Escape from the Legion*, 95.

47. Harris, *Escape from the Legion*, 98.

CHAPTER 17

1. Unpublished memoir by Reid, 16, HIA, W. Stafford Reid Papers.

2. Interview with King, February 24, 1948, USAHEC, OCMH Collection, Sidney Matthews Papers, Interviews.

3. Dave King's Report, July 19, 1944, NARA, RG 226, Entry A1–99, Box 49, TORCH Anthology.

4. Letter, King to Wright, March 16, 1951; Personal History Statement, HIA, David Wooster King Papers, Personal Data; "Other Weddings: King-Appleton," *New York Times*, September 25, 1932; "W. H. Appleton and Noel Johnston Wed," *New York Times*, April 15, 1915; King, *The French Foreign Legion*, 145–146; "King, Mr. David W.," *New York Social Register, 1920*, 393.

5. Personal History Statement, HIA, David Wooster King Papers, Personal Data.

6. Dave King's Report, July 19, 1944, USNA, RG 226, Entry A1–99, Box 49, TORCH Anthology.

7. Murphy, *Diplomat Among Warriors*, 119.

8. Murphy, *Diplomat Among Warriors*, 120.

9. Murphy, *Diplomat Among Warriors*, 121.

10. Unpublished memoir by Reid, 4–6, HIA, W. Stafford Reid Papers.

11. Placement questionnaire completed by Reid, July 10, 1943, USNA, RG 226, Entry 224, Personnel, Stafford Reid; from the *New York Times*, "Margaret Knott Feted, October 26, 1928; "Debutante Party for Marion Carter," December 1, 1929; "Dinner for Miss Carolyn Storrs," April 9, 1930; "Notes of Social Activities in New York and Elsewhere," July 19, 1931; "Southampton Club Holds Horse Show," July 30, 1930; "Mrs. M. L. Gould Gives Dinner Party," April 4, 1934; "Miss Joy Schnell Has Birthday Fete," February 13, 1935; "Brilliant Throng at Opera's Opening," December 17, 1935; "Large Society Attendance Adds to Color of Show in the Garden," November 5, 1936; "Brilliant Throng at Opera Opening," December 22, 1936; "Notables Gather at Opera Opening," November 30, 1937; "Horseshow Opens New Social Season," November 6, 1938; "Brilliant Throng Is Present as Metropolitan's Season Gets Under Way," November 22, 1938; "Brilliant Throng at Opera Premiere," November 28, 1939.

12. Dave King's Report, July 19, 1944, NARA, RG 226, Entry A1–99, Box 49, TORCH Anthology; Unpublished memoir by Reid, 9, HIA, W. Stafford Reid Papers.

13. Unpublished memoir by Reid, 10, HIA, W. Stafford Reid Papers.

14. Unpublished memoir by Reid, 14, HIA, W. Stafford Reid Papers.

15. Unpublished memoir by Reid, 21, HIA, W. Stafford Reid Papers.

16. Unpublished memoir by Reid, 18–21, HIA, W. Stafford Reid Papers.

17. Unpublished memoir by Reid, 19, HIA, W. Stafford Reid Papers.

18. Unpublished memoir by Reid, 21, HIA, W. Stafford Reid Papers.

19. Vaughan, *FDR's 12 Apostles*, 47.

20. Dave King's Report, July 19, 1944; John Knox's Report, August 2, 1944, NARA, RG 226, Entry A1–99, Box 49, TORCH Anthology.

21. Unpublished memoir by Reid, 30, HIA, W. Stafford Reid Papers.

22. Letter, Shaw to Murphy, April 30, 1941, HIA, Robert Murphy Papers, Box 45.

23. Jackson, *France: The Dark Years*, 159.

24. Singer, *Maxime Weygand*, 153; Paxton, *Vichy France*, Kindle location 1959; Jackson, *France: The Dark Years*, 160.

25. Weygand, *Recalled to Service*, 334.

26. Unpublished memoir by Reid, 10, HIA, W. Stafford Reid Papers.

27. Vaughan, *FDR's 12 Apostles*, 47.

28. John Knox's Report, August 2, 1944, NARA, RG 226, Entry A1–99, Box 49, TORCH Anthology; Telegram 235, Algiers to State, 1941, *FRUS*, 1941, 3:314.

29. Telegram 134, State to Algiers, June 11, 1941, *FRUS*, 1941, 3:315; Telegram 235, Murphy to Sec State (125.283H3), June 10, 1940, NARA, RG 59, Dec File 1940–1944, Box 846.

30. Pendar, *Adventure in Diplomacy*, 21.

31. Murphy, *Diplomat Among Warriors*, 121.

32. Letter, Childs to Goold, February 21, 1941; Letter, Goold to du Gardier, February 21, 1941; Note, Goold to du Gardier, February 28, 1941, NARA, RG 84, Entry 2997, Box 41.

33. Letter, Childs to Sec State, March 5, 1941; Telegram 107, Stanton to Sec State, March 21, 1941; Telegram 77, Sec State to Stanton, March 27, 1941; Letter, Russell to Murray, August 4, 1941, NARA, RG 59, Dec File 1940–1944, Box 846.

34. Telegram 331, Murphy to Sec State, July 20, 1941, NARA, RG 59, Dec File 1940–1944, Box 846.

35. Interview with Stafford Reid, June 17, 1943, NARA, RG 226, Entry A1–99, Box 49, TORCH Anthology; Unpublished memoir by Reid, 30, HIA, W. Stafford Reid Papers.

36. Interview with Stafford Reid, June 17, 1943, NARA, RG 226, Entry A1–99, Box 49, TORCH Anthology.

37. Interview with Stafford Reid, June 17, 1943, NARA, RG 226, Entry A1–99, Box 49, TORCH Anthology; Unpublished memoir by Reid, 22–25, HIA, W. Stafford Reid Papers.

38. Message No. 19 by 347, April 23, 1943, NARA, RG 226, Entry 97, Box 4.

39. Letter, Murphy to Wallace, October 13, 1941, *FRUS*, 1941, 3:317.

CHAPTER 18

1. Unpublished memoir by Reid, 50–51, HIA, W. Stafford Reid Papers.

2. Unpublished memoir by Reid, 54, HIA, W. Stafford Reid Papers; Harris, *Escape from the Legion*, 132.

3. Unpublished memoir by Reid, 56, HIA, W. Stafford Reid Papers.

4. Unpublished memoir by Reid, 59, HIA, W. Stafford Reid Papers.

5. Harris, *Escape from the Legion*, 120, 125.

6. Harris, *Escape from the Legion*, 125–126.

7. Reid memoir, 40–49, NARA, RG 226, Entry A1–99, Box 45.

8. Harris, *Escape from the Legion*, 117–118.

9. Harris, *Escape from the Legion*, 118.

10. Harris, *Escape from the Legion*, 119.

11. Harris, *Escape from the Legion*, 119.

12. Harris, *Escape from the Legion*, 128–129.

13. Harris, *Escape from the Legion*, 146–147; Report on Foreigners' Work Camp, no. 12: Settat, July 16, 1942, USHMMA, RG-67.008M, box 1, folder 15.

14. Unpublished memoir by Reid, 60, HIA, W. Stafford Reid Papers.

15. Unpublished memoir by Reid, 61, HIA, W. Stafford Reid Papers.

16. Unpublished memoir by Reid, 62, HIA, W. Stafford Reid Papers; Reid memoir, 40–49, USNA, RG 226, Entry A1–99, Box 45.

17. Unpublished memoir by Reid, 63, HIA, W. Stafford Reid Papers.

18. Unpublished memoir by Reid, 64, HIA, W. Stafford Reid Papers.

19. Unpublished memoir by Reid, 66, HIA, W. Stafford Reid Papers; Reid memoir, 40–49, USNA, RG 226, Entry A1–99, Box 45.

CHAPTER 19

1. "Ce matin à Casablanca dix mille légionnaires," *La Vigie marocaine*," June 22, 1941.

2. Sweets, *Choices in Vichy France*, 64.

3. Hoisington, *Casablanca Connection*, 188.

4. Béthouart, *Cinq années d'espérance*, 97–98, 101; Entry for Antoine Béthouart, Chemins de Mémoire, http://www.cheminsdememoire.gouv.fr/fr/antoine-Béthouart.

5. Béthouart, *Cinq années d'espérance*, 97–98, 110.

6. Béthouart, *Cinq années d'espérance*, 112.

7. Béthouart, *Cinq années d'espérance*, 113.

8. Kitson, *The Hunt for Nazi Spies*, Kindle location 855, 1600–1608.

9. Testimony by Weygand, October 24, 1956, in *Le procès du général Noguès*.

10. Maghraoui, "The Moroccan *'Effort de Guerre'* in World War II," 95.

11. Maghraoui, "The Moroccan *'Effort de Guerre'* in World War II," 96.

12. Paxton, *Vichy France*, Kindle locations 3240–3241.

13. Abitbol, *Les juifs d'Afrique du Nord sous Vichy*, 344–346; Letter, Russell to Childs, July 17, 1941, NARA, RG 84, Entry 2997, 1941, Box 48.

14. Letter, Russell to Childs, July 17, 1941, NARA, RG 84, Entry 2997, 1941, Box 48.

15. Laskier, *North African Jewry in the Twentieth Century*, 61–62; Assaraf, *Mohammed V et les Juifs du Maroc*, 148–149. Letter, Russell to Childs, August 13, 1941, NARA, RG 84, Entry 2997, 1941, Box 49.

16. Laskier, *North African Jewry in the Twentieth Century*, 63; Letter, Russell to Childs, August 19, 1941, NARA, RG 84, Entry 2997, 1941, Box 49.

17. "Sultan of Morocco Orders Ghetto for Jews; Vichy Registers Jews in Indochina," *Jewish Telegraphic Agency*, August 21, 1941.

18. Wyrtzen, *Making Morocco*, 208.

19. Bénatar Papers, USHMM.

20. Satloff, *Among the Righteous*, 109.

21. Memo by Bagby, October 17, 1941, NARA, RG 84, Entry 2997, Box 49. Schroeter, "Vichy in Morocco," Location 5869. Satloff, *Among the Righteous*, 110–111.

22. Letter, Russell to Childs, December 13, 1941; Memo by Bagby, October 17, 1941, NARA, RG 84, Entry 2997, Box 49.

23. Article translated in Memo by Bagby, October 17, 1941, NARA, RG 84, Entry 2997, Box 49.

CHAPTER 20

1. Weygand, *Recalled to Service*, 379; Telegram 1356, Leahy to Sec State, October 21, 1941, *FRUS*, 1941, 2:477–479.

2. Weygand, *Recalled to Service*, 380.

3. Weygand, *Recalled to Service*, 380; Telegram 1356, Leahy to Sec State, October 21, 1941, *FRUS*, 1941, 2:477–479.

4. Levisse-Touzé, *L'Afrique du Nord dans la guerre*, 173; Weygand, *Recalled to Service*, 381.

5. Telegram 1417, Leahy to Sec State, November 7, 1941, *FRUS*, 1941, 2:456.

6. Levisse-Touzé, *L'Afrique du Nord dans la guerre*, 174.

7. Telegram 153, Leahy to Sec State, November 18, 1941, *FRUS*, 1941, 2:460.

8. Telegram 1454, Leahy to Sec State, November 19, 1941, *FRUS*, 1941, 2:464.

9. Telegram C-129x, WSC to FDR, November 20, 1941, in Kimball, *Churchill and Roosevelt*, 1:269–270.

10. Weygand, *Recalled to Service*, 386; Clayton, *General Maxime Weygand*, 127.

11. Clayton, *General Maxime Weygand*, 126–127; Levisse-Touzé, *L'Afrique du Nord dans la guerre*, 177.

12. Hoisington, *Casablanca Connection*, 189.

13. Kitson, *The Hunt for Nazi Spies*, Kindle location 1606.

14. Béthouart, *Cinq années d'espérance*, 116.

15. King report, 19 July 1944, NARA, RG 226, A-199, Box 49, TORCH Anthology.

16. Vaughn, *FDR's 12 Apostles*, 54.

17. King report, 19 July 1944; Note by Carleton Coon on King's Report, NARA, RG 226, A-199, Box 49, TORCH Anthology.

CHAPTER 21

1. US Congress. *Investigation of the Pearl Harbor Attack*, 64–65.

2. "A Date Which Will Live in Infamy," National Archives, http://www.archives.gov /education/lessons/day-of-infamy/#documents.

3. Weinberg, *A World at Arms*, Kindle location 6289.

4. Churchill, *The Grand Alliance*, 511.

5. Kimball, *Forged in War*, 123.

6. Telegram C-138-x, WSC to FDR, December 9, 1941, in Kimball, *Churchill and Roosevelt*, 1:283.

7. Telegram C-139-x, WSC to FDR, December 10, 1941, in Kimball, *Churchill and Roosevelt*, 1:283.

8. Telegram R-73 drafts, FDR to WSC, December 10, 1941, in Kimball, *Churchill and Roosevelt*, 1:285–286.

9. Telegram C-139x, WSC to FDR, December 10, 1941, in Kimball, *Churchill and Roosevelt*, 1:284.

10. Telegram R-73, FDR to WSC, December 10, 1942; Kimball, *Churchill and Roosevelt*, 1:286.

11. Churchill, *The Grand Alliance*, 533.

12. Waller, *Wild Bill Donovan*, 87–88.

13. Memo, Donovan to FDR, December 22, 1944, USEHAC, Donovan Collection, Box 99A.

14. Waller, *Wild Bill Donovan*, 90.

15. Meecham, *Winston and Franklin*, 139; Gilbert, *Winston S. Churchill*, 7:23.

16. Meecham, *Winston and Franklin*, 141.

17. Kimball, *Forged in War*, 131.

18. "Yule Messages of Roosevelt and Churchill," *New York Times*, December 25, 1941.

19. "Churchill Introduced to Typical US Dinner," *Los Angeles Times*, December 26, 1941.

20. "Churchill 'V' Sign Brings U.S. Cheers," *Christian Science Monitor*, December 26, 1941; "Text of Address by Winston Churchill," *Atlanta Constitution*, December 27, 1941.

21. Bland and Stevens, *Papers of George Catlett Marshall*, 3:xxiii–xxiv.

22. Kimball, *Forged in War*, 128.

23. Telegram Grey 73, WSC to War Cabinet and Chiefs of Staff, December 24, 1941, TNA, FO371/31909.

24. Kimball, *Forged in War*, 129.

25. Stoler, *Allies and Adversaries*, 64–65.

26. "Dr. William Eddy to Head Hobart," *New York Times*, January 5, 1936.

27. Lippman, *Arabian Knight*, 26, 32.

28. Waller, *Wild Bill Donovan*, 134.

29. Letter, Wm. Eddy to Mary Eddy, April 11, 1942, Princeton Mudd Library, William A. Eddy Papers, Box 10.

30. Letter, Wm. Eddy to Bill Eddy, January 30, 1942, Princeton Mudd Library, William A. Eddy Papers, Box 10.

31. Langer, *Our Vichy Gamble*, 238.

32. Letter, Wm. Eddy to Jack Eddy, February 12, 1942, Princeton Mudd Library, William A. Eddy Papers, Box 10.

33. Letter, Eddy to Bill, March 24, 1942, Princeton Mudd Library, William A. Eddy Papers, Box 10.

34. Letter, Wm. Eddy to Bill Eddy, February 8, 1942, Princeton Mudd Library, William A. Eddy Papers, Box 10.

35. Letter, Wm. Eddy to Cita, February 10, 1942, Princeton Mudd Library, William A. Eddy Papers, Box 10.

36. Letter, Wm. Eddy to Cita, February 10, 1942, Princeton Mudd Library, William A. Eddy Papers, Box 10.

37. Letter, Wm. Eddy to Bill Eddy, February 8, 1942, Princeton Mudd Library, William A. Eddy Papers, Box 10.

CHAPTER 22

1. Letter, Eddy to Jack, March 1, 1942, Princeton Mudd Library, William A. Eddy Papers, Box 10.

2. Drake, *Paris at War*, 237–239.

3. Letter, Eddy to Mary, March 8, 1942, Princeton Mudd Library, William A. Eddy Papers, Box 10.

4. Memo, Donovan to Roosevelt, December 22, 1941, USAEC, William J. Donovan Papers, Box 99A.

5. Waller, *Wild Bill Donovan*, 131.

6. Vaughan, *FDR's 12 Apostles*, 67–68.

7. Letter, Wm. Eddy to Bill Eddy, February 18, 1942, Princeton Mudd Library, William A. Eddy Papers, Box 10; Memo, Eddy to Murphy, March 2, 1942, HIA, Robert Murphy Papers, Box 46.

8. Reid memoir, 60, NARA, RG 226, Entry A1–99, Box 45; Murphy, *Diplomat Among Warriors*, 108.

9. Reid memoir, 62–65, NARA, RG 226, Entry A1–99, Box 45.

10. Reid memoir, 62–65, NARA, RG 226, Entry A1–99, Box 45.

11. Interview with Stafford Reid, July 1943, 17, NARA, RG 226, Entry A1–99, Box 49, TORCH Anthology.

12. Reid memoir, 68, NARA, RG 226, Entry A1–99, Box 45.

13. Letter, Eddy to Reid, March 28, 1942, reprinted in Reid memoir, 68, NARA, RG 226, Entry A1–99, Box 45.

14. Reid memoir, 69, NARA, RG 226, Entry A1–99, Box 45.

15. King report, July 19, 1944, NARA, RG 226, Entry A1–99, Box 49, TORCH Anthology.

16. Pinkeye's Tale, dictated to CSC by Michel Despax, July 15, 1944, NARA, RG 226, Entry A1–99, Box 49, TORCH Anthology.

17. Pinkeye's Tale, dictated to CSC by Michel Despax, July 15, 1944, NARA, RG 226, Entry A1–99, Box 49, TORCH Anthology.

18. Pinkeye's Tale, dictated to CSC by Michel Despax, July 15, 1944, NARA, RG 226, Entry A1–99, Box 49, TORCH Anthology.

19. King report, July 19, 1944, NARA, RG 226, Entry A1–99, Box 49, TORCH Anthology.

20. Pinkeye's Tale, dictated to CSC by Michel Despax, July 15, 1944, NARA, RG 226, Entry A1–99, Box 49, TORCH Anthology.

21. Pinkeye's Tale, dictated to CSC by Michel Despax, July 15, 1944, NARA, RG 226, Entry A1–99, Box 49, TORCH Anthology.

22. King report, July 19, 1944, NARA, RG 226, Entry A1–99, Box 49, TORCH Anthology.

23. Pinkeye's Tale, dictated to CSC by Michel Despax, July 15, 1944, NARA, RG 226, Entry A1–99, Box 49, TORCH Anthology.

24. Pinkeye's Tale, dictated to CSC by Michel Despax, July 15, 1944, NARA, RG 226, Entry A1–99, Box 49, TORCH Anthology.

25. Memo, Colette to Murphy, King, Eddy, February 12, 1942; Letter, Murphy to Dunn, February 18, 1942, HIA, Robert Murphy Papers, Box 46.

CHAPTER 23

1. Letter, Murphy to Dunn, January 8, 1942, HIA, Robert Murphy Papers, Box 46; Funk, *Politics of TORCH*, 13–14, 19.

2. Letter, Murphy to Dunn, January 8, 1942; Memo by Murphy, February 23, 1942, HIA, Robert Murphy Papers, Box 46; Letter, Murphy to Welles, December 7, 1941, *FRUS*, 1941, 3:494–496; Letter, Murphy to Welles, January 12, 1942, *FRUS*, 1942, 229–236; Funk, *Politics of TORCH*, 39.

3. Letter, Murphy to Dunn, January 8, 1942, HIA, Robert Murphy Papers, Box 46; Telegram 25, Murphy to State, January 10, 1942, *FRUS*, 1942, 228–229.

4. Memo by Eisenhower, January 4, 1942, in *PDDE: The War Years*, 1:29.

5. Memo, Eisenhower to Wilson, February 25, 1942; Letter, Welles to Murphy, March 5, 1942, HIA, Robert Murphy Papers, Box 46.

6. Circular 405, Loi du Janvier 18, 1941, Chantiers del Jeunesse, April 25, 1941; Annex of law signed by Darlan, April 15, 1941, CADN, 1MA.15/706; Letter, Murphy to Welles, March 14, 1942, HIA, Robert Murphy Papers, Box 46; Austin, "The Chantiers de la Jeunesse in Langedoc," 108–109.

7. Letter, Murphy to Welles, March 14, 1942, HIA, Robert Murphy Papers, Box 46.

8. Letter, Murphy to Welles, March 14, 1942, HIA, Robert Murphy Papers, Box 46.

9. Letter, Eddy to Murphy, March 1, 1942; Memo, Eddy to Donovan, March 1, 1942; Letter, Eddy to Murphy, March 17, 1942, HIA, Robert Murphy Papers, Box 46.

10. Memo, King to Eddy, March 18, 1942, HIA, Robert Murphy Papers, Box 46.

11. Memo, King to Eddy, March 18, 1942; Letter, Murphy to Eddy, March 23, 1942; Memo, King to Eddy and Murphy, March 19, 1942; Letter, Eddy to Donovan, March 18, 1942, HIA, Robert Murphy Papers, Box 46.

12. Memo, King to Murphy and Eddy, March 2, 1942, HIA, Robert Murphy Papers, Box 46; Letter, Eddy to Donovan, April 8, 1942, HIA, Preston Goodfellow Papers.

13. Memo, Donovan to FDR, April 10, 1942; Letter, Eddy to Donovan, April 8, 1942, HIA, Preston Goodfellow Papers.

14. Memo, Donovan to Smith, April 12, 1942; Memo, Donovan to FDR, April 16, 1942, HIA, Preston Goodfellow Papers.

15. Letter, Donovan to Eddy, April 23, 1942; Letter, Eddy to Murphy, May 4, 1942, HIA, Robert Murphy Papers, Box 46; Langer, *Our Vichy Gamble*, 244.

16. Letter, Eddy to Murphy, May 4, 1942, HIA, Robert Murphy Papers, Box 46.

17. Letter, Donovan to Eddy, April 23, 1942, HIA, Robert Murphy Papers, Box 46.

18. Letter, Murray to Murphy, April 28, 1942, HIA, Robert Murphy Papers, Box 46.

19. Letter, Eddy to Murphy, May 4, 1942, HIA, Robert Murphy Papers, Box 46.

20. Telegram, Murphy to Eddy, May 6, 1942; Telegram 48, Eddy to COINFORM, copy from May 18, 1942; Letter, Eddy to Murphy, May 12, 1942, HIA, Robert Murphy Papers, Box 46.

21. Telegram, Murphy to Eddy, May 6, 1942; Telegram 48, Eddy to COINFORM, copy from May 18, 1942, HIA, Robert Murphy Papers, Box 46.

22. Letter, Eddy to Murphy, May 11, 1942, HIA, Robert Murphy Papers, Box 46.

23. Letter, Solborg to Murphy, May 20, 1942, HIA, Robert Murphy Papers, Box 46.

24. Record of discussion regarding collaboration between British and American SOE, June 22, 1942, HIA, Preston Goodfellow Papers; Waller, *Wild Bill Donovan*, 159.

25. Waller, *Wild Bill Donovan*, 115.

CHAPTER 24

1. Transcript of oral report by Eddy, June 11, 1942, HIA, Preston Goodfellow Papers, Box 3.

2. Telegram C-101, WSC to FDR, June 13, 1942, in Kimball, *Churchill and Roosevelt*, 1:510.

3. Telegram R-158, FDR to WSC, June 13, 1942, in Kimball, *Churchill and Roosevelt*, 1:511.

4. Telegram R-52, FDR to WSC, May 31, 1942, in Kimball, *Churchill and Roosevelt*, 1:503.

5. Matloff and Snell, *Strategic Planning for Coalition Warfare*, 236.

6. Excerpt from Stimson diary, June 17, 1942, *FRUS, The Conferences at Washington, 1941–1942, and Casablanca*, 1943, 421.

7. Churchill, *Hinge of Fate*, 376; Gilbert, *Winston S. Churchill*, 126.

8. Alanbrooke, *War Diaries*, xvi.

9. Alanbrooke, *War Diaries*, 267.

10. Churchill, *Hinge of Fate*, 327.

11. Editorial note, *FRUS, The Conferences at Washington, 1941–1942, and Casablanca, 1943*, 422.

12. Churchill, *Hinge of Fate*, 327.

13. Pawle, *The War and Colonel Warden*, 168.

14. Churchill, *Hinge of Fate*, 327.

15. Memo, WSC to FDR, June 20, 1942, *FRUS, The Conferences at Washington, 1941–1942, and Casablanca, 1943*, 461.

16. Ismay, *The Memoirs of General the Lord Ismay*, 254.

17. "Offensive Operations in 1942 and 1943," Report by the Combined Chiefs of Staff (CCS 83), June 21, 1942, *FRUS, The Conferences at Washington, 1941–1942, and Casablanca, 1943*, 465.

18. Meeting of the Combined Chiefs of Staff (CCS 28th meeting), June 20, 1942, *FRUS, The Conferences at Washington, 1941–1942, and Casablanca, 1943*, 429.

19. Alanbrooke, *War Diaries*, 267–268.

20. Churchill, *Hinge of Fate*, 332; Alanbrooke, *War Diaries*, 267.

21. Gilbert, *Winston S. Churchill*, 128.

22. Ismay, *The Memoirs of General the Lord Ismay*, 254–255.

23. Weinberg, *A World at Arms*, 223.

24. Churchill, *Hinge of Fate*, 332.

25. Roosevelt-Churchill meeting, June 21, 1942, *FRUS, The Conferences at Washington, 1941–1942, and Casablanca, 1943*, 433–435.

26. Alanbrooke, *War Diaries*, 269.

27. Memorandum by Prime Minister Churchill's Chief Staff Officer, June 21, 1942, *FRUS, The Conferences at Washington, 1941–1942, and Casablanca, 1943*, 435.

28. Editorial note (3–228) on Allied Strategic Debates, June 1942, *Papers of George Catlett Marshall*, 3:242–246.

29. Memo (3–229), Marshall to Roosevelt, June 23, 1942, *Papers of George Catlett Marshall*, 3:246–248.

30. Churchill, *Hinge of Fate*, 335.

31. "Churchill Sees American Might in Visit to Camp," *Chicago Tribune*, June 28, 1942.

32. Churchill, *Hinge of Fate*, 336–337; Letter, Churchill to Stimson, June 25, 1942, *FRUS, The Conferences at Washington, 1941–1942, and Casablanca, 1943*, 479.

33. Alanbrooke, *War Diaries*, 272.

34. Pawle, *The War and Colonel Warden*, 170.

35. Radiogram 98259, Brooke to Marshall, June 29, 1942; Radiogram, Marshall to Brooke, June 29, 1942, *Papers of George Catlett Marshall*, 3:257.

36. Alanbrooke, *War Diaries*, 272.

37. White House Press Release, June 27, 1942, *FRUS, The Conferences at Washington, 1941–1942, and Casablanca, 1943*, 482–483.

38. Gilbert, *Winston S. Churchill*, 135.

39. Ismay, *The Memoirs of General the Lord Ismay*, 257.

40. Gilbert, *Winston S. Churchill*, 139.

CHAPTER 25

1. Freud, *Living in the Shadow of the Freud Family*, 276; Spinage, *African Ecology*, 551.

2. D. L. Smith, *The Most Dangerous Animal*, 33.

3. Freud, *Living in the Shadow of the Freud Family*, 137.

4. Freud, *Living in the Shadow of the Freud Family*, 206.

5. Freud, *Living in the Shadow of the Freud Family*, 237.

6. Freud, *Living in the Shadow of the Freud Family*, 259.

7. Freud, *Living in the Shadow of the Freud Family*, 261.

8. Freud, *Living in the Shadow of the Freud Family*, 267.

9. Freud, *Living in the Shadow of the Freud Family*, 269.

10. Freud, *Living in the Shadow of the Freud Family*, 269–270.

11. Freud, *Living in the Shadow of the Freud Family*, 271, 273, 278.

12. Freud, *Living in the Shadow of the Freud Family*, 275.

13. Laskier, *North African Jewry in the Twentieth Century*, 67.

14. Freud, *Living in the Shadow of the Freud Family*, 279.

15. Freud, *Living in the Shadow of the Freud Family*, 287.

CHAPTER 26

1. Waller, *Wild Bill Donovan*, 132.

2. Memo by King, "Further Notes on Port Lyautey Organization," June 2, 1942, HIA, Robert Murphy Papers, Box 46.

3. Pinkeye's Tale, dictated to CSC by Michel Despax, July 15, 1944, NARA, RG 226, Entry A1–99, Box 49, TORCH Anthology; King report, July 19, 1944, NARA, RG 226, Entry A1–99, Box 49, TORCH Anthology; Memo by King, "Further Notes on Port Lyautey Organization," June 2, 1942, HIA, Robert Murphy Papers, Box 46.

4. King report, July 19, 1944, NARA, RG 226, Entry A1–99, Box 49, TORCH Anthology.

5. Pinkeye's Tale, dictated to CSC by Michel Despax, July 15, 1944, USNA, RG 226, Entry A1–99, Box 49, TORCH Anthology.

6. King report, July 19, 1944, NARA, RG 226, Entry A1–99, Box 49, TORCH Anthology; Telegram 543, Russell to Sec State, July 15, 1942, *FRUS*, 1942, 2:338.

7. Letter, Murphy to Atherton, July 6, 1942, HIA, Robert Murphy Papers, Box 46.

8. Paillat, *L'échiquier d'Alger*, 318; Ryder, *Edith Cavell*, 138.

9. Hoisington, *The Assassination of Jacques Lemaigre Dubreuil*, 55; Painton, "Giraud's Brilliant Escape from a Nazi Prison," 39.

10. Scheck, *French Colonial Soldiers in German Captivity During World War II*, 85.

11. Churchill, *Hinge of Fate*, 527.

12. Letter, Murphy to Atherton, July 6, 1942, HIA, Robert Murphy Papers, Box 46.

13. Harris, *Escape from the Legion*, 194.

14. Harris, *Escape from the Legion*, 177.

15. Harris, *Escape from the Legion*, 168–169.

16. Harris, *Escape from the Legion*, 197.

17. Harris, *Escape from the Legion*, 198.

18. Harris, *Escape from the Legion*, 200.

19. Harris, *Escape from the Legion*, 203–204.

20. Harris, *Escape from the Legion*, 201.

21. The biography that accompanies Harris's papers at Churchill College, Cambridge, indicates that he signed up with the Royal Air Force. A personnel file for him in the British National Archives, however, indicates that he worked for the Special Operations Executive.

CHAPTER 27

1. Letter, Eisenhower to Hartle, *PDDE: The War Years*, July 20, 1942. 1:40.

2. Jordan, *Brothers, Rivals, Victors*, 65.

3. Letter, Marshall to Eisenhower, July 30, 1942, *Papers of George Catlett Marshall*, 3–263.

4. Telegram 962, Eisenhower to Marshall, August 7, 1942, in *PDDE: The War Years*, 1:450; Eisenhower, *Crusade in Europe*, Kindle locations 1502–1508; Howe, *Northwest Africa*, 25; Letter, Marshall to Eisenhower, July 30, 1942, *Papers of George Catlett Marshall*, 3–263; Radio No. 3318, Marshall to Eisenhower, August 14, 1942, *Papers of George Catlett Marshall*, 3–278.

5. Letter, Marshall to Eisenhower, July 30, 1942, *Papers of George Catlett Marshall*, 3–263.

6. Matloff and Snell, *Strategic Planning for Coalition Warfare*, 284.

7. Patton diary, August 5, 1942, LOC, Patton Papers.

8. D'Este, *Patton*, 418.

9. John Walsh, "Claridge's: An Opulent Hotel Where Every Corner Tells a Story," *Independent*, December 9, 2012.

10. Patton diary, August 7, 1942, LOC, Patton Papers; Telegram 962, Eisenhower to Marshall, August 7, 1942, in *PDDE: The War Years*, 1:450.

11. Eisenhower, *Crusade in Europe*, Kindle locations 1621–1622.

12. Cable 823, Eisenhower to Marshall, August 1, 1942, in *PDDE, The War Years*, 1:433–436.

13. Eisenhower, *Crusade in Europe*, Kindle locations 1536–1540.

14. Eisenhower, *Crusade in Europe*, Kindle locations 1540–1548; Cable 823, Eisenhower to Marshall, August 1, 1942, in *PDDE, The War Years*, 1:433–436.

15. Eisenhower, *Crusade in Europe*, Kindle location 1557.

16. Patton diary, August 9, 1942, LOC, Patton Papers.

CHAPTER 28

1. Abtey, *La guerre secrète de Joséphine Baker*, #.

2. Rose, *Jazz Cleopatra*, 196; Baker and Bouillon, *Josephine*, 126–128; "Peritonitis," Medline Plus, National Library of Medicine, https://medlineplus.gov/ency/article /001335.htm (retrieved July 16, 2016); "Sepsis," Medline Plus, National Library of Medicine, https://medlineplus.gov/sepsis.html (retrieved July 16, 2016).

3. Haney, *Naked at the Feast*, 225.

4. "The Discovery and Development of Pencillin," American Chemcial Society, https://

www.acs.org/content/acs/en/education/whatischemistry/landmarks/flemingpenicillin.html#us
-penicillin-production.

5. Rose, *Jazz Cleopatra*, 197.

6. Abtey, *La guerre secrète de Joséphine Baker*, 123.

7. Vaughan, *FDR's 12 Apostles*, 112.

8. Abtey, *La guerre secrète de Joséphine Baker*, 123, 125.

9. Abtey, *La guerre secrète de Joséphine Baker*, 126.

10. Vaughan, *FDR's 12 Apostles*, 113, 124; Pendar, *Adventure in Diplomacy*, 20–21; King report, July 19, 1944, NARA, RG 226, Entry A1–99, Box 49, TORCH Anthology.

11. Riding, *And the Show Went On*, Kindle location 1876, 1935.

12. Rosbottom, *When Paris Went Dark*, 124.

13. Riding, *And the Show Went On*, Kindle location 1803, 1885.

14. Riding, *And the Show Went On*, Kindle location 1489.

15. deRochemont, "The French Underground," *LIFE*, 86.

16. Abtey, *La guerre secrète de Joséphine Baker*, 142; Rose, *Jazz Cleopatra*, 197.

17. "Child of Charm," *Chicago Defender*, December 5, 1942.

18. "Chevalier Slated," *Northern Miner*, June 2, 1943.

CHAPTER 29

1. Churchill, *Hinge of Fate*, 413.

2. Telegram C-126A, WSC to FDR, August 4, 1942; Telegram R-173, FDR to WSC, August 5, 1942, in Kimball, *Churchill and Roosevelt*, 1:553.

3. Churchill, *Hinge of Fate*, 414.

4. Churchill, *Hinge of Fate*, 415; Telegram C-129, WSC to FDR, August 13, 1942, in Kimball, *Churchill and Roosevelt*, 1:560.

5. Braithwaite, *Moscow 1941*, 190.

6. Churchill, *Hinge of Fate*, 414.

7. Churchill, *Hinge of Fate*, 415; Telegram C-129, WSC to FDR, August 13, 1942, in Kimball, *Churchill and Roosevelt*, 1:560–561.

8. Kimball, *Forged in War*, Kindle locations 2754–2761.

9. Churchill, *Hinge of Fate*, 415, 420; Telegram C-129, WSC to FDR, August 13, 1942, in Kimball, *Churchill and Roosevelt*, 1:560–561.

10. Alanbrooke, *War Diaries*, 303.

11. Telegram C-131, WSC to FDR, August 15, 1942, in Kimball, *Churchill and Roosevelt*, 1:564–567; Kimball, *Forged in War*, Kindle locations 2779–2788.

12. Telegram C-133, WSC to FDR, August 17, 1942, in Kimball, *Churchill and Roosevelt*, 1:569–570.

13. Churchill, *Hinge of Fate*, 433.

14. Telegram C-134, WSC to FDR, August 18, 1942, in Kimball, *Churchill and Roosevelt*, 1:571; Kimball, *Forged in War*, Kindle locations 2779–2788.

15. Alanbrooke, *War Diaries*, 307.

16. Telegram C-136, WSC to FDR, August 26, 1942, in Kimball, *Churchill and Roosevelt*, 1:575.

17. Howe, *Northwest Africa*, 26; Radio No. R-84, Marshall to Eisenhower, August 24, 1942, Marshall Papers, vol. 3., document 3–291.

18. Alanbrooke, *War Diaries*, 314–315.

19. Alanbrooke, *War Diaries*, 316; Butcher, *My Three Years with Eisenhower*, 49.

20. Churchill, *Hinge of Fate*, 468.

21. Telegram C-140, WSC to FDR, August 30, 1942; Telegram R-180, FDR to WSC, August 30, 1942; Telegram R-181, FDR to WSC, August 30, 1942; Telegram C-141, WSC to FDR, August 31, 1942; Telegram C-142, WSC to FDR, September 1, 1942; Telegram R-182, FDR to WSC, September 2, 1942; Telegram C-143, WSC to FDR, September 3, 1942; Telegram R-183, FDR to WSC, September 4, 1942; Telegram R-184, WSC and FDR, September 4, 1942; Telegram C-144, WSC to FDR, September 5, 1942, all in Kimball, *Churchill and Roosevelt*, 1:576–592.

CHAPTER 30

1. Entries for September 3–8, 1942, "Franklin D. Roosevelt Day by Day," FDR Library, http://www.fdrlibrary.marist.edu/daybyday/timeline/#1942-09-03. Murphy's meeting, like his last one with Roosevelt, is not mentioned in the diaries.

2. Murphy, *Diplomat Among Warriors*, 101.

3. Murphy, *Diplomat Among Warriors*, 102.

4. Murphy, *Diplomat Among Warriors*, 99, 101.

5. Murphy, *Diplomat Among Warriors*, 102–103; Eisenhower, *Crusade in Europe*, Kindle locations 1699–1701. There are different spellings of Murphy's secret identity ("MacGowan" or "McGowan"). I decided to use "MacGowan," as Murphy uses in his memoir and it was his secret identity.

6. Vaughan, *FDR's 12 Apostles*, 113.

7. Murphy, *Diplomat Among Warriors*, 103; Vaughan, *FDR's 12 Apostles*, 112. The two men didn't get on, prompting Coster's reassignment to OSS in Washington, DC.

8. Butcher, *My Three Years with Eisenhower*, 103.

9. Murphy, *Diplomat Among Warriors*, 103–104.

10. Butcher, *My Three Years with Eisenhower*, 106–107.

11. Murphy, *Diplomat Among Warriors*, 103.

12. Eisenhower, *Crusade in Europe*, Kindle location 1708.

13. Murphy, *Diplomat Among Warriors*, 104–105; Eisenhower, *Crusade in Europe*, Kindle locations 1724–1729.

CHAPTER 31

1. Shoemake, *Tangier*, 90–92.

2. Letter, Eddy to Cita, September 14, 1942, Mudd Library Princeton, William A. Eddy Papers, Box 10.

3. Letter, Eddy to Mary, July 25, 1942, Mudd Library Princeton, William A. Eddy Papers, Box 10.

4. Reid memoir, 73, NARA, RG 226, Entry A1–99, Box 45.

5. Murphy, *Diplomat Among Warriors*, 107.

6. Reid memoir, 75, NARA, RG 226, Entry A1–99, Box 45.

7. Interview with King, February 24, 1948, USAHEC, OCMH Collection, Sidney Matthews Papers, Interviews.

8. Interview with King, February 24, 1948, USAHEC, OCMH Collection, Sidney Matthews Papers, Interviews.

9. King report, July 19, 1944, NARA, RG 226, Entry A1–99, Box 49, TORCH Anthology.

10. Brady, *Twelve Desperate Miles*, Kindle location 1073.

11. Brady, *Twelve Desperate Miles*, Kindle locations 1123–1125.

12. Brady, *Twelve Desperate Miles*, Kindle location 1130.

13. Tangier JIC Report, No. 63, TNA, FO371/31914. Note 553, Commissaire spécial du port à Vice-Admiral commandant, March 29, 1941, CADN, 11MA/900/83.

14. Brady, *Twelve Desperate Miles*, Kindle locations 1469–1471.

15. Brady, *Twelve Desperate Miles*, Kindle location 1493.

16. Brady, *Twelve Desperate Miles*, Kindle location 1609.

17. Letter, Eddy to unknown, August 1942, Princeton, Eddy Papers, Box 10.

18. King report, July 19, 1944, NARA, RG 226, Entry A1–99, Box 49, TORCH Anthology.; Memo, Donovan to Joint Security Control, October 7, 1942, USAHEC, William J. Donovan Papers, Box 99A; Waller, *Wild Bill Donovan*, 155.

CHAPTER 32

1. Message (Tangier No. 140), Eisenhower to Clark, October 20, 1942; HIA, Robert Murphy Papers, Box 47.

2. Clark, *Calculated Risk*, 64–66; Key, *Admiral Jerauld Wright*, 140.

3. Atkinson, *An Army at Dawn*, 43; Eisenhower, *Crusade in Europe*, Kindle locations 1491, 1714; Patton diary, September 28, 1942, LOC, Patton Papers; Churchill, *Hinge of Fate*, 335.

4. Clark, *Calculated Risk*, 66.

5. Murphy, *Diplomat Among Warriors*, 111–112.

6. Murphy, *Diplomat Among Warriors*, 112.

7. Murphy, *Diplomat Among Warriors*, 113.

8. Leahy, *I Was There*, 92.

9. Murphy, *Diplomat Among Warriors*, 114.

10. Murphy, *Diplomat Among Warriors*, 115.

11. Letter, Murphy to Giraud, October 27, 1942, HIA, Robert Murphy Papers, Box 45. Langer, *Our Vichy Gamble*, 323–327.

12. Clark, *Calculated Risk*, 67; Key, *Admiral Jerauld Wright*, 143.

13. Clark, *Calculated Risk*, 68; Key, *Admiral Jerauld Wright*, 144.

14. Murphy, *Diplomat Among Warriors*, 119; Clark, *Calculated Risk*, 68–69. Message 6912, Eisenhower to Murphy, October 28, 1942, HIA, Robert Murphy Papers, Box 47.

15. Murphy, *Diplomat Among Warriors*, 119; Clark, *Calculated Risk*, 69.

16. Murphy, *Diplomat Among Warriors*, 119; Clark, *Calculated Risk*, 71.

17. Key, *Admiral Jerauld Wright*, 146.

18. Clark, *Calculated Risk*, 72–73.

19. Clark, *Calculated Risk*, 74. Telegram 95, GIB to London, October 10, 1942, HIA, Robert Murphy Papers, Box 47.

CHAPTER 33

1. Patton diary, October 24, 1942, LOC, Patton Papers; Hewitt, *The Memoirs of Admiral H. Kent Hewitt*, 151.

2. Howe, *Northwest Africa*, 69; Morison, *Operations in North African Waters*, 43–44; Tomblin, *With Utmost Spirit*, Kindle location 356–365.

3. Morison, *Operations in North African Waters*, 41–42.

4. Carter and Duvall, *Ships, Salvage, and Sinews of War*, 145.

5. Morison, *Operations in North African Waters*, 44.

6. Morison, *Operations in North African Waters*, 44; Hewitt, *The Memoirs of Admiral H. Kent Hewitt*, 150.

7. Atkinson, *An Army at Dawn*, 21–22; Howarth, *Men of War*, 313–315.

8. Patton diary, October 26, 1942, LOC, Patton Papers.

9. Blumenson, *The Patton Papers*, Kindle locations 1926–1938.

10. Harold Taylor, "In Service of My Country," 10, USAHEC, Donald J. Peel Papers.

11. Taylor, "In Service of My Country," 10.

12. King report, July 19, 1944, NARA, RG 226, Entry A1–99, Box 49, TORCH Anthology.

13. King report, July 19, 1944, NARA, RG 226, Entry A1–99, Box 49, TORCH Anthology.

14. King report, July 19, 1944, NARA, RG 226, Entry A1–99, Box 49, TORCH Anthology.

15. Reid memoir, 78–79; Pendar, *Adventure in Diplomacy*, 99.

16. Béthouart, *Cinq années d'espérance*, 142, plus Annex II, 343–349; Interview with King, February 24, 1948, USAHEC, OCMH Collection, Sidney Matthews Papers, Interviews.

17. Béthouart, *Cinq années d'espérance*, 142–143; King report, July 19, 1944, NARA, RG 226, Entry A1–99, Box 49, TORCH Anthology; Telegram 78, King to Eddy, November 5, 1942, HIA, Robert Murphy Papers, Box 47.

18. Telegram 79, King to Eddy, November 5, 1942, HIA, Robert Murphy Papers, Box 47; Interview with King, February 24, 1948, USAHEC, OCMH Collection, Sidney Matthews Papers, Interviews.

19. Telegram, Eddy to King, November 6, 1942, HIA, Robert Murphy Papers, Box 47.

20. King report, July 19, 1944, NARA, RG226, Entry A1–99, Box 49, TORCH Anthology; Telegram, Murphy to Eddy for Kingpin, November 7, 1942, HIA, Robert Murphy Papers, Box 47.

21. Telegram 79, King to Eddy, November 5, 1942, HIA, Robert Murphy Papers, Box 47.

22. Telegram, London to Gibraltar (184) and Tangier (126), November 2, 1942, HIA, Robert Murphy Papers, Box 47.

23. King report, July 19, 1944, NARA, RG 226, Entry A1–99, Box 49, TORCH Anthology.

24. Telegram 78, King to Eddy, November 5, 1942, HIA, Robert Murphy Papers, Box 47; King report, July 19, 1944, NARA, RG 226, Entry A1–99, Box 49, TORCH Anthology.

25. Patton diary, November 7, 1942, LOC, Patton Papers.

26. Message by Patton, November 1942, LOC, Patton Papers, Box 45, Folder 16.

27. USS *Augusta*, War Diary for November 1–30, 1942, NARA, RG 38, via Fold3.com.

28. Patton diary, November 7, 1942, LOC, Patton Papers.

CHAPTER 34

1. Clark, *Calculated Risk*, 81; Eisenhower, *Crusade in Europe*, Kindle location 1734.

2. Eisenhower, *Crusade in Europe*, Kindle location 1709; Murphy, *Diplomat Among Warriors*, 122–123.

3. Clark, *Calculated Risk*, 81–82; Atkinson, *An Army at Dawn*, 63–64.

4. Clark, *Calculated Risk*, 82.

5. Telegram 113, London to Agwar, November 8, 1942, FDRL, Map Room, Box 105.

6. Eisenhower, *Crusade in Europe*, 1959.

7. Telegram 132, London to Agwar, November 8, 1942, FDRL, Map Room, Box 105.

8. Clark, *Calculated Risk*, 83.

9. Clark, *Calculated Risk*, 84; Telegram 138, London to Agwar, November 8, 1942, FDRL, Map Room, Box 105.

10. Telegram 113, London to Agwar, November 8, 1942, FDRL, Map Room, Box 105.

11. Eisenhower, *Crusade in Europe*, Kindle locations 1971–1972.

12. Telegram 113, London to Agwar, November 8, 1942, FDRL, Map Room, Box 105.

13. Pinkeye's Tale, dictated to CSC by Michel Despax, July 15, 1944, and King report, July 19, 1944, NARA, RG 226, Entry A1–99, Box 49, TORCH Anthology.

14. King report, July 19, 1944, NARA, RG 226, Entry A1–99, Box 49, TORCH Anthology.

15. Reid interview, NARA, RG 266, Entry A1–99, Box 49, TORCH Anthology; Reid memoir, 76–78, NARA, RG 226, Entry A1–99, Box 45.

16. King report, July 19, 1944, NARA, RG 226, Entry A1–99, Box 49, TORCH Anthology.

17. King report, July 19, 1944, NARA, RG 226, Entry A1–99, Box 49, TORCH Anthology.

18. King report, July 19, 1944, NARA, RG 226, Entry A1–99, Box 49, TORCH Anthology.

CHAPTER 35

1. Béthouart, *Cinq années d'espérance*, 145–146.

2. Levisse-Touzé, *L'Afrique du Nord dans la guerre*, 246.

3. Béthouart, *Cinq années d'espérance*, 149; Béthouart testimony, October 24, 1956, *Le procès du général Noguès*, 31–32.

4. Hoisington, *Casablanca Connection*, 225.

5. Hoisington, *Casablanca Connection*, 226–227.

6. Hoisington, *Casablanca Connection*, 225; Interview with David King, February 24, 1948, USAHEC, OCMH Collection, Sidney Matthews Papers.

7. Levisse-Touzé, *L'Afrique du Nord dans la guerre*, 246.

8. Hoisington, *Casablanca Connection*, 226.

9. Hoisington, *Casablanca Connection*, 226.

10. Morison, *Operations in North African Waters*, 70.

11. Reid memoir, 81, NARA, RG 226, Entry A1–99, Box 45.

12. Reid memoir, 83, NARA, RG 226, Entry A1–99, Box 45.

13. *Foreign Office List*, 1939, 330.

14. Reid memoir, 84, NARA, RG 226, Entry A1–99, Box 45.

15. Reid memoir, 89, NARA, RG 226, Entry A1–99, Box 45.

16. Unpublished memoir by Reid, 233, HIA, W. Stafford Reid Papers.

17. Letter, Russell to Hull, November 12, 1942, NARA, RG 59, 740.0011EW/26336, Roll 142.

18. Letter, Russell to Hull, November 12, 1942, NARA, RG 59, 740.0011EW/26336, Roll 142; Béthouart, *Cinq années d'espérance*, 150.

19. Levisse-Touzé, *L'Afrique du Nord dans la guerre*, 246.

CHAPTER 36

1. Report (A16–3/0047) by Commander of Southern Attack Group, "Operation TORCH, Assault on Safi, French Morocco, November 8, 1942," November 24, 1942, NARA, RG 38, via Fold3.com.

2. Letter, Patton to Harmon, October 10, 1942, LOC, Patton Papers, Box 45, Folder 16.

3. Morison, *Operations in North African Waters*, 137.

4. Park and Boum, *Historical Dictionary of Morocco*, 313–314.

5. Morison, *Operations in North African Waters*, 137.

6. Howe, *Northwest Africa*, 97.

7. Howe, *Northwest Africa*, 99–100; Morison, *Operations in North African Waters*, 138.

8. Howe, *Northwest Africa*, 102.

9. Report (A16–3/0047) by Commander of Southern Attack Group, "Operation TORCH, Assault on Safi, French Morocco, November 8, 1942," November 24, 1942, NARA, RG 38, via Fold3.com.

10. Morison, *Operations in North African Waters*, 59; Howe, *Northwest Africa*, 123.

11. Morison, *Operations in North African Waters*, 140; Howe, *Northwest Africa*, 103.

12. Howe, *Northwest Africa*, 104; Report (A16–3/0047) by Commander of Southern Attack Group, "Operation TORCH, Assault on Safi, French Morocco, November 8, 1942," November 24, 1942, NARA, RG 38, via Fold3.com; Carter and Duvall, *Ships, Salvage, and Sinews of War*, 176.

13. Report (A16–3/0047) by Commander of Southern Attack Group, "Operation TORCH, Assault on Safi, French Morocco, 8 November 1942," November 24, 1942, NARA, RG 38, via Fold3.com.

14. Morison, *Operations in North African Waters*, 145.

15. Morison, *Operations in North African Waters*, 145; Report (A16–3/0047) by Commander of Southern Attack Group, "Operation TORCH, Assault on Safi, French Morocco, November 8, 1942," November 24, 1942, NARA, RG 38, via Fold3.com.

16. Morison, *Operations in North African Waters*, 146.

17. Morison, *Operations in North African Waters*, 146; Howe, *Northwest Africa*, 105.

18. Morison, *Operations in North African Waters*, 147; Report (A16–3/0047) by Commander of Southern Attack Group, "Operation TORCH, Assault on Safi, French Morocco, 8 November 1942," November 24, 1942, 9, NARA, RG 38, via Fold3.com.

19. Report (A16–3/0047) by Commander of Southern Attack Group, "Operation TORCH, Assault on Safi, French Morocco, 8 November 1942," November 24, 1942, NARA, RG 38, via Fold3.com.

20. Morison, *Operations in North African Waters*, 146; Howe, *Northwest Africa*, 105.

21. Report (A16–3/0047) by Commander of Southern Attack Group, "Operation TORCH, Assault on Safi, French Morocco, 8 November 1942," November 24, 1942, NARA, RG 38, via Fold3.com.

22. Howe, *Northwest Africa*, 107.

23. Howe, *Northwest Africa*, 109.

24. Carter and Duvall, *Ships, Salvage, and Sinews of War*, 178.

25. Carter and Duvall, *Ships, Salvage, and Sinews of War*, 179.

26. Morison, *Operations in North African Waters*, 149; Report (A16–3/0047) by Commander of Southern Attack Group, "Operation TORCH, Assault on Safi, French Morocco, 8 November 1942," November 24, 1942, 3, NARA, RG 38, via Fold3.com.

CHAPTER 37

1. Action Report (CA31/A16–3), "U.S.S. *Augusta*, Casablanca-Fedala Area, French Morocco, 8–10 November 1942," November 29, 1942, NARA, RG 38, via Fold3.com; Morison,

Operations in North African Waters, 59; Howe, *Northwest Africa*, 123; Hewitt, *The Memoirs of Admiral H. Kent Hewitt*, 171.

2. Morison, *Operations in North African Waters*, 59; Howe, *Northwest Africa*, 123.

3. Morison, *Operations in North African Waters*, 142; Howe, *Northwest Africa*, 102–103.

4. Quoted in Morison, *Operations in North African Waters*, 72.

5. Howe, *Northwest Africa*, 125; "General Eisenhower's Proclamation," *New York Times*, November 8, 1942.

6. Atkinson, *An Army at Dawn*, 106.

7. Morison, *Operations in North African Waters*, 78; Letter, Patton to Anderson, October 10, 1942, LOC, Patton Papers, Box 45, Folder 16.

8. Howe, *Northwest Africa*, 117; *Les guides bleu: Maroc* (1936), 107–110.

9. Howe, *Northwest Africa*, 118; Interview with David King, February 24, 1948, USAHEC, OCMH Collection, Sidney Matthews Papers.

10. Morison, *Operations in North African Waters*, 58.

11. Morison, *Operations in North African Waters*, 56; Howe, *Northwest Africa*, 118.

12. Morison, *Operations in North African Waters*, 65.

13. Report (0F7–26/A4–3/A16–3) by Commander Destroyer Division 26, "Action Against Vichy French Forces Off Fedhala, French Morocco," December 9, 1942, NARA, RG 38, via Fold3.com.

14. Morison, *Operations in North African Waters*, 73.

15. Morison, *Operations in North African Waters*, 65; Action Report (CA31/A16–3), "U.S.S. *Augusta*, Casablanca-Fedala Area, French Morocco, 8–10 November 1942," November 29, 1942, NARA, RG 38, via Fold3.com.

16. Howe, *Northwest Africa*, 123–124.

17. Morison, *Operations in North African Waters*, 74.

18. Morison, *Operations in North African Waters*, 76; Tomblin, *With Utmost Spirit*, Kindle locations 519–520.

19. Action Report (CA31/A16–3), "U.S.S. *Augusta*, Casablanca-Fedala Area, French Morocco, 8–10 November 1942," November 29, 1942, NARA, RG 38, via Fold3.com.

20. Report (0F7–26/A4–3/A16–3) by Commander Destroyer Division 26, "Action Against Vichy French Forces Off Fedhala, French Morocco," December 9, 1942, NARA, RG 38, via Fold3.com.

21. Action Report (CA31/A16–3), "U.S.S. *Augusta*, Casablanca-Fedala Area, French Morocco, 8–10 November 1942," November 29, 1942, NARA, RG 38, via Fold3.com.

22. Citation for William H. Wilbur's Medal of Honor, bestowed January 13, 1943, US Army Center of Military History, http://www.history.army.mil//html/moh/wwII-t-z.html #WILBUR; Howe, *Northwest Africa*, 96; Morison, *Operations in North African Waters*, 110; Atkinson, *An Army at Dawn*, 137.

23. Howe, *Northwest Africa*, 128.

24. Patton diary, November 8, 1942, LOC, Patton Papers; Hewitt, *The Memoirs of Admiral H. Kent Hewitt*, 162–163.

CHAPTER 38

1. Morison, *Operations in North African Waters*, 88; Action Report (CA31/A16–3), "U.S.S. *Augusta*, Casablanca-Fedala Area, French Morocco, 8–10 November 1942," November 29, 1942, NARA, RG 38, via Fold3.com.

2. Morison, *Operations in North African Waters*, 89.

3. Morison, *Operations in North African Waters*, 89.

4. Auphan and Mordal, *The French Navy in World War II*, 230; Action Report (CA31/A16–3), "U.S.S. *Augusta*, Casablanca-Fedala Area, French Morocco, 8–10 November 1942," November 29, 1942, NARA, RG 38, via Fold3.com.

5. Auphan and Mordal, *The French Navy in World War II*, 230.

6. Morison, *Operations in North African Waters*, 91, 93.

7. Auphan and Mordal, *The French Navy in World War II*, 228.

8. Morison, *Operations in North African Waters*, 96.

9. Tomblin, *With Utmost Spirit*, Kindle locations 539–545; Morison, *Operations in North African Waters*, 96.

10. Morison, *Operations in North African Waters*, 96–97.

11. Morison, *Operations in North African Waters*, 99; Auphan and Mordal, *The French Navy in World War II*, 232.

12. Action Report (CA31/A16–3), "U.S.S. *Augusta*, Casablanca-Fedala Area, French Morocco, 8–10 November 1942," November 29, 1942, NARA, RG 38, via Fold3.com.

13. Patton diary, November 8, 1942, LOC, Patton Papers.

14. D'Este, *Patton*, 434.

15. Morison, *Operations in North African Waters*, 101; Action Report (CA31/A16–3), "U.S.S. *Augusta*, Casablanca-Fedala Area, French Morocco, 8–10 November 1942," November 29, 1942, NARA, RG 38, via Fold3.com.

16. Morison, *Operations in North African Waters*, 104.

17. Morison, *Operations in North African Waters*, 105; Action Report (CA31/A16–3), "U.S.S. *Augusta*, Casablanca-Fedala Area, French Morocco, 8–10 November 1942," November 29, 1942, NARA, RG 38, via Fold3.com.

18. Morison, *Operations in North African Waters*, 106; Auphan and Mordal, *The French Navy in World War II*, 233.

19. Action Report (CA31/A16–3), "U.S.S. *Augusta*, Casablanca-Fedala Area, French Morocco, 8–10 November 1942," November 29, 1942, NARA, RG 38, via Fold3.com.

20. Morison, *Operations in North African Waters*, 107; Auphan and Mordal, *The French Navy in World War II*, 233; Action Report (CA31/A16–3), "U.S.S. *Augusta*, Casablanca-Fedala Area, French Morocco, 8–10 November 1942," November 29, 1942, NARA, RG 38, via Fold3.com.

21. Morison, *Operations in North African Waters*, 107–108.

22. D'Este, *Patton*, 435.

23. Interview of Lieutenant Colonel Francis M. Rogers by Lieutenant Porter, February 4, 1944, NARA, RG 38, via Fold3.com.

24. Morison, *Operations in North African Waters*, 110.

25. Interview of Lieutenant Colonel Francis M. Rogers by Lieutenant Porter, February 4, 1944, NARA, RG 38, via Fold3.com.

26. Morison, *Operations in North African Waters*, 108.

27. Morison, *Operations in North African Waters*, 109; Action Report (CA31/A16–3), "U.S.S. *Augusta*, Casablanca-Fedala Area, French Morocco, 8–10 November 1942," November 29, 1942, NARA, RG 38, via Fold3.com.

28. Unpublished memoir by Reid, 240, HIA, W. Stafford Reid Papers.

29. Auphan and Mordal, *The French Navy in World War II*, 233.

30. Morison, *Operations in North African Waters*, 111.

31. Auphan and Mordal, *The French Navy in World War II*, 234.

32. Morison, *Operations in North African Waters*, 79, 82.

33. Patton diary, November 8, 1942, LOC, Patton Papers.

CHAPTER 39

1. Reid memoir, 89, NARA, RG 226, Entry A1–99, Box 45; Letter, Russell to Hull, November 12, 1942, NARA, RG 59, 740.0011EW/26336, Roll 142; Message 3495, AFHQ to AGWAR, October 13, 1942, HIA, Robert Murphy Papers, Box 47. Leaflet in personal collection.

2. Letter, Russell to Hull, November 12, 1942, NARA, RG 59, 740.0011EW/26336, Roll 142.

3. Reid memoir, 90, NARA, RG 226, Entry A1–99, Box 45; Letter, Russell to Hull, November 12, 1942, NARA, RG 59, 740.0011EW/26336, Roll 142.

4. Reid memoir, 90–91, NARA, RG 226, Entry A1–99, Box 45; King report, July 19, 1944, NARA, RG 226, Entry A1–99, Box 49, TORCH Anthology.

5. Unpublished memoir by Reid, 238–241, HIA, W. Stafford Reid Papers.

6. Reid memoir, 91, NARA, RG 226, Entry A1–99, Box 45; Letter, Russell to Hull, November 12, 1942, NARA, RG 59, 740.0011EW/26336, Roll 142.

7. Reid memoir, 93, NARA, RG 226, Entry A1–99, Box 45; Unpublished memoir by Reid, 242, HIA, W. Stafford Reid Papers.

8. Letter, Russell to Hull, November 12, 1942, NARA, RG 59, 740.0011EW/26336, Roll 142.

9. Reid memoir, 94, NARA, RG 226, Entry A1–99, Box 45.

10. King report, July 19, 1944, NARA, RG 266, Entry A1–99, Box 49, TORCH Anthology.

11. Reid memoir, 91–92, NARA, RG 226, Entry A1–99, Box 45.

12. Reid memoir, 92, 96, NARA, RG 226, Entry A1–99, Box 45.

13. Letter, Russell to Hull, November 12, 1942, NARA, RG 59, 740.0011EW/26336, Roll 142.

14. King report, July 19, 1944, NARA, RG 266, Entry A1–99, Box 49, TORCH Anthology; Interview with King, February 24, 1948, USAHEC, OCMH Collection, Sidney Matthews Papers, Interviews.

15. Letter, Russell to Hull, November 12, 1942, NARA, RG 59, 740.0011EW/26336, Roll 142.

16. King report, July 19, 1944, NARA, RG 226, Entry A1–99, Box 49, TORCH Anthology.

17. Reid memoir, 97, NARA, RG 226, Entry A1–99, Box 45.

18. King report, July 19, 1944, NARA, RG 226, Entry A1–99, Box 49, TORCH Anthology.

CHAPTER 40

1. Report (FB7–5/A16–3) by Commander Transport Division Five, "Operation TORCH; Action Report," December 3, 1942, 1–2, NARA, RG 38, via Fold3.com.

2. Morison, *Operations in North African Waters*, 121; Truscott, *Command Missions*, Kindle location 1820; Interview with General Harry Semmes, March 9, 1950, USAHEC, OCMH Collection, Sidney Matthews Papers.

3. Truscott, *Command Missions*, Kindle location 1823.

4. Tomblin, *With Utmost Spirit*, Kindle location 446; Truscott, *Command Missions*, Kindle location 1803; Operation TORCH Action Report (FB7–5/A16–3), Commander Transport Division Five, December 3, 1942, NARA, RG 38, via Fold3.com.

5. Memo, Patton to Truscott, October 10, 1942, LOC, Patton Papers, Box 45, Folder 16.

6. *Le guide bleu: Maroc*, 260.

7. Howe, *Northwest Africa*, 153; Morison, *Operations in North African Waters*, 121.

8. Morison, *Operations in North African Waters*, 122; Tomblin, *With Utmost Spirit*, Kindle locations 432–446; Howe, *Northwest Africa*, 152; Report (FB7–5/A16–3) by Commander Transport Division Five, "Operation TORCH; Action Report," December 3, 1942, NARA, RG 38, via Fold3.com.

9. Morison, *Operations in North African Waters*, 122.

10. Morison, *Operations in North African Waters*, 123; Tomblin, *With Utmost Spirit*, Kindle location 457; Truscott, *Command Missions*, Kindle location 1837.

11. Morison, *Operations in North African Waters*, 123.

12. Morison, *Operations in North African Waters*, 123.

13. Howe, *Northwest Africa*, 154–155; Truscott, *Command Missions*, Kindle location 1740.

14. Howe, *Northwest Africa*, 154–155; Atkinson, *An Army at Dawn*, 143.

15. Morison, *Operations in North African Waters*, 124.

16. Tomblin, *With Utmost Spirit*, Kindle location 490.

17. Truscott, *Command Missions*, Kindle location 2127; Howe, *Northwest Africa*, 160.

18. Howe, *Northwest Africa*, 160.

19. Interview with General Harry Semmes, March 9, 1950, USAHEC, OCMH Collection, Sidney Matthews Papers.

20. Truscott, *Command Missions*, Kindle locations 2184–2185.

CHAPTER 41

1. Mayars, *FDR's Ambassadors and the Diplomacy of Crisis*, 154.

2. Telegram 685, Vichy to State, November 8, 1942, FDRL, Map Room, Box 105.

3. Telegram 1651, Tuck to State, November 8, 1942, FRUS, 1942, 2:202.

CHAPTER 42

1. Carter and Duvall, *Ships, Salvage, and Sinews of War*, 178–179.

2. Report (A16–3/0047) by Commander of Southern Attack Group, "Operation TORCH, Assault on Safi, French Morocco, 8 November 1942," November 24, 1942, NARA, RG 38, via Fold3.com.

3. Howe, *Northwest Africa*, 110; Report (A16–3/0047) by Commander of Southern Attack Group, "Operation TORCH, Assault on Safi, French Morocco, 8 November 1942," November 24, 1942, NARA, RG 38, via Fold3.com.

4. Howe, *Northwest Africa*, 110.

5. Report (A16–3/0047) by Commander of Southern Attack Group, "Operation TORCH, Assault on Safi, French Morocco, 8 November 1942," November 24, 1942, NARA, RG 38, via Fold3.com.

6. Tomblin, *With Utmost Spirit*, Kindle locations 784–791.

7. Béthouart, *Cinq années d'espérance*, 146.

8. Howe, *Northwest Africa*, 111.

9. Howe, *Northwest Africa*, 112; Memo, Lemeitzer to C-in-C, November 13, 1942, NARA, RG 331, AFHQ, Box 73.

10. Howe, *Northwest Africa*, 114.

11. Tomblin, *With Utmost Spirit*, Kindle locations 773–780.

12. Patton diary, November 9, 1942, LOC, Patton Papers.

13. Tomblin, *With Utmost Spirit*, Kindle locations 762–764.

14. Howe, *Northwest Africa*, 139.

15. Truscott, *Command Missions*, Kindle location 2209.

16. Howe, *Northwest Africa*, 161; Morison, *Operations in North African Waters*, 127.

17. Morison, *Operations in North African Waters*, 126.

18. Howe, *Northwest Africa*, 161.

19. Interview with General Harry Semmes, March 9, 1950, USAHEC, OCMH Collection, Sidney Matthews Papers; Howe, *Northwest Africa*, 161; Tomblin, *With Utmost Spirit*, Kindle locations 780–784.

20. Truscott, *Command Missions*, Kindle locations 2214–2225.

21. Truscott, *Command Missions*, Kindle locations 2233–2242.

22. Truscott, *Command Missions*, Kindle locations 2257–2262.

23. Howe, *Northwest Africa*, 162; Letter, Patton to Cannon, October 10, 1942, LOC, Patton Papers, Box 45, Folder 16.

24. Truscott, *Command Missions*, Kindle locations 2270–2271; Howe, *Northwest Africa*, 163.

25. Truscott, *Command Missions*, Kindle locations 2294–2299.

26. Howe, *Northwest Africa*, 141.

27. Hoisington, *Casablanca Connection*, 228–229.

CHAPTER 43

1. Reid memoir, 97, NARA, RG 226, Entry A1–99, Box 45; Unpublished memoir by Reid, 247, HIA, W. Stafford Reid Papers.

2. King report, July 19, 1944, NARA, RG 226, Entry A1–99, Box 49, TORCH Anthology.

3. Radio log of American invasion of French Morocco, November 8–10, 1942, NARA, RG 226, Entry A1–99, Box 45.

4. Letter, Russell to Hull, November 12, 1942, NARA, RG 59, 740.0011EW/26336, Roll 142.

5. Reid memoir, 98, NARA, RG 226, Entry A1–99, Box 45; Letter, Russell to Hull, November 12, 1942; NARA, RG 59, 740.0011EW/26336, Roll 142.

6. King report, July 19, 1944, NARA, RG 226, Entry A1–99, Box 49, TORCH Anthology; Interview with Stafford Reid, July 1943, 17, NARA, RG 226, Entry A1–99, Box 49, TORCH Anthology.

7. Unpublished memoir by Reid, 250, HIA, W. Stafford Reid Papers; Letter, Russell to Hull, November 12, 1942, NARA, RG 59, 740.0011EW/26336, Roll 142.

8. Reid memoir, 99, NARA, RG 226, Entry A1–99, Box 45; Letter, Russell to Hull, November 12, 1942, NARA, RG 59, 740.0011EW/26336, Roll 142.

9. Reid memoir, 100, NARA, RG 226, Entry A1–99, Box 45; Telegram 871, Russell to State, November 14, 1942, FRUS, 1942, 2:440.

10. Unpublished memoir by Reid, 199–200, HIA, W. Stafford Reid Papers.

11. Unpublished memoir by Reid, 250–251, HIA, W. Stafford Reid Papers.

12. Reid memoir, 102, NARA, RG 226, Entry A1–99, Box 45.

13. Reid memoir, 103, NARA, RG 226, Entry A1–99, Box 45; Unpublished memoir by Reid, 253, HIA, W. Stafford Reid Papers.

14. Reid memoir, 103, NARA, RG 226, Entry A1–99, Box 45; Letter, Russell to Hull, November 12, 1942, NARA, RG 84, Entry 2997, Box 63.

15. King report, July 19, 1944, NARA, RG 226, Entry A1–99, Box 49, TORCH Anthology.

16. Letter, Russell to Hull, November 12, 1942, NARA, RG 59, 740.0011EW/26336, Roll 142.

17. Reid memoir, 104–105, NARA, RG 226, Entry A1–99, Box 45.

18. Interview with Stafford Reid, July 1943, 17, NARA, RG 226, Entry A1–99, Box 49, TORCH Anthology.

19. Statement by President Roosevelt, November 9, 1942, *FRUS*, 1942, 2:202.

CHAPTER 44

1. Howe, *Northwest Africa*, 142; Noguès proclamation, *La Vigie marocaine*, November 8, 1942.

2. Howe, *Northwest Africa*, 142–143.

3. Morison, *Operations in North African Waters*, 163.

4. Howe, *Northwest Africa*, 145.

5. Report (A16–3/0047) by Commander of Southern Attack Group, "Operation TORCH, Assault on Safi, French Morocco, 8 November 1942," November 24, 1942, NARA, RG 38, via Fold3.com; Howe, *Northwest Africa*, 114–115.

6. Howe, *Northwest Africa*, 164.

7. War Diary, USS *Dallas*, November 1942, NARA, RG 38, via Fold3.com.

8. Tomblin, *With Utmost Spirit*, 48; Howe, *Northwest Africa*, 165; Morison, *Operations in North African Waters*, 129; War Diary, USS *Dallas*, November 1942, NARA, RG 38, via Fold3.com.

9. Morison, *Operations in North African Waters*, 131; Howe, *Northwest Africa*, 165; War Diary, USS *Dallas*, November 1942, NARA, RG 38, via Fold3.com.

10. Howe, *Northwest Africa*, 166.

11. Tomblin, *With Utmost Spirit*, 48.

12. Brady, *Twelve Desperate Miles*, 282.

13. Howe, *Northwest Africa*, 167; Truscott, *Command Missions*, Kindle location 2329.

14. Howe, *Northwest Africa*, 169; Truscott, *Command Missions*, Kindle location 2350.

15. Howe, *Northwest Africa*, 171; Hoisington, *Casablanca Connection*, 229.

16. Hoisington, *Casablanca Connection*, 230.

17. Howe, *Northwest Africa*, 171.

CHAPTER 45

1. King report, July 19, 1944, NARA, RG 226, Entry A1–99, Box 49, TORCH Anthology.

2. Howe, *Northwest Africa*, 145.

3. King report, July 19, 1944, NARA, RG 226, Entry A1–99, Box 49, TORCH Anthology.

4. Letter, Russell to Hull, November 12, 1942, NARA, RG 59, 740.0011EW/26336, Roll 142.

5. Letter, Russell to Hull, November 12, 1942, NARA, RG 59, 740.0011EW/26336, Roll 142.

6. Reid memoir, 108, NARA, RG 226, Entry A1–99, Box 45.

7. Letter, Russell to Hull, November 12, 1942, NARA, RG 59, 740.0011EW/26336, Roll 142.

8. Reid memoir, 110, NARA, RG 226, Entry A1–99, Box 45.

CHAPTER 46

1. Howe, *Northwest Africa*, 171.

2. Telegram 251, Eisenhower to Patton, November 10, 1942, *PDDE: The War Years*, 2:684–685.

3. Morison, *Operations in North African Waters*, 164; Howe, *Northwest Africa*, 171.

4. Patton diary, November 11, 1942, LOC, Patton Papers.

5. Reid memoir, 111, NARA, RG 226, Entry A1–99, Box 45; Unpublished memoir by Reid, HIA, W. Stafford Reid Papers, 261.

6. Unpublished memoir by Reid, HIA, W. Stafford Reid Papers, 262.

7. Unpublished memoir by Reid, HIA, W. Stafford Reid Papers, 263.

8. Letter, Heath to Helen, November 22, 1942, USHMM, AFSC, North Africa, Box 1, Folder 29.

9. Letter, Russell to Hull, November 12, 1942, NARA, RG 59, 740.0011EW/26336, Roll 142.

10. Reid memoir, 112–113, NARA, RG 226, Entry A1–99, Box 45.

11. Telegram 871, Russell to State, November 14, 1942, *FRUS*, 1942, 2:440; Telegram, Culbert to Gibraltar, November 12, 1942, HIA, Robert Murphy Papers, Box 47; Unpublished memoir by Reid, HIA, W. Stafford Reid Papers, 264.

12. King report, July 19, 1944, NARA, RG 226, Entry A1–99, Box 49, TORCH Anthology.

13. Interview with King, February 24, 1948, USAHEC, OCMH Collection, Sidney Matthews Papers, Interviews.

14. Hewitt, *The Memoirs of Admiral H. Kent Hewitt*, 165.

15. Hewitt, *The Memoirs of Admiral H. Kent Hewitt*, 165–166; Interview with Captain Leo S. Bachman, January 16, 1951, USAHEC, OCMH Collection, Sidney Matthews Papers.

16. Patton diary, November 11, 1942, LOC, Patton Papers.

17. Letter, Patton to Stimson, December 7, 1942, in Blumenson, *The Patton Papers*, Kindle locations 2216–2217.

18. Patton diary, November 11, 1942, LOC, Patton Papers.

19. Howe, *Northwest Africa*, 173–174; Hoisington, *Casablanca Connection*, 233.

20. Telegram 363, Eisenhower to CCOS, November 12, 1942, in *PDDE: The War Years*, 2:696–697.

21. Letter, Patton to Stimson, December 7, 1942, in Blumenson, *The Patton Papers*, Kindle locations 2216–2217; Letter, Patton to Beatrice Patton, November 11, 1942, in Blumenson, *The Patton Papers*, Kindle locations 2204–2210.

22. Letter, Patton to Eisenhower, November 14, 1942, in Blumenson, *The Patton Papers*, Kindle location 2284.

23. Unpublished memoir by Reid, 266, HIA, W. Stafford Reid Papers.

24. Reid memoir, 112–113, NARA, RG 226, Entry A1–99, Box 45, 116.

25. Reid memoir, 112–113, NARA, RG 226, Entry A1–99, Box 45, 117.

26. Letter, Russell to Hull, November 12, 1942, NARA, RG 59, 740.0011EW/26336, Roll 142.

CHAPTER 47

1. Howe, *Northwest Africa*, 249; Pendar, *Adventure in Diplomacy*, 101.

2. Murphy, *Diplomat Among Warriors*, 125.

3. Howe, *Northwest Africa*, 249.

4. Murphy, *Diplomat Among Warriors*, 128.

5. Murphy, *Diplomat Among Warriors*, 129.

6. Murphy, *Diplomat Among Warriors*, 129.

7. Murphy, *Diplomat Among Warriors*, 130.

8. Murphy, *Diplomat Among Warriors*, 130; Howe, *Northwest Africa*, 249.

9. Pendar, *Adventure in Diplomacy*, 107.

10. Murphy, *Diplomat Among Warriors*, 131.

11. Murphy, *Diplomat Among Warriors*, 131; Pendar, *Adventure in Diplomacy*, 109; Letter, Murphy to Murray, June 7, 1943, HIA, Robert Murphy Papers, Box 44.

12. Letter, Murphy to Murray, June 7, 1943, HIA, Robert Murphy Papers, Box 44.

13. Pendar, *Adventure in Diplomacy*, 110.

14. Telegram 117, London to Agwar, November 8, 1942; Telegram 129, London to Agwar Washington, November 8, 1942, FDRL, Map Room, Box 105; Murphy, *Diplomat Among Warriors*, 133–134.

15. Howe, *Northwest Africa*, 251.

16. Murphy, *Diplomat Among Warriors*, 132.

17. Murphy, *Diplomat Among Warriors*, 133; Message Agwar 31, London to Agwar, November 9, 1942, FDRL, Map Room, Box 105.

CHAPTER 48

1. Clark, *Calculated Risk*, 88; Key, *Admiral Jerauld Wright*, 165; Message 361, Eisenhower to Agwar, November 12, 1942, FDRL, Map Room, Box 105.

2. Langer, *Our Vichy Gamble*, 351.

3. Murphy, *Diplomat Among Warriors*, 135–136.

4. Clark, *Calculated Risk*, 89.

5. Letter, Eisenhower to Murphy, November 9, 1942, HIA, Robert Murphy Papers, Box 44.

6. Message 203, London to Agwar, November 9, 1942, FDRL, Map Room, Box 105.

7. Telegram 4862, November 8, 1942, FDRL, Map Room, Box 105.

8. Murphy, *Diplomat Among Warriors*, 136.

9. Key, *Admiral Jerauld Wright*, 167; Clark, *Calculated Risk*, 89.

10. Clark, *Calculated Risk*, 91.

11. Langer, *Our Vichy Gamble*, 353; Message 286, London to Agwar, November 11, 1942, FDRL, Map Room, Box 105.

12. Murphy, *Diplomat Among Warriors*, 138.

13. Langer, *Our Vichy Gamble*, 354.

14. Langer, *Our Vichy Gamble*, 355.

15. Message, Eisenhower to Marshall, November 11, 1942, FDRL, Map Room, Box 105; Ambrose, *Supreme Commander*, 122.

16. Langer, *Our Vichy Gamble*, 355.

17. Cable 363, Eisenhower to CCS, November 12, 1942, in *PDDE: The War Years*, 2:696.

18. Murphy, *Diplomat Among Warriors*, 138.

19. Langer, *Our Vichy Gamble*, 356.

20. Message 286, London to Agwar, November 11, 1942, FDRL, Map Room, Box 105.

21. Clark, *Calculated Risk*, 100.

22. Pendar, *Adventure in Diplomacy*, 119.

23. Message 506, Eisenhower to Agwar, November 14, 1942, FDRL, Map Room, Box 105; Eisenhower, *Crusade in Europe*, Kindle location 2062.

CHAPTER 49

1. Message 431, London to Agwar, November 13, 1942, FDRL, Map Room, Box 105.

2. Cable 613, Eisenhower to Clark, November 12, 1942; Cable 425, Eisenhower to Marshall, November 13, 1942, in *PDDE: The War Years*, 2:698, 2:705.

3. Message 442, Eisenhower to Agwar, November 13, 1942, FDRL, Map Room, Box 105.

4. Message 527, Eisenhower to Agwar, November 14, 1942, FDRL, Map Room, Box 105; Murphy, *Diplomat Among Warriors*, 140.

5. Eisenhower, *Crusade in Europe*, Kindle locations 2082–2083.

6. Butcher, *My Three Years with Eisenhower*, 190–193.

7. Eisenhower, *Crusade in Europe*, Kindle locations 2063–2068; Murphy, *Diplomat Among Warriors*, 139.

8. Message 527, Eisenhower to Agwar, November 14, 1942, FDRL, Map Room, Box 105.

9. Message 527, Eisenhower to Agwar, November 14, 1942, FDRL, Map Room, Box 105.

10. Cable 722, Eisenhower to CCS, November 16, 1942, in *PDDE: The War Years*, 2:722.

11. Cable 623, Eisenhower to Churchill, November 14, 1942, in *PDDE: The War Years*, 2:711.

12. Message, WSC to FDR, November 17, 1942, *FRUS*, 1942, 2:445.

13. Telegram, Foreign Office to State Department, November 17, 1942, *FRUS*, 1942, 2:445–447.

14. Rosenman, *Public Papers and Addresses of Franklin D. Roosevelt*, 479–480.

15. Message 1229, Gibraltar to Agwar, November 24, 1942; Message R-3657, Marshall to Eisenhower, November 27, 1942, FDRL, Map Room, Box 105.

16. Cable 836, Eisenhower to Smith, November 18, 1942, in *PDDE: The War Years*, 2:732–734.

17. Eisenhower, *Crusade in Europe*, Kindle location 2094.

18. Murphy, *Diplomat Among Warriors*, 139.

19. Clark, *Calculated Risk*, 90.

CHAPTER 50

1. *La Vigie marocaine*, November 11, 1942.

2. "Télégramme adressé par M. P. Laval au général Noguès" and "Message de Maréchal Pétain au Président Roosevelt," *La Vigie marocaine*, November 8, 1942.

3. Front page banner of *La Vigie marocaine*; "Le S.O.L. est pour la pureté française contre la lèpre juive," *La Vigie marocaine*, November 9, 1942.

4. "Proclamation du chanceller Hitler et message au Maréchal Pétain," *La Vigie marocaine*, November 11, 1942.

5. "Une proclamation du général Noguès," *La Vigie marocaine*, November 12, 1942.

6. Edition speciale, *La Vigie marocaine*, November 14, 1942.

7. French-English Words and Phrases, Supply Plans and Data, Western Task Force, vol. 1, August to November 1942, HIA, Walter Muller Papers, Box 1.

8. Arabic-English Words and Phrases, Supply Plans and Data, Western Task Force, vol. 1, August to November 1942, HIA, Walter Muller Papers, Box 1.

9. Supply Plans and Data, Western Task Force, vol. 1, August to November 1942, HIA, Walter Muller Papers, Box 1.

10. Patton diary, November 18, 1942, LOC, Patton Papers.

11. Alanbrooke, *War Diaries*, 360.

12. Blumenson, *The Patton Papers*, Kindle Locations 2357–2358.

13. Howe, *Northwest Africa*, 179–180.

14. Cable 977, Eisenhower to OPD, November 20, 1942, in *PDDE: The War Years*, 2:742.

15. Hewitt, *The Memoirs of Admiral H. Kent Hewitt*, 169.

16. Leighton and Coakley, *Global Logistics and Strategy*, 452.

17. "Avis aux employés des forces militaires des Etats-Unis," HIA, Walter Muller Papers, Box 1; Cable 836, Eisenhower to Smith, November 18, 1942, in *PDDE: The War Years*, 2:733.

18. War Diary, USS *Augusta*, November 15, 1942, NARA, RG 38, via Fold3.com.

19. Supply Plans and Data, Western Task Force, vol. 1, August to November 1942, HIA, Walter Muller Papers, Box 1; Craven and Cate, *Europe: TORCH to POINTBLANK*, 83. The 31,790 number comes from Howe, *Northwest Africa*, Appendix A.

20. Message 928, London to Agwar, November 19, 1942, FDRL, Map Room, Box 105.

21. Message 940, London to Agwar, November 19, 1942, FDRL, Map Room, Box 105.

22. Summary of Events by Patton, November 22, 1942, FDRL, PSF, Series 4, War Department, Patton; Leighton and Coakley, *Global Logistics and Strategy*, 449–451; Supply Plans and Data, Western Task Force, vol. 1, August to November 1942, HIA, Walter Muller Papers, Box 1.

23. This was Private Thomas J. Plourde, 23rd QM Regiment, a soldier-passenger on the USS *Hermitage*.

24. Supply Plans and Data, Western Task Force, vol. 1, August to November 1942, HIA, Walter Muller Papers, Box 1.

25. Memo, Miller to Muller, December 3, 1942, Supply Plans and Data, Western Task Force, vol. 1, August to November 1942, HIA, Walter Muller Papers, Box 1.

26. "The Sultan's Anniversary" by Patton, November 22, 1942, FDRL, PSF, Series 4, War Department, Patton.

27. Supply Plans and Data, Western Task Force, vol. 1, August to November 1942, HIA, Walter Muller Papers, Box 1.

28. Memo No. 1 by Lt. Col. Burdge, December 2, 1942, HIA, Walter Muller Papers, Box 1.

29. Oren, *Power, Faith, and Fantasy*, 447.

30. Memo No. 1 by Lt. Col. Burdge, December 2, 1942, HIA, Walter Muller Papers, Box 1.

CHAPTER 51

1. Radio 593, Eisenhower to Clark, November 15, 1942, in *PDDE: The War Years*, 2:713.

2. Letter, Eisenhower to Patton, November 15, 1942, in *PDDE: The War Years*, 2:716.

3. Letter, Eisenhower to Noguès, November 15, 1942, in *PDDE: The War Years*, 2:714.

4. Letter, Eisenhower to Patton, November 15, 1942, in *PDDE: The War Years*, 2:715. Message, King to Murphy, November 11, 1942, HIA, Robert Murphy Papers, Box 47.

5. Letter, Noguès to Eisenhower, November 17, 1942, in *PDDE: The War Years*, 2:715.

6. Message 1067, Gibraltar to Agwar, November 21, 1942, FDRL, Map Room, Box 105.

7. Message 2247, London to Agwar, November 19, 1942, FDRL, Map Room, Box 105.

8. "Description of the Visit of the Commanding General and Staff to General Noguès and the Sultan of Morocco," November 16, 1942, USAHEC, George S. Patton Papers, Box 4.

9. "Description of the Visit of the Commanding General and Staff to General Noguès and the Sultan of Morocco," November 16, 1942, USAHEC, George S. Patton Papers, Box 4. In this account, Patton misidentifies the chef de protocol as the grand vizier. In a latter account, he notes his mistake.

10. "Description of the Visit of the Commanding General and Staff to General Noguès and the Sultan of Morocco," November 16, 1942, USAHEC, George S. Patton Papers, Box 4.

11. "The Sultan's Anniversary, November 18, 1942," November 22, 1942, USAHEC, George S. Patton Papers, Box 4.

12. *La Vigie marocaine*, November 18, 1942.

13. *La Vigie marocaine*, November 23, 1942; "Description of Requiem Mass Honoring American and French Dead, Held at Casablanca," November 23, 1942, USAHEC, George S. Patton Papers, Box 5.

14. "Description of Requiem Mass Honoring American and French Dead, Held at Casablanca," November 23, 1942, USAHEC, George S. Patton Papers, Box 5.

15. Letter, Patton to Beatrice Patton, December 8, 1942, LOC, Patton Papers, Box 10.

16. Jordan, *Brothers, Rivals, Victors*, 100; Letter, Patton to Beatrice Patton, December 5, 1942, LOC, Patton Papers, Box 10.

17. Letter, Patton to Beatrice Patton, November 27, 1942; Letter, Patton to Beatrice Patton, December 15, 1942, LOC, Patton Papers, Box 10.

CHAPTER 52

1. Letter, Gova to Schauffler, July 29, 1942, USHMM, AFSC, Case File 7275.

2. Letter, Haynes to AFSC, July 7, 1941, USHMM, AFSC, Case File 7275.

3. Information about Ruth Lueck, October 28, 1941, USHMM, AFSC, Case File 7275.

4. Letter, Nobel to Thiemann, February 18, 1942, USHMM, AFSC, Case File 7275; Letter, Gova to Thieman, October 8, 1941, USHMM, AFSC, Case File 7275.

5. Letter, Haynes to AFSC, July 7, 1941, USHMM, AFSC, Case File 7275.

6. Memo by Heath, September 30, 1942, USHMM, AFSC, Case File 7275.

7. Letter, Szamatolski to Schauffler, December 1, 1942, USHMM, AFSC, Case File 7275.

8. Letter, Schauffler to Szamatolski, November 30, 1942, USHMM, AFSC, Case File 7275.

9. Letter, Thieman to Kimber, July 3, 1942; Letter, Thieman to Szamatolski, February 12, 1942; Letter, Kimber to Schauffler, September 11, 1942; Letter, Haynes to Schauffler, August 9, 1942, USHMM, AFSC, Case File 7275.

10. Telegram, Schwartz to Bénatar, December 8, 1942, USHMM, RG 68.115, Folder 63.

11. Telegram, Bénatar to AJJDC Lisbon, November 28, 1942, USHMM, RG 68.115, Folder 63.

12. Telegram AJJDC Lisbon to Bénatar, November 23, 1942; Telegram, AJJDC Lisbon to Bénatar, November 28, 1942; Letter, Mayerson to Bénatar, December 15, 1942, USHMM, RG 68.115, Folder 63.

13. Telegram, Bénatar to AJJDC Lisbon, December 5, 1942; USHMM, RG 68.115, Folder 63; Cable 127, Schwartz to Leavitt, January 7, 1943; Letter, Oettinger to HICEM, December 29, 1942, AJJDC Archives.

14. Letter, Heath to Voizard, January 14, 1943, USHMM, AFSC, Box 3, Folder 34.

15. Cable 159, Schwartz to Leavitt, January 20, 1943; Cable, Leavitt to Schwartz, January 22, 1943; Expenses, January 1943, Refugiés Étrangers; Refugees Financially Assisted, January 1943, AJJDC Archives.

16. Report of the Joint Commission on Political Prisoners and Refugees in French North Africa, August 26, 1943, USHMM, AFSC, Box 3, Folder 31.

17. Memo, Swett to ACS, G-2, HQ, Fifth Army, March 20, 1943, NARA, RG 338, Entry A1–42853, Box 2; Memo by Bagby, "Internment of the Italians in French Morocco," June 21, 1943, USHMM, AFSC, Box 3, Folder 31.

18. Letter, Culbert to Murphy, June 19, 1943, NARA, RG 338, Entry A1–42853, Box 2

CHAPTER 53

1. Howe, *Northwest Africa*, 177; Pinkeye's Tale, dictated to CSC by Michel Despax, July 15, 1944, NARA, RG 226, Entry A1–99, Box 49, TORCH Anthology.

2. Dave King's Report, July 19, 1944, NARA, RG 226, Entry A1–99, Box 49, TORCH Anthology.

3. Pinkeye's Tale, dictated to CSC by Michel Despax, July 15, 1944, NARA, RG 226, Entry A1–99, Box 49, TORCH Anthology.

4. Waller, *Wild Bill Donovan*, 141.

5. Vaughan, *FDR's 12 Apostles*, 225; Pendar, *Adventure in Diplomacy*, 123.

6. Atkinson, *An Army at Dawn*, 251.

7. Murphy, *Diplomat Among Warriors*, 142.

8. Clark, *Calculated Risk*, 107.

9. Murphy, *Diplomat Among Warriors*, 142–143.

10. Jordan, *Brothers, Rivals, Victors*, 87.

11. Jackson, *France: The Dark Years*, 427; Atkinson, *An Army at Dawn*, 252.

12. Murphy, *Diplomat Among Warriors*, 125.

13. Clark, *Calculated Risk*, 107.

14. Atkinson, *An Army at Dawn*, 256.

15. Atkinson, *An Army at Dawn*, 257.

16. Thomas, *Britain and Vichy*, 169–170; Ricks, "Who Whacked Admiral Darlan?"

17. Clark, *Calculated Risk*, 109.

18. Churchill, *Hinge of Fate*, Kindle locations 10025–10027.

19. Clark, *Calculated Risk*, 108; Thomas, *Britain and Vichy*, 166.

20. Fifth Army, *Fifth Army History*, 1.

21. Jordan, *Brothers, Rivals, Victors*, 101.

22. Letter, Patton to Beatrice, December 5, 1942, LOC, Paton Papers, Box 10.

23. Ambrose, *Supreme Commander*, 138, 164; Barr, *Eisenhower's Armies*, 270–271.

24. Clark, *Calculated Risk*, 123.

CHAPTER 54

1. "'Invasion Padre' at Casablanca," *Rattle of the Theta Chi*, December 1943, 22.

2. "Boxing Bouts as Part of Chaplin's Job," *Rattle of the Theta Chi*, June–August 1945, 9.

3. Office of the Chief of Naval Operations, *History of the Naval Armed Guard Afloat*, 114; "Ack-Ack Fire at Casablanca," *LIFE*, March 15, 1943.

4. "Le bombardement de Casablanca," *La Vigie marocaine*, January 1, 1943; "January 1943" by Patton, USAHEC, George S. Patton Papers, Box 5.

5. Sherwood, *Roosevelt and Hopkins*, 665.

6. Harmetz, *The Making of Casablanca*, 270; Isenberg, *We'll Always Have Casablanca*, 201.

7. Telegram, FDR to WSC, November 26, 1942.

8. Telegram, WSC to FDR, November 26, 1942.

9. Telegram 224, FDR to WSC, December 3, 1942, TNA, CAB120/75.

10. Telegram T1648/2, Churchill to Stalin, December 3, 1942; Telegram, Churchill to Roosevelt, December 7, 1942, TNA, CAB120/75; Telegram, Stalin to Roosevelt, December 17, 1942; Churchill, *Hinge of Fate*, 580.

11. Letter (R-234-1), Roosevelt to Churchill, December 14, 1942, in Kimball, *Churchill and Roosevelt*, 2: 73–74.

12. Telegram 3324, Jacob to Ismay, December 28, 1943, TNA, CAB120/75.

13. Sherwood, *Roosevelt and Hopkins*, 664; Telegram 3500, Eisenhower to Ismay, December 29, 1942, TNA, CAB120/75; Message 248, Churchill to Roosevelt, December 30, 1942, TNA, CAB120/75.

14. Telegram 251, Churchill to Roosevelt, January 2, 1943, *FRUS, The Conferences at Washington, 1941–1942, and Casablanca, 1943*, 503.

CHAPTER 55

1. Telegram 224, FDR to WSC, December 3, 1942, TNA, CAB120/75.

2. Cover plans for Operation Symbol, LO(43)1[?], January 4, 1943, TNA, CAB120/75; Ismay, *The Memoirs of General the Lord Ismay*, 284.

3. Sherwood, *Roosevelt and Hopkins*, 672.

4. Meecham, *Winston and Franklin*, 3947.

5. Churchill, *Hinge of Fate*, 587.

6. "Notes on Anfa Camp," January 1943, TNA, CAB120/75; Report on Casablanca arrangements, American Heritage Center, Frank Wilson Papers, Box 7.

7. Pawle, *The War and Colonel Warden*, 218.

8. Report on Casablanca arrangements, American Heritage Center, Frank Wilson Papers, Box 7.

9. Report on Casablanca arrangements, American Heritage Center, Frank Wilson Papers, Box 7.

10. "Casablanca Conference," February 1, 1943, TNA, CAB120/75.

11. Sherwood, *Roosevelt and Hopkins*, 664; Telegram 3500, Eisenhower to Ismay, December 29, 1942, TNA, CAB120/75; Message 248, Churchill to Roosevelt, December 30, 1942, TNA, CAB120/75.

12. Anfa Conference Security memo, TNA, CAB120/75.

13. Report on Casablanca arrangements, American Heritage Center, Frank Wilson Papers, Box 7.

14. Hindley, "Glamorous Crossing."

15. McCrea, *Captain McCrea's War*, 133.

16. Sherwood, *Roosevelt and Hopkins*, 669.

17. Roosevelt, *As He Saw It*, 64.

18. Report on Casablanca arrangements, American Heritage Center, Frank Wilson Papers, Box 7; McCrea, *Captain McCrea's War*, 134.

19. Sherwood, *Roosevelt and Hopkins*, 672; McCrea, *Captain McCrea's War*, 134.

20. McCrea, *Captain McCrea's War*, 135.

21. Alanbrooke, *War Diaries*, 359.

22. Churchill, *Hinge of Fate*, 587.

CHAPTER 56

1. Matloff and Snell, *Strategic Planning for Coalition Warfare*, 21; Stoler, *Allies and Adversaries*, 99–100.

2. COS meeting with Roosevelt and Churchill, January 15, 1943, *FRUS, The Conferences at Washington, 1941–1942, and Casablanca, 1943*, 573.

3. COS meeting with Roosevelt and Churchill, January 15, 1943, *FRUS, The Conferences at Washington, 1941–1942, and Casablanca, 1943*, 577.

4. COS 57th meeting, *FRUS*, 1943, 3:569.

5. Eisenhower, *Crusade in Europe*, Kindle locations 2592–2608.

6. Eisenhower, *Crusade in Europe*, Kindle locations 2622–2637.

7. Eisenhower, *Crusade in Europe*, Kindle locations 2622–2637.

8. Eisenhower, *Crusade in Europe*, Kindle locations 2637–2647.

9. Sherwood, *Roosevelt and Hopkins*, 678.

10. Ambrose, *Supreme Commander*, 160–161; Barr, *Eisenhower's Armies*, 223.

11. Clark, *Calculated Risk*, 124.

CHAPTER 57

1. Entry for William H. Wilbur, "Medal of Honor Recipients—World War II (Recipients T–Z)," US Army Center for Military History, http://www.history.army.mil/moh/index .html.

2. Roosevelt, *As He Saw It*, 88; Sherwood, *Roosevelt and Hopkins*, 689.

3. Notes of meeting, January 17, 1943, *FRUS, The Conferences at Washington, 1941–1942, and Casablanca, 1943*, 609.

4. Roosevelt, *As He Saw It*, 88.

5. Notes of meeting, January 17, 1943, *FRUS, The Conferences at Washington, 1941–1942, and Casablanca, 1943*, 609; Breitman and Litchman, *FDR and the Jews*, 249.

6. Katznelson, *Fear Itself*, 57; Persico, *Roosevelt's Centurions*, 44.

7. Dallek, *Franklin D. Roosevelt and American Foreign Policy*, 366.

8. Notes of meeting, January 17, 1943, *FRUS, The Conferences at Washington, 1941–1942, and Casablanca, 1943*, 609.

9. Notes of meeting, January 17, 1943, *FRUS, The Conferences at Washington, 1941–1942, and Casablanca, 1943*, 607; Meeting of Roosevelt with the Joint Chief of Staff, January 15, 1943, *FRUS, The Conferences at Washington, 1941–1942, and Casablanca, 1943*, 558.

10. Meeting of Combined Chiefs of Staff, Roosevelt, and Churchill, January 18, 1943, *FRUS, The Conferences at Washington, 1941–1942, and Casablanca, 1943*, 628.

11. Meeting of Combined Chiefs of Staff, Roosevelt, and Churchill, January 18, 1943, *FRUS, The Conferences at Washington, 1941–1942, and Casablanca, 1943*, 631.

12. Telegram 1423A, Churchill to Atlee, January 19, 1943, TNA, CAB120/75; Meeting of Combined Chiefs of Staff, Roosevelt, and Churchill, January 18, 1943, *FRUS, The Conferences at Washington, 1941–1942, and Casablanca, 1943*, 629.

13. Meeting of Combined Chiefs of Staff, Roosevelt, and Churchill, January 18, 1943, *FRUS, The Conferences at Washington, 1941–1942, and Casablanca, 1943*, 636.

14. McCrea, *Captain McCrea's War*, 138.

15. Cadogan, *The Diaries of Sir Alexander Cadogan*, 504; Churchill, *Hinge of Fate*, 592–593.

CHAPTER 58

1. Roosevelt, *As He Saw It*, 83, 89.

2. Patton diary, January 20, 1943, LOC, Patton Papers.

3. Clark, *Calculated Risk*, 124.

4. Patton diary, January 21, 1943, LOC, Patton Papers.

5. Clark, *Calculated Risk*, 125.

6. McCrea, *Captain McCrea's War*, 143; "President Roosevelt Reviews American Troops in Casablanca, Morocco During World W . . . HD Stock Footage," video posted by CriticalPast to YouTube, May 14, 2014, https://www.youtube.com/watch?v=YNNGIx2QSvI.

7. Sherwood, *Roosevelt and Hopkins*, 685.

8. Clark, *Calculated Risk*, 126.

9. Patton diary, January 21, 1943, LOC, Patton Papers.

10. Clark, *Calculated Risk*, 126; McCrea, *Captain McCrea's War*, 143; "Churchill-Roosevelt Casablanca Conference Aka Churchill—Roosevelt Casablanca Meeting (1943)," video posted by British Pathé to YouTube, April 13, 2014, https://www.youtube.com/watch?v=l0cojFJ5UYc.

11. Images of the dagger, tiara, and braclets given by Sidi Mohammed to Franklin Roosevelt,

FDRL Tumlbr, posted January 14, 2015, http://fdrlibrary.tumblr.com/post/108080581639/ourpresidents-on-this-day-in-1943-the.

12. Sherwood, *Roosevelt and Hopkins*, 690; Patton diary, January 22, 1943, LOC, Patton Papers.

13. Murphy, *Diplomat Among Warriors*, 173.

14. Roosevelt, *As He Saw It*, 111.

15. Murphy, *Diplomat Among Warriors*, 173.

16. Sherwood, *Roosevelt and Hopkins*, 690.

17. Patton diary, January 22, 1943, LOC, Patton Papers.

18. McCrea, *Captain McCrea's War*, 146.

19. Sherwood, *Roosevelt and Hopkins*, 690.

20. Murphy, *Diplomat Among Warriors*, 173.

21. Patton diary, January 22, 1943, LOC, Patton Papers.

22. Patton diary, January 23, 1943, LOC, Patton Papers.

23. Hopkins–el Mokhri conversation, January 23, 1943, *FRUS, The Conferences at Washington, 1941–1942, and Casablanca, 1943*, 701.

CHAPTER 59

1. Cadogan, *The Diaries of Sir Alexander Cadogan*, 505.

2. De Gaulle, *The Complete War Memoirs of Charles de Gaulle*, 386.

3. De Gaulle, *The Complete War Memoirs of Charles de Gaulle*, 387.

4. De Gaulle, *The Complete War Memoirs of Charles de Gaulle*, 389.

5. Murphy, *Diplomat Among Warriors*, 174.

6. President's Log, January 22, 1943, *FRUS, The Conferences at Washington, 1941–1942, and Casablanca, 1943*, 694.

7. De Gaulle, *The Complete War Memoirs of Charles de Gaulle*, 391.

8. Sherwood, *Roosevelt and Hopkins*, 686.

9. McCrea notes on Roosevelt–de Gaulle conversation, *FRUS, The Conferences at Washington, 1941–1942, and Casablanca, 1943*, 694–695.

10. Churchill, *Hinge of Fate*, 592.

11. Churchill, *Hinge of Fate*, 593.

12. CCOS meeting with Roosevelt and Churchill, January 23, 1943, *FRUS, The Conferences at Washington, 1941–1942, and Casablanca, 1943*, 708.

13. CCOS meeting with Roosevelt and Churchill, January 23, 1943, *FRUS, The Conferences at Washington, 1941–1942, and Casablanca, 1943*, 697, 708.

14. De Gaulle, *The Complete War Memoirs of Charles de Gaulle*, 392–395; Memo, Murphy to Hopkins, January 23, 1943, *FRUS, The Conferences at Washington, 1941–1942, and Casablanca, 1943*, 700.

CHAPTER 60

1. Churchill, *Hinge of Fate*, 580–581; Telegram R-22, FDR to WSC, November 25, 1942, in Kimball, *Churchill and Roosevelt*, 2:41–42.

2. Report on Casablanca arrangements, American Heritage Center, Frank Wilson Papers, Box 7.

3. McCrea, *Captain McCrea's War*, 147.

4. Churchill, *Hinge of Fate*, 603.

5. McCrea, *Captain McCrea's War*, 147.

6. Sherwood, *Roosevelt and Hopkins*, 693.

7. Transcript of press conference, January 24, 1943, *FRUS, The Conferences at Washington, 1941–1942, and Casablanca, 1943*, 727.

8. McCrea, *Captain McCrea's War*, 147.

9. Gilbert, *Road to Victory*, 300, 309; Sherwood, *Roosevelt and Hopkins*, 696; Kimball, *Forged in War*, Kindle location 3327.

10. Meeting of Combined Chiefs of Staff, Roosevelt, and Churchill, January 18, 1943, FRUS, 1943, 635; Kimball, *Forged in War*, Kindle locations 3320–3339.

11. Sherwood, *Roosevelt and Hopkins*, 696.

12. Churchill, *Hinge of Fate*, 598–599.

13. Transcript of press conference, January 24, 1943, *FRUS, The Conferences at Washington, 1941–1942, and Casablanca, 1943*, 728.

14. Churchill, *Hinge of Fate*, 603. Meeting of Roosevelt with the JCS, January 15, 1943, *FRUS, The Conferences at Washington, 1941–1942, and Casablanca, 1943*, 558. Telegram 4746, Algiers to USFOR London, 8 January 1943. TNA, CAB120/75.

15. Pawle, *The War and Colonel Warden*, 221. Sherwood, *Roosevelt and Hopkins*, 694. Churchill, *Hinge of Fate*, 603.

16. Pawle, *The War and Colonel Warden*, 222. Pendar, *Adventure in Diplomacy*, 43. Alanbrooke, *War Diaries*, 368.

17. Churchill, *Hinge of Fate*, 603–604. Alanbrooke, *War Diaries*, 368. McCrea, *Captain McCrea's War*, 149. Pendar, *Adventure in Diplomacy*, 149–150. Sherwood, *Roosevelt and Hopkins*, 694.

18. Churchill, *Hinge of Fate*, 603–604. McCrea, *Captain McCrea's War*, 149. Sherwood, *Roosevelt and Hopkins*, 694.

19. Letter, Patton to Sprigg (undated), in Blumenson, *The Patton Papers*, Kindle locations 3270–3271.

20. Sherwood, *Roosevelt and Hopkins*, 695.

21. Murphy, *Diplomat Among Warriors*, 177.

CHAPTER 61

1. Rose, *Jazz Cleopatra*, 199.

2. "Josephine Baker Is Safe," *New York Times*, December 6, 1942.

3. "Sidney Williams: Headed Chicago Urban League," *Chicago Tribune*, March 25, 1992.

4. Rose, *Jazz Cleopatra*, 199.

5. "Friends of Jo Baker Organize to Aid Her Orphans," *Jet*, May 15, 1975.

6. Baker and Bouillon, *Josephine*, 130.

7. Baker and Bouillon, *Josephine*, 130; Crawford, *Report on North Africa*, 43.

8. Crawford, *Report on North Africa*, 43.

9. Baker and Bouillon, *Josephine*, 131.

10. Baker and Chase, *Josephine Baker*, 251–252.

11. Crawford, *Report on North Africa*, 44.

12. Jones, *The Sonarman's War*, Kindle location 4002.

13. "Jim and Nikki in Casablanca: An American Navy Flier Meets a French Refugee Girl in Morocco," *LIFE*, February 1, 1943.

14. Staszak, "Colonial Tourism and Prostitution: The Visit to Bousbir in Casablanca, 1924–1955," *Via@* 2, no. 8 (2015).

15. Jones, *The Sonarman's War*, Kindle locations 661–667; Carlson, *The Wonder of It All*, xx.

16. Jones, *The Sonarman's War*, Kindle locations 716–717.

17. Message 15, March 25, 1943; Flash, "Incident at Jockey-Bar," March 25, 1943; Intelligence report, late March 1943, on "Jockey Bar Affair," NARA, RG 226, Entry 97, Box 4.

18. Message 19 by 347, April 23, 1943, NARA, RG 226, Entry 97, Box 4.

CHAPTER 62

1. Letter, Patton to Nita, December 24, 1942, in Blumenson, *The Patton Papers*, Kindle locations 2856–2857.

2. Cable, Eisenhower to Marshall, November 17, 1942, in *PDDE: The War Years*, 2:731; Jordan, *Brothers, Rivals, Victors*, 95.

3. Murphy, *Diplomat Among Warriors*, 153.

4. Eisenhower, *Crusade in Europe*, Kindle locations 2866–2867.

5. D'Este, *Patton*, 461–463.

6. D'Este, *Patton*, 454; Letter, Patton to Beatrice, March 2, 1942, in Blumenson, *The Patton Papers*, Kindle location 3525.

7. Fifth Army, *Fifth Army History*, 2.

8. Fifth Army, *Fifth Army History*, 5–11.

9. Clark interview, May 19, 1948, NARA, RG 319, Entry 138, Box 9.

10. Leighton and Coakley, *Global Logistics and Strategy*, 485, Table 13; War Diary, USS *New York*, March 18, 1943, NARA, RG 338, via Fold3.com.

11. Clark, *Calculated Risk*, 133; War Diary, USS *New York*, March 18, 1943, NARA, RG 338, via Fold3.com.

12. Clark, *Calculated Risk*, 133.

13. Cable 409, Murphy to State, March 17, 1943, NARA, RG 338, Entry A1–42853, Box 3.

14. Memo, Knight to Sutherland, March 28, 1943, NARA, RG 338, Entry A1–42853, Box 3.

15. Memo, Lambert to Lagemann, March 5, 1943, NARA, RG 338, Entry A1–42853, Box 3.

16. "Disbelief in the Allies in Morocco," *New York Times*, January 28, 1943; Message 3, January 19, 1943, NARA, RG 226, Entry 97, Box 4.

17. Memo, Press interview with General Noguès, March 23, 1943, NARA, RG 338, Entry A1–42853, Box 3; Ferro, *Pétain*, Kindle location 10195.

18. Letter, Holmes to Saltzman, March 18, 1943, NARA, RG 338, Entry A1–42853, Box 3.

19. Letter, Clark to Ike, March 20, 1943, NARA, RG 338, Entry A1–42853, Box 3.

20. Cable 54, Gordon to Victor, February 21, 1943, NARA, RG 226, Entry 88, Box 491.

21. Message 18, by 347, April 14, 1943, NARA, RG 226, Entry 97, Box 4.

22. Memo, Lambert to Lagemann, March 5, 1943, NARA, RG 338, Entry A1–42853, Box 3.

CHAPTER 63

1. Franklin D. Roosevelt, "Statement on Temporary Political Arrangements in Africa," November 17, 1942, American Presidency Project, http://www.presidency.ucsb.edu/ws/index.php?pid=16204.

2. Murphy, *Diplomat Among Warriors*, 150.

3. The commission was chaired by the Allied consul generals in Algiers: J. E. M. Carvell (Britain) and S. H. Wiley (United States). They were appointed January 11, 1943.

4. Letter, Doolittle to Murphy, March 2, 1943, NARA, RG 338, Entry A1–42853, Box 3.

5. Memo, Codman to Saltzman, March 10, 1943, NARA, RG 338, Entry A1–42853, Box 3.

6. Report of the Joint Commission on Political Prisoners and Refugees in French North Africa, August 26, 1943, USHMM, AFSC, Box 3, Folder 31.

7. "La suppression de camps d'internés politiques étendu aux camps d'internés étrangers," *La Presse marocaine*, May 6, 1943.

8. "Kenneth Crawford, 80; Newsweek Columnist," *New York Times*, January 14, 1983.

9. Crawford, *Report on North Africa*, 101.

10. Crawford, *Report on North Africa*, 103.

11. Crawford, *Report on North Africa*, 104.

12. Crawford, *Report on North Africa*, 110.

13. Crawford, *Report on North Africa*, 109–110.

14. Crawford, *Report on North Africa*, 112.

15. Crawford, *Report on North Africa*, 113.

16. Crawford, *Report on North Africa*, 133.

17. Wriggins, *Picking Up the Pieces from Portugal to Palestine*, 21.

18. Memo by Joint Commission, May 5, 1943, USHMM, AFSC, Box 3, Folder 31.

19. Wriggins, *Picking Up the Pieces from Portugal to Palestine*, 67.

20. Wriggins, *Picking Up the Pieces from Portugal to Palestine*, 68.

21. Memo, Johnson to Hartley and Kimberland, May 11, 1943, USHMM, AFSC, Box 3, Folder 31.

22. Addition to minutes, Joint Commission, May 8, 1943; Minutes, Joint Commission, May 8, 1943, USHMM, AFSC, Box 3, Folder 31.

23. Memo, Kimberland to Heath, May 8, 1943, USHMM, AFSC, Box 3, Folder 31.

24. Letter, Rains to Bernstein, May 24, 1943; Report of the Joint Commission on Political Prisoners and Refugees in French North Africa, August 26, 1943, USHMM, AFSC, Box 3, Folder 31.

25. Memo, Johnson to Kimberland and Hartley, May 11, 1943; Memo, Heath to Kimberland and Hartley, May 6, 1943; Minutes, Meeting Regarding Labor Problems, May 11, 1943, USHMM, AFSC, Box 3, Folder 31.

26. Report of the Joint Commission on Political Prisoners and Refugees in French North Africa, August 26, 1943, USHMM, AFSC, Box 3, Folder 31.

27. "Paul Henreid, Who Gained Fame in 'Casablanca,' Dies," *Los Angeles Times*, April 3, 1992.

28. Harmetz, *The Making of Casablanca*, 151–152.

29. Harmetz, *The Making of Casablanca*, 157–160.

30. Harmetz, *The Making of Casablanca*, 211

31. Harmetz, *The Making of Casablanca*, 213–214

32. Harmetz, *The Making of Casablanca*, 216–217.

33. Letter, Leavitt to Warner Brothers, May 10, 1943, AJJDC Archives; Receipt for transfer of Warner Brothers funds (500,000FR), May 10, 1943, USHMM, RG 68.115, Folder 72.

34. Cable 218, Katzki to Leavitt, February 14, 1943, AJJDC Archives, Roll 745. Letter, Heath to Bénatar, March 10, 1943; Letter, Heath to Bénatar, February 8, 1943, USHMM, RG 68.115, Folder 69.

35. Cable 385, Katzki to Leavitt, April 14, 1943, AJJDC Archives, Roll 745.

36. "Report on Moroccan Trip of Inspection" by Joseph Schwartz, July 19, 1943, AJJDC Archives, Roll 745.

37. Letter, Bénatar to AJJDC, May 30, 1942, USHMM, RG 68.115, Folder 63.

38. "Report on Moroccan Trip of Inspection" by Joseph Schwartz, July 19, 1943; Accounting Letter No. 253, Lisbon to New York, August 26, 1943; Letter, Bénatar to AJJDC, October 5, 1943; Minutes, meeting of the Comité d'assistance aux réfugiés étrangers, October 30, 1943, AJJDC Archives, Roll 745.

39. Letter, Gova to Schauffler, June 21, 1943; Letter, Johnson to Lueck, January 18, 1944; Letter, Koehler to Gova, April 10, 1944, USHMM, AFSC, Case File 7275.

40. Memo, Kimberland to Heath, June 20, 1943, USHMM, AFSC, Box 3, Folder 31.

41. Memo, Kimberland to Heath and Johnson, June 23, 1943; Report of the Joint Commission on Political Prisoners and Refugees in French North Africa, August 26, 1943, USHMM, AFSC, Box 3, Folder 31

42. Report of the Joint Commission on Political Prisoners and Refugees in French North Africa, August 26, 1943, USHMM, AFSC, Box 3, Folder 31.

CHAPTER 64

1. "Open Letter to M. Noguès, Ex-General, *Liberation: Organ of the National Front of Liberation*, no. 6, March 24, 1943, NARA, RG 338, Entry A1–42853, Box 3.

2. Message 16, March 27, 1943, NARA, RG 226, Entry 97, Box 4.

3. Memo, Knight to Sutherland, March 28, 1943, NARA, RG 338, Entry A1–42853, Box 3.

4. Message 16, March 27, 1943, NARA, RG 226, Entry 97, Box 4; Memo, Knight to Sutherland, March 28, 1943, NARA, RG 338, Entry A1–42853, Box 3.

5. Cable 76–79, Gordon to Victor, March ?, 1943, NARA, RG 226, Entry 88, Box 491; Message 16, March 27, 1943, NARA, RG 226, Entry 97, Box 4.

6. Memo, Knight to Sutherland, April 8, 1943, NARA, RG 338, Entry A1–42853, Box 2.

7. Memcon, Murphy and Noguès, April 15, 1943, NARA, RG 338, Entry A1–42853, Box 3.

8. Memo, Macmillan to Murphy, April 15, 1943, NARA, RG 338, Entry A1–42853, Box 3.

9. Memocon, Eisenhower and Noguès, April 16, 1943, NARA, RG 338, Entry A1–42853, Box 3.

10. Baker and Chase, *Josephine Baker*, 252–253.

11. Baker and Bouillon, *Josephine*, 131.

12. Baker and Bouillon, *Josephine*, 131, 133.

13. Baker and Bouillon, *Josephine*, 131; Baker and Chase, *Josephine Baker*, 252–253.

CHAPTER 65

1. Memo, Knight to Sutherland, May 2, 1943, NARA, RG 338, Entry A1–42853, Box 2.

2. Vigneras, *Rearming the French*, 55.

3. Vigneras, *Rearming the French*, 62; Fifth Army, *Fifth Army History*, 11–12.

4. Vigneras, *Rearming the French*, 65; Tomblin, *With Utmost Spirit*, 110.

5. Atkinson, *An Army at Dawn*, 511; Howe, *Northwest Africa*, 665–666.

6. "L'enthousiasme de Casablanca à la cérémonie du réarmement," *La Vigie marocaine*, May 10, 1943.

7. Report, "Casablanca's 9 of May Celebration," May 11, 1943, NARA, RG 226, Entry 97, Box 5.

8. Quote from movie poster of *Desert Victory*; "Desert Victory," Wikipedia, https://en.wikipedia.org/wiki/Desert_Victory (accessed December 1, 2016).

9. Reeves, *The Power of Film Propaganda*, 173–174.

10. Letter, Culbert to Murphy, May 16, 1943, NARA, RG 338, Entry A1–42853, Box 2.

11. Letter, Culbert to Murphy, May 16, 1943; Letter, Knight to Saltzman, May 14, 1943, NARA, RG 338, Entry A1–42853, Box 2.

12. Letter, Knight to Saltzman, May 14, 1943, NARA, RG 338, Entry A1–42853, Box 2.

13. Message 22, May 29, 1943, NARA, RG 226, Entry 97, Box 4.

14. Cable 53, Jacquet to Wash/Algiers, May 28, 1943, NARA, RG 226, Entry 136, Box 7; Memo, Exp. Det g-3 to JICA/PWB, May 30, 1943, NARA, RG 226, Entry 97, Box 5.

15. Memo by Sutherland, "Propaganda and Moroccan Nationalism," May 5, 1943, NARA, RG 338, Entry A1–42853, Box 3.

16. Memo, "Arab Nationalist Movement," April 10, 1943, NARA, RG 338, Entry A1–42853, Box 3.

17. De Gaulle, *The Complete War Memoirs of Charles de Gaulle*, 422.

18. Hoisington, *Casablanca Connection*, 242.

19. Letter, Noguès to Giraud, June 4, 1943, NARA, RG 338, Entry A1–42853, Box 2.

20. Letter, Sutherland to Clark, 10 June 10, 1943; Cable 61, Mayer to Sec State, 8 June 8, 1943, NARA, RG 338, Entry A1–42853, Box 2.

21. Address from General Noguès to the People of Morocco, June 5, 1943, NARA, RG 338, Entry A1–42853, Box 2.

22. Address from General Noguès to the People of Morocco, June 5, 1943, NARA, RG 338, Entry A1–42853, Box 2.

23. Memo, Knight to Sutherland, June 28, 1943, NARA, RG 338, Entry A1–42853, Box 2.

24. Hoisington, *Casablanca Connection*, 290n56.

25. Cable 61, Mayer to Sec State, June 8, 1943, NARA, RG 338, Entry A1–42853, Box 2.

26. Letter, Sutherland to Clark, June 10, 1943, NARA, RG 338, Entry A1–42853, Box 2.

CONCLUSION

1. *La Vigie marocaine*, August 6–7, 1943.

2. De Gaulle, *The Complete War Memoirs of Charles de Gaulle*, 446–447.

3. "Rabat fait au général de Gaulle un accueil delirant d'ethousiasme," *La Vigie marocaine*, August 7, 1943.

4. "Le discours du général de Gaulle," *La Vigie marocaine*, August 8, 1943.

5. M. Thomas, *The French Empire at War*, 173.

6. Baker and Bouillon, *Josephine*, 134.

7. Baker and Chase, *Josephine Baker*, Kindle locations 4961–4979.

8. Haney, *Naked at the Feast*, 235–236, 278–284.

9. M. Thomas, *The French Empire at War*, 182.

10. Blair, *Western Window into the Arab World*, 98.

11. Pennell, *Morocco Since 1830*, 264.

12. Miller, *A History of Modern Morocco*, Kindle location 3330.

13. Pennell, *Morocco Since 1830*, 266.

14. Jackson, *France: The Dark Years*, 557.

15. Noguès testimony, October 23–26, 1956, in *Le procès du général Noguès*.

16. "Un grand praticien du 'protectorat," *Le Monde*, April 23, 1971; "Une carrière mouvementée," *Le Monde*, April 23, 1971.

17. Singer, *Maxime Weygand*, 180.

18. Jackson, *France: The Dark Years*, 568; "Madame Pétain: On Lonely Fisherman's Island She Stays Near Husband's Prison," *LIFE*, March 10, 1947.

19. Brody, *The Trial of Pierre Laval*, 246.

20. W. Stafford Reid personnel file, NARA, RG 226, Entry 224.

21. Report by King, 31 October 1943, NARA, RG 226, Entry A1–97, Box 8; Letter, King to Gallary, 30 November 1943, NARA, RG 226, Entry 108C, Box 16.

22. Lippman, *Arabian Knight*, 133.

23. Memo, Eddy to Acheson, April 17, 1947, FRUS (history.state.gov), Emergence of the Intelligence Establishment, 1945–1950, document 221.

24. Application form for CIA employment, HIA, David Wooster King Papers.

25. Craven and Cate, *Army Air Forces in World War II*, Vol. 7: *Services Around the World*, 213–220.

26. Ricks, *The Generals*, 68.

27. Murray and Millett, *A War to Be Won*, Kindle location 5213.

28. Jordan, *Brothers, Rivals, Victors*, 266.

29. Jordan, *Brothers, Rivals, Victors*, 543.

30. Murphy, *Diplomat Among Warriors*, vi.

31. Memo, "Refugee Situation at APO 759," by Henry Scattergood, AFSC, Refugee Services, French Morocco, Unnumbered Letters from Casablanca, 1944.

32. Biography of Bénatar, USHMM, RG 68.115, Folder 1.

33. Satloff, *Among the Righteous*, 110. Schroeter, "Vichy in Morocco: The Residency, Mohammed V, and His Indigenous Jewish Subjects," 5624–5661. Abitbol, *Les juifs d'Afrique du Nord sous Vichy*, 162–164.

34. Laskier, *The Alliance Israélite Universelle*, 321; Buom, *Memories of Absence*, 1.

Bibliography

ARCHIVES

American Heritage Center, University of Wyoming, Laramie, Wyoming
American Jewish Joint Distribution Committee, New York, New York
Centre des archives diplomatiques de Nantes, Nantes, France
    1MA/15/59   11MA/900   11/MA/900/83
    1MA/15/706   11/MA/49   11/MA/844
    1MA/15/707
Churchill College, Cambridge University, Cambridge, United Kingdom
    HARS (The Diaries of Fedor Minorsky, alias Theodor Harris)
Frank Wilson Papers
Franklin D. Roosevelt Presidential Library, Hyde Park, New York
    Map Room Files
    President's Secret Files, Series 1, 3,4, 5
Gallica, Bibliothèque nationale de France (http://gallica.bnf.fr)
Hoover Institution Archives, Stanford University, Stanford, California
    M. Preston Goodfellow Papers
    David Wooster King Papers
    Walter J. Muller Papers
    Robert D. Murphy Papers
    W. Stafford Reid Papers
Library of Congress, Washington, DC
    H. Kent Hewitt Papers
    George S. Patton Papers
Naval Heritage and History Command, Washington, DC
National Archives, Richmond, United Kingdom
    ADM116   FO371   PREM3
    CAB65   FO836   PREM4
    CAB120   KV2
National Archives and Record Administration, College Park, Maryland
    RG 38   RG 226
    RG 59   RG 331
    RG 59, 740.0011EW   RG 338
    RG 84
Seeley G. Mudd Manuscript Library, Princeton University, Princeton, New Jersey
    William A. Eddy Papers
United States Holocaust Memorial Museum, Washington, DC
    1997.A.0050 (Herman F. Reissig Memorandum)
    2002.296 (American Friends Service Committee Case Files)
    2010.401.1 (Sophie Freud Papers)
    ITS 2.3.5.1 (International Tracing Service)
    RG 67.008M (American Friends Service Committee)
    RG 68.115M (Hélène Bénatar Papers)
    RG 81.001M (National Library of Morocco)

US Army Heritage and Education Center, US Army War College, Carlisle Barracks, Pennsylvania
    George S. Patton Papers
    J. Donald Peel Papers
    OCMH Collection, Sidney Matthews Papers
    William J. Donovan Papers

SECONDARY SOURCES

Abitbol, Michel. *Les juifs d'Afrique du Nord sous Vichy*. Paris: CNRS, 2012.

Adam, André. *Casablanca: Essai sur la transformation de la société marocaine au contact de l'Occident*. Paris: Éditions de Centre national de la recherche scientifique, 1968.

Adams, Henry. *Years of Deadly Peril, 1939–1941*. New York: McKay, 1969.

Ambrose, Stephen. *Supreme Commander: The War Years of General Dwight D. Eisenhower*. New York: Anchor Books, 2012.

Assaraf, Robert. *Mohammed V et les Juifs du Maroc à l'époque de Vichy*. Paris: Plon, 1997.

Atkinson, Rick. *An Army at Dawn: The War in North Africa, 1942–1943*. New York: Henry Holt, 2002.

Auphan, Paul, and Jacques Mordal. *The French Navy in World War II*. Annapolis, MD: Naval Institute Press, 1959.

Austin, Roger. "The Chantiers de la Jeunesse in Langedoc, 1940–1944." *French Historical Studies* 13, no. 1 (spring 1983).

Baker, Jean-Claude, and Chris Chase. *Josephine Baker: The Hungry Heart*. New York: Cooper Square Press, 2001.

Barr, Niall. *Eisenhower's Armies: The American-British Alliance During World War II*. New York: Pegasus, 2015.

Bartrop, Paul. *Resisting the Holocaust: Upstanders, Partisans, and Survivors*. Santa Barbara, CA: ABC-Clio, 2016.

Bauer, Yehuda. *American Jewry and the Holocaust: The American Jewish Joint Distribution Committee, 1939–1945*. Detroit, MI: Wayne State University Press, 1981.

Bell, A. C. *A History of the Blockade of Germany, 1914–1918*. London: HMSO, 1937.

Blair, Leon Borden. *Western Window into the Arab World*. Austin: University of Texas Press, 2011.

Boum, Aomar. *Memories of Absence: How Muslims Remember Jews in Morocco*. Stanford, CA: Standford University Press, 2013.

Brady, Tim. *Twelve Desperate Miles: The Epic World War II Voyage of the SS Contessa*. New York: Crown, 2012. Kindle Edition.

Braithwaite, Rodric. *Moscow 1941: A City and Its People at War*. London: Profile Books, 2006.

Breitman, Richard, and Alan Kraut. *American Refugee Policy and European Jewry, 1933–1945*. Bloomington: Indiana University Press, 1988.

Breitman, Richard, and Allan Litchman. *FDR and the Jews*. Cambridge, MA: Harvard University Press, 2013.

Brody, J. Kenneth. *The Trial of Pierre Laval: Defining Treason, Collaboration and Patriotism in World War II France*. New York: Transaction Publishers, 2010.

Budd, Lucy. "Global Networks Before Globalisation: Imperial Airways and the Development of Long-Haul Air Routes," *GaWC Research Bulletin* 253 (December 2007).

Butler, J. R. M. *Grand Strategy*. Vol. 2: *September 1939–June 1941*. London: HMSO, 1957.

Byfield, Judith A., Carolyn Brown, Timothy Parsons, and Ahmad Alawad Sikainga. *Africa and World War II*. New York: Cambridge University Press, 2015.

Carlson, Howard. *The Wonder of It All: A Memoir of an Armored Field Artillery Officer in World War II*. Seattle: iUniverse, Inc., 2005.

Carter, Worrall Reed, and Elmer Duvall. *Ships, Salvage, and Sinews of War: The Story of Fleet Logistics Afloat in Atlantic and Mediterranean Waters During World War II*. Washington, DC: Department of Navy, 1954.

Cesarani, David, *Arthur Koestler: The Homeless Mind*. New York: Free Press, 1999.

Churchill, Winston S. *The Second World War*. Vol. 2: *Their Finest Hour*. New York: Bantam, 1965.

———. *The Second World War*. Vol. 3: *The Grand Alliance*. New York: Bantam, 1965.

———. *The Second World War*. Vol. 4: *Hinge of Fate*. New York: Bantam, 1965.

Clayton, Anthony. *General Maxime Weygand, 1867–1965: Fortune and Misfortune*. Bloomington: Indiana University Press, 2015. Kindle Edition.

Cohen, Jean Louis, and Monique Eleb. *Casablanca: Colonial Myths and Architectural Adventures*. Los Angeles: Monacelli Press, 2003.

Craven, Wesley, and James Cate. *Army Air Forces in World War II*. Vol. 7: *Services Around the World*. Washington, DC: Office of Air Force History, 1983.

———. *Europe: TORCH to POINTBLANK, August 1942 to December 1943*. Washington, DC: Government Printing Office, 1949.

Crawford, Kenneth. *Report on North Africa*. New York: Farrar & Rinehart, 1943.

D'Este, Carlo. *Patton: A Genius of War*. New York: Harper Perennial, 1996. Kindle Edition.

Dallek, Robert. *Franklin D. Roosevelt and American Foreign Policy, 1932–1945*. New York: Oxford University Press, 1994.

Davis, Belinda J. *Home Fires Burning: Food, Politics, and Everyday Life in World War I Berlin*. Chapel Hill: University of North Carolina Press, 2000.

deRochemont, Richard. "The French Underground." *LIFE*, August 26, 1942.

Drake, David. *Paris at War: 1939–1944*. Cambridge, MA: Belknap Press, 2015.

Favreau, Bertrand. *Georges Mandel: Ou la passion de la République, 1885–1944*. Paris: Fayard, 1996.

Fenby, Jonathan. *The General: Charles De Gaulle and the France He Saved*. New York: Skyhorse, 2012.

Ferro, Marc. *Pétain*. Paris: Fayard, 1987. Kindle Edition.

Finlayson, T. J. *The Fortress Came First: Story of the Civilian Population of Gibraltar During the Second World War*. Leatherhead, UK: Ashford, Buchan & Enright, 1996.

Ford, Corey. *Donovan of the OSS*. New York: Little, Brown, 1970.

France, Haute Cour de justice. *Procès du Maréchal Pétain: Compte rendu in extenso des audiences transmis par le Secrétariat général de la Haute Cour*. Paris: Imprimerie des Journaux Officiels, 1945.

Funk, Arthur. *The Politics of TORCH: The Allied Landings and the Algiers Putsch, 1942*. Lawrence: University of Kansas Press, 1974.

Gates, Eleanor. *End of the Affair: The Collapse of the Anglo-French Alliance, 1939–40*. Berkeley: University of California Press, 1981.

Gibbs, N. H. *Grand Strategy*. Vol. 1: *Rearmament Policy*. London: HMSO, 1976.

Gilbert, Martin. *Winston S. Churchill*. Vol. 7: *Road to Victory, 1941–45*. Hillsdale, MI: Hillsdale College Press, 2015. Kindle Edition.

Goda, Norman. "Hitler's Demand for Casablanca in 1940: Incident or Policy?," *International History Review* 16, no. 3 (August 1994).

———. *Tomorrow the World: Hitler, Northwest Africa, and the Path Toward America*. College Station: Texas A&M Press, 1998.

Haney, Lynn. *Naked at the Feast: A Biography of Josephine Baker*. New York: Dodd Mead, 1981.

Harmetz, Aljean. *The Making of Casablanca: Bogart, Bergman, and World War II*. New York: Hachette, 2002.

Herwig, Holger H. *The First World War: Germany, Austria-Hungary, 1914–1918*. New York: Arnold, 1997.

Hindley, Meredith. "Glamorous Crossing: How Pan Am Airways Dominated International Travel in the 1930s," *Longreads*, February 10, 2015, https://longreads.com/2015/02/10/glamorous-crossing-how-pan-am-airways-dominated-international-travel-in-the-1930s/.

Hoisington, William. *The Assassination of Jacques Lemaigre Dubreuil: A Frenchman Between France and North Africa*. New York: Routledge, 2004. Kindle Edition.

———. *The Casablanca Connection: French Colonial Policy, 1936–1943*. Chapel Hill: University of North Carolina Press, 1984.

———. "The Selling of Agadir: French Business Promotion in Morocco in the 1930s." *International Journal of African Historical Studies* 18, no. 2 (1985).

Howarth, Stephen, ed. *Men of War: Great Naval Leaders of World War II*. New York: St. Martin's Press, 1993.

Howe, George. *Northwest Africa*. Washington, DC: Government Printing Office, 1957.

Imlay, Talbot, *Facing the Second World War: Strategy, Politics, and Economics in Britain and France, 1938–40*. Oxford: Oxford University Press, 2003.

Isenberg, Noah. *We'll Always Have Casablanca*. New York: W.W. Norton, 2017.

Jackson, Julian. *The Fall of France: The Nazi Invasion of 1940*. New York: Oxford University Press, 2004. Kindle Edition.

———. *France: The Dark Years, 1940–1944*. New York: Oxford University Press, 2003.

Jackson, William Godfrey Fothergill. *The Rock of Gibraltarians: A History of Gibraltar*. Teakneck, NJ: Fairleigh Dickinson University Press, 1988.

Jennings, Eric. "'The Best Avenue of Escape': The French Caribbean Route as Expulsion, Rescue, Trial, and Encounter." *French Politics, Culture & Society* 30, no. 2 (summer 2012).

———. *Free French Africa in World War II: The African Resistance*. New York: Cambridge University Press, 2015.

Jordan, Jonathan. *Brothers, Rivals, Victors: Eisenhower, Patton, Bradley and the Partnership That Drove the Allied Conquest in Europe*. New York: Berkley Caliber, 2011. Kindle Edition.

Katznelson, Ira. *Fear Itself: The New Deal and the Origins of Our Time*. New York: Liveright, 2014.

Kennedy, David M. *Freedom from Fear: The American People in Depression and War, 1933–1945*. New York: Oxford University Press, 1999.

Key, David M. *Admiral Jerauld Wright: Warrior Among Diplomats*. Manhattan, KS: Sunflower University Press, 2001.

Kimball, Warren. *Forged in War: Roosevelt, Churchill, and the Second World War*. New York: William Murrow, 1997.

———. *The Most Unsordid Act: Lend-Lease, 1939–1941*. Baltimore: Johns Hopkins, 1969.

Kitson, Simon. *The Hunt for Nazi Spies: Fighting Espionage in Vichy France*. Chicago: University of Chicago Press, 2008.

Lahure, Auguste. *Sur la route du Congo: Lettres d'Afrique, Maroc et Sahara occidental*. Bruxelles: O. Lamberty, 1905.

Langer, William. *Our Vichy Gamble*. New York: Knopf, 1947.

Laskier, Michael M. *The Alliance Israélite Universelle and the Jewish Communities of Morocco, 1862–1962*. Buffalo: State University of New York Press, 1984.

———. *North African Jewry in the Twentieth Century: The Jews of Morocco, Tunisia, and Algeria*. New York: New York University Press, 1997.

Lazareff, Pierre. "The Fall of France," *LIFE*, August 26, 1940.

Leahy, William D. *I Was There: The Personal Story of the Chief of Staff to Presidents Roosevelt and Truman Based on His Notes and Diaries Made at the Time*. New York: Whittlesey House, 1950.

Leighton, Richard M., and Robert Coakley. *Global Logistics and Strategy, 1940–1943*. Washington, DC: Government Printing Office, 1955.

Lemprière, William. *Tour from Gibraltar to Tangier, Sallee, Mogodore, Santa Cruz, and Tarudant*. Philadelphia: Dobson, 1794.

Lesser, Jeffrey. *Welcoming the Undesirables: Brazil and the Jewish Question*. Berkeley: University of California Press, 1995.

Levisse-Touzé, Christine. *L'Afrique du Nord dans la guerre, 1939–1945*. Paris: Albin Michel, 1998.

Lippman, Thomas W. *Arabian Knight: Colonel Bill Eddy USMC and the Rise of American Power in the Middle East*. Vista, CA: Sewla Press, 2008.

Maghraoui, Driss. "The Moroccan '*Effort de Guerre*' in World War II." In *Africa in World War II*. Edited by Judith A. Byfield, Carolyn A. Brown, and Timothy Parsons, 89–108. Cambridge: Cambridge University Press, 2015.

Matloff, Maurice, and Edwin M. Snell. *Strategic Planning for Coalition Warfare, 1941–1942*. Washington, DC: Government Printing Office, 1953.

Mayers, David. *FDR's Ambassadors and the Diplomacy of Crisis*. New York: Cambridge University Press, 2013.

Meecham, Jon. *Winston and Franklin: An Intimate Portrait of an Epic Friendship*. New York: Random House, 2003.

Metzger, Chantal. *L'empire colonial français dans la stratégie du Troisiéme Reich*. Vols. 1–2. Paris: Peter Lang, 2002.

Miller, Susan Gilson. *A History of Modern Morocco*. New York: Cambridge University Press, 2013. Kindle Edition.

Morison, Samuel Eliot. *Operations in North African Waters: October 1942–June 1943*. Annapolis, MD: Naval Institute Press, 2010.

Motadel, David. *Islam and Nazi Germany's War*. Cambridge, MA: Harvard University Press, 2014.

Murray, Williamson, and Allen R. Millett. *A War to Be Won: Fighting the Second World War*. Cambridge, MA: Harvard University Press, 2009. Kindle Edition.

Nicosia, Francis R., and David Scrase, eds. *Jewish Life in Nazi Germany: Dilemmas and Responses*. New York: Berghahn, 2010.

Offer, Avner. *The First World War: An Agrarian Interpretation*. New York: Oxford University Press, 1989.

Oren, Micheal B. *Power, Faith, and Fantasy: America in the Middle East, 1776 to the Present*. New York: W.W. Norton, 2007. Kindle Edition.

Paillat, Claude. *L'échiquier d'Alger*. Paris: Robert Laffont, 1966.

Painton, Frederick C. "Giraud's Brilliant Escape from a Nazi Prison." *Reader's Digest*. September 1943.

Park, Thomas K., and Aomar Boum. *Historical Dictionary of Morocco*. New York: Scarecrow Press, 2006.

Paxton, Robert. *Parades and Politics at Vichy*. Princeton, NJ: Princeton University Press, 2015.

———. *Vichy France: Old Guard and New Order*. New York: Knopf, 2015. Kindle Edition.

Pennell, C. R. *Morocco Since 1830*. New York: New York University Press, 2001.

Persico, Joseph. *Roosevelt's Centurions: FDR and the Commanders He Led to Victory in World War II*. New York: Random House, 2013.

Porch, Douglas. *The Conquest of Morocco*. New York: Farrar, Straus and Giroux, 2013.

———. *The French Foreign Legion: A Complete History of the Legendary Fighting Force*. New York: Skyhorse Publishing, 2010.

———. *The Path to Victory: The Mediterranean Theater in World War II*. New York: Farrar, Straus, and Giroux, 2004.

Rearick, Charles. *The French in Love and War: Popular Culture in the Era of the World Wars*. New Haven, CT: Yale University Press, 1997.

Reeves, Nicholas. *The Power of Film Propaganda*. London: Bloomsbury, 2004.

Richards, Brook. *Secret Flotillas: Clandestine Sea Operations to Brittany, 1940–44*. Yorkshire, UK: Pen and Sword Press, 2013.

Ricks, Thomas E. *The Generals: American Military Command from World War II Until Today*. New York: Macmillan, 2013.

———. "Who Whacked Admiral Darlan?," *Foreign Policy*, December 16, 2014, http://foreign policy.com/2014/12/16/who-whacked-admiral-darlan-my-guess-is-that-winston -churchill-ordered-it.

Riding, Alan. *And the Show Went On: Cultural Life in Nazi-Occupied Paris*. New York: Vintage, 2011.

Roberts, Andrew. *The Storm of War: A New History of the Second World War*. New York: Harper Collins, 2011.

Rosbottom, Ronald C. *When Paris Went Dark: The City of Light Under German Occupation, 1940–1944*. New York: Little, Brown and Company, 2014.

Rose, Phyllis. *Jazz Cleopatra: Josephine Baker in Her Time*. New York: Vintage, 1991.

Ryder, Rowland. *Edith Cavell*. London: Stein and Day, 1975.

Satloff, Robert. *Among the Righteous*. New York: Public Affairs, 2006.

Scammell, Michael. *Koestler: The Literary and Political Odyssey of a Twentieth-Century Skeptic*. New York: Random House, 2009.

Scheck, Raffael. *French Colonial Soldiers in German Captivity During World War II*. New York: Cambridge University Press, 2014.

Schroeter, Daniel. "Vichy in Morocco: The Residency, Mohammed V, and His Indigenous Jewish Subjects." In *Colonialism and the Jews*. Edited by Ethan B. Katz, Lisa Moses Leff, and Maud S. Mandel. Bloomington: Indiana University Press, 2017. Kindle Edition.

Schiff, Stacy. *Saint-Exupéry: A Biography*. New York: Random House, 2011. Kindle Location.

Sherwood, John M. *Georges Mandel and the Third Republic*. Palo Alto, CA: Stanford University Press, 1970.

Sherwood, Robert. *Roosevelt and Hopkins: An Intimate History*. New York: Bantam, 1948.

Shoemake, Josh. *Tangier: A Literary Guide for Travellers*. London: I. B. Tauris, 2013.

Singer, Barnett, and John Langdon. *Cultured Force: Makers and Defenders of the French Empire*. Madison: University of Wisconsin Press, 2008.

Singer, Barnett. *Maxime Weygand: A Biography of the French General in Two World Wars*. Jefferson, NC: McFarland, 2008.

Smith, David Livingstone. *The Most Dangerous Animal: Human Nature and the Origins of War*. New York: Macmillan, 2009.

Smith, James. *British Writers and MI5 Surveillance, 1930–1960*. London: Cambridge University Press, 2012.

Social Register Association. *Social Register, 1920*. New York: Social Register Association, 1920.

Spinage, Clive A. *African Ecology: Benchmarks and Historical Perspectives*. Berlin: Springer, 2012.

Staszak, Jean-François. "Colonial Tourism and Prostitution: The Visit to Bousbir in Casablanca, 1924–1955. *Via@* 2, no. 8 (2015).

Stevenson, William. *Spymistress: The True Story of the Greatest Female Secret Agent of World War II*. Washington, DC: Arcade Publishing, 2011.

Stockey, Chris, and Gareth Crocott. *Gibraltar: A Modern History*. Chicago: University of Chicago Press, 2012.

Stoler, Mark. *Allies and Adversaries: The Joint Chiefs of Staff, the Grand Alliance, and US Strategy in World War II*. Chapel Hill: University of North Carolina Press, 2004.

Sweets, John. *Choices in Vichy France: The French Under Nazi Occupation*. New York: Oxford University Press, 1986.

Taraud, Christelle. "Urbanisme, hygiénisme, et prostitution à Casablanca dans les années 1920." *French Colonial History* 7 (2006).

Thomas, Martin. *The French Empire at War, 1940–1945*. Manchester, UK: Manchester University Press, 2007.

———. *The French Empire Between the Wars: Imperialism, Politics, and Society*. Manchester, UK: Manchester University Press, 2007.

———. "The Vichy Government and French Colonial Prisoners of War, 1940–1944," *French Historical Studies* 25, no. 4 (fall 2002).

Thomas, R. T. *Britain and Vichy: The Dilemma of Anglo-French Relations, 1940–42*. London: Palgrave, 1979.

Tomblin, Barbara Brooks. *With Utmost Spirit: Allied Naval Operations in the Mediterranean, 1942–1945*. Louisville: University of Kentucky, 2004. Kindle Edition.

United States Holocaust Memorial Museum. "Emigration from Germany." *Holocaust Encyclopedia*. https://www.ushmm.org/wlc/en/article.php?ModuleId=10007455.

Vaughan, Hal. *FDR's 12 Apostles: The Spies Who Paved the Way for the Invasion of North Africa*. Guilford, CT: Lyons Press, 2006.

Vigneras, Marcel. *Rearming the French*. Washington, DC: Government Printing Office, 1957.

Vinen, Richard. *The Unfree French: Life Under the Occupation*. New Haven, CT: Yale University Press, 2006.

Waller, Douglas. *Wild Bill Donovan: The Spymaster Who Created the OSS and Modern American Espionage*. New York: Free Press, 2011.

Walsh, John. "Claridges: An Opulent Hotel Where Every Polished Corner Tells a Story." *Independent*. December 9, 2012. http://www.independent.co.uk/travel/hotels/claridges -an-opulent-hotel-where-every-polished-corner-tells-a-story-8395674.html.

———. *Germany, Hitler, and World War II: Essays in Modern Germany and World History*. New York: Cambridge, 1996.

———. "Hitler's Image of the United States," *American Historical Review* 69, no. 4 (July 1964).

Weinberg, Gerhard. *A World at Arms: A Global History of World War II*. New York: Cambridge University Press, 1994.

Weisbrode, Kenneth. *The Atlantic Century: Four Generations of Extraordinary Diplomats Who Forged America's Vital Alliance with Europe*. New York: Da Capo, 2009.

West, Nigel. *The A to Z of British Intelligence*. New York: Scarecrow Press, 2009.

Wharton, Edith. *In Morocco*. New York: Charles Scribner & Sons, 1920.

Wyrtzen, Jonathan. *Making Morocco: Colonial Intervention and the Politics of Identity*. Ithaca, NY: Cornell University Press, 2016.

Yahil, Leni. *The Holocaust: The Fate of European Jewry, 1932–1945*. New York: Oxford University Press, 1991.

Young, Robert J. "'La guerre de longue durée': Some Reflections on French Strategy and Diplomacy." In *General Staffs and Diplomacy Before the Second World War*. Edited by Paul Preston, 41–64. London: C. Helm, 1978.

Zisenwine, Daniel. *Emergence of Nationalist Politics in Morocco: The Rise of the Independence Party and the Struggle Against Colonialism After World War II*. London: I. B. Tauris, 2010.

MEMOIRS AND EDITED DIARIES

Abtey, Jacques. *La guerre secrète de Joséphine Baker*. Paris: Editions Siboney, 1948.

Alanbrooke, Field Marshall Lord. *War Diaries, 1939–1945*. Edited by Alex Danchev and Daniel Todman. Berkeley: University of California Press, 1998.

Baker, Josephine, and Jo Bouillon. *Josephine*. New York: Da Capo, 1995.

Béthouart, Antoine. *Cinq années d'espérance: Mémoires de guerre, 1939–1945*. Paris: Plon, 1968.

Butcher, Harry C. *My Three Years with Eisenhower: The Personal Diary of Captain Harry C. Butcher, USNR, Naval Aide to General Eisenhower, 1942 to 1945*. New York: Simon and Schuster, 1946.

Cadogan, Sir Alexander. *The Diaries of Sir Alexander Cadogan, O.M., 1938–1945*. Edited by David Dilks. London: Faber and Fabers, 2010.

Clark, W. Mark. *Calculated Risk*. New York: Enigma Books, 2007.

De Gaulle, Charles. *The Complete War Memoirs of Charles de Gaulle*. London: Carroll & Graf Publishers, 1998.

Eisenhower, Dwight D. *Crusade in Europe*. New York: Doubleday, 2013. Kindle Edition.

Freud, Sophie. *Living in the Shadow of the Freud Family*. Westport, CT: Praeger, 2007.

Fry, Varian. *Surrender on Demand*. New York: Johnson Books, 1997.

Harris, Ted. *Escape from the Legion*. London: John Murray, 1945.

Hewitt, H. Kent. *The Memoirs of Admiral H. Kent Hewitt*. Newport, RI: Naval War College Press, 2002.

Hooker, Joseph Dalton, and John Ball, *Journal of a Tour in Morocco and the Great Atlas*. London: Macmillan and Co., 1878.

Ismay, Baron Hastings Lionel. *The Memoirs of General the Lord Ismay*. London: Heinemann, 1960.

Jones, H. G. *The Sonarman's War: A Memoir of Submarine Chasing and Mine Sweeping in World War II*. Jefferson, NC: McFarland, 2010.

King, David. *The French Foreign Legion: David King's Ten Thousand Shall Fall*. Edited by Paul Rich. Washington, DC: Westphalia Press, 2013.

Koestler, Arthur. *Scum of the Earth*. London: Eland Publishing, 2012. Kindle Edition.

Lyautey, Louis Hubert Gonzalve. *Paroles d'action, Madagascar—Sud-Oranais—Oran—Maroc (1900–1926)*. Paris: A. Colin, 1944.

McCrea, John. *Captain McCrea's War: The World War II Memoir of Franklin D. Roosevelt's Naval Aide and USS Iowa's First Commanding Officer*. Edited by Julia C. Tobey. New York: Skyhorse, 2016.

Murphy, Robert. *Diplomat Among Warriors*. New York: Doubleday, 1964.

Pawle, Gerald. *The War and Colonel Warden*. London: Corgi, 1965.

Pendar, Kenneth. *Adventure in Diplomacy*. New York: Cassell, 1966.

Ricard, Prosper. *Maroc. Les guides bleus, sous la direction de Marcel Monmarché*. 5th ed. Paris: Hachette, 1936.

Roosevelt, Elliott. *As He Saw It*. New York: Duell, Sloan and Pearce, 1946.

Saint-Exupéry, Antoine de. *Flight to Arras*. New York: Mariner Books, 1969.

Saint-Exupéry, Antoine de. *Wind, Sand, and Stars*. Translated by Lewis Galantière. New York: Harcourt Brace & Co., 1967.

Schechter, Edmund. *Viennese Vignettes: Personal Recollections*. New York: Vantage, 1983.
Spears, Sir Edward. *Assignment Catastrophe: Prelude to Dunkirk, July 1939–May 1940*. London: A. A. Wyn Inc., 1954.
Truscott, Lucian. *Command Missions: A Personal Story*. New York: Pickle Partners Publishing, 2013. Kindle Edition.
Weygand, Maxime. *Recalled to Service*. New York: Doubleday, 1952.
Wriggins, Howard. *Picking Up the Pieces from Portugal to Palestine: Quaker Refugee Relief in World War II*. Washington, DC: University Press of America, 2004.

EDITED DOCUMENT COLLECTIONS

Bland, Larry I., and Sharon Ritenour Stevens, eds. *The Papers of George Catlett Marshall: "The Right Man for the Job,"* December 7, 1941–May 31, 1943. Vol. 3. Baltimore: Johns Hopkins University Press, 1991.
Blumenson, Martin. *The Patton Papers: 1940–1945*. New York: De Capo, 2009. Kindle Edition.
Fifth Army. *Fifth Army History*. Part 1: *From Activation to the Fall of Naples*. Italy: Headquarters Fifth Army, 1944.
Galambos, Louis. *The Papers of Dwight David Eisenhower*. Vols. 1–5: *The War Years*. Baltimore, MD: Johns Hopkins University Press, 1970.
Great Britain. *Naval Intelligence Division, Morocco*. London: HMSO, 1942.
Kimball, Warren F., ed. *Churchill and Roosevelt: The Complete Correspondence*. Vol. 1. Princeton, NJ: Princeton University Press, 1987.
Ministère des affaires étrangères. *Documents diplomatiques français: 1940 (11 juillet–30 décembre)*. Vol. 2. London: Peter Lang, 2015.
———. *Documents diplomatiques français: VICHY (1 er janvier–31 décembre 1941)*. Vol. 3. London: Peter Lang, 2015.
Noguès, Charles, Ministère public, and Haute Cour de justice. *Le procès du général Noguès devant la Haute Cour de justice: Ministère publique*. October 1956.
Rosenman, Samuel, ed. *Public Papers and Addresses of Franklin D. Roosevelt, 1942*. New York: Harper and Brothers, 1950.
US Congress. *Investigation of the Pearl Harbor Attack: Report of the Joint Committee on the Investigation of the Pearl Harbor Attack*. Washington, DC: Government Printing Office, 1946.
US Department of State. *Foreign Relations of the United States*. Washington, DC: Government Printing Office, 1939.
———. 1940, vol. 2.
———. 1941, vol. 2.
———. 1941, vol. 3.
———. 1942.
———. *The Conferences at Washington, 1941–1942, and Casablanca, 1943*.
———. 1943, vol. 3.
Vital Speeches of the Day, 1940. Vol. 6. New York: City News Pub. Co., 1940.

NEWSPAPERS AND MAGAZINES

Atlanta Constitution
Chicago Defender
Chicago Tribune
Christian Science Monitor
Independent (UK)
Jet
Jewish Telegraphic Agency
La Vigie marocaine (Casablanca)
Le Journal (Paris)
Le Matin (Paris)
Le Monde (Paris)
Le Monde colonial illustré (Paris)
Le Petit marocain (Casablanca)
LIFE
Los Angeles Times
New York Times
Northern Miner
Rattle of the Theta Chi
Reader's Digest
Time

Index

MEREDITH HINDLEY is a historian and senior writer for *Humanities*, the quarterly review of the National Endowment for the Humanities. Her work has also appeared in the *New York Times*, *Salon*, *Christian Science Monitor*, and *Barnes & Noble Review*. Hindley received her PhD from American University. She lives in Washington, DC.

PublicAffairs is a publishing house founded in 1997. It is a tribute to the standards, values, and flair of three persons who have served as mentors to countless reporters, writers, editors, and book people of all kinds, including me.

I. F. STONE, proprietor of *I. F. Stone's Weekly*, combined a commitment to the First Amendment with entrepreneurial zeal and reporting skill and became one of the great independent journalists in American history. At the age of eighty, Izzy published *The Trial of Socrates*, which was a national bestseller. He wrote the book after he taught himself ancient Greek.

BENJAMIN C. BRADLEE was for nearly thirty years the charismatic editorial leader of *The Washington Post*. It was Ben who gave the *Post* the range and courage to pursue such historic issues as Watergate. He supported his reporters with a tenacity that made them fearless and it is no accident that so many became authors of influential, best-selling books.

ROBERT L. BERNSTEIN, the chief executive of Random House for more than a quarter century, guided one of the nation's premier publishing houses. Bob was personally responsible for many books of political dissent and argument that challenged tyranny around the globe. He is also the founder and longtime chair of Human Rights Watch, one of the most respected human rights organizations in the world.

·   ·   ·

For fifty years, the banner of Public Affairs Press was carried by its owner Morris B. Schnapper, who published Gandhi, Nasser, Toynbee, Truman, and about 1,500 other authors. In 1983, Schnapper was described by *The Washington Post* as "a redoubtable gadfly." His legacy will endure in the books to come.

Peter Osnos, *Founder*